Revolutionary Change in Cuba

Revolutionary Change in

CUBA

Carmelo Mesa-Lago

Editor

UNIVERSITY OF PITTSBURGH PRESS

This book is one product of a continuing research seminar on Cuba made possible by a grant from the Carnegie
Corporation of New York to five institutions of higher
learning in Pittsburgh: Carlow College, Carnegie-Mellon
University, Chatham College, Duquesne University, and
the University of Pittsburgh.

Library of Congress Catalog Card Number 73–158190
ISBN 0–8229–3232–6
Copyright © 1971, University of Pittsburgh Press
Henry M. Snyder & Co., Inc., London
Manufactured in the United States of America

Contents

I. POLITY

II. ECONOMY

III. SOCIETY

IV. CONCLUSIONS

Illustrations

Tables

Preface

THIS volume seeks to present a comprehensive, well-documented, up-to-date, and relatively objective study of the revolutionary changes that have taken place in Cuba from 1959 to 1970. The contributors represent a variety of academic specialties in the social sciences and the humanities with viewpoints toward the Revolution ranging from sympathetic to critical.

All revolutions are profoundly complex social phenomena and certainly the Cuban Revolution is no exception. A single social scientist using the limited tools and training of his specialty is seldom equipped to undertake a comprehensive and sophisticated analysis of the multiple facets of a revolutionary process. Moreover, one's academic field often influences the evaluation of social phenomena. Thus an economist may tend to be skeptical about the Cuban experiment with moral incentives particularly in view of its negative impact on output, whereas a sociologist may be enthusiastic because of the experiment's potential for changing values. A collection of essays written by a group of scholars in several disciplines has been a traditional approach to handle the problem. However, already published multi-disciplinary studies on the Cuban Revolution are now out of date by several years or cover only a few aspects of the revolutionary process. The eighteen chapters in this volume break new ground by describing in a coordinated manner the structural transformations that have occurred in Cuba in the last twelve years in the most relevant areas of politics, economy, and society, and analyzing their effects.

This section on politics opens with Suárez's examination of three main components of Cuba's political system: charismatic leadership, ideology, and party. Next Malloy applies to Cuba his model of conflict in a developmental revolution (derived from the Bolivian case), analyzing sources of political support (such as affection, demand satisfaction, and coercion) and sectors of the population bearing the social costs of the process. In an insightful study, Blasier explores the conflict of interests between Cuba and the United States both before and after 1959, as well as the politico-economic strategy followed by both governments. Gonzalez, in turn, analyzes how Castro has maximized, in Cuba's favor, the convergent and divergent

interests that unite and separate Cuba and the USSR. Why Cuba's attempts
to export its revolution have failed in Latin America in spite of conditions
favoring success is one of the questions that Betancourt poses. The section
closes with Horowitz's comprehensive, analytical piece in which he makes
an analogy between the Stalinist and *Fidelista* political models.

The section on economics begins with an essay, written by the editor in
collaboration with Zephirin, explaining how the revolutionary leaders decided among the alternative economic models that were available to them
at the onset of the Revolution, and describing the current macroeconomic
organization, as well as the planning mechanisms, techniques, and functions. This is followed by Bernardo's analysis of the microeconomics of
Cuban state enterprise and managerial organization. Next Hernández and
the editor describe the organization of labor and wages and discuss the role
of the workers and unions both in the overall decision-making process and
in regulating their own labor conditions. Baklanoff's chapter relates the
changes in Cuba's international relations: direction, composition, and balance of trade; sources and volume of foreign aid and external debt; and
the brain drain. This section closes with the editor's chapter in which he
describes the shifting economic policies and analyzes their effectiveness and
impact on output and growth.

Opening the section on social life, Amaro and the editor study prerevolutionary social inequalities based on location, race, and occupation,
as well as rural and urban interest groups, and the evolution of these inequalities and groups throughout the revolutionary process. Paulston then
examines the changes in social organization and educational functions in
the prerevolutionary and revolutionary periods and the characteristics,
problems, and trends of the current educational system. The study of the
conflict between church and state in revolutionary Cuba, the causes of this
conflict and the future possibilities for cooperation are undertaken in
Jover's essay. In the next two chapters in a socio-political context, Matas
discusses the changes that have taken place in theater and cinematography
and Casal explores the literary scene. Finally, Moreno analyzes the developing value system in Cuba in an attempt to detect whether the revolutionary policies are more conducive to modernization than the former policies.

The book closes with an evaluation of the achievements and failures of
the Revolution and their interconnections, followed by a theoretical discussion of the various alternatives open to the Revolution.

The contributors have based their work on perhaps the most complete
assembly of Cuban statistics and information ever employed before in research on the subject. Vital sources were the Central Planning Board's
(JUCEPLAN) publications *Boletín Estadístico* (covering the period 1962–
1966) and *Compendio Estadístico de Cuba* (annual issues from 1965 to

1968). Innumerable official reports on planning, education, the guerrillas, social conditions, economic development, agriculture, and sugar were also used. Collections of the newspapers *Revolución, Hoy,* and *Granma,* and of monitored and transcribed transmissions from Havana radio were the main sources of speeches and news reports. Most of the legislation cited was taken from *Gaceta Oficial* or from newspapers. Some thirty-five Cuban specialized journals and magazines provided substantial technical data.

The available literature on the Cuban Revolution commonly covers events up to 1964. However, the period from 1964 to 1970 is crucial to the understanding of the Revolution because it is a period in which dramatic decisions were made—decisions to change economic policy, reorganize planning, establish the Communist party, support moral incentives, launch the Revolutionary Offensive, endorse the Soviet invasion of Czechoslovakia, and harvest ten million tons of sugar. All of these subjects are examined in detail in this book. Every effort was made to cover the latest events in Cuba; most contributors include data up to mid-1970; a few chapters, up to mid-1971.

The sixteen contributors of the book are among the most knowledgeable specialists in the field. All their essays are published here for the first time, the majority of which were presented at the seminar "Cuba: A Decade of Revolution, 1959–1968" held at the University of Pittsburgh in 1969–1970. Invitations were extended to other scholars (among them Edward Boorstein, Carlos Díaz Alejandro, Richard Fagen, Joseph Kahl, James Petras, Jaime Suchlicki, and Maurice Zeitlin), most of whom also presented papers at the seminar. Unfortunately, previous commitments for publication prevented the inclusion of their papers in this book.

In a sizeable number of cases, books and articles on Cuba have reflected two contradictory approaches, either rabid praise or outrageous criticism. Typical of the literature in the field are journalistic reports, hastily written by two-week visitors to the island—in most cases strong sympathizers of the Revolution who emphasize the positive aspects of the process and conveniently ignore the negative side. The literature of the exiles, on the other hand, commonly suffers similar defects in reverse, the interpretation being biased against the Revolution by stressing the negative features and neglecting the positive ones. Lacking solid data these works have at least something in common: ideological considerations or subjective interpretation prevail over objectivity and serious analysis. Two radically opposed pictures of the Cuban phenomenon confuse the layman: before the Revolution everything was wrong but now everything is right, or before 1959 Cuba was a paradise and now it is hell.

Fortunately this Manichean vision of the phenomenon is slowly being corrected by a more accurate vision. Serious writers favorable to the Revolution (e.g., René Dumont, Richard Fagen, Irving Louis Horowitz, K. S. Karol, Paul Sweezy, Maurice Zeitlin) have pointed out some problems that have been obstructing the political institutionalization and satisfactory economic performance of the Revolution and/or have indicated certain positive aspects of the prerevolutionary society, which were actually instrumental in the rapid socialization of Cuba. Conversely, Cuban émigré scholars teaching in universities or working on research (e.g., Luis Aguilar León, Boris Goldenberg, Andrés Suárez), together with a new breed of young Cuban graduates of universities in the United States, Europe, and Latin America (e.g., Nelson Amaro, Rolando Bonachea, Lourdes Casal, Carlos Díaz Alejandro, Roberto Hernández, Mateo Jover Marimón, Jaime Suchlicki, Nelson Valdés), have developed a more objective approach, digging into the roots of Cuba's problems and/or going through the often costly but revitalizing process of accepting positive revolutionary reforms.

In the light of these tendencies the editor sought to balance the contributions ideologically combining both sides but mainly recruiting scholars who would play down subjective coloration in the search for truth. (One myth that the book should destroy is that all émigrés are right-wingers. The reader will find that some of the chapters most sympathetic toward the Revolution are written by Cuban-born scholars.)

The list of institutions and persons who helped the editor is extensive. The University Center for International Studies at the University of Pittsburgh and its director, Carl Beck, provided generous and continuous funds for the organization of the 1969–1970 Cuban seminar and its public lecture series as well as for research assistance, typing, and professional editing of this book. The University of Pittsburgh Student Union helped in financing the visit of specialists to the Cuban seminar. Cole Blasier, director of the Center for Latin American Studies encouraged the editor to undertake the project and made helpful comments on various parts of the book. The Center's personnel, especially Shirley Kregar and June Belkin, were very useful in various stages of the project. The immense task of typing two versions of the manuscript was efficiently handled by Clemencia Prieto and Donna Bobin. Translations into English of chapters 12 and 14, originally written in Spanish, were beautifully done by Barbara Handler. The Latin American bibliographer at the University of Pittsburgh libraries, Eduardo Lozano, patiently answered innumerable requests for information. Professors James Malloy, Julio Matas, José Moreno, Rolland Paulston, and Reid Reading made useful suggestions on the content of the book. The editor's research assistant, Eduardo Masferrer, gave him a hand in the computations and the completion of footnote data. Professional copy editing was a task accomplished with excellence by Arlene Abady. The final editing and the index were done by Karilyn Bouson. Finally, as it is customary in these cases, the editor wants to express his gratitude to his wife Elena for the Job-like patience that she displayed in the apparently endless period of eight months in which the manuscript was put together. Now that the work is over, it will be easy to go back to the task of eroding her suspicion that research and books are her competitors.

C.M.L.

Abbreviations

ANAP	National Association of Small (Private) Farmers
CDR	Committees for the Defense of the Revolution
CTC	Confederation of Cuban Workers
EIR	Schools of Revolutionary Instruction
FMC	Federation of Cuban Women
ICAIC	Cuban Institute of Cinema Arts
INPF	National Institute of Physical Planning
INRA	National Institute of Agrarian Reform
JUCEI	Coordination, Execution, and Inspection Boards
JUCEPLAN	Central Planning Board
MINAZ	Ministry of the Sugar Industry
MINCEX	Ministry of Foreign Trade
MINCIN	Ministry of Domestic Trade
MININD	Ministry of Industries
MINTRAB	Ministry of Labor
OAS	Organization of American States
OLAS	Latin American Solidarity Organization
UJC	Communist Youth League
UNEAC	National Union of Writers and Artists of Cuba

POLITICAL PARTIES

PSP	Popular Socialist Party (1925–1961)
ORI	Integrated Revolutionary Organizations (1961–1963)
PURS	United Party of the Socialist Revolution (1963–1965)
PCC	Communist Party of Cuba (1965–)

I
Polity

1 Andrés Suárez

Leadership, Ideology, and Political Party

THE Cuban Revolution is too near in time to allow us to draw definitive conclusions about its nature. The task of this chapter is to contribute to a better understanding of the deep transformation that has taken place in Cuba in the last twelve years by describing and analyzing the main elements of interest to the political analyst.

Most studies of the politics of the Revolution stress sociological factors. Regarding the origins of the Revolution, the standard attitude has been to explain everything as the result of tensions, conflicts, and a disequilibrium in the prerevolutionary social structure. Another approach has been to focus on the classes or groups that integrated the revolutionary movement, mainly prior to their ascension to power. In discussing the revolutionary process itself, attention has been centered on an analysis of social groups, such as workers, peasants, etc. There are few scholarly studies analyzing such political elements as the leadership, the party, or the struggle for power by the various political factions. These problems have been more commonly discussed in a journalistic fashion with little sophistication.

Recently two scholars in the field of political development, Samuel P. Huntington and Aristide R. Zolberg, have concentrated their attention on the "creation of political order."[1] Huntington identifies political development with the creation of political institutions and gives a decisive role in the developmental process to the political party and the party system. Zolberg emphasizes the obstacles faced in the creation of political order and, besides the party, analyzes the role of leadership and ideology. This approach selects elements of the political system that are also present in the Marxist-Leninist analysis of political development, although the latter usually plays down personal leadership by referring to it as "personality

3

cult."[2] Therefore this chapter concentrates its attention on the three mentioned political elements: leadership, ideology, and political party.

The Leader

Notwithstanding the disparate character of the normative judgments about the Cuban Revolution, there is general consensus about the decisive role played by Castro in the movement. According to Lockwood, Castro "has been at once the creator, motor force, guide and spokesman for the Revolution."[3] In spite of the obvious preeminence of Castro, very little of note, with the exception of Lockwood's book, has been written about this fascinating personality.[4] A promising approach to the study of Castro is to employ the concept of charismatic leadership as developed by Weber.[5] The characteristics of the Weberian ideal charismatic type are summarized below.[6]

1. It is only in times of crisis that the conditions for the appearance of charismatic leadership are ripe and, especially, at times when the other two types of legitimate leadership studied by Weber—the traditional and the rational—have lost their hold on the people.

2. There is an interaction between the leader and his disciples or followers. The leader, endowed with exceptional qualities and under the increasing conviction that a "mission" has been assigned to him, performs extraordinary activities that set him apart from the ordinary man, thus winning the devotion of the masses. Contemporarily at least, the most significant quality of the leader, proving his charismatic power, is the ability to produce powerful results in the absence of apparent power.

3. The leader not only reinforces his authority by expressing popular grievances, but also by identifying himself with past heroes, exploiting popular myths, and, last but not least, by using modern means of communication.

4. Administrators who serve the leader do not occupy a job in the usual sense, but are personal disciples, inspired to work by loyalty and enthusiasm. The leader determines the limitations of the disciples' authority, usually in terms of the exigencies of the moment.

5. Charismatic leadership can be established, and maintained, only through success; it is essentially unstable and is subject to the process of "routinization," so called by Weber. Through this process, the followers, especially the members of the new administrative staff, try to institutionalize the new regime, securing their positions, whereas the leader strives for the fulfillment of his "mission."

The vagueness of the charismatic concept has permitted its application to such different characters as Napoleon, Hitler, Nkrumah, and even Eisenhower, thus casting doubts upon its utility. But more concrete typologies have not been created, and the Weberian concept—together with other elements to be discussed later—can help us emphasize some features that, in our judgment, have made Castro's charisma credible.

It does not seem necessary to go to great lengths to "prove" that Castro's leadership, in the early years of the Revolution, corresponds to elements of the Weberian ideal type. His leadership was established at a time of profound crisis and during a vacuum of authority. His magnetism and strong personality cannot be denied and he has taken advantage of a modern communications system to spread his word to the masses. Castro was able to produce powerful acts (in spite of his apparent absence of power), such as defeating the Batista dictatorship, defying U.S. corporations and U.S. government restrictions, and winning the battle of the Bay of Pigs. He has proven his talents as the articulator of the anxieties and expectations accumulated by his fellow citizens with a low level of income and education through long years of national frustration, and has been capable of partially satisfying some of these expectations, such as education and medical care. The effort of the Cuban news media to identify Castro's goals with those of José Martí are obvious. But there are two elements in Weber's ideal type with which Castro's leadership appears to correspond only slightly: the leader's belief in a "mission" and his *continuing* production of powerful actions.

Fagen stated in 1965 that Castro was strongly possessed by a sense of "mission," which according to the latter consisted of perceiving the Revolution "as part of a greater historical movement against tyranny and oppression."[7] This is an interpretation, among many others, based on the vague word "mission," used by Weber as applied to Castro. But despite differences in objectives, one characteristic of "mission" is the performance with a sense of permanency of a special duty or task in which the leader believes. This author has profusely illustrated elsewhere the multiple shifts in Castro's apparent beliefs and duties from 1959 to 1966.[8] In contrast to his earlier views about dictatorship and national independency, in his most recent turn Castro has endorsed the Soviet invasion of Czechoslovakia, manifested a close relationship with the USSR, poured scorn upon those who do not share his admiration of the Soviets (including some leftist adherents of the Cuban Revolution abroad), and has given his support to military regimes in Latin America. Thus, unless one is willing to define "mission" in the very broadest of terms, the identification of Castro as a leader with a particular, permanent "mission" seems hazardous.

To arrive at such a conclusion is not necessarily to imply a negative value judgment. It is quite possible that the repetition of sudden political turns was produced by the gigantic problems created by the small size of the island, the closeness of the United States, and the nature and goals of the Revolution. But whatever the causes may be, our contention is that the available data do not allow us to characterize Castro's performance in terms of a stable and continuous "mission," but rather the opposite.

With reference to the continuous performance of extraordinary activities, it has clearly become more and more difficult for Castro to exploit significant victories, especially after his climactic triumph at the Bay of Pigs. In fact, there have been serious setbacks for Castro's image: the failure of the rural guerrillas and their attempts to extend the Revolution in Latin America; the inability to lift the rationing system as promised; and most recently, the nonfulfillment of the ten-million-ton sugar target. Thus, Castro has attempted to capitalize on events of lesser importance to maintain his prestige or to distract public attention when significant failures have occurred. Note the extensive media coverage recently given to the victory of the Cuban sport team in the Eleventh Central-American and Caribbean games, the defeat of a tiny force of exiles that landed in Baracoa, in the province of Oriente, and the successful pressure exerted on British authorities in the Bahamas and on the Swiss embassy in Havana to obtain the release of eleven fishermen captured by counterrevolutionaries. The latter event is particularly significant because it coincided with the announcement of the failure of the ten-million-ton sugar goal.[9]

If the leader no longer performs powerful acts and does not have a well-defined mission, either these two elements of the model are not indispensable for charisma or there is some erosion in Castro's charismatic leadership. We will return to this point later.

The Ideology

The term "ideology" has a long history and its use is far from being clear or uniform. To Marx, ideology was a part of the general process of alienation by which the mental products of human activity assume a life of their own, a case of "false consciousness."[10] To Lenin, ideology was a belief implemented by an elite of class-conscious leaders among a mass of potentially class-conscious workers. In present Soviet doctrine, the central feature of ideology is not any specific theoretical formulation, but the basic demand for belief in the party itself.[11]

Among these and other present uses of the concept of ideology, the one offered by Daniel Bell seems to us particularly useful. Bell, after distinguishing between values, norms, and ideologies, states: "In societies (or social movements) that seek to mobilize people for the attainment of goals, some sharper specification of doctrine is necessary. The function of an ideology, in its broadest context, is to concretize the values, the normative judgments of the society."[12]

There are several factors that make it a difficult task to assess the nature and role of ideology in the Cuban Revolution. Castro is not an ideologist and he has shown little concern for ideology. Before its triumph, the July 26 movement produced neither a coherent program nor an ideological scheme. Actually, the movement's goals were so similar to the goals of Cuba's populist and progressive political parties that they did not generate ideological discussion.[13] After his ascension to power, Castro not only radically changed the movement's goals but later modified his political line many times, both internally and externally.

Recently, it has been speculated that Castro's lack of clear ideology may lead him to surprising internal changes, such as dropping the current revolutionary emphasis on moral incentives if confronted with failure of the experiment. Apparently, important Cuban personalities such as Osvaldo Dorticós, Raúl Castro, Haydeé Santamaría, and Raúl Roa share this belief.[14] Fagen has somewhat changed his previous views and has recently stated, "While hardly consistent over the years in some of his policies and public pronouncements he [Castro] has been *extremely* consistent in reasserting his dominance over the shifting revolutionary power struggle."[15]

If we exclude the early efforts made by Ernesto (Che) Guevara, it was only at the end of 1966, more than seven years after being in power, that the revolutionaries produced a formulation of a hemispheric ideology. This ideology is contained in the last of Guevara's works, Regis Debray's essays, Castro's speeches of the period 1966–1968, and the resolutions adopted by both the Tricontinental Conference of 1966 and the First Conference of the Latin American Solidarity Organization (OLAS) held in Havana in 1967.

The Cuban report to the OLAS conference is a sort of blueprint of Cuba's ideological formula for the hemisphere.[16] The report is actually "a declaration of war against imperialism and the oligarchies of Latin America."[17] Applying a general Marxist approach (e.g., use of class struggle to explain historical events), and ascribing to the revolutionary potential of the Latin American masses (as continuously shown since the Wars of Independence), the report asks for a radical transformation of the current economic, social, and political structures in Latin America. The immediate program, which does not present any radical departure from the common position of the Latin American left, is synthesized in five points: (a) elimination of *latifundia*, (b) nationalization of foreign monopolies, (c) development of broad agricultural and industrial plans, (d) assurance of a stable and fair price and financial system, and (e) improvement of the mass educational system. The ultimate goal, however, is to make "a single revolution of the oppressed peoples which will not stop until it becomes a socialist revolution."[18] The guerrilla band established in rural areas was to be the only instrument to achieve such a goal. The report pointed out as most promising sources for recruitment peasants, workers, middle-class intellectuals, students, and finally "in certain countries certain strata of the bourgeoisie."[19]

Other documents and speeches publicized at the time refer to economics and social change, for example, the use of moral incentives and the attempt to build a "New Man." But the Cuban report to OLAS "concretizes" an additional new set of political values, for example, the total dedication to revolution ("the duty of every revolutionary is to make revolution"), the identification of this task with violence, and the exaltation of the guerrilla as a way of life. If internalized, these political values are to result in a radical transformation of the present "bourgeois" values prevalent in the hemisphere.

However, recent events make unnecessary any discussion on whether such a process of internalization is taking or has taken place. Cuba's ideological blueprint of 1967 is today undergoing drastic revision. Nothing is heard about the OLAS, the organization founded to implement the new ideology. No Cuban documents reiterating the heroic themes of those glorious days are now circulating. Guevara's attempt to implement the theory failed in Bolivia. Castro has turned to domestic economic problems, postponing or neglecting his external "revolutionary duty," as the Venezuelan guerrilla leader Douglas Bravo has reproached.[20] Castro has also offered his support to Peru's military junta, manifesting his belief that the guerrilla road to power is not really the only road to revolution in Latin America.[21] Finally, in 1970, Carlos Rafael Rodríguez introduced new clarifications that significantly changed some of the basic ideological principles of 1967.[22]

Obviously, if the ideology is so elusive as to be hardly ascertainable in terms of content, it is difficult to claim a significant role for it in the regime. Therefore, let us look at the third political element, the political party, in relation to the Cuban political system.

The Party

Although the concept of party seems much more definite than the concept of ideology, nevertheless, the appraisal of its role in Cuba requires some previous clarifications. First, we must say that the concept of political party prevalent in the West (according to which the party is a "part of the whole," competing with similar organizations for political power) is difficult to apply to single-party states such as those of Communist countries. This single-party type rejects competition, monopolizes power, demands ideological loyalty, and imposes strict conditions of both admission and militancy upon its members. One quotation from Lenin will help to clarify the characteristics of such parties, which are relevant to this essay. A party can only be called Communist, wrote the founder of Bolshevism,

> if it is really the vanguard of the revolutionary class, if it really contains all its best representatives, if it consists of fully conscious and loyal Communists who have been educated and hardened by the experience of the persistent revolutionary struggle, if this Party has succeeded in linking itself inseparably with the whole life of its class, and through it, with the whole mass of exploited, and if it has succeeded in completely winning the confidence of this class and this mass.[23]

Once Bolshevism took power, such leaders as Sun Yat-sen and Kemal Atatürk tried to emulate the single-party model stripped of the Leninist requirements. And after the Soviet Union achieved great economic and political power, the same imitation has been attempted by a large number of underdeveloped countries. Space does not permit a discussion of these experiences, but Richard Lowenthal, for one, has written on this subject.[24] His conclusions can be compared to those arrived at by Harry Bretton in Ghana, after the fall of Kwame Nkrumah. According to Bretton, the Convention People's Party never was anything other than the personal political machine of Nkrumah.[25]

Theoretically, Cuba should be a different case because the formal model of the Leninist organization has been imported, the party has taken the title of Communist, and the leaders call themselves Marxist-Leninists. Yet it must be seriously questioned whether there is in Cuba a real Communist party, fulfilling the characteristics stressed by Lenin and playing the role typical of a single party in Communist countries. This author has documented extensively the antecedents of the Communist Party of Cuba (PCC).[26] Here we will refer to these antecedents only briefly and then discuss the more recent data in attempting to answer this question.

There have been several predecessors to the current PCC in Cuba. The traditional Communist party was founded in 1925 and, after various changes, became the Popular Socialist Party (PSP). The PSP and other revolutionary organizations (i.e., the July 26 movement, the Student Revolutionary Directorate) merged loosely into the Integrated Revolutionary

Organizations (ORI) in 1961. The affair against Aníbal Escalante, then main organizer of ORI, led to some changes and ORI became the United Party of the Socialist Revolution (PURS) in 1963. In October 1965 the party was finally organized and became officially the Communist Party of Cuba (PCC). The PCC lacks a program or bylaws, has never held a congress, and only very rarely is something published about its activities or decisions. The first congress of the PCC was announced for 1967, but it did not take place.[27] The congress was then scheduled for 1969 but was cancelled without public debate on the allegation that all the nation's efforts had to be concentrated on the production of sugar.[28] With the exception of some declaration of solidarity or endorsement of political communiqués, mainly for external consumption, the last public activity of the PCC (and perhaps the only relevant one) took place in January 1968, when the "microfaction" of the PCC was purged (see chapter 4).

Current members of the Central Committee were not chosen in 1965 by the rank and file of the old PURS and, according to Zeitlin, there seems to be no inclination to carry out such elections within the party in the future.[29] Even the vacancies in 1967–1968 in the Central Committee produced by the Marcos Rodríguez affair and the microfaction purge (e.g., Ameijeiras, Calcines, and Matar) or the killing of some of its members in Bolivia (e.g., Acuña, Sánchez, and Reyes) had not been filled by mid-1970.[30]

There are no official figures on the PCC rank-and-file membership. According to Blas Roca, a member of the PCC Secretariat and former secretary general of the PSP, in 1969 the party had some 55,000 members.[31] In the province of Havana, party membership increased slightly in 1967–1968 from 11,179 to 11,824 members.[32] These figures should be contrasted to a total population of more than 8 million inhabitants and a labor force of some 2.6 million workers.

How well does the PCC fulfill the requirements set by Lenin for truly Communist parties? For simplicity, two factors will be analyzed: whether the working class supplies its best representatives to the party; and whether the party members are "fully conscious and loyal Communists who have been educated and hardened by the experience of the persistent revolutionary struggle."

At the highest levels of the party hierarchy, that is, the Politburo and the Secretariat, there were no labor leaders in 1965 and only four of the one hundred members of the Central Committee were labor leaders: Lázaro Peña, Ursinio Rojas, Ramón Calcines, and Miguel Martín. Since then, Calcines has been purged. Two of the remaining members (Peña and Rojas) come from the PSP and only one (Martín) has emerged after the triumph of the Revolution. The PSP faction defeated in the Tenth Labor

Congress held in November 1959 now has two representatives in the Central Committee; the delegates elected by the majority of workers at the congress are now either in jail, exile, or in oblivion; and only one among the new leaders has been promoted to the Central Committee.

The percentage of workers who are rank-and-file members of the party seems to be very small, as suggested by the sample presented in table 1. Scattered data reinforce the previous impression. Thus, the delegate of the Politburo in the province of Matanzas has given examples of sugar mills in which the party cell is composed of three or four members.[33] And sugar is the basic industry of the country.

TABLE 1
A SAMPLE OF WORKERS' MEMBERSHIP IN THE PCC: 1968

Factories and Industries	Number of Workers	Members of the Party	Percentage
Automatic loading dock (Cienfuegos)	240	40	17%
"Venezuela" sugar mill (Camagüey)	1,500	74	5
Fertilizer construction site (Cienfuegos)	1,583	533	34
Machine-building shop (Santa Clara)	1,700	200	12
Fertilizer industry (national)	2,363	140	6
Electric industry (national)	8,340	404	5
Machine-building industry (national)	12,743	367	3
Total	28,469	1,758	6%

Sources: Armando Hart, "El proceso de crecimiento y de construcción del partido," Granma Revista Semanal, May 25, 1969, p. 3; and Gil Green, Revolution Cuban Style (New York, 1970), p. 82.

In evaluating the fulfillment of the requisite that party members should be "fully conscious and loyal Communists who have been educated and hardened by the persistent revolutionary struggle," three sets of data will be analyzed. One pertains to the ideological education of the party members. In August 1968, 1,649 members were enrolled in the "Schools of Study and Work," which apparently were the successors of the Schools for Revolutionary Instruction (EIR) closed in February of the same year.[34] Although the figure increased to 5,622 in March 1969, this represents little more than 10 percent of the total party membership.[35]

The second set of data pertains to the party "cadres" in charge of ideological instruction. In 1966, out of a total of 573 cadres, 109 came from the July 26 movement, 27 from the PSP, 13 from the Socialist Youth Party branch, 6 from the Student Revolutionary Directorate, and 418 had no political or revolutionary record before 1959.[36] In other words, 73 percent of the personnel entrusted with the teaching of Marxism-Leninism and with ideologizing the new generation did not participate at all in the revolutionary struggle against Batista. Furthermore, only 7 percent—the former members of the PSP and the Socialist Youth—could be considered "fully conscious and loyal Communists."

The third set of data pertains to the party leadership. Out of eight members of the Politburo, none was a "conscious and loyal Communist" before 1959, and only two among the six members of the Secretariat, and twenty-two out of the one hundred members of the Central Committee have such qualifications. If we take into consideration the guerrilla experience of many other members of the top party hierarchy, the situation substantially improves. However, these members lack the condition of permanency and loyalty to the Marxist-Leninist ideology, being principally followers of and loyal to Castro throughout his numerous ideological shifts.

What is the role of the PCC as an institution in Cuban politics? A sympathizer of the Revolution, Lockwood, who has recently visited Cuba and has studied Castro's personality, asserts that the party and other political institutions have no real power and that the administrative-political apparatus is constructed as a pyramid, at the top of which Castro's power remains undisturbed and supreme.[37]

Castro, in addition to holding the title of first secretary of the party, is also premier, commander in chief of the armed forces, and, usually, the only one who speaks in the name of the PCC. The strong asymmetry in the distribution of power within the party is obvious. In fact, the most important officials of the administration and the armed forces in Cuba also hold the top positions in the PCC. The consequence of this dual role is the lack of defined, separated political and administrative functions in the Cuban government. In 1962, Aníbal Escalante, a prominent member of the PSP and main organizer of the ORI, was denounced by Castro for attempting to subordinate the administration to the party, but today it is obvious that the party is subordinated to Castro and a group of his inner circle who are in charge of the administration. In spite of this situation, in May 1970 Castro blamed the party's intervention into administrative affairs as one of the causes of the failure in achieving the ten-million-ton sugar goal and announced that in the future the party's role will be restricted to the stimulation, coordination, and supervision of the administrative function.[38] In actuality, Castro personally directed the sugar campaign and his first step after its failure was to dismiss an administrative official, the minister of the sugar industry. In a more realistic speech on July 26, 1970, Castro seemed to accept his own responsibility for the failure, said that the masses might change their leadership if they wanted to, and admitted that there were problems, discontentments, and irritations. Although he announced that there would be changes in the party, he did not elaborate on them.[39]

Problems in the Classification of Cuba's Political System

The previous analysis of three political elements is helpful to characterize the Cuban political system by, first, the prominence of a leader with charismatic attributes and, second, the rather elusive and ancillary—if not insignificant—role played by both ideology and party in that system. It is obvious that the analysis of these three elements does not exhaust the analytical possibilities, but to attempt a further description of the Cuban regime that would be useful for the comparative study of politics is a difficult task. Neither Western political science nor Soviet doctrine provides more than meager help.

Robert Dahl, for example, has offered a typology of political systems by following such criteria as the distribution of power, the level of legitimacy, and the number of subsystems.[40] According to this classification, the Cuban regime probably would be placed among those characterized by a personal autocracy and a relatively low level of subsystem autonomy and legitimacy.[41] To recognize the inadequacy of Dahl's classification, it is enough to point out that Trujillo's former regime in the Dominican Republic could be put in the same group.

Gabriel Almond's typology is more complex but no more satisfactory to our purpose. According to Almond, among the "authoritarian systems" (a subgroup of the "mobilized modern systems"), there is a variety of "radical totalitarian systems" whose paradigm is the Soviet Union. Almond, however, adds that "the Communist systems of Eastern Europe and Cuba . . . are by no means identical with that of the Soviet Union." Although he then explains that the Eastern European systems are more representative of the "conservative totalitarian type of systems" (another variety of the authoritarian systems), he does not discuss at all what makes the Cuban system different from the Soviet model.[42]

The recent studies on comparative communism are no more illuminating. Skilling, Tucker, Little, Jacobs, Kautsky, Sharlet, and Meyer simply ignore Castro.[43] Nevertheless, Meyer has written before, "If Cuba is a Communist country, then the meaning of 'communism' has become exceedingly vague."[44] Shoup shows more prudence, "Cuba comes to mind as a country whose claim to be Communist is still open to question."[45] And Lowenthal follows him, "It is still an open question how far Castro's regime has really become a communist party regime in the classical sense."[46]

Hauptmann, after trying a typology of Communist systems based on the criteria of "rationality" and "sophistication," includes Cuba in the group of Communist regimes called "non-rational" and "non-sophisticated." He goes even further by saying that "Cuba is an exception to nearly every generalization made above," and more, "One may even sometimes wonder whether the Castro phenomenon cannot best be explained by reference to the traditional Latin American caudillism."[47]

Soviet doctrine is not very helpful either. According to this doctrine, there are four "basic features" or "principles" that characterize the countries of the socialist commonwealth.[48] They are (a) the significance of the role of the people led by the working class and under the guidance of the Communist party; (b) an economy founded on the public ownership of the means of production; (c) a new social structure characterized by two social groups, the toiling classes of workers and peasants, and the people's intelligentsia; and (d) a new culture based on the Marxist-Leninist ideology. Evidence accumulated in this paper shows the absence of the first feature in today's Cuba. The second, however, is clearly present in Cuba. In the case of the third feature, workers, peasants, and intelligentsia all exist in Cuba. However, the latter term, although it could be extended to cover highly specialized technicians, is difficult to apply to other significant sectors such as the military who are neither workers nor peasants. (This objection, of course, is applicable to the USSR also.) There is the additional problem of whether these groups are actually fully integrated into the new social structure. Finally, it has been clearly established that Cuba has not developed the fourth feature, that is, a "new culture" or set of values based on the Marxist-Leninist ideology. Frequent ideological shifts have impeded the development of a firm base to build a "new culture," although such a thing could yet occur. Perhaps it is not so surprising, in light of these observations, that the Soviets and their domestic group of old-guard Communists have been constantly pushing for the development of party and ideology within the last nine or ten years; they apparently feel that Cuba has some distance to travel before it can be accepted as a Communist state.

The analysis of this special external factor (Soviet pressure) may help to further explain why it is so difficult to classify the Cuban political system. Our contention is that the Cuban leadership did not have an original commitment to adopt the Soviet model but accepted it under particular international circumstances and, since then, there has been a permanent conflict between the Soviet desire to have its model fully implemented in Cuba and the Cuban leadership's resistance to such full implementation. Thus, this factor has operated, together with the personalistic factor represented by Castro, as a deterrent to the political institutionalization of the socialist revolution. This aspect requires more detailed discussion.

The Castroite regime emerged in 1959 as a consequence of the following essential factors: a long-standing crisis of legitimacy that became acute with the coup of March 10, 1952, and climaxed with the military collapse of December 1958; the appearance of Castro as a charismatic leader; and the international situation in which the Soviet Union decided to explore the value of Cuba as a pawn in its conflict with the United States. The power formula discovered by Castro under such circumstances was based on his own leadership and massive popular support, but also on Soviet external protection and aid.

However, Soviet help had not been granted with the extension and thoroughness demanded by the Cubans. Furthermore, the Soviets, in exchange for their help, asked for internal reforms, such as a significant role for the party, greater ideological rigor, and domestic-economic and foreign-political policies congruent with their own.

Neither the July 26 movement, the Student Revolutionary Directorate, the Cuban people, nor, perhaps, even Castro, fought against Batista for the purpose of establishing a regime of the Soviet model in Cuba. What happened was that, at a certain stage of the process, Castro was able to capitalize on Cuba's international position to make the Revolution a much more intense and profound phenomenon than previously projected. The Cuban people followed the charismatic leader in his decision. But when the costs of the decision began to materialize in the form of rationing, regimentation, hemispheric isolation, etc., popular support entered into a process of contraction. At the same time, the Soviets asked for the reforms mentioned above, and Castro faced a dilemma: to resist or to yield to Soviet pressure. In spite of the risks involved, Castro chose the first alternative, at least until 1968.

It is not our purpose here to discuss the ability shown by Castro both to delay the process of contraction of popular support and to resist Soviet pressure. These aspects are documented in other chapters of this book. The significant point for our study is that, in this process, the original Castroite power formula—charismatic leadership, popular support, and external protection—began to weaken and conflict with each other. Another important point is that the armed forces have been very helpful to Castro in this difficult process, working as an instrument of "routinization" and regimentation.

Although very little is known about the armed forces, the scant data available seem to indicate an increase in its personnel and role in the Cuban political system.[49] Three conditions explain this phenomenon: (a) both the leader and his closest followers feel a strong vocation for military life, (b) the U.S. threat justifies the presence of a powerful military instrument, and (c) diminishing popular support makes it advisable to substitute regimentation and coercive means for voluntary adhesion in the Castroite tripartite power formula.

Thus, in the summer of 1970, the Cuban political system could be characterized as a variant of the charismatic model, in which ideology and party play a minimal role and in which the process of institutionalization is very weak, obstructed by the personality of the leader and his resistance to accept a foreign model of routinization. Institutionalization does not appear to be taking place at the level of the top leadership, the formal state apparatus, the party, or even the mass organizations, but it does seem to be present in the armed forces, which has been given an increasingly large role in the regime. If the transition to direct military rule should become the case in Cuba, not only would the system become easier to classify, but we might also be able to draw on the increasing literature about the behavior patterns of the military in developing nations that could help us to understand the Cuban phenomenon better.

Future Outlook

There are too many variables involved in the Cuban phenomenon to make valid predictions about the future. Hence, the hypotheses presented here should be considered with this caution in mind. If our previous remarks are substantially correct, that is, if the USSR is exerting pressure in the indicated direction, thereby increasing the difficulties of the leader in trying to keep his popular following, and if the other factors (especially U.S.–Cuban relations) remain constant, then the preservation of the present structure of power in Cuba is improbable.

If this juncture is reached, three alternatives are available: (a) an open confrontation with the Soviets, with unforeseeable consequences; (b) nominal subordination, but practical resistance to fully implement the Soviet model as practiced in 1966–1968; and (c) subordination and growing acceptance of the Soviet model. The first alternative would be suicidal because it would result in a cut of Soviet supplies and external protection. The second alternative may no longer be possible since the 1966–1968 situation has led to the current state of affairs. There were indications visible in 1968–1969 (which will be discussed in chapter 4) and in 1970 (which are discussed below) suggesting that the Soviet influence in Cuba is increasing and that the leader's charismatic power may be eroding.

The failure to achieve the ten-million-ton goal of sugar placed Castro in a difficult bargaining position to negotiate with the USSR for the renewal of the Cuban sugar treaty that expired as of 1970. In his speech of July 26, 1970, Castro apparently accepted part of his responsibility for the failure and said, "The best would be to tell the people that they should find another leader . . . the people may substitute us whenever it is convenient, right now if they wish."[50] (In later speeches, however, Castro has managed to avoid his own responsibility by emphasizing the negative role that, according to him, the administration and the party played in the failure.)

Uncommonly, in his speech before the Central Committee of the Soviet Communist party, President Dorticós did not mention Castro's name even once. In a press release on the Dorticós-Brezhnev meeting, the same omission was noticeable. In this release, the Cuban president emphasized that, in the course of socialist construction, the Cuban Communists "consider Marxist-Leninist theory to be of the greatest importance."[51]

Blas Roca, former secretary general of the PSP, reappeared after a long silence to strongly criticize "the anarchists," that is, those who "do not want to accept the dictatorship of the proletariat" (reference to the leading role of the working class), and refuse to recognize that there is "a period of transition between capitalism and communism."[52] (Another article with the same theme was published almost at the same time by Fabio Grobart, also a member of the old guard.)[53] Castro and his closest followers refused to accept such a transition in 1966–1968, trying to get rid of mechanisms— necessary in such periods according to the Soviets—such as economic incentives, monetary calculation, etc.

At about the same time, Carlos Rafael Rodríguez maintained that Castro learned to be a revolutionary not only by making the Revolution, but also with the help of theoretical or ideological readings. Rodríguez did not say very much about the guerrilla's way but recommended a policy flexible enough to attract the Latin American rebel military men and the priests. In a recent speech by Castro, the leader clarified Guevara's wish to create "two, or three, or more Vietnams" in this hemisphere, by saying that Guevara was not inciting "tragedy" but thinking "in terms of glory, dignity and justice."[54] In another speech, Castro introduced substantial revisions in the 1966–1968 political line concerning the exportation of the Revolution, the guerrilla as the only way to power, etc., and hailed and defended the USSR vis-à-vis radical-left criticism.[55]

As it has been stated before, it is extremely difficult to make concrete predictions on the immediate future of Cuba's political regime. The only two things that seem to be fairly sure are that the role of the armed forces will continue to be of primary importance, regardless of any change, and that Castro will have to share his power with the military. If the Soviet model is finally accepted, however, the party will increase its power, sharing it with the leader and the armed forces.

NOTES

1. Samuel P. Huntington, *Political Order in Changing Societies* (New Haven, 1968); and Aristide R. Zolberg, *Creating Political Order: The Party States of West Africa* (Skokie, Ill., 1966). Although Huntington's book is more ambitious, his

information about Latin America is unsatisfactory and, in my view, he emphasizes too much the role of the party. Zolberg's book is more modest, but its treatment of the three elements is more balanced, and the author has the obvious advantage of being a specialist in the area.

2. See Alfred G. Meyer, "Historical Development of the Communist Theory of Leadership," in *Political Leadership in Eastern Europe and the Soviet Union,* ed. Robert B. Farrell (Chicago, 1970).

3. Lee Lockwood, *Castro's Cuba, Cuba's Fidel* (New York, 1969), p. 329.

4. The two more recent biographies of Castro, Enrique Meneses, *Fidel Castro* (New York, 1968) and Herbert L. Matthews, *Fidel Castro* (New York, 1969), have not filled the existing vacuum.

5. Max Weber, *The Theory of Social and Economic Organization* (New York, 1947).

6. The literature on the topic has grown enormously. Recent works include Peter M. Blau, "Critical Remarks on Weber's Theory of Authority," *American Sociological Review,* 28 (June 1963), pp. 305–16; W. G. Runciman, "Charismatic Legitimacy and One-Party Rule in Ghana," *Archives Européenes de Sociologie,* 4 (first half 1963), pp. 148–65; William A. Friedland, "For a Sociological Concept of Charisma," *Social Forces,* 43 (October 1964), pp. 18–25; Ann R. Willner and D. Willner, "The Rise and Role of Charismatic Leaders," *The Annals of the American Academy of Political and Social Science* (March 1965), pp. 77–88; Edward Shils, "Charisma, Order and Status," *American Sociological Review,* 30 (April 1965), pp. 199–212; Robert C. Tucker, "The Theory of Charismatic Leadership," *Daedalus,* 97 (Summer 1968), pp. 731–56; Dankwart A. Rustow, "Atatürk as Founder of a State," ibid., pp. 793–828; and Shmuel N. Eisenstadt, *Max Weber on Charisma and Institution Building* (Chicago, 1968). Applications of the Weber model to Cuba have been made by Richard R. Fagen, "Charismatic Authority and the Leadership of Fidel Castro," *Western Political Quarterly,* 18 (June 1965), pp. 275–84; and Ward M. Morton, *Castro as Charismatic Hero* (Lawrence, Kan., 1965).

7. Fagen, "Charismatic Authority," n. 10.

8. Andrés Suárez, *Cuba: Castroism and Communism, 1959–1966* (Cambridge, Mass., 1967). Castro's recent dramatic turns in his political line or "mission" have been documented by J. Clark, "Thus Spoke Fidel Castro," *Dissent* (January–February 1970), pp. 38–56.

9. See *Granma Revista Semanal,* March 29, April 26, May 14 and 21, 1970.

10. See George Lichtheim, *The Concept of Ideology and Other Essays* (New York, 1967); and Norman Birnbaum, "The Sociological Study of Ideology (1940–1960)," *Current Sociology,* 9, no. 2 (1960), pp. 91–172.

11. Daniel Bell, "Ideology and Soviet Politics," *Slavic Review,* 24 (December 1965), pp. 591–603. On the concept of ideology see Mary Matossian, "Ideologies of Delayed Industrialization," *Economic Development and Cultural Change,* 6 (April 1958), pp. 217–28; G. Geertz, "Ideology as a Cultural System," in *Ideology and Discontent,* ed. David E. Apter (London, 1964); Alfred G. Meyer, "The Function of Ideology in the Soviet Political System," *Soviet Studies,* 17 (January 1966), pp. 273–85; and comments by David Joravsky, Frederick C. Barghoorn, Robert V. Daniels, and Morris Bornstein, ibid., 18 (July 1966), pp. 1–80; David W. Minar, "Ideology and Political Behavior," *Midwest Journal of Political Science,* 5 (November 1961), pp. 317–31; and Giovanni Sartori, "Politics, Ideology, and Belief Systems," *American Political Science Review,* 63 (June 1969), pp. 398–411.

12. Bell, "Ideology and Soviet Politics," n. 21. See also the comments by George Lichtheim and Carl J. Friedrich and the reply by Bell in the same issue—*Slavic Review*, 24 (December 1965), pp. 604–21.

13. José Manuel Otero, "El escritor en la revolución cubana," *Casa de las Américas*, 6 (May–August 1966), pp. 203–09, among others, has acknowledged this weakness of the revolutionary movement. President Osvaldo Dorticós, in his speech before the Cultural Congress (*Granma Weekly Review*, January 14, 1968) admitted the low level of "anti-imperialist consciousness" during the insurrectional stage.

14. As quoted in Matthews, *Fidel Castro*, pp. 32–33, 37, 318–19, 328–29.

15. Richard R. Fagen, "Revolution for Internal Consumption Only," *Trans-action*, 6 (April 1969), p. 13.

16. The report has been included in the study prepared by the Special Consultative Committee on Security of the OAS on the *First Conference of the Latin American Solidarity Organization* (OEA/Ser. L/X/II.18).

17. Ibid., p. 63.

18. Ibid., p. 103.

19. Ibid., p. 102.

20. *Le Monde*, January 15–21, 1970.

21. See Fidel Castro's "Discurso en conmemoración del Centenario del Natalicio de Lenín," *Granma Revista Semanal*, May 3, 1970, pp. 2–5.

22. Carlos Rafael Rodríguez, "Lenín y la cuestión colonial," *Casa de las Américas*, 10 (March–April 1970), pp. 7–33.

23. Vladimir I. Lenin, "Thesis on the Fundamental Tasks of the Second Congress of the Communist International," *Selected Works*, 10 (New York, 1938), p. 165.

24. Richard Lowenthal, "The Model of the Totalitarian State," *The Impact of the Russian Revolution: 1917–1967*, Royal Institute of International Affairs (London, 1967).

25. Henry L. Bretton, *The Rise and Fall of Kwame Nkrumah* (New York, 1966).

26. Suárez, *Cuba*.

27. The announcement was made by Castro in his speech closing the Twelfth National Congress of the Confederation of Cuban Workers (CTC), see *El Mundo*, August 30, 1966, pp. 7–9.

28. As reported by Maurice Zeitlin, "Inside Cuba: Workers and Revolution," *Ramparts*, 8 (March 1970), p. 70

29. Ibid.

30. Marcos, a member of the old PSP, was tried by the revolutionary government for denouncing a group of revolutionary student leaders to Batista's police. This trial and Marcos's eventual execution were used by Castro to discredit the PSP.

31. Quoted in Gil Green (member of the National Committee of the U.S. Communist party), *Revolution Cuban Style* (New York, 1970), p. 76. Another estimate of 250,000 members given by Juan de Onís (*New York Times*, January 12, 1969), section IV, p. 7E, seems to be a gross exaggeration in view of Roca's figures and other data presented later.

32. Armando Hart, secretary of organization of the party, "El proceso de crecimiento y de construcción del partido," *Granma Revista Semanal*, May 25, 1969, p. 3. It should be clarified that Hart included the party candidates in those figures.

33. José R. Machado, "Frente a todas las dificultades . . . ," June 29, 1969, p. 5.

34. On the rise and fall of the EIR, see Richard R. Fagen, *The Transformation of Political Culture in Cuba* (Stanford, 1969), ch. 5.

35. Armando Hart, "La primera necesidad de la producción es la superación . . . del nivel ideológico de los cuadros y militantes," *Granma Revista Semanal,* July 20, 1969, p. 10.

36. Lionel Soto, "Lo importante es que desarrollemos nuestro camino," *Cuba Socialista,* 7 (January 1967), pp. 37–61.

37. Lockwood, *Castro's Cuba,* pp. 329–31, 353.

38. See Fidel Castro, "Discurso en el acto de recibimiento a los 11 pescadores secuestrados . . . ," and "Comparecencia . . . sobre la zafra azucarera de 1970," *Granma Revista Semanal,* May 31, 1970, pp. 2–5, 7–12.

39. See Fidel Castro, "Discurso en el décimo séptimo aniversario del asalto al Cuartel Moncada," *Granma Revista Semanal,* August 2, 1970, pp. 6–7.

40. Robert A. Dahl, *Modern Political Analysis* (Englewood Cliffs, N.J., 1964), pp. 25–38.

41. There is no confident way to estimate the legitimacy of the Castro regime. *Legitimacy* is defined here, following S. M. Lipset, as "the capacity of the system to engender and maintain the belief that the existing political institutions are the most appropriate ones for the society." See Seymour M. Lipset, *Political Man* (New York, 1963), p. 64. The estimation given in the text is based on the arguments to be introduced later when discussing the dynamics of the system.

42. Gabriel Almond and Bingham Powell, *Comparative Politics: A Developmental Approach* (Boston, 1966), pp. 279–80.

43. H. Gordon Skilling, "Soviet and Communist Politics: A Comparative Approach," *Journal of Politics,* 22 (May 1960), pp. 300–14; Robert C. Tucker, "On the Comparative Study of Communism," *World Politics,* 19 (January 1967), pp. 242–57; D. Richard Little, "Communist Studies in a Comparative Framework: Some Unorthodox Proposals," in *Communist Studies and the Social Sciences,* ed. Frederick J. Fleron, Jr. (Skokie, Ill., 1969); John A. Armstrong, Alfred G. Meyer, John H. Kautsky, Daniel N. Jacobs, and Robert S. Sharlet, "Symposium" [on Comparative Politics and Communist Systems], *Slavic Review,* 25 (March 1967), pp. 1–28.

44. Alfred G. Meyer, *Communism,* 3d ed. (New York, 1967), p. 198.

45. Paul Shoup, "Comparing Communist Nations: Prospects for an Empirical Approach," *American Political Science Review,* 62 (March 1968), pp. 185–204.

46. Lowenthal, "Model of the Totalitarian State," p. 351.

47. O. H. Hauptmann, "The Communist-Ruled States," in *Aspects of Modern Communism,* ed. Richard F. Starr (Chapel Hill, N.C., 1968), pp. 10, 12.

48. For a recent formulation, see I. Pomelov, "Common Principles and National Characteristics in the Development of Socialism," *Pravda,* August 14, 1968. Compare this with the Suslov formulation of November 1956, and the one given by the Moscow Declaration of November 1957, both in Zbioniew K. Krzezinski, *The Soviet Bloc: Unity and Conflict* (New York, 1961), pp. 273, 300.

49. An estimate of Cuba's armed forces in 1966 placed its total at 121,000 men distributed as follows: 90,000 in the army, 25,000 in the air force, and 6,000 in the navy. The militia was not included. See UCLA, Latin American Center, *Statistical Abstract of Latin America, 1968* (Los Angeles, 1969), p. 138, table 47. A more recent estimate places the total number at 175,000, plus 80,000 on reserve and 200,-000 militiamen. See *El Mercurio* (Santiago de Chile), July 5, 1970. Commenting on the latter estimate, the July 7 Radio Habana-Cuba broadcast said that such computations were well below the actual figures. Castro has recently stated, "If analyzed from the point of view of the number of men and weapons, our army is without doubt the

strongest in Latin America." See "Speech to the Soldiers and Officers in the Armed Forces . . . ," *Granma Revista Semanal,* November 6, 1969, p. 1.

50. Castro, "Discurso en el décimo séptimo aniversario."

51. *Granma Revista Semanal,* May 3, p. 6, and May 10, p. 1.

52. Blas Roca in *Bohemia,* March 27, 1970.

53. Fabio Grobart, "Lenín y la fundación del primer Partido Comunista de Cuba," *Granma Revista Semanal,* May 10, 1970, pp. 2–3.

54. Fidel Castro, "Discurso en la inauguración del pueblo Doce y Medio," *Granma Revista Semanal,* June 7, 1970, pp. 2–4.

55. See Castro, "Discurso en conmemoración del Centenario . . . "

2 James M. Malloy

Generation of Political Support
and Allocation of Costs

POVERTY and economic backwardness may create conditions that motivate men to rise in violence. Such a violent insurrection may destroy a preexistent social order. But the task of "making the revolution" is a problem of a different magnitude than that of simply destroying the old. It is a problem of creating a new social order out of the fragments of the old. All indications are that the Cuban revolutionaries have successfully erected such a new order. Moreover, they have done so with such speed and relative lack of bloodletting that the Cuban experience stands in stark contrast to all other modern revolutions, which went through long and bloody epochs before new orders were built. For these reasons alone, the Cuban Revolution is one of the most significant phenomena of the twentieth century. But the Cuban experience is significant for many other reasons as well.

Viewed in its proper third-world context, the Cuban Revolution can be seen as a modern "developmental" revolution—an attempt by means of revolution to pull a society out of economic backwardness and set it on a course of rapid economic development. In this context, the task of creating a new order is basically one of stripping previously dominant groups of the resources under their control and of reorganizing those resources within a new political and economic framework with the avowed aim of national development. The aim of this paper is to analyze this process as it has been played out thus far in Cuba. Our intention is not to generate new information about the Cuban Revolution, but to develop an interpretation of existing knowledge within the terms of a frame of analysis originally developed to study aspects of the Bolivian Revolution. Our aim is not to develop precise hypotheses, but rather to point out what we consider to be

23

a common set of problems confronting revolutions in the third world and, hopefully, thereby contribute to ongoing comparative studies of modern developmental revolutions.

Problems of Support, Social Costs, and Mobilization in Developmental Revolutions

The phenomenon of the modern developmental revolution can be delimited in terms of three major factors: (a) the existence of elites committed to the goal of rapid economic development, (b) the mobilization of groups confronting economically problematic personal situations, and (c) the underdeveloped context itself in which resources (in the broadest sense) for development are, to one degree or another, in short supply. These factors not only help to define the phenomenon, but also act as concrete contextual factors that limit the area in which revolutionary behavior can be played out.

It seems undeniable that rapid economic development is one of the chief goals of emergent elites throughout the third world. While ideologies vary, in the main, control and use of the state apparatus is seen as the chief means to the goal. Concomitantly, it is also evident that the process of mobilization of marginal social groups is increasing in speed, breadth, and intensity in these countries. This dual process of the mobilization of marginal groups and the emergence of elites committed to rapid state-sponsored economic development in environments of relative (in some cases, extreme) scarcity is fraught with a number of points of contradiction and, hence, potential conflict.

First is the contradiction between the development goals of elites and the aspirations of mobilized groups. The goal of development in environments of scarcity demands that an investable surplus be accumulated primarily by means of restricting the consumption of local groups. The bulk of the mobilized groups, on the other hand, are responding to real situations of often extreme economic deprivation. Hence, their aspirations are translated into increasing demands for consumption of goods and services. This contradiction is often exacerbated by the fact that elites in their drive to power spur the process of mobilization through rhetoric and programs that create anticipation among the masses of alleviation of their needs once the leaders they follow achieve formal power. Thus, revolutionary leaders often arrive at power with a large debt to their supporters.

In areas such as Latin America, the situation is further confounded by the makeup of reform and revolutionary movements. Most often, such movements are formed out of a diversity of groups—ranging across segments of the middle class, peasants, and urban and rural workers, led by a counterelite derived from the preexistent elite and subelite of the society. This was clearly the case in Mexico, Bolivia, and Cuba. These agglomerations have been called by many "national popular movements." These movements are usually held together by loose populist ideologies that reject simple notions of class conflict and project, instead, a concept of "nation" versus "antination." Basically, the operative logic is that the various sectors of the society have a common set of interests because they are oppressed equally by external powers operating through a local elite, which has sold out the nation as a whole. Thus, the aim is to unseat the *status quo* elite, assert national independence, and call forth the remainder of the nation to achieve its destiny of development.

Whatever the tactical validity of such ideologies, it is evident that the assumption of a common set of interests among middle sectors, workers, and peasants is illusory. This becomes most clear when such movements successfully achieve power and immediately face the problem of distributing rewards among supporters. This situation becomes even more serious in the underdeveloped context in which the available store of goods is limited and the question of distributing rewards inevitably gives way to the thornier issue of the distribution of costs. Euphoria rapidly turns into dissidence and the revolutionary family is racked by intense internal conflict.

These multiple points of contradiction and conflict result in a central problem common to all instances of the modern developmental revolutionary situation, namely, an ongoing tension between what we may call *political* and *economic logics*. In such situations, political logic is clear—gain support for a new order and specific governments to run it. But, given the developmental goal, economic logic is also quite clear—accumulate an investable surplus to stimulate development. Both must be done, but the question is, how?

In very general terms, there are three ways support can be generated for a political system: (a) mobilization of commitment, that is, affective identification, (b) force, and (c) satisfaction of demands. The first is the ideal, but, given the fact that a revolutionary situation is by definition one in which affective commitment to various orders is in question, it is rather problematic. Within the revolutionary movement there may be fervor, especially in the early days, but since the movement is usually based on mobilization by means of slogans and ideologies expressing previously frustrated demands for gratification, the fervor is usually based on anticipation of gratification soon after an insurrection has succeeded. Supportive behavior, if not identification, could be achieved by force, but this raises moral questions for some types of projected orders; it is unstable and uneconomical over the long run; and presupposes that contending elites have the wherewithal to use force, which is not always the case. Thus, we are left with the satisfaction of demands, which puts us right back to the clash between consumption and investment, but in an even more serious context.

Actually, the problem of support is even more complex in the developmental revolutionary situation, for the amount and kinds of support necessary will be further shaped by the types of goals the elite defines for the society. In this situation, the goal the elite defines for the society is rather grandiose: to progress rapidly from a state of relative economic backwardness to a developed state. Given the resource situation of the underdeveloped environment, often the most available resource is sheer human energy, mobilized, organized, and directed toward the development goal. Passive support or acquiescence is not sufficient to sustain a development-oriented revolutionary regime. The regime needs the active support, physical and mental, of large sectors of the society. Whether it employs positive or negative techniques to achieve support, a key problem of political economy confronting the elite is the need to sustain, over time, controlled mobilization. The ongoing need for mobilization in an environment of scarcity feeds back into the continuing problem of reconciling political and economic logics.

After a successful insurrection, such as that in Cuba in 1959, revolutionary movements split into rival elite factions struggling not only over power but, more fundamentally, over how to reorder, redefine, and reorganize society. In the situation defined here, that struggle is basically one of alternative political courses to the goal of rapid state-sponsored economic development, or what we might call "political models" for rapid economic development. The limiting factors and sources of contradiction discussed above set the stage upon which that battle is waged.

The fashioning of specific political models is the result of the resolution of two basic problems: control and social costs. The problem of control concerns the issue of which of the contending elites—identified with which segments of the society—will play the major role in reordering the society. The second problem involves the inevitable and tragic question of which groups will bear the brunt of the burden of the overall society's drive to development. These questions can only be resolved through a process of struggle. Whereas the chief strategic question of the battle is one of political models, elites continually confront the tactical problem of creating alliances of social groups powerful enough to impose a "development solution" on the society. Such a "political model" will reflect the imposition of the values and interests of some groups to the exclusion of others. The latter literally pay the costs of development, simply because they are forced to do so.

Political Models of Development in Latin American Revolutionary Societies

Although there is no necessary limitation on the kinds of political models of development a revolutionary country may adopt, the issue in Latin America has tended to revolve around variations of the themes of state capitalism and state socialism. Mexico is a case of implementation of the former model, and Cuba, a case of the latter. In Bolivia, Latin America's third real revolutionary society, the issue has yet to be clearly resolved, although since 1960 Bolivia has leaned toward the state-capitalist solution.

In the state-capitalist model, control is in the hands of a new elite of entrepreneurs, technocrats, political professionals, and, often, top labor leaders. Their power rests on an alliance of powerful groups in the public and private sectors led by an agglomerated party, such as the Mexican Revolutionary Institutional Party (PRI) or, as has been the recent case in Peru and Bolivia, by a nationalist-oriented military. Costs are primarily allocated through bargaining in a nationally regulated market, with those groups capable of organizing and deploying political or economic power holding the upper hand. Hence, the bulk of the costs tend to fall on peasants, urban marginals, and the less well organized workers. Although an unequal position in the market is the primary means of allocating costs, these allocations are often backed up by force in cases of protest—for example, the Bolivian army's occupation of the mines in 1965. Thus, the process of cost allocation is partially masked by the market mechanisms and commonly does not appear to be a product of official decision.

In the state-socialist model, control is in the hands of a bureaucratized elite formally identified with the interests of the masses of workers and peasants. Lacking the market mechanism, the state-socialist model is, of necessity, a command system. Cost allocations must be formulated in the national plan and transmitted to groups as central-command decisions. The cost-allocation process is, therefore, much more open (e.g., wage rates, rationing) and appears as the direct result of official decisions. Hence, the government can be specifically blamed for privation, and conflict between the government and sectors of the populace is highly possible.

Therefore, the government must be in a position to back its commands with force when more voluntaristic means fail to elicit compliance. The nature of the command system, the problem of costs, and the necessity of maintaining mobilization in an environment of scarcity are factors that, to a large part, account for the predilection of state-socialist systems in the third world to elaborate "totalitarian" control structures. Indeed, one might argue—and the case of Cuba tends to confirm—that the successful establishment of a state-socialist model of development is predicated upon the construction and coordination of such a centrally dominated control structure.

The Cuban Case

For purposes of analysis, the revolutionary process in Cuba can be broken into three stages defined by shifts in the balance between economic and political logics and the patterns of generating support and allocating costs among sectors of the society.

In the first stage (1959–1961), the leadership simultaneously tried to pursue consumptionist and developmental policies with emphasis of the former over the latter. Although revolutionary enthusiasm was at its highest (particularly throughout 1959 and early 1960), political support was mainly achieved through means of demand satisfaction. Force was used to a relatively small degree (as compared with other revolutions) to crush the opposition, but not to generate support. Social costs were allocated to foreign investors and domestic upper and middle sectors.

In the second stage (1962–1965), the developmental goal was given priority over the consumptionist one. There was, therefore, a reduced reliance on demand-satisfaction means, and these became collectivistic and egalitarian through minimum equal rations and free social services for all. There was also a limited use of individual economic incentives. Social costs were transferred to the masses, particularly to the urban groups. There was a gradual increase in the use of mobilization, regimentation, and compulsive means.

In the current stage (1966–) the developmental goal has become obsessive, further reducing consumption. An attempt is being made to substitute moral stimuli and commitment for demand satisfaction. The rural sector has become a bearer of social costs also. Mobilization has reached a climax, and there is an increasing militarization of the society.

Political Support Through Means of Demand Satisfaction (1959–1961)

Similar to most revolutions, the Cuban Revolution first went through a period of ideological effervescence and confusion as various sectors of the revolutionary movement split into rival hostile cliques. However, unlike most other revolutions, this period was inordinately short and, by the end of 1961, the main features of the state-socialist model were evident.

Many factors contributed to the brevity of this period, not the least of which was the Cuban environment itself. In confronting the task of consolidating power and constructing a new system, the Cuban revolutionaries were in a significantly better position than their Mexican and Bolivian forerunners. Mexico and Bolivia are large countries split into myriad regions separated by formidable natural barriers. In addition, they are racially and culturally diverse societies, which, previous to their revolutions, had not achieved a coherent national cultural system. Although Mexico was more developed in 1910 than its neighbors (Bolivia was one of the least developed Latin American states in 1952), neither it nor Bolivia had developed a nationwide system of communications or transportation. Finally, neither had established an effective "national" system of governance, but, rather, were agglomerations of semisovereign fragments held together by alliances of regionally based strong men. Thus, in each case when the central authority was overthrown, the societies collapsed and fragmented along regional, class, and racial lines. Mexico had to go through more than fifteen years of civil war before the parts were put back together, whereas, in many respects, Bolivia, after more than eighteen years, has yet to accomplish the task.

In contrast, Cuba is a small island and, despite some racial prejudice, was considerably more integrated both culturally and racially before its Revolution. Moreover, in 1959 Cuba was among the more highly developed Latin American countries by almost all social and economic indicators. This was particularly apparent in a relatively well articulated system of communications and transportation, which facilitated the overall integration of the country. Although the political system was venal and unstable, the government, whoever possessed it, was at least national in scope with its administration and vital services centered around the capital city. On the eve of the Revolution, Cuba, unlike Mexico and Bolivia, was effectively a nation, although a somewhat backward one in comparison to the advanced industrial states. Thus, when Batista was overthrown, a man and a government fell, but the Cuban society did not disintegrate. By seizing Havana, the rebels seized the hub of an intact national system.

One must also, of course, take note of the phenomenon of Fidel Castro, who by performing a number of "miracles"—surviving in the Sierra, defying the Yankee titan, and rapidly elevating the material and psychological condition of the masses—became a charismatic leader in the true sense of that much used and abused term. The prophetlike position that Castro assumed provided a critical focal point, bridging the gap between the old and the new systems. However, his ability to develop and project his charisma was aided considerably by the homogenity of the Cuban culture and the existence of a national system of communications. What other twentieth-century revolutionary leader had, from the moment of his ascension to power, such an opportunity to project both his voice and image— through radio and television—into almost every corner of the country he sought to rule?

The first three years of the Cuban Revolution have aptly been called the period of guerrilla mentality. Stimulated by their successful campaign against Batista, the revolutionaries approached the tasks of governance with the same attitudes and tactics they used in the military struggle. The operative attitude was that all problems would fade in the face of their enthusiasm and effort. There is little evidence that they had a plan for the future other than a firm commitment to overhaul Cuban society drastically and to eliminate the abuses of the past. This "renovationist" spirit was the major line separating the radicals around Castro and the other more conservative leadership groups. The early struggle among rival factions was not, properly speaking, an ideological dispute; rather, it was a battle over the degree and tempo of projected change.

The issue of the ideology of the Revolution arose only when the Castroites, frustrated by the cautious and reformist approach of their other allies, accepted the Communist party's offer of support for a true revolutionary program. The Castroites, at that point, were neither Communists nor socialists; they remained, essentially, radical renovationists. However, when groups opposed to drastic change seized the Communist issue to justify their opposition, the Castroites began to equate anticommunism with being antirevolutionary. Thus, there quickly emerged a "revolutionary" alliance between the radical Castroites and the old-line Communists.

The Castroite-Communist alliance quickly divided and emasculated their opponents and achieved a preponderant position in defining policy. An important factor contributing to their ascending power was their ability to mobilize massive worker and peasant support for the renovationist line. Worker and peasant support increased primarily because the reforms imposed by the radicals were to the direct material benefit of these groups. Under the slogan of social justice, the radicals courted worker and peasant support by meeting the concrete economic needs and demands of these strategic groups. Thus, during this period, the political logic of mobilizing support outweighed any accumulationist economic logic. The primary means used to achieve political support was demand satisfaction. Social expenditures outweighed economic expenditures and the overall level of consumption of the Cuban society rose rapidly.

Although the politically motivated consumptionist policy was dominant, it was not exclusive. Simultaneously, the now firmly entrenched radicals sought to stimulate a broad-based process of economic development. Significant investments were made in a concerted attempt to stimulate industrialization and agricultural diversification. The radicals were, in effect, burning the candle at both ends by pursuing a dual policy of investment and consumption. The resource outlay involved in the dual policy put a tremendous strain on Cuba's economic base; the effects of which were manifested in an incipient inflation and, more importantly, in the deterioration of the country's balance of payments. Cuba was accumulating a large foreign debt, and the short-term question became, who was going to pay the immediate bill?

The immediate costs of the dual policy were imposed on foreign interests, and the old upper and middle classes. Through a variety of mechanisms, these groups were systematically stripped of their share of social resources in order to increase the consumption level of the masses and underwrite the investment program. Not unexpectedly, these groups recoiled against this drastic leveling-off process and turned against the Revolution. However, they were powerless in face of the revolutionary alliance that was forming. Unable to resist, they were forced to bear the costs of the dual policy thrust. They had little choice but to acquiesce, resist and be crushed, or to get out. Most chose exile, thereby eliminating rapidly and with little bloodshed, upper- and middle-class resistance as a significant factor in the unfolding revolutionary process.

At the beginning of 1961, the ideology of the Revolution was still undefined, but the policies of the previous two years had set in motion a dynamic that was becoming increasingly difficult to reverse. The elite alliance of Castroites and Communists had subdued most of their rivals. The problem of control, therefore, was being resolved by the emergence of a new elite sprung from previously dominant groups, but identified with the aspirations of workers and peasants. Through the politically motivated strategy of demand satisfaction, the new elite succeeded in mobilizing workers and peasants into a solid revolutionary bloc, powerful enough to impose costs on the old upper and middle groups. The alienation of these groups, followed by their steady withdrawal from Cuba, reinforced the logic of the process. The possibility of turning the Revolution in the state-capitalist direction was more and more remote, for these groups would have been the essential human base of such a model, both as a critical skill group and as a power base to impose the state-capitalist solution on other groups. The movement toward state socialism was all but inevitable.

Throughout 1961, the drift to state socialism became patent. If there had been any question of deflecting that drift, it was dashed on the beaches of the Bay of Pigs. The abortive invasion of April 1961 was one more "miracle" confirming the "superhuman" skills of Castro. The euphoria of victory cemented the masses' identification with the leader and his revolution. Thus, he was able to give the *coup de grâce* to his opponents and consolidate the Castroites' control vis-à-vis challenges from within and abroad. The extension of the Soviet umbrella confirmed and solidified the new reality.

A crucial development of this transition period was the steady elaboration of a set of centrally dominated control mechanisms. Military control reached out of the rebel army confines into the larger society with the formation of the militia. Unlike Bolivia, these units did not represent an arming of sectors of the society on an independent basis, but the formation of a centrally controlled paramilitary organization, the members of which were subjected to vigorous military discipline. Through this mechanism, the revolutionary elite brought under their control a massive force capacity for mobilization purposes.

Central control was elaborated further with the establishment and rapid growth of the INRA, which in a short time brought the bulk of rural Cuba under national direction. A system of new central ministries, together with the Central Planning Board, completed economic control. To these instrumentalities were added the national system of Committees for the Defense of the Revolution (CDR), which scrutinized local affairs on a day-to-day basis; state control of labor unions and other associations; and governmental control of the communications media. Finally, in an attempt to integrate and coordinate the new control structure, the first steps toward the creation of a single dominant party (ORI) were taken. At the end of 1961, the Marxist nature of the Revolution was proclaimed by Castro.

As mentioned previously, the elaboration of such a total control structure is probably inevitable in any attempt to establish a state-socialist model of development. The modern developmental revolution seeks development through a process of stripping previously dominant groups of their resources and organizing those resources into a new framework. The ability to carry out the process within any political model depends, to a great extent, on the previous level of development, for that level will determine what can be wrenched from the past in the name of the future. But, though there are degrees of underdevelopment, it is axiomatic that in an underdeveloped society the past cannot totally underwrite the future; at the same time, internal economies must be generated from the present primarily through restrictions on consumption. The question of social costs, therefore, is considerably more complicated than the billing of previously dominant groups.

Cuba, for example, had a relatively well developed economic base. However, the dual policy followed in the first three years of the Revolution, although politically successful, ate deeply into the country's resource base. The resources forcefully taken from the old upper and middle groups bought time, but were hardly enough to underwrite the entire bill. Cuba could not continue to burn the candle at both ends: sooner or later accumulationist economic logic would have to take precedence over consumptionist political logic. Moreover, with the old power groups bled dry, the revolutionary directorate would have to shift the costs onto their prime support groups—the workers and peasants. Such a turn of events was hardly likely to have been received with enthusiasm.

The Cuban revolutionary elite—as its counterpart in other under-developed countries—faced the real possibility of a clash with its original support groups once the harsh realities of the situation became apparent. Once the point of revolutionary euphoria and consumption gave way to the inevitable necessity of sacrifice in the name of the future, the revolu-tionary elite had to be in a position to enforce its commands and maintain a high level of mobilization by using force, if necessary. In view of that need, the control structure had been established.

Reduced Demand Satisfaction and Increasing Regimentation (1962–1965)

By 1962, the strategic problem of which political model of development the Revolution would follow had been resolved in favor of the state-socialist model. In self-definition, as well as in practice, Cuba became a socialist society and a member of the socialist bloc. The problem then shifted to the tactical reality of how to make the state-socialist model function and achieve success over time. This tactical problem still revolved around the delicate issues of balancing political and economic logics and the imposition of costs.

It was obvious that the dual policy of consumption and investment followed during the previous three years was no longer feasible. If develop-ment was to be achieved, accumulationist policies would have to override consumptionist policies, economic logic would have to take precedence over political logic. As it was no longer possible to wrench resources from the past by imposing costs on the old middle and upper groups, future costs would have to be levied on the groups that had been, thus far, the major supporters of the Revolution. Such a shift in policy, however, could dampen enthusiasm for the Revolution and turn supporters into opponents. Given the fact that mere passive support is not sufficient to underpin a developmental regime, the potential problem was even more serious. In the developing environment, sustained mobilization of human energy is essential to both the political and economic health of the regime. Within the state-socialist model, the critical task of the political economy is to achieve and sustain a high level of controlled mobilization. But, the eco-nomic realities were such that the elite could no longer lean primarily on the mechanism of demand satisfaction to elicit the requisite levels of sup-port. Henceforth, the revolutionary elite would have to deploy a variety of mechanisms in its attempt to walk the line between maintaining support and squeezing an investable surplus out of the masses.

In confronting this new dilemma at the beginning of 1962, the revolutionary elite was in a significantly better position than a year before. In the first place, all serious domestic contenders for power had been eliminated and Soviet power diminished any threat from the outside. Thus, potential dissidents faced the reality that there were virtually no sources of support to turn to. Moreover, the population confronted a still-expanding set of control mechanisms, which gave the new elite the capacity to exercise forceful sanctions, if necessary. Finally, the charismatic power of Castro and the consumptionist policies of the three previous years had built up a large store of affective commitments for the new regime among the masses. The regime and its leaders had a significant legitimate base from which to call for collective sacrifice. Hence, the fledging socialist regime was in a position to utilize force as well as the somewhat eroded but still significant revolutionary fervor as basic mechanisms of generating support. The situation was not as bright concerning demand satisfaction.

The shift in favor of economic logic induced the imposition of rationing in March 1962. Rationing, which gradually expanded to embrace all essential consumer goods, had its greatest impact first on the urban sector, particularly among those who used to have, even before the Revolution, levels of consumption higher than the quota. This sector consisted mainly of the lower-middle-class segments, skilled and some semiskilled workers, etc. Furthermore, many unskilled workers and the former unemployed who, prior to the Revolution, possibly had a level of consumption lower than that assigned by rationing, nevertheless, had been able to improve this level during the first stage of the Revolution. Hence, they were affected also. The situation in rural areas was different. It is true that the rapidly increasing number of state farms and the imposition of the *acopio* (part of the private farms' production that had to be sold to the state at official prices set below market prices) were mechanisms to squeeze a surplus out of the rural sector. Yet, the rationing system, at the beginning at least, did not greatly affect the rural masses, mainly because their prerevolutionary level of consumption was very low and they were capable of offsetting a possible loss by increasing their production. However, when the rationing system expanded to cover most manufactured goods, the rural sector was also affected.

Although consumption was cut, the network of social services (stable employment, education, health) remained intact. Yet, as emphasis shifted from "nonproductive" to "productive" investment, the rate of expansion of social services declined. Thus, services, such as housing, which were provided in large quantity and at low costs in the consumptionist period, were drastically reduced.

If the overall level of consumption was cut, at least the available scarce goods, as well as services, were equally distributed. Outside of this collective consumption, there was an attempt to use a limited number of material rewards as a work incentive for individuals. A minority of workers could win bonuses, refrigerators, motorcycles, automobiles, and trips in the socialist competition for surpassing output quotas. In summary, although the mechanism of demand satisfaction was played down considerably, the regime made sure that all were submitted to it; the government continued to meet a minimal general level of demand for services and used limited individual demand satisfaction—material incentives—as a means of gaining political and economic support.

The complex shifts in economic policy in Cuba will be dealt with in chapter 11 of this book. It is enough to say that in 1963 Cuba discovered that it could not escape from its role as an exporter of agricultural products by revolutionary fiat and, to cope with the situation, it had to swing back to sugar as the potential savior and provider of the Revolution. For our purposes, the important point is that in the last part of the industrialization phase, and particularly in the return-to-sugar phase, the dominant logic was that of accumulation and investment primarily paid for by increasing restrictions on mass consumption.

During this stage, Cuba followed the classic state-socialist model. The guerrilla spirit disappeared as Cuba rather mechanistically adopted the Soviet and East European socialist model. The governmental structure was highly centralized and all the features of a command system were established, for example, central planning, central allocation of resources, and central wage-fixing. The breadth of socialization was also extended as the state progressively eliminated, particularly in agriculture, more and more private economic activity.

This centralization and organization of the economy was accompanied by a parallel process in the political field. The control mechanisms mentioned above were broadened and streamlined. The two most significant developments of the period, however, came in regard to the organization of the army, and the, as yet undefined, national party.

In 1963, compulsory military service was established in Cuba. With that measure, the size of the regular army swelled and became the largest single standing army in the hemisphere, outside of the United States. At the same time, the regime moved to downgrade the power and role of the militia, thereby establishing the regular army as the predominant manager of force in Cuban society. The new army is, however, considerably more than an instrument for organizing and deploying military force. Large sections of the army are not armed. These sections have no military function, but are militarized labor brigades that work in agriculture and on construction projects. Even those army sections that are given weapons and trained in warfare perform economic tasks such as cutting sugar cane.

The draft system is a mechanism of political and economic mobilization. On the one hand, it generates a significant amount of cheap labor (a form of cost allocation), whereas, on the other, it is a mechanism of control and surveillance of political dissidents and other "antisocial" types. Thus, the regime introduced a form of compulsive mobilization controlled and organized by the new multifunctional army. The assignment of these mobilization and production functions to the regular army was to have profound significance for the course of the Revolution, particularly after 1966.

The implementation of the state-socialist model in Cuba was a result of the Castroite-Communist alliance. Once the outlines of the model were established, the alliance began to crack and a new intraelite struggle ensued. The lines of cleavage were complex, involving personal ambition, intersectoral struggles, and stylistic differences; intimately intertwined with these was the tactical problem of the specific implementation of the model. As early as 1962, a prominent member of the old Communist group, Aníbal Escalante, was publicly denounced for his "sectarianism," purged from the government and ORI, and sent abroad. In early 1963, the ORI (which had been organized mainly by Escalante) was transformed into the PURS under the control of Castroites. Soon, the Soviet model itself came under increasing attack from within the regime. The guerrilla spirit symbolized by Ernesto (Che) Guevara emerged and became the basis for a powerful assault on the Soviet orthodoxy and the groups and institutions associated with it. Unresponsive trade unions, rigid bureaucrats, and arrogant officials came under fire. The old Communists and the "older" Soviet socialism they stood for were also assailed: the aesthetic revolutionary spirit of China was contrasted with the bureaucratic materialism of the Soviets. The proponents of orthodoxy fought back, contrasting their "realistic" approach to development with the "infantile idealism" of their opponents.

At one level, at least, the debate raised the question of the "political morality" of the Revolution. Central to this dimension was the concept of the socialist "New Man"—a new selfless creature dedicated to the good of his collectivity. The debate over how to create such a man eventually centered around the question of material versus moral incentives, which, in turn, raised a number of complex issues regarding demand satisfaction: would a man respond only to concrete material rewards or did he have other moral needs, the satisfaction of which would motivate him to work and, in the process, transform himself into a New Man? Aside from the moral issue, the debate also raised pragmatic questions of political control and economic production.

Throughout the period, Castro acted as arbiter, leaning now to one side and then to the other, but never committing himself completely to either line. In many ways, it was reminiscent of the right-left struggle in the Soviet Union manipulated by Stalin. This is not the place to detail the struggle. Suffice it to note that with these complex shifts, Castro succeeded in either controlling or eliminating the major figures on both sides of the debate.

This period of political consolidation and construction came to an end in 1965 with the final formalization of the PCC. Although Cuba was now officially a single-party state, the new party organization did not, in fact, have total political primacy; it had a very potent rival in the highly politicized regular army. The elimination of the powerful faction leaders and the existence of two powerful political instrumentalities—the army and the party—that could be played off one another magnified Castro's position as maximum leader of the Revolution even further.

In summary, 1962 to 1965 was a period of the consolidation of the state-socialist model, both politically and economically. In the political sphere, Castro brought the major factions of the Revolution to heel and brought into being two powerful instrumentalities, the army and the party, astride which he established his undisputed role as definer of the future course of the Revolution. Economically, there was a shift in priorities from consumption to development. Support was generated by a complex interplay of three means: (a) the manipulation of, perhaps, declining affective commitment, based on the charismatic appeal of Castro and the store of commitment built during the consumptionist years of 1959–1961; (b) a severely reduced but equalized level of demand satisfaction and social service, plus a limited policy of individual demand satisfaction; and (c) an increasing use of negative sanctions in the form of suppression of opponents and forced and semiforced mobilization.

Moral Incentives and Militarization of Society (1966–)

Prior to 1966, Castro skillfully avoided committing himself on the substantive issue of the material incentives versus moral incentives controversy. Then, in August 1966, with the political structure consolidated and his own position secure, the maximum leader announced his and the Revolution's commitment to the path of moral incentives. This move was followed in 1968 by the announcement of the Revolutionary Offensive, aimed not only at an impressive increase in investment (at the cost of consumption), but also at a simultaneous construction of socialism and communism in Cuba. Castro had accepted the logic of the previous Guevarist line. In so doing, he launched the Revolution on a new course; one that veered sharply from the orthodox socialist forms of the Soviet Union and Eastern Europe.

In announcing the new course, Castro made an attack on the kind of socialism (as practiced in the Soviet Union and Eastern Europe) that relies on material incentives and other market devices, because such a path was in danger of ending in capitalism instead of socialism. As in China, the "political morality" of the Revolution became of primary concern in Cuba. In our view, the Cuban new course is indicative of a general deviance from orthodoxy common to countries of the third world, both capitalist and socialist. The working out of a new variation on the state-socialist model springs from the common problems confronting third-world countries. They face the dilemma of development in a new historical era and within a world context dominated by the industrial states of both the capitalists and the orthodox socialists. Their common dependence on one or the other of the dominant blocs—due to their being exporters of primary goods and importers of manufactured goods—forces third-world states to seek new solutions to their problems, even as they often ideologically identify themselves with the formal systems of the dominant blocs.

Perhaps, due to the extended experience of invidious comparison, there is a great sense of urgency among the socialitst states of the third world. Be it a Chinese "Great Leap Forward" or a Cuban "Revolutionary Offensive," there exists a holier-than-thou attitude toward the USSR, expressed in the desire to build a purer form of socialism than the Soviets, and in half the time. There is a desire to achieve development, socialism, and, ultimately, communism all at the same time. The holier-than-thou attitude is translated into a tremendous concern with the morality of the Revolution in all its aspects. This "moral imperative" was the basis of the justification for the shift to moral incentives in Cuba after 1966.

Whatever the moral basis of the new emphasis, it must also be considered in practical economic and political terms. By the mid-1960s, Cuba was in a dismal economic position. The previous consumptionist policies and the abortive attempt at industrialization had cost dearly. In spite of the sacrifice in consumption and the gradual increase in accumulation, the average proportion of GNP devoted to investment in 1962–1965 was about equal to the prerevolutionary proportion. In spite of the return to agriculture, the accumulated debt of miscalculations was quite serious and continued to exert a negative influence, evident, for instance, in the growing balance of trade. The tasks of the late 1960s were to minimize imports of consumer goods even more, and to keep imports of capital goods flowing while attempting to expand exports by increasing production and maximizing the surplus to be squeezed out of the population.

In 1968, the sector of private farmers that had managed to escape from bearing the costs of development received their own share. The Revolutionary Offensive eliminated, or at least sharply reduced, the agricultural free market, both a source of extra income to the farmers and of supplies for the black market. It also crushed a small but rapidly growing urban sector composed of tiny businesses, handicrafts and service shops that had benefited from the scarcity, black market, and the state inefficiency. Rationing was expanded even more in the late 1960s to include gasoline, sugar, and bread.

Labor mobilization gradually increased, reaching a peak with the Revolutionary Offensive. This was in preparation for the climactic mobilization of the 1970 sugar harvest, a species of holy war in which every Cuban was viewed as a crusader engaged in a great moral-political-economic task. In the political arena, all dissidency within the official criteria was to be rapidly suppressed, as the "microfaction" affair against the old-guard Communists, led again by Escalante, exemplified (for details see chapter 4).

But before all these increased pressures were built up, the Cuban government had managed to open a safety valve for the potential dissident or discontent: the Miami airlift sponsored by the U.S. government. Certainly, this was an efficient, nonviolent alternative to that of using force.

From a purely economic point of view, the combination of mobilization and moral stimuli could be viewed as a functional adaptation to the realities of an economy that had to restrict its consumption and increase its production: a policy designed for a situation of scarcity in which material incentives are no longer available or are considered too expensive. By meeting moral demands, one seeks to maintain mobilization, while simultaneously increasing the cost burden the society must bear.

From the political point of view, moral incentives can be seen as a way out of the dilemma of substituting traditional coercive methods for demand satisfaction as a means for achieving political support, by creating a mental state of generalized affectivity and commitment. It completely reverses the classical-liberal theory of political obligation, which sees affective commitment as a product of a previous incremental process of material reward: instead of authority being based on a social contract entered into by advantage-seeking individuals, it is based on a preexistent "moral community," which transcends the individual members.

The notion of a moral community is critical to an understanding of the control role of moral incentives, for the moral incentive is a double-edged sword. On the one hand, it is a positive noncoercive means of generating support; on the other, it has a high coercive potential. Due to the secularization of social relations in the West, we tend to forget the tremendous coercive potential of moralized communities. Indeed, in such a community, moral pressure is often a more potent sanction than force. In a moral community, conformity is rewarded by abstract moral signs of approval, whereas deviance is punished by public shame, or, in the extreme, excommunication. Thus, in Cuba today the various revolutionary organizations maintain a moral vigilance on the population and hold up to public criticism all signs of deviant behavior, whereas those who reject the Revolution are excommunicated—they become *gusanos* ("worms"), who are stripped of their material possessions, sent to work in agriculture, and subjected to humiliation before they leave the "Cuban Paradise" for the "Miami Hell."

Moral communities, of course, cannot be simply declared; they must be constructed. In contemporary Cuba, this end is sought in the dual process known as mobilization and formation. This process is applied on a generational basis. If there is a privileged class in contemporary Cuba, it is the youth. One of the social services that continues to be heavily supported is education, through the building of schools, granting of scholarships, free student housing and dining halls, etc. One of the chief goals of the educational apparatus is formation: the creation of a social consciousness that will convert the young person into a self-mobilizing adult. He learns that his present privileged position carries with it the moral obligation to form himself into a selfless man morally committed to struggle for the good of his collectivity. Ideally, he will be motivated by this moral commitment alone, thus rendering force or material reward unnecessary.

With adults, the process is reversed. Through various means, they are mobilized into collective work projects, the experience of which it is hoped will create formation. But, as they are products of the previous "degenerate" society, their mobilization is more complex and their formation of consciousness is expected to be imperfect. Positive and negative moral incentives are employed. These are supported by a much diminished, but nonetheless real, level of material reward in the matter of job security and social services. In a few cases, individual material incentives may be used when their need is urgent; such is the case of housing built for farmers (in the Green Belt around Havana) who decided to integrate their private farms with the state program, or that of professional cane cutters whose services were badly needed in the 1970 sugar crop and as an incentive received higher, guaranteed annual wage rates. Finally, if these means fail, the more direct coercive powers of the state are brought to bear. Thus, in the concerted attempt to create a new type of moral community, the Cuban elite is betting first of all on the youth. Whereas there has been a decided shift to moral incentives, in dealing with adults the more classic carrot-and-stick approach to social control is employed, although recent years have seen more and more reliance on the stick.

The increasing utilization of coercive means points up another aspect of contemporary Cuba. At the same time that there is an increasing attempt to moralize the society, it is also being increasingly militarized. As stated, the proclamation of the Revolutionary Offensive was also a declaration of quasi-moral war. In a real sense, all Cubans are now considered to be soldiers in a vast producing army. As such, they are expected to adhere to the traditional military values of discipline and devotion to duty. Each is a soldier on permanent alert ready to join his brigade and fight with muscle and tool to win the economic war. The image of the army has become the image of society.

The militarization of the Cuban society is evidenced not only in rhetoric and style, but in the pivotal position that the regular army has assumed in all spheres. The new Cuban army is a multifunctional entity, which performs critical political and economic tasks as well as its traditional military role of national defense. The army is an important institution of social control; an important instrumentality for the mobilization of human and material resources; and an important source of technological skill and expertise. It has become a critical social institution and, therefore, an important source of political power.

In the orthodox socialist states, military institutions are subordinate instrumentalities subjected to strict party control. In Cuba, if anything, the roles have been reversed. All indications are that the army is the real locus of political power. The party is ostensibly the chief organ of political coordination, but its command structure is permeated at all levels by military men. Cuba's top military men hold key positions in both the army and the party, thereby guaranteeing not only the interests of the military institution, but a preponderance of military style and values.

Conclusion

Although Cuba is undoubtedly a state-socialist system, it is different from the older orthodox socialist states of Eastern Europe in many respects. In Cuba, as in other third-world socialists countries, we are witnessing the emergence of an important new variation of the classic socialist model. Although there are many important dimensions of this new phenomenon, two critical features appear to be: (a) a concerted attempt to moralize society in a profoundly new way and (b) the primacy of military organizations and values. Cuba, under the leadership of Fidel Castro, chose to attempt to resolve the multiple problems of development within the state-socialist framework. In attempting to secure that framework and cope with the ongoing problems of control, mobilization, and social costs, the Cuban leadership appears to be attempting to anchor the new state in a militarized moral community.

If the current methods of youth formation and mobilization are effective in the long run, and the government manages to keep a minimum of adult commitment by noncoercive methods in the short run, the future means of generating political support will be that of affective commitment. Furthermore, the realization (even if imperfect) of moral incentives should result in increased production and services and increased consumer goods and social services available for demand satisfaction. The state-socialist model will prove to be operative and successful, and increased demand satisfaction and affective commitment to the Revolution will make unnecessary some of the coercive methods actually used today. We may also expect a deemphasis on militarization.

On the other hand, if the experiment of moral incentives proves to be a failure with the youth or if the government is not able to keep a minimum productivity among the adults, either militarization and coercive means will increase or the leadership will be forced to return to the orthodox state-socialist model.

3 Cole Blasier

The Elimination of United States Influence

CUBA is the first Latin American country in the twentieth century to break decisively out of the United States sphere of influence.[1] Argentina, Mexico, and other Latin American nations have sometimes charted an independent course, but they have not developed such close political, economic, and military ties with a great power rival of the United States as Cuba has with the Soviet Union. The Cuban–United States break may be the single most politically significant aspect of the Cuban Revolution. Enough information is now available to explain how, and to advance hypotheses explaining why, U.S. influence was eliminated from Cuba.

Overt opposition to U.S. domination has been common in Latin America in the twentieth century, but its expression has tended to be sporadic and spotty. A few countries, such as Chile, have had a long and fairly continuous tradition of "standing up to Uncle Sam," ordinarily while maintaining a friendly or neutral relationship. However, the strongest opposition seems to come from social movements with an antiimperialist character. The most powerful of these, that is, those which actually seized the government and carried through a social revolution, in addition to the Cuban, are the Mexican and the Bolivian movements.

The Mexican Revolution had strong anti-American currents and Mexico defied U.S. intervention during World War I. Mexican independence, however, has been expressed mainly in domestic rather than foreign affairs. The Bolivian revolutionaries (MNR) had a long history of opposition to

Ernesto Betancourt, Rolando Bonachea, Philip W. Bonsal, and Carmelo Mesa-Lago were especially helpful in the preparation of this chapter, as was my research assistant, Gerald Lemega.

43

and conflict with the U.S. government before they seized power in 1952. But within less than two years, the Bolivian revolutionary government was receiving emergency assistance from the United States and, thereafter, the two countries developed a closer relationship than ever before in history.[2]

Until the Castro take-over in Cuba, Argentina had perhaps been the country most independent of U.S. influence and was sometimes a rival of the United States for leadership of the hemisphere. The two countries had a falling out during World War II when Argentina flirted with Nazi Germany, but Nazi defeats and Allied pressures eventually caused Argentina to declare war on Germany in April 1945. Thus, Cuba, led by Castro, remains the only Latin American country that has not only defied the United States but has directly opposed U.S. policies for more than a decade.

The U.S.–Cuban diplomatic break in January 1961 was comparable in many ways to Yugoslavia's break with the Soviet Union in 1948. In both cases, the junior partner withdrew from participation in a community bound together by close economic, military, and political ties. However, the USSR's commanding influence in Eastern Europe was scarcely four years old at the time, whereas by 1959 the United States had dominated the Caribbean, and, less so, South America, for more than half a century. Castro's defection may have been more costly economically and strategically for the United States than Tito's defection from the USSR. But up to 1970, Castro's defiance had not yet had the political repercussions in the Western Hemisphere comparable to Tito's in Eastern Europe.

An explanation can be found for the break between Cuba and the United States through an examination of developments between the years 1956 and 1961, interpreted in the light of the relationship between the two countries as it developed after 1898. The year 1956 is selected as a starting point because, in December of that year, Castro landed his small force on the island of Cuba to overthrow Batista, an effort that was eventually brought to a successful conclusion on January 1, 1959, when the dictator fled the country. The year 1961 is selected as the end of the period of study, since in January of that year, the United States and Cuba broke diplomatic relations, and U.S.–Cuban tensions culminated in the Bay of Pigs invasion some three months later. The latter event left U.S. policies aimed at overthrowing Castro in ruins.

Castro and the United States Before 1959

In view of the often decisive role the United States has played in Cuba, Castro devoted little attention to the United States in his public statements before 1959. Castro, who apparently did not know a great deal about U.S.–Cuban relations, was ideologically immature in terms of his views on foreign policy, as the Marxists might put it, or "idealistic" and "utopian," as he himself has put it.[3] More important, Castro seemed to know instinctively how dangerous it was to attack the United States openly. As he explained later, "radical revolutionaries . . . do not announce programs that might unite all our enemies on a single front."[4]

Castro dealt briefly with U.S. agricultural and public utility interests in Cuba in his speech, *La historia me absolverá,* in 1953 and in his political program from the Sierra Maestra published in 1957. In the speech, Castro points out that "over half of the best lands under cultivation are in the hands of foreigners" and that "the lands of the United Fruit Company and the West Indian Company stretch from coast to coast in the [Oriente] province."[5] In the program announced from the Sierra, Castro called for land grants to tenant farmers working less than 170 acres, indemnifying owners out of rents over a ten-year period. He also added a provision to guarantee small sugar growers a minimum share of the annual quota at a minimum price. Similarly, without mentioning the United States itself, Castro called for the nationalization of the power and telephone companies.[6] Such provisions could be interpreted as a foreshadowing of the profound impact the Revolution was to have on U.S. private interests, although direct attacks on U.S. imperialism were notably absent from Castro's statements. His assertion that "the country cannot continue to beg, on bended knee, for miracles from a few 'golden calves'," suggests that he "felt" more than he said.[7]

Castro succeeded in bolstering his position in the United States by a series of sympathetic articles in U.S. magazines, such as *Life, Look,* and *Coronet. Castro* appealed to the democratic idealism of the U.S. middle class in *Coronet* by stressing his struggle for freedom and "representative government" against the Batista dictatorship. He said that civic associations, including the Lions and Rotarians, would help in preparations for honest elections for the new government. Castro solemnly added, "Let me say for the record that we have no plans for the expropriation or nationalization of foreign investment here," explicitly calling for a halt to talk of the nationalization of public utilities.[8] Castro tried at that time not to arouse the animosity of foreign investors in Cuba. Later, he explained, "Naturally we were in the middle of a struggle where it was not at all practical to say exactly what we intended to do with those businesses. So what we did was to treat them with all the cunning that was necessary under the circumstances."[9]

Castro wanted a sympathetic public in the United States partly because the country served as one of the major bases for mounting resistance to Batista. When his men were training in Mexico for a landing in Cuba, Castro raised funds among anti-Batista Cuban exiles in Bridgeport, Union

City, New York, Miami, Tampa, and Key West.[10] Former Cuban President
Prío Socarrás supplied forty or fifty thousand dollars, part of which was
used to buy the ship *Granma* (which carried the revolutionaries to Cuba in
1956) from U.S. residents in Mexico.[11] Batista never ceased to make official complaints about rebel activities in the United States and U.S. authorities convicted some 170 Cubans of violating U.S. neutrality legislation and
seized arms, munitions, and other materials valued at in excess of half a
million dollars.[12] However, Ernesto Betancourt, a Castro spokesman in
Washington, estimates that collections in the United States for the July 26
movement did not exceed $100,000 and that most arms shipments arrived
too late to be of much help.[13] Castro relied heavily on U.S. arms captured
or stolen from Batista's troops.

The February 1958 indictment of former President Prío for conspiring
to violate neutrality laws dramatically focused public attention on U.S.
military assistance to Batista. The assistance was under the terms of the
mutual defense assistance agreements signed with Prío in 1952, just before
he was forcefully deposed by Batista. Under its terms, the United States
made military assistance grants to Batista of about one and a half million
dollars a year from 1954 through 1956, and the amounts doubled to over
three million dollars each in 1957 and 1958.[14] The equipment supplied included rifles, grenades, rockets, tanks, machine guns, and bombs.[15] In 1958,
the U.S. military mission in Havana included about eleven men from the
army, nine from the navy, and eleven from the air force.[16] The agreement
provided that this military assistance was for the "defense of the Western
Hemisphere" and would not be used for other purposes without the prior
agreement of the United States.

Castro had long expressed his strong opposition to "mediation or intervention of any kind from another nation in the internal affairs of Cuba"
and had openly called on the United States "to suspend all shipments of
arms to Cuba."[17] In September 1957 the Department of State and Ambassador Earl E. T. Smith brought the matter of the possible misuse of
U.S. military assistance to the attention of Cuban officials in Washington
and Havana, and U.S. concern was already delaying the implementation
of the agreement.[18] Ernesto Betancourt and other Cubans in the United
States who opposed Batista informed such congressmen as Charles Porter
and Adam Clayton Powell of the fact that Batista was using U.S. arms
against the Cuban resistance in contravention of the provisions of the mutual defense agreement. Also, public opinion in the United States had been
aroused against Latin American dictators by revelations of Trujillo's role
in the assassination of Jesús Galíndez, an anti-Trujillo author residing in
the United States, and against Batista because of censorship, his abrogation
of constitutional guarantees, and his sometimes brutal political tactics.

The foregoing set the stage for the confrontation that took place in a meeting of the Senate Foreign Relations Committee on March 5, 1958. Senator Mike Mansfield closely questioned Roy R. Rubottom, the assistant secretary of state for American Republic Affairs, about arms support for Batista. Mansfield put his finger on the contradictions in U.S. policy of arming Batista and imprisoning Prío: "A government which came into power in Cuba by usurpation, and which maintains a military dictatorship, can buy arms or have arms given to it by the United States, but a constitutionally elected President is put in jail for trying to assist in the overthrow of that government."[19] Under pressure from the Foreign Relations Committee and in the light of other political considerations, the Department of State suspended a shipment of arms to Batista on March 14, 1958. The suspension took on the more permanent character of an arms embargo in April when Secretary Dulles announced publicly: "We allow arms to go to other countries primarily to meet international defense requirements. . . . We don't like to have those go where the purpose is to conduct a civil war."[20]

However, the Cuban Resistance movement failed to terminate the U.S. military missions in Havana, which "train and support the armed forces of the dictatorship to kill Cubans and to fight against those who struggle to liberate the fatherland." The Department of State refused to stop the missions on the grounds that "governments and administrations change . . . but hemispheric defense needs present a constant problem the solution of which calls for a cooperative program carried out on a steady, long-range basis."[21]

United States policy remained, for the most part, indecisive all through 1958. After the arms embargo in March, substantial U.S. support to bolster Batista was no longer possible, and President Eisenhower himself had ruled out supporting a "self-enriching and corrupt dictator."[22] The possibility of U.S. armed intervention arose when U.S. nationals became involved in the Cuban civil war. United States troops occupied the water supply source just outside the limits of Guantánamo naval base very briefly and then were withdrawn, neither the rebels nor the United States wanting a confrontation. Also, forty-three U.S. nationals were kidnapped in July when Castro became suspicious that the United States might be directly involved in military operations against the guerrillas, but they were gradually released when the United States protested. Tension arose in October, too, when other U.S. nationals fell into the guerrillas' hands. Since the United States and Castro both wanted to avoid U.S. entanglement, the incidents blew over.

Another, though less likely, possibility would have been to swing U.S. support behind Castro. However, the strategy and tactics of Castro and the

United States were never harmonious, and the latter's long-time collaboration with Batista made that almost impossible. Moreover, Ambassador Smith's indiscreet confidence to the press in January 1958 that the United States would never "be able to do business with Castro" made such a possibility doubly unlikely.[23] United States officials had long been concerned about what might happen in Cuba after Batista's inevitable fall from power. They hoped for an orderly transition to a successor government, and Castro was not their choice to lead it.

The United States decided tentatively and too late to promote the establishment of a third force, an alternative to both Batista and Castro. Ambassador Smith had hoped, many thought naïvely, that this could be accomplished through free elections, but the fraudulent elections of November 1958 put even his hopes to rest. As a kind of desperate, last-minute try, on December 9 the Department of State sent former Ambassador William D. Pawley on an unofficial and secret mission to talk Batista into resigning in favor of a military junta. Pawley said the men "we had selected . . . were Colonel Barquín, Colonel Borbonnet, General Díaz Tamayo, Bosch of the 'Bacardi' firm and one other . . . all enemies of Batista."[24] Pawley blamed the Department of State for not permitting him to link the proposal directly to the U.S. government, which allegedly caused Batista to refuse the offer. On December 15, the department sent Ambassador Smith to ask Batista to resign, indicating that "there were Cuban elements which could salvage the rapidly deteriorating situation."[25] Ambassador Smith, however, was not authorized to tell Batista who they were.

Castro had long feared and spoken out against the imposition of a military junta or any form of foreign mediation. As a Castro representative in Washington, Betancourt protested the efforts of Ambassador Smith and U.S. military officers to change what the United States described as a policy of nonintervention.[26] As further evidence of U.S. efforts to block Castro, Betancourt quoted William Wieland, director of the Office of Caribbean and Mexican Affairs, as remarking on the eve of his departure for Cuba on December 23 that the government that succeeded Batista should be independent of Castro.[27]

By the end of 1958, the revolutionary forces had gained the upper hand and Batista decided to flee, setting up in his place a provisional military government under General Cantillo and headed by a civilian. When Castro first heard the news, he reportedly "exploded": "This is a cowardly betrayal. They are trying to prevent the triumph of the Revolution."[28] In his first broadcast after Batista's flight, Castro violently protested that the coup snatched "victory away from the people" and he called for a general strike to force the unconditional surrender of Batista's forces.[29] Given his

personal history and recent years in the Sierra, Castro probably felt alienated from the Cuban and U.S. establishments. No doubt, too, he feared the
United States as a likely obstacle to his political objectives, however amorphous they may have been at that time. In unsuccessfully attempting to
deny Castro's political victory, the United States confirmed and solidified
his suspicions.

Implications of Castro's Early Strategies for the United States

Batista's flight led to popular rejoicing throughout the island and Castro,
the symbol of forceful resistance against Batista, became the undisputed
hero of the moment. Castro capitalized on the popular euphoria by receiving the plaudits of the populace in an overland procession to Havana which
lasted the better part of a week. The Department of State decided to make
the best of the *fait accompli* despite its misgivings and lingering doubts. Besides, Castro had committed himself squarely to the implementation of the
Cuban Constitution of 1940, had denied any plans for expropriating foreign property, and had said little for or against the United States. As a
result, the United States promptly recognized the new government, headed
by Castro's designee, Manuel Urrutia, and recalled Ambassador Smith
whose antipathy for Castro was already well known. Philip W. Bonsal,
then U.S. Ambassador to Bolivia, was selected to succeed him.

The insurrectional phase of the Cuban Revolution came to an end with
Batista's flight, but it was only the first major phase. At that time, Castro
had several vital assets, the most important of which was control of an effective, though relatively small, guerrilla force. (Castro's armed units numbered only a few hundred men until the concluding months of the resistance.[30] And even toward the end, when their numbers mushroomed as
Cubans rushed to Castro's bandwagon, the regular army was still far
larger.) Also, Castro was widely recognized as the leader of the armed
resistance against Batista. He had achieved this position by his astute use
of the foreign press and through the resistance radio, "Radio Rebelde," as
much as through the guerrilla action against Batista. No other person enjoyed his immense personal prestige.

However, Castro was weak in many respects. In the first place, he had
never controlled the Cuban resistance, particularly in the cities and in rural
areas other than those occupied by his own forces at the eastern end of
the island. Secondly, he did not control a political party as such. Several
of the anti-Batista political parties, the students, and even organized labor
had larger and more firmly established organizations. Castro lacked a
clearly defined base of popular support in the sense of a political program

tied to the interests of specific Cuban groups. Toppling Batista was one thing, gaining control of the government and establishing his political authority in Cuba were quite another.

It is doubtful that Castro had initially planned any grand domestic political strategy. In fact, hindsight suggests that he developed his strategy incrementally during the early months of 1959. In any case, the strategy he developed placed important limits on the nature of his relations with the United States, not to mention the domestic course of the Revolution.

First, Castro sought to secure control of the armed forces and to destroy the remnants of Batista's influence in Cuba. The rebel army arrested General Cantillo who Batista had left in charge of the armed forces. Colonel Ramón Barquín took charge briefly. He was a former Batista official who had been imprisoned after an unsuccessful military coup to depose the dictator, and a man the United States had once considered as a possible alternative to Castro. Castro ordered Camilo Cienfuegos, his representative, to take over from Barquín. In the next few weeks, Castro's forces conducted a series of spectacular trials leading to the imprisonment or execution of hundreds of persons charged with crimes under Batista. Widespread popular revulsion toward Batista and the euphoria following his flight made the political elimination of the *Batistianos* relatively easy. The procedures used in the trials, some conducted in public in the heat of national emotion, were widely criticized in the United States. In fact, the trials were among the first important sources of friction in Castro's formal relations with the United States, and Castro demonstrated great sensitivity to criticism of the conduct of the trials by U.S. journalists and politicians.

Much more difficult was establishing his primacy over other groups in military and political opposition to Batista. By using his immense personal prestige and the rebel army, and by skillfully manipulating the public media, Castro faced down other armed units, including those of the Student Revolutionary Directorate. Many of the leaders of the political opposition to Batista who were not part of the July 26 movement were needed and quite naturally took over posts in the government in early 1959. At first, Castro's strategy was to remain outside the civilian government and exercise power as head of the armed forces. However, early in February a decree concentrated legislative and executive power in the cabinet, and Castro took over as prime minister on February 16. During the course of the year he discredited and separated leaders from their popular bases of support one by one. By the end of the year, the once independent student and labor movements were bent to his will. Many of the eliminated leaders were well thought of in or had close ties with the United States.

Castro gained control of the government without recourse to free elections. Few people have doubted that Castro could have been elected by an overwhelming majority of Cubans, at least initially. However, Castro may have reasoned that to follow such a course would have meant a return to the corrupt politicking of the past and would have established his dependence on the traditional electoral and legislative process, a dependence he was not prepared to accept. In order to carry through his audacious challenge to the old system and to other groups of the political center and left, he needed to develop other sources of popular support. Identifying with the needs and aspirations of the rural and urban poor, Castro put through a series of economic measures at the expense of the middle class. In addition, he moved closer to and made use of the PSP (the Cuban Communist party), at that time one of the best organized parties in the country, though with limited popular support.

All of the above developments were viewed first with concern and later with alarm in the United States. The public trials and executions of the so-called *Batistianos* shocked Americans whose historical traditions and personal experience made it difficult for them to understand the passionate and violent forces unleashed by a social revolution. Many of the leaders of government in 1959 who became the political victims of Castro's maneuvers were the very persons on whom U.S. leaders had counted for cooperation. Castro's cavalier postponement of his pledge to hold free elections flew in the face of U.S. political ideals. And his willingness to collaborate with the Cuban Communists alarmed public opinion in the United States where the cold war psychology prevailed.

In April 1959, Castro first visited the United States as Cuba's undisputed leader. This came about in an unusual way. The American Society of Newspaper Editors invited him to give a luncheon address without discussing the matter with appropriate officials in the Department of State. The visit might have gone smoothly if Castro had simply come to Washington for the day, given the luncheon address, and then returned home. Instead, he brought with him a planeload of high-ranking officials, particularly those concerned with financial and economic matters, and remained for several days, thus giving the impression of an official visit. The Department of State did not have much time to prepare for the visit nor did it have the opportunity to pick its own date for a meeting, as is usually the case when one country plays host to the head of another government. President Eisenhower was irritated over the invitation and was out of town when Castro was in Washington. Nevertheless, the Department of State arranged several meetings at which opportunities were provided to discuss substantive issues of mutual interest.

There was much speculation in Cuba about whether the visit would result in a U.S. program of economic assistance for Cuba, since the issue would serve as an indicator of future relations between the two countries.

Cuban Minister of Finance Rufo López-Fresquet hoped to arrange for economic assistance and was encouraged when he and other officials with economic responsibilities were asked to make the trip. However, on the way to the United States, Castro dampened his hopes about any immediate results when he told him:

> Look Rufo, I don't want this trip to be like that of other new Latin American leaders who always come to the U.S. to ask for money. I want this to be a good-will trip. Besides, the Americans will be surprised. And when we go back to Cuba, they will offer us aid without our asking for it. Consequently, we will be in a better bargaining position.[31]

In any case, as López-Fresquet recounted later, Assistant Secretary of State Roy R. Rubottom, "offered to help us carry out our economic plans," but "not being able to say anything else, I told him we had already solved our immediate problems and we preferred to wait until we made our long-term plans before making a presentation of needs."[32] Apparently, the United States did not push the matter further and neither did the Cubans. (On his visit to Buenos Aires shortly thereafter, Castro publicly proposed a U.S. economic assistance plan of $30 billion to Latin America, but without specific reference to aid for Cuba.)

Actually, during Castro's visit, Vice President Richard Nixon had a three-hour talk with Castro on Capitol Hill and wrote a confidential memorandum asserting that Castro was "either incredibly naive about Communism or under Communist discipline." At that time, however, Nixon believed that his view was a minority of one within the administration and, particularly, within the Latin American branch of the Department of State.[33] In any event, the Department of State's willingness to talk about economic assistance was one thing, and the granting of authorization for aid was another. United States suspicion and distrust of Castro during his resistance years lingered on and was heightened by the events of early 1959. The United States may well have been prepared to consider seriously large-scale aid to Cuba at this time, but no doubt only after a clarification of a number of pending issues and guarantees with regard to Castro's political direction.

The whole issue of aid is purely academic since the two parties never sat down to serious negotiations on this point. For his part, Castro could hardly have been oblivious to U.S. suspicions, given his pre-1959 experience and the interview with Vice President Nixon. And, surely, he must have suspected that certain conditions would have to be fulfilled before large-scale aid would be extended. Nevertheless, it is difficult to find conclusive evidence to bear out the conclusion expressed by López-Fresquet that Castro never intended to ask for U.S. aid.[34] It would be interesting to know just when Castro decided that close political relations with the United States, a *sine qua non* of extensive economic assistance, were incompatible with his revolutionary objectives.

The United States: Obstacle to Castro's Revolutionary Goals?

Castro's objectives for Cuba, that is, the shape he hoped Cuban society would take after Batista's fall, were vague not only before 1959 but during the early months of the new regime as well. In fact, the Castro regime developed less from advance blueprints than through day-to-day accretion. Nevertheless, by the end of 1959, Tad Szulc of the *New York Times* was able to report:

> In the year since the demise of the Batista dictatorship, Cuba has become a full-fledged revolutionary state whose regime is determined to refashion the country in a new image as speedily as possible. . . . The Cuban revolution addressed itself . . . to the task of initiating sweeping economic and social changes at the expense of the restoration of democratic institutions battered by the Batista dictatorship.[35]

As Castro admitted later, his early political ideas were not truly Marxist and his position in coming to power was still somewhat "idealistic" and "utopian." He did not announce in early 1959 the revolutionary reforms introduced later, probably because they had not yet crystallized in his mind. And, in any case, he believed, and it appears correctly, that it was politically astute not to elaborate his ideas at that time (see earlier discussion). Yet it is already clear that Castro's vague objectives vaulted high and that he would not be content with the gradual reform of traditional Cuban institutions. Instead, he sought to establish a commanding place in Cuban history through a comprehensive social transformation. Some sense of his aspirations comes through in his claim to the multitudes who assembled in Central Park during his visit to the United States in April 1959, "The Cuban Revolution has been, in our opinion, the most generous and the purest Revolution which has been carried out in the history of the World."[36]

However, any comprehensive transformation of Cuban society faced not only the opposition of entrenched Cuban interests, but U.S. vested interests as well. Castro gave his own slant to this matter in August 1959:

The campaigns in the U.S. and the constant charge of communism form part of a grand conspiracy of vested interests against the effort of a nation to move ahead, to achieve its economic independence and political stability.[37]

Whether the Castro version was correct or not, few would deny that U.S.–Cuban relations for more than half a century had resulted in closely interlocking social structures. The two societies were intimately related, especially in trade and investment. In a sense, U.S. interests occupied, to use a Soviet expression, the "commanding heights" of the Cuban economy. The United States bought about two-thirds of Cuba's exports and paid, under the quota system, large premiums, sometimes approaching nearly twice the world-market price for Cuban sugar. In exchange, Cuba offered the United States tariff preferences, which was only one of several reasons why the U.S. sold Cuba nearly 70 percent of its imports. United States interests controlled a declining, but still large, percentage (about 40 percent) of raw sugar production, 90 percent of telephone and electric services, and 50 percent of public service railroads. In addition, U.S. banks had about 25 percent of all bank deposits in the nation.[38] Clearly, these powerful U.S. interests stood in the way of any comprehensive economic transformation undertaken at their expense with the full weight of tradition, law, and U.S. policies to back them up.

It gradually became clear that Castro was not only seeking a fundamental transformation of Cuban society, but also of the character of that society's relationship with the United States. For reasons of its historical origins, its propinquity to the United States, and the nature of its economy, Cuba had fallen under U.S. influence more than almost any other Latin American country, with the possible exception of Panama. Cuba had grown so dependent on the United States as to raise doubts about the long-term stability of the arrangement in a world of rising nationalist sentiment.

Take, for example, the special relationship created under the sugar quota. In the 1950s the United States consistently took the largest share of the Cuban sugar crop, ordinarily at prices above those of the world market. The U.S. government fixed this quota from year to year in accordance with the law, and the amount purchased and the price paid had an immense impact on the Cuban economy. Except during the Korean and Suez crises, Cuban exporters benefited from the price differential during the 1950s. The benefit to Cuban exporters of quota price arrangements often totaled $100 million a year, and rose to $153 million in 1959.[39] The political power that the United States wielded on the quota issue put the Cuban government at the mercy of the U.S. authorities. The U.S. government secured this negotiating advantage partly through this "subsidy" paid by the North American consumer to the Cuban sugar industry. Furthermore, the quota system had several aspects: one was that the quota assigned to domestic U.S. producers and the tariff barrier protected high-cost producers in the United States. Also, the premium prices paid Cuban sugar producers went, in part, to U.S.-owned sugar companies in Cuba, which accounted for about 40 percent of Cuba's raw sugar production.

In the early negotiations, the United States secured, as a concession from the Cubans for the quota and premium price arrangements, preferential entry of U.S. goods in the Cuban market. The results of this arrangement, and more importantly, the U.S. competitive advantage in many products, even in the absence of tariff protection, were Cuban dependence on U.S. manufactures and limited development of domestic industry in the face of U.S. competition.

The United States exercised an overriding political influence in Cuba from the time of the Spanish-American War up to January 1, 1959, when President Batista fled the island. General Leonard Wood, the U.S. commander in the occupation of Cuba after the Spanish-American War, presided at the first session of the Cuban constitutional convention, and the United States government forced the delegates to include the so-called Platt Amendment as part of their constitution by convincing them that refusal to accept American demands insured the continuation of the American occupation.[40] The Platt Amendment made Cuba a protectorate of the United States by limiting Cuba's treaty-making and fiscal powers, and gave the United States "the right to intervene for the preservation of Cuban independence, the maintenance of government adequate for the protection of life, property, and individual liberty."

The United States exercised these rights through military intervention, military and civilian advisers, or through the U.S. ambassador from 1902 until 1934 when the Platt Amendment was officially abrogated. The United States made and unmade Cuban governments up to 1934. The unwillingness of the United States to recognize the Grau San Martín government in 1933 and early 1934 was an important reason for its downfall, and the U.S. ambassador contributed to Fulgencio Batista's rise to political dominance in the mid-1930s.[41] The U.S. ambassador continued to be regarded, by many at least, as the "second most important man in Cuba" and the last U.S. ambassador to Cuba before Castro made a formal call on President Batista to request his resignation.[42]

In view of the above, is it any wonder that Castro aspired to a fundamental change in U.S. relations with Cuba? Observers of many different political persuasions believe that the U.S.–Cuban relationship before 1959 was fundamentally inequitable. But, whether it was or not is less significant than the fact that many Cubans, including Castro, passionately and profoundly believed that it was. Castro put the Cuban nationalist attitude in a nutshell in his visit to the U.S. in 1959: "In economic and political matters relations have been solely unilateral . . . because one party had decided our political principles and always the arduous economic problem."[43]

Castro perceived the United States as a potential threat to his revolutionary aspirations in a more ominous sense. After Batista's fall and the prompt dispatch of his followers through execution, imprisonment, and exile, the major initial threats to Castro were the leaders of other groups in opposition to Batista. Within a year, Castro had largely subjected them to his will or eliminated them from influence in the government or politics. Yet these elements still represented a potential threat in the event of serious political or economic difficulties. And this threat would be magnified should such groups secure the support of the United States and attempt to overthrow Castro by force.

Castro soon developed what appeared in the United States to be almost a paranoiac fear of enemies at home and abroad. As time progressed, he described the threats to Cuba in increasingly strident and dramatic tones, lashing back at his opponents frequently and with vehemence. When asked by a journalist in January 1960 why Cuba had introduced militias, Castro replied, "Because of the obvious international conspiracy against Cuba, the insolent threats, the plans of the monopolists, war criminals and the international oligarchy to approach and destroy us."[44] Castro stressed that militias were needed not simply to deal with domestic oppositions, "The large landowners and war criminals do not have sufficient strength . . . to threaten danger, . . . the only hope is to mobilize . . . foreign resources."[45]

Castro was well aware of the threat the United States could pose, as demonstrated by U.S. support of counterrevolutionaries in Guatemala in 1953 and 1954. It must be remembered, too, that Castro had struck out on an audacious and risky course in the face of much opposition within the Cuban middle classes that formed the traditional cadres of Cuban government and politics. Also, his political and economic measures put him under immense personal and political pressures. All this helps to explain his extreme sensitivity to criticism from U.S. politicians, journalists, and others.

Nor were the attacks on his regime purely verbal. Mounting opposition among émigrés took the form of incursions on Cuba territory and anti-Castro propaganda, which paralleled the crystallization of the opposition in Cuba. Castro played up these incidents and U.S. involvement in them in order to mobilize support at home. In response to Castro's accusations, the United States argued in a lengthy press statement on October 27, 1959, that extensive efforts had been made to enforce the neutrality act and deal with specific Cuban charges, including the question of air incursions. On November 2, 1959, the Department of Justice announced that special measures were being undertaken to enforce these laws. In late October and early November, the departments of State and Justice arranged to tighten up the enforcement of U.S. laws to prevent aliens from using U.S. territory as a "base of operations for starting or futhering civil strife in Cuba."[46] And yet, Castro remained skeptical about U.S. intentions with regard to forays from the mainland. Having once mounted a revolutionary expedition against Batista himself, he was well aware of his own vulnerability in this respect. In fact, Castro contrasted his own isolation in organizing the *Granma* expedition with the immense resources that he believed lay at the disposal of the rapidly growing Cuban opposition.

An analysis of Castro's position in terms of the balance of international and national forces, after he had overthrown Batista and subdued his rivals, shows that the greatest potential threat was the United States. Quite apart from possible links with the anti-Castro underground, the United States was the only power in the Western Hemisphere that could threaten him. No other great power friendly to the United States could so so, the United States could see to that. Other Latin American countries were either unwilling to oppose Castro or, as in the case of Trujillo in the Dominican Republic, lacked the capacity. To be sure, the United States became the main enemy, taking over in this sense the role assigned Batista earlier, against which Castro could rally and unite the Cuban people.

The fact that the United States posed the greatest *potential* threat to Castro, regarding the possible links with his domestic opposition as well as the external pressures the former was capable of exerting, does not mean that the United States actually did threaten Castro or use these pressures in 1959 and early 1960. There were many critical voices in Washington during these months but the United States government was relatively accommodating, certainly in comparison with the policies inaugurated in March 1960 (see below). Castro's reason for concern during this early period was not so much due to what the United States had done, as to what it could do. Castro surely knew better than Washington what he wanted and he estimated, correctly as it turned out, that his policies would encounter stubborn resistance. In a way, he was already responding to what the United States would do, not to what it had done, thereby helping to fulfill his own dire prophecies.

Castro's opposition at home also anticipated strong U.S. opposition to Castro's revolutionary innovations. Like Castro, his opponents over-estimated U.S. effectiveness in opposing the revolutionary drive. Both sides expected more of the United States than the bankrupt policies that ended in the Bay of Pigs fiasco. As Ambassador Bonsal has put it, "A conviction that the U.S. would take care of the situation sapped the activism of much of the opposition."[47] Mr. Bonsal believes that this fact helps explain why Castro was able to "revolutionize" Cuban society with so little domestic resistance.

Castro's Independent Course

Castro inherited the complex and intimately related web of interests and practices that constituted the U.S.–Cuban relationship. He found that relationship unacceptable, and Castro, not the United States, first sought to change it. In his efforts to resist what he felt was unwarranted U.S. interference, Castro had several means of opposing U.S. pressure or, if you wish, retaliating.

The first was his capacity to regulate and seize U.S. private investments in Cuba. According to his count, these were worth some $800 million, and according to U.S. figures about $1 billion.[48] United States investments in Cuba were at Castro's mercy—hostages, so to speak. The second major weapon was his potential for getting extrahemispheric support, that is, for bringing Soviet economic, political, and military power into play against the United States. The following pages deal with Castro's implementation of these two means of opposition to the United States.

There are some observers who believe that fomenting social revolution and guerrilla wars in other Latin American countries was another means Castro had of resisting the United States. Be that as it may, Castro has actually had little success fomenting revolutions elsewhere in Latin America (see chapter 5).

Seeking Extrahemispheric Support

In view of Cuba's political, strategic, and economic vulnerability, and Castro's ambitious social and national objectives, it is no wonder that he sought an extrahemispheric counterweight to U.S. influence. What is surprising is that he did not cultivate relations with the USSR, or the latter with him, earlier. The first official Soviet representative in residence, a Tass correspondent, did not come to Cuba until December 1959. Diplomatic relations—broken by Batista in early 1952—were not formally restored until May 1960, nearly a year and a half after Castro's march into Havana.

Castro needed arms to realize his larger purposes, one of which was to protect himself against domestic opposition and possible foreign intervention as the Revolution deepened. Another was that Castro's objectives of supporting revolutionary forces in the Caribbean, especially against traditional military dictatorships, meant arming expeditionary forces against neighboring governments. Early expeditions, such as that against the Dominican Republic in mid-1959, became a heightening source of friction with the United States.

Castro opened negotiations for arms in Europe in the early spring of 1959, and with the United States shortly thereafter.[49] In fact, he wished to spend some $9 million to purchase U.S. destroyers and other military equipment. The United States, however, insisted on keeping the arms embargo (introduced under Batista) in full effect. In a press statement on October 27, 1959, the Department of State explained why it had introduced in March 1958, and continued to maintain in force, an embargo against the shipment of arms to Cuba: "Armed expeditions were organized and launched against various countries, an armament race appeared imminent, and armed civil strife and terrorism continued. . . . This policy was made known to allied and friendly governments."[50]

Although accepting an embargo on U.S. arms, Castro complained bitterly about U.S. efforts to prevent Cuba from buying arms in Western Europe in a speech on March 5, 1960, the day after the French merchant ship, *La Coubre,* blew up at a Havana dock (the Cubans estimating some seventy-five dead and twice that number injured). While admitting the absence of conclusive evidence, Castro made a strong case for U.S. sabotage. Castro said that the British, referring to U.S. statements on the subject, had refused to sell him arms, and that a U.S. consul and military attaché had tried unsuccessfully to persuade an arms dealer in Belgium not to sell to Cuba. Then he warned that Cuba would buy arms where it thought best, an only slightly veiled allusion to later Soviet arms deliveries.[51]

The Department of State sharply repudiated Castro's "irresponsible" charges of U.S. participation in the *La Coubre* explosion, and tempers flared in a meeting between Secretary of State Christian Herter and the Cuban ambassador. The *New York Times* featured a report in Washington from "reliable sources" in Havana that Castro had spent more than $120 million for arms in 1959.[52]

Dependence on foreign supplies of arms was not Castro's only strategic liability. Cuba also needed imported oil since island production only covered a small fraction of domestic consumption. United States and British-owned refineries in Cuba were supplying Cuba's needs with crude oil from Venezuela and elsewhere. Cuba was falling behind in foreign exchange payments to cover these purchases and on April 19, 1960, received the first shipment of Soviet crude oil in exchange for Cuban products.[53]

Finally, Castro sought to lessen Cuba's extreme dependence on U.S. sugar purchases and to diversify its sugar markets. Talk in the United States about cutting the sugar quota made finding new markets more urgent. President Eisenhower indicates in his memoirs that cutting the quota came under consideration late in 1959.[54] In a news conference on December 10, Secretary Herter declined to discuss "punitive action" against Cuba but left no doubt that this was a possibility. One result was that Castro was complaining about "daily threats" to cut the sugar quota in January.[55] During December and January, arrangements were made for the Soviet trade exhibitions in Havana. The arrival of Soviet First Deputy Chairman Mikoyan on February 4, 1960, set the stage for Castro's negotiations with the USSR. On February 13, the two countries announced the conclusion of a trade agreement including a five-year contract by which Cuba would sell to the Soviet Union 425,000 tons of sugar in 1960 and one million tons a year from 1961 to 1964. The Soviets also granted a credit of $100 million to Cuba for the purchase of plants, machinery, materials, and technical assistance. Agreements followed with East Germany in February and Poland in March (for more details, see chapters 4 and 10).

In a television interview on March 28, Castro publicly repudiated Cuba's obligation under the Rio Treaty of 1947, a hemispheric agreement designed in part to protect the Americas from external aggression. The Rio Treaty was and is the cornerstone of U.S. security arrangements in the Western Hemisphere, and adherence to it has perhaps been, from the U.S. point of view, the most important political component of the inter-American system. Castro's overt flaunting of that agreement cut the United States to the quick, as the Department of State indicated in a press release of March 30, 1960. A few weeks later, Cuba reestablished diplomatic relations with the USSR, broken by Batista soon after his *coup d'état* in 1952.

From a purely Cuban and nationalistic point of view, there is no question that Castro could strengthen his hand vis-à-vis the United States with extracontinental support. Other Latin American leaders have strengthened their ties with extracontinental powers in order to lessen their economic and political dependence on the United States. In view of the overwhelming power of the United States, the issue was not so much whether this might be a useful political ploy in the abstract, but whether Castro or Cuba could or should pay the price that challenging traditional U.S.–Cuban relationships might entail.

Seizing U.S. Investments

It would be inaccurate to describe all, or probably even most of the seizures of property in 1959, as primarily directed against U.S. interests. The first Agrarian Reform Law, however conceived and applied, aimed at improving the lot of tenant farmers and agricultural wage laborers and attracting their political support as part of a broad program of social reform. The "interventions" in public utilities owned by U.S. interests similarly sought to supply inexpensive services to the less affluent in the cities and, to a lesser extent, in the countryside. The fact that Castro may have taken a nationalist's satisfaction in depriving U.S. interests of control of these important public services does not mean that anti-American action was his fundamental purpose. North American property owners suffered but so, too, did the Cubans.

Most damaging to U.S. private interests in Cuba, initially, were seizures of land following the promulgation of the Agrarian Reform Law of May 17, 1959. Many large American-owned properties were seized by the Cuban authorities and no compensation was paid. The burden of the U.S. case was not to deny the Cuban government the right of expropriation, but simply to insist on "prompt, adequate, and effective compensation." Thus, the Department of State protested

> the numerous actions taken by officials of that Government [the Cuban] which are considered by the United States Government to be in denial of the basic rights of ownership of United States citizens in Cuba—rights provided under both Cuban law and generally accepted international law. . . . The actions in question involve principally the seizure and occupation of land and buildings of United States citizens without court orders and frequently without any written authorization whatever, the confiscation and removal of equipment, the seizure of cattle, the cutting and removal of timber, the plowing under of pastures, all without the consent of the American owners. In many cases no inventories were taken nor were any receipts proferred nor any indication afforded that payment was intended to be made.[56]

To my knowledge the Cuban government did not then, nor has it since, provided compensation for the lands and other property seized from American citizens. Castro justified the land seizures under the Agrarian Reform Law in his speech to the United Nations in 1960:

> No one can deny that agrarian reform is one of the essential conditions for the economic development of the country. . . . More than 200,000 peasant families lived in the countryside without land on which to grow essential food crops. . . . It was an agrarian reform which was to solve the problems of the landless peasants, the problem of supplying basic foodstuffs, the problem of rural unemployment, and which was to end, once and for all, the ghastly poverty which existed in the countryside of our native land. . . .
>
> How could we solve the problem of payment? Of course, the first question that should have been asked was what were we go-

ing to pay with, rather than how. Can you gentlemen conceive of a poor, underdeveloped country, with 600,000 unemployed and such a large number of illiterates and sick people, a country whose treasury reserves have been exhausted, and which has contributed to the economy of a powerful country with one billion dollars in ten years—can you conceive of this country having the means to pay for the land affected by the Agrarian Reform Law, or the means to pay for it in the terms demanded?

What were the State Department aspirations regarding their affected interests? They wanted prompt, efficient, and just payment. . . . This means "pay now, in dollars, whatever we ask for our land."

We were not one hundred percent Communist yet [1959]. We were just becoming slightly pink. We did not confiscate land; we simply proposed to pay for it in twenty years, and in the only way in which we could pay for it: in bonds, which would mature in twenty years at four and one-half percent, or be amortized yearly.

How could we pay for the land in dollars? And the amount they asked it? It was absurd. Anyone can readily understand that, under those circumstances, we had to choose between making the agrarian reform and not making it. If we chose not to make it, the dreadful economic situation of our country would have continued indefinitely. If we decided to make it, we exposed ourselves to the hatred of the government of the powerful neighbor in the north.[57]

Actions against U.S.-owned property were not confined to agriculture. On March 3, 1959, the Cuban government took over the management of the Cuban Telephone Company formerly controlled by the International Telephone and Telegraph Corporation, and revoked a rate increase authorized toward the end of Batista's government. The Cuban government also lowered the rates for electric power charged to rural consumers by the U.S.-owned Cuban Electric Company. One year later, on March 9, 1960, Castro took over ("intervened") the management of the Moa Bay Mining Company, a wholly-owned subsidiary of the Freeport Sulphur Company. On June 10, four hotels in Havana (Hilton, Capri, National, and Havana Riviera) owned by U.S. citizens or corporations were nationalized also.

The official Cuban interpretation of "nationalization" as an international legal concept was discussed by Miguel A. D'Estéfano Pisani, a Cuban lawyer, "It is absolutely inadmissible, in view of the coexistence of two economic systems, to enunciate the principle of the sanctity of private property as a norm of international law." D'Estéfano cited numerous cases and international legal precedents to show that "there exists in international law no principle universally accepted . . . which makes adequate compensation obligatory for expropriations of a general and impersonal character." He described negotiations on indemnifications as "pending."[58]

The U.S. Response to Castro's Actions

Throughout 1959 and early 1960 the United States remained largely passive, responding through established channels to Castro's various moves, often with diplomatic protests. On January 26, 1960, President Eisenhower issued a public statement on U.S. policy, which Ambassador Philip W. Bonsal has described as one of "continued moderation and restraint on our part, denying Castro the chance to make political capital out of alleged American economic aggression."[59] The statement expressed U.S. determination to do its best to enforce the laws against anti-Castro exiles, to show its sympathy with the aspirations of the Cuban people for social reform, its continuing interest in the rights of its citizens under international law, and its willingness to resolve any conflicts in this respect through negotiations. Above all, the statement led off with a short but unequivocable reaffirmation of the policy of nonintervention in Cuban domestic affairs.

With regard to the Agrarian Reform Law of 1959, the Department of State's protests were lodged not primarily against the law itself, but against arbitrary seizures without payment. Dispossession of land from owners was made purportedly under the authority of the law, whereas, in practice, the provisions of the law regarding the procedures for seizure and compensation were flaunted. The Department of State did not insist, as Castro charged in his 1960 speech at the United Nations, on immediate cash payments in full at an U.S. evaluation, but rather sought to negotiate arrangements for compensation. The two governments never achieved sufficient mutual understanding to begin serious negotiations. As it turned out, the Castro government did not begin payments to either U.S. or Cuban owners under the provisions of the 1959 law. (A second Agrarian Reform Law was issued in 1963 and most confiscated lands—not all—ended up as part of large state owned and operated farms.)

The policy of forbearance of late 1959 and early 1960 lasted only a few months. In February and March 1960, significant events, already discussed, had taken place, for example, the conclusion of trade agreements between Cuba and the USSR and other Eastern European countries; Castro's warning that he would buy weapons from any country, implying Communist sources; the expropriation or intervention of some U.S.-owned businesses; and the growing domestic alignment of Castro with the Cuban Communists.

The furor was at its height in Cuba and the United States when President Eisenhower returned from his trip to South America in March. At this time, the United States ceased what had been an essentially defensive posture and assumed the initiative. The Eisenhower administration began to ready important measures for "bringing Castro into line." Taken together, these measures posed a mortal threat to Castro's government.

Training a Counterrevolutionary Force

The Central Intelligence Agency (CIA) began to recruit anti-Castro exiles in December 1959, if not earlier. On December 14, Americans from the U.S. embassy in Cuba engineered the escape from Cuba of Manuel Artime, who later became one of the leaders of the abortive Bay of Pigs invasion.[60] The actual decision, however, to organize a counterrevolutionary force under the auspices of the CIA was not taken until March 17, 1960. At this time, President Eisenhower gave orders "to begin to organize the training of Cuban exiles, mainly in Guatemala, against a possible future day when they might return to their homeland."[61]

How President Eisenhower came to make this sharp reversal in his policy towards Cuba has not been revealed to the public as yet, and his memoirs are not very illuminating. Ambassador Bonsal, a strong advocate of the earlier policy and critic of the latter, was not consulted in advance of the change. Vice President Nixon, who had warned President Eisenhower about Castro during the latter's visit to the United States, claims to have been in the "minority" within the administration in opposing the initial policy of forbearance. In *Six Crises* Nixon explains, "Early in 1960, the position I had been advocating for nine months finally prevailed, and the CIA was given instructions to provide arms, ammunition, and training for Cubans who had fled the Castro regime."[62] The information available to the public, however, probably tells only a small part of the story. Little is known about how this decision was reached, partly because it involved intelligence operations that are ordinarily "held close," with limitations on coordination with other government agencies. The U.S. president apparently did not consider his decision to arm exiles an irrevocable commitment, but the U.S. government may not have fully appreciated the impact the knowledge of official U.S. involvement would have on Castro and his policies.

The Refusal of the Oil Companies

Cuba was dependent on two U.S. companies, Esso and Texaco, and one Dutch company, Shell, for petroleum, the refining capacity for which had been sharply increased during Batista's last administration. Under the provisions of the February 1960 trade agreement with the USSR, Soviet crude oil was one of the Soviet products that could be exchanged for Cuban sugar. An initial shipment of Soviet crude oil arrived in Cuba in April and the Cuban government insisted that the companies refine it. Representatives of the American companies met with Secretary of the Treasury Robert Anderson, who urged the companies to refuse to refine Soviet crude oil.[63] Early in June, the three companies communicated their refusal to refine Soviet oil to the Cuban government. That refusal posed an unprecedented challenge to the Castro government, not only with regard to its foreign exchange and commercial policies, but on strategic grounds as well.

Cutting the Sugar Quota

Pressure mounted within the United States during 1960 to cut the Cuban sugar quota. The argument ran that Cuba should no longer enjoy preferential treatment in the purchase of sugar and, particularly, the benefit of the quota premium, which amounted to $150 million in 1959, while the Cuban government was seizing or "intervening" U.S.-owned property and otherwise damaging U.S. private business interests. Draft legislation authorizing the U.S. president to cut the sugar quota was formally presented to the Congress early in March.

Late in June 1960, the Eisenhower administration pressed the Congress hard for authority to reduce the Cuban sugar quota for 1960. A hearing of the House Committee on Agriculture on June 22, 1960, together with the debates in the House and the Senate about a week later, throw much light on the purposes underlying the government's decision.

In his testimony on June 22, Secretary Herter said that a primary purpose of the administration's request "was to safeguard consumers in this country from possible interruptions in supply and fluctuations in price," and the administration reiterated this contention time and again to answer charges that the cut was a form of economic sanction, or as the Cubans charged, "economic aggression."[64] In fact, the administration's justification was neither internally consistent nor convincing. The immediate problem was not to protect the United States from domestic shortages, and the administration, as congressional debate showed, was trying to rush through the legislation to prevent Castro from completing stepped-up deliveries under the quota arrangements. One of the major impulses behind the quota cut was the clamor of various foreign and domestic interests for part of the Cuban quota. Castro's interest was to sell as much sugar as he could for high prices, and the United States continued to be a prime market. Eventually, Cuba might decline to sell the United States as much sugar as the latter might want as Cuba developed other markets, including those in

Communist countries. But this eventual possibility could hardly justify eliminating all purchases in Cuba, accomplished by administrative decision in less than a year, and was the kind of abrupt and emergency adjustment this act presumably sought to avoid.

The debate in both the House and Senate was carried out in an atmosphere of urgency, haste, and high emotion. In spite of its immense foreign policy implications, the bill was not considered by the Senate Foreign Relations Committee. Much of the pressure for enactment of the bill came from members of the House Committee on Agriculture and other congressmen with ties to sugar interests. The chairman of the committee, Congressman Cooley, in the following statements gives some idea of the atmosphere in which the bill was considered: "I have been on this committee 26 years . . . more or less grown up with the sugar law . . . and I can truthfully say that never before in more than 25 years, has this legislation become involved in partisan politics."[65] One congressman appeared to be more concerned that his vote on the issue would be interpreted as a "vote for communism" than with its effect on the national interest.

Powerful vested interests in the United States and in some Latin American countries hoped to profit from Cuba's political difficulties and get part of the Cuban quota. President Eisenhower was aware of these influences, and explicitly disassociated himself from the decision to give part of the Cuban quota to the Dominican Republic.[66] There seems little doubt that other sugar interests capitalized on Cuba's difficulties and contributed to the pressures on the Congress and the president to cut the quota for reasons not related exclusively to public interests.

Whatever may have been the administration's motives, the congressmen who backed the legislation gave forthright explanations of their positions. Congressman Rivers said: "Think of what is happening—Castro and Communism—both must be destroyed. . . . Let us take a little of the Rivers' backbone. . . . God Save America."[67] Congressman Haley said, "The time had come to deal with Castro where it hurts: in the pocketbook."[68] Congressman McDowell said, "It is high time that the bluff of the Cuban Prime Minister and his colleagues was called."[69] Congressman Conte said: "I am a patient man, but I am also an American. I cannot allow my country to continue to suffer the constant humiliations and opprobrium heaped upon her in an irresponsible manner. . . . We are, in fact, supporting the rapid growth of international communism at our very door step."[70]

The bill was passed overwhelmingly in the House, 396 yeas, no nays, and 36 not voting. The bill had more difficulty in the Senate, but the conference report passed easily: 32 to 24, with 44 not voting. Congressman Cooley and Senator Morse frequently expressed their concern about the implications of the bill, the latter primarily on the grounds that it would immensely complicate our relations with many friendly Latin American countries. One member of the House expressed concern that the bill might make a martyr out of Castro.

In his memoirs, President Eisenhower comments, "It was silly, for example, to continue to give Cuba favored treatment regarding its sugar exports."[71] This suggests that the president had in mind the premium prices paid for Cuban sugar. But what was at stake was not simply the premiums, but the total U.S. purchase, some three million tons, or more than half the Cuban sugar crop, the bulk of its exports, and the main contributor to its gross domestic product. The U.S. sugar quota was Cuba's principal source of foreign income.

Armed with authority from Congress, President Eisenhower cut the Cuban sugar quota by 700,000 tons on July 6 for the balance of 1960, permitting new authorization of only 39,752 short tons. On December 16, 1960, the president fixed the Cuban quota at zero for the first quarter of 1961, thus establishing the policy of eliminating the Cuban quota entirely, a policy confirmed by the Kennedy administration.

Some observers have mistakenly attributed the sugar quota cut to the large-scale nationalizations that took place thereafter, partly because the announcements of the two actions took place almost simultaneously. Actually, the nationalizations, which were not effected until August, were a response to, not a cause of, the sugar quota cut. On the other hand, it would be a serious error to assert that Castro did not make major moves against U.S. private interests prior to the sugar quota cut. The Department of State estimates, for example, that prior to the cut Castro had seized about half of U.S.-owned properties, mainly in agriculture, mining, public utilities, and tourist facilities.[72] Seizures of most U.S. investments in manufacturing, commerce, finance, and transportation were not made until August and September.

I have been able to find no instances in the hearings or in the debate in Congress that cutting the Cuban sugar quota might have an effect diametrically opposite to that intended, namely, instead of combatting communism in Cuba, its result would in fact strengthen Soviet influence there. If such a concern existed, it did not seem to receive much attention. Several congressmen appeared to believe that Castro would have difficulty surviving the quota cut. Congressman McDowell said, "If Cuba's splendid people understand that they must sell their sugar or their economy will be destroyed, they will themselves find a way to deal with the present misleaders and fomenters of hatred." He was prepared to let the Cubans sell their sugar elsewhere, but expressed the belief that the Russians would "not find Cuban sugar sufficiently important to them or their economy to take the place of the United States as the largest consumer of Cuban sugar in the world."[73]

Why did the United States take such severe measures against Cuba with all the risks these entailed? As suggested above, there were a number of pressures at work in the Congress not directly related to U.S.–Cuban bilateral relations per se. As for the administration, Castro's seizures of U.S. property was an important element, as well as the growing totalitarian and socialist nature of the new Cuban regime. But perhaps the decisive motivation was not primarily that Castro threatened U.S. private interests and the traditional Cuban political structure, but that Castro was becoming a channel for the introduction of Soviet political and military influence into the Western Hemisphere.

As will be shown below, Castro had already made arrangements in June or earlier to receive large shipments of arms from socialist countries. In the debate on the sugar quota issue on the floor of the House of Representatives, Congressman Brook expressed his great apprehension of Soviet activities in Cuba, "Arms are being purchased by the Castro government, airports are being built by the Soviets and I have read of submarine activities unloading arms and munitions of war."[74] It would be interesting to know, too, whether the confidential part of Secretary Herter's testimony before the Committee on Agriculture in late June mentioned Cuban purchases of arms from Eastern Europe. In any case, the preceding evidence is sufficient in light of all the pertinent circumstances to justify the inference that the Department of State was already deeply concerned about Castro's strategic and military ties with Communist countries on the eve of the sugar quota cut. These considerations, coupled with Castro's open and belligerent defiance of U.S. political primacy in the hemisphere, caused the president to take this economic measure apparently designed to eliminate Castro politically.

Whether the decision to arm anti-Castro exiles and stop buying Cuban sugar helped or hindered the achievement of the administration's objectives is an entirely different question, indeed. This subject, together with a consideration of the broader causes for the U.S.–Cuban split will be taken up in the conclusions. First, let us examine the immediate repercussions of the president's anti-Castro measures.

The Elimination of U.S. Influence

Any one of the Eisenhower administration's anti-Castro measures—the counterrevolutionary force, the refusal to refine Soviet crude oil, the cut in the sugar quota—might have led to the fall of the Castro government. Castro reasoned, not implausibly, that he was in mortal peril. In his reflex reaction to protect himself, he turned first to the Soviet Union and other socialist countries for the means to counter Eisenhower's punitive policies.

Once Soviet help was assured, he was then able to strike back against the United States. \

Castro feared U.S. armed intervention long before Eisenhower reached his decision in March 1960 to arm a counterrevolutionary force, and Castro had been seeking sometimes with bitter frustration, to buy arms to protect himself, as well as for armed attacks against other Caribbean countries such as Trujillo's regime nearby. Acquisition of arms became doubly urgent when he learned about Eisenhower's decision. It is difficult to pinpoint that date, but Castro said on May 1, 1960, nearly one year before the Bay of Pigs invasion, "We have reports that the foreign office of the United States is preparing an aggression against Cuba through the Government of Guatemala."[75] Apparently, the first group of Cuban exiles arrived at the Retalhuleu Base in Guatemala in May 1960, and arrangements to set up that base had to have been made sometime before.[76] Therefore, it seems reasonable to assume that Castro had knowledge of the CIA's operations in May and acted on the basis of that knowledge.

No doubt, Castro intensified his efforts to secure arms from the Communist countries and could cite the CIA's Guatemalan operations to strengthen his case. Castro stated publicly on July 8, 1960, that the arrival of an arms shipment was imminent and confirmed later that they had arrived by July 26. Thus, Suárez's suggestion that the Castro government had already arranged for the purchase of arms from Czechoslovakia and possibly the USSR no later than June, if not sooner, is plausible.[77] A report of the Department of State made public on November 18 described how Castro had built up an army "ten times" the size of Batista's and lists the number of rifles, submachine guns, mortars, tanks, helicopters, etc., received from Communist countries, most beginning in July.[78] Thus, by mid-1960 Castro had arranged for a source of arms and munitions independent of U.S. controls and was rapidly bolstering his capacity to resist an armed attack. To do this, however, Cuba became militarily and strategically dependent on the Communist countries.

Castro followed a similar strategy with regard to the oil companies' refusal in early June, under official U.S. encouragement, to refine Soviet crude oil. No doubt after assuring himself that he could count on the Communist countries as a regular source of supply, Castro took over the American and Dutch refineries (Texaco, Esso and Shell) beginning on June 29. As a result, the companies lost not only their properties but also some $50 million in back payments from the Cuban government. It would be ironic if foreign exchange held back from payments due the oil companies had been used to pay for Cuban arms purchased from Eastern Europe.

The Cubans were worried about a possible cut in the sugar quota long before it actually happened, and certainly as early as December 1959 when it was made a matter of public discussion at Secretary Herter's press conference. In March, when the administration formally asked Congress for discretionary authority over the Cuban quota, Ernesto (Che) Guevara made a statement which attracted much public attention at the time:

> Why are we not a developed country? . . . The Northamericans take many pains so that the country does not make progress in other branches of industry [besides sugar] so that we have to buy the majority of manufactured products abroad. The Northamericans dispose of the greater share of the Cuban import market . . . they afford us good prices for our sugar and even concede us preferential tariffs in exchange for which we reciprocate with preferential tariffs for the products the country needs for its consumption and which the North produces. . . . This influx of Northamerican capital is translated into political dependence even after the abolition of the Platt Amendment. . . . When we struggle with all our strength to get out of this situation of economic vassalage and sign an agreement with the USSR, the representatives of the colony . . . try to sew confusion. . . . They try to show that by selling to another country we enslave ourselves and they don't stop to consider how much slavery for our country the three million tons which we sell at supposedly preferential prices represents.[79]

Guevara found the United States a handy scapegoat to explain Cuban underdevelopment, although even he would have surely admitted that there were many other reasons why Cuba had not made greater economic and social progress. Tariff protection for U.S. products in Cuba was part of the story, especially in earlier years, but Cuban dependence was also due to the much larger and sometimes more efficient productive capacity of the United States. Much of Cuban development had theretofore taken place under the impulse of trade with and investment by the United States. United States resources, including premiums on sugar sales, offered one source for capital accumulation.

The Cubans were caught on the horns of a dilemma. They wanted to rid themselves of U.S. leverage from the sugar quota, but the loss of the Cuban market would have deprived the nation of its lifeblood. Castro certainly could not have expected to survive long without help from some third party. Even if Castro was ready to break ties with the United States, it is doubtful at that date that he had commitments from the USSR to take up the slack. One would not be surprised if even Castro feared the immense risks involved. And, in view of those risks, how much better to leave responsibility for cutting the quota to the United States rather than assuming it himself!

In June as the United States moved closer to a decision on the sugar quota, Castro said, "We will exchange the quota for investments" and estimated U.S. investments as being worth $800 million.[80] Most of the property seizures up until the sugar quota cut early in July were agricultural properties. Some of the nonagricultural seizures included the Moa Bay Mining Company in March and hotels in June. Up to the time of the sugar quota cut, the seizures were either explained as temporary interventions or expropriations, and theoretically, at least, were subject to negotiation and eventual compensation.

The U.S. action in cutting the Cuban sugar quota on July 6 brought the USSR dramatically and prominently into the picture. Soviet Chairman Nikita Khrushchev declared on July 9, 1960: "Figuratively speaking, in case of need, Soviet artillerymen can support the Cuban people with their rocket fire if the aggressive forces in the Pentagon dare to launch an intervention against Cuba. . . . This, if you will, is a warning to those who would like to settle international issues by force and not by reason."[81] Castro was inclined to interpret Khrushchev literally rather than "figuratively," and Soviet "complete support in maintaining Cuban independence against unprovoked aggression" was reaffirmed in a Soviet-Cuban communiqué on December 19, 1960.

According to Suárez, Castro pressed a suitor's case for Soviet military and economic support after the quota cut in the face of Soviet reluctance. The USSR hedged on the question of military guarantees, but was prepared to say enough to give the United States pause. After a delay of more than five months, the USSR, prodded by the Chinese example, finally agreed to buy 2.7 million tons of sugar in 1961. This figure, plus agreements to buy 1 million tons by the Chinese and 300,000 tons by other socialist countries, meant that Cuba was guaranteed the sale of four million tons in "socialist markets."[82] In this fashion, the Communist countries came to buy the sugar the United States had spurned.

Meanwhile, Castro carried out his threat to seize remaining U.S. properties. After a delay of nearly a month, on August 6, Castro seized twenty-six companies wholly or partially owned by U.S. citizens; on September 17, he seized U.S.-owned banks; and on October 24, he seized 166 additional U.S.-owned properties, which largely fulfilled Castro's pledge to seize U.S. investments to compensate for Cuba's loss of the sugar quota. Unlike his early seizures, Castro's expropriation measures of August 1960 were openly directed against U.S. properties, discriminating explicitly on the basis of nationality and with compensation linked to sugar sales in the United States. Castro's post-sugar-quota-cut expropriations made the prospect of compensation so remote as to make eventual reconciliation on this issue virtually impossible. At this time, perhaps, the process had become irreversible.

The elimination of the sugar quota cast the die in U.S.–Cuban relations. As Eisenhower himself said: "This action amounts to economic sanctions against Cuba. Now we must look ahead to other moves—economic, diplomatic, and strategic."[83] On October 19, the United States prohibited exports to Cuba except for nonsubsidized foodstuffs, medicines, and medical supplies. Alarmed by the mounting activities of the counterrevolutionary invasion forces, Castro proclaimed his fear of a U.S.-sponsored invasion and on January 2 demanded that U.S. embassy persons assigned to Havana be cut down to eleven, the same number as in the Cuban embassy in Washington. President Eisenhower responded by announcing the severance of diplomatic relations on January 3.

Castro's conduct from May 1960 to January 1961 when diplomatic relations were severed, emerges in a totally different light when viewed from the perspective of Havana. Castro must have considered himself in deadly peril, literally fighting for his life during this period, and so he was. He almost surely knew about the U.S.-sponsored organization of the counterrevolutionary force beginning in May 1960, a development that most Americans could not take seriously until almost a year later when the Cuban exiles actually landed. Nor was the American public upset about the mounting preparations to cut the sugar quota, already a real menace to Havana. Thus, the U.S. president's announcement of the cut may have come as a surprise to the uninformed North American, but it simply confirmed fears Castro expressed publicly six or more months earlier. In this light, many of Castro's acts are more understandable: his seizure of the oil companies for refusing to refine Soviet crude oil beginning June 29, 1960; his seizure of much American property in August and later; and his restrictions on the size of the American embassy staff to conform to the size of the Cuban staff in Washington in January 1961. The Castro government, let it be remembered, was not the first to take actions leading to a diplomatic break with a country mounting a hostile invasion force!

Meanwhile, the Cuban Revolution was being dramatically "radicalized" and the Communist party became increasingly prominent. There were, no doubt, many domestic reasons to explain this development, but an important consideration for Cuban foreign policy was the desirability of attracting Soviet support against the impending U.S.-sponsored invasion. One of the best ways to secure such support was to identify Cuba with communism and the USSR, thereby increasing the odds that the USSR might support Cuba in some way, morally or materially. Perhaps, this as much as any other factor explains why Castro characterized the Cuban Revolution as "socialist" on April 16, the day before the Bay of Pigs invasion.

During the presidential election campaign the preceding fall, the two candidates, Richard Nixon and John F. Kennedy, had vied with one another in their attacks on Castro. Kennedy inherited the CIA-sponsored Cuban exile invasion from the previous administration. He permitted the invasion to take place, while refusing to permit the direct participation of U.S. troops. From March 17, 1960, until the failure at the Bay of Pigs, the United States had embarked on a policy of overthrowing Castro. The unwillingness of the Kennedy administration to use its own military might against Castro at that time made that objective unrealizable, while at the same time, tempting the Cubans and the Soviet Union to establish nuclear rockets in Cuba. Kennedy's success in having the rockets removed during the missile crisis resulted in mutual recognition of the impasse and a tacit agreement to a standoff. Under the provisions of the agreement, the United States committed itself not to overthrow Castro by force, whereas the Soviet Union agreed not to attempt to use Cuba for rocket-launching sites. The ground rules of the U.S.–Cuban relationship, fixed in 1963, have remained largely in effect until today (fall 1970). The rupture—economic, political, and cultural—continues to be almost complete.

From time to time, there has been talk about a possible *rapprochement* with Cuba. Former Ambassador Philip Bonsal referred to the matter briefly in his article in the January 1967 issue of *Foreign Affairs*. Richard Fagen led a discussion group on the subject for the Council on Inter-American Relations in late 1968 and early 1969. John N. Plank discussed the subject in the Sunday magazine of the *New York Times* on March 30, 1969. Irving Louis Horowitz made a case for the renewal of diplomatic relations in *Trans-action,* April 1969. On the Cuban side, Miguel D'Estéfano Pisani discussed some of the technical aspects of issues separating the two countries in the October 1964 issue of *Política Internacional.* However, almost no progress has been made. Up to 1970 the question has usually been dismissed for apparent lack of genuine interest on either side.

Conclusions

Many of the best-known interpretations of recent U.S.–Cuban relations follow the "devil" theory of politics. Castro is portrayed as a Communist devil or the United States as an imperialist devil. For purposes of analysis neither approach is of much use.

Every proud nation must ultimately accept responsibility for its fate, and the Cubans are no exception. The all-too-common habit in Latin America of blaming everything on the United States sometimes obscures reality. Another way of saying this is that "internal" factors are vital to understanding developments in individual countries, and are usually more important than "external" factors. This generalization is probably true even in the Cuban case, that is, in explaining the origins of the Cuban Revolution and the rupture in U.S.–Cuban relations. I mention this by way of preface since what follows deals primarily with external factors. I admit that these external factors are only part of the story, and not necessarily the most important part.

Fundamental to understanding the Cuban Revolution is the recognition that the U.S.–Cuban relationship that has developed since the Spanish-American War was inequitable and, therefore, potentially vulnerable and unstable. The political expression of that inequity was symbolized by the Platt Amendment, which was based on U.S. military power. The Platt Amendment arose out of the military occupation of Cuba and was sustained by military force at least until 1934.

After 1934 the juridical basis of the inequity was removed, but U.S. dominating influence continued partly due to the overwhelming weight of the U.S. economy and Washington's military potential—two facts of international life for which, in themselves, the United States could not properly be blamed. Cubans criticized the United States for misusing this immense power, sometimes justifiably, and sought ways to strengthen Cuba's hand against its powerful neighbor. United States influence was manifested in the Cuban sugar quota in which U.S. purchasing power and premium prices gave U.S. authorities immense leverage over the Cuban government. Within Cuba, U.S. capital controlled a declining, but still large, share of Cuban production and a large sector of finance, manufacturing, public utilities, and mining. Trade and investment patterns made Cuba an appendage of the U.S. economy. Some might say that inequalities are inevitable between parties of unequal power, and equal distribution of power between nations is rare. Perhaps, but the very fact that Castro was able to challenge the foundations of the U.S.–Cuban relationship, and survive after its destruction, shows that that particular "inequity" was not immutable.

The former U.S.–Cuban relationship also helps to explain why the Cuban Revolution came about. Compared to other Latin American countries, Cuba came nearly a century late to "self-government," and U.S. interference was decisive at major junctures of Cuban politics at least until the mid-1930s. From 1898, when Generals Máximo Gómez and Calixto García put themselves unconditionally under the orders of the U.S. generals, to 1933 and 1934, when Sumner Welles and Jefferson Caffery helped make and unmake Cuban presidents, U.S. authorities called most of the major turns in Cuban politics. Vestiges of that pattern survived until 1958 when

William Pawley, unofficially, and Ambassador Earl E. T. Smith, officially, asked President Batista to resign.

Perhaps the only years before 1959 that "democratic-capitalism" had much chance to flower in Cuba were from 1944 to 1952. Not only was the time short, but corruption and gangsterism had discredited the Grau and Prío administrations, as the failure of popular support to rally behind Prío against Batista in 1952 showed. The roots of representative government were not deep or strong enough to resist Batista's 1952 *coup d'état,* to supply an effective alternative to Castro in 1958, or to check his rapid accretion of power in 1959. The reason for the fragility of Cuba's "democratic-capitalism" must be sought on Cuban soil, but U.S. involvement cannot be rightly denied.

Castro deserves the credit, or blame, for challenging the foundations of the U.S.–Cuban relationship and is no doubt proud to claim it. He not only wanted to assert for Cuba a genuinely independent role vis-à-vis the United States, but private U.S. interests linked with the Cuban middle classes were an obstacle to the history-making social transformation to which Castro aspired. Once his domestic enemies, first Batista and then the "democratic" Cuban opposition were overcome, the United States, though largely passive at this early stage, became the major potential threat to his continued control of Cuba. There were psychological reasons for opposing the United States as well, and Castro gave free reign to his own and his countrymen's pent-up resentment of what they considered more than a half century of U.S. domination. Castro capitalized on Cuban nationalism to bolster his political position and carry the Revolution forward. From the beginning, Castro did violence to U.S. private interests, publicly defied U.S. political leaders, and moved in the direction of foreign policies independent of the United States, first with tentative and later persistent moves toward the Communist countries.

The actions of the United States are harder to explain than Castro's, although explanations of either suffer from the limitations of any effort to derive motivations. For the first year, the Eisenhower administration sought to adjust flexibly to Castro's unprecedented challenges. Some charge that the United States did not try hard enough during 1959 to accommodate Castro and thereby retain some capacity for influencing his behavior. Such comment assumes a commonality of interests between Castro and the United States that was, and is, hard to find, plus an expectation of greater adaptability of U.S. political processes than heretofore attainable. In any case, the United States maintained a relatively accommodating posture through January 1960.

The sharp reversal in policy was marked initially by the decision to arm anti-Castro exiles in March 1960 and culminated in the cut in the Cuban sugar quota in July. Its causes are elusive and complex. If Castro over-reacted to the United States in 1959, the United States overreacted to Castro in 1960. Castro's treatment of U.S. private business interests was shameful by U.S. standards in 1959, but, thus far, the damage had been limited mainly to seizures in agriculture and to interference in public utili-ties and mining. Castro's ties with the Communist countries were minimal, and what seemed menacing to the United States about the sugar purchase and credit agreements with the USSR was not the quantities involved as much as their potential for mischief. President Eisenhower's own descrip-tion of events and the statements of congressmen suggest that the U.S. decision to overthrow Castro was an emotional reaction by the United States, a kind of personal animosity to Castro's defiance coupled with the United States's almost pathological fear and hatred of "communism." Also, the role of sugar interests seeking a slice of the Cuban quota should not be discounted.

President Eisenhower never seemed to realize that his decision to sponsor a counterrevolutionary invasionary force, a fact which could not be kept from Castro long, caused Castro to take extraordinary measures to defend himself. Ambassador Bonsal maintains, "We did not force them into the arms of the Communists, but we were, in my judgment, unwisely coopera-tive in removing the obstacles to his chosen path."[84] Mr. Bonsal apparently believed that Castro wanted to break off with the United States anyway and desired closer economic relations with the USSR. With domestic opposition crystallizing and the exiled community growing, Eisenhower placed Castro in grave jeopardy, and Castro interpreted it thus. Therefore, it is difficult to see what more menacing move could have been made to insure Castro's turning elsewhere for help, and where else could he go but to the Russians and Chinese?

Similarly, the cut in the sugar quota literally put Castro at the Commu-nists' mercy, and logically led to the radicalization of the Cuban Revolu-tion and his close political and military ties with the Communist countries. What is puzzling, and disturbing, is that there is little or no evidence that leaders in the Department of State or in the Congress seemed to have been aware that their own actions would lead precisely to the circumstances they claimed they were trying to avoid. One of the only dissenting voices in the United States, perhaps because others are not in a position to speak, was that of former Ambassador Bonsal who testifies to his own strong opposi-tion to the reversal of the January 1960 nonintervention policies. Candi-dates Nixon and Kennedy competed to see who could be most anti-Communist and anti-Castro during the 1960 presidential campaign, and Kennedy, as president, confirmed the main lines of the Eisenhower policy.

Almost from the beginning, Castro and the United States expected the worst from one another, and neither was disappointed. In retrospect, Castro emerged from the dispute remarkably well. The Cuban middle class was destroyed, and that, perhaps, was a natural result of the kind of revolution Castro sought. The shock of the total reorientation to the Cuban economy at the time of the break with the United States and the radicalization of the Revolution was truly shattering; it was a shock from which the economy has not yet recovered. Broader social changes involving an improvement in the living standards of the rural and urban poor were achieved at immense costs to other economic and social sectors. Castro completed a literally epoch-making revolution while surviving as the continuing and dominant political power in Cuba. There is still insufficient evidence about the extent of Soviet influence over Castro to validate the overly facile U.S. dismissal of Castro as a leader who has exchanged American for Soviet domination.

The fruits of U.S. policy are bitter indeed. United States private interests have lost investments valued at about one billion dollars, larger than losses suffered earlier in Russia or China. Cuba now has a Marxist-Leninist system with close ties to the Communist countries, serving as a focus of hostility to the United States in Latin America. Castro may have sought these results initially, but whether he did so or not, the United States inadvertently helped enormously in their achievement.

NOTES

1. *Sphere of influence* means here "a territorial area within which the political influence or the interests of one nation are held to be more or less paramount." P. B. Gove, ed., *Webster's Third New International Dictionary of the English Language, Unabridged,* 1968. The United States has successfully asserted its paramount interests in Latin America from 1896, when U.S. President Grover Cleveland forced the British to arbitrate their dispute with Venezuela, until Castro's time. In the missile crisis, the Soviet Union implicitly reaffirmed the primacy of U.S. interests in Cuba with regard to missiles and nuclear weapons. For comment and references, see contributions of Kalman H. Silvert and Raymond Carr in *Cuba and the United States: Long Range Perspectives,* ed. John Plank (Washington, D.C., 1967). Other contributions are also pertinent, particularly J. Wilmer Sundelson's chapter on U.S. business in Cuba.

2. See Cole Blasier's "The United States and the Revolution" in *Beyond the Revolution: Bolivia Since 1952,* eds. James M. Malloy and Richard S. Thorn (Pittsburgh, Pa., 1971).

3. Lee Lockwood, *Castro's Cuba, Cuba's Fidel* (New York, 1969), p. 141.

4. Ibid., p. 142.

5. Fidel Castro, *La historia me absolverá* (La Habana, 1961), pp. 59–60.

6. Fidel Castro, "What the Rebels Want," *The Nation,* November 30, 1957.

7. Ibid.

8. *Coronet*, February 1958, pp. 84–85.

9. Lockwood, *Castro's Cuba*, p. 142.

10. Jules Dubois, *Fidel Castro: Rebel-Liberator or Dictator?* (Indianapolis, 1959), p. 105.

11. Ibid., pp. 133, 136; and Herbert L. Matthews, *Fidel Castro* (New York, 1969), p. 90.

12. U.S. Congress, Senate, Subcommittee of the Committee on the Judiciary, *Hearing on State Department Security, Testimony of William Wieland,* 87th Cong., January 9, 1961, pt. 5, p. 554.

13. Personal interview with Ernesto Betancourt, Washington, D.C., June 9, 1970.

14. Worksheets, Office of Statistics and Reports, Bureau for Program and Policy Coordination, Agency for International Development, 1954: 1.1, 1955: 1.5, 1956: 1.7, 1957: 3.2, 1958: 3.6.

15. U.S. Congress, House, *Congressional Record,* 85th Cong., 2d sess., 1958, 104, pt. 4, pp. 4948, 5496.

16. Ibid., p. 5497.

17. Dubois, *Fidel Castro,* p. 169.

18. U.S. Congress, Senate, *Hearing on State Department Security,* p. 554.

19. U.S. Congress, Senate, Committee on Foreign Relations, *Hearing on Review of Foreign Policy, 1958,* 85th Cong., 2d sess., 1958, pt. 1, p. 359.

20. U.S. Department of State, *American Foreign Policy: Current Documents, 1958* (Washington, D.C., 1962), no. 7322, p. 343.

21. The first quote comes from a letter from J. Miró Cardona to President Eisenhower, dated August 26, 1958; the second is from the reply of William A. Wieland, Director, Office of Caribbean Affairs, Department of State, dated October 13, 1958. Both can be found in Dubois, *Fidel Castro,* pp. 299, 312.

22. Dwight D. Eisenhower, *The White House Years: Waging Peace, 1956–1961* (New York, 1965), p. 520.

23. Earl E. T. Smith, *The Fourth Floor* (New York, 1962), p. 60.

24. U.S. Congress, Senate, Committee on the Judiciary, Subcommittee to Investigate the Administration of the Internal Security Act and Other Internal Security Laws, 86th Cong., 2d sess., Sept. 2 and 8, 1960, p. 739.

25. Smith, *Fourth Floor,* p. 182.

26. *New York Times,* November 2, 1958, p. 11.

27. Personal interview with Ernesto Betancourt, Washington, D.C., June 9, 1970.

28. Dubois, *Fidel Castro,* p. 345.

29. Ibid., pp. 345, 347.

30. Cole Blasier, "Studies of Social Revolution: Origins in Mexico, Bolivia, and Cuba," *Latin American Research Review,* 2 (Summer 1967), p. 43, discusses conflicting estimates of the numbers of armed guerrillas.

31. Rufo López-Fresquet, *My Fourteen Months with Castro* (Cleveland, 1966), p. 106.

32. Ibid., p. 108.

33. Richard M. Nixon, *Six Crises* (New York, 1962), p. 352.

34. López-Fresquet, *My Fourteen Months,* p. 106.

35. *New York Times,* December 17, 1959, p. 1.

36. *Revolución,* April 25, 1959.

37. *Revolución,* January 1, 1960, quote reprinted from original article entitled "Ante la prensa," in the August 14, 1959, issue.

38. U.S. Department of Commerce, Bureau of Foreign Commerce, *Investment in Cuba: Basic Information for United States Businessmen* (Washington, D.C., 1956), p. 10.

39. International Sugar Council, *The World Sugar Economy,* vol. 2, *The World Picture* (London, 1963), pp. 176, 181–82.

40. David F. Healy, *United States in Cuba: 1898–1902* (Madison, Wis., 1963), pp. 150, 178.

41. Bryce Wood, *The Making of the Good Neighbor Policy* (New York, 1967), pp. 81 ff, 101 ff.

42. Smith, *Fourth Floor,* p. 172.

43. *Revolución,* April 18, 1959, p. 10.

44. *Revolución,* January 21, 1960, p. 2.

45. Ibid.

46. U.S. Department of State, *American Foreign Policy: Current Documents, 1959* (Washington, D.C., 1963), no. 7492, pp. 383–84.

47. Letter to author, October 1, 1970.

48. Castro's estimate is quoted in *Revolución,* June 25, 1960. An official U.S. figure for 1960 can be found in U.S. Department of Commerce, *Balance of Payments: Statistical Supplement, 1961* (Washington, D.C., 1961), p. 215.

49. López-Fresquet, *My Fourteen Months,* p. 82; Andrés Suárez, *Cuba: Castroism and Communism, 1959–1966* (Cambridge, Mass., 1967), p. 72.

50. U.S. Department of State, *Current Documents, 1959,* p. 380.

51. *Revolución,* March 7, 1960, pp. 5–6.

52. *New York Times,* March 11, 1960, p. 1.

53. U.S. Congress, Senate, Committee on Foreign Relations, *Events in United States–Cuban Relations: A Chronology from 1957 to 1963,* 88th Cong., 1st sess., 1963, p. 12. Prepared by the Department of State for the Committee on Foreign Relations and quoted in Suárez, *Cuba.*

54. Eisenhower, *White House Years,* p. 524.

55. *Revolución,* January 21, 1960.

56. *Department of State Bulletin,* 42, no. 1075, (February 1, 1960), p. 158.

57. Martin Kenner and James Petras, eds., *Fidel Castro Speaks* (New York, 1970), p. 4. The Department of State rebuttal to Castro's speech is contained in a memorandum written to the United Nations on October 12, 1960. See U.S. Department of State, *American Foreign Policy: Current Documents, 1960* (Washington, D.C., 1964), no. 7624, p. 222.

58. Miguel A. D'Estéfano Pisani, "Las nacionalizaciones del Gobierno Revolucionario y el Derecho Internacional," *Política Internacional,* 1, no. 3, (Havana, 1963), pp. 53, 63, 88.

59. Philip W. Bonsal, "Cuba, Castro and the United States," *Foreign Affairs,* 45 (January 1967), p. 271.

60. Haynes Johnson, *The Bay of Pigs* (New York, 1964), p. 26.

61. Eisenhower, *White House Years,* p. 533.

62. Nixon, *Six Crises,* p. 352.

63. Bonsal reported that the oil companies "would probably have reluctantly gone along with the government's request, seeking remedies through the courts and eventually, if necessary, through channels provided under international law." He reported, however, that the secretary of the treasury had strongly urged the companies to refuse to refine the Soviet crude oil. See Bonsal, "Cuba," p. 272.

64. U.S. Congress, House, Committee on Agriculture, *Extension of Sugar Acts in 1948 as Amended,* 86th Cong., 2d sess., June 22, 1960, HR12311, HR12534, HR12624, p. 4.

65. Ibid. p. 8.

66. Eisenhower, *White House Years,* p. 535.

67. U.S. Congress, House, *Congressional Record,* 86th Cong., 2d sess., 1960, 106, pt. 11, p. 15228.

68. Ibid., p. 15230.

69. Ibid., p. 15232.

70. Ibid., p. 15245.

71. Eisenhower, *White House Years,* p. 535.

72. U.S. Congress, Senate, *Events in United States–Cuban Relations,* p. 16. As of December 31, 1968, 8,368 Cuban claims totaling $3,275,286,076.33 have been filled with the Foreign Claims Settlement Commission of the United States. Of these, 1,071 were corporate claims, and 7,297, individual claims. No funds are currently available to compensate claimants; the procedure provides an opportunity to make claims a subject of judicial record and review, thereby strengthening such claims should compensation become a matter for negotiation. By the end of 1968, the Commission had issued final decisions on 3,230 claims, of which 2,514 were favorable and totaled $58,594,463.27. See the Commission's *Annual Report to the Congress for the Period January 1–December 31, 1968* (Washington, D.C., 1969), pp. 12–13.

73. U.S. Congress, House, *Congressional Record,* 86th Cong., 2d sess., 1960, 106, pt. 11, p. 15232.

74. Ibid., p. 15245.

75. *Revolución,* May 2, 1960.

76. Gregorio Selser, *De Dulles a Raborn* (Buenos Aires, 1967), p. 97.

77. Suárez, *Cuba,* pp. 92 ff.

78. U.S. Department of State, *Current Documents, 1960,* p. 246.

79. *Revolución,* March 3, 1960, p. 12.

80. *Revolución,* June 25, 1960.

81. U.S. Department of State, *Current Documents, 1960,* p. 207.

82. Suárez's interpretation can be found in Suárez, *Cuba,* pp. 113, 119.

83. Eisenhower, *White House Years,* p. 535.

84. Bonsal, "Cuba," p. 272.

4 Edward Gonzalez

Relationship with the Soviet Union

THE relations between Cuba and the Soviet Union from 1960 to 1970 show how a small state can exploit to maximum advantage its relations with a superpower. Since he came to power in 1959, Fidel Castro pursued two foreign policy objectives in order to safeguard the development of the Cuban Revolution. First, he sought to overcome revolutionary Cuba's isolation within a hostile hemispheric environment. Secondly, he sought to realize this objective without sacrificing Cuba's independent status. Beginning in 1960, Castro worked toward the first objective by securing and then maximizing Cuba's ties with the Soviet Union as the extracontinental guarantor of his Revolution. The Soviets provided the indispensable political, economic, and military lifeline over the years, which enabled the Cuban regime to break out of its revolutionary isolation and to offset its vulnerability to the United States. Moreover, Castro achieved considerable success in realizing his second objective throughout most of the 1960s. Despite Cuba's increasing economic and military dependence on the Soviet bloc, Castro was able to maintain an independent and often deviant position within the socialist camp on a number of critical issues.

This analysis begins by examining the constellation of convergent and divergent interests that have both united and separated the two states, making for sometimes harmonious and sometimes strained relations between Havana and Moscow. Next, it conceptualizes the bargaining relationship that existed between the two actors, identifying the bargaining weapons that enabled Castro to increase his leverage in dealing with the Soviets. It then traces the development of Cuban-Soviet relations over the decade of the 1960s. This part of the analysis will attempt to show how Castro capitalized on shared interests, exploited favorable circumstances, and utilized available bargaining counters to Cuba's full advantage. It also attempts to

81

demonstrate how he maneuvered for advantage by relying on the politics of accommodation when Soviet commitments to Cuba seemed strong, and by employing confrontation politics when Soviet solidarity began to weaken. Finally, the analysis concludes with an examination of the *détente* reached between Cuba and the Soviet Union after 1968, discussing its significance for future Cuban-Soviet ties and the way in which Castro may reduce his present dependency on the Soviet Union.

Convergence and Divergence of Interests

The dispatch of First Deputy Premier Anastas Mikoyan to Havana in early February 1960 marked the beginning of the Soviet Union's commitment to the Cuban Revolution. The initial and continuing basis of the Cuban-Soviet relationship was pragmatic. Havana required external protection for the Revolution against interference by the United States, whereas Moscow sought to realize cold war and strategic objectives in the Western Hemisphere by rendering support to revolutionary Cuba.[1] In addition, the ensuing ties between the two countries were reinforced by a commonality of interests. Cuba and the USSR shared the same international enemy— the United States. Moreover, both states professed their support for revolutionary movements throughout the third world. Furthermore, with Castro's adoption of Marxism-Leninism in 1961, both Havana and Moscow shared a common ideology and a common commitment to the building of communism in their respective countries. Paradoxically, Cuban-Soviet relations were recurrently strained by conflicts and divergencies over their interests in four main areas: (a) internal security of both states, (b) degree of involvement in Latin America, (c) revolutionary strategy in this area and relations with native Communist parties, and (d) ideology and operational models for achieving communism.

Internal Security

The most important source of friction developed out of the different security interests and needs of the two countries. To be sure, both Havana and Moscow viewed the United States as their main enemy. But the Cuban regime remained much more vulnerable to the United States and saw the latter as posing a constant and overwhelming threat to the Revolution. The Soviets, on the other hand, possessed the strategic capabilities with which to deter direct U.S. aggression. They also had buffer areas and pressure points in Europe, the Middle East, and Asia with which to ward off or counter hostile moves by Washington.

The Castro regime, therefore, always sought to maximize the Soviet commitment to Cuba, preferably through the latter's entry into the Warsaw

Pact or through a security pact.[2] However, such a formal commitment would have burdened the Soviets with a strategic liability. Hence, they avoided any type of entangling alliance with Cuba.[3] Only in the missile buildup in 1962 did Moscow assume a momentary strategic risk in Cuba. However, this risk was incurred for Soviet strategic and political objectives, whereas the promotion of Cuba's security interests appear to have been a by-product of Moscow's decision to install strategic missiles.[4] In turn, Castro never forgave the Soviets for Premier Khrushchev's peremptory and unilateral withdrawal of the missiles during the October 1962 crisis.[5] Together with more recent examples of Soviet equivocation, as in Vietnam, Moscow's unwillingness to risk Soviet security interests for the sake of Cuba became a permanent source of recurrent tension.

Involvement in Latin America

The separate revolutionary interests of the two regimes became a second issue of contention. For Castro, Latin America remained the prime target area for revolutionary expansion during most of the 1960s. The continental revolution would have ended Havana's hemispheric isolation and maintained Soviet interest in Cuba as a revolutionary base. Hence, until 1968, when the Revolution turned inward following Guevara's death, the Cuban regime directly and indirectly promoted the armed struggle in Latin America.[6] In contrast, Latin America traditionally had been in the backwaters of Soviet revolutionary interests.[7] Rather than communization of the region, Moscow's objectives in the Western Hemisphere were of a limited cold war nature—to undermine and minimize U.S. influence by establishing ties with independent regimes led by the national bourgeoisie.[8]

The consolidation of the Cuban Revolution, together with the rising influence of *Fidelismo* in Latin America, led Moscow to reevaluate the prospects for revolution elsewhere in the hemisphere in the early 1960s. The outcome of the missile crisis, however, demonstrated the limits of Soviet power and precipitated Moscow's gradual disengagement from the continental revolution. Moreover, the very existence of Communist Cuba reduced the likelihood of new Cubas emerging, as was illustrated by Washington's armed intervention during the Dominican revolt in 1965. Finally, Soviet economic, technical, and military support for the Castro regime turned into a costly venture, which presumably Moscow did not care to repeat elsewhere in Latin America.[9]

The Soviets, therefore, reverted to their traditional limited aims in Latin America by the mid-1960s. They continued giving qualified endorsement to the armed struggle in selected countries and paid lip service to the Cuban strategy of armed struggle.[10] But, beginning in 1965, they moved to normalize relations with various Latin American regimes as the principal means for promoting Soviet foreign policy aims, thereby requiring that Moscow disassociate itself from the *Fidelista* movements.[11] As a result, Cuban-Soviet relations were increasingly strained as both countries pursued their divergent interests.

Revolutionary Strategies and Latin American Communists

Another source of tension involved the different revolutionary strategies of Havana on the one hand, and Moscow and the Latin American Communists on the other. The Castro-Guevara thesis on armed struggle was a maximum strategy for the revolutionary overthrow of existing regimes. The strategy maintained that, with a rural peasant base, a revolutionary group could ultimately seize power by waging armed struggle in the countryside. It stressed subjectivism, such as the will to triumph, and minimized objective political, economic, and military factors for the existence of a revolutionary situation. And, it substituted the guerrilla band, or guerrilla *foco,* for the urban-based party organization and mass movement.[12]

Before the Cuban Revolution, Moscow and the Communists adhered to a minimalist, nonviolent, and urban-oriented strategy. The Communists denied that conditions existed for the successful waging of armed revolution in the hemisphere. Thus, they sought increased influence within the established political systems through electoral participation, party alliances, and trade union influence. The Communist strategy also stressed the necessity of both favorable objective and subjective conditions as preconditions for a revolutionary situation. Moreover, it emphasized the pivotal importance of party organization and allied mass movements in waging any revolutionary struggle.[13] The Communist urban-oriented strategy thus aimed at organizational survival and limited political gains within existing regimes, whereas the Cuban rural-oriented strategy proposed the toppling of established regimes by means of armed struggle.

In order to remain in the revolutionary mainstream, however, Moscow and the Communists were compelled to give qualified endorsement to the Cuban strategy in the early 1960s, and to support some of the guerrilla bands. But Communist association with the guerrilla movements became self-defeating by the mid-1960s as the prospects for armed revolution receded. Such ties exposed the Communist parties to government repression and precluded Communist efforts to gain legal status and political power through the established electoral process. As a result, the Communist movement abandoned the line of armed revolution after 1965, adopting, instead, the alternative Chilean Communist strategy of "the peaceful road to socialism."[14] These developments increasingly strained Havana's relationship with Moscow and the Latin American Communists, particularly when the Communist Party of Venezuela (PCV) scuttled the

Fidelista insurgent movement after 1965. Consequently, Castro bitterly denounced the PCV on March 13, 1967. And the following August, at the first conference of the Latin American Solidarity Organization (OLAS), Havana openly broke with the Soviets and Communists on the question of revolutionary strategy.

Ideology and Operational Models

Ideology became the final point of divergency and conflict. The Cubans and Soviets approached communism from different perspectives, had different conceptions of the Communist society, and had different operational models for realizing communism. The Castro leadership saw the socialist system as the vehicle for guaranteeing Cuba's national liberation, rapid economic development, and societal redemption. The Cuban conception of the Communist society minimized the institutional, economic, and technological requisites for attaining communism. Instead, it placed primary importance on the psychic transformation of man, the negation of the market and the law of value in the transitional stage, and the eradication of bourgeois vices from society. As to means, the Cubans did not legitimatize their practices in Marxist-Leninist doctrine, but, rather, freely adopted dogma to their own purposes. Thus, Castro announced the "socialist" character of his revolution in 1961, despite the absence of a ruling Communist party; and he proclaimed the parallel construction of socialism and communism in 1966, despite the low level of Cuba's development, thereby telescoping the two stages.

Moreover, the Cuban model of socialism-communism is distinguished from the Soviet bloc systems by its continued charismatic and noninstitutionalized character, by its high level of state ownership and centralization, and by its heavy emphasis on moral incentives.[15] In contrast, the Soviets viewed communism from the perspective of attained independence and modernity. They emphasized institutional, economic, and technological development as preconditions for achieving the Communist threshold. In this connection, they were not adverse to employing some market practices, such as profits, interest, material incentives, and administrative decentralization for managing the economy. However, they saw the realization of Communist consciousness as the result of, and not the means to, the Communist millennium. Finally, leaning on Marxist-Leninist dogma and their own experience, the Soviets viewed socialism and communism as a necessary two-stage historical process.

These ideological differences became politically relevant and constituted a source of friction in Cuban-Soviet relations. Briefly put, the Cuban regime was a late convert to communism, possessed questionable Communist credentials, and ruled over an underdeveloped agrarian state. Yet

Castro's model implied, at the very least, that Cuba was approaching communism as rapidly as the Soviets; or even more, that the Soviets had adopted state capitalism, whereas the Cubans were constructing "genuine communism."[16] Equally important, the Soviet bloc countries were caught in subsidizing Cuba's often costly and unproductive economic and social experiments under Castro's model of communism. Hence, Soviet bloc criticism of the Cuban model, along with bloc economic pressures, became another irritant in Cuban-Soviet relations.[17]

In sum, there were divergencies and conflicts over interests, which strained the Cuban-Soviet axis. What, therefore, kept the two states together? To be sure, there were the core pragmatic considerations that continued to bind Havana and Moscow. However, these considerations in themselves do not reveal why and how Castro was able to maximize the Soviet commitment to Cuba despite the tension that existed on several key issues. The answer lies in the bargaining relationship that was in operation between the two states. And it was precisely these conflicting interests that enabled Castro to increase his leverage with the Soviets.

The Cuban-Soviet Bargaining Relationship

Castro maximized Cuba's bargaining position by exerting ideological and political pressures based on the available opportunities, resources, and issues at his disposal. There were limitations to Castro's bargaining advantage because he could not go so far as to precipitate a rupture in the crucial Soviet lifeline to Cuba. By the same token, however, the Soviets could not afford to scuttle Cuba because of their heavy ideological, economic, and military investment in the Castro regime. Moreover, Moscow's abandonment of revolutionary Cuba would have undermined its international position in the Communist camp and in the third world. Although careful to avoid the final provocation, Castro was able to maintain considerable pressure on Moscow in order to obtain maximum Soviet concessions.

The opportunities, issues, and resources that Castro used to increase his leverage fall into four categories. The first were ideological weapons. These included the internationalist obligations of the Soviet Union as the leading Communist and antiimperialist power, and Cuba's liberationist and, subsequently, socialist revolution. Together, they meant that Moscow was duty bound to render all necessary support to the Castro regime in order to ensure the survival of the antiimperialist and socialist government in Cuba.

The second weapon was the Sino-Soviet conflict and the emergence of polycentricism, which deprived Moscow of its unchallengeable hegemony over the international Communist camp. Until Havana's denunciation of the Chinese in 1966, Peking's militancy and bid for international leadership provided the Castro regime with a bargaining counter in pressing for maximum Soviet assistance.[18] Similarly, polycentricism within the international Communist camp provided Castro with additional leverage as Cuba's support or neutrality on key and controversial issues became increasingly important to the Soviets.

The third weapon was the promotion of the continental revolution. The insurgent *Fidelista* movements in Latin America not only offered the means by which Cuba could overcome its hemispheric isolation, but also provided Castro either with the means for maintaining and revitalizing Soviet interest in Cuba as a revolutionary base, or with a negotiable issue with which he could bargain for major Soviet concessions.

The fourth was an overlapping category consisting of symbolic deviation and political extortion. On the one hand, it involved Castro's sharp deviations from the Soviet line on such major issues as the construction of communism or revolutionary strategy. On the other hand, it involved Castro's public challenge of Moscow's professed support for revolutionary movements, questioning the extent of Soviet solidarity with Vietnam and Cuba, or exposing the conspiracies of old Moscow-line Communists in the Escalante affair of 1962, the Marcos Rodríguez affair of 1964, and the "microfaction" affair of 1968.[19]

Castro thus possessed an array of weapons in promoting his twin objectives of (a) overcoming Cuba's isolation through his lifeline with the Soviets, and (b) retaining his regime's independence. He could pursue an accommodation with Moscow as long as Cuban-Soviet relations remained satisfactory. In this stage of the relationship, trade offs were obtainable through mutual concessions and a convergence of interests. Once Soviet solidarity weakened, however, Castro could resort to the politics of confrontation in order to recommit Moscow. Hence, he could deviate on politically and ideologically sensitive issues, and avail himself of internal and external bargaining counters, in an effort to refashion Cuban-Soviet ties. These bargaining relationships will now be examined in greater detail by analyzing Cuban-Soviet developments over the last decade.

Forging the Cuban-Soviet Relationship

Soon after Castro came to power in 1959, he had to contend with the manifest and anticipated opposition of the United States to his profoundly radical revolution. But in turning to the Soviets for help, he found Moscow to be equivocal toward the Revolution and fearful of involvement in Cuba. From Moscow's vantage point, the island was remote, strategically vulnerable, and outside the Soviet security sphere. The Soviets also feared that the Guatemalan precedent of 1954 could be repeated in Cuba (see note 7). They mistrusted the class character of the Castro regime, since it was composed of the radical but adventuristic petty bourgeoisie. Finally, Khrushchev's efforts to reach a personal accommodation with Eisenhower at the Camp David meeting in September 1959 precluded Soviet involvement in Cuba at the time. At best, therefore, Moscow might have considered extending limited aid to Castro as it had with other nationalist regimes, such as those of Nasser and Sukarno.

This prospect, however, offered Castro no assurance that Soviet assistance would be substantial and permanent under such an arrangement, nor that it would act as a deterrent to future U.S. aggression. Thus, Castro had to find a way of engaging Soviet involvement in Cuba to a degree that would assure the survival of the Revolution. He succeeded, in effect, by choosing the socialist camp, beginning in the last months of 1959.

In the ensuing bargaining process, Castro utilized ideology, political extortion, and the Sino-Soviet rift in exerting pressure on Moscow to comply with its international obligations. Ideologically, he radicalized the Revolution in the fall of 1959 by reorienting it politically along a pro-Communist course, by redirecting it economically toward socialism, and by intensifying its anti-American content. He thus confronted the Soviets not only with a "national-liberationist" revolution, but also with an emerging socialist and pro-Communist revolution that, sooner or later, they would be compelled to support. In turn, having secured their alliance with Castro, the Cuban Communists became aggressive brokers for Havana in bargaining for Soviet support. They publicly assessed and verified the socialist potential of the Cuban Revolution; publicly questioned Khrushchev's policy of peaceful coexistence with the United States at a time when Cuba was under threat; openly courted Chinese support for the Revolution; and, in effect, demanded Moscow's fulfillment of its internationalist obligations toward revolutionary Cuba. In the end, Mikoyan was dispatched to Cuba in February 1960, resulting in the first long-term Soviet trade pact with Cuba and marking Castro's first successful step in opting to join the socialist camp.[20]

In the 1960s, Castro consolidated his ideological, military, and economic ties with the Soviet Union, which in turn ensured the survival of the Cuban Revolution. In this way, he secured Moscow's ideological recognition of Cuba's "socialist" status, thereby strengthening the Soviet obligation toward his regime. He obtained massive Soviet bloc military assistance— amounting to $1.5 billion by 1970—for the equipping and training of the revolutionary armed forces, which ensured the internal and external security of his regime.[21] Although Castro was unable to obtain a security pact with the USSR, Cuba's ties with the Soviets nevertheless provided a sufficient deterrent to Washington, giving his regime a further sense of security against direct U.S. aggression. Finally, Castro gained economic concessions from the Soviet bloc that supported Cuba's otherwise faltering economy during the mid-1960s and its ambitious development programs in more recent years. In this respect, the Soviet Union supplied Cuba with the bulk of its imports between 1961 and 1967, with the USSR alone absorbing more than $1.1 billion in Cuban trade deficts over that same period (see chapter 10, tables 2 and 5).

These bonds were forged by using the politics of accommodation and confrontation. The early 1960s saw a period of mutual accommodation in which both Cuban and Soviet interests converged. Castro moved rapidly into the socialist camp once the Bay of Pigs fiasco in April 1961 demonstrated to the Russians the survivability of the Cuban Revolution and the unlikelihood of direct U.S. armed aggression. The highpoint in this accommodative period was reached in mid-1962 with the Soviet decision to install medium- and intermediate-range ballistic missiles in Cuba. Such a strategic investment in the island not only implied that Moscow would not forsake Cuba, but also that Soviet security interests would be directly tied to those of Cuba. However, Moscow's precipitous withdrawal of the missiles during the October 1962 crisis severely strained Cuban-Soviet relations and prompted Castro's reliance on confrontation politics.[22]

In the first place, the outcome of the 1962 missile crisis demonstrated the weakness of the Soviet commitment to Cuba. In the second place, it abruptly reduced Soviet interest in Cuba as both a strategic base and revolutionary beachhead in the Western Hemisphere. Castro was thus faced with the prospect of lagging Soviet interest toward his regime. This development was made all the more critical by the need to negotiate a new Cuban-Soviet trade agreement and by the impending small output of sugar in the 1963 harvest.

To revitalize Soviet support, therefore, Castro challenged Moscow on several political and ideological issues in the months following the October 1962 crisis: (a) He maintained a highly and publicly critical posture toward Khrushchev's withdrawal of the missiles and his policy of "peaceful coexistence." (b) He exploited the deepening Sino-Soviet schism by openly courting the Chinese. (c) He created the United Party of the Socialist Revolution to gain recognition as a full-fledged Communist regime. (d) He roundly castigated the Moscow-oriented Latin American Communist parties for their lack of revolutionary activity. And (e) he renewed Cuba's support for the *Fidelista* movement and armed struggle in Latin America. In the end, Moscow responded with important economic and political concessions to Cuba. New and favorable trade agreements were signed in

1963, in which the Soviets extended new trade credits to Havana and agreed to purchase Cuban sugar at the prevailing world-market price of six cents a pound. Equally important, Castro paid a lengthy visit to the Soviet Union in May 1963, at which time he received Moscow's recognition as a full-fledged Communist leader.[23] The politics of confrontation had thus come to an end and were replaced by a new harmony and intimacy in Cuban-Soviet relations.

Indeed, the 1963–1965 period was one of mutual accommodation between Havana and Moscow. Castro returned to the Soviet Union in January 1964. He obtained Khrushchev's assurance of Soviet aid to Cuba in the event of U.S. aggression. He also secured a new long-term trade treaty which committed the Soviet Union to purchase increasing amounts of Cuban sugar, up to five million metric tons in 1969 and 1970, at the fixed price of 6.11 cents per pound. In return, Castro endorsed Khrushchev's policy of peaceful coexistence and the Soviet position in the Sino-Soviet conflict.[24] Moreover, a temporary compromise was reached between Castro on the one hand, and Moscow and the Latin American Communists on the other, concerning the divisive issue of revolutionary strategy. At the November 1964 Havana Conference of Communist parties, called to reconcile differences between the three actors, the strategy of armed struggle was endorsed as one road to revolution for selected Latin American countries; in turn, Havana supported Moscow and its Latin American Communist parties in their rivalry with Peking.[25] Shortly thereafter, Moscow also voiced renewed interest in the Venezuelan guerrilla struggle led by the *Fidelista* Armed Forces of National Liberation (FALN).[26]

Renewed Crisis and Confrontation

The accommodation between Havana and Moscow, however, was intrinsically unstable. The Soviets had not given Castro firm security guarantees despite their pledges of solidarity with Cuba. Moreover, the 1964 trade treaty required that the yearly level of trade between the two countries be renegotiated in annual trade protocols, thereby leaving Cuba vulnerable to Soviet economic leverage. Finally, the separate and divergent interests of the Soviets and Cubans pulled the two parties apart. Hence, a new period of crisis and confrontation ensued after 1965 as four developments heightened the Castro regime's sense of global isolation, reduced its external leverage, and strained the Cuban-Soviet axis as Castro manuevered to regain his bargaining advantage with the Soviets.

The first development, the U.S. armed intervention in the Dominican revolt in April–May 1965, along with the effectiveness of counterinsurgency efforts in other countries, led Moscow to discard its revolutionary objectives in Latin America and to soft-peddle the Castro line of armed struggle.[27] Returning to their traditional strategy, the Soviets sought to advance the interests of the USSR through the normalization of diplomatic and commercial relations with Latin American governments. Thus, Moscow established diplomatic and trade relations with the Christian Democratic government of Chile in April 1965. It extended $100 million in industrial credits to the Brazilian military regime of Castello Branco in August 1966, which had sent a large Brazilian contingent to the Organization of American States (OAS) peace-keeping force in Santo Domingo the previous year. And most galling to the Cubans, the Soviets made overtures for trade and financial assistance to the Colombian and Venezuelan governments during 1966 and 1967—precisely the two regimes under threat from *Fidelista* insurgent forces. In short, Moscow appeared not only to be abandoning Havana's revolutionary interests, but also to be directly subverting these interests.

The second disturbing development was the course of the Vietnam War and Soviet-American relations. Moscow had not deterred "imperialist aggression" in Vietnam nor actively responded to the U.S. bombing of a bona fide Communist state as demanded by the Cuban leadership.[28] Given its searing memories of the missile crisis, the Vietnam War reinforced the Cuban regime's fears that Moscow was capable of sacrificing its allies. Indeed, Cuban apprehensions over a Moscow-Washington accord at Cuba's, as well as North Vietnam's, expense was heightened by the Kosygin-Johnson talks at Glassboro in June 1967. Consequently, the Soviet leader was coldly received during his stopover in Havana following his U.S. visit.[29]

The third development was the scuttling of the *Fidelista* insurgent forces by most of the Communist parties. Responding to local conditions as well as to the Dominican development, the Communists moved to work within their respective political systems following the example of the Chilean Communist party. Nowhere was the Communist abandonment of armed insurgency of more critical importance for the Cubans than in Venezuela, which had long been the prime target for the Castro regime. The Communist Party of Venezuela (PCV) began to disengage itself from the FALN after mid-1965, seeking legal status and a broad political alliance under its program of "democratic peace." Thereafter, the position of the FALN continued to deteriorate, leading to the rupture between the *Fidelistas* and the PCV in April–May 1966, and to Castro's open break with the PCV the following year.[30]

The last development contributing to Cuba's sense of increasing isolation was the clear demise of the *Fidelista* insurgent forces after mid-1965 in Venezuela, Colombia, and Peru; only in Guatemala did the guerrilla movement hold out for some possibility of limited success. The continued deterioration of the position of the insurgent groups, therefore, dimmed Havana's hopes of maintaining a viable and supportive revolutionary movement in the hemisphere, and accordingly reduced Castro's bargaining leverage with Moscow.

Consequently, Castro moved to revitalize the moribund guerrilla movement as a means of overcoming Cuba's hemispheric isolation and regaining his international leverage. A key step was Cuba's support for the new guerrilla *foco* in Bolivia, established by Ernesto (Che) Guevara in late 1966, and staffed by seven former members of the Cuban Communist Party's Central Committee. Another step was to inject new doctrinal support for armed struggle through Havana's publication in early 1967 of Regis Debray's *Revolution in the Revolution?*, which condemned orthodox Communist strategy and developed the Castro-Guevara thesis on armed struggle. The final step was to establish a new institutional base for the revolutionary struggle through the convening of the first conference of the Latin American Solidarity Organization (OLAS) in Havana in August 1967, attended by some 160 pro-Castro delegates from Latin America.

The OLAS conference signified the final split between Castro, and the Soviets and Communists on the issues of revolutionary expansion and strategy.[31] At the closing session of the conference, Castro defiantly challenged Moscow's professed revolutionary commitment by citing its offers of assistance to the Venezuelan and Colombian governments. "If internationalism exists, if solidarity is a word worthy of respect," he declared, "the least that we can expect of any state of the socialist camp is that it refrain from giving any financial or technical aid to those regimes."[32] This attack on the Soviets was paralleled by extreme acts of ideological-political deviation by the OLAS conference as the Cubans completely divorced *Fidelismo* from the prevailing Moscow-Communist line. The OLAS conference militantly reaffirmed armed insurrection in the countryside as being virtually the only road open for revolution in Latin America. It proclaimed that the revolution would be made with or without the Communist party and that the status of revolutionary vanguard would be assigned to *any* group that took up the armed struggle. And it established a permanent OLAS executive committee, with its seat in Havana, to co-ordinate and extend support to the guerrilla movements—the intent of which was subversive to Moscow's interests and policies in Latin America.[33]

Castro's efforts to revitalize the insurgent movement, however, failed with the death of Che Guevara in Bolivia in October 1967. Guevara's death and the collapse of the Bolivian *foco* was a traumatic development for the Cuban leadership. It ended any illusion of rebuilding a viable revolutionary movement in the hemisphere, thereby forcing the Cuban regime to turn the Revolution inward. In turn, it deprived the Castro regime of its principal leverage in dealing with Moscow precisely at the time when Cuban-Soviet relations were most strained, and when Havana was about to enter into negotiations with Moscow on the 1968 trade protocol. Indeed, evidently expecting hard and prolonged bargaining, the Cuban minister of foreign trade arrived in Moscow in mid-October 1967, some three to four months before the expected signing of the protocol.

Escalated Confrontation and New Accommodation

Nevertheless, Castro was not without bargaining counters in resisting Soviet pressures and in pressing for a new accommodation with Moscow. He could still employ extreme acts of ideological-political insubordination, symbolic deviation, and political extortion in an attempt to restructure Cuban-Soviet relations. Thus, throughout most of 1968, Castro maneuvered close to the breaking point, although avoiding a final rupture in Cuban-Soviet ties.

The pattern was already set in late 1967 when Havana cancelled its high-level delegation to Moscow's fiftieth anniversary celebration of the Bolshevik Revolution. The insignificant minister of health, who was not a member of the Politburo or Secretariat of the Communist Party of Cuba, replaced President Osvaldo Dorticós as head of the Cuban delegation. Moreover, along with China and Albania, Cuba was conspicuously absent from *Pravda*'s list of fraternal greetings from ruling Communist parties, while in Havana neither Castro nor Dorticós attended the anniversary celebrations at the Soviet embassy. These humiliating snubs were only a prelude to Havana's escalating acts of political defiance.

In January 1968, the "microfaction" affair was exposed and used by the Castro regime as a deterrent move against the Soviets. Thirty-five members of the disolved PSP, led by Aníbal Escalante, were arrested, tried and sentenced to prison terms ranging from two to fifteen years for conspiring against the Revolution. The principal charges against this microfaction were that it had opposed Castro's economic and foreign policies; and most importantly, that, through its Soviet and Eastern European contacts, it had urged the withdrawal of Soviet bloc support as a means of bringing about Castro's downfall and replacement by trusted old-line Communists. Although Soviet bloc officials were disassociated from the subversive activities of the microfaction, the arrest and sentencing of this pro-Soviet faction nevertheless served as a preemptive warning to Moscow. That is, Havana had signaled its readiness to oppose increased Soviet influence in Cuban affairs, and its readiness to retaliate against cutbacks in Soviet assistance, by its ability to carry out additional actions that would be embarrassing to Moscow.[34]

A further act of defiance came with Havana's boycott of the Soviet-sponsored meeting of Communist parties in Bucharest in February 1968, at which Moscow had hoped to garner international support against Peking. This was followed by the launching of the Revolutionary Offensive in mid-March, whereby the Castro regime accelerated the simultaneous construction of socialism and communism in Cuba. Consequently, the Castro regime could publicly claim the distinction of having "the socialist country with the highest percentage of state-owned property," thereby implying that Cuba had reached a more advanced state of Communist development than either the USSR or the Eastern European states.[35] Then, at the United Nations in May, the Cuban foreign minister pointedly denounced the nuclear nonproliferation treaty that had been jointly sponsored by Moscow and Washington.[36]

These acts of defiance, however, were not entirely effective in warding off Soviet retaliation, not to speak of restructuring the Cuban-Soviet relationship. The long-delayed 1968 trade protocol that was finally signed on March 22, 1968, for example, reflected a tightening up of Soviet economic assistance. Reportedly, the volume of trade for 1968 was to increase by only 10 percent as opposed to 23 percent the previous year; moreover, Moscow would henceforth charge an undisclosed rate of interest on the $327.8 million credit extended to Cuba to help finance its trade imbalance with the Soviet Union.[37] The effectiveness of Soviet economic denials, in turn, was enhanced by the condition and needs of the Cuban economy.

The performance of the Cuban economy had been erratic and sluggish after 1965.[38] Beginning in 1966, however, the regime moved to accelerate the tempo of development by allocating additional resources into development projects necessarily having a delayed payoff and by restricting personal consumption for the populace. An increasingly higher share of Cuba's gross disposable material product was thus devoted to total investments (see chapter 11, table 10) requiring an increasingly severe regimen of austerity to be imposed upon the populace. Hence, the Cuban regime needed to obtain maximum levels of external assistance to support its ambitious developmental programs and to tide it over the lean period of austerity until the expected upturn in the economy in the early 1970s. Moreover, the immediate situation became even more pressing for the Cubans, with the poor 1968 sugar harvest of 5.2 million tons, almost 3 million tons below the target, and the commitment to sell 5 million tons to the USSR in 1969–1970. For the moment, therefore, the Soviets seemed to have gained a stranglehold over the Cuban regime against which further countermoves by Havana would have been extremely risky.

The Soviet bloc occupation of Czechoslovakia in August 1968, however, gave Castro the opportunity to recover his bargaining advantage. In his speech of August 23, Castro used the Czech crisis to air Cuban grievances toward the Soviet bloc and to demand a redefinition of Cuban-Soviet ties in exchange for his endorsement of the Warsaw Pact occupation. First, he voiced Cuban displeasure over internal developments within the Soviet bloc (and by implication within the USSR) and over the state of Soviet bloc relations with Cuba. Thus, he charged that Communist ideals had been corrupted by the bureaucratism and revisionism of the Novotny and Dubcek regimes, respectively; and that the spirit of true internationalism had been violated by the poor quality and disadvantageous terms of Czech trade with Cuba. Next, he both condemned and approved the Warsaw Pact occupation. On the one hand, it was a "flagrant" violation of Czech sovereignty and thus illegal; but on the other, it was politically justified because, "Czechoslovakia was moving toward a counterrevolutionary situation . . . and into the arms of imperialism . . . [and] it was absolutely necessary, at all costs, in one way or another, to prevent this eventuality from taking place." Castro was thus basing his justification for Soviet intervention on ideological and not geopolitical grounds.[39] Accordingly, he demanded that the same Soviet bloc protection be extended to North Vietnam, North Korea, and Cuba: "Will they send the divisions of the Warsaw Pact to Cuba if the Yankee imperialists attack our country, or even in the case of the threat of a Yankee imperialist attack on our country, if our country requests it?"[40]

In effect, Castro was pressing for the desired trade off with the Soviets. On the one hand, he was goading Moscow into fully committing itself to genuine proletarian internationalism toward Cuba. In other words, Cuba should be given the economic support and security guarantees commensurate with its status as a full-fledged socialist state. On the other hand, in exchange for this expected solidarity, Castro had given his qualified endorsement of the armed Soviet bloc intervention in Czechoslovakia. Indeed, Cuba's support of the Warsaw Pact invasion came at a time when the Soviets were facing mounting opposition within as well as outside the international Communist movement. Only fourteen nonbloc Communist parties supported the invasion; seven of these were from Latin America, of which Cuba represented the only ruling Communist party. Hence, although neither *Pravda* nor *Izvestia* reprinted excerpts from Castro's Czech speech, the Soviets surely must have appreciated Cuba's support.

Castro's speech on the Czech crisis thus proved to be the turning point in Cuban-Soviet affairs. The earlier tension and confrontation gave way to a new accommodation by 1969, characterized by mutual concessions and new bonds of solidarity between the two countries. The Soviets, for their part, signed new trade protocols with Havana in 1969 and 1970 that evidently were satisfactory to the Cubans. Soviet Vice President Vladimir

Novikov visited Cuba in January 1969. A Soviet naval squadron paid a highly publicized visit to the Havana harbor on the occasion of the July 26 anniversary of the Revolution, marking the first time the Soviet fleet had honored Cuba with an official visit. In November, 650 Soviet technicians and diplomats, headed by the Soviet ambassador, spent a day cutting sugar cane as a gesture of international solidarity with the push for the ten-million-ton harvest. Marshal Andrei Grechko, Soviet minister of defense, also visited Havana the same month, stirring speculation about a new Soviet arms agreement with Cuba.[41]

On its side, Havana moved back into line behind Moscow, establishing the Cuban-Soviet Friendship Society in April 1969, and fully endorsing the Soviet Union in its domestic and foreign policies.[42] Cuba attended the Conference of Communist Parties held in Moscow in June, at which it was expected that the USSR would attempt to expel China. Conspicuously, China, Albania, North Korea, and North Vietnam did not attend the conference. The Cubans also ceased their polemical attacks on the pro-Moscow Latin American Communist parties, and backed off from their promotion of the strategy of armed struggle.[43] Finally, the Cubans began to share a new area of agreement with the Soviets as Havana moderated its policy toward Latin America. Since July 14, 1969, Castro has praised the nationalist and reformist posture of the Peruvian military regime on several occasions, and a trade agreement with Chile was signed early in 1970.

These shifts in Castro's foreign policy were clearly evident in his speech of April 22, 1970, honoring Lenin's birth. Castro paid tribute to the Soviet state by noting that its existence had made it possible for Cuba to become "the first socialist country in Latin America." He severely attacked the leftist critics of the Soviet Union in Latin America and Europe for their condemnation of the Warsaw Pact invasion of Czechoslovakia. He acclaimed the Soviet Union's supportive role in resisting imperialism in Vietnam, the Middle East, and Cuba. Finally, he vowed that Cuba would not give up its support for the revolutionary movement in Latin America. However, he qualified this in an apparent reference to Peruvian developments by adding that Cuban

> support *does not necessarily have to be expressed exclusively in favor of guerilla movements, but includes any government* which sincerely adopts a policy of economic and social development and of liberating its country from the Yankee imperialist yoke; *no matter by what path that government has reached power, Cuba will support it.* [italics added][44]

The Cuban-Soviet *détente,* therefore, was manifested by renewed evidence of mutual solidarity and by new points of agreement.

The Future Basis for Cuban-Soviet Ties

The *rapprochement* between Havana and Moscow since 1968 appears to rest on a more stable and broader basis than was the case with prior accommodations. No longer are the two states separated by as many divergent and conflicting interests that characterized the relationship during most of the 1960s. Instead, Cuba and the Soviet Union not only continue to share common and reinforced ideological ties, but also their respective revolutionary and political interests converge due to developments in Latin America and Cuba. The collapse of the guerrilla struggle in the hemisphere following Guevara's death compelled the Castro regime to give up its illusions of expanding a Cuban-type revolution in Latin America and to focus, instead, on building socialism within the island. As a result, the devisive questions of divergent revolutionary interests and separate revolutionary strategies no longer strained the Cuban-Soviet relationship. In turn, the demise of the *Fidelista* movement left the Cuban leadership with no alternative but to shore up its relationship with Moscow as a means of safeguarding Cuba's security interests. Similarly, the regime's accelerated program of economic development required that Cuba refashion its ties with the Soviet bloc in order to ensure the success of this new and critical stage of the Revolution. Finally, the emergence of assertive nationalist tendencies among non-*Fidelistas* ruling circles, such as the Peruvian military regime, not only provided Cuba with prospects for overcoming its isolation in Latin America, but also broadened the area of agreement between Cuba and the Soviets.

Nevertheless, the new Cuban-Soviet *détente* signified a fundamental alteration in the bargaining relationship that Castro had exploited so effectively in the past. As was demonstrated, the new accommodation was reached only after hard bargaining. But, unlike in the past, it was an extraneous occurrence within the socialist camp—the Warsaw Pact intervention in Czechoslovakia—that gave Castro the singular opportunity to press for a trade off with Moscow. Moreover, even though Guevara's death and the demise of the guerrilla movements made it possible for Havana to concede its line on armed struggle, this reality also left Cuba with less leverage in its relations with the Soviets. Finally, as was noted, Moscow's position was strengthened by the Cuban economy's need for maximum Soviet assistance.

In fact, the deteriorating state of the Cuban economy became the critical variable in the Havana-Moscow relationship, with the turning point being reached with the 1970 sugar harvest setback. Beginning in 1968, Castro had staked his personal reputation on an all-out drive to achieve his much heralded goal of a 10-million-ton sugar harvest for 1970 despite Soviet reservations if not criticisms to the contrary. Although a new historic record of 8.535 million tons was set over the old record of 7.290 million tons in 1952, Castro had fallen considerably short of winning this "historic battle" and "decisive test" for the Revolution. Equally if not more important, the harvest drive had contributed greatly to a whole series of production setbacks in other sectors of the economy.[45] These developments reflected adversely on Castro's authority and on his ability to make the Revolution economically viable, while at the same time leaving the Cuban economy even more dependent on the Soviets. Combined with the expiration of the 1964 Soviet-Cuban trade treaty at the end of 1970, the harvest and other economic setbacks in 1970 thus further reduced Havana's leverage and its ability to limit Soviet influence in Cuba.

For example, the establishment of an intergovernmental Soviet-Cuban Scientific, Technical and Economic Cooperation Commission in December 1970 evidently signifies a heightened and perhaps direct role for Soviet technicians in running Cuba's economic affairs. The commission provides for joint collaboration in Cuba's long-range planning, and it will study Cuba's economic management and ways for improving economic efficiency. Such a corrective is needed from Moscow's point of view if only because Cuba has run up a cumulative debt to the Soviet Union that is now estimated at more than $3 billion as of the end of 1970.[46] A further sign of Cuba's weakening position is seen by its failure to renegotiate a long-term trade treaty following the lapse of the 1964 treaty. After three months of negotiations in Moscow, an annual trade and payment agreement was signed in February 1971 which will provide for an increase of $110 million in Soviet exports to Cuba in 1971 over the previous year. Nevertheless, the new year-to-year basis for Soviet-Cuban trade will henceforth increase the precariousness of Havana's position, making the latter even more susceptible to Moscow's pressures than in the past. Finally, the Soviets may well have called in Castro's long-standing debts on still another issue. The establishment of a Soviet submarine servicing and personnel facility in the Bay of Cienfuegos in the fall of 1970 evidently means that Cuba has become a forward base of operations—albeit in the form of a "minibase"—for the expansion of Soviet naval power in the Caribbean without, however, obtaining commensurate security guarantees in return. The bitter irony for Cuba, therefore, is that it now provides military bases for the two rival superpowers—the USSR in Cienfuegos and the United States in Guantanamo.

This state of increased foreign dependency and penetration may continue to characterize Cuba's relations with the Soviet Union until there is a marked upturn in the Cuban economy and/or until there is a relaxation of U.S. policy toward the Castro regime. Such future contingencies would lessen Cuba's need to depend so heavily upon the Soviets for its economic well-being and security requirements. However, as he has proven time and again, Castro has a remarkable aptitude for salvaging his position by making the most of his limited resources. Hence, one way for him to lessen Cuba's new dependency upon the Soviets is to explore new alternatives in his policy toward Latin America.

In November 1969, for example, Castro noted that the year-old Peruvian military regime was playing a "revolutionary role" in Latin American politics. Consequently, he said, "We are watching with great interest the development of the political process in Peru, where, without the slightest doubt, a new phenomenon has developed."[47] Indeed, he may have looked upon the anti-Communist but reformist and nationalistic armed forces in Peru as his potential anchor for realigning right-wing and left-wing nationalism in Latin America.[48] The establishment of relations between Cuba and Peru, of course, would require that Havana associate itself with military circles that had vigorously prosecuted a counterinsurgency campaign in the recent past, thereby cutting Castro off from the remnants of the revolutionary left in that country. Nonetheless, Castro has previously overlooked ideological differences when it was to his advantage, as has been the case with Cuba's close economic ties with Franco's Spain. Moreover, the Cuban leader can foresake his militant revolutionary line in order to permit the normalization of relations on a selective basis with such states as Peru, while simultaneously endorsing violent revolution in other countries that are closely aligned with the United States such as Argentina, Brazil, Uruguay, and the Central American states. This dual track policy in turn could enable Cuba to overcome its hemispheric isolation, thereby giving the Castro regime a greater sense of security.

The rendering of earthquake relief to Peru and the courting of the Peruvian military regime by Havana, however, have not led to the restoration of relations between the two countries as of mid-1971. Only Chile has thus far provided the Castro regime with a tangible diplomatic success. The first break occurred with the signing of a trade agreement between Havana and the Christian Democratic government of Eduardo Frei in early 1970. This was followed by the election of the Socialist candidate, Salvador Allende, as President of Chile in September 1970 which in turn was acclaimed by Havana as a legitimate step in the road to socialism in Chile. The restoration of diplomatic and trade relations came in November, upon Allende's assumption to the presidency. Early 1971 also saw the signing of agreements on air travel between the two countries and new trade exchanges valued in the neighborhood of some $17 million. While these developments are of psychological importance in reducing Cuba's sense of hemispheric isolation, they nevertheless are of limited value in lessening Cuba's economic dependence upon the Soviet Union. Such a contingency turns upon Havana broadening its ties with still other Latin American countries that can better supply Cuba with needed raw materials and manufactured products, such as Venezuela and Colombia, and ultimately upon the restoration—at a minimum—of trade relations with the United States.

NOTES

1. Initially, the Soviets saw the Cuban Revolution as a means of disturbing inter-American solidarity, weakening U.S. hegemony in Latin America, and diverting Washington's attention to the Western Hemisphere. Rather than revolutionary objectives, however, these were cold war objectives, which Moscow evidently hoped to achieve through a minimum of direct involvement in Cuba and with the Castro regime retaining a liberationist but non-Communist character. On the other hand, Cuba began to acquire strategic and revolutionary significance for the Soviets once the permanency of the Castro regime seem assured after 1961, and *Fidelista* armed insurgency appeared as a viable force in Latin America.

2. Although there is no evidence that Cuba has ever applied for admission to the Warsaw Treaty Organization, "Cuban leaders and the Cuban press have always maintained a high interest in the organization and its activities. It is likely that from 1962 to 1964 the Cuban leaders would have welcomed an opportunity to become a signatary to the mutual defense treaty. Under such an arrangement, Cuba's military defenses would have been far more secure vis-à-vis the United States and the Cuban exiles than through bilateral pledges of assistance." David Ronfeldt and Daniel Tretiak, "Cuba's Integration Into the World Communist System, 1962–1966: A Preliminary Assessment," in *The World Communist System: International and Comparative Studies,* ed. J. F. Triska (New York, 1969), p. 209.

3. The Soviet leadership thus found it necessary to hedge on the extent of Soviet military commitments with Cuba. For example, three days after Washington cut the Cuban sugar quota, on July 9, 1960, Khrushchev announced that in a figurative sense, if it became necessary, the Soviet military could support the Cuban people with rocket weapons. Despite the inherent qualifications in this threat, Moscow studiously avoided making any references to military assistance in the event of aggression in its official communiqués, while Khrushchev subsequently stressed the "symbolic" character of his missile threat.

4. In brief, the missile installations in Cuba offered the Soviets a shortcut and a less expensive method for closing the imbalance in strategic weapons between the USSR and the United States. See Arnold L. Horelick, "The Cuban Missile Crisis: An Analysis of Soviet Calculations and Behavior," *World Politics,* 16 (April 1964), pp. 363–89.

5. In his speech of March 13, 1968, for example, Castro spoke derisively of "the

famous intercontinental missiles" in 1962 that had produced an attitude of complacency and led many a Cuban "to count on them as if he had them in his pocket." *Granma Weekly Review,* March 24, 1968, p. 2.

6. See chapter 5, this volume.

7. Soviet revolutionary expansion and probing in the postwar period had occurred in the contiguous regions of Eastern and Central Europe, the Middle East, and the Far East. Only Guatemala in the early 1950s offered some possibility of a Communist take-over in Latin America, but this evidently was the result of local conditions rather than of Soviet intentions. See Ronald M. Scheneider, *Communism in Guatemala, 1944–1954* (New York, 1959).

8. For the Soviet perspective, see M. Antyasov and A. Glinkin, "New Trends in Pan Americanism," *International Affairs* (Moscow), no. 12 (December 1957), pp. 90–100; V. Volsky, "Argentina—An Important Victory," ibid., no. 4 (April 1958), pp. 95–96; and V. Vasilyev, "Growing Resistance to U.S. Colonialist Policy in Latin America," ibid., no. 8 (August 1958), pp. 29–36.

9. Referring to Brazilian developments under Goulart, for example, a Soviet affairs specialist has pointed out that "the Soviet Union could not support Brazil economically on anything like the scale on which it was supporting Cuba. A Communist regime under Goulart would pose very serious problems for the Soviet Union while it existed, and its viability was uncertain." Herbert S. Dinerstein, "Soviet Policy in Latin America," *The American Political Science Review,* 61 (March 1967), p. 85.

10. The Soviets maintained that the violent or nonviolent path to revolution depended on local circumstances. Armed struggle was not to be used against liberal reformist regimes. However, where dictatorships were in power and allied with foreign monopolies, "the development of the struggle on a broad front, including armed struggle, and the creation of partisan detachments in some areas, is a completely justified course." A. Sivolobov, "Krestianskoe dvizhenie v Latinskoi Americke" [The Peasant Movement in Latin America], *Kommunist* (August 1964), p. 107.

11. For an analysis of these developments see Dinerstein, "Soviet Policy," pp. 86–90.

12. The most cogent exposition of the Castro-Guevara thesis is contained in Ernesto (Che) Guevara, "Guerrilla Warfare: A Means," *Peking Review* (January 10, 1964), pp. 14–21; and Regis Debray, *¿Revolución en la revolución?* (La Habana, 1967). For a discussion of this theme see chapter 5, this volume.

13. The orthodox Communist position at the time of the Cuban Revolution is represented by Rodney Arismendi, "On the Role of the National Bourgeoisie in the Anti-Imperialist Struggle," *World Marxist Review* (May 1959), pp. 29–39, and (June 1959), pp. 31–39. See also the summary analysis of the Chilean Communist party's strategy by Ernst Halperin, *Nationalism and Communism in Chile* (Cambridge, Mass., 1965), pp. 42–117.

14. The Chilean Communists formed an electoral front with the Socialists whose candidate was the main though unsuccessful contender in the 1964 presidential elections against the Christian Democrats.

15. For a description of these aspects see chapters 1, 2, and 7, this volume.

16. In 1965, for example, Ernesto Guevara in effect criticized the Soviet bloc countries for not building communism because "the adapted economic base [from capitalism] has undermined the development of consciousness. To build communism, a new man must be created simultaneously with the material base." *Man and Socialism in Cuba* (Havana, 1967), p. 22. Castro later took up the Guevarist thesis. See, for example, *Granma Weekly Review,* July 28, 1968, p. 6.

17. The main criticisms of the Cuban economy came from Czechoslovakia which had been delegated the job of supplying technical assistance to Cuba. See the critical articles by Valtr Komarek appearing in *Hospodarske Noviny* (Prague), August 18 and August 25, 1967, as summarized by Carmelo Mesa-Lago, "Economic, Political and Ideological Factors in the Cuban Controversy on Material Versus Moral Incentives" (Paper delivered at the Latin American Studies Association Second National Meeting, Washington, D.C., April 17–18, 1970), pp. 25–26.

18. Cuban-Chinese relations deteriorated throughout 1965, culminating with Castro's denunciation of Peking in January 1966 for reducing rice exports to Cuba and meddling in its internal affairs. The dispute, however, evidently stemmed from the pro-Soviet position taken by Castro at the Havana conference of Communist parties in November 1964.

19. The Escalante affair has been documented by Andrés Suárez, *Cuba: Castroism and Communism, 1959–1966* (Cambridge, Mass., 1967), pp. 146–53. For the trial of Marcos Rodríguez see Janette Habel, *Proceso al sectarismo* (Buenos Aires, 1965). The "microfaction" affair is discussed later in this chapter.

20. For a more detailed analysis of the 1959–1960 developments, see Edward Gonzalez, "Castro's Revolution, Cuban Communist Appeals, and the Soviet Response," *World Politics*, 21 (October 1968), pp. 39–68.

21. *Granma Weekly Review*, May 3, 1970, p. 3.

22. In settling the missile crisis, and without Castro's prior consent, Washington and Moscow agreed to the international inspection of Cuba to verify that the missiles had been withdrawn. Castro never accepted inspection and insisted that five conditions would first have to be met: the United States must (a) end the naval blockade and economic embargo, (b) cease subversive activities in Cuba, (c) stop the armed attacks by exiled groups, (d) terminate U-2 overflights, and (e) withdraw from the Guantanamo naval base. It was not until November 1, 1962, four days after the resolution of the crisis, that *Izvestia* announced the Soviet Union's support of Castro's conditions.

23. See the analysis by Suárez, *Cuba*, pp. 171–83.

24. Ibid., p. 193.

25. See Dinerstein, "Soviet Policy," p. 87.

26. The January 14, 1965, issue of *Pravda*, for example, editorially endorsed the "just struggle" of the FALN in Venezuela.

27. Following the Dominican revolt, which was not Communist led, Moscow and the Latin American Communists backed away from their qualified endorsement of armed struggle. They argued, instead, for the avoidance of provocative and premature actions by revolutionaries, and for the formation of "broad national anti-imperialist fronts" to include the progressive bourgeoisie and their political parties. See V. Listov, "Big Stick Against a Small Nation," *New Times*, May 17, 1965, p. 11; and the August 1965 issue of *World Marxist Review*, containing the assessments of Latin American Communists.

28. Armando Hart, head of the Cuban Communist delegation to the Twenty-third Congress of the Communist Party of the Soviet Union (CPSU) in 1966, affirmed that the socialist states had "the right and the duty" to hurl back the U.S. aggressors. He also quoted Castro's speech of March 13, 1965, in which the Cuban leader had demanded armed intervention by the socialist camp in Vietnam. Armando Hart, "Saludo del CC del PCC at XIII Congreso del PCUS," *Cuba Socialista*, 6 (May 1966), pp. 38–39.

29. *Granma,* for example, matter-of-factly announced the arrival of the Soviet premier, mentioned no honor guard or state reception for Kosygin, and carried a terse biographical sketch of the Soviet leader. See *Granma,* June 27, 1967, pp. 1, 3.

30. On the Venezuelan affair, see D. Bruce Jackson, *Castro, the Kremlin, and Communism in Latin America* (Baltimore, 1969), pp. 40–119.

31. On the eve of the OLAS conference, the July 30, 1967, issue of *Pravda* reprinted a leading article by the Chilean Communist, Luis Corvalán, upholding the "peaceful road" and criticizing *Fidelismo.* Regarding the latter, Corvalán declared, "The revolutionary current which emerges on a petty bourgeois basis usually underrates the proletariat and the communist parties, is more disposed toward nationalism, adventurism and terrorism, and sometimes permits anti-communist and anti-Soviet attitudes."

32. *Granma Weekly Review,* August 20, 1967, p. 5.

33. See Castro's speech and the OLAS Resolution, ibid., pp. 2–7.

34. See the testimony by Raúl Castro and others concerning the "microfaction" in ibid., February 11, 1968, pp. 2, 4–5, 7–11. It should be pointed out that the microfaction affair was also a warning to internal "reformist" currents. See Castro's speech of March 13 in ibid., March 24, 1968, p. 2.

35. See the editorial, "Somos socialistas" [We Are Socialists], *Granma,* March 29, 1968, p. 1. For a complete discussion of these events see Carmelo Mesa-Lago, "The Revolutionary Offensive," *Trans-action,* 6 (April 1969), pp. 22–29.

36. Among the reasons for Cuba's not signing the treaty, according to Foreign Minister Raúl Roa, was that it provided the small states with no protection against U.S. nuclear aggression. For Roa's full indictment, see *Granma,* May 19, 1968, pp. 2–3.

37. Kevlin Devlin, "The Soviet-Cuban Confrontation: Economic Reality and Political Judo," pub. by the research departments of Radio Free Europe, April 1, 1968, pp. 15–16.

38. See Edward Gonzalez, "Castro: The Limits of Charisma," *Problems of Communism,* 19 (July–August 1970), pp. 12–24.

39. By inference, therefore, Castro was saying that the United States also had no legal right to intervene in Cuba. But if Washington did aggress Cuba, or if it provoked a counterrevolution, then the Soviet Union was equally obligated to rescue socialism in Cuba as it had done in Czechoslovakia.

40. *Granma Weekly Review,* August 25, 1968, pp. 1–4.

41. Raúl Castro paid a six-week return visit to the Soviet Union in April–May, 1970. According to one report, the Soviets agreed to reequip the Cuban armed forces, including supplying it with improved SA-2, a defense missile, and a 25-plane squadron of F model Mig-21s. *Time,* July 27, 1970, p. 17.

42. Beginning in November 1968, *Granma Weekly Review* began to give full coverage to past and recent Soviet accomplishments, and to give extraordinary publicity to gestures of Soviet solidarity with Cuba.

43. See chapters 1 and 5, this volume.

44. *Granma Weekly Review,* May 3, 1970, pp. 2–5.

45. See Castro's speech of July 26, 1970, in ibid., August 2, 1970, pp. 2–6.

46. *New York Times,* February 28, 1971, p. 3.

47. *Granma Weekly Review,* November 16, 1969, p. 2. Castro also acclaimed the Peruvian phenomenon and Chile's decision to trade with Cuba in his April 22, 1970, speech. See ibid., May 3, 1970, p. 5.

48. The Cuban-Peruvian alignment would be facilitated by the increased militarization of the Cuban Revolution. In addition to their assertive nationalism, the two regimes would thus share institutional, generational, and developmental similarities that could help overcome ideological differences.

5

Ernesto F. Betancourt

Exporting the Revolution to Latin America

"HOW bright and near would the future seem were two, or three, or more Vietnams to emerge throughout the years . . . with their repeated blows to imperialism, with the inevitable dispersal of its forces this would entail!" Thus spoke Ernesto (Che) Guevara in his last political manifesto, the "Message to the Peoples of the World," released in April 1967 by the Tricontinental Secretariat in Havana.[1] Guevara's death is emerging as the turning point that brought to an end his hope of promoting several Vietnams in Latin America. Yet, all along, the threat from the exporters of revolution, such as Guevara, has not amounted to much in this hemisphere. Rather, we believe it is the inadequacy of the efforts undertaken so far through the Alliance for Progress to cope with the conditions conducive to revolution that constitutes the real threat.

In any case, in writing on the subject of exporting the Cuban Revolution to Latin America, it is easy to appear as either an accuser of the Castro regime or as an advocate of revolutionary solutions. Neither of the two *clisés* applies. In the first place, there is no need to accuse Castro of encouraging revolutionary activities in other Latin American countries. It is a fact that Cuba has tried to export its revolution. At times, even the Cuban leaders have boldly admitted their subversive activities and some have been caught red-handed. After all, what was Guevara doing in Bolivia with his entire Cuban staff if not exporting revolution? In the second place, to agree with the advocates of revolution in their diagnosis of the conditions that may be conducive to revolutionary outbreaks does not necessarily mean that we agree with their prognosis on how to cope with the diagnosed situation.

Keeping this in mind, in this essay we will attempt to present the rationale behind the Cuban policy of external subversion, the events necessitating a change of tactics, and the formulation of a revolutionary strategy. We will also discuss the revolutionary potential of Latin America and the conditions under which a revolutionary propensity develops. Finally, we will attempt to explain why Cuba's revolutionary strategy has failed in Latin America in spite of the conditions favoring success.

Changing Rationale for Exporting the Revolution

From Castro's point of view, Cuba is a beleaguered and isolated outpost of socialism only ninety miles from the United States, subject to the hostility of the hemisphere, and at the mercy of the doubtful support of the Soviet Union. Castro believed that only the promotion of revolution in other countries in Latin America could assure the survival and consolidation of his regime. This was, in essence, the objective pursued with increasing boldness in the last few years. However, the death of Guevara in 1967 was a serious setback, and as will be shown, it has forced Castro to resort to a different revolutionary policy to achieve his aims. In examining the internal struggle in Cuba over the issue of exporting the revolution, it is useful to understand the evolution of that policy.

Revolutionary Romanticism and Solidarity

During what we shall call the romantic period of the Revolution, from 1959 to 1961, the Cuban leadership was motivated by the feeling of solidarity all revolutionaries have for their own breed. Cuban exiles had lived throughout the region and brought back with them a network of contacts with people of similar inclination in those countries. Venezuela and Costa Rica had been the source of arms shipments under the tolerant eyes of sympathetic authorities. When the revolutionaries took over in Cuba it was not only natural, but moral to want to do the same in other countries.

In fact, the roots of this attitude went even deeper, both in historical terms and in the personal experience of the leaders. The history of Latin America's independence is rich in episodes showing this type of regional solidarity. The history of Cuba's independence provides many examples of Latin Americans going to fight for the freedom of another land in the hemisphere. And, coming to the personal experience of Cuba's leaders, Castro was part of the Cayo Confites expedition of 1947 against Trujillo in the Dominican Republic and also participated in the uprising in 1948 in Bogota, where he was attending a student meeting sponsored by Perón. Furthermore, while in exile in Mexico, he met exiles from many other countries. It was there that he met Guevara, who had been in Bolivia, Peru, Ecuador, Panama, and Guatemala. In Guatemala, Guevara arrived at the tail end of the Arbenz regime and participated briefly in the futile effort to prevent Arbenz's overthrow.[2]

Perhaps we could also speculate on other subjective motivations of these two leaders. Castro and Guevara can be seen as the kind of men who enjoy playing a historical role. The success of the Cuban Revolution was a surprise even to themselves, particularly in relation to the U.S. response to it. Guevara himself wrote an article in April 1961 with the very significant title, "Cuba: Historical Exception or Vanguard in the Anti-Colonial Struggle?"[3] It is not too farfetched to assume that both of them felt that Cuba was at the vanguard of such a struggle and, therefore, that they could repeat the Cuban experience in a much larger theater, as in Latin America. Success in such an undertaking would place them in history along with the great liberators of the previous century, José de San Martín and Simón Bolívar.

Increasing Need of Exporting the Revolution

Whatever the initial motivations, by 1962 the Cuban leadership had more objective reasons to export revolution to Latin America. In fact, in response to Cuban actions and also because of the ideological stance taken by Castro, the hemisphere was moving to isolate Cuba. The Bay of Pigs in April 1961 had pushed Cuba into the Soviet sphere of influence, thus bringing to an abrupt end whatever possibility had existed before for the Cuban Revolution to steer a middle course between the two great powers, the United States and the Soviet Union. When Castro announced in December 1961 that the Cuban Revolution was Marxist-Leninist, the hemisphere reacted by banning Castro's government from the OAS Eighth Meeting of Consultation in Punta del Este held in January of 1962.[4]

Up to that time, the Cuban Revolution enjoyed widespread sympathy in Latin America, which served to offset the hostility of the United States and of the Latin American ruling classes. Now it was clear that sympathy was no longer a sufficient deterrent.

At Punta del Este, Cuban President Osvaldo Dorticós stated: "We know, on the basis of our own experience, that it is impossible to have in any country an exported revolution. We do not pretend, and shall never pretend, to export our revolution."[5] However, upon Dorticós's return to Havana, Castro organized a mass rally on February 4, 1962, at which time the Second Declaration of Havana was ratified. In this document, the ruling groups of Latin America are bypassed with a direct appeal to revolution by the Latin American masses. The Latin Americans present at the rally were asked to join in voting for the Declaration. In a subtle way, they were asked to commit themselves as true revolutionaries by words and, hopefully, by deeds.

The Declaration states, "The United States cannot use Cuba against Latin America, but is using its domination of Latin America to attack Cuba with the force of these countries."[6] It then proceeds to explain how this could be prevented only by the unavoidable revolution that would sweep the continent. In essence, Castro was abandoning any hopes that the governments of Latin America could or would be willing to help him lessen American hostility and, therefore, their replacement by revolutionary forces in those societies became a basic goal of Cuban foreign policy.

After the missile crisis in October 1962, this goal acquired a greater degree of urgency in the minds of the Cuban leadership. The Soviet Union had reached the brink and wavered. Cuba had become a pawn in the cold war and could be bargained away by the Soviets. As Ricardo Rojo relates in his book, *My Friend Che,* he was summoned to Havana by Guevara in early 1963 to discuss revolutionary possibilities in Latin America. In summarizing Guevara's reaction to the gloomy prospect for Cuba, Rojo says: "Since capitalist Latin America rejected coexistence with socialist Cuba, Cuba would help all revolutionaries wipe out capitalism in their countries."[7]

By July 26, 1963, Castro was announcing that the "Andes would become the Sierra Maestra of Latin America." In September of that year, Guevara wrote an article for *Cuba Socialista,* the theoretical organ of the regime, on guerrilla warfare as the method to be applied to carry the revolution throughout Latin America.[8]

Plans are easier to make than to carry out, however. By the end of 1964, Hugo Blanco had failed in Peru, and Masetti in northern Argentina. In Venezuela, the Armed Forces of National Liberation (FALN) had failed completely in its efforts to prevent the election of Raúl Leoni, and in Brazil, the Goulart regime had been overthrown. United States intervention in the Dominican Republic of 1965 reduced even further the hopes harbored by the Cuban leadership of the feasibility that the Cuban experience could be repeated.

In the process, Cuba had been caught red-handed exporting the revolution. On November 1, 1963, the Venezuelan army had uncovered a shipment of arms in the Paraguaná Peninsula of Falcón State, which provided material evidence against Cuba presented at the OAS Ninth Meeting of Consultation. Cuba was found guilty of aggression and sanctions were approved requesting member states to sever diplomatic, economic, and transportation links with Cuba.[9] Thus, rather than attaining the goal sought by Guevara, the policy of exporting the revolution was further isolating Cuba.

Reconsideration and Guevara's Disappearance

It is clear that during this period, either as a result of pressure from the Soviet Union, under prodding from the pro-Soviet Communist parties in

Latin America, or on the basis of Castro's own political instinct, there were serious doubts within the regime as to whether it was wise to continue this exportation policy. However, for Castro, such a turnabout would involve serious risks to his status. For one, he could hardly afford to continue to appear subservient to the Soviets. Besides, to acknowledge the failure of such a vital policy was to renounce the goal of breaking the increasing isolation of Cuba, particularly in view of the reluctance of the rest of the hemisphere to accept a socialist Cuba within the general trend toward peaceful coexistence.

The most dramatic indication that something was brewing inside the regime was Guevara's disappearance early in 1965 upon his return from an extended trip to the United Nations and Africa. Since Guevara was known as the advocate of an internal economic policy of industrialization, based on moral incentives, and of an external policy of exporting the revolution, his disappearance could have been the result of a disagreement with Castro on either policy or on both. In a letter to his mother, Guevara apparently was considering withdrawing to a humble job as factory manager.[10] However, the fact that he resigned his post as minister of industries to go abroad to promote revolution, first in the Congo and then in Bolivia, points to the export of revolution issue as perhaps the most significant cause of his cleavage with Castro. This impression is strengthened by his letter to Castro dated April 7, 1965, in which he broke his official ties with Cuba to free his country of any responsibility for what he was about to do.[11] In other words, Castro was hesitant to continue that policy so Guevara was going to pursue it on his own.

Regis Debray, furthermore, made an enigmatic reference to this question in his essay, "Latin America: Some Problems of Revolutionary Strategy," written in 1965. He refers to the initial hopes of new revolutions in Latin America harbored by the Cuban leadership and makes comparisons with similar statements by Lenin, adding, "Lenin, unlike Trotsky, soon abandoned his illusion, just as the Cuban leaders, so it would appear, have abandoned it today."[12] In that same essay, right at the beginning, he recognizes that Cuba has been at the vanguard of Latin American revolution "to the extent that the Cuban people and their leaders, after six years of struggle, have abandoned none of their proletarian internationalism." Why this contradiction as to abandoning the illusion of revolutions but not their proletarian internationalism? What was going on within the inner ruling group of Cuba to leave such a contradictory impression on Debray?

Adolfo Gilly, a Latin American Trotskyite, wrote in 1965: "The Cuban people have this conviction, that can be perceived by any visitor: there is no stable outcome for Cuba without the revolution spreading to the rest of the continent. That conviction is felt as a tremendous pressure everywhere on the island. It is foolish to think that the Cuban government can act independently of that opinion (that is, in case it wanted to do so)."[13] Who had those foolish thoughts, Castro or his detractors? Was this a veiled revelation of wavering determination at the top or was this a defense of the Cuban leadership against their detractors?

After the Tricontinental Conference in January 1966 (held in Havana by revolutionaries from Africa, Asia, and Latin America), the issue came out into the open. In his closing speech at the meeting, Castro accused Trotskyite elements of slandering him over Guevara's disappearance and for his lack of support of the Dominican rebellion when the United States intervened. He also brought into the open his disagreement with the MR-13 guerrilla organization in Guatemala, whose leader he accused of having become an instrument of the Trotskyites. At the same time he proclaimed, "The revolutionary movement anywhere on earth can count on Cuban fighters."[14] Behind the scenes, Castro was also involved in a bitter struggle with the Chinese over control of the Tricontinental meeting. The conflict with the Chinese became public on January 2, when Castro unleashed his oratory on them for meddling in Cuba's internal affairs and failing to deliver rice as agreed. The pro-Chinese parties in Latin America reacted against Castro by accusing him of belatedly siding with the Soviets in the Sino-Soviet split.

In March 1966, the Communist party of Brazil—of Chinese affiliation —sent Castro an open letter that accuses him of having been dishonest in his words at the Tricontinental and of stacking the conference with pro-Soviet revisionists. The letter states, "By these actions you have displayed an abominable bias in favor of the opponents of revolution in this Hemisphere."[15]

Castro Changes Tactics

As later events showed, Castro may not have abdicated his revolutionary goals. His move perhaps was tactical rather than strategic and based on rivalry with the Chinese for control of Latin American revolutionary movements, more than on a weakening of his revolutionary fervor. One source reports that while this debate was going on, Castro asked Guevara, then abroad, to repeat the 1963 attempt by Masetti to set up a guerrilla *foco* in northern Argentina.[16] Again, one of the motivating factors could have been distrust of Soviet intentions. If this is true, it could mean that the Soviets may have attempted to use the Cubans at the Tricontinental, as the pro-Chinese were saying, and later reverted to their peaceful coexistence line.

Whatever the reason, it is obvious there was a change of policy between Guevara's departure for the Congo and his return early in 1966. Castro's goal of exporting the revolution may have not changed during the period. But, as Debray and Gilly pointed out, Castro must have expressed some doubts as to the feasibility of promoting revolutions. At the same time, the increasing and bogged-down American entanglement in Vietnam was providing a new ray of hope for guerrilla movements. That Vietnam was very much in the minds of the Cuban leadership, both as an example and as a tactical opportunity, is explicitly indicated in Guevara's "Message to the Peoples of the World," when he spoke in April 1967 of "one, two, three Vietnams" and not of one, two, or three Cubas. The year 1967 was proclaimed in Cuba as the year of the "Heroic Vietnam" and, at the Latin American Solidarity Organization (OLAS) meeting in August 1967, point 15 of the report presented by the Cuban delegation says, "Vietnam shows that our victory is unavoidable." The reasoning being that if a small country like Vietnam can "successfully" fight American imperialism, a whole continent, like Latin America, stands an even better chance.

The OLAS meeting took place at a time when Cuba had been caught again red-handed. A small group of Cuban army officers were smuggling arms and guerrillas into Machurucuto Beach on the Barlovento coast of Venezuela when their boat capsized. Two officers died and two were captured. Castro's response was defiant. In reply to the corresponding accusation made by the Venezuelan government, the Central Committee of the Communist Party of Cuba issued a statement on May 18, saying, "We are accused of helping the revolutionary movement and, it is true, we are helping and shall help, whenever we are asked, all revolutionary movements that fight imperialism anywhere in the world."[17] Later on, this policy was further ratified by the presence of sixteen Cuban officers in the guerrilla force in Bolivia, of which four were members of the Central Committee of the Communist Party of Cuba.[18]

At the OLAS meeting, Cuba tried to gain some control over the guerrilla forces it was helping. The mechanism set for achieving such control was related to the organizational structure of OLAS. This structure included three bodies: the OLAS conference (which would meet only occasionally), the National Committees representing each country involved in the conference, and the Permanent Committee. The secretariat of the latter, under Castro's control, was entrusted to and headquartered in Cuba and had the function, among others, "to maintain control over the composition of the National Committees in order to assure their dynamism."[19]

However, in Venezuela and in Bolivia, as well as in the previously referred to situation in Guatemala in 1965, the attempt to impose external control was a source of conflict. The forces of nationalism seem to resent revolutionary imperialism as much as the more conventional variety of imperialism. This is evident in the violent exchange of charges with the Venezuelan Communist party in Castro's speech at the OLAS meeting.[20] In Bolivia, at that same time, Guevara's failure was being sealed by his inability to gain national support. His insistence on being the supreme political and military authority did not help.[21]

The Failure of Revolution à la Cuba in Latin America

In the end, the policy of exporting revolution had failed. In failing, it has given an answer to Guevara's own question as to whether Cuba was the historical exception or the vanguard of an anticolonial struggle. In pursuit of this revolutionary policy, Castro had awakened the forces of reaction, alienated reformist elements, disagreed violently with traditional Communist parties, and even antagonized some among the extreme radicals of the New Left. Cuba was no nearer than it was in 1963 to establishing revolutionary governments in Latin America that would break its isolation from the hemisphere.

In the aftermath of Guevara's death, Castro tried to make the best of things in propaganda terms. However, the coup of publishing Guevara's diary and the conversion of Guevara into a myth contrasted with the reality of Castro's actions. Actual support of guerrilla movements was reduced, if not discontinued. Thus, by January 15, 1970, Douglas Bravo accused Castro of having abandoned his Venezuelan guerrillas.

At the same time, a different policy toward the Soviets became evident. On August 23, 1968, the "Year of the Heroic Guerrilla Fighter," Castro went on television and, after acknowledging that what he was about to say "ran against the emotions of many," he endorsed the Soviet intervention in Czechoslovakia.[22] In Latin America, where intervention is a dirty word, this speech tarnished Castro's image as a revolutionary figure. How could he be considered a revolutionary, while defending intervention of a great power in a small country? Castro was buckling down to the realities of power. He had become part of the establishment. In his speech, Castro was very explicit as to his real concern. After quoting at length from dispatches on Latin American comments indicating the possibility of reopening the Cuban issue in the light of the Soviet response to the Czech heresy, Castro conditioned his support to the Soviets to a more orthodox Marxist line. He asked whether Soviet divisions would also be sent to Cuba, North Vietnam, or North Korea should there be an imperialist aggression there, and added, "We accept the bitter necessity that required the dispatch of these troops to Czechoslovakia . . . but we have the right to demand that a consequent position be taken in all the other matters affecting the international revolutionary movement."[23]

In the face of the failure to export his revolution, Castro had no recourse to assure the security of his regime other than to submit to Soviet policy, regardless of how much it ran against the grain of Castro's revolutionary followers. In June 1969, Cuba was represented just as an observer at the conference of Communist parties in Moscow by Carlos Rafael Rodríguez, an old-time Communist party hand. In the Declaration of Moscow passed at the conference, exporting revolution, armed struggle, the guerrilla as vanguard, and all the other shibboleths of Guevara and Debray were given a subordinated role within the overall Soviet strategy to promote Marxism-Leninism. It is true, Cuba did not sign the document by hiding behind the observer status. However, in contrast with the bravado of the past, it was left to the Dominican representative to say that he could not sign because the document was not revolutionary enough. Carlos Rafael Rodríguez did not challenge the Soviets, but meekly went along finding points of agreement where, before, there was bitter controversy.[24]

On the surface, the Cuban leaders, as Lenin and Stalin before them, seem to have abandoned the hope for other revolutions. The doubts expressed in Debray's 1965 paper seem to have become a reality. What had gone wrong with Cuba's revolutionary strategy? A deeper look into the development of this strategy may help answer this question.

The Revolutionary Strategy Advocated by Cuba

Castro's appraisal of the correlation of forces at the international level, particularly since the American entanglement in Vietnam, led him to the conclusion that a new opportunity had opened in this hemisphere for the establishment and consolidation of revolutionary regimes. His assumption was that the United States was too overextended, internally and externally, to be able to react effectively should a new Cuba arise. As a precautionary measure, the idea was to have revolutionary situations develop simultaneously in several countries, thus preventing the United States from concentrating its forces in one country, as was the case at the time of the intervention in the Dominican Republic. Consequently, a protracted process of erosion on a multinational basis was to take place, avoiding isolated revolts.

The essence of the strategy advocated to pursue this objective was the use of violence. It may have been called armed struggle or guerrilla warfare, but willingness to resort to violence was its first principle. Marxism as an ideology became secondary. In other words, violence was to be the primary ideology, with Marxism taking over after victory, just as it happened in Cuba. The slogan that served as the theme for the 1967 meeting of

OLAS, a slogan first used in the Second Declaration of Havana, is an excellent synthesis of the intended strategy.[25] This slogan says, "The duty of
every revolutionary is to make revolution."

The Initial Absence of Strategy

In the early or romantic period of the Revolution, there was no deep
strategic concept guiding the exportation policy. It was assumed that somehow, with some outside help, other groups in Latin America could reproduce the Cuban experience.

The first action of this nature took place in April 1959. A landing force
of eighty-four men disembarked in a small Panamanian locality named
"Nombre de Dios." According to the Inter-American Peace Commission
report, eighty-two of the invaders were Cubans, one was American, and
one was Panamanian.[26] Obviously, such an expeditionary force had little
chance for success and was captured without great difficulty. During the
rest of 1959, similar adventures against Nicaragua, Haiti, and the Dominican Republic were equally unsuccessful and provoked the corresponding
diplomatic actions at the inter-American level.[27]

Parallel with this direct and rather amateurish approach to exporting
the revolution, the Castro regime took advantage of the ground swell of
hemispheric sympathy for the Revolution to meddle in the internal affairs
and politics of Latin American countries. Thus, by the time of the OAS
Eighth Meeting of Consultation in 1962, Cuban diplomats had been expelled from Venezuela, Guatemala, Nicaragua, Peru, El Salvador, Bolivia,
Panama, Uruguay, and Honduras as a result of their subversive activities
in those countries.[28] But, here again, no strategic concept was involved and,
in many cases, the objective was to mobilize support for Cuba within
the established order rather than to pursue a coherent strategy to export
the revolution.

Inception of the Strategy

However, during the same period, Guevara was already working on developing some generalizations from the Cuban experience that could be applied to the whole of Latin America. Probably, one of his earliest efforts to
put his ideas down is his already mentioned article, "Cuba: Historical Exception or Vanguard in the Anti-Colonial Struggle?" published in 1961 in
the official journal of the Cuban armed forces. In this article, Guevara
recognizes a few clear differences between what happened in Cuba and the
Latin American situation. One of them was the surprise factor. Neither the
Cuban ruling classes nor the United States perceived the threat to their
interests and they delayed action against the Cuban Revolution until it was
too late; and then, only with halfhearted efforts. Castro's charismatic per-

sonality is pointed out as a key factor difficult to reproduce. In Guevara's opinion, the moving force for revolution is the peasant class, perhaps even more in Latin America as a whole than it was in Cuba. As additional factors on the plus side, he points to the demonstration effect Cuba had as to the feasibility of success and to the fact that the "masses already are aware of their destiny." At the end of this article, Guevara compares the possible performance of Latin American armies to the performance of Batista's army, an assumption that, as later events show, was one of the weakest in his strategy.[29]

In 1962, the Second Declaration of Havana provides a background for a more comprehensive analysis of the possible strategy. This was at the end of the romantic period of exporting the revolution, a period requiring more thorough strategic concept. In this document, the so-called *objective* conditions are analyzed in fatalistic terms. "In many countries of Latin America revolution is today unavoidable. This fact is not determined by the will of anyone. It is determined by the horrible conditions of exploitation under which Latin Americans live, the awakening conscience of the masses, the world-wide crisis of imperialism and the universal struggle of subjugated people."[30]

The strategy proposed to create the *subjective* conditions was based on using social resentment and the psychological factor of the feasibility of success for the mobilization of the peasant class by a revolutionary vanguard, the guerrilla. The inadequacy of the armed forces to cope with the resulting armed struggle was to result in a process of escalating terror that eventually would alienate all classes and demoralize the forces of repression. This is basically the same prescription given by Guevara in his book, *La guerra de guerrillas.*[31]

In fact, in his 1963 publicized essay on the use of guerrilla tactics in Latin America, Guevara quotes both from his book and from the Second Declaration of Havana to reiterate the above points. The possibility of reformist, electoral, or evolutionary solutions is rejected. Furthermore, in this instance, he openly discusses the need to destroy the armed forces and to make the struggle continental rather than isolated in one country.[32]

Guevara's prescription varies greatly with what actually happened in Cuba, where neither the army, the bourgeois, nor the United States was basically threatened by the revolutionaries in the stage of armed struggle against Batista. Obviously, with the surprise element lost in Latin America, total war had to be waged. The validity of this whole strategy in view of the additional resources needed to wage such a war escaped Guevara's attention, at least in this essay.

It is not until Regis Debray wrote his previously mentioned essay that the experience in the application of the initial strategy was discussed. Debray took exception to some of the points advanced by Guevara. To start with, his assumptions were the complete opposite of Guevara's. Debray recognized the refreshing impact of Cuba on Latin American communism, "Cuba has liquidated geographic fatalism." But he realized that "Cuba has condemned to failure every attempt at a merely mechanical repetition of Sierra Maestra." In his opinion, the awakening of the forces defending the *status quo* had made it more difficult to repeat the Cuban experience, particularly in military terms. Another point in which he pointedly disagrees with Guevara concerns the continental revolution. "The revolutionary struggle can only be a fight for *national* liberation. To assign . . . the prior condition of continental unity is equivalent to sending them to the Greek calends." However, Debray agrees with Guevara in rejecting reformism, in the need for armed struggle, and in the reliance on the peasants for the long fight ahead.[33]

Guevara's "Message to the Peoples of the World" reflects a much broader international outlook. Written in April 1967, after his departure for Bolivia, it must be assumed that it reflected Guevara's experience in Africa and the impact of Vietnam. Here he reiterates his concept of the continental struggle but shows an increasing awareness of the difficult road ahead and of the more intensive resistance to be met. At the same time, whether in anticipation of this intensive resistance, or exasperated at the failure of his previous efforts, he reflects great bitterness. He says, "Our soldiers must hate; a people without hatred cannot vanquish a brutal enemy."[34] The lines were drawn. The strategy was aimed at the maximum objective, total destruction of the opposite forces, while the correlation of forces made advisable more prudent objectives.

Also in 1967, Debray published his famous handbook, *Revolution in the Revolution?*, based on the Cuban revolutionary experience. It is a great irony that after what he wrote in his first essay on the unfeasibility of repeating the Cuban experience, Debray became the propagandist of the lessons of the Sierra Maestra. Even more, the man who challenged Guevara on his continental approach and insisted on the nationalist nature of the struggle ended by making the prophesy that Guevara was going to appear as "the head of a guerrilla movement, as its unquestioned political and military leader."[35] What happened to Debray's own perception of the nationalist nature of the revolution in Latin America is left for us to wonder. Since Guevara was not a Bolivian, it was precisely this insistence on being the "unquestioned political and military leader" that prevented him from reaching agreement to obtain local support in that country. In trying to prove his theories, Debray was also caught with the Bolivian guerrillas and was imprisoned.

The Strategy Blueprint

The most comprehensive summary of these strategic ideas, however, came out of the OLAS meeting in the summer of 1967. As expressed both in the report of the Cuban delegation and in the introductory section of the general resolution, the strategic concept as evolved through the years, based on the writings of Guevara and Debray as well as on Castro's own ideas, can be summarized as follows:

1. Latin America is rapidly reaching the point at which the objective conditions for a socialist revolution exist.

2. The example of Cuba creates a subjective condition by replacing the old fatalistic notion that it was not possible to succeed with an equally fatalistic notion that success is unavoidable.

3. To neutralize the anticipated U.S. response, simultaneous action and continental coordination of the struggle are advocated.

4. Violence, rather than electoral or evolutionary means, is to be used.

5. The main goal is to destroy the armed forces—a substantial deviation from the Cuban model in which this was never spelled out in advance as an objective.

6. The destruction of the armed forces will be attained by mobilizing the masses through a process of interaction starting around a vanguard core of leadership, the guerrilla.

7. The role of the guerrilla is threefold: to make propaganda through warfare, setting an example of violent action; to act as the catalytic agent for further alienation of the masses from the regime by forcing repressive measures; and to provide a hard core of leaders for the new regime.

8. The scenario of the struggle is the countryside where the population is more exploited and space can be used to offset military weakness, but the ideology of the struggle is proletarian and not peasant oriented.

9. In the final stages, a people's army shall emerge from the guerrilla forces and, counting on their protection, other sectors of the population in the urban centers will join the last battle against the repressive forces.[36]

So far, the experience in Latin America shows that, in practice, the problem is a lot more complicated than the advocates of this strategy made it appear in their theoretical papers. However, if this were a problem of romantic rhetoric against military realities, subversive efforts to promote revolution would not arouse so much concern. What is really surprising is that these subversive attempts have failed despite the increasing revolutionary potential of Latin America.

The Revolutionary Potential of Latin America

The efforts of the promoters of revolution depend for their success on the revolutionary propensity of the society upon which they are acting. This revolutionary propensity is the consequence of a certain number of conditions, which can be reduced to five for purposes of analysis. We realize that they are an oversimplification of the reality being represented, but they do provide a meaningful framework in which to consider the situation: (a) there must be a segment of the population that is victim of some injustice or arbitrariness; (b) this group must also become aware of the injustice of its predicament; (c) a leadership has to emerge, capable not only of awakening consciousness of injustice among these individuals, but also of organizing them effectively to redress their grievances; (d) the prevailing political system must be inflexible enough to block the peaceful satisfaction of their new aspirations within a reasonable enough span of time; and (e) finally, the repressive capacity of the regime—and by this is meant adequate force and the will to use it resolutely—must be smaller than the violence generated within the oppressed group by frustration or slowness in satisfying their new level of aspirations.

Each of these conditions should be explained in more detail.

Injustice

In Latin America only the most indifferent observer would not perceive the solid base for feelings of injustice among the mass of the population. In fact, in view of the appalling misery prevailing among the majority of the Latin American masses, it is surprising that we have not witnessed a revolutionary explosion already. This is explained to some extent by the lack of awareness on the part of the mass of the people of any alternative thereof and by cultural factors, such as the paternalistic tradition.

Awareness

However, the situation is changing, and at a rapid pace indeed. The mass exodus to the cities in the last two decades, which at first satisfied a craving for better opportunities, in a second stage when the initial impact wears off, creates a more explosive situation. The city, with its neon lights, store windows, and mass propaganda media generates more aspirations for comfort and consumption than the countryside. It also breaks the social relationships that breed paternalistic responses. Moreover, popular revolts increase in danger the higher the concentration of the potentially rebellious population. By 1975, the urban population of Latin America is expected to be greater than the total population of the region in 1950. In a continent that has an annual overall population growth rate of 3 percent, with a growth rate of 15 percent in so-called marginal neighborhoods, the revolutionary potential is in the cities. The dogmatic insistence of Guevara, Debray, and Castro on the peasant base for their strategy seems to be one of the reasons for their failure. Their efforts ignore the most favorable scenario for the resentment to be organized into a revolutionary movement.

As to the rural masses, the situation of injustice is worse than in the cities. It is interesting to note that, in making agrarian reform, which is one of the key concepts of the Alliance for Progress, the governments of the hemisphere agreed, at least in principle, with the importance given to the situation of the landless peasant in the strategy of the exporters of revolution. Here, however, lack of social, economic, and political awareness and submissive patterns of behavior are stronger than in the urban centers and are, therefore, greater obstacles to population mobilization.

The potential dissatisfaction of the population is being awakened also by the revolution in mass communications brought about by the transistor radio. Today, it is no longer necessary for a man to be literate to be exposed to new ideas and to an increasing awareness of the injustice surrounding him. The United States Information Agency reported in 1967 before the Subcommittee on Inter-American Affairs of the U.S. House of Representatives that there were an estimated 38,592,000 radios in Latin America.[37] Between eighteen and twenty million of these are shortwave sets, which gives an idea of the vast audience accessible to the broadcasts of Radio Havana.

Education is another qualitative factor to be taken into consideration. As was the case with the exodus to the cities, expanded educational opportunities do satisfy growing aspirations initially. However, for people in the lower and middle classes, education is a means to an end—a way to improve their economic well-being and their social status. To the extent that the economic situation of the countries or their social structures are not capable of satisfying the new aspirations emerging from the obtained education, the degree of dissatisfaction could increase rather than decrease.

Registration at the secondary and university levels throughout Latin America increased at annual rates of 11.4 percent and 9.8 percent, respectively, from 1960 to 1969.[38] Therefore, should the same levels of retention that prevailed in the past be maintained, the output of graduates into the labor market will be double the rate of pre-Alliance years. As to the adequacy of the economic system to provide employment for this growing mass of graduates, the 1969 report on problems and perspectives for economic and social development presented to the Interamerican Economic and Social Council meeting in Trinidad and Tobago concluded that economic growth rates have not been adequate to provide the estimated 2.5 million new jobs needed every year.[39] Unemployment is one of the most dangerous factors eroding the social system of Latin America.

Leadership

It is obvious from these very general observations that the first two conditions for the development of a revolutionary situation, injustice and awareness by the affected groups, do exist in Latin America to an increasing degree. The emergence of a leadership capable of directing and organizing the resulting frustration is the next condition that has to be satisfied. Neither the peasants nor the proletariat has produced this revolutionary leadership. For historical reasons, the universities are the breeding grounds for the revolutionary vanguard in Latin America. This could be compounded by the frustrated hopes of an unemployed or underemployed intelligentsia.

Castro knows this very well. He himself started his revolutionary career at Havana University. No wonder that after the January 1966 meeting of the Tricontinental Conference in Havana, the first organizational step taken was the establishment of OCLAE (Continental Organization of Latin American Students) in August 1966.[40] However, to date, there is no indication of any move to call similar conferences of labor or agrarian leaders.

Despite the many failures and setbacks suffered, perhaps it is in this area that efforts to promote revolution could pay more dividends to Castro. The training of Latin American youngsters in the art and technique of violent social change may plant a seed that could yield its harvest. In the brutal school of revolution, those who fail to make the grade die or go to prison. They provide the needed martyrs for the cause. It is from among the hardened survivors that a battle-tested leadership emerges. That is why abortive or smoldering situations of violence—although leading to temporary setbacks—could be critically important in the long run.

However, one of the shortcomings of Castro's strategy is the communications gap between this urban vanguard and the peasants whom they are to lead. The synthesis between leaders and followers is not easy. According to Debray, "In order not to usurp a role to which they have only a provisional title, this progressive petty bourgeoisie must, to use Amilcar Cabral's phrase, commit suicide as a class in order to be restored to life as revolutionary workers, totally identified with the deepest aspirations of their people."[41] Up to now the suicidal risk has not been precisely in terms of the petty bourgeoisie class background of the leaders, but in their own survival potential.

Rigidity Toward Change

The ability of societies to adapt to the growing demands forced by the developments described so far has been uneven throughout the region. In some countries the forces of the *status quo* are so deeply entrenched that they have been able to resist successfully the reformist pressure generated at one time by the Alliance for Progress. Just to give one example, from 1962 to 1969 only between 800,000 and one million farmers out of a potential ten million benefited from land reform programs and, of these, two-thirds are in three countries: Mexico, Bolivia, and Venezuela.[42]

On the other hand, there are countries in which the will to reform has been severely restrained by the structural weaknesses of their economies. Colombia, Peru, and Chile, in which inflation and balance of payments difficulties act as constraints to the reformist efforts of their administrations, are good examples of this predicament. In some other countries, such as Uruguay, Costa Rica, and, in some respects, Bolivia, social reforms made in the past have created economic problems which are difficult to solve without antagonizing broad sectors of the population. Perhaps, only Venezuela and Mexico offer the pushing combination of the will to carry out social reforms and the financial means to accomplish them.

In general, it can be said that Latin American societies have shown themselves to be either too rigid to make the necessary concessions to the growing aspirations of their populations or economically too weak to finance them. In this respect, the assumption made in the strategy of the exporters of revolution as to the implausibility of reformist solutions has unquestionable validity.

Repressive Capacity

Coming to the last condition—failure of the repressive capacity of the established order—the experience already gathered indicates that there has been an excessive dependency on repressive capacity to prevent the development of revolutionary situations in Latin America. It could be said that the overdevelopment of military institutions in relation to the overall institutional development of the countries has reduced the flexibility of these societies. Confidence in the effectiveness of the repressive capacity of the system discourages the willingness to make concessions.

In the long run, this could lead to military radicalism. A soldier in Latin America usually comes from the lower classes and, in many countries, is of peasant origin. The officer corps, contrary to the general impression, comes, in the majority of the countries, from the middle class and not from the upper class. Thus, the armed forces of Latin America are not completely immune to public opinion. The military's reaction to political situations will depend on how intense the feelings of the population are on one issue and on how deep the crisis is confronting the respective society.

For example, in Cuba the defeat of the Batista regime was by no stretch of the imagination a military victory of the guerrillas over the regular armed forces. Rather, it was the collapse of the will of the regular armed forces to repress efficiently the violent manifestation of popular resistance against a regime that had alienated the majority of the population that brought Castro to power. In the case of the Dominican Republic, we find again that, in a really deep social crisis, important segments of the armed forces decided to cast their fate with popular political groups rather than with their more conservative comrades-in-arms. In fact, there are serious doubts that, had there been no intervention in the Dominican Republic, the armed forces of that country would have been able to cope with the situation facing them, despite their overwhelming numerical superiority.

This caveat on the excessive dependency on the military in no way detracts from the fact that, so far, the Latin American military, with the previously mentioned exceptions of Cuba and the Dominican Republic, have shown they have the necessary repressive capacity to keep under control whatever violence has been generated by the frustration of the dissatisfied elements within their societies.

This brief review of the potential for revolution in Latin America shows that the region may be in for a period of turmoil. The growing population is awakening to its predicament and a potential leadership from the ranks of students and unemployed intelligentsia could emerge to lead a revolt. So far, societies have not been too willing to make reforms, particularly after the Dominican Republic intervention restored the confidence of the Latin American ruling classes that if the worst came, the United States would not tolerate another Cuba. Meanwhile, the growing number of military dictatorships is a clear indication that in Latin America the lid on revolutionary pressure is being kept on by resorting, to an increasing extent, to the repressive capacity of their armed forces.

Why Has the Revolutionary Strategy Failed?

In summary, we can say that Castro perceived the revolutionary potential of Latin America correctly. However, both he and Guevara, as well as Debray later on, fell under the spell of their own version of the success of the Cuban Revolution. This led to the formulation of a strategy that was not suitable to the Latin American situation as a whole.

This seems to be a case of subjectivism. First of all, it is not true that Batista was overthrown by a successful guerrilla war. Batista was overthrown through nationwide political warfare, particularly in Havana and Santiago de Cuba, with the guerrillas serving as a symbol to keep the will to fight alive. The effort to belittle the role of the urban fighters against Batista was a political necessity for Castro. These groups included urban workers, the middle class, the professionals, and some of the upper class who feared and resented Batista's terroristic methods. These people had the means and the know-how to provide leadership and could not be as easily manipulated as the illiterate farmers from the Sierra Maestra. Therefore, to displace these rivals for leadership, the best tactic was to deny the importance of the role they had played in overthrowing Batista.

Guevara, on the other hand, had never been to a Cuban city. His perception of Cuba was shaped by his first contact with the Sierra Maestra peasants. Besides, the peasant cult fitted very well with his own ideological preconceptions. Thus, out of political expediency and social and historical ignorance, the myth of the military victory of the guerrilla in the countryside was created.

Obviously, once this was done, the need to upgrade the military performance of Batista's army follows as a corollary. That is why the conspiracies and rebellions against Batista within the armed forces, which deprived them of their most competent officers and demoralized the ranks, were practically ignored. It must be remembered that Batista first came to power in 1933 through a sergeants' revolt that destroyed the officer corps. By 1956, however, a new professional officer corps had been formed that resented Batista's own political military appointees. No serious analysis of Castro's success can be made without taking all of these factors into account. Having distorted the nature of the struggle in Cuba and the performance of their opponents, the whole strategy used to export the revolution was based on false assumptions.

Furthermore, Cuba is not Latin America. In Cuba the large-scale commercial operation of the sugar industry had created a rural proletariat, not landless peasants. The sugar workers union included 400,000 agricultural workers who had been unionized since the 1930s. Therefore, in Cuba there was a large mass of rural workers with experience in organized collective action. In the document presented to OLAS by the Cuban delegation, reference is made to a peasant war, but a proletarian mentality.[43] As can be seen, this was a situation peculiar to Cuban production relationships. Whether peasants in areas not experiencing this type of productive relationship can be given a proletarian mentality is doubtful.

And, finally, we have the element of surprise. We must ask ourselves how much better Batista's army would have performed if they had been warned in advance that the aim of the rebels was to destroy them. Never during the period of the struggle against Batista was such a warning statement, as the following made by Guevara, heard by Batista's army.

> We must carry the war as far as the enemy carries it: to his home, to his centers of entertainment, in a total war. It is necessary to prevent him from having a moment of peace, or a quiet

moment outside his barracks or even inside; we must attack him wherever he may be, make him feel like a cornered beast whenever he may move.[44]

It is doubtful that such rhetoric would frighten the Latin America military into surrendering. However, it certainly would persuade them to fight with more bitterness against the guerrillas than Batista's forces had fought.

Cuba has been forced to abandon its policy of exporting revolution. Not only did Che Guevara give his life for his ideas, but many more who trusted Guevara and his leadership also paid with their lives for his mistaken strategy. At least for the time being, more reliance will have to be placed by Cuba on Soviet support for the internal security and economic consolidation of the regime. This policy will be followed even at the price of losing the independence that made Cuba so attractive to rebels everywhere. And, although the revolutionary potential of Latin America is great, Cuba can no longer be considered the model for successful revolution throughout the area.

NOTES

1. Published as Ernesto Guevara, "Mensaje a la Tricontinental," *Verde Olivo* (Havana), September 1, 1968, p. 58. Also published in English as "Message to the Tricontinental," in *Latin American Radicalism,* ed. I. L. Horowitz (New York, 1969).

2. Ricardo Rojo, *My Friend Che* (New York, 1968), p. 62.

3. Ernesto Guevara, "Cuba: Historical Exception or Vanguard in the Anti-Colonial Struggle?" in *Marxism in Latin America,* ed. Luis E. Aguilar (New York, 1968), pp. 174–79.

4. Organization of American States, *Documentos Oficiales,* OEA/Ser.F/III.8 (Washington, D.C., 1963), p. 299.

5. Ibid., p. 183.

6. "II Declaración de la Habana," *Verde Olivo* (Havana), September 1, 1968, pp. 21–30.

7. Rojo, *My Friend Che,* p. 133.

8. Ernesto Guevara, "Guerra de guerrillas: un método," *Cuadernos de Marcha* (Montevideo, November 1967), pp. 58–67.

9. Instituto Interamericano de Estudios Jurídicos, *El sistema interamericano* (Madrid, 1966), p. 219.

10. Rojo, *My Friend Che,* p. 174.

11. Ibid., p. 180.

12. Regis Debray, "Latin America: Some Problems of Revolutionary Strategy," in *Latin American Radicalism,* ed. I. L. Horowitz (New York, 1969), pp. 499–531.

13. Adolfo Gilly, *Cuba: coexistencia o revolución* (Buenos Aires, 1965), p. 35.

14. Organization of American States, *Documentos Oficiales,* OEA/Ser.G/IV (esp.), II (Washington, D.C., November 28, 1966), p. 56.

15. Foreign Broadcast Information Service (FBIS), May 6, 1966.

16. Rojo, *My Friend Che*, p. 186.

17. *Verde Olivo*, May 28, 1967, pp. 15–18.

18. Comisión Especial de Consulta sobre Seguridad, *Estudio del "Diario del Che Guevara en Bolivia,"* OEA/Ser.L/X/II.23 (Washington, D.C., December 20, 1968).

19. Comisión Especial de Consulta sobre Seguridad, OEA/Ser.L/X/II.18 (Washington, D.C., 1967), p. 256.

20. Ibid.

21. Rojo, *My Friend Che*, p. 204.

22. *Verde Olivo*, September 1, 1968.

23. Ibid., p. 14.

24. Comisión Especial de Consulta sobre Seguridad, OEA/Ser.L/X/II.25 (Washington, D.C., 1969), p. 15.

25. *Verde Olivo*, September 1, 1968, p. 30.

26. Instituto Interamericano de Estudios Jurídicos, *El sistema interamericano,* p. 200.

27. Ibid., p. 203.

28. Informe de la Comisión Interamericana de Paz, OEA/Ser./III.CIP/1/62. Corr. (Washington, D.C., 1962), p. 39.

29. Guevara, "Cuba: Historical Exception or Vanguard," p. 174.

30. *Verde Olivo*, September 1, 1968, p. 23.

31. Guevara, *La guerra de guerrillas* (Havana, 1961).

32. Guevara, "Guerra de guerrillas," p. 67.

33. Debray, "Latin America," p. 506.

34. *Verde Olivo*, September 1, 1968, p. 64.

35. Regis Debray, *Revolution in the Revolution?* (New York, 1967), p. 119.

36. See both documents in Comisión Especial de Consulta sobre Seguridad, OEA/Ser.L/X/II.18 (Washington, D.C., 1967), pp. 93–106, 201–05.

37. U.S. Congress, House, Subcommittee on Inter-American Affairs of the Committee on Foreign Affairs, *Communist Activities in Latin America, 1967,* p. 69.

38. Fondo Fiduciario de Progreso Social, *Progreso socio-económico en América Latina: noveno informe anual, 1969* (Washington, D.C., 1969), pp. 141–43.

39. Consejo Interamericano Económico y Social, *Problemas y perspectivas del desarrollo económico y social,* OEA/Ser.H/X.14, CIES/1380 (May 19, 1969), p. 61.

40. Comisión Especial de Consulta sobre Seguridad, OEA/Ser.G/IV-C-i-769 Rev., II (Washington, D.C., November 28, 1966), p. 305.

41. Debray, *Revolution in the Revolution,* p. 112.

42. Fondo Fiduciario de Progreso Social, *Progreso socio-económico en América Latina,* p. 170.

43. Comisión Especial de Consulta sobre Seguridad, OEA/Ser.L/X/II.18 (Washington, D.C., 1967), p. 104.

44. See English version, Guevara, "Message to the Tricontinental," p. 618.

6
Irving Louis Horowitz

The Political Sociology
of Cuban Communism

THIS essay discusses the theory of the Stalinization of the Cuban Revolution. The very first point to clarify is what the term *Stalinization* means. We
are now so distant from the Stalinist period in Russia that it is easy to conceive of Stalin as an earthly assistant of the Devil, as the modern-day re-
incarnation of Ivan the Terrible or as a generalized specter that haunted
the Soviet Union. But the emotive use of the term will herein be eschewed.
Stalinization refers to specific forms of social and political behavior and
institutions.

First, Stalinization historically means the bureaucratization of the Communist party machinery, which, in turn, signifies severe limits to inner party
disputes and the termination of the period of factionalism. In broader
terms, it means the subordination of society to the party state. Secondly,
Stalinization means the emergence of a leader and his small coterie as exclusive spokesmen for the Communist party. The nation reduces *itself* to
himself. The party state is subordinated to the party leader. Thirdly, Stalinization means the promotion of inner political struggle as a substitute for
class struggle, the politics of debate, and the passion for socialist democracy. Fourthly, Stalinization means the elimination or at least abandonment of all roads to socialism save one: the economic growth road set
and defined by the maximum leader. The fifth, most characteristic point
of Stalinism is a nearly exclusive concentration of energies on national
rather than international problems. This might be called the domestication
of the revolutionary movement under the above conditions.

This definition of Stalinization is introduced in order to make plain what
appears to be a new stage in the development of the Cuban Revolution.
This new stage, in comparison to the early years, represents an utter sim-

plification of the sociological problem; that is, we have the "advantage" of being able to pay attention to what the leader says and having it stand for what the nation ostensibly believes. There is no longer a problem of pluralization: alternative spokesmen, alternative newspapers, or even of alternative responses to selective problems. There is no longer an empirical problem—a world to be interpreted on the basis of information—only an ideological problem—a world to be acted upon on the basis of imaginary demands by outside forces. The task of political interpretation and analysis is remarkably simplified, since access to the ideas of the leader becomes equivalent to the national essence, no less than the political truth.

The Stalin-Castro phenomenon has a shared organizational basis in patrimonial restorationism. Revolution is conducted in the name of collective leadership principles, but the charismatic element, far from being enveloped by the bureaucratic organization, becomes transformed into a super-government. Traditional Latin American personalism resolves itself in private government. From this stems the social origins of terrorism of the socialist type. The parallel structures of social system and state system are parallel in name only. In fact, the superstate system mediates the claims of all social sectors. In this way, the forms of legality are kept intact, but the actual conduct of affairs is channeled into totalitarian directions.

What we attempt here is a difficult argument by analogy. Even with safeguards distinguishing and separating Castro from Stalin, it rests on an argument by historical analogy. Clearly, this type of argument is not the strongest framework for casting theories. But it is at least a framework. It takes on added weight when we realize that Castro is guiding an ideological state, along lines laid down by Marxism-Leninism. This very fact makes the analogy into a set of guidelines within which, and through which, Castro desires to realize his goals—such as they may be.

Socialist Cuba finds itself in a double bind (what some might insist on terming a "dialectical situation"). On one hand, it is being subjected to strangulation from external sources, primarily the United States; and is suffering stagnation as a result of internal sources, primarily the oligarchical political elite directed by Premier Fidel Castro. The process of Stalinization is partly the result of Castro's personality and of the oppressive nature of the United States policy toward Cuba, which has provided the milieu for the worst possible features of the Cuban regime to come to the fore.

Cuba's Adoption of the Stalinist Model

Between 1966 and 1969 there were three proclamations issued by Fidel Castro which, we submit, bear out our contention that he has accepted the premises of Stalinism. Given the ideological assumptions of the leading players in the international power game, Castro perhaps had little alternative than to become what he became. But what is at issue here is whether the deterministic framework out of which Castro operates is a consequence of social forces or of personal ideology. The assumptions he now makes about the condition of the world deserve further scrutiny.

First, there is the stated need for rapid development and the internal obstacles to such development, for example, the rise of absenteeism and slower work schedules developing among even the loyal workers. This requires both tremendous labor mobilization of a military type and repressive legal measures. Secondly, there is the belief that Cuba is surrounded by hostile forces, led by the United States. Also, that this ring of bases makes impossible the normalization of trade and aid agreements with the capitalist bloc generally or with other "captive" Latin American nations. Third is the growing dissatisfaction with any other "roads to socialism," particularly those of the more extreme variety, as existing in Yugoslavia, Czechoslovakia (1968), and China. Hence, the continued emphasis on independent forms of political expression invariably creates the basis for leadership ideology derived from within rather than from international Communist leaders such as Mao Tse-tung or Tito. In other words, the "socialism in one country" slogan is not so much a cause as a consequence of the practice of Stalinization.

It should now be said that the 1966 denunciation of the Tricontinental Conference (held in Havana in 1966 by revolutionists from Africa, Asia, and Latin America) by all member nations of the Organization of American States (OAS), including the usually recalcitrant Chileans and Mexicans, seriously missed the vital political point. Behind the talk of hemispheric revolution is a deep transformation. The rhetoric of world revolution adopted at the Tricontinental Conference disguised the intense nationalism of the Castro revolution, a disguise which fails to conceal its growing criticism of other Latin American revolutionists—if not yet revolutions. This conference saw the debut of a new Cuba, one which no longer had confidence in hemispheric revolution and one which, in fact, had transformed itself from the first stage of a high-risk Latin American revolution into the conduct of a low-risk Cuban Revolution.

There is as major a difference between a Latin American revolution and the Cuban Revolution in the sixties as there was between a world revolution and the Bolshevik Revolution in the twenties. The Lenin period was characterized by a faith not so much in a Russian revolution, but rather a Soviet revolution. Stalin transformed its character from a working-class Soviet movement to a national Russian movement. The degree of terrorism, if not the fact of it, is a secondary consideration, whatever its human import. Just as fascism is not defined by the number of Jews it killed, Stalinism cannot be defined by the number of people in Asian concentration camps. These are historical variations in the slaughter and blood of the innocent, but not the essence of a definition.

The core of the Stalinist system is, first, left-wing nationalism, or the rightward drift of revolutionism. Furthermore, it successfully pervades the society, as can be seen in the loyalty that the Russian people manifested for their homeland during the Nazi attacks, and that the Cuban people displayed during the American-supported invasion of Playa Girón (Bay of Pigs). In other words, paradoxically, the survival of the revolution in Russia and Cuba depended in some measure on the abandonment of certain internationalist pretensions or ambitions. However, the rhetoric of internationalism is so firmly established in the socialist tradition that at the very period the Russian Revolution was being nationalized, international organizations, such as the Comintern Bureau, were hatched. The same seems to be the case with the Cuban Revolution. The more conservative its practices, the more noisy are its ideological pronouncements.

The various maneuverings within the Cuban party system, while ostensibly an effort to "balance" old and new Communist militants, is, at its core, an effort on Castro's part to shape the party system in his own image. It is reminiscent of Stalin's technique in dealing with "right" and "left" wings within the Soviet Communist party.

There are four clearly demarcated stages in the political transformation of Cuba's political party life. The first was the movement stage in which the July 26 movement was to have performed party tasks without the party bureaucracies. The second was the united front stage in which the Communists from the urban centers and revolutionists from the rural (and also urban) sectors were fused in the ORI. Third came the socialist stage represented by the PURS, which, while hastened by the internal machinations and intrigues of the various factions of the united front groupings, was inevitable in light of the socialist-Marxist ideology in the name of which Cuba came to be ruled by the fifth year. The fourth was the Communist stage represented by the PCC. While this final stage was accelerated by internal organizational dilemmas, the clear evidence is that the PCC is a direct reflection of Castro's personal will and charismatic authority. The decline of internationalist pretensions, meshed as it is with the growth of a tight-knit political party bureaucracy, characterizes the new Castro regime just as assuredly as it did the prewar Stalin period between 1929 and 1941.

Peculiar Features of Cuban Stalinism

What do we find in Cuba leading to the unique conditions that give its form of Stalinism special properties? Most important is that Cuba is a small nation dependent on the world economy and dependent on a single crop. By contrast, Russia in 1918 was relatively advanced industrially. Geographically, Russia dominates Europe while Cuba is dominated by the Americas. Given these conditions, plus the fact that Cuba is engaged not in forced industrialization but in forced collectivization, the possibilities of liberalism in the Cuban situation are minimized. Industralism coupled with balanced urban growth have opened up tendencies of pluralization and diversification in the Soviet Union. The Cuban situation, on the contrary, lacking, at this point, the basis of industrial diversification or even the possibility of crop diversification, has collectivization in place of industrialization as the essence of its economic program.

The social ecology and geography of an island economy, which puts severe limits on natural resources, also places sharp limits on any heavy industrialization process. Even were these natural barriers to industrialization overcome, the sociological barriers remain: peasant dominance, the absence of a strong proletarian tradition, and the flight of professional and commercial expertise along with the other "remnants of the bourgeois past." The strain on the Castro regime produced by these problems motivates even harsher political repression. The steady rise of police informants and the street-by-street spy system (CDR) is an augury of things to come. This is particularly significant since internal political and cultural repression is taking place at precisely a point in Cuban history when anti-Castro guerrillas have been practically eliminated and when oppositional influence has been drained off by the "airlift" arranged with the United States.

Precisely because the possibilities of pluralization at the economic level are far more restricted than in Stalinist Russia, the potential for extreme repression increases rather than decreases over time. The collectivization of a single-crop economy is necessarily a more severe act than industrialization. In Russia, the destruction of the kulak class was designed to break the back of the agricultural class as part of a campaign for industrialization. This industrialization did, in fact, enable the country to flower in economic ways, even in a severely repressive political atmosphere. This is one reason why the Stalinist system had sufficient resilience to outlive its tormentor. It is doubtful whether the same could be said of the Cuban situation.

There is an absence of a strong factory proletariat in Cuba, and a heavy reliance on the peasant-agrarian sector for Cuban economic well-being. Analysts make the frequent mistake of equating industrialization with urbanization. The fact that 56 percent of the Cuban population has been urbanized (measures of urbanization are themselves subject to examination) has little to do with the degree to which a nation depends on industrialization. Correlations between the two broad indicators of modernization vary extensively. In Cuba, there is a relatively low correlation between urbanization and industrialization. Indeed, this is itself an important element in the cause of the Cuban Revolution. The fact that there was a high degree of unionization under Batista only indicates organizational strength, not size or, for that matter, effectiveness; for example, the factory workers of Shanghai made the Chinese Revolution.

It is plain to all concerned that socialist Cuba is primarily an agricultural society. Sugar is the most important single item in the economy. Although the role of sugar was downgraded in the early sixties, when various industrialization programs failed to lead to diversification, the role of sugar was once again made central. After sugar comes cattle, tobacco, coffee, fruits, rice, cacao, corn, and turbes. Despite the stagnation in this sector, the powerful agricultural base provided a great deal more in the way of a self-sustaining economy than the imagined benefits of rapid industrialization. To examine the *Statistical Yearbook* of the United Nations is to be struck by the even greater stagnation of industrial production. Not only is there a seeming absence of production increase, but an equal absence of growth of new plant equipment. At the same time, it is interesting to note the increase in the national budget. The pressures on the Cuban economy compelled the reestablishment of agricultural preeminence in the economic sector, that is, a return to single-crop socialism. The size of the Communist party under Batista, or the degree of trade unionism in the fifties, is as irrelevant to a serious general characterization of the economy as these two factors were to a general characterization of the polity at the time of the Castro takeover.

The question of sugar production and single-crop socialism reached altogether new proportions in the drive announced in 1969, and gotten underway in 1970, for the production of ten million tons of sugar. In point of fact, whether or not this target was achieved signifies less than the character of the drive as such. As Robert Daland shrewdly noted in connection with developmental programs in Brazil during the *SUDENE* period, the latent purpose of such short-term economic planning is less connected with economic reforms than with political mobilization.[1] Furthermore, the sugar production goals in Cuba have precisely this aim of mobilizing the entire Cuban population around the single-crop economy.

More exactly, sugar production norms underscore the Stalinist character of the Cuban political leadership in several critical ways:

1. As mentioned above, they mobilize the population for a single achievable goal, without regard to the economic costs or consequences of that goal.

2. They artificially sustain a high energy output by the society at a

period, more than a decade after the Revolution, when most forms of struggle have either been achieved or abandoned.

3. The sugar production norms sustain a permanent interest in Cuba in place of a permanent revolution. Nationalistic norms are emphasized in place of internationalist goals.

4. The sugar drive stimulates international "brigade" participation, with agrarian "troops" recruited from all parts of the "imperialist" and third worlds, and does so on a low- to no-risk basis, since farming in Cuba is, after all, far less risky than fighting in Bolivia.

5. The sugar drive is part of the larger deemphasis on urbanization and industrialization and serves to provide a meaningful rationale for keeping people from flocking to Havana, while minimizing the high risks involved in any extended period of industrialization.

It should, however, be noted in all fairness that the agrarian policies of the Castro regime are quite at variance with the industrialization policies pursued by Stalin between 1929 and 1941. In some measure, Stalinism refers to forced industrialization. This only underscores the relatively ambiguous nature of any "model." In the larger sense, the search for high mobilization and collective consensus produced the agrarian policies of Castro just as assuredly as it produced the industrial policies of Stalin. The focus on specific mechanisms of producing high social cohesion is, in this sense, less important than the ultimate values implicit in this sort of nation-building conception of socialist construction.

Consequences of Cuban Stalinism for the Latin American Revolution

Let us turn from the economic to the political consequences of having the first socialist system in the Western Hemisphere organized in one of the smallest and least representative of nations. We would have to say that the most singular fact of the revolution taking place in Cuba is that it raises the ante of revolutions everywhere else. Revolution becomes more expensive in every other country of the Americas, and, at the same time, the impotence of the first socialist republic itself becomes more manifest.

Bearing out this contention, it could be said that the U.S. action in the Dominican Republic was an opening salvo informing the Latin American nations: "We are here in the Dominican Republic. The Cubans are not. Nor will they come. Their revolution, you see, is not a Latin American revolution. They are impotent, and we are not." That lesson was not lost. Quite the reverse, the invasion of the Dominican Republic in 1965 had immense value for the United States in terms of the schisms and splits that resulted throughout the rest of Latin America, particularly in Cuba. And, it made possible subsequent hemispheric adventures.

What does this mean? Simply that many revolutionists have brought to the attention of Cuba that it was indeed impotent during the invasion of the Dominican Republic by the United States. Castro's response to this criticism was immediate and vigorous: such action would have been precipitous, costly, and would have opened up Cuba to immediate invasion from the United States. This is likely to have been the case and, hence, calls for joint participation in revolutionary action were prime examples of adventurism. The next phase of the dialogue went something like this: "That may very well be the case. A Cuban intervention to save Caamaño's rebel forces would have been a form of adventurism, but if Cuba cannot do that for its Caribbean neighbor, what can it do for anyone else?"

What then becomes the character of a Latin American revolution is a kind of pathetic slogan that every nation has to come to its own revolution in its own way, in its own time. Indeed, if the Cuban Revolution raises the question of cost in starting a revolution, then not only has it failed in its stated task to assist revolutionary movements elsewhere, but its very existence jeopardizes other forms of revolutionary activity in the hemisphere. Cuba becomes a paper tiger which makes the real tiger even more alert. The Cuban response to this, as Castro himself has put it, is an accusation of "Trotskyism."

What Castro means by Trotskyism is not clear in his pronouncements. Dotted through documents and dozens of speeches are attacks on all sorts of left-wingers who have been identified with the Cuban Revolution. For example, in the Tricontinental Conference, the Uruguayan Adolfo Gilly, the American Marxists Leo Huberman and Paul Sweezy, and various Mexican leftists were denounced as Trotskyists. Castro's speech supporting the Soviet invasion of Czechoslovakia provoked a negative reaction among European leftists, who in turn were attacked by Cuba. In his speech commemorating Lenin's centennial, Castro attacked the "pseudo-revolutionaries" and "super-leftists" of Paris and Rome that were asking a more radical position of the Cuban Revolution.[2] This was a clear criticism of René Dumont and K. S. Karol who, in 1970, published books criticizing the Cuban Revolution.[3] (Karol accused Castro of abandoning Guevara's ideals, militarizing the island, and returning to the Soviet style of the 1930s. Dumont pointed to the militarization of society as the most distinctive feature of today's Cuba.) What is the dispute about?

On inspection, it turns out that Castro strongly resents the call for revolution as a permanent entity, at least until the entire Latin American area is liberated from the American "imperialists." There is a further rejection of the idea that the Cuban Revolution must have as an aim the revolution of the hemisphere as a whole in order to make sure that the Cuban "stage" will not become bureaucratized and corrupt. This is an idea reminiscent of Trotsky's view of the Russian Revolution in his years of exile.

Castro's response was much the same as was Stalin's. The role of Cuba as a springboard for international revolution may be tactically halted, but its function as an exemplary case of a nation breaking its links with the colonial past is said to remain firmly intact. In this sense, Cuba is said to remain a model for Latin American revolutionaries. What this approach tends to underestimate drastically is that a "model" for revolutionists can also serve as a warning for the established order. It leads to a heightened emphasis on counterrevolutionary programs. The Stalinist concept of the Soviet Union as a model for Western Europe to follow quite obviously proved a failure. Yet, underlying Stalin's response to advocates of the permanent revolution is the mere existence of the Soviet Union to serve as a rallying point for European revolutionists. In this respect, Stalinism was as erroneous in its theory as it was conservative in its practice. To the extent that Castro seems bound by similar ideological patterns, there is a rightful doubt that he will have more success.

Evidence of this Stalinization process is not only known indirectly, such as the case of the Dominican Republic, but directly, as in the case of Ernesto (Che) Guevara. Guevara's role was obviously that of the surrogate Trotskyist. He was the Gray Eagle of the Cuban Revolution because what he primarily believed in was total revolution in the hemisphere. Trotsky, too, believed in revolution in Europe and not just in Russia. Thus, the roles of these two leaders are remarkably striking. Both had divergences with the maximum leader and both died in a foreign country trying, like twentieth-century Quixotes, to achieve continental revolution.

An event of some moment was Castro's attack on China in January 1966. It is extremely important to keep in mind that for the orthodox Communist parties, China, in its ideological approach, represents not Stalinism but Trotskyism; that is, the Chinese position supports the necessity of world revolution, not just of any revolution, but of socialist revolution. This is one reason why the Chinese have encountered difficulty in Africa, where the Africans believed that they had already had their revolution. The concept of the permanent revolution is embodied in the Chinese doctrine. From the point of view of ideology, Castro's attack on China was yet another attack on Trotskyism in its most "insidious" form, that of Chinese communism.

Interestingly enough, at the same time Castro openly broke with China, the Soviet ideologists were resuming their condemnation of Trotskyism. Particularly striking are the subtle hints relating Trotsky to the Chinese position. The title of a feature article in *Pravda* (March 1966) indicated this, "Behind the Red Dragon Mask of Trotskyism." But lest the analogy be lost, Trotsky's position is described unmistakably in Chinese terms: the falsity of the claim that socialism cannot be built in one country (especially in the USSR), the falsity of any concept of permanent revolution; the falsity of the claim that peaceful coexistence entails class capitulation. The concluding point in the Soviet attack on Trotskyism is a reference to the Maoist position held by *Frente Obrero* (Uruguay) on the need to prepare for nuclear war or preparing a preventive war before imperialism unleashes it. Given the increased reliance of the Maoists on nonparty organs, there can be little doubt that the critique of Maoism will be increasingly linked to the "bankrupt" Fourth International established by Trotsky.

The severity of the Castro critique can best be appreciated by keeping in mind that it is harsher in tone than any Soviet document ever released on the question of Chinese communism. "From the first moment we understood the obvious opportunistic position taken by China in trade relationships. . . . A much more important and fundamental question than food is whether the world of tomorrow can assume the right to blackmail, extort, pressure, and strangle small peoples."[4] This comment by Castro, directed as it is toward China, can be viewed as a response of those who believe in legality and dignity, a Latin American rather than a Communist response.

It cannot be said that Castro's critique made economic sense. In bartering agreements, one cannot make the assumption that direct political attack is an effective method for gaining national ends. From an economic point of view, Castro's attack on China was hopelessly absurd. There are two ways of interpreting his pronouncement. First, that it represented an outcry of a poor nation against a wealthy nation. Secondly, that it represented a rejection of the notion of permanent revolution and, therefore, is an extension of the Stalinist perspective. The idea that Castro's critique is a psychological phenomenon can be accepted only as a last resort. It is possible to end with a theory of personal madness, but political analysis cannot start with it. Cuba has been exploited in many ways with equal impunity by the Soviet Union, but there have been no parallel attacks on Russian propagandists, on Russian trade practices, or on the Russian abandonment of Cuba during the missile crisis. Further, whether China can be considered even remotely a "rich" nation is dubious. Finally, to assume that Castro's anti-China declaration is the response of a man who believes in law is to ignore his capacity previously to suppress commentary on departures from "socialist legality."

Let us take one step further in our survey and examine Castro's attitude toward revolutionists elsewhere in the hemisphere. This, after all, is a decisive test of Stalinism. What is the attitude of Castro toward other Central American revolutionists? It turns out that it is of two kinds: patronizing and censorious—patronizing when the revolution agrees with the Cuban position and censorious when it does not. The closing address to the Tricontinental Conference by Castro was largely taken up with a critique of the leader of the guerrilla movement in Guatemala, Yon Sosa. Ironically enough, the attack was not much different from the attack of the Communists against Castro when he was a guerrilla in the mountains: Castro accused Yon Sosa of being a romantic, of being ignorant of revolutionary strategies and of ways to win the people, and he accused him of allowing himself to be captivated by agents of imperialism, by Trotskyists. The arguments that were presented by the Communist Party of Cuba (PSP) prior to 1959 were used by Castro against Yon Sosa in 1966. The man he defended was Turcios, who represented Guatemala at the Tricontinental Conference. Simultaneous with the attack on Yon Sosa (who was killed in action in 1970), Luis Augusto Turcios was upheld as the "orthodox" revolutionist, believer in the national rather than in the socialist character of revolution.

Early in 1970, the Venezuelan guerrilla leader Douglas Bravo accused Castro of abandoning the continental revolution for Cuban economic development. The premier's answer was given in his speech in commemoration of Lenin's centennial: he warned that guerrilla fighters would have to define themselves very closely if they were to get Cuban aid in the future, and defended vehemently Cuba's right and duty to consolidate its own economy.[5]

The attack on revolutionary romanticism, which up to now has been limited to revolutionists in Latin America, when generalized becomes an attack on any other hemispheric revolution as premature or adventuristic. The United front position taken by the Soviets during the thirties has now become Castro's tactic—for revolutions being fought elsewhere. For example, Castro's attitude toward events in Peru amounts to an acceptance of "revolution from above"; or military leftism—on a united front position—irrespective of mass support.

Castroite Personalism

A special characteristic of Castro is his growing reliance on nepotism, on familial contacts as political leaders. The steady rise in position of his brother Raúl Castro, the influence of other members of his extended family, all serve to surround him with nonthreatening figures. Personalism in Latin America has traditionally served to enhance the direct link of the leader to the people. In the case of Castro, it enables him, when necessary, to bypass the only stable party apparatus remaining in the country—the Communist party. By this tactic, he is striving to make over the image of the party into his own.

Castro's humiliation of old-line associates and their displacement either by himself or nonentities cannot be made light of. The family power held by Fidel Castro, Raúl Castro, Vilma Espín, along with Dorticós, is the only visible power left in the new Cuba. The politics of the purge, the dismemberment of any possible opposition, is clear.

The purging of Aníbal Escalante and Ramón Calcines, and the removal of or attacks against Joaquín Ordoqui, Edith García Buchaca, Manuel Luzardo, and Lázaro Peña, had nothing to do with their collective competences, but simply with their politics. The resignation of Carlos Rafael Rodríguez as head of the National Institute of Agrarian Reform (INRA) in 1965 and Castro's assumption of this post is illustrative of his organizational concentration of power in himself. It should be remembered that Castro is also prime minister, commander in chief of the armed forces, president of the Central Planning Board, and first secretary of the PCC. The general militarization of the Cuban society is manifested by the fact that ten out of the twenty ministries are headed by military men of Castro's inner circle, who control the most strategic sectors, that is, agriculture, the sugar industry, mining, transportation, communications, labor, the armed forces, and internal order. All members of the party Politburo, except two, and 66 percent of the Central Committee members are also military men.

Indeed, Castro has even cast his alter ego as president—Osvaldo Dorticós—much as the late Joseph Stalin could boast his in the person of Klementi Voroshilov. The trusted political lieutenant serves to legitimatize the remarks of the *caudillo*. The lieutenant provides the slogans; the leader provides the cement linking doctrines to slogans.

Related to this emergent nepotism is the increased demand for proletarian puritanism. First, in 1965 there was a concerted attack on alleged examples of homosexuality among government officials (featured by a "parade" of deviants in Havana); and in 1966 this was widened to include all those engaged in "antisocial" activities. The dismissal of Efigenio Almeijeiras as armed forces vice minister and his court martial, along with several dozen others in government life "for activities contrary to revolutionary morals," indicates that such puritanism has the dimensions of a full-scale purge.

The fusion, or rather the fudging, of personal and political aspects of behavior has served to justify an increased politicalization of the military and, no less, of the diplomatic corps. Changes in the army Chiefs of Staff, commander of the navy, and the leadership of the Ministry of Interior represent not simply a tightening of the political net, but an increased penetration by the maximum leader into middle echelons of power. With each series of dismissals, the actual power lodged in both civil and military agencies seems to become correspondingly weaker; the replacements are less able (or willing) to make decisions independently.

Conclusions

What do we make of the current Cuban position? The most important thing is that it announces that Castro is no longer a significant threat to the United States. Any government bent on national redemption, on the national road to salvation, on national socialism, on a concentration upon internal problems, can hardly threaten the international position of the United States. It is not that Castro is seeking a *rapprochement* with the United States any more than Stalin was interested in obtaining such a *rapprochement* with Europe. This is a *realpolitik* phase. *Rapprochement* would be neither sought nor spurned. But it would be no more shocking to have an agreement between Nixon and Castro than it was to have one between Molotov and Von Ribbentrop. It may be viewed as shocking from the point of view of the Latin American revolutionists and their expectations (just as the Russo-German pact of 1939 shocked and chagrined the world Communist movement), but not from the logic of the Stalinist position.

Cuban-United States relations are in a period of self-imposed isolation for both nations. The Cubans hope to make this a period of national economic growth. A newspaper headline every January first will announce the unswerving allegiance of the Castro regime to an antiimperialist alliance; and July 26 will headline the celebration of the anniversary of the Revolution, embellished by rhetorical antiimperialist vows. Other than that, we would expect to see little in the way of Cuban action or Cuban behavior at the international plane. In this, Castro is not only pursuing a Stalinist position, but also a classical Latin American disregard of hemispheric needs as a whole. The Cuban Revolution of 1959 announced that Latin America will become a consolidated reality; post-Che Cuba announced a return to twenty nations.

The differences between Stalin and Castro—both as ideologists and personality types—can hardly be minimized. Stalin was bureaucratic; Castro is charismatic. Stalin was enmeshed with all phases of Soviet cultural life; Castro—at least up to 1971—has limited himself to platitudinous comments on the cultural apparatus. Stalin was, above all, a figure of immense international significance, and Castro has little possibility of performing a similar world role. There are, indeed, other aspects indicating differences. But beneath the military tunic of Castro is a man concerned with consolidation and absolute loyalty—the same properties which made "socialism in one country" the rallying party slogan in the Soviet Union for over two decades and served to weld the military and political elites into a united phalanx for economic development.

This is not to deny in any way that the Cuban Revolution is an authentic revolution; only that it has little chance of becoming hemispheric in character. The Cuban Revolution is of such major consequence that no leader can capture it, not even a man as powerful as Castro. It is inconceivable that there can be a restoration of Cuban barracks revolutionists, since democracy of arms still exists. The Cuban Revolution represents a total rupture with the past. There is no gain in saying that. Castro led as complete a revolution as ever took place in Europe. What is at stake is the character and purpose of that revolution; the strategy of Stalinism versus that of Trotskyism. What we are observing is the consolidation of a socialist Cuba and an indefinite postponement of a socialist Latin America.

The Stalinization of Cuba should occasion small comfort for Washington "Castrologists." As in so many aspects of political life, the degeneration of socialism in Cuba was sharpened and accelerated by an American hard line; by support of counterinsurgency operations, however disreputable; by constant violations of Cuban air and sea space; by a virtual embargo on basic industrial and consumer goods; and above all, by the manipulation of the international economy to the disadvantage of Cuba. "War Communism" has indeed come to an end in Cuba—replaced by two steps backward and one step forward. But whether the new turn in Castroism would have taken place without the emergence of "War Capitalism" in the United States is impossible to say.

In summary then, Cuban communism has achieved special dimensions: (a) There is a subordination of society to the party and the army. (b) There is in Cuba the emergence of a leader and his small coterie as exclusive spokesmen for the Communist party. (c) There is the promotion of inner political struggle as a substitute for class struggle. (d) The passion for economic development displaces the politics of debate and the passion for socialist democracy. (e) The Stalinization of the Cuban regime has brought to a halt discussion of alternative strategies for economic development, letting the matter rest with single-crop socialism. (f) Stalinization in Cuba has meant the nearly exclusive concentration of energies on national rather than international problems.

Clearly, like any model built upon analogy, there are notable exceptions in the linkage between the organization and ideology of Stalinism and the present political and social structure of Cuban communism. Yet this effort at fusing historical information with the actual functioning of the Cuban regime may permit scholars to achieve a fully integrated statement of the nature of Cuban communism—a task which has been tragically ignored by most specialists on international development thus far.

NOTES

1. Robert Daland, *Brazilian Planning: Development, Politics and Administration* (Chapel Hill, N.C., 1967).

2. Fidel Castro, "Speech in the Ceremony to Commemorate the Centennial of the Birth of V. I. Lenin," *Granma Weekly Review,* May 3, 1970, pp. 2–5.

3. René Dumont, *Cuba est-il socialiste?* (Paris, 1970); and K. S. Karol, *Les Guérrilleros au pouvoir* (Paris, 1970).

4. Fidel Castro, *Betrayed by Chinese Government of Cuban People's Good Faith* (Havana, February 6, 1966).

5. Castro, "Speech in the Ceremony," pp. 2–5.

II
Economy

7

Carmelo Mesa-Lago and Luc Zephirin

Central Planning

THIS essay attempts to describe and analyze the evolution of the planning system in Cuba throughout the revolutionary period. Since 1959, at least three different planning models have been tested by the Cuban leadership. They are now searching for an original planning model that can be adapted to the peculiarities of the country rather than simply following the Soviet pattern.

As an alternative to the prerevolutionary market system, the establishment of planning (with a varying degree of centralization) was a prime task faced by the revolutionary government. By reviewing the many alterations that have taken place in the operational planning machinery to meet the requirements of the economy, the nature of the difficulties involved in the process will be brought out. Hopefully, this will expand the still primitive body of knowledge on this matter and be useful to developing countries that face similar problems.

This chapter first describes the alternative planning models available to the Cuban leaders at the revolutionary onset, followed by a brief history of the evolution of planning in the 1960s. Next the current structure and organization of planning, the mechanism and techniques for the preparation of the plan, and the various functions of the planning system (e.g., capital and labor allocation) are described and analyzed. The essay concludes with a summary of the current situation and discussion of main problems.

Mr. Zephirin prepared drafts of the material up to the section on planning apparatus under Dr. Mesa-Lago's guidance. The final version of the entire paper was written by the latter.

Alternative Models of Planning

Not too long ago, economists engaged in heated debate concerning the advantages and disadvantages of the planned economy versus the market economy. The debate is still going on, but its character has undergone a significant change. For developing countries, particularly in Latin America, the need for developmental planning has been recognized as the result of a combination of internal and external factors. At the Punta del Este conference of 1961, Latin American governments agreed that planning should be the fundamental instrument for mobilizing national resources, bringing about necessary structural changes, and securing more international financial cooperation.[1] The need for state intervention in the overall allocation of resources to speed up development has been accepted also. Thus, the question is not whether to plan or not, but how to plan.

Planning theory does not offer an appropriate framework for evaluating the success or failure of program implementation in developing countries. Very often, theory underestimates political, administrative, and other practical problems that constrain the planning process in those countries. The Cubans claim that for planning to be operational it is first necessary that the state controls (collectivizes) the means of production in order to eliminate internal and external obstacles. Within the limits of this chapter, it is not possible to tackle this crucial question. A more modest objective is to describe how the Cuban leaders tested, selected, implemented, and adapted a particular model of economic organization from among three different alternatives: indicative planning, central planning, and decentralized (market socialism) planning.[2]

Indicative Planning: The Sierra Programs

In prerevolutionary Cuba, there were several institutions dedicated to the promotion of economic development. The objectives of the National Economic Council founded in 1943, transformed in 1949 into the National Economic Board and in 1955 into the National Planning Board, were to prepare an inventory of natural resources and make recommendations on production and urban plans, but these objectives had little compulsory character. In the financing field, there were the National Bank (created at the turn of the 1940s as a central bank), the Bank of Agrarian and Industrial Development (BANFAIC: founded in 1950 as a credit institution to promote diversification of agriculture and new industries), the Bank of Economic and Social Development (BANDES: established in 1953 as a credit institution to promote development), and the Cuban Bank of Foreign Trade (founded in 1954 to supervise foreign trade operations). Other agencies included the Institutes for the Stabilization of Sugar, Coffee, and

Rice, which regulated domestic production in agreement with agencies devoted to stabilize the international market price of these products.[3] However, none of these agencies ever prepared and implemented a comprehensive plan of development; hence, it may be said that prior to the Revolution only features of indicative planning were in operation.

Both at the Sierra and at the onset of the revolutionary take-over, Castro stated that the Revolution was not socialistic but democratic-nationalistic. It seems that at the time Cuban policy makers had no economic blueprint; hence, planning efforts followed initially the only pattern and techniques available in the continent, that is those promoted by the U.N. Economic Commission for Latin America (ECLA).

In none of the documents signed by Castro or members of the July 26 movement was there a clear idea of the planning model to be followed by the revolutionaries, but all the proposed economic reform measures suggested a market economy under indicative planning.[4] The economic program of the July 26 movement, prepared by two economists (who in the early period of the Revolution became the president of the National Bank and the minister of economics), recommended (a) the establishment of a Ministry of Economics to be in charge of economic development, (b) the introduction of planning measures compatible with the use of markets (e.g., the use of fiscal and monetary incentives), and (c) the participation of all sectors or groups in the elaboration of planning. The program also endorsed a state campaign to mobilize idle capital and other resources for industrialization through the National Bank and the BANFAIC. It also suggested the need for planned GNP growth rates, and estimated the amount of investment necessary to wipe out unemployment in a ten-year period. Although this program and other documents of this period mentioned the need of nationalization in strategic industries (e.g., electric power, telephone) and of the expropriation of *latifundia,* the willingness to pay compensation was acknowledged and, in general, private domestic enterprise, as well as private ownership of land (and Western-style cooperatives) were defended. Participation of workers in the profits of enterprises and sugar mills was also recommended.

In spite of some socialistic features, all of these documents suggested a program for a "mixed economy" in which market elements (private ownership of the means of production, reliance on private capital as a guiding force in production, resource allocation through market and prices) and state control elements (planning, nationalization, government-directed agrarian reform, and government-sponsored industrialization) were present. The vagueness of the economic program of the July 26 movement was an asset in that it helped to bind together the diverse tendencies that opposed Batista. Both Castro and Ernesto (Che) Guevara acknowledged later that those programs could not have been more concrete or radical at the time because they could have alienated important segments in the revolutionary struggle.[5]

Central Planning: Guevara-style

The organizational alternative of a comprehensive, highly centralized planning system (typical of the Soviet Union under Stalin) was strongly supported by Guevara, possibly under the influence of a group of Marxist experts from the United States, France, and Belgium who visited Cuba in the early 1960s. These experts were Leo Huberman and Paul Sweezy (in early and late 1960), Paul Baran (in late 1960), and Ernest Mandel (in 1963).[6]

Having held the key posts of head of the Department of Industrialization of the National Institute of Agrarian Reform (INRA), president of the National Bank, and minister of industry, Guevara was, since late 1959, in a position to influence the Cuban economic organization according to his views. He wanted to implement a command economy in Cuba in which the basic decisions regarding the allocation of resources would be the prerogative of central planners responding to broad policy goals laid down by the political leadership. Guevara envisaged all the enterprises in the public sector as a single state enterprise; the enterprise's freedom of action was to be limited so as to harmonize its goals with the objectives of the central plan. Adopting a pure Marxist conception, Guevara advocated a kind of socialism that would transform not only the economy, but also human values and consciousness. Therefore, he emphasized the need for moral incentives to increase production, build a new society, and stimulate the worker to improve his professional training. He dreamed of a "New Man" with superior consciousness who could be mobilized in labor-intensive projects without being motivated by material reward. In such a society, money, profit, rent, and interest would be eliminated and wage egalitarianism would be encouraged.

Another important characteristic of the model was the financing system (budgetary financing), based on the national budget as the principal tool for allocating funds and controlling financially the operations carried out by the enterprises. The state enterprises, in practice, would depend totally on the state budget to receive the capital necessary for their expansion. Their revenue or profit would automatically go into the state treasury, whereas their expenditures would be covered by budgetary appropriations. Hence, the budget became functionally a financial plan for the mobilization and distribution of funds. The planners would decide how to invest these funds by taking into account, not the profitability of the enterprises, but, rather, the programs and targets of the different economic and social sectors. In a small country with a good communications system, such as Cuba, it would be easy to plan centrally by using mathematical and computer techniques.

Guevara and his followers defended the above-explained model in available Cuban journals or they created new ones sponsored by the Ministry of Industry. They also answered the arguments of the supporters of a more liberal, decentralized system of planning in this way.[7]

Decentralized Planning: Market Socialism

A third alternative available to Cuban leaders for the shaping of the economy was the model proposed since the late 1920s and early 1930s by Fred Taylor, Oscar Lange, and Abba P. Lerner. In replying to the arguments of Ludwig von Mises and Frederick Hayek concerning the practical impossibility of economic calculation in socialism, Lange, following Taylor's ideas, launched his well-known proposal for market socialism.[8] According to Lange, private enterprise may well continue to have a useful social function (in small-scale industry and farming) by being more efficient than a socialized enterprise may be. Market forces would set the price of consumer goods and wages, whereas a Central Planning Board would compute "accounting or parametric prices" for capital goods and would fix the interest rate. Capital accumulation would be the result of both communal savings (handled by the Central Planning Board) and individual savings. A "social dividend" would be distributed to households to reduce inequality resulting from market-determined wages. Finally, free exchange in international relations was to be favored instead of a state monopoly of trade.[9]

Lerner adopted a similar, although more elaborated and promarket, approach. He called his system a controlled economy to contrast it with both capitalism and Soviet socialism. Lerner stressed the necessity of keeping both market and price mechanisms in proper relation to consumer goods in order to enhance individual freedom. He also supported the use of the market in the distribution of goods and transportation.[10]

Market socialism, or at least most of its features, was adopted by Yugoslavia in the 1950s and influenced economic reform in Eastern Europe and Libermanism in the Soviet Union after Stalin's death. In Cuba, this model was partially endorsed in 1963–1965 by members of the old PSP, as well as by a small group of young revolutionaries and a few foreign specialists who served as advisers to the government. In a public debate with the Guevarists, they defended the use of market mechanisms (and acknowledged the functioning of the law of value) in the transition stage, the method of self-finance to permit state enterprises to reinvest part of their profits, profitability as the best indicator of managerial performance, and the use of material incentives to motivate workers and managers.[11]

René Dumont, a French Marxist agronomist who was an adviser to the Cuban government in mid-1960 and late 1963, apparently had some influence also. Dumont criticized Cuba's acceleration of collectivization, the highly centralized system of planning, the nationalization of small enterprises, the elimination of agricultural cooperatives, the gigantic size of state farms, the lack of financial autonomy of enterprises, the growing bureaucracy and inefficiency, and the disdain for material incentives. Dumont's proposals, based on the principle of a decentralized management system, urged the restoration of market prices as regulators of consumer-goods allocation, of profit as a measurement of enterprise efficiency, and of cooperatives in agriculture and small industries to increase production. He also urged the use of differential rent on land provided by the state, of decentralization in state-owned large and heavy industry, of interest on state-bank loans and credit, and of monetary and fiscal measures in long-range planning.[12]

Along the same line, but with some differences, Charles Bettelheim, a French planner who also went to Cuba as adviser in 1961 and 1962, made a major theoretical contribution about the organizational system of the Cuban economy. He argued that the economy was suffering not only from administrative deficiencies, but also from a fundamental malady due to the fact that productive relations were not as developed as the productive forces. The result was a lack of real economic control, which was not actually corrected by multiplying regulatory measures and bureaucracy. According to Bettelheim, Cubans should abandon the vain hope of reducing the different forms of social ownership to one common notion of state ownership. He thought it would also be wise not to force the progress from "lower" (cooperative) forms to "higher" (collectivist) forms of socialism and, instead, to try to adopt those forms that best corresponded to the level of development of the productive forces at that time.[13]

The principles of this model were temporarily and partially applied in two vital sectors of the Cuban economy: agriculture and foreign trade. Cuba is essentially an agrarian country which depends heavily on foreign trade. Traditionally, agriculture has been the Achilles' heel of socialist countries, and most of these are industrialized with small dependence on trade. Central planning could be more easily applied to concentrated industry in which labor is commonly skilled and disciplined. But in agriculture, there are natural factors impossible to predict, and production is dispersed and in the hands of thousands of unskilled, undisciplined workers and peasants who are difficult to control. Market mechanisms (e.g., prices) and private ownership seemed to be more appropriate to this sector. Concerning foreign trade, Cuban officials were faced with foreign markets, productivity, and market prices, as well as the need for foreign exchange. It is understandable that they also sided with the market-socialist approach.[14]

Historical Evolution of Planning in Cuba

There are three stages in the evolution of Cuban planning since the Revolution in which the three models explained above were in operation at least partially and temporarily. In the presocialist stage, which began in 1959 and ended in early 1961, some features of indicative planning were present, but, in general, this was a period of confusion and lack of coordination (although the basis for socialism was laid down through collectivization and increasing state control of the economy). The second stage, which began by mid-1961 and terminated in 1965, was one of experimentation. Thus, centralized planning Soviet-style was mechanically applied in 1961–1962, decentralization measures typical of market socialism were partially tested in 1964–1965 in some sectors, and features of the Guevarist model were also present. In the third stage, which began in late 1965 and is still developing, the Guevarist model has been thoroughly applied to the economy, but with the Castroite addition of the so-called special plans, which operate somewhat outside of the central plan.

Presocialist Stage: Increasing Collectivization and Economic Control

On January 2, 1959, Castro was appointed chief of the armed forces, which soon became a powerful administrative arm of the Revolution. Members of the rebel army were placed in key positions, particularly in the countryside, and played an important role in the application of the agrarian reform. The first Agrarian Reform Law became effective on June 3, and, in the same month, Castro was appointed as prime minister. As a state corporation, the INRA received broad functions and powers that transformed it into the main agency for a vast development program, not only agricultural but also industrial. In November, the Department of Industrialization was created under the INRA and Guevara was appointed as its director. This department became one of the key nerves of the program of economic development, and its Section of Planning and Studies was the *foco* of the first genuine experiment on central planning.[15]

In January 1960, several measures were adopted by the National Bank aimed at achieving selective control of the credit facilities of commercial banks, including control over foreign exchange. After February 1960, official credit institutions in existence began to disappear. In March, the Central Planning Board (JUCEPLAN) was created at the ministerial level to coordinate policies of various governmental agencies and to guide the private sector. Although the possibility of physical planning was opened up, there were many obstacles to its practical implementation. At the time, most of the economy was still under private control and a substantial portion of the state apparatus still had the prerevolutionary organizational structure. Within the context of democratic reformism, JUCEPLAN tried to develop the planning techniques (such as budgetary programming and global projections) suggested by a team of economists sent to Cuba by the ECLA. (The mission was headed by the Mexican Juan Noyola, and included the Chileans Jacques Chonchol and Jorge Ahumada.) Since the 1950s, the ECLA had influenced the ideology and techniques for the economic and social development in Latin America, emphasizing the role of planning.[16]

In the second half of 1960, the nationalization of foreign and domestic enterprises and banking practically destroyed the market system. Theoretically, state control and planning were to replace market mechanisms, but in practice the existing state institutions were not able to perform this task and the economy became disorganized. By the end of the year, President Osvaldo Dorticós headed a committee for administrative reorganization and, as a result of its work, new ministries and regulations were implemented, most of them in February 1961.

JUCEPLAN was charged with the responsibility of formulating development plans in the short and long run, to be submitted for consideration to the Council of Ministers, and of regulating and orienting the activity of the private sector. Soon JUCEPLAN became the hub of a vast network of agencies connected at all levels with the administrative machinery. Its organization consisted of a plenary council with an executive secretariat, an executive committee and six directorates. The plenary council presided over by the prime minister included all ministers dealing with economic matters. It was an agency of broad revision and control. The executive committee was concerned primarily with policy and directives for the elaboration of plan and budgets. The six directorates were the working staff of JUCEPLAN and part of the technical secretariat headed by the Ministry of Economics. These directorates were Central Administration; Agriculture; Industry; Domestic Trade, Transport, and Construction; Balances; and Statistics.

New ministries were also created and given important planning functions. The new Ministry of Foreign Trade established a state monopoly over foreign trade and attempted to bring order and control to a field that is vital to the economic relations with other socialist countries. The new Ministry of Industry was to govern, direct, supervise, and carry out the policy of industrial development of the nation and administer the state industrial enterprises in accordance with central planning directives. The new Ministry of Domestic Trade was in charge of the state's stores and had the responsibility to plan and administer the distribution system.

A new structure was also given to the financing system. The Ministry of Finance was made responsible for the preparation of the budget that became, in fact, the national financial plan for investment. A new organic law of the National Bank entrusted it with a monopoly for all banking operations through its network of offices in the country. The bank, besides the usual functions of central banks, such as the emission of money, also had control of short-term credit and all payment operations, as well as custody of the working capital of the enterprises and the savings of the people. It was used as a main economic weapon to bring about the necessary increase in reserves, and, in coordination with the Ministry of Foreign Trade (MINCEX) to face the acute problems of foreign payments, and to stop the high speed of money circulation as well as the outflow of foreign exchange.

The Ministry of Labor was reorganized according to its second organic law to make it part of the new planning machinery. A new office of planning was in charge of the preparation, in coordination with the planning agencies, of the systems of work measurements or output standards. The ministry was also empowered to fix salaries of workers in the state sector, and was given increased control over collective bargaining and social security funds.[17]

The planning and central administration machinery was reinforced with the creation of a network of regional agencies—the Coordination, Execution and Inspection Boards (JUCEI)—whose functions were to coordinate, inspect, and exercise vigilance over state policy at provincial and local levels. According to JUCEI's president in Havana, the board's objective was to eliminate "personalism and capricious individual decision-making" that was the consequence of the disorganized mixed economy of 1959–1960.[18]

In the agricultural sector, the private farmers were integrated into the National Association of Small Farmers (ANAP), tied in turn to the INRA and JUCEPLAN. The management of the state farms and sugar-cane cooperatives was centralized in the INRA through the creation of general administration offices. In the industrial sector, Guevara was appointed as minister of industries; and he rapidly implemented the system of consolidated enterprises by line of production. A more detailed discussion of these changes can be found in the next chapter.

The new ministries were hastily organized with a great deal of improvisation, and staffed with inadequate personnel. Most technicians, managers, and administrators fled the country in big waves after mid-1960, when the process of socialization required an increased need for skilled workers and qualified decision makers to do the job that was automatically done before by the market. Consequently, organizational deficiencies became evident. There was an increase in the bureaucracy of the planning apparatus and in paper work, and a decline in productivity.

According to Edward Boorstein, an American Marxist economist who worked for Cuban planning and foreign trade agencies in 1960–1963, the method of administration and work that prevailed from 1959 to 1961 was known to the Cubans as *por la libre*.[19] Little attention was paid to the need for coordination and systematic plans, and the state ministries and agencies operated in a kind of freewheeling way with no control procedures. Productivity was of secondary importance. Top priority was given to breaking the power of the ruling classes and to providing social benefits to the masses, two necessary steps for the consolidation of the Revolution. The economic chaos of these years made urgent the development of central planning.

The Experimentation Stage: Centralism Versus Decentralization

The preliminary work for the 1962 plan (1962 was going to be declared the "Year of Planning") began by the end of March 1961, but was interrupted by the Bay of Pigs invasion, and was not resumed until the end of April. A mission from the Czechoslovakian State Planning Commission cooperated with JUCEPLAN officials in the preparation of the plan. The Czech methodology, based on orthodox principles, relied on some 500 material balances derived from a series of sector projections and global balances, "the latter not very different from the national account system used in bourgeois economies."[20] The Czech model was applied rigidly and mechanically, with no effort to adapt it to Cuban peculiarities. It required both detailed and accurate statistics and trained cadres. In spite of the lack of qualified personnel, planning offices were rapidly staffed, and when data were not available, figures were grossly estimated or even invented to comply with JUCEPLAN's pressures. Hence, goals were excessively optimistic with no basis in reality. The first variant of the plan was completed in September of 1961, but a total of seven variants were made, the last one in May 1962. By the time the plan was ready, its gross miscalculations were so obvious (e.g., rationing had to be established in March 1962) that it never was given the force of law.[21]

In fact, it was difficult with few trained people, no previous experience, and inadequate data to convert the chaotic Cuban economy into a planned one in such a short period of time. In contrast to the previous stage when administrative problems were left to the free will of managers, this stage was characterized by excessive centralism and rigidity. Deep concern was given to norms and procedures to the detriment of decision-making attitudes.

Almost parallel with the preparation of the first annual plan, various attempts were made to elaborate a long-range plan for 1962–1965. Polish planner Michael Kalecki prepared the first one by the end of 1960, and French planner Charles Bettelheim and Russian planner A. Efinov prepared the other two by mid-1961; all these models followed Soviet techniques.[22] But according to Cuban publications, several shortcomings made these plans theoretical studies divorced from reality, impeding their practical usage: (a) there was a lack of sectorial studies, statistics were incomplete and deficient, and the planners did not have a real knowledge of the Cuban economy; and (b) the leadership had not defined the economic directives enough to allow for the preparation of concrete targets. After 1962, new attempts were made to elaborate medium-range plans (from three to four years), but, in spite of some improvement in the degree of disaggregation, their scope and degree of concretion was limited and they never became official. Because of the lack of qualified cadres, most of whom were concentrating on the preparation of annual plans or on other economic studies, the Cuban leadership decided not to devote more effort to prepare medium- or long-range plans.[23]

Changes in the organizational structure accentuated even more the previous tendency toward centralization. A law enacted in early 1962 introduced strict control of prices and rationing by the Ministry of Domestic Trade in coordination with JUCEPLAN. The system of budgetary finance spread throughout state-controlled industrial enterprises. In private agriculture, the system of *acopio,* state procurement quotas fixed to small farmers at official prices, was introduced. The National Institute of Physical Planning (INPF) was established to prepare physical plans for the principal cities and the location of new investment. In mid-1962, sugar-cane cooperatives were transformed into state farms and centrally directed by the INRA. In the same month, the National Institute of Water Resources (INRH) was entrusted with the elaboration of water control plans and similar projects. The Ministry of Labor was reorganized so that it would prepare uniform output standards and wage scales for all workers in the nation. In 1963, the office of planning at the Ministry of Public Health was empowered to elaborate short- and long-term health plans for the country.

Serious administrative problems plagued the economy in 1963, making it the worst agricultural year of the revolutionary period. Agricultural plans were determined centrally without allowing lower echelon agencies to participate in their discussion and preparation.[24] Because of their rigidity and the absence of competent managers, these plans ended in failure. The decision to reduce the land devoted to sugar cultivation resulted in the lowest sugar crop of the Revolution. In October, the second Agrarian Reform Law was passed and Carlos Rafael Rodríguez announced a drastic reorganization of state agriculture (see chapter 8).[25]

Albán Lataste, a Chilean economist who worked as an adviser to Cuban planning institutions in 1960–1966, has made an evaluation of the principal problems faced in this period. Lataste states that economic decisions were taken by the political leadership in a casuistic manner and without consultation with JUCEPLAN. Hence, central planning could not play a relevant role in improving economic decision-making, and serious inconsistencies resulted. Because long-range planning never materialized, the economy could not function properly. Investment was made in a casuistic manner without integration into a concrete plan of development. Annual plans were unrealistic and had neither a legal bounding nor a compulsive nature. Land collectivization and the system of *acopio* in agriculture induced a dislocation in the flow of supplies from the countryside to the towns. Millions of economic microrelations were destroyed at once, breaking the automatic mechanism of market distribution when the state system was not ready to take over these functions. Lataste also states that, due to the lack of information, agricultural products often badly needed in the cities were lost in the ground or, after harvested, were spoiled due to a lack of transportation. Because of price rigidity, many state stores that did not reduce their prices lost perishable products. The irrationality of the price system encouraged private farmers to decrease the output of badly needed crops. Due to lack of interest and profit, the effectiveness of investment was poor and some enterprises had a negative productivity.[26] The state apparatus of economic direction was too concentrated, rigid, and overloaded.

In a brief attempt to solve these problems in 1964–1965, some features of the market-socialist model were applied to one-third of the state enterprises, mainly in agriculture and foreign trade, and to a few industrial enterprises. Theoretically, the system called for self-finance, charged interest for repayable loans, reinvested part of the enterprise profit, and called attention to cost and profitability. In practice, the system was adulterated so that it resembled the budgetary-finance model more than the market-socialist model.

Another attempt to decentralize also began in 1964 with the deconcentration of the power of the INRA and Ministry of Industries (MININD) and the initiation of a system of "combines." These combines are central ministries or agencies that vertically integrate several functions, in some cases from planting to manufacturing and exporting. The Ministry of the Sugar Industry was created by merging the manufacturing functions formerly entrusted to MININD, as well as the INRA's sugar-cane farms and foreign trade functions of MINCEX. In addition, the INRA's poultry sector was organized independently as the National Poultry Combine. The system of *agrupaciones* (clustering of state farms at the regional level) was also implemented in 1964, helping to decentralize somewhat the direction of agriculture. However, these were partial changes that did not solve the overall problem. In mid-1964, President Dorticós took over the direction of JUCEPLAN and, early in 1965, the Commission of Economic Organization (COE) was created to elaborate a project of reorganization of the state apparatus in charge of planning. The commission depending directly on the president, was headed by one of JUCEPLAN's vice ministers, and was composed of two officials each from JUCEPLAN, the National Bank, and the Ministry of Finance. By mid-1965, the COE presented a project that was approved in October by the government. This "marked a state of profound change ranging from the concept of economic relations to organizational forms."[27]

The Current Stage: Centralism and Special Plans

According to Lataste, the classic Soviet model of planning and economic organization was definitely replaced in Cuba toward the end of 1965 by another model, one that radically departs from the directives of the socialist countries of Eastern Europe. This move was preceded by a concentration of economic functions by political leaders, exemplified by Dorticós's take-over of JUCEPLAN and Castro's take-over of the INRA. "In the second half of 1965, practically all economic power was concentrated in one hand [referring to the political leadership] which now performs both political and administrative-economic decisions."[28]

As a result of the 1965–1966 reorganization, the Ministry of Finance was abolished and its functions transferred to the National Bank, which became the sole agency dealing with financing. (Just a few months before, most functions of the Ministry of Finance had been transferred to other agencies, e.g., customs were assigned to MINCEX, computation of expenses by sector of activity went to JUCEPLAN, and tax and budgetary operations were passed to the National Bank.)[29] The experiment of self-finance was stopped and the system of budgetary finance spread throughout the economy. The combine models rapidly expanded. The Ministry of Food Industry, created at the end of 1965, absorbed the INRA's enterprises that produced food and MININD's enterprises that produced beverages. The *Cubatabaco* combine founded in 1966 integrated tobacco storing, manufacturing, and exports. *Instituto del Libro* established in 1967 controlled printing, distribution, and exports of publications. In 1967, MININD was dismembered into three new ministries—Basic Industry, Light Industry, and Mining-Metallurgy.[30] *Cubacafé,* a combine organized in 1968 within the Ministry of Food Industry, integrated coffee and cocoa crops, and the manufacturing of these products. This process of ministerial compartmentalization and vertical integration into combines was closely tied to the movement away from central planning and toward miniplanning which is explained below.

A law passed in April 1966 provided for the third reorganization of JUCEPLAN. Apparently, JUCEPLAN kept its function of preparing annual and medium- and long-range plans. JUCEPLAN's structure became integrated into three vice ministries, one in charge of economic development, another, sectorial planning, and a third in charge of national balances; plus two departments, one in charge of statistics, and the other, organization and methodology. But by the end of 1966, the Vice Ministry of Economic Development was eliminated and the preparation of long-range plans was assigned to the Economic Commission of the PCC. At the same time, the Vice Ministry of Sectorial Planning, in charge of the preparation of annual and medium-range plans for agriculture, industry, etc., was merged with the Vice Ministry of National Balances. Hence, by the end of that year, JUCEPLAN functions were mainly limited to research and computation of global and material balances for the annual plan, and the economic strategy became an exclusive function of the political leadership. Furthermore, the annual plan lost a great deal of its directive nature and became mainly a tool for internal calculation. JUCEPLAN's work was reduced to the logistical functions of assuring the needed inputs to meet the output targets fixed by the political leadership and of solving eventual discrepancies.[31]

In place of medium- and long-range macroplans, medium-range miniplans for special sectors (e.g., sugar, cattle-raising, fishing, electricity) have proliferated since 1965. The official reasoning supporting this move is that, due to the lack of cadres and background studies, as well as common unforeseen contingencies in agriculture and frequent structural changes, it is better to concentrate all efforts on sectorial, practical plans instead of highly abstract macroeconomic interrelations.[32]

However, the lack of overall coordination seems to be a major cause of low productivity and inefficiency in the Cuban economy. The well-known planner and inventor of input-output analysis, Wassily Leontief, commented on this after a visit to Cuba in 1969: "Fidel apparently has for some time emphasized what he calls 'mini-planning,' that is separate planning of the operations of each individual sugar mill, textile plant, or electric station. No wonder bottlenecks develop everywhere, inventories run down, and unforeseen shortages occur resulting in frequent extremely costly shutdowns."[33]

A second type of plan used since 1965 is the so-called special or extra plan, which is casuistically decided by the political leadership in order to tackle a particular problem or develop a concrete project. The administrator of these plans, directly appointed by the top hierarchy, is usually a loyal person from the inner circle, who does not have connections with the regular economic apparatus (JUCEPLAN, central ministries), but is dependent on those who appointed him. The allocation of resources to the special plan is done by "superior order," outside of central-plan specifications. This often results in the reduction of allocations made to central projects already in operation but ranked lower in priority than the special plan. Since there is neither a central agency nor a set of rules to deal *ex ante* with coordination problems and incompatibilities resulting between special and central plans, these conflicts are solved *ex post* in an arbitrary manner by the top hierarchy, mainly the prime minister.[34]

Another type of "extra plan" results from modifications and additions to current plans. This case has been explained in detail by the French agricultural economist Isy Joshua, who worked in Cuba from 1963 to 1967. According to Joshua, the annual sectoral plan for agriculture is commonly unrealistic, and, hence, cannot be fulfilled and has to be modified. Alterations in the plan may also result from changes in the decisions of the leadership. Often, when one part of the plan is changed (e.g., production), other parts are not modified in a similar manner (e.g., investment, supplies). Sometimes, there are so many important modifications that it is impossible to remake the whole plan, but additions or extra plans must be made. Joshua indicates that the multiplication of this usage could cause the abandonment of all planning, leaving the administrators satisfied to conduct production activities on a daily basis.[35]

Lataste believes that the above-explained situation has created a serious danger—the economy will not be capable of maximizing the possibilities open to a socialist system. Due to the lack of central planning, advances in certain areas may be offset by a decline in others, thus the overall performance of the economy could be below its actual potentiality, "This [the Cuban experience] could result in the first exception against the rule set by the socialist countries which have been capable of showing enormous success in economic growth during the first decade of their regimes, even when starting under extremely unfavorable conditions."[36]

A report sent in 1968 by JUCEPLAN to the ECLA's seminar on administrative aspects of the execution of development plans, diminished the importance of the problems pointed out by Leontief, Lataste, and Joshua.[37] This report argues that the Cuban leadership could not wait until macroeconomic long-range planning had been prepared in order to take steps to develop the economy. Although acknowledging the current lack of macroeconomic long- and medium-range plans, the report asserts that there is a strategy for development and a set of programs in the essential branches of the economy and states that "daily decisions in the economic process are those which ultimately allow the real and effective implementation of the strategy for development."[38]

The Planning Apparatus

The Cuban planning apparatus is organized vertically into national planning and horizontally into regional planning. This section attempts to describe the current organization of both schemes.[39]

National Planning

The national planning apparatus has a pyramidal shape and embraces four levels, as may be seen in figure 1. The first level or apex corresponds to central global agencies (e.g., JUCEPLAN, National Bank) in charge of planning, supervision, or control that are not engaged in execution tasks. The second level includes the sectorial central ministries or *combinados* devoted to the direction of a given type of either productive (agriculture, industry) or service activities. The third level deals with regional or sectorial clusterings such as the agricultural *agrupación,* the industrial *consolidado,* or the provincial service branches set up as vincula to the central ministries and responsible for the execution of the plan. The fourth level or base is composed of farms, factories, and local agencies whose managers and workers execute the planned targets. Supporting this apparatus are other institutions of a political, trade union, or mass-mobilization nature that help in the orientation or implementation of the plan.

Central planning agencies. JUCEPLAN is the institution placed at the top of the planning hierarchy. In theory it is supposed to be a superministry, which provides orientation, allocates resources, and coordinates economic activities. Since late 1966, JUCEPLAN is no longer in charge of either long- or medium-range planning, but prepares the annual plan following leadership directives and in consultation with the central ministries, and controls the execution of the plan. Other JUCEPLAN tasks relate to technical studies and compilation of statistics. Its most important departments today are the Vice Ministry of National Balances and the Central Statistics Department.

The National Bank is the treasury, investment bank, issuer and controller of currency, national budget office, and depository bank. All enterprises must secure their funds from the bank and transfer their profits or revenues to it. Transactions among state enterprises are done through bank compensation in special accounts. The bank also grants credits to private

ORGANIZATION OF CUBAN PLANNING: 1967

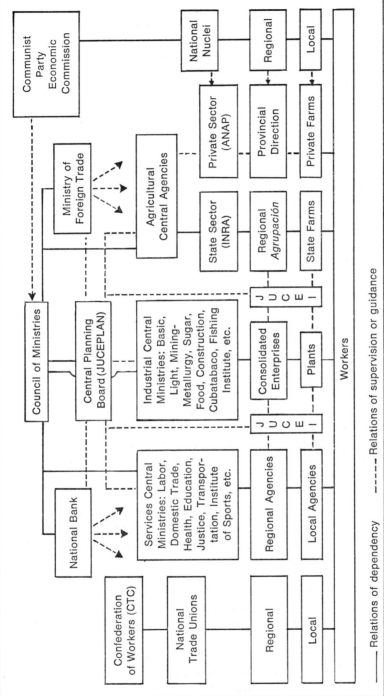

Prepared by Carmelo Mesa-Lago, based on Osvaldo Dorticós, "Avances institucionales de la revolución," *Cuba Socialista*, 6 (January 1966), pp. 2–23; "El desarrollo industrial de Cuba," ibid., 6 (May 1966), pp. 122–27; and "New Economic-Industrial Organization in Cuba," *Cuba Economic News*, 2 (September 1967), pp. 6–8.

— Relations of dependency   ----- Relations of supervision or guidance farmers through ANAP, collects payments from the public (e.g., electric and telephone bills), pays social security pensions, and it is the depository of saving accounts. The central office of the bank has three vice presidencies (finance, international operations, and administration) and three departments (auditing, methods and systems, and global analysis). There are 250 branches of the bank dispersed throughout the country.

The Ministry of Foreign Trade (MINCEX) exerts a monopoly on trade with a few exceptions (e.g., some combines). Most imports and exports have to be processed through MINCEX, which controls the foreign-trade plan, the supply plan, and the foreign-exchange plan. In 1969, there were twenty-six enterprises (either within MINCEX or other ministries or independent) that took care of exports or imports. Exports include *Cubaexport* (food, liquor, marbles, minerals); *Cubazúcar* (crude and refined sugar and derivatives); *Cubatabaco* (leaf and pipe tobacco, cigars, cigarettes); and *Exportadora del Caribe* (fresh and canned seafood). Imports include *Alimport* (foodstuffs, alcoholic beverages); *Consumimport* (durable consumer goods and other manufactured goods); *Construimport* (construction equipment); *Maquimport* (industrial equipment); *Cubapesca* (ships and fishing equipment); *Ferrimport* (hardware, ceramics); and *Cubatex* (natural and synthetic yarns and fibers, footwear).[40]

The Ministry of Labor (MINTRAB) functions as both a planning agency and a service central ministry. It controls the labor market, fixes output standards (labor quotas) and wage scales for all workers, regulates working conditions (e.g., work schedules, vacations) through models for collective contracts, directs the system of social security (except for medical care), supervises emulation plans, endorses safety and hygienic measures in the enterprises, and handles occupational accidents. Its main planning function, done in coordination with JUCEPLAN, pertains to the disaggregation of output targets and the material balances between income and consumption.

Central ministries. Each central ministry, combine, or agency embraces a particular sector of the economy or branch of production or services. For simplicity, figure 1 divides these into three broad categories: industry, agriculture, and services.

In the industrial sector, there are six ministries as well as a few combines that control practically all industrial output. The type of production, the size of existing plants, total investment, and the importance of the industry in the national economy determine whether an industry is classified as "basic" or "light."[41]

The Ministry of the Sugar Industry (MINAZ) is the most important ministry of Cuba. It contributed 16 percent of the state industrial output in 1966, excluding the agricultural sector. It embraces 161 sugar mills and their plantations, as well as transportation equipment; it controls bulk-sugar terminals and handles sugar exports in coordination with MINCEX. The Cuban Research Institute of Sugar Cane Derivatives (ICIDCA) controls twenty-eight laboratories engaged in research on sugar by-products.

The Ministry of Basic Industry, the second in importance in Cuba, deals with some 288 factories that in 1966 provided 23 percent of Cuba's state industrial output. It is in charge of such industries as electric power, petroleum, chemicals, fertilizer, machine construction, industrial equipment, and metal assembly.

The Ministry of Light Industry is responsible for 640 factories, which in 1966 contributed 16 percent of the state industrial output. Its enterprises are printing, hard fibers, clothing, shoes, furniture, packing, soap and cosmetics, tires, glass, plastics, and leather.

The Ministry of Mining-Metallurgy embraces forty-seven enterprises. It covers mining plants—mainly nickel, copper, manganese, and chrome—oil extraction, and one or two small metallurgical plants. In 1966, the ministry generated 6 percent of the state industrial output. The Cuban Petroleum Institute is a combine that controls enterprises from oil refining to service stations.

The Ministry of Food Industry (MINAL) is composed of seven enterprises (five for production and two for services) devoted to canning (vegetables, fruits, milk, fish), dairy products, pastes, beverages, etc. It contributed 6 percent of the state industrial output in 1966. The ministry has several divisions for control and marketing.

The Ministry of Construction (MINCON) executes all construction activities of a productive or nonproductive (service) nature. It directs the enterprise that produces construction material, which contributed 6 percent of the state industrial output in 1966.

Cubatabaco is the combine composed of eight enterprises that manufacture tobacco (cigars, cigarettes, leaf and pipe tobacco) and matches. It contributed 6 percent of the state industrial output in 1966.

Other industrial agencies are the Cuban Institute of Cinema Arts (ICAIC) in charge of film production; the *Instituto del Libro* composed of nine enterprises in charge of book and journal production; the Institute of Tourist Industry (INIT), which administers hotels, night clubs, and some restaurants; and the National Institute of Fishing, which controls the fishing fleet, shipyards, and the wholesale distribution of fish caught.

The Ministry of Agrarian Reform, now in charge of INRA, embraces all nonsugar agricultural production. The planning department of the INRA prepares medium-range and annual agricultural plans. The INRA administers state farms through the system of regional delegations and *agrupaciones.* The private sector is integrated through ANAP into the INRA's Vice-Ministry of Agrarian Production. The latter fixes production targets and controls the *acopio* and the supply of seeds, fertilizer, and machinery to private farms.

The Sugar Cane Research Institute under the Cuban Academy of Sciences conducts research on biology, soils, and meteorology. The Institute of Animal Science is also a research center engaged in improving cattle-breeding, animal husbandry, etc. The Institute of Artificial Insemination administers the insemination of cattle, sheep, turkey, etc. The National Institute of Forestry Development takes care of reforestation and conservation plans.

The National Poultry Combine (CAN) is engaged in the production of fowl and eggs, as well as fodder. Two important research departments of CAN deal with poultry genetics and animal nutrition.

The agency for Agricultural and Livestock Development (DAP) was formed in 1969 as an outgrowth of the former Institute of Water Resources. DAP controls the mechanical equipment (excavators, bulldozers, trucks, cranes) and 41,000 workers for the construction of irrigation systems, small dams, wells, highways, railways and bridges, and the cleaning of fields and terracing of mountains.[42]

In the service sector, the Ministry of Domestic Trade (MINCIN) takes care of the distribution of intermediate and consumer goods, administering the rationing system, state stores, and warehouses. The Ministry of Transportation (MINTRAN) controls railroad, bus, air, and river transportation. The Ministry of Merchant Marine and Ports takes care of the merchant fleet, maritime transportation, and docks. The Ministry of Public Health (MINSAP) directs all state hospitals as well as the small numbers of medical cooperatives still functioning. It also administers vaccination campaigns, the rural two-year medical service of newly graduated physicians (800 in 1969), the Committees of Hygiene and Labor Protection (in cooperation with MINTRAB), etc. The Ministry of Education (MINDED) directs the educational system at all levels: elementary, secondary, vocational, higher, and adult education. Other ministries and agencies in this sector administer communications, justice, sports and recreation, etc.

Sectorial, or regional, and local agencies. The system of agricultural *agrupaciones* and industrial *consolidados,* as well as the organization of the local enterprise (farms and plants), is explained in detail in the next chapter.

Supporting institutions. The Economic Commission of the PCC is in charge of the strategy of development and theoretically should trace the general directives for the plan. In practice, it seems that the decisions are concentrated in the Politburo and the Council of Ministers. PCC cells are organized in factories, farms, service agencies, the armed forces, etc., exerting functions of control, orientation, supervision and transmission of information. Besides the PCC national bodies (Politburo, General Secretariat, Secretariat of Organization, Special Commissions, and the Central Committee), there are committees in each province and at the local level. The PCC is an important vehicle for implementing planned goals through mass mobilization and control at all organizational levels of the administrative structure.

The CTC does not participate in the elaboration of national planning (see chapter 9). Decisions concerning what to produce, how much to produce, how to produce, and how much to pay are made at the first and second levels of planning, in consultation with the third level and, occasionally, with local managers (see figure 1). The CTC has the job of mobilizing the labor force in the implementation of the plan. Other tasks include recruitment of unpaid voluntary labor, raising of workers' skills and education, improving factory conditions and safety measures and, in general, exhorting the workers to fulfill output targets and increase productivity.

The ANAP helps in the implementation of agricultural plans, handling of supplies and credit (through its credit department) organization of productive associations, control of *acopio,* and provision of technical advice. Other mass organizations that cooperate in the implementation of planning are the FMC (recruitment of idle women into the labor force, participation in special campaigns, and education), the CDR (helping in the rationing system, seizing of houses of those leaving the country, vaccination and health campaigns, and education), and the Communist Youth League (UJC: recruitment of youth into labor brigades, education, sports, and recreation).

Regional and Urban Planning

The National Institute of Physical Planning (INPF) is a regional planning agency originally assigned to the Ministry of Construction in charge of city planning. Later, the INPF absorbed part of the Cuban Institute of Cartography and Land Registration and became engaged in the study of territorial organization, land distribution, and agricultural production and productivity. The INPF regional administrations have replaced the former municipal governments. The INPF has a staff of 470 professionals working in cooperation with JUCEPLAN and some central ministries, and has helped to prepare important sectorial plans, such as the one for the sugar sector, the prospective agricultural plan, and the housing and road plans. Some INPF studies have been useful in the rationalization of production;

for example, an evaluation of the distribution of sugar mills, cane plantations, highways and roads, and transportation facilities resulted in a report
to improve the organization of this sector. Other important functions of
the INPF are to help in making optimum decisions regarding the location
of new investments and to help in the study of the politico-administrative
division of the island.

Due to the concentration of investment and rapid development of some
regions (Nuevitas, Cienfuegos, North Oriente, Isle of Pines), coordination
centers have been founded to help in regional planning. These agencies
are responsible for developing the investment plan, whereas other state
agencies perform special tasks (e.g., MINCON executes construction).
The need for coordination became evident when bottlenecks appeared
because the demand for labor, construction materials, etc., was greater
than the available resources in the area. In trying to solve the problem, an
integrated programming model has been developed to show interdepend-
encies and design schedules, and to predict potential delays. Finally, the
Coordination, Execution, and Inspection Boards (JUCEI) work at the
provincial and local levels in an attempt to coordinate several plans, to
help in their implementation, and to transmit information to the center.

Planning Techniques

The Current Technique: Material Balances

The process of preparing the annual plan may be divided into five
different steps: (1) basic directives, (2) global model, (3) control figures,
(4) directive figures, and (5) control of execution and revisions. What
follows is a description of the ideal or theoretical mechanism of planning
in Cuba as explained by Cuban officials.[43]

Basic directives. The basic politico-economic directives of development (e.g., desirable rate of GNP growth, the distribution of GNP between
investment and consumption, the distribution of investment between production and services) are drawn by the premier and the Council of Ministries under party guidance. Actually, the political decision on directives is
made out of a consideration of various potential alternatives prepared by
the Ministry of Economics, based on historical data, and an economic
diagnostic for the planned year.

Global model. This model is composed of a set of highly aggregative,
macroeconomic projections prepared by JUCEPLAN, beginning in January and completed in February. A set of these global projections for the
planned year includes volume of GNP; volume of foreign trade and balance
of payments (estimated in coordination with MINCEX); investment vol-

ume and structure (estimated amount of investment and its distribution by sectors—industry, agriculture, services); labor force; and the population's income and consumption. Another set of projections refer to needed total inputs in the economy both domestically produced or imported (e.g., power, fuel, raw materials, labor) and expected outputs of the chief productive sectors (e.g., sugar, nickel, electricity).

In order to assure the consistency of all these projections, physical "material balances" are computed for a group of the most important products (some 200 in Cuba) of the national economy. A *material balance* is an accounting technique by which the estimated total supply of one product for the planned year (e.g., metric tons of oil that will be available from stock, domestic production, and imports) is balanced with the estimated total demand of the same product for that year (e.g., needs of enterprises, exports, and population's consumption). Consistency checks in value terms (money) are also made (e.g., estimated value of the demand and supply of investment or the population's income and available consumer goods).

Control figures. Based on the highly aggregative global model, JUCEPLAN in consultation with the central ministries and agencies begins a process of disaggregation by successive approximation, in the course of which the desired targets are transformed into more concrete indicators. The first disaggregation of the global model, known as control figures, include concrete targets for each central ministry, combine, or agency. For example, MINAZ will have estimates for import of machinery from Eastern Europe, for total investment in sugar mills, for the total area of sugar cane to be harvested, the total number of cane cutters, the total sugar output, etc. These control figures should be ready by the second half of March and constitute the first version of the plan.

Based in the control figures, a process of even greater disaggregation begins within each central body. For example, each sugar mill within MINAZ must estimate the needed inputs to fulfill its assigned target of output; in other words, how much capital, import of equipment, power, sugar cane, labor, etc., will be necessary to produce its assigned quota of sugar. A second stage of this process consists of determining the interrelations between enterprises from different central ministries, for example, how much power should be supplied by the consolidated enterprise of electricity or how much oil by the petroleum enterprise to each sugar mill. Enterprises and plants should determine not only gross output, but also the quality, assortment, and schedule of production. Thus, a sugar mill must report the estimated monthly output (and eventually weekly and daily output) of raw sugar, molasses, and other by-products, as well as the schedule for transporting sugar to the sugar-bulk stations and ports. This information is vital for MINCEX's export plan, trade negotiations with the socialist countries, ship schedules, etc.

In agriculture, control figures are estimated for both the state and the private sectors, and are disaggregated down through the state *agrupación* and its farms, and through the ANAP and its provincial delegations and farms. These figures should estimate the land to be cultivated by crop (here the INPF enters the picture with maps, measurements, etc.); the physical amount of the *acopio* by product, farm, etc.; the necessary inputs (measured both in physical terms—metric tons—and value or money) that will come from imports; and investment. Then, the figures go up again to the ANAP and INRA, and then to JUCEPLAN in a process of reaggregation.

In industry, control figures are estimated for the five ministries and other minor agencies, including physical output of basic products; physical inputs to be imported for each basic-product output; value of industrial input and output by economic sector; and volume of investment. These figures go down to the enterprises and plants for disaggregation, and then up the pyramid in a process of reaggregation.

Directive figures. JUCEPLAN must seek maximum consistency among the revised control figures to avoid possible discrepancies that may result in bottlenecks, shortages, or surpluses. For instance, if provisions are not made for the necessary import of fuel, the electric enterprise will not be able to produce the planned output, there will be stoppages in sugar mills, the expected output of sugar will not be produced; this, in turn, will reduce exports, and an unplanned deficit in the balance of payments will result.

Cross-checks should be made, for example, between production, foreign and domestic trade, construction, and transportation figures. Discrepancies may show, for instance, insufficient output in view of demand or insufficient resources in view of planned targets. All these consistency checks permit the readjustment of estimates and targets, generating a new set of data called directive figures. These should be ready by the second half of August, allowing their use in the foreign trade negotiations with other socialist countries that often take place in September or October.

The directive figures are integrated into the plan, which is submitted to the government and approved by December. The plan is then sent back to the enterprises and operation begins in January.

Control of execution and revisions. No matter how carefully the plan has been elaborated, it means nothing until it is implemented. Control is exercised by JUCEPLAN and the National Bank. The latter mainly relies on financial control techniques based on accounting and auditing methods.

Calculations are made in money, which currently is the only tool that permits aggregation, control, and analysis. But the Cuban leaders hope to substitute physical control for financial control in the future in order to eliminate the use of money.

JUCEPLAN's control is exerted both in physical and financial ways. The actual allocation of key products, supply of consumer goods to the population, and output are measured in physical terms (tons, weight, volume) against the planned targets. Control of investment, balance of payments, monetary circulation, wage fund, budgetary deficits or surplus, inventories, and output is made by financial means. Frequent unforeseen contingencies make necessary the revision of the plan by JUCEPLAN in consultation with the central ministries, and, if the changes are relevant, with the political leadership.

The Future: Input-Output Techniques?

From the historical background discussed earlier, it is obvious that the above-explained planning mechanism (which copies the Soviet technique of planning with material balances) is more ideal than real. In view of the increasing significance of miniplans, as well as special and extra plans, it is clear that the annual plan has lost most of its compulsory nature. Hence, it is difficult to accept that, today, the elaboration and implementation of the annual plan evolves in the perfectly coordinated manner alleged by Cuban planners. For example, the 1965–1970 sugar prospective plan, a vital component of the annual sugar output targets was only met in the first year, with nonfulfillment reaching in some years 50 percent of the planned target. Certainly, this unforeseen nonfulfillment had to have a serious impact on the extremely complex network of plan interrelations. How the Cuban planners have solved the problem is not known. Yet, by using our knowledge of the Soviet experience, it may be guessed that a scale of priorities has been established, and those necessities ranked lower on the scale must have been sacrificed to satisfy those at the top.[44]

Cuban planners have been experimenting with both input-output and lineal programming techniques as potential substitutes for material balances, and as a better tool for achieving efficiency, coordination, and control.[45] When Leontief visited Cuba in 1969, he reported high interest in input-output among planners, university professors, and students at the Institute of Economic Investigation. According to him, those attending his lectures in Havana were able to follow his explanations and ask coherent questions. He saw a Cuban edition of two of his books and several other monographs on input-output analysis.[46]

Leontief also reported that Minister without portfolio Carlos Rafael Rodríguez (former member of the PSP and former head of the INRA) has organized an input-output team of eleven statisticians and economists. In May 1969, they had completed the computation of an input-output table for part of the industrial sector of the Cuban economy. Some 600 plants (60 percent of the total) were combined into a balanced table consisting of 171 vectors, in addition to several columns of final demand. The table, however, did not include adequate labor input data, but only the total wage bill, and agriculture and service enterprises were relegated to the final bill of goods. However, Leontief was informed that in the near future, the compilation will be extended to embrace sugar and other important agricultural products. Rodríguez also told Leontief that the input-output team had been transferred to JUCEPLAN's headquarters.

Considerable interest was also shown by Cubans in the potential application of input-output techniques to regional and sectorial planning. For example, Leontief discussed the use of this technique in the developmental program of the Isle of Pines and the possibility of computing an input-output table for this region. The application of input-output in special plans or combines (that resemble U.S. corporations, where Leontief's techniques were first applied) was discussed with the head planning officer of Cuba's electric enterprise, who explored the possibility of using input-output in projecting the demand for electric power, and determining an optimal mix of alternative sources of supply.[47]

Can Guevara's dream of developing central planning through cybernetic techniques be realized in Cuba? This would be an alternative to that of decentralization (market socialism) combined with input-output techniques. Either of these two alternatives would be more efficient than that of central planning with the old method of material balances in operation in Cuba.[48] The current possibility of developing input-output tables for the whole economy continues to be a dream. It took four years for the Cuban experts to compile an incomplete table for one-fourth of the Cuban economy. Statistics are not developed fast enough, there are not enough trained cadres to even take care of managerial functions, and the instability of the Cuban economy, its large dependency on sugar (a factor difficult to control), and the tendency toward special plans would be insurmountable obstacles. Leontief was surprised to learn that Cuba does not yet possess a well-articulated budgeting system, and that there is no overall investment planning. He also observed from his talks with administrators that the accounting aspects of some projects were rather primitive. One of these administrators told him that "the state of our economy [referring to Cuba's planning and administrative techniques] today is similar to that of Russia in the year 1921."[49] However, input-output and lineal programming techniques could be used in planning relevant sectors of the economy such as electricity, sugar, poultry, etc., in order to improve efficiency and implementation.

Planning Functions

Problems of allocation and distribution of resources were kept at manageable dimensions in the first two years of the Revolution by the partial operation of the market and the existence of a large amount of stocks, idle capital equipment, and surplus labor. As the process of collectivization increased, the market mechanisms gradually disappeared. As development and consumptionist policies of the Revolution used up all the available resources and increased the foreign debt, the need to rationalize the allocation and use of scarce capital goods and labor became crucial. The planning system attempts to be a substitute for the abolished market functions. Because Cuba has rejected the market socialism model, its planning model has to rely mainly on physical or administrative allocation of resources (capital, land, power, raw materials, intermediate products, labor, consumer goods) in a degree similar or higher to that employed in the USSR in the early period of planning. Furthermore, the Cubans have expressed their intention to wipe out the already restricted use of monetary calculation and to replace it with physical units, such as labor hours. The following describes how Cuban planning performs the functions of allocation, organization, and distribution of resources and production.

Capital

Since the mid-1960s, the Cuban leadership has gradually increased the proportion of GNP (actually "gross material product") devoted to investment by sacrificing consumption, reaching a record of 30 percent in 1968. The pattern of investment is oriented toward productive sectors (mainly sugar, mining, cattle, and fishing), whereas outlays for infrastructure and social services (hospitals, schools, recreation facilities) have been declining. The structure of investment has reflected an increasingly high priority for quick-yield investments rather than deferred growth.

The equilibrium between the demand and supply of capital is achieved by the National Bank through financial balances. Allocation of capital in the state sectors is done by the bank, according to the plan, by opening accounts to the enterprises. These are free capital grants; hence, interest is not charged and the funds do not have to be repaid. This creates a serious problem of investment efficiency.

In a market economy (or in market socialism à la Yugoslavia), the interest rate operates as a rationing device to allocate capital to the most profitable users, thus maximizing the use of capital. But, according to the Marxist theory of value, only labor creates value; hence interest, rent, and profit do not have a place in an orthodox socialist economy. The Soviet Union, in trying to find a formula for selecting the best technical investment projects—those which maximize production and minimize costs, and those which allow the fastest recuperation of invested funds—introduced in the 1950s a sort of disguised interest rate, the so-called coefficient of investment effectiveness based on a "payoff period." But the system was cumbersome and only partially efficient, and in 1965, under Liberman's influence, the interest rate was reintroduced throughout most of the Soviet economy.[50]

Apparently, Cuba has not used the payoff period, but there are indications that lineal programming is being considered to help make investment decisions in vital sectors.[51] The INPF helps in making decisions concerning the location of new investment. Difficult problems to solve are those regarding plant scale and expansion. Investment efficiency is also difficult to estimate due to Cuba's neglect of profitability.

Due to the lack of an overall investment plan and supportive studies, and the little or no observance of technical economic indices to measure investment effectiveness, speculative and arbitrary decisions have been made in this field, resulting in waste and poor investment efficiency. Gigantism in agriculture and in some industrial projects, dispersion of investment among too many projects, insufficient provision of investment funds, and the proliferation of extra plans have resulted in a large number of uncompleted projects, which are nonproductive and, hence, reduce investment productivity. Also, poor planning in construction schedules has induced the piling up of equipment and machinery.[52]

Capital is allocated to the only existing private sector, the small farmers, through credit extended by the National Bank in coordination with ANAP. In 1963–1966, the overall amount of this credit was stagnant (some one hundred million pesos annually), but declining as a percentage of annual state investment from 14.5 percent to 10.7 percent. It could be speculated that credit to small farmers had been reduced after the Revolutionary Offensive of 1968. Interest rates are charged in a declining percentage according to the degree of socialization (integration into productive associations) of the small farms: 4 percent for those outside of any cooperative or association, 3.5 percent for members of credit-and-service cooperatives, and 3 percent for members of agricultural societies (a sort of commune). Financing covers from 60 percent to 80 percent of the estimated value of the crop, and the loan has to be repaid after the harvest. (Apparently, there are also investment loans granted for a period of from three to seven years.) The rate of repayment seems to be good, although in exceptional cases (unforeseen natural phenomena such as Hurricane Flora in 1963) the bank has cancelled the debts.[53]

Capital and Consumer Goods

Capital and intermediate goods (machinery, fuel, raw materials) are centrally allocated in a physical manner following a strict scale of priorities. The criteria for allocation among the various economic sectors are set according to the economic strategy designed by the political leadership.

Scarce durable consumer goods are physically allocated among consumers according to lists prepared by the CTC and other mass organizations. Ranking is based in the merits accumulated by the consumer (e.g., title of "Vanguard Worker," hours of voluntary labor).

All essential, nondurable consumer goods are allocated through rationing by MINCIN and the system of state stores. Since 1962, the population's available income has largely surpassed available consumer goods. Faced with a critical shortage of consumer goods, the leadership had three alternatives: (a) to let market forces operate so that prices would have to increase to reach equilibrium; (b) to freeze prices but use a sales tax to achieve the same equilibrium, as the Soviets with the "turnover tax"; or (c) to freeze prices and ration scarce products. The first two alternatives would have benefited the remaining wealthy people as well as highly-paid government technicians. Striving for egalitarianism, the third alternative was chosen. The black market, however, soon began to operate, and rapidly expanded in 1962–1968 as a nonofficial consumer-goods allocator favoring high-income groups. These groups were the only ones able to pay black-market prices, set from five to ten times higher than official ones. However, in 1968, the government gave a severe blow to the black market.

Besides the *de jure* rationing system, there is a *de facto* system: the queue. Often, the quota of consumer goods allocated to a state store is insufficient to cover the rations of the population assigned to that zone. Hence, the long queues in front of state stores. Compensators for rationing are the various organizations that provide free (or very cheap) meals to groups that the government wants to protect or favor, such as nursery schools, workers' cafeterias, and students' dining rooms. Restaurants also constitute a safety valve for those who have enough money and time to make the long queues. Most social services (education, medical care) are provided free and equal to all. In summary, it may be said that consumer sovereignty does not exist in Cuba and that consumer choice is seriously limited.

Labor

Elimination of unemployment, ambitious projects of economic and social development, and decline in labor effort and productivity have made labor scarce for the first time in modern Cuba. Departing from current practice in socialist countries (China being an exception), labor allocation and distribution is made increasingly by physical means. Unpaid labor is a common sector of administrative allocation. Military recruits, prisoners, students, workers, and housewives are recruited (either through compulsive means, social pressure, or moral stimulation) to participate in the most important economic tasks: the sugar crop, road construction, the coffee crop, etc. The organization of unpaid workers follows militaristic lines, for example, battalions and brigades.[54] The FMC is engaged in a permanent campaign to incorporate idle females into the labor force. In some professions, as medicine and dentistry, a compulsory two-year service in rural areas is in operation. Since 1963, there has been also an increasing trend to abolish the private practice of some professions, such as medicine, and, since the 1968 Revolutionary Offensive, it has been a crime to work in private activities or businesses outside of agriculture. Pressures on private farmers to eliminate hired laborers are mounting. Vagrancy is severely repressed and vagrants sent to labor camps.

All state workers are under control of the corresponding enterprise, central ministry, and MINTRAB. Since 1969 no one can change his place of employment without the prior authorization of the regional office of MINTRAB. The latter has issued a labor identity booklet with the worker's record and is empowered to effect labor transfers. The 1964–1967 campaign against bureaucracy was a tool to eliminate the labor surplus in urban areas and services, and transfer it to agriculture. The campaigns, such as the signing of three-year contracts among urbanites to go to the countryside, are additional tools for the physical reallocation of labor. Moral stimulation is a middle-of-the-road technique, between physical and market allocation, which appeals to feelings of national solidarity.[55]

The Ministry of Labor attempts to achieve equilibrium between national output and income by the system of output standards (work quotas) and wage scales. The wage fund (total wage bill) is centrally calculated by JUCEPLAN in coordination with MINTRAB. The fund is then distributed among central ministries, and, within these, among enterprises according to the number and skill of the workers required by each plant or farm. Wage scales are closely related to output standards; thus, in order to receive full pay the worker has to fulfill his quota. There are no wage differences according to enterprise profitability. Bonuses for overfulfillment of output quotas and overtime pay, in operation in 1963–1968, have been drastically reduced or eliminated.

The system of emulation is quite formal and relies on the use of moral incentives and penalties instead of material rewards. Unemployment is no longer a check. The leadership dream for the future is total egalitarianism and the elimination of money and wages. Still, wages and material incentives are occasionally used to mobilize workers when the government faces urgent problems. Thus, a serious shortage of professional cane cutters during the 1970 sugar harvest was alleviated by offering permanent jobs at the highest wage rate to these workers.[56]

The system has created serious disturbances, such as surpluses of labor in certain areas and shortages in others, low labor productivity, and absenteeism (see chapter 9). On the other hand, physical allocation of labor has contributed to the solution of some of these problems, and the government hopes to avoid increased administrative regulation by the use of moral stimuli. According to an official report of 1967, little or no participation of local managers and workers in the elaboration of planning had negatively affected the plan on labor and wages. The report suggested increasing plant participation in planning so that the knowledge of local circumstances and conditions could improve the quality of the plan.[57]

Land

At the beginning of the Revolution, the assumption of relative land abundance was undisputed. As a result, there was a relevant extension of the cultivated area, often to the detriment of valuable pastures and forests, without achieving noticeable increases in output due to the poor methods employed. Because of this assumption and the early developmental emphasis on industry rather than on agriculture, intensive methods of cultivation received little attention. With the return to agriculture in 1963–1964, the government had realized that, despite Cuba's rich soils and good rainfall, arable land is limited. Extensive methods of cultivation are still being used, but there is a definite move toward more intensive techniques, such as improved seeds (sugar, rice), irrigation and fertilizers, and advanced techniques in planting, fumigating, and harvesting. Cattle-raising has been characterized by the same type of development. The leadership expects to secure a large increase in meat and milk output in the future through artificial insemination, improved pastures and fodder, and animal husbandry. As stated earlier, various research agencies are devoted to these tasks.

Land rent has been abolished in Cuba. Some 200,000 small farmers work their own land (30 percent of the total), which according to government reports is the most fertile, and the rest is state owned. Since there is no differential rent, problems of efficiency and productivity are approached by other methods. The INPF plays an important role in this area.

In 1965, *acopio* prices were apparently the same as those fixed for state-farm products, with a few exceptions such as sugar cane, for which a higher price was paid to private farmers. In the formation of agricultural prices, steps have been taken to fix farm prices "at the level corresponding to the quantity of socially necessary labor embodied in the product." However, in view of the shortages and surpluses experienced in the first half of the 1960s, other factors are taken into account. Prices are now seasonally adjusted, depending on the product supply (e.g., the price of mangoes is reduced at the seasonal time of highest yield). Prices are also manipulated to discourage or encourage the output of a product. Thus, in 1965 prices of some vegetables were reduced because supply exceeded demand, whereas prices of turbes (like malanga) were increased due to the acute shortage of this product. Finally, prices are also manipulated to try to encourage the increase of yields.[58] Since 1968, the small farmers' free market, where supply and demand used to set prices for one-third of the products turned out by private farms, has been greatly reduced. On the other hand, reports of recent visitors to the island indicate that barter trade among farmers is quite significant.

Management

The most significant feature of the Cuban management system is the tendency to eliminate economic calculation and the function of money as a medium of exchange. The use of money is limited to a standard of value for aggregation, control, and analysis, and for foreign trade computations. State enterprises do not pay taxes over their output or profits, money is not used for payments, credit and interest have been eliminated, and, instead, these enterprises receive capital gifts from the National Bank. The principle of profit is kept only for accounting purposes, but not as a success indicator of managerial performance. The Cubans believe that profitability has lost significance as a tool for measuring enterprise efficiency; this is now essentially determined by the enterprise's capability to fulfill output targets and reduce costs. As previously stated, one of the features of the system of budgetary finance is that all profits from state enterprises are automatically transferred to the state treasury.

There are no bonuses for managers who fulfill or overfulfill output targets as in the Soviet system. Managerial decisions on what and how much to produce, quality and assortment, and size of the labor force are extremely limited by central directives and the physical allocation of resources. Inefficiency, defective goods, piling up of inventories, and other negative effects of the system are expected to be solved by the combined use of cybernetic methods and moral stimuli (see next chapter).

Prices

Cuban planners have officially recognized that their price system is deficient and have urged total reform.[59] All prices were frozen by a law enacted in late 1961, and regulated in 1962–1963, but this was done without integrating a new price system. Current price formation is highly distorted. For example, the prices of several products have been unified, but lack proportionality with other prices. There are different prices for the same imported goods according to the country of origin. A study conducted in 1966 on the system of prices of the consolidated enterprises of pharmaceutical products shows that (a) raw materials were undervalued, (b) containers and the product itself were of low quality because of the low price fixed to the final product, (c) scarcity of certain inputs led the enterprises to buy these products from the private sector at prices over official rates in order to fulfill output quotas, and (d) prices charged to enterprise products often ignored current regulations, exceeing official pricing. In order to solve these problems, Cuban planners faced two alternatives: to adopt the price system being used in socialist countries, or to develop a new method based on Cuban peculiarities.[60]

The Cuban leadership has rejected the possibility of adopting a price system either of a market-socialist or current Soviet variety. The necessity of using the law of value has been denied, "There is no reason for using interest, rent, and profit because financiers, *latifundia* owners, and merchants no longer exist in Cuba."[61] Cuban planners do realize that there are important market mechanisms that could be partially used in a socialist system in which the essential means of production have been collectivized. Capital, land, and most goods are scarce in present-day Cuba and interest, rent, and profit could help in the more efficient allocation and administration of resources. Yet, the Guevarist approach presently in operation drastically rejects these techniques, arguing that their usage could generate the danger of reintroducing capitalism.

The proposed price reform in Cuba is based on the "planned cost" of a product, which is the average cost computed from all costs of producing the same product in the state enterprises. This is no real innovation, but is actually the application of the prereform Soviet system of industrial price formation. Industrial production costs would be integrated by direct costs (the Russian *sebestoimost'*), such as raw materials, labor, power, and depreciation, and indirect costs, which the Cubans call *carga fabril*. Although the latter phrase has not been defined, it apparently refers to the Marxist "surplus product" or Soviet "profit markup."[62] To the cost of production, MINCIN would add an amount for administration, distribution, and selling. "Planned cost" prices would be used, without alteration, for a period of five years. The new system would begin by computing prices of imported goods and raw materials and, then, of intermediate goods, wholesale goods, and consumer goods. The proponents of the new price system hope that it will make financial controls, determination of enterprise costs, comparison of domestic prices with international prices, and investment decisions easier. The new price system would provide a better basis for estimation of real costs of exports and would eliminate any potential surplus income that private farmers currently may receive from *acopio* prices.[63]

Foreign Trade

How significant is the distortion of current prices in determining the efficiency of Cuban exports and imports? On the one hand, the island's heavy dependency on foreign trade (some one-third of GNP) should increase the decision problems of what to export and what to import and from where. On the other hand, the traditional concentration of Cuba's exports in a few primary products (sugar, tobacco, nickel), as well as its enormous dependency on imports, reduce the present magnitude of the problem. But in the long run, the seriousness of the problem will increase as Cuba will have to decide what new lines of production should be developed to reduce imports and expand exports.[64] The proposed price reform might be of some help, although the Soviet experience with this kind of approach did not prove too successful in the 1950s. Another possibility is the application of lineal programming to maximize revenue from exports and make decisions on optimal imports. Several technical papers have been published in Cuba on such topics as the export coefficient of profitability, the application of input-output techniques to determine the needs of imports, the application of mathematical techniques for optimal imports, and the connection between domestic investment and foreign trade.[65]

Conclusions

Rapid collectivization of the means of production and ambitious developmental problems presented the Cuban leadership with an early necessity to substitute planning for the market. The dilemma was not whether to plan or not, but how to plan. Three alternatives were available (indicative, central, and decentralized market-socialism planning). Each one received domestic support and was under external influences. Some features of indicative planning, ECLA style, were present in 1959–1960, but ideological confusion, lack of coordination, and constant changes did not permit the institutionalization of such measures. From the economic anarchy of these years, the pendulum moved to the other extreme; thus, in 1961–1963 there was an attempt to introduce a highly centralized model of planning, Soviet-Czech style. But the Cuban basis (statistics, personnel) was insufficient and the model was rigidly and mechanically applied, ending in failure. Excessive administrative centralization and economic deterioration in 1963 led to an attempt to test market socialism techniques in the following two years. There was some ministerial decentralization, the combines appeared, and the system of self-finance was introduced in agriculture and foreign trade enterprises. But again, not enough time was given to the system to mature and, in practice, it was adulterated. An overall reform of the planning apparatus and economic administration was undertaken by the end of 1965, resulting in the current system in which characteristics of the pre-reform Soviet model of planning are mixed with features of the Guevarist model (moral incentives, thorough application of budgetary enterprise, tendency to eliminate money and equalize wages) with Castroite additions, such as the increasing use of miniplans, extra, and special plans and the disregard of medium- and long-range planning.

The annual plan is elaborated in Cuba by using the Soviet technique of material balances, with declining use of economic calculation and financial balances and increasing use of physical balances. In the future, the leadership hopes to substitute totally a physical unit of measurement, such as man-hours, for money. The central plan in practice has lost much of its relevance and compulsive nature and is mainly used as an overall guide and a tool for internal calculations and consistency. Political leaders seem to be interested in, and planners are experimenting with, mathematical and cybernetic techniques as means to improve economic decision-making and managerial efficiency. An input-output table has been computed for one-fourth of the 1965 Cuban economy, and the application of both input-output and lineal programming has been proposed in the selection of investment projects, optimalization of imports and exports, projections in vital sectors of the economy, and regional planning. Although the possibility of centralized macroeconomic planning with cybernetic techniques seems to be realistically impossible today, it is evident that this could be applicable and useful in sectorial planning and in specific tasks.

The allocation and distribution of resources (capital; capital, intermediate, and consumer goods; labor; land) is essentially made by physical means. Although there are still some areas in which market mechanisms operate, such as private agriculture and wages, their application is limited and their use is in clear decline. There is no such thing as a planned system of prices in Cuba, because a thorough reform has never been made in this area. Prices are distorted because they do not include interest, rent, and profit; hence, they are not scarcity prices, nor do they seem to operate as rational allocators. The leadership has rejected the possibility of solving this problem by following the current model of price formation in Eastern Europe. Instead, they have announced the development of an autochthonous system in which the main features appear to be based on the prereform Soviet price model.

When confronted with economic difficulties, the Cuban leadership has commonly resorted to changes in the planning apparatus and administrative structure, as well as shifts in positions of responsibility. It is obvious that, in a period of two or three years, it is quite difficult for sound economic reforms to take root, mature, and show effects. Although the latest organizational change (implemented at the turn of 1965) is the one that has lasted the longest, the Cubans are still experimenting with it, and organizational difficulties have been pointed out as recently as 1970 as being responsible for economic difficulties (i.e., the nonfulfillment of the target of ten million tons of sugar). Since the second half of 1968, the Cubans have been moving closer to the Soviet Union, and recent leaders' statements emphasizing technology and productivity could be a sign of a new round of changes.[66]

In September 1970, Premier Castro criticized the excessive centralization of the administration and the "superplanning." He said that plans had been prepared by skilled technicians and mathematicians who lack knowledge of the Cuban reality: "Several schemes [and plans] have been made and often presented as miraculous solutions to solve our problems but ultimately have contributed to worsen the situation. [Planners and administrators] ignored the low levels of both the culture of our people and the development of our productive forces. Some of those formulas [schemes, plans] required super-perfect planning and this was unrealistic. . . . If one really cares for the people, more thinking should be given to such formulas before trying them."[67]

One of the crucial aspects of Cuban planning is the lack of participation of the lower echelons in the hierarchical structure (workers, private farmers, local managers) in the elaboration of planning. Decisions are made at the top of the hierarchy in coordination with the second and third levels, and the function of trade unions and farmer associations is mainly to endorse the plan and mobilize their membership for its implementation. The concentration of decision-making power in the hands of the political leadership, chiefly Premier Castro, has been instrumental in keeping the Revolution in power but, apparently, has also impeded the necessary institutionalization and stability of the economy. The original lack of economic training on the part of the Cuban leaders (Castro, Dorticós, and Armando Hart, former minister of education and secretary of organization of the PCC, are lawyers and Guevara was a physician) has been partially solved by on-the-spot training, but there still seems to be a tendency to oversimplify complex problems, improvise solutions, and ignore the experience of other socialist countries. The combination of the concentration of power in the hands of the political leadership, their lack of solid economic training and disregard for similar economic experiences, and the lack of local participation by those who are really in touch with production has resulted in the subordination of economics to politics, the constant administrative changes that are not given enough time to solve the structural problems, and the inability of the planning system to materialize as a realistic and efficient tool for economic development.

NOTES

1. See ECLA, "Planning in Latin America," *Economic Bulletin for Latin America,* 12 (October 1967), pp. 1–32.

2. Pioneering work in this field has been made by Roberto M. Bernardo, "Central Planning in Cuba" (Ph.D. diss., University of California, Berkeley, 1968). Part of Bernardo's dissertation has been incorporated into *The Theory of Moral Incentives in Cuba* (University, Ala., 1971).

3. For a description of these agencies, their functions, and historical evolution see Cuban Economic Research Project, *Study on Cuba* (Coral Gables, 1965).

4. The main documents were Castro's 1953 speech *La historia me absolverá,* Felipe Pazos' and Regino Boti's *Tesis económica del Movimiento 26 de Julio* (1956), and Castro-Pazos-Chibás's *Manifesto de la Sierra Maestra* (1957). For original sources and discussion see Theodore Draper, *Castroism: Theory and Practice* (New York, 1965), pp. 4–21.

5. Fidel Castro, *Revolución,* December 2, 1961; and Ernesto Guevara, *Pasajes de la guerra revolucionaria* (La Habana, 1963).

6. Bernardo's "Central Planning" maintains that Guevara had an antimarket ideology, and that both he and Castro were utopian Marxists before the Revolution. Matthews has pointed out that Castro had a contempt for money and now lives "outside the money economy." See Matthews, *Fidel Castro* (New York, 1969), pp. 34–35.

7. See Ernesto Guevara's "Sobre la concepción del valor: réplica a ciertas declaraciones sobre el tema," *Nuestra Industria Revista Económica,* 1 (October 1963), pp. 3–9; "Sobre el sistema presupuestario de financiamiento," ibid., 2 (February 1964), pp. 3–23; "La banca, el crédito y el socialismo," *Cuba Socialista,* 4 (March 1964), pp. 23–42; and "La planificación socialista, su significado," ibid. (June 1964), pp. 13–24. See also Alvarez Ron, "El contenido político y económico del presupuesto estatal," *Trimestre de Finanzas al Día* (April–June 1963), pp. 31–40, and "Sobre el método de análisis de los sistemas de financiamiento," *Cuba Socialista,* 4 (July 1964), pp. 64–79; "¿Renuncia el sistema presupuestario de financiamiento a la utilización de los estímulos materiales?" *Nuestra Industria,* 4 (June 1964), pp. 2–3, (July 1964), pp. 43–47, and (August 1964), pp. 2–3; and Mario Rodríguez, "La concepción . . . y el sistema presupuestario de financiamiento en el período de transición," *Nuestra Industria Revista Económica,* 2 (December 1964), pp. 13–40.

8. See Frederick A. Hayek, ed., *Collectivistic Economic Planning* (London, 1935).

9. Oscar Lange and Fred M. Taylor, *On the Economic Theory of Socialism* (New York, 1965). Most of Lange's works were published in Cuba in 1963–1965 in a serialized manner in *Comercio Exterior* and *Trimestre de Finanzas al Día.*

10. Abba P. Lerner, "Economic Theory and Socialist Economy," *Review of Economic Studies,* 2 (1934–1935), pp. 51–61.

11. See Alberto Mora, "En torno a la cuestión del funcionamiento de la ley del valor en la economía cubana en los actuales momentos," *Comercio Exterior,* 1 (June 1963), pp. 2–10; Marcelo Fernández, "Desarrollo y funciones de la banca socialista en Cuba," *Cuba Socialista,* 4 (February 1964), pp. 32–50, and "Planificación y control de la circulación monetaria," ibid. (May 1964), pp. 79–97; and Joaquín Infante, "Características del funcionamiento de la empresa autofinanciada," ibid. (June 1964), pp. 25–50.

12. René Dumont, *Cuba: Socialisme et développement* (Paris, 1964), pp. 95–142.

13. Charles Bettelheim, "Formas y métodos de la planificación socialista y nivel de desarrollo de las fuerzas productivas," *Cuba Socialista,* 4 (April 1964), pp. 51–78.

14. See José M. Barros, "Observaciones sobre las posibilidades de implantación del cálculo económico en las empresas operativas del comercio exterior," *Comercio Exterior*, 1 (June 1963), pp. 47–49. See also Bernardo, "Central Planning."

15. Background information for this section comes from Edward Boorstein, *The Economic Transformation of Cuba* (New York, 1968), pp. 37–151; and Cuban Economic Research Project, *Study on Cuba*, pp. 728–39.

16. See ECLA, *Análisis y proyecciones de desarrollo económico: introducción a la técnica de programación* (México, 1955).

17. Cuban Economic Research Project, *Labor Conditions in Communist Cuba* (Coral Gables, 1963).

18. José A. Naranjo, *Revolución*, October 2, 1961.

19. *Por la libre* is loosely translated as "freewheeling" by Boorstein. Boorstein, *Economic Transformation*, p. 135.

20. "Planning in Cuba," *Panorama Económico Latinoamericano*, 8 (1967), pp. 11–13.

21. Boorstein, *Economic Transformation*, pp. 151–66.

22. See James O'Connor, *The Origins of Socialism in Cuba* (New York, 1970), pp. 255–56.

23. "Planning in Cuba," p. 13; and JUCEPLAN, "La planificación económica en Cuba," *Aspectos administrativos de la planificación: documentos de un seminario* (New York, 1968), pp. 161–64.

24. See Michel Gutelman, *L'Agriculture socialisée à Cuba* (Paris, 1967), pp. 90–102.

25. James O'Connor, "Agrarian Reforms in Cuba, 1959–1963," *Science and Society*, 32 (Spring 1968), p. 209.

26. Albán Lataste, *Cuba: ¿hacia una nueva economía política del socialismo?* (Santiago de Chile, 1968), pp. 31–32, 42–50.

27. "Planning in Cuba," p. 11.

28. Lataste, *Cuba*, pp. 12, 51. See also René Dumont, *Cuba est-il socialiste?* (Paris, 1970), pp. 70–73.

29. "Planning in Cuba," p. 11.

30. "Planning in Cuba," pp. 11–12; and Osvaldo Dorticós, "Avances institucionales de la Revolución," *Cuba Socialista*, 6 (January 1966), pp. 2–23, and "Tareas importantes de nuestros organismos económicos," ibid. (March 1966), pp. 26–42.

31. Lataste, *Cuba*, pp. 51, 67, 69.

32. "Planning in Cuba," p. 13. For a description of various miniplans see Dumont, *Cuba est-il socialiste?*, pp. 63–67.

33. Wassily Leontief, "Notes on a Visit to Cuba," *New York Review of Books*, 13 (August 21, 1969), p. 19.

34. Lataste, *Cuba*, pp. 40–45, 52–54.

35. Isy Joshua, "Organisation et rapports de production dans une économie de transition (Cuba)," *Problems de Planification*, 10 (Centre D'Etude de Planification Socialiste, Paris, 1968), pp. 64–66.

36. Lataste, *Cuba*, p. 53.

37. See also Leo Huberman and Paul Sweezy, *Socialism in Cuba* (New York, 1969), pp. 171–72.

38. JUCEPLAN, "La planificación económica en Cuba," pp. 161, 164–65. On Cuba's development strategy and plans for 1970–1980, see *Informe de la Delegación Cubana* (Santiago, 1969), pp. 44–45, 50–63. See also chapter 11, this volume.

39. Background information on this section, unless otherwise stated, comes from

JUCEPLAN, "La planificación económica en Cuba," "Planning in Cuba," and *Cuba Economic News* (1965–1969).

40. *Cuba Economic News*, 5 (1969), pp. 7–14.

41. See "El desarrollo industrial de Cuba," *Cuba Socialista*, 6 (April and May 1966), pp. 128–83 and 94–127; "New Economic-Industrial Organization in Cuba," *Cuba Economic News*, 3 (September 1967), pp. 6–8; Rolando Alvarez, "Problemas actuales y planes futuros de la industria alimenticia en Cuba," *Cuba Socialista*, 6 (August 1966), pp. 38–62; and JUCEPLAN, *Boletín Estadístico, 1966* (La Habana, n.d.), pp. 27, 78–79.

42. *Informe de la Delegación Cubana*, p. 53. See also F. Castro, "Discurso con motivo de la fusión del Instituto de Recursos Hidráulicos y de Desarrollo Agropecuario," *Granma Revista Semanal*, June 1, 1969, pp. 2–3.

43. Background information on this section comes from "Planning in Cuba," pp. 12–13; JUCEPLAN, "La planificación económica en Cuba," pp. 129–56; and Lataste, *Cuba*, pp. 65–69.

44. See Robert W. Campbell, *Soviet Economic Power* (New York, 1966), pp. 47–48.

45. See Ricardo Rodas, "Aplicación de las tablas de insumo-producto al sector industrial cubano," *Comercio Exterior*, 2 (July–September 1964), pp. 2 ff; Roberto Pérez, "Aplicación de la programación lineal a . . . la industria del petróleo en Cuba," *Nuestra Industria Revista Económica*, 3 (February 1965), pp. 56–62; and Nestor Lavergne and Pedro Sáenz, "Experiencias en Cuba, en la aplicación de métodos matemáticos en el análisis económico y en la planificación de empresas," *Comercio Exterior*, 3 (October–December 1965), pp. 13–91.

46. Leontief, "Notes," pp. 15–16.

47. Ibid., p. 19.

48. See C. A. Knox Lovell, "Profits and Cybernetics as Sources of Increased Efficiency in Soviet Planning," *The Southern Economic Journal*, 34 (January 1968), pp. 392–405.

49. Leontief, "Notes," p. 16. In September 1970, Castro referred to a project concerning a Center for National Computation, but warned that, currently, there was a lack of knowledge of natural and human resources and a lack of precise economic controls. See "Debate obrero sobre ausentismo y trabajo voluntario," *Granma*, September 8, 1970, p. 5.

50. For more details see Campbell, *Soviet Economic Power*, pp. 55–59.

51. JUCEPLAN, "La planificación económica en Cuba," p. 156. See also Albán Lataste, "El proceso de inversiones en Cuba," *Comercio Exterior*, 1 (October–December 1963), pp. 23–27; Angel A. Pernas, "Criterios para la selección de proyectos industriales en Cuba," *Nuestra Industria Revista Económica*, 4 (February 1966), pp. 16–27; and Gerardo Ortega, "Programación de inversiones," *Nuestra Industria Revista Tecnológica*, 4 (March–April 1966), pp. 33 ff, and "Selección de procedimientos de ejecución de inversiones," ibid. (September–October 1966), pp. 64 ff.

52. Lataste, *Cuba*, pp. 70–86.

53. *Cuba Economic News*, 2 (November 1966), pp. 1–2.

54. See Carmelo Mesa-Lago, "Economic Significance of Unpaid Labor in Socialist Cuba," *Industrial and Labor Relations Review*, 22 (April 1969), pp. 339–57.

55. Robert M. Bernardo, "Moral Stimulation as a Nonmarket Mode of Labor Allocation in Cuba," *Studies in Comparative International Development*, 6 (1970–1971).

56. Carmelo Mesa-Lago, *The Labor Sector and Socialist Distribution in Cuba* (New York, 1968), and "Economic, Political and Ideological Factors in the Cuban Controversy on Material Versus Moral Incentives" (Paper presented at the Latin American Studies Association Second National Meeting, Washington, D.C., April 17–18, 1970).

57. Fernando González Quiñones, "Algunas experiencias acerca de la planificación de trabajo y salarios en nuestra industria," *Nuestra Industria Revista Económica,* 5 (August 1967), pp. 3–18.

58. Carlos Rafael Rodríguez, "The Cuban Revolution and the Peasantry," *World Marxist Review,* 8 (October 1965), pp. 17–18.

59. See JUCEPLAN, "La planificación económica en Cuba," p. 156; Raul León, "Algunas cuestiones relativas a la formación de los precios en la economía cubana," *Comercio Exterior,* 1 (May 1963), pp. 3 ff; and Dirección Económica, "Proposición de un sistema de precios utilizando los costos planificados como precios de entrega del sector estatal," *Nuestra Industria Revista Económica,* 5 (June 1967), p. 71.

60. Dirección Económica, "Proposición de un sistema," pp. 71–72, 85–91.

61. Ibid., pp. 73–75.

62. See Morris Borstein, "The Soviet Price System," in *The Soviet Economy,* eds. Morris Borstein and Daniel Fusfeld (Homewood, Ill., 1965), pp. 278–309.

63. Dirección Económica, "Proposición de un sistema," pp. 76–81.

64. Lataste, *Cuba,* p. 91.

65. Julio González Noriega, "Las inversiones desde el punto de vista del comercio exterior," *Comercio Exterior,* 2 (January–March 1964); Juan Bárcenas and Antonio Bebelagua, "Aplicación de un modelo matemático para optimalizar el flujo de las importaciones de materias primas," ibid., 3 (January–June 1965), pp. 129–35; and Enrique González and Zoila González, "Algunas contribuciones al análisis y utilización de la matriz de insumoproducto," *Nuestra Industria Revista Económica,* 3 (December 1965), pp. 3–25.

66. In his speech of July 26, 1970, Premier Castro stated that it was no longer possible to direct national production through the Council of Ministers. He announced a coordination of activities of various groups of central ministries by a team of seven or nine cadres in each group, e.g., a group of ministries engaged in consumer-goods production and distribution (as food and light industries, INIT, MINCIN), another group of ministries that deal with manpower (as MINTRAB, MINED, MINFAR). Castro strongly criticized the present lack of coordination and emphasis on sectors: "The tendency of sectorialism is absurd, is inadmissible, is stupid, is a crime!" See Fidel Castro, "Discurso en commemoración del XVII aniversario del asalto al Cuartel Moncada," *Granma Revista Semanal,* August 2, 1970, pp. 2–6.

67. "Debate obrero sobre ausentismo y trabajo voluntario," p. 5.

8

Roberto M. Bernardo

Managing and Financing the Firm

ONE of the major aims of the economic and cultural offensive launched in Cuba in late 1966 was the construction of communism in its organizational sense. This meant intensifying the campaign to inculcate the productive mechanism of moral incentives in every major sphere of production. *Estímulo moral* ("moral stimulus") or *conciencia comunista* ("Communist consciousness") is viewed by Cuban policy makers not only as a main goal of Cuban society but as a means of partially decentralizing the administrative planning system. Ideally, it is a nonmarket decentralist device whereby managers and workers voluntarily intensify their work efforts and choose alternative tasks that are more beneficial to the community than their own private interest. In contrast to this technique of partial decentralization, the Libermanist way so popular in Eastern Europe relies mainly on the greater use of market incentives and institutions for partially decentralizing the administrative planning system. In Cuba and China, Libermanism is thought of as a retreat backward toward capitalism. Managers in Cuba and China are, no doubt, reminded not to disregard profits entirely and careful accounting of costs is emphasized. But in Cuba and China, profit-making and cost minimization stand for different sets of firm behavior, which is not what these terms would indicate in a market setting. Rent and interest are not included in cost estimates and, in regard to their production activities, firms in Cuba and China have output physically prescribed, and inputs are

I am grateful to Franz Schurmann, but particularly to Benjamin Ward, Jr., and Gregory Grossman, all of the University of California at Berkeley, for their comments on a much earlier version. My main debt is to Carmelo Mesa-Lago whose substantive and editorial work greatly improved this version. He generously added several pages of information and insight from his thorough and vast knowledge of the Cuban reality.

185

similarly laid down. And, unlike Libermanist countries, there are no material incentive funds out of profits, and salaries bear little relation to the firm's profitability.

In this paper, we will stress the importance of the previous points in the organizational evolution of the Cuban firm. Whereas moral incentives in the allocation of labor have received serious attention from economists doing research on Cuba, little has been published on the organizational structure and management of the socialist firm in Cuba. In this field as a whole, Cuba has made an innovation worthy of attention. The Cuban firm is run as a government office by salaried staff from budgetary grants independent of their revenues in the manner that classical antimarket and equalitarian Marxists have extolled.

Very early in the formative years of Cuban socialism, Ernesto (Che) Guevara and his followers claimed that moral incentives in the sphere of managerial behavior could be implemented best in a particular type of centralized planning in which the firm was made to act as a government office by staff whose salaries were not made to vary with the services they provided the public. By so acting, managers (and workers) would behave in a way compatible with the Communist allocative rule of "from each according to his ability, to each according to his need." Thus, the Guevarists showed an early preference for a form of enterprise management reminiscent of Soviet War Communism in which firms were incorporated into the state budget, receiving investment and operating funds from it and delivering their receipts and net earnings to it. In contrast to the method of enterprise management just described, the Guevarists reluctantly tolerated an alternative, but really only slightly different, method of centralized management: self-finance or *khozraschet,* a method in which the firm was regarded as an independent accounting unit responsible for its profits and losses. The latter is the general method used in China, but as we shall see in subsequent discussion, both methods of centralized management are quite compatible with the ideological aim of preserving a non-Libermanist productive system.

One's view point depends on one's meaning of self-finance: the system of self-finance has various degrees of development ranging from the severely limited form, which was practiced by a significant number of Cuban enterprises, to its Libermanist form in the Soviet Union, to its climactic development in Yugoslavian market socialism, in which the firm is not only a separate accounting unit, but is separated from the administrative planning structure as well by means of an ever greater use of private material incentives and markets. In the Soviet Union, self-finance is associated with managerial and worker bonuses for fulfilling the centrally laid plan, which often produced income disparities larger than in many capitalist countries;

and it is associated with labor recruitment through the market. This is not the case in either Cuba or China. Although a vigorous attempt was earlier made in Cuba to widen the sphere of application of a limited form of self-finance, the predominant practice is that of budgetary finance, under which the firm is directly incorporated into the state budget. We shall show, however, that the two divergent modes of financing the Cuban firm are different merely on a superficial level. Analysis reveals that they are the same in essence, and that essence is defined by the fact that all state firms are run as government offices from state finances independent of their revenues.

This paper describes the main changes in the structure of the Cuban firm from the revolutionary triumph in 1959 to 1970 in the framework of the preceding discussion. Although Cuba has not embarked on serious innovations in the organization of the nonagricultural firm, it has in agriculture in the large-scale use of state combines. We know that agriculture has been a political and economic problem in socialist countries, and Cuba has had some interesting experiences in this regard.

Managerial Organization

Structure of the Nonagricultural Firm

The consolidated enterprise or *consolidado* is the basic administrative unit of production in the nonagricultural sector. It is essentially a group of industrial factories and firms of the presocialist period, which were merged under a common management on the basis of the horizontal criterion of "sameness" of products. The *consolidado* appeared from late 1960 to early 1961 in the wake of the previous massive nationalization. Guevara's description of it on May 1, 1961, is our earliest available source in print:

> The consolidated [enterprise] for sugar administers the 160 mills which are operating in the country. The central office is in Havana and is answerable directly to the Minister [of Industries] for the functioning of this industry. Each enterprise is responsible to the undersecretariat which controls it and plans for it. Each enterprise has a plan, a budget, and quotas. It must surrender its production to the Ministry of Internal Commerce or to the other industries of the state apparatus. These enterprises make no profits. All profits they produce belong to the Cuban state.[1]

The first regulations of the consolidated enterprise were enacted in mid-1961. Various departments took care of the functions of planning, account-

FIG. 1

ORGANIZATIONAL CHART OF A CONSOLIDATED ENTERPRISE IN CUBA: 1963–1964

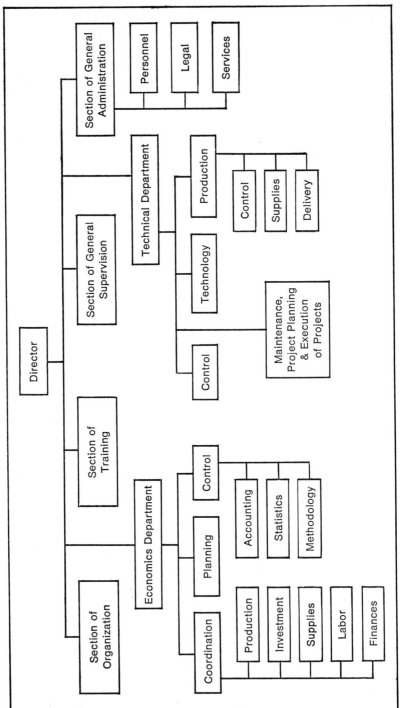

Data from *Gaceta Oficial*, November 21, 1963.

ing, inputs, output, labor, and sales. A minor reorganization took place one year later.[2] In late 1963, the Ministry of Industries, which had been empowered to create, restructure, and govern the activities of the *consolidado*, released the organizational operational charts (*organogramas*) of some of its consolidated enterprises, that is, transport, wood, and printing.[3] Figure 1 shows a typical *organograma*.

The number of factories or firms in each *consolidado* varied from a few units to several hundred. In the mid-1960s, the Hard Fibers Consolidated Enterprise had 5 factories; the beer and malt enterprise had 15; but the flour enterprise had 800, and the soaps and perfume enterprise, 843. In such sectors where the numbers of factories or workshops reached into the several hundreds, an intermediate body was created between the *consolidado* and the factories to reduce the administrative problem to manageable proportions. As an average, the *consolidado* administered from ten to fifteen factories.[4]

TABLE 1
DISTRIBUTION OF INDUSTRIAL PRODUCTION BY
CONSOLIDATED ENTERPRISES IN CUBA: 1966

Output (in Millions of Pesos)	Number of Enterprises	Percentage of Gross Industrial Output
0–10	17	4.7%
11–25	13	9.4
26–50	12	19.8
51–100	10	30.5
Over 100	4	35.6

Source: "El desarrollo industrial de Cuba," *Cuba Socialista*, 6 (May 1966), p. 104.

A comparison of the market structure of the presocialist period with the number of *consolidados* suggests the extent of the merging process. Up to around 1958, there were about 38,300 industrial firms of all types and sizes, 74,391 commercial firms, 23,932 firms in the professional services, and 42,893 owner-operated farms.[5] By March 1961, long before socialization had reached its final point, 18,500 industrial enterprises, accounting for 80 percent of industrial production, had been combined into several dozen *consolidados*.[6] In 1966, about 90 percent of the gross industrial output was generated by 56 consolidated enterprises. As table 1 shows, some 66 percent of industrial output was produced by the largest 14 consolidated enterprises, that is, one-fourth of the total number.

In 1963, the Ministry of Industries controlled 68 percent of the consolidated enterprises and 76 percent of the state industrial output. The rest of the *consolidados* were mainly under the supervision of the INRA and the Ministry of Construction and, in a minor degree, under the Ministry of Transportation, the Institute of Cinema Arts, the Institute of Hydraulic Resources, and the National Institute of Fishing.[7]

The formation of industrial *consolidados* was partially motivated by managerial considerations: (a) the task of central management is easier when there are several dozen big enterprises instead of several thousand; (b) the ban on rent and interest charges and the fact that most firms did not amortize capital made it possible to run the *consolidados* as "budget units," as other government offices were run; (c) the nationalization of previous capitalist firms into one single owner, the state, induced the concentration of direction in order to save labor, administrative expenses, and other operational costs; and (d) allocation and supervision of scarce skilled manpower was made easier through centralized control.

Besides managerial considerations, ideological factors (or the position of the various groups struggling for power) were significant in the inception and growth of the *consolidado*.[8] Thus, the Guevarists were strongly in favor of this institution and it is obvious that in 1961–1964, the Ministry of Industries headed by Guevara, was in tight control of most of the *consolidados*. But with the decline of Guevara's influence, the dismembering of the Ministry of Industries began, its formerly controlled *consolidados* going to newly created ministries, that is, Sugar Industry (1964), Food Industry (1965), and Basic Industry, Light Industry, and Mining-Metallurgy (1967).[9]

Decentralization of the control of the *consolidado* from the Ministry of Industries was not only the result of the above-explained movement, but the consolidated enterprise itself became a target of attacks. Premier Fidel Castro in mid-1963 made the first criticism against the gigantism, inefficiency, and waste of some *consolidados*.[10]

A new type of firm organization, the *combinado,* appeared in the mid-1960s in an attempt to achieve vertical (instead of horizontal) integration. In the *combinado,* the whole chain of industrial input-output and distribution activities is entrusted to a single combine, such as *Cubatabaco* of the tobacco industry. The tobacco combine takes care of the whole manufacturing process, plus storage, distribution, and exports.[11] More on the combine will be said in the following section.

Structure of the Agricultural Firm

In the agricultural sector, four types of ownership and organization are found: state farms, private farms, cooperatives, and communes. The state-farm type embraces 70 percent of the land area available for cultivation, whereas most of the rest is owned and operated by small farmers who are integrated into the National Association of Small Farmers (ANAP), which, in turn, is under the control of the INRA's Vice Ministry of Private Production. The number of people and land belonging to cooperatives sharply declined in mid-1962 and today is negligible. There are now only a few communes in operation (e.g., San Andrés in the Pinar del Rio province with 900 families) and, although this type of organization is expected to be the scheme for the future, the commune still is in an experimental stage. Due to the dominance of the state-farm system, this study will concentrate on this type of organization.

The first Agrarian Reform Law (1959) divided the island into twenty-eight "Agricultural Development Zones" (ZDAs). Although, theoretically, the ZDAs were under the INRA's control, they operated with almost absolute autonomy. The anarchical operation of the ZDAs and the dramatic increase of state-owned plantations after the huge nationalization drive of late 1960 made effective central control necessary. The expropriated *latifundia* (mainly sugar plantations and cattle ranches) were organized in early 1961 into (a) sugar cooperatives, supervised by the INRA's General Administration of Sugar Cooperatives; and (b) state farms, directed by the INRA's General Administration of People's Farms. In mid-1961, there were 11,675 sugar-cooperative members, who also hired 44,897 wage workers; and 298 state farms that gave employment to 105,-000 wage earners.[12] The ZDAs were dropped altogether in 1962.

The organization of cooperatives in the sugar sector was chosen due to the peculiarities of the plantation economy, its large number of workers and high trade unionization. But cooperatives were, in fact, managed directly by the INRA as state enterprises. Their manager and secretariat were appointed by and were responsible to the INRA. The INRA office, usually in Havana, prescribed the output targets in physical terms of the various farms it administered. This included such central instructions as those pertaining to the crop to be planted and the times of planting and harvesting. There was strict control of investment also. Although a wage was not guaranteed, the cooperative's workers were paid a minimal sum and shared in the profits after all debts and obligations to the INRA were settled. The INRA also controlled all the cooperative's machinery and had exclusive rights to sell its output.[13] The INRA, too, had the legal power to borrow money with or without interest, open and close current accounts of any kind with any bank, and a continuous supply of funds were available to meet the costs of all its enterprises, which at this time showed little concern for costs. Thus, a very strong preference for administrative central planning was already shown by Cuba's central planners during this early period of the Revolution, since the firms and all other enterprises run by the INRA, including its industrial enterprises, were by then state enterprises in real form.

In August 1962, sugar cooperatives were formally renamed and converted into state farms, although until late 1963, they were kept under separate administration (i.e., the renamed General Administration of Sugar Farms of the INRA). In 1962, there were 220,000 workers in general state farms and 110,000 in sugar state farms. At this time, the state agricultural sector owned from 50 percent to 60 percent of the total arable land in Cuba.[14]

The excessive administrative centralization of the state farms in Havana came under attack in 1963 with charges of bureaucratism, excessive and rigid control, inefficient operation, and erroneous decisions because of the lack of knowledge of local conditions. As a result of the second Agrarian Reform Law, a new type of agricultural structure, the *agrupación* (*Agrupaciones Básicas de Producción Agropecuaria*) replaced the general administrations. Carlos Rafael Rodríguez, head of the INRA, defined the new institution:

> The *agrupación* is integrated by several state farms [located in the same region] under a common management. Each farm forms an administrative unit but it is under the direction of the *agrupación* in economic and technological matters. Each *agrupación* is considered a large agricultural and livestock enterprise under general control of the INRA's Vice Ministry of Agrarian Production.[15]

The criterion for integration of the original thirty-six *agrupaciones* was a horizontal one based on the concentration around a type of crop (as in the *consolidado*), but also based on geographical proximity.

The new administrative regulations for the state agricultural sector were published in early 1964. The island was divided into several regions (in remembrance of the former ZDAs), each embracing one or more *agrupaciones* and headed by a delegate from the INRA. Each *agrupación* had a director in charge of executive matters, assisted by an administrative council. The latter included three departments—economics, technology, and machinery. There were also several offices, for example, organization, supervision, stores, supply and sales, and construction. The *agrupación* embraced several state farms, each having an administrator and council, as well as departments in charge of land, economics, machinery, and supply and sales. Each farm, in turn, was divided into lots, the size of which varied depending on the type of cultivation. Lots were headed by a chief and were allocated a permanent "brigade" of workers who took responsibility for land preparation, cultivation, and harvesting (see figure 2).[16]

The average size of the state farm in 1961 was 8,870 hectares, although there were some farms with as much as 25,000 hectares. The average size increased to about 10,000 hectares in 1963. A relatively small state farm in the Havana province at this time had 3,640 hectares, grew a chief crop (mainly sugar cane, but also turbes, tomatoes, and corn) and raised animals (e.g., cattle and hogs). It employed 298 workers and had its own farm machinery.[17]

The Cuban state farm is similar to the Soviet *sovkhoz*.[18] The main income of state-farm workers is their wage, regulated by the wage-scale system. Workers are also granted subsidized housing, free medical services, and social security protection. Until 1967, they were allowed a small vegetable garden for their own consumption, but selling produce from this source and raising livestock were illegal.

In addition to the state farms there is a state enterprise (*Empresa de Servicios de Maquinarias a los Pequeños Agricultores*) similar to the Machine Tractor Stations (MTS) of Soviet experience. This operates heavy equipment and tractors and services the private sector of small producers as well.

A comparison of the factory in the *consolidado* and the farm in the *agrupación* shows differences and similarities. On the one hand, it seems that in the agricultural sector there is (or at least there was in 1964–1965) more autonomy at the local level in the decision-making process and more participation of the workers in farm revenue than in the industrial sector. All the orders of the director of the *agrupación* concerning a state farm are coursed through the farm's administrator. Although state-farm administrators are formally appointed by the provincial delegate of the INRA's Agricultural Production Department, the administrator of the *agrupación* may suspend them for serious reasons. The administrator of the *agrupación* may decide how to handle administrative expenses within the margins of a ceiling of 0.8 percent of the value of production and a maximum annual limit of $80,000.[19] The system of self-finance was to be introduced at the level of the *agrupación* first and at the level of the farm as soon as technical and accounting facilities had improved. Some sources have stated that the institution of profit-sharing was introduced in agriculture at this time.[20] This, however, is quite vague and the nearest to such a profit-sharing scheme was the establishment of prizes and economic incentives (as well as the vegetable garden) for brigade members who fulfilled and overfulfilled planned targets in their lots.[21] On the other hand, the *agrupación* had to receive capital from the Central Bank, profits of the state farms went to the state in most cases, output standards (work quotas) were set by the

FIG. 2

ORGANIZATIONAL CHART OF THE AGRICULTURAL *AGRUPACIÓN*
IN CUBA: 1964

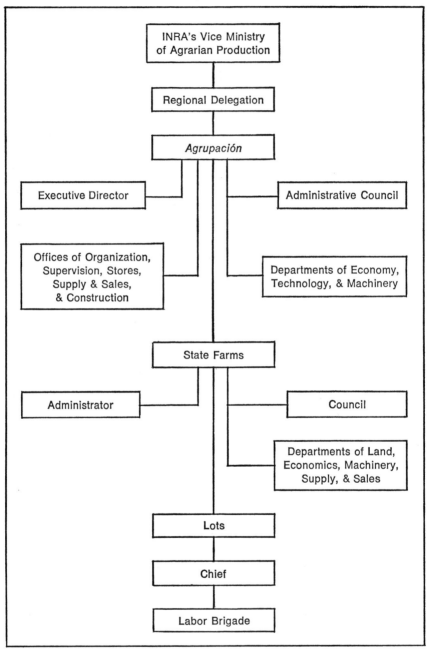

Data from "Reglamento tipo de la granja del pueblo," and "Reglamento tipo de
la unidad de dirección de la Agrupación Agropecuaria," *Hoy,* March 18, 1964.

INRA and JUCEPLAN, and workers were under wage rates decided centrally by the Ministry of Labor and the INRA.

Estimates on the number of *agrupaciones* and state farms by the mid-1960s ranged respectively from 56 to 80 and from 577 to 800.[22] In February 1965, Carlos Rafael Rodríguez was removed as president of the INRA and a new organizational change that actually had begun two years before definitely spread throughout state agriculture. This change was parallel to the introduction of the combine in the industrial sector. However, the organization of agrarian combines in Cuba is a more significant experiment because this scheme is rarely applied in the agricultural sector of Soviet-type economies. The "national combine" is an agro-industrial trust that vertically integrates numerous functions from the planting-harvesting stage through the industrial-manufacturing stage to the distribution stage, both domestically and internationally. Therefore, functions previously assigned to central ministries (e.g., INRA, Industries, Domestic Trade, Foreign Trade) are now integrated into the combine. The first experiment was initiated in 1963 with the poultry combine that allegedly resulted in a huge increase in the production of eggs. This was followed by the sugar combine in 1964, which organized itself as a ministry and which embraced all sugar activities from the cutting stage to the shipping stage. We have referred already to the tobacco combine organized in 1965.[23] Unfortunately, very little is known outside of Cuba about the structure and operations of these combines.[24]

Financing Systems

In 1961–1965, three different types of enterprise-financing coexisted in Cuba: budgetary finance, self-finance, and special budgetary finance à la Cuba. Private financing will not be discussed here. The budgetary system started in industry and was the method used in all state enterprises in 1961–1963. At the start of 1964, elements of the self-finance system were introduced in agriculture and foreign trade, although they never matured. In 1965, a degeneration of the budgetary system, embellished with Cuban features, was developed and it spread throughout the economy in 1966. In 1967, only budgetary types of financing were present, together with a mixture of private and public finance limited to private agriculture and in clear decline. This section concentrates on these three methods of financing the state firm.

Budgetary Finance

This system (called *sistema presupuestario* by the Cubans) began late in 1960 in the INRA's Department of Industrialization, controlled by

Ernesto (Che) Guevara. The nationalized industrial firms' bank accounts were lumped together under one centralized fund in the National Bank, into which enterprises made direct deposits of their revenues and from which they withdrew funds to cover their costs. In 1961, at the time the consolidated enterprises were set up, the centralized fund was incorporated into the general state budget, administered through the branches of the National Bank by the Ministry of Finance. Four laws enacted in 1961 organized the structure of the National Bank, the Ministry of Finance, JUCEPLAN, and the new Ministry of Industries around the budgetary finance system. The budgetary law of 1962 centralized practically all finances into the national budget, administered by the Ministry of Finance. Finally, the regulation of the state enterprises under budgetary financing was enacted in mid-1963. An important point to note at this time is that the *consolidados* (as well as agricultural enterprises) continued to be centrally and financially managed as before, depositing their revenues directly to the budget in accounts at the National Bank and, similarly, withdrawing funds to cover their firms' costs. The new regulation merely shifted power over the nation's financial and credit plans from both the National Bank and the INRA to the Ministry of Finance.

In the budgetary system, all economic activities of the nation are viewed as a huge, single state enterprise in which factories, farms, and workshops are mere branches.[25] These branches (state enterprises) do not own property or capital but are run as a ministry office. Transactions among enterprises cannot, in theory, assume the form of purchases and sellings (there is no "real" change of property because all belongs to the state), but only of transfers. The minister of finance at the time, Luis Alvarez Ron, explained these aspects in detail:

> The receipts and payments among enterprises, in our view, are nothing more than compensating acts in which the monetary expression shown by the use of a bank document is purely of an arithmetic or accounting nature. It is the instrument used by the bank in its role as the center of social accounting to register the flow of the receipt and delivery of products.[26]

The enterprise receives all its funds from the state and all its profits go to the state. There is no relationship between enterprise income and expenditures, the two being independent. If there is a surplus, it goes automatically to the national budget; if there is a deficit, it is cancelled in the national budget. The enterprise receives the allocation of funds for its expenses for every trimester, before producing its own revenue. Expenditures may exceed the established limits, whereas revenue may fall below expectations.

Capital allocations for all purposes (investment, wages, other expenditures) are granted from above, independently of enterprise performance or profitability. These allocations are considered budgetary "gifts" and, hence, are not repayable. The enterprise is not allowed to receive credit from the banking system, other enterprises, or private sources. Since the enterprise does not retain or accumulate funds of its own, it is unnecessary to tax it or charge interest to its capital allocations. Depreciation charges are imputed to sale prices and, hence, ultimately go to the state budget.

The enterprise takes initiative in preparing its financial plan within rules laid down by JUCEPLAN, the National Bank (up to 1966 this was a function of the now defunct Ministry of Finance), and the ministry or central agency to which the firm is associated. The financial plan regulates four accounts: income, expenses, wages, and investment. There is also a section that describes the financial relationship between the enterprise and the state budget. The financial plan is reviewed and eventually approved or modified by the central ministry or agency (e.g., Ministry of Light Industry), which, in turn, submits it to the National Bank (formerly to the Ministry of Finance). Enterprise accounts are all handled through branches of the National Bank as "budget units." Enterprise transactions are consummated by means of debits to the receiver's expense account and credits to the supplier's income account. All accounts are automatically cancelled by December 31. The enterprise cannot change its financial plan without JUCEPLAN's consent.

Money is used mainly as a unit for accounting purposes in order to reduce divergent elements (wages, physical input and output, etc.) to a common denominator. (Eventually money as a standard of value, not a medium of exchange, should be substituted by a better accounting unit such as a man-hour of socially necessary labor.) Accounting concerning capital funds is used for auditing purposes, but not as a means for assessing profitability, for example. Monetary calculation is used only for international trade relations.

Because there is no set of economic levers and incentives to increase productivity, improve quality, meet deliveries on schedule, use investment in an efficient manner, reduce costs, and make innovations, the only internal motivation to achieve these objectives is the worker's or manager's degree of consciousness and regard for the community's welfare.

Since there is no monetary calculation of production costs, prices, and profitability, no market mechanism is used to achieve supply and demand equilibrium; and, consequently, this task must be fulfilled through physical measurement and control as in the technical coefficients that determine the input-output relationship in physical terms. The enterprise must register, physically speaking, supplies and transfers of output. Labor efficiency is controlled through the system of output standards, that is, work quotas measured in physical terms (e.g., weight, volume, number of units). Managers must fulfill planned output targets, which are assigned to their enterprises and measured in physical terms.

Guevara was hopeful that the above task would be achieved: "All our work ought to be directed in making the administrative task of control and supervision ever simpler. . . . When all the indices and the methods and habits of control are established . . . modern planning methods will become important and it will then be possible to approximate the ideal of managing the economy by means of mathematical analysis."[27] Guevara preferred the audacious mathematical planner's variant of socialism to the various versions of market socialism, and encouraged the preparation and use of mathematical and computerized methods of planning in his ministry. By using sophisticated mathematical models of the allocation process, central administrators would be able to calculate the imputed efficiency (scarcity) prices of inputs from a predetermined, comprehensive final output plan. Soviet mathematician and founder of linear programming L. V. Kantorovich at one time advocated a comprehensive scheme of central mathematical planning.[28] Guevara pinned great hopes on the feasibility of using such a system for a small country favored with a good communications system, such as Cuba. A small nation, he thought, could approximate the centralized administrative ideal resting chiefly on budgetary finance and on moral incentives without having to resort to radical self-financing methods within the administrative system envisioned in Libermanist reforms elsewhere or in the Yugoslavian full-market solution.

Self-finance

The decision to experiment with a limited form of self-finance was induced by the unintended results of enterprise functioning in 1961–1963, which were partially blamed on the system of budgetary finance. During this period, state administrators of industrial and agricultural enterprises behaved as if their main objective was to maximize their budgets. They were essentially committed to the maximizing of physical output and, hence, neglected costs and even the collection of payments from their customers as required by law. Thus, deficits mounted and administrators were constrained to request increases in their budget allocations. The president of the National Bank complained in early 1964 that "some of these enterprises do not appear motivated in collecting payment for their merchandise and services because their costs are covered and, for them, it only means not depositing revenues to the budget." The rules obliging firms to pay and collect promptly were violated at a weekly average of 20,000 times, at a value of twenty million pesos.[29] With neither an obligation to repay grants nor a pressure to show profitability, there was also a tendency to inflate enterprises' requests for investment capital and to store often low-quality inventories.[30]

This disorganization among firms resulted in a directive by the revolutionary government, made in mid-1963, to restore "financial order in the enterprises, reduce costs of production and raise labor productivity."[31] Part of the solution was the initiation at the beginning of 1964 of the first rules of self-finance, mainly in agricultural and foreign and domestic trade enterprises. According to table 2, by the end of 1964, a little less than one-

TABLE 2
DISTRIBUTION OF ENTERPRISES BY ECONOMIC SECTOR
AND FINANCING SYSTEM IN CUBA: 1964

Sectors	Self-finance		Budgetary Finance	
	Number	Percentage[a]	Number	Percentage[a]
Agriculture	25	11.3%	—	—
Industry	11	5.0	—	—
Foreign trade	14	6.3	—	—
Domestic trade	9	4.1	—	—
Others	10	4.5	—	—
Total	69	31.2%	152[b]	68.8[b]%

Source: Based on Salvador Vilaseca Forne, "El Banco Nacional de Cuba y los sistemas de financiamiento," Nuestra Industria Revista Económica, 3 (February 1965), p. 8.
a. Of the total 221 enterprises.
b. Mainly concentrated in the industrial sector.

third of the state enterprises were under self-finance, mainly concentrated in agriculture where the system was applied on the level of the agrupación with the distant hope of extending it to the state-farm level when technical resources permitted.

These initial rules pertained to the grant of power to firms to make use of bank credit on terms set by the bank. These terms concerned the use of the loan, its amortization schedule, and material guarantees (such as raw materials, goods-in-process, fuel, and the like), as well as exhortation to enterprises to be solvent.[32]

The system of self-finance (called khozraschet in the USSR; autofinanciamiento in Cuba) works within the same administrative planning framework that budgetary finance does. Nevertheless, under self-finance the conception of a huge, single state enterprise was changed in favor of the development of as many enterprises as necessary and as autonomous as possible. According to Carlos Rafael Rodríguez, former president of the INRA, this system

> requires socialist enterprises to cover their [current] costs with their own revenues and insure the profitability of production. The state supplies the financing for centralized investments. However, part of the enterprise profits are earmarked for decentralized investments proposed by the enterprise and approved by the central planning bodies. This method, also presupposes the use of bank credits [as repayable loans] to finance working capital [due to unforeseen factors.] It permits the establishment of an additional control of the economic activities of the enterprises by means of supervision by the banks [monetary control or calculation].[33]

The partial use of money in self-finance facilitates communication of information and evaluation of production, which helps to make the information available to the center complete. The evaluation of managerial performance is made in large measure by using monetary-mercantile indices (e.g., costs and profits). Managers are empowered to determine the ultimate specifications of their output and input orders from the center. Because managers possess some command power over resources, they are able to subspecify their instructions from any number of ultimate products and ultimate technologies as long as they are guided in this by profitability. In practice, however, output and input plans leave little room for choice. With a given product goal, profit maximization reduces to cost minimization, and since input-utilization plans severely limit the scope for input substitution, the latter rule approximates the technical (physical) rule of obtaining the largest output from each input taken singly.[34]

Self-finance permits direct contacts among enterprises. This party allows managers to decide the ultimate specifications of products they require from suppliers and, to a certain extent, their output in view of the needs of other enterprises. However, these interenterprise contacts take place within the limits of supply and delivery plans set administratively from above.

In regard to the leading role of material incentives, Guevara seemed to be right in thinking that the system of self-finance would enhance group individualism biased toward the search for private material gain.[35] This was admitted by his critics but justified as historical necessity. The reasons seem obvious. Any decentralization that bolsters the decision power of managers is likely to release individual and material impulses unless dampened by unusually strong and contrary cultural factors. Also, to make the firm's residual goal of profit-making meaningful, the director's and worker's salary may need to be tied to that success indicator, either in the form of a director's fund for amenities, or an individual bonus or material award system.

Other ideal characteristics of the system of self-finance were that managers were theoretically held responsible for unjustified nonfulfillment of national production plans or delays in deliveries to other enterprises; that production costs should be realistically estimated in order to provide a solid basis for a rational price system; and that proper accounting methods and financial balances should be used. The supervision of enterprise finances was exerted by the central ministry or production agency in relation to output, and by the banking system in relation to credits and budget (the latter function was assigned to the Ministry of Finance until late 1965).

The efficient functioning of self-finance required certain conditions that were not present in Cuba at the time, such as institutionalization and stability in production, prices, and investment, as well as rigorous discipline in management. Hence, in practice, the application of self-finance was highly formal, the system never had a real chance of maturing and evolving into a more liberal form; in practice, it operated as a disguised budgetary finance system. Thus, enterprise expenditures were actually disconnected with its revenues; deficits were covered with grants or bank "loans" that were not repaid; investment funds were completely financed through the state budget; and there was no fully developed system of economic incentives tied to plan fulfillment. In the second half of 1965, the idea of self-finance itself was officially devalued in favor of budgetary finance.[36]

Special Budgetary Finance à la Cuba

Two Cuban peculiarities have seemed to play a significant role in the adoption and expansion of the budgetary system. The development of modern accounting methods and of monopolistic corporations, mainly U.S. subsidiaries, prior to the Revolution offered both the technique and the experience that other socialist revolutions did not have at the time of their take-overs. Some of those U.S. subsidiaries used computers in their operations. Furthermore, reciprocal debits among them were often offset through accounting compensation by the central administration. According to a Cuban official, this was an important basis for expanding budgetary finance in the industrial sector.[37] This may also explain Guevara's dream of computerized centralized management.

Another peculiarity is the concentration of economic, administrative, and political powers in the hands of one person or small coterie. To some extent the debate over budgetary versus self-finance systems was a power struggle among key persons (represented by Guevara and Rodríguez) in central positions for control over national financial planning. This seems clear from

the descriptions of the two forms given by the protagonists, which give un-
due emphasis to the relative primacy of the Ministry of Finance (in the
hands of budgetary supporters) or the National Bank (controlled by self-
finance supporters) in granting credits to enterprises and receiving revenues
from them. In the second half of 1965, both factions in the struggle had
been seriously weakened by the substitution of Castro for Rodríguez in the
INRA and by the departure of Guevara. Thus, the prime minister became
the most powerful figure and the arbiter in the polemic.[38]

In 1966 the Ministry of Finance was abolished and all its functions consolidated into the National Bank. This act by no means signaled the demise
of the system of budgetary enterprise. It actually signaled its expansion, although in a slightly different way. The Cuban firm is now managed in a
purely administrative and highly centralized manner in the style of a government office described, for example, in V. I. Lenin's *State and Revolution*. The supporters of budgetary finance imply that the firm's allocational
functions can be very nearly completely specified and structured with responsibility thereby delegated and evaluated in the style of a Weberian
rational bureaucracy. In practice, as in many countries, the administrative
official is chosen more for his political loyalty than for his technical expertise. This is the case with the Cuban manager whose total monthly salary
is often below his technical section chief or his most skilled worker. As
with many government functionaries, his responsibilities are not very clearly
specified nor is there a clear quantitative measure of his principal output.
For example, a manager in a market economy is judged principally by his
contribution to the firm's profits, and in producing this principal output, he
can fire and transfer unproductive or incompetent subordinates. The Cuban
manager, as the typical government administrator, does not possess as
much power. His power to hire is subject to the consent of his industrial
ministry and the Ministry of Labor and the latter's regional office; his
power to fire and transfer workers even for justified cause is subject to veto
by the Communist party nucleus in the firm, by union leaders and members
of his administrative staff, and by the relevant ministry.

The exact characteristics of the current system and the degree to which
the *pure* budgetary system has been embellished with Cuban additives are
difficult to ascertain. The main sources that provided information on the
polemic are no longer in publication. All of them (e.g., *Cuba Socialista,
Nuestra Industria Revista Económica, Comercio Exterior*) disappeared between 1965 and 1967. Copies of the *Gaceta Oficial* are difficult to obtain
since the Cuban combine that controls publications and their exports
(*Instituto Cubano del Libro*) has banned its exportation. But it is obvious
that nonmarket (mobilization) means of allocating labor, socialization of
the means of production, and moral incentives were further enhanced in

1967–1968, and so was the office-like physical management of the firm, without using either economic incentives or monetary calculation. The secretary of organization of the party stated in late 1968:

> How can we, under socialism, insure efficiency and the good or-
> ganization and management of production? . . . Sometimes an
> attempt is made to apply the mechanism of economic control
> using the monetary procedure. We have rejected this mechanism
> and we want to go on leaving it aside; we do not want to measure
> efficiency by it. So how can we insure efficiency? . . . by or-
> ganizing efficiency plans, pinpointing tasks, defining responsibili-
> ties, effectively controlling inventories, constantly concerning
> ourselves with the problems of maintenance. That is, we must go
> directly to the root of the problem, discarding monetary mech-
> anisms, capitalist-type economic controls . . . technological
> skill must be applied in order to insure a centralized control es-
> pecially in large industries.[39]

The 1966–1967 reforms emphasized the necessity of perfecting the administrative organization by improving technical efficiency; in keeping with this principle, an increase of emphasis was placed in the control of the sources and uses of funds by the firm. Each was assigned a fixed maximum of finances for circulating capital, the main ones were for inventories of raw material, goods-in-process, finished products, and the number of days allowed for the collection of payments from customers. Methods of de-preciation-costing, previously neglected, were established, as well as for other scarce materials. In all these, various input-utilization norms amounted to more than a dozen. The main task in 1967 was the enforce-ment of these circulating capital indicators down to the level of depart-ments and shops.[40]

Another feature of this new stage, explained in detail by Albán Lataste, is the development of extra or special miniplans, somewhat connected with the organization of combines. The assumption was made that there were some unutilized reserves that the central plan was incapable of mobilizing, as well as some urgent problems that required special treatment. Several of the characteristics of these plans are as follows (see also chapter 7): (a) some of the special plans regulate in an individual manner the structure and functioning of agro-industrial combines; (b) the financing system fol-lowed by the special plans is the budgetary system, but without the disci-pline and rigor applied to the enterprises under the central plan; and (c) there is an attempt to solve the efficiency problems created by the new system through the use of computers, but, given the current level of technology and availability of data, more hope seems to be put in the development of consciousness.[41]

An Outlook for the Future

Summarizing the previous pages, four stages in the organization of the firm and its financing system seem evident. First, a transitional stage (1959–1960) of relative disorganization and independence from the center, in which there were both private and state firms, the latter without a clear organization. Secondly, a stage of consolidation and centralization (1961–1963) in which the state factories were integrated into *consolidados* under the huge Ministry of Industries, the cooperatives were transformed into state farms, all of which became centrally directed by the INRA, and in which the system of budgetary finance was introduced and reigned supreme. Thirdly, there was a brief stage (1964–first half of 1965) in which an attempt to decentralize was made but never matured—the Ministry of Industries was dismembered, its *consolidados* were distributed among five new ministries, the agrarian *agrupación* was developed, and the system of self-finance was introduced and rapidly embraced one-third of all state enterprises. Fourth is the current stage, still in experimentation, in which the agro-industrial combines based on vertical integration, the special plans, the expansion of the budgetary system à la Cuba, and the gradual elimination of self-finance, monetary, and mercantile relations are the main features.

The Cuban managerial model for the future appears as a paradoxical combination of two different factors: technology and consciousness. On the one hand, it is expected that the problems of a highly centralized administration resulting from the elimination of all market mechanisms will be solved, in as small an island as Cuba, by applying cybernetic methods. On the other hand, the development of consciousness, through the increasing use of moral incentives, is expected to avoid the necessity of extremely detailed and possibly coercive methods. Economic reality, however, may be more complex than is envisioned in the dreams of daring mathematical planners. The mathematically efficient (scarcity) prices of the factors of production can be derived only if the relative prices of the final consumer goods are known in advance. These consumer prices are the relative weights of the goods whose value is said to be maximized. In theory, these consumer prices can be stated and communicated by consumers without the aid of a monetized consumer market. In practice, this is impossible due to the enormous cost and rapidity required in gathering, processing, and communicating the needed information. The usual mathematical methods of allocation assume fixity of input-output norms and the linear proportionality between inputs and outputs—both unrealistic in a modern setting. This system oversimplifies the complexity and constantly changing nature of the allocational field, of technological choices, and of consumer tastes.

Even if the computers and mathematical methods were perfected and made more realistic (e.g., dynamic and nonlinear methods) within the next few decades, the enormous load of data fed to computers and the orders that need to be issued back raise doubts as to the ability of the communications media to transmit these large masses of information. Central managers with the latest computers may not respond quickly enough and communicate instructions fast enough to handle constant changes in the allocational material. Given the proliferation of special plans, given the fact that Cuba is essentially relying on agriculture (a problematic sector for planning), given that planners may not have sufficient information and time to devote to coordinative planning, the computerized budgetary system may not be an adequate substitute for establishing direct links among firms, either through a more radical form of self-finance or through some market varieties. At any rate, the preference for officelike management of the firm with reliance on technical norms may be made at the price of a lower growth rate in GNP.

The intractability and natural failings of human beings may prove to be a serious obstacle. As far as the processing and aggregating of raw data are concerned, Professor Ragnar Frisch states that "this processing is an immense practical task that demands great understanding, accuracy and feeling of responsibility on the part of the large staff that takes part in the work." In regard to enforcement and checking of instructions sent from computers, he states, "Not only downright corruption, but also a lack of understanding and the general shortcoming of humans will put definite limits to what can be achieved."[42] The considerations mentioned above do not, of course, imply that mathematical programming cannot be useful for intraenterprise use and even in highly concentrated and homogenous sectors; indeed, these are their proper fields of application.

Managing the firm almost like a government office may be seen as the managerial counterpart of moral incentives in the intensification and deployment of labor to various geographical places and work centers. Moral incentives may be considered an organizational building block based on feelings of solidarity with others. By unleashing a cultural revolution to instill it, the policy makers hope to reconcile managerial and worker values with centralized requirements. One indicator of its workability is the near elimination of taxes in Cuba (to a lesser extent in China) in 1970, funds which were hitherto needed to finance investment. This indicates that managers and workers have been motivated sufficiently by a combination of administrative and psychological pressure to work more for the community's profit than for their own private salaries. By not collecting their increasing additional products in the form of higher salaries, they show more willingness to give resources voluntarily than to have their extra income involuntarily taxed away.

Although moral stimulation has worked relatively well in mobilizing labor to solve the manpower shortage in the key agricultural harvests, the managerial performance of the system has not been convincing. Remarkable success in some productive sectors (e.g., eggs, fishing, and sugar in 1970) is commonly achieved at the cost of failure in other sectors, and overall results, in terms of GNP, are disappointing. There are increasing signs that centralized regimentation is filling the gap of frustrated expectations in the matter of moral stimuli.

The Cuban model of management aspires to eliminate all monetary-mercantile relations, whereas most of the socialist countries are using these means more and more and trying to improve on them. The latter model is supposed to be based on "objective" scientific laws tested by half a century of practice. Both models allege that theirs is the easier and fastest way to complete the transitional stage of socialism and enter that of communism. The two models are based on mutually exclusive hypotheses.[43] If the use of some market mechanisms in the socialist stage correspond to a real need, then the eradication of monetary-mercantile relations in Cuba is anti-scientific, and will result in grave inefficiency and eventual stagnation or decline in economic growth. On the other hand, if the Cuban model proves in the immediate future that monetary-mercantile relations can be abolished and egalitarianism enforced with positive results, then the current socialist economic theory would prove to be erroneous, at least as a general theory. Herein lies the significance of the Cuban experiments.

NOTES

1. Ernesto (Che) Guevara, *Economic Planning in Cuba* (New York, 1961), p. 3.

2. "Reglamento orgánico de las empresas consolidadas del Ministerio de Industrias," *Gaceta Oficial,* August 9, 1961; and "Restructuración del reglamento orgánico," ibid., July 3, 1962.

3. *Gaceta Oficial,* November 5 and 21, 1963.

4. See Juan M. Castiñeiras, "La industria ligera en la etapa actual," *Cuba Socialista,* 4 (June 1964), pp. 4–5; and "El desarrollo industrial de Cuba," ibid., 6 (May 1966), p. 103.

5. Cited in *Primer simposio de recursos naturales de Cuba* (La Habana, 1958).

6. Aníbal Escalante, public speech of March 1961, as quoted in Cuban Economic Research Project, *Labor Conditions in Communist Cuba* (Coral Gables, 1963), p. 7.

7. See ECLA, *Economic Survey for Latin America, 1963* (New York, 1965), part four: "The Cuban Economy."

8. See Jorge I. Domínguez, "Sectoral Clashes in Cuban Politics and Development,"

mimeographed (Paper presented at the Conference of the American Association for the Advancement of Science, Boston, December 29, 1969).

9. On monopolization of industrial activities by the Ministry of Industries, see Osvaldo Dorticós, "Tareas importantes de nuestros organismos económicos," *Cuba Socialista*, 6 (March 1966), pp. 26–42.

10. *Organogramas* were made fun of by the prime minister for their alleged bureaucratic proliferation; he proudly mentioned having abolished one (the office of the prime minister itself) by reducing its staff to a handful. See *Granma*, February 26, 1967, p. 3.

11. "Planning in Cuba," *Panorama Económico Latinamericano*, 8 (1967), pp. 11–12.

12. For sources and opposing points of view on agrarian developments in 1959–1963, see Cuban Economic Research Project, *Cuba: Agriculture and Planning* (Miami, 1965), pp. 213–41; and Sergio Aranda, *La revolución agraria en Cuba* (Mexico, 1968), pp. 169–94.

13. See Irving P. Pflaum, *American Universities Field Staff Reports Service*, 5 (August 1960); Leo Huberman and Paul Sweezy, *Cuba: Anatomy of a Revolution* (New York, 1961); and Carlos Rafael Rodríguez in *Revolución*, August 18, 1962.

14. Antero Regalado, "El camino de la cooperación agraria en Cuba," *Cuba Socialista*, 3 (June 1963), p. 47; and Blas Roca, *El Mundo*, August 16, 1962.

15. Carlos Rafael Rodríguez, "El nuevo camino de la agricultura cubana," *Cuba Socialista*, 3 (November 1963), p. 83.

16. "Reglamento tipo de la granja del pueblo," *Hoy*, March 18, 1964; and "Reglamento típico de la unidad de dirección de la agrupación agropecuaria estatal," ibid.

17. Said Usnanov and Boris Kidrin, "La aplicación experimental de las cartas tecnológicas en la Granja Rubén Martínez Villena," *Cuba Socialista*, 3 (August 1963), pp. 57–58.

18. Castro acknowledged this fact in *Revolución*, December 17, 1961.

19. Rodríguez, "El nuevo camino," p. 92.

20. *Hispanic American Report* (July 1964), p. 416; Ernest Mandel, "Defend the Cuban Revolution," *International Socialist Review* (Summer 1964), p. 61.

21. Rodríguez, "El nuevo camino," p. 96.

22. G. L. Beckford, "A Note on Agricultural Organization and Planning in Cuba," *Caribbean Studies*, 6 (October 1966), pp. 45–46; *Hispanic American Report* (August 1964), p. 513; Carmelo Mesa-Lago, *The Labor Sector and Socialist Distribution in Cuba* (New York, 1968), p. 55.

23. See Michel Gutelman, *L'Agriculture socialisée à Cuba* (Paris, 1967), pp. 128–40.

24. René Dumont devotes only a couple of lines of his last book to the combine. See Dumont, *Cuba est-il socialiste?* (Paris, 1970), p. 72.

25. Most information in this section comes from Albán Lataste, *Cuba: ¿hacia una nueva economía política del socialismo?* (Santiage del Chile, 1968), pp. 17–53. Lataste, a Chilean, worked as an economic adviser to the Cuban government until 1966. Other sources used are "Ley reguladora del sistema presupuestario de financiamiento de las empresas estatales," *Gaceta Oficial*, August 26, 1963; Marcelo Fernández Font, "Desarrollo y funciones de la banca socialista en Cuba," *Cuba Socialista*, 4 (February 1964), pp. 32–50; Ernesto (Che) Guevara, "La banca el crédito y el socialismo," *Cuba Socialista*, 4 (March 1964), pp. 23–42; Luis Alvarez Ron, "Sobre el método de análisis de los sistemas de financiamiento," *Cuba Socialista*, 4 (July 1964), pp. 64–79; and Gilberto Gutiérrez Núñez, "El sistema presupuestario

de financiamiento: descripción de su funcionamiento y objetivo," *Nuestra Industria Revista Económica,* 5 (June 1967), pp. 44–70.

26. Alvarez Ron, "Análisis de los sistemas de financiamiento," p. 77.

27. Guevara, "La banca," pp. 35–36. See also his "Consideraciones sobre los costos de producción, . . ." *Nuestra Industria Revista Económica,* 2 (June 1963), pp. 4–12.

28. Described in Benjamin Ward, "Kantorovich on Economic Calculation," *Journal of Political Economy,* 68 (December 1960), pp. 546–48.

29. Fernández, "Desarrollo de la banca," pp. 45–46.

30. Lataste, *Cuba,* p. 35.

31. Israel Talavera, "La organización del trabajo y la rentabilidad en las empresas agropecuarias," *Cuba Socialista,* 3 (December 1963), p. 23.

32. Fernández, "Desarrollo de la banca," p. 39.

33. Rodríguez, "El nuevo camino," p. 88.

34. This argument is found in Gregory Grossman, "Notes Towards a Theory of the Command Economy," in *Comparative Economic Systems,* ed. M. Bornstein (Homewood, Ill., 1965), pp. 135–55.

35. Guevara, "La banca," pp. 36–37.

36. Lataste, *Cuba,* pp. 36–39.

37. Gutiérrez, "El sistema presupuestario de financiamiento," p. 44–46.

38. See Carmelo Mesa-Lago, "Cuba: teoría y práctica de los incentivos," *Aportes* (Paris), 20 (April 1971), pp. 84–85.

39. Armando Hart, *Granma,* November 10, 1968, p. 2.

40. See the report of the Vice Ministry of Economics, "El análisis económico como instrumento de control del plan de eficiencia industrial," *Nuestra Industria Revista Económica,* 5 (February 1967), pp. 3–23.

41. Lataste, *Cuba,* pp. 40–45, 52–54.

42. Ragnar Frisch, "Economic Planning and the Growth Problem in Developing Countries," *Øst-Okonomi* (Special Number, 1961), pp. 60–61.

43. Lataste, *Cuba,* pp. 17–18.

9
Roberto E. Hernández and Carmelo Mesa-Lago

Labor Organization and Wages

THIS chapter describes the changes in labor philosophy and organization that have taken place in Cuba under the Revolution, particularly since 1961 when the socialist system began to be introduced. The authors do not consider it appropriate, within the framework and space limitations of the essay, to discuss in detail the state of labor conditions and union rights on the eve of the Revolution. It should be enough to call the reader's attention to the fact that practically all studies on Cuban labor agree on the following points: by 1958, the Cuban labor movement was one of the best organized and most powerful in Latin America and unionized workers enjoyed, in general, conditions that were above average in the area. However, at the same time, as in other Latin American countries, a very high proportion of the labor force suffered from either unemployment or underemployment, and most rural workers did not enjoy the same benefits as those of their counterparts in the city, especially those of the privileged members of the stronger unions.

Furthermore, this essay will not discuss the problem of how, positively or negatively, the Revolution has affected substantive labor conditions such as employment, equal job opportunities, work schedules, vacations, labor safety, and social security. Other chapters of this book discuss some of these problems and serious studies are available elsewhere that deal with matters not covered in the book, such as social security.[1]

What this chapter does propose to do is to explore what has been and is (at the end of the summer of 1970) the role of the workers and their unions in the decision-making process and regulation of labor conditions, and how the labor force is integrated into national planning through the system of work quotas and wage scales. At this point, the reader may think that we are avoiding central issues by centering our attention on either formal or procedural aspects that have an ancillary importance, or on obscure economic intricacies. Our contention is, however, that the topic selected is of maximum significance because it deals with the key problem of whether or not the Cuban proletariat is actually a decisive force in the nation, and how the workers' effort is channeled and remunerated by the government.

One final warning to the reader: Cuban statistics on labor matters (e.g., trade union affiliation, labor conflicts, wage structure, etc.) are among the worst in terms of availability, accuracy, and continuity. In the *Boletín Estadístico* prepared by JUCEPLAN for the 1962 to 1966 period, only 3 out of 170 pages were devoted to labor, and the only published data which deal with employment and wages were incomplete and obscure. In the annual *Compendio Estadístico,* consisting of fifty-four pages in its 1968 issue, no tables on labor matters had been published since publication began in 1965. Thus, we have had to rely on very scanty quantitative data, a selective number of technical studies, and legal provisions. To avoid the potential danger of "coolness" or lack of reality, a profusion of statements from government and union officials and direct observations made by researchers of the Cuban phenomenon have been used. Therefore, the nature of our findings must be essentially qualitative and subject to further sharpening.

Concrete topics to be discussed in the essay include the role and structure of trade unions; the scope and content of collective bargaining; the regulation of labor conflicts; the system of work quotas and wage scales; and the organization of socialist emulation. At the end, an attempt is made to evaluate the participation of the workers in decision-making and in the regulation of labor conditions.

Role and Structure of Trade Unions

Since the mid-1930s, Cuba's trade unionism had shown a history of activism, struggles for workers' rights, and gains in its economic objectives. The Confederation of Cuban Workers (CTC) was founded in 1939, heavily dominated by Communist leaders. Its secretary general in 1939–1947, Lázaro Peña, was a member of the PSP. This was a period in which Batista and the Communists were united in a popular front. Under *Auténtico* party rule the Communists lost control of the CTC in the mid-1940s and their influence rapidly declined. The labor movement became more and more centered around the goal of improving labor conditions. When Batista took power again in 1952, he was quite careful not to alter workers' rights during his dictatorship; hence, it is not difficult to explain why the labor unions did not actively participate in the political movement that overthrew his regime. However, there were many union leaders who belonged to the urban underground, and they took control of the CTC and the unions in the early days of 1959. Most of these leaders came from revolutionary organizations such as the July 26 movement, but some were also members of the Catholic Workers' Youth (JOC) and labor leaders of the *Ortodoxo* and *Auténtico* parties that had opposed Batista. Communist control of the unions at this time was minimal.

Elections held in all unions in late 1959 backed most of the new labor leaders and defeated the Communist candidates. An executive council was to be elected during the Tenth National Congress of the CTC held in November of that year by representatives of the local unions. At this time, it was obvious that the new labor leaders would be ratified in their positions and the old-guard Communists defeated. However, the personal intervention of Prime Minister Fidel Castro led to the approval of a single "unity" state (with the presence of pro-Communist labor leaders) in spite of strong opposition among members of the congress. Shortly after the congress had ended, purges began and, as a result, "antiunity" leaders were gradually eliminated, usually after being accused either of being Batista's collaborators or of participating in counterrevolutionary activities. The purge wave reached the top of the CTC hierarchy when, in May 1960, Secretary General David Salvador resigned (or was expelled) and was later imprisoned. For more than a year, the secretary of organization of the CTC, Jesús Soto, a loyal *Fidelista,* led the organization in a *de facto* manner. During the Eleventh National Congress of the CTC, held in November 1961, Lázaro Peña returned to the CTC as secretary general, since there was only one list of candidates presented to all the unions.[2] Peña remained as the top official of the CTC throughout the period 1962–1966, a period in which Castro closely followed the Soviet model of economic organization. At the Twelfth National Congress of the CTC (an occasion taken by Prime Minister Castro to announce his position in the controversy on incentives—favoring moral incentives), a loyal *Fidelista* (although former member of the PSP youth section), Miguel Martín replaced Peña as secretary general. The new secretary general fervently endorsed Cuba's new line of thought. In August 1968 Castro supported the Soviet invasion of Czechoslovakia, a move that some observers believe was a milestone in his return to closer relations with the USSR. On November 18, Martín was given a leave of absence as secretary general of the CTC and was appointed delegate of the provincial branch of the PCC in Camagüey, a job of secondary importance. The second man in the CTC's hierarchial line, Héctor Ramos Latour, took Martín's former position and was ratified in it at the Fifth National Council Meeting of the CTC held in September 1970 (National Congresses and National Councils will be discussed in more detail later).

At the same time that the Cuban Revolution became more collectivistic in nature, trade unions were subjected to increasing pressure in order to conform their structure and role to the new ideology and objectives. Theoretically, in a socialist country the government is run by the workers through their leaders, the means of production are collectively owned, and managers are government appointed. Thus, the goals of government, managers and workers should coincide and unions should no longer need to defend workers' interests. In fact, unions must cooperate with government and management in order to fulfill and protect collective interests, "Before the owner was the capitalist who took advantage of the workers' effort; now the owner is the people, is the whole community, and only they take advantage of labor and production."[3]

By August 1961, a new legal system for the organization of trade unions was implemented in Cuba. In its preamble, the new law explained that the old legislation corresponded "to a period that had been surpassed by the Revolution" and that, the old law hampered "the realization of the government's plans to construct a society in which man does not exploit man."[4] Furthermore, the Declaration of Principles and Union Statutes approved by the Twelfth National Congress of the CTC in mid-1966 stated that "the labor movement, directed and guided by the Party, must effectively contribute to the mobilization of the masses in fulfillment of the tasks assigned by the Revolution and to strengthening Marxist-Leninist ideology." The labor leaders should be "at the vanguard of the masses in the effort requested to the latter in behalf of the Revolution."[5]

According to the 1961 law, the main objectives of trade unions in Cuba are to assist in the fulfillment of the production and development plans of the nation; to promote efficiency and expansion of social and public services; to improve the administration in all fields; and to organize and carry out political education activities. The 1966 Declaration of Principles added more concrete tasks: (a) organization of socialist emulation and voluntary (unpaid) labor; (b) strict application of the labor legislation, work quotas, wage scales, and labor discipline; (c) increase of output, improvement of quality of production, reduction of costs and maintenance of the equipment; (d) development of political consciousness; and (e) expansion of recreational, sports, and cultural facilities.

Adding to the cold phrasing of the legislation and in order to convey precisely the new situation to the workers, Cuban authorities elaborated on the new role of the unions. Blas Roca, former secretary general of the PSP, declared in 1962, "If previously, the fundamental function of the unions was to fight for the partial and immediate demands of each labor sector (an instrument to defend the rightful interest of the workers against the capitalists), today the fundamental task of the unions is to fight for an increase in production and productivity."[6] Vice Premier Raúl Castro ex-

panded the previous idea: "Yesterday it was necessary [for unions] to struggle continuously in order to gain certain advantages, to obtain a little more
from the profits being made by the magnates. Today the great task confronting the CTC and the unions is to increase production, recruit voluntary
workers, tighten labor discipline, push for higher productivity, and improve the quality of what is produced."[7] In spite of these explanations, it
seems that a sector of the workers did not accept the new union role and
came under criticism from Premier Castro: "The working people gave the
impression that they did not understand the new role they have to play
[and] . . . obstacles existed between the revolutionary government and
the workers in general."[8]

Since 1965 the role of the unions had been sharply reduced by the
establishment of the Labor Councils (see below). In mid-1966, during
the meetings of the Twelfth National Congress of the CTC, the newly
appointed secretary general of that body was asked what was left to the
unions. He answered that the unions could help in the organization of
labor discipline and the avoidance of negligence, in compelling those
workers who still had "ideas from the past" to change their attitude, and
in fighting selfish workers who only think of their own interests and thus
contribute to the lack of discipline and organization in production.[9]

By the turn of the 1960s, the trade unions seemed "to have withered
away" in the words of an American scholar and sympathizer of the Revolution, Maurice Zeitlin: "The workers do not have an independent organization which takes the initiative in the plant, industry or country as a
whole, to assure—let alone to demand—improved working conditions.
. . . No organization exists, as an autonomous force, to protect and advance the immediate interests of the workers as they see them, independent
of the prevailing line of the Communist Party or policies of the Revolutionary government."[10] Another sympathizer of the Revolution, the internationally known economist, Joan Robinson, said, "The [Cuban] trade
unions . . . represent the view of the Party and the government rather
than that of the workers."[11]

Two questions are important in relation to the new role of the unions.
One relates to how efficiently in the views of the administration the unions
have performed their newly assigned tasks, particularly those pertaining
to production. The second is whether the abandonment of the former,
traditional role of the unions, that is, the defense of the workers' interests,
has not induced negative effects. In 1969, two highly ranked Cuban officials
made significant statements that are useful in answering these questions.

Armando Hart, secretary of organization of the PCC, referred to the
role of the unions in increasing labor productivity. Hart acknowledged
that the unions do not intervene in the direction of production, a function

reserved for the administration, and that the main task of the labor movement is "to further the Revolution plans, to raise productivity." Hart criticized the poor performance of the unions in fulfilling this task, and presented to them, as an example, the work of the militarized Centennial Youth Column. Then, he stated that if such an example would be followed, the labor leaders would be doing something "more useful than what they are doing today: they would be decisively aiding production." The PCC official mentioned structural problems that were impeding the unions in assuming their production role and predicted that "new revolutionary structures [without further elaboration] will have to be established in the future by the labor movement, more related to the needs of production, to assure greater efficiency in work and to raise productivity."[12]

Carlos Rafael Rodríguez, member of the old guard, minister without portfolio, and the best-known economist in the present Cuban government, candidly said to Zeitlin in 1969 that the unions had been inadequately concerned with defending the interests of the workers relative to their emphasis on spurring them to meet production targets, and added: "The unions are transmission belts of the Party directives to the workers but have insufficiently represented the workers to the Party or Revolutionary Government. They cannot be merely instruments of the Party without losing their purpose."[13] More will be said later concerning this matter.

Let us now discuss other salient features of the current union organization. Former unionization by crafts and occupations has been substituted by unionization along industrial lines or economic sectors. In this way, all the employees of a factory, state farm, or agency belong to the same union regardless of occupation. Unionization by occupation tends to result in the development of pressure groups with strong solidarity in defending their interests. As a reason for the shift, the 1961 trade union law states, "The multiplicity of different organizations by occupation and professions within the same work center caused difficulties to the collective effort required by Cuba's development."

As a result of the new type of unionization, professionals ("intellectual workers") joined manual workers in the same local union. Civil servants who had been barred from organizing a union prior to 1961 were given this right. The only sectors of the labor force who are excluded from unionization are the private farmers (integrated into ANAP), the armed forces, and the police.

Another feature of the new organization is union monopoly rights, that is, only one charter of the union is allowed to be established in each enterprise, one national union in each economic sector, and one central union in the country. Since union affiliation is optional, the worker either belongs to the official organization or to no union at all. However, unionized workers receive certain benefits and considerations (e.g., lists for housing and consumer durable goods distribution) that are not granted otherwise; hence, most workers join the union. By the mid-1960s, out of a labor force of 2.5 million, and of 1.9 million state-employed workers (excluding private farmers, the armed forces, police, political executives, etc.) there were some 1.5 million workers unionized, that is, 60 percent of the labor force and almost 80 percent of those allowed to join unions.[14]

Other basic rights such as those of assembly, free speech, voting, and running for office are specifically mentioned in the legislation. The contents and exercise of these rights, however, have to be judged within the framework of a socialist state and the explained role of the unions. The following description of the meetings of the union sections (see below) made by the secretary general of the CTC and the minister of labor, respectively, in a true example of self-criticism are illustrative:

> The meetings of the local union are predominantly meant to activate and inform. They are not devoted to examining and discussing labor matters. There is generally little time between the notice of meeting and the date it is held, which consequently limits the possibility of preparing matters for discussion. . . . The speaker generally talks at great length. He ends with verbal propositions that are approved without discussion—or at most discussed slightly—and *ipso facto* the meeting is dissolved. . . .[15]
>
> At times waiving [of certain benefits such as overtime pay or bonuses] has not been conducted properly, either because meetings have not had a large number of workers, or because the situation has not been well explained. . . . Any worker can stand up at a meeting and state that the attendants must waive such and such benefits. He shouts: "Fatherland or Death!" and everybody agrees.[16]

The structure and relationships at various levels of union organization, which were quite complex under the 1961 law, have been simplified somewhat by the 1966 Union Statutes but still remain complicated. At the local (enterprise) level, there is the "union section" composed of a minimum of fifteen workers. All union sections are integrated into municipal (county), regional, and provincial branches of the CTC. But the union sections are also affiliated with a national union, according to the type of industry or economic branch to which the enterprise belongs. (There were fourteen national unions in 1966). For example, the union section of a sugar mill will be affiliated with the National Union of Sugar Workers (together with all sections functioning in the 152 sugar mills), but at the same time it will be affiliated at the municipal level with all union sections of different enterprises located in the same county, and so on in the regional and provincial branches (see figure 1).

According to current regulations, the National Congress of the CTC is the body that decides the overall policy and elects the members of the executive bureau, which is actually the directive body of the CTC. The regularity of the congress meetings is not specified by the law; the latest congress was held in mid-1966, and the next one is currently scheduled for the second half of 1972. The National Council's main function is to check the fulfillment of the National Congress's resolutions; it has met regularly every year since 1966. National unions do not have executive functions, but are, rather, dedicated to consultation and study of productive problems. The local sections are expected to implement most objectives discussed above. Sections should hold elections every two years. The CTC is affiliated to the World Federation of Trade Unions (WFTU).

The revenue supporting the CTC and trade unions is generated by a contribution of 1 percent of the affiliated worker's salary. Since 1966, budgetary financing has been the technique used to handle the union funds, through an account opened in the National Bank. It is not known whether the general principles of budgetary financing are applied to this fund (i.e., if all revenues go to the state treasury and all expenses are covered by the state budget) or whether the union funds are handled separately.

Collective Bargaining

Beginning in 1934, a steady development of collective bargaining took place in Cuba, although minimum labor conditions (e.g., eight-hour workday) were regulated by law. The collective contract was a means to regulate labor conditions above the minimum stipulated by the law through direct negotiation between the union and the employer. At the beginning of the 1960s, the International Labour Office (ILO) estimated that collective bargaining in Cuba had reached one of the highest levels of development in Latin America.

During 1959, collective agreements reached record proportions. Most of the existing agreements were subject to negotiation, and firms that previously had no agreements were faced with demands from their employees, who felt encouraged by the government. Many of the problems that arose were resolved within the framework of collective bargaining. However, in other situations, when agreements were not reached, the intervention of officials from the Ministry of Labor was required and a backlog of cases developed within the ministry. In December 1959, collective bargaining activities were suspended by the government alleging

FIG. 1
UNION STRUCTURE IN CUBA: 1966

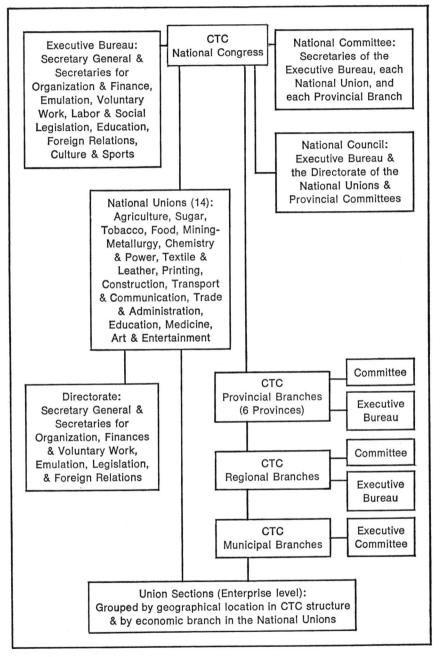

From "Estatuto de la CTC," *El Mundo,* July 6, 1966, p. 6. In 1971, important changes took place in this structure.

that the procedures were excessively time-consuming and were resulting in the accumulation of a large number of cases that only served to make settlements more difficult to achieve.[17] Although the suspension was decreed for a period of 120 days, in actuality, the traditional process of collective bargaining ceased completely at this time.

Between 1960 and 1962, three organic laws of the Ministry of Labor and three laws of labor procedures were enacted. Each of these laws was more restrictive than its precedent in allowing direct collective bargaining between the union and management of the enterprises. These laws facilitated the gradual assumption by the government of the function of regulating labor conditions. By mid-1962, the majority of enterprises had been collectivized and were subject to centralized planning. Hence, the Ministry of Labor was empowered to determine wages, work schedules, and other labor conditions, as well as to suspend or revoke any collective agreement that, in the ministry's opinion, was against government regulations.[18]

In September 1962, the National Council of the CTC met. On this occasion, the Minister of Labor publicized the new orientations for collective bargaining following the socialist pattern:

> Under capitalism, where the means of production are the capitalists' property and workers are compelled to sell their labor force in order to survive, collective bargaining reflects the irreconcilable positions of capital and labor. When a socialist revolution takes place, the working class assumes the reins of power and the means of production, thereby liquidating the exploitation of man by man. Under these conditions, collective agreements take on a new significance and content. The bargaining of collective agreements turns into an important measure addressed to guarantee the fulfillment and surpassing of production plans, the increase in labor productivity, the improvement of labor organization. It is also addressed to increase the responsibility of government agencies and unions on the improvement of the material living and cultural conditions of workers.
>
> The Ministry of Labor has designed a model collective agreement which is to serve as the basis for the beginning of a mass collective-bargaining campaign in each enterprise throughout the country. These collective discussions are to be accompanied by a revolutionary enthusiasm on the part of the workers such as will demand that the union and the enterprises accept those obligations which are designed to surpass the economic plans.[19]

After the meeting, a model collective agreement, as well as instructions on how to discuss and approve it, was issued by the Ministry of Labor.[20]

This document followed closely the 1947 Soviet regulations on collective bargaining. The statements of the minister of labor made during the CTC meeting became part of the preamble of the document. The model contract was studied by the workers and, in special assemblies held in November, they gave their approval.

The Cuban model of collective agreement is similar in composition and content to its Soviet counterpart. It starts with an introduction in which the general political tasks of the Revolution are exposed, together with the general economic tasks that the party and the government set for that particular sector of the national economy. The core of the contract covers the following points: (a) obligations of the enterprise administration and the national union on the fulfillment and surpassing of the production plan and on the development of socialist emulation, (b) wages and work quotas, (c) preparation and increase of workers' qualifications, (d) work discipline, (e) work protection, (f) housing conditions, (g) cultural and sports activities, and (h) control measures and the term of agreement (one year).[21]

In spite of the fact that one section of the collective contract deals with wages and work quotas, in fact, these are centrally fixed by the planning apparatus, as will be explained later. The contract actually aims at the implementation of the wage scales as well as the fulfillment and overfulfillment of the work quotas, as Ernesto Guevara stressed in 1963: "Each work quota has to be bound together with the consciousness that it is a social duty and not a minimum level with which the agreement between the enterprise and the union is fulfilled. This contract does not exist, because enterprise and workers are not different, and ownership is only one."[22]

Labor Conflicts

Prior to 1959, labor conflicts were solved in Cuba through tripartite (unions, management, and goverment) Commissions of Conciliation and Arbitration. Workers have been granted the right to strike since 1934. During the six years from 1959 through the beginning of 1965, five laws were enacted for regulating labor conflicts and their procedures.[23] Rapid changes took place as the government found that the regulations in effect were no longer suitable for its purposes. More effective government control was apparent throughout this period. The last of the five laws, *Ley de Justicia Laboral,* enacted in 1964, came into effect on January 1, 1965.[24]

In accordance with the socialist system, which was fully established by this time, collective conflicts (e.g., strikes) simply could not exist and, therefore, the 1965 law did not even mention them. This was a logical consequence of the theoretical premise that the workers are the owners of the means of production and, therefore, cannot strike against themselves and the whole people, who are represented by the government. In fact, the right to strike was mentioned only in the regulations in force through 1960. Already in June 1961, Ernesto Guevara said, "The Cuban workers have to get used to living in a collectivistic regime and therefore, cannot strike."[25] In a similar fashion, Blas Roca made the following statement: "Before, a sector could call a strike . . . now such a procedure is not permissible. The problem is not solved by strikes but by production, by an increase of production."[26]

In 1961–1964, the primary bodies to hear individual conflicts induced by workers' claims (e.g., alleged violations by the administration of regulations on wages, transfers, discharge) were the so-called Grievance Commissions (*Comisiones de Reclamaciones*). These commissions handled the conflict at the enterprise level, although the Ministry of Labor reserved to itself the final decision. In 1963, the commissions were criticized by government officials. Minister of Industries Guevara stated: "The grievance commissions are a barrier creating contradictions, . . . [they] will be able to accomplish a very useful task only provided that they change their attitude. Production is the fundamental task."[27] Later, Premier Castro charged, "Many members of the grievance commissions seem to be on the side of absenteeism and vagrancy."[28] It seems, therefore, that in spite of their limited power, some grievance commissions were backing the plaintiff's point of view vis-à-vis the administration at the cost of undermining the manager's authority and increasing enterprise costs.

When the 1965 law was enacted, Minister of Labor Augusto Martínez Sánchez made it clear that one of the reasons to abrogate the then existing system was its permissiveness and he explained how this problem would be corrected:

> The law will correct the mistakes and weaknesses of the former bodies of labor justice . . . but not by the way of forgiveness. . . . The new law will strengthen labor discipline and will increase production and productivity . . . [it will be applied to] that kind of worker who is a residue of the exploiting society . . . who is still found in working places as a residue of capitalism. . . . We have to admit that in the working places there are still undisciplined workers and for them we have to have discipline measures. . . . We still find workers who have not taken a revolutionary step and tend to discuss and protest any measure coming from the administration.[29]

Violations of labor discipline penalized by the law include, among others: tardiness, absenteeism, disobedience, negligence, lack of respect to superiors (back talk), physical offenses, damage to the equipment, fraud, and robbery. Sanctions regulated by the law have increasing severity according to the seriousness of the offense: admonition, loss of honors granted for meritorious work, disqualification from occupying certain posts, wage deductions (up to 25 percent for a maximum of four months), postponement of vacations (for a maximum of four months), transfer to another job, temporary discharge for a month, and definite discharge.

Labor Councils (*Consejos de Trabajo*) introduced by the law deal with these violations in the first instance. The councils are established within all enterprises and are composed of five members elected by the workers. Requirements specified by the law for council members are to have a socialist attitude toward work, to be disciplined, and to have a good record showing no faults for absenteeism. (Each worker in Cuba has to have an identification labor card with his occupational record, e.g., merits such as voluntary work and demerits such as absenteeism.) Besides the local councils, there are two superior bodies that hear cases in appeal: the Regional Appeal Commissions (composed of three persons, representing, respectively, the Ministry of Labor, state management, and the unions), which constitutes the second instance; and the National Revision Commission (composed of two representatives of the Ministry of Labor, two from state management, and one from the CTC), which constitutes the supreme appeal or third instance.

According to the law, the manager of the enterprise has power to impose disciplinary measures directly (such as wage deductions, postponement of vacations, transfers, and temporary discharge) without the intervention of the councils. In exceptional cases, the sanction of definitive discharge may be applied also by the manager without any right of the worker to appeal. Zeitlin, however, has reported that in practice the authority to fire does not reside in the administration and that even the decision to transfer a worker (the most typical one, according to Zeitlin) requires the approval of the union, the party cell, and the Ministry of Labor, and, hence, it is rare that the offense is punished with a transfer. Zeitlin's comment was based on isolated observation in only seven plants in Cuba and, hence, has a limited value.[30]

The law empowered the Ministry of Labor (a) to dismiss and change members of the council, (b) to recall a case being heard by a council (or commission) and solve it without any further right to appeal, and (c) to annul a decision of a council or commission, also without further right to appeal. In mid-1966, a decree of the Ministry of Labor ordered a national restructuring of the Labor Councils. Members of the councils were elected in January 1965 for a three-year period, but the decree explained that many such members "had been promoted to administrative and trade-union positions" and that these vacant posts had to be filled. The restructuring was made under the direction of the Ministry of Labor and aided by the unions.[31] New elections for members of the councils were reported in 1971.

In view of the qualifications required to be a member of the Labor Councils, the composition of the Regional Appeal Commissions and the National Revision Commission (in which the combined number of representatives from the Ministry of Labor and state management is in the majority), and the broad powers given to the Ministry of Labor by the law, it seems that government control on the matter of labor discipline and conflicts is quite strong.

In a national meeting on labor procedure held in August 1969, Minister of Labor Jorge Risquet explained that some legal sanctions, such as wage deductions and temporary discharge, were obsolete because their effects were contradictory to revolutionary objectives. For example, penalties on salaries stress a material factor in opposition to Cuba's attempt to develop a "New Man" not motivated by this type of incentive or disincentive. Temporary discharge, on the other hand, led the fired worker to the worst of evils being attacked by the regime, that is, vagrancy. Thus, the minister exhorted the Labor Councils not to apply that type of legal sanction and instructed them on the implementation of other sanctions, such as transfers, suspensions of vacations, and definite discharge. The latter, for instance, should be applied as a transfer to another job, "taking into account both the manpower needs of the region and the worker's physical fitness and skills." The Ministry of Labor should see that the place where the sanctioned worker goes is no better than the place he left. The time that is lost in absences should be deducted from paid vacations. Risquet said that reeducation instead of penalties should be the best tool to eliminate "antisocial" behavior and announced that the 1965 law would soon be replaced by new legislation.[32]

The apparent cause of this shift seems to be the failure of the previous system in coping with increasing absenteeism, diminution of labor effort, and negligence. As shown in table 1, these violations of labor discipline constituted 58 percent of the total number of conflicts that went to appeal in 1969. Minister Risquet indicated three main causes for this phenomenon: (a) the absorption by the state sector of hundreds of thousands of workers who were previously employed in the private sector, workers still influenced by "capitalist values and attitudes"; (b) the annual incorporation into the labor force of thousands of youngsters and females who need to acquire work habits and discipline; and (c) the negligence and permis-

TABLE 1
LABOR CONFLICTS IN CUBA

A. *Cases That Go to Appeal: 1967–1969*

Years	Labor Councils	Regional Appeal Commissions	National Revision Commission	Percentage
1967	—	5,077	1,469	28.9%
1968	—	4,040	1,206	29.8
1969[a]	—	3,406	742	21.7

B. *Ratio of Workers to Cases That Go to Regional Appeal: 1969*

Economic Sectors	Number of Workers in Each Sector to One Case That Goes to Appeal
Transportation	181
Public health	188
Basic industry	224
Food industry	233
Tourist industry	235
Light industry	254
National	550

C. *Cases That Go to Appeal by Cause of Conflict: 1969*

Cause of Conflict	Number of Cases	Percentage
Wage disputes	375	11%
Absenteeism Negligence Disobedience	1,975	58
Physical offenses Damage to equipment Fraud and robbery	1,056	31
Total	3,406	100%

Source: "En la clausura de la Plenaria Nacional de Justicia Laboral," *Granma Revista Semanal*, August 17, 1969, p. 2.

Note: State sector only.

a. Year projection based on the figure of 1,703 and 371 cases respectively for the first half of 1969.

siveness of some managers who do not request from their subordinates (the workers) "with maximum rigor" the "strict fulfillment of their labor duties."[33] Another cause not directly referred to by the minister is the declining importance of money in a situation of extreme scarcity of consumer goods, as is the case of today's Cuba. This factor has been acknowledged as a cause of absenteeism in a report released by the party in late 1969. The report states, "Every worker knows that he can live on what he is paid for working 15 or 20 days a month," and, thus, he stays at home the rest of the month. Such measures as wage deductions or temporary discharge cannot solve the problem. The report also recommends the use of educational tools and stricter managerial supervision as the only ways to correct the situation.[34] The instructions given by Minister Risquet to the Labor Councils should be interpreted in light of this situation. An absentee worker would certainly fear a transfer to the sugar fields much more than a discount in his wage or a temporary discharge.

Official statistics on the number of labor conflicts, shown in table 1, do not include data on the cases heard by the local Labor Councils (which would be the most significant), but only on those heard on appeal. According to these figures, in 1967–1969, the number of conflicts that went on appeal declined by 34 percent in the second instance and by 50 percent in the third instance. The proportion of cases that went from the first to the second instance is not known, but the proportion of cases that went from the second to the third instance was 29 percent in 1967–1968, declining to 22 percent in 1969. It is quite difficult to make an accurate evaluation of these changes based on such incomplete data. However, the decline of cases could be the result of several factors including (a) a sharp decline in wage claims, (b) an increase of "consciousness" on the part of the workers, or (c) an increased control of the government over the procedures and bodies dealing with labor conflicts.

Perhaps the most significant aspect of the data presented in table 1 pertains to the ratio of the number of workers to conflicts that go to appeal. Again, although caution should be exerted in making conclusions based on such incomplete data, the table indicates that the ratio in sectors such as transportation and public health triplicates the national ratio, whereas the ratio in sectors such as basic, light, food, and tourist industries duplicates the national ratio. Minister Risquet did not offer any explanation for this phenomenon but announced that a study will be conducted to determine its causes. It should be noted, however, that the sectors that today show a higher frequency of labor conflicts are those which were among the best organized prior to 1959—sectors in which unions enjoyed more power and, hence, in which collective bargaining was strong, allowing for exceptional benefits.

Work Quotas and Wage Scales

Prior to the Revolution, minimum wages at national, regional, local, and occupational levels, were primarily fixed by the National Commission of Minimum Wages. This was a public body composed of representatives of the workers, the employers, and the government, and its decisions were binding. Over the minimum rates, collective agreements were negotiated for higher wages in the various enterprises and occupations.

During the first two years of the Revolution, significant wage increases were obtained by groups of workers through collective bargaining. However, in March 1960, the National Commission of Minimum Wages was dissolved and the power to determine wages was basically entrusted to the Ministry of Labor. Almost at the same time, a movement among trade unions aimed at restraining wage increases was initiated. The National Union of Sugar Workers was the first to support a wage freeze and other sectors followed. This move to stop demands for wage increases was paired with another coming from most white-collar employees of large enterprises requesting a "waiver" of certain wage privileges, which, in practice, meant a reduction of income. These white-collar workers had been enjoying comparatively higher wages and fringe benefits. As the government began seizing the enterprises they worked for, these employees were induced to make sacrifices for the sake of the Revolution. The practice finally reached the agricultural sugar workers, who also gave up part of their remuneration.[35] Although this policy's immediate goal was to curb inflation, it was also aimed, in the long run, to induce a new pattern in the wage structure: government-fixed wage scales, typical of centrally planned economies.

According to orthodox socialist theory, the establishment of wage scales eliminates the "capitalist wage anarchy," consisting of paying different wages to workers performing the same task, though employed in different enterprises of varying productivity and profitability. In a socialist country— at least in theory—all enterprises are state owned and the benefits of productivity and profitability should be shared collectively by all the workers and not only by a privileged few. The theory, however, has many unorthodox variations as in the case of Yugoslavia, which has a well-developed system of wages connected with varying enterprise profits.

The system of uniform, centrally determined wage scales eliminates all wage differences among workers performing the same job in different state enterprises. The Cuban official statements quoted below follow the orthodox line of thought:[36]

> The anarchic state of worker's salaries and wages (the capitalist system left us 90,000 different types of wages and 25,000 classifications) is an obstacle to the proper organization of labor and is contrary to the socialist principle demanding that each individual be paid according to his work. . . .[37]
>
> [From now on], worker, you are going to earn according to

your capacity, according to your work, and not depending on the profit of this or that enterprise, because . . . all of these enterprises are already yours, they belong to the people, and all workers must be equally evaluated.[38]

Preliminary studies to establish wage scales in Cuba were conducted during 1962 and the early months of 1963. These studies were made with the assistance of several Soviet technicians as well as skilled Cubans trained in the USSR. At the end of April 1963, Castro announced the immediate establishment of wage scales and several weeks after, on May 15, the minister of labor disclosed a pilot plan to be immediately implemented as the initial step.[39] The system was established throughout the country by the end of 1965, in spite of the reservations that Guevara had in 1962, "The wage scale will provide the solution to the problem of wages within ten years; we estimate that in less than that time it will be very difficult to achieve."[40]

Together with wage scales, and because of their interrelationship, a system of work quotas, labor norms, or output standards was also put into effect. Work quotas specify how many items of a given quality a worker must produce in a given work schedule (quantity norm) or within how much time a worker must produce an item of standard quality in a given work schedule (time norm).[41] In this way, a worker must fulfill the individual work quota corresponding to his job in order to draw the corresponding wage rate from his scale. As explained in chapter 7, the system of work quotas is centrally determined and is an important tool for achieving balance between the amount of work done, the income of the workers, and their consumption. Work quotas are also instrumental in attaining the socialist goal of equal payment for equal work because they standardize work measurements at a national level.

Early studies to implement the system of work quotas in Cuba began in 1962 and a pilot plan was tested in 1963. The Ministry of Labor designed the methodology and controlled the national system, while the central ministries and agencies helped in the fixing of the quotas, their implementation, and revision. In 1964 the system was introduced and a thorough check was done in 1965.[42] By late 1969, however, there were still serious difficulties, particularly in the agricultural sector. By this time, due to the absence of uniform methods and the excessive reliance on the arbitrary criteria of the administration in each region for setting the quotas, workers doing the same type of job (under the same labor conditions) but in enterprises or farms located in different places, had divergent labor norms: "The linking between the norm and wages and its arbitrary application cause serious problems with workers. Moreover, the low technical level of many of our cadres [officials setting and administering the system] contributes to making the application of agricultural norms not as just as should be."[43]

Although complete and detailed data are not available concerning the Cuban wage-scale system, it is possible to describe the system to a certain extent from piecemeal information. We will discuss various aspects such as the occupational sectors, the various wage scales, and the additional income of the workers, as well as the basic wage-scale rate and the problem of income differentials.

Workers in the state sector (private workers are excluded from the system) are grouped in four major occupational sectors for wage-scale purposes: agricultural workers, nonagricultural workers, administrative employees, and technicians and executive personnel. A worker in one of the first two groups could be either unskilled, semiskilled, or skilled, for example, a peon, cane cutter, tractor operator, factory operator, ditch-digger, truck driver, etc., but not a technician. Administrative employees include bookkeepers, typists, stenographers, and other clerical employees. Technicians are professionals working in technological, economic, socio-logical, agrarian, industrial, educational, legal, or artistic fields. These activities require a college education, or training in a technological school, or creative capabilities applied to literature or art. Examples of specialists in this group are physicians, engineers, architects, scientists, economists, teachers, electricians, refrigeration experts, mechanics, writers, musicians, and painters. An executive is anyone who plans, organizes, directs, or coordinates under his own responsibility, or within the limits of functions received, the activities of government bodies such as ministries, combines, *agrupaciones, consolidados,* enterprises, farms, unions, mass organizations, etc. Included here are government officials, planners, party activists, enter-prise managers, trade union leaders, etc. It is interesting to note that per-sons from the four groups may coincide within a single enterprise.[44]

There are four types of wage scales applicable to the occupational sectors described above. In the scales for workers (both agricultural and nonagricultural), wage rates are measured by the hour, whereas in the other two scales, rates are computed by the month. To allow comparisons, in table 2 the first two scales have been recomputed on the basis of a monthly wage. After this computation, it is evident that scales II and III (nonagricultural workers and administrative employees) are alike, thus they have been clustered in table 2. Wage scale IV is an estimate based on recent information on the highest annual wage paid in Cuba by 1968 to highly specialized technicians (about $10,000 a year), the wage paid to ministers of the government ($8,400 a year), and the methodology used elsewhere by Carmelo Mesa-Lago.[45]

TABLE 2
WAGE SCALES IN CUBA
(*In Pesos per Month*)

Grades	Scale I: Agricultural Workers		Scales II and III: Nonagricultural Workers and Administrative Employees		Scale IV: Technical and Executive Personnel	
	Coef.	*Rate*	*Coef.*	*Rate*	*Coef.*	*Rate*
1	1.00	64	1.00	85	1.00	272
2	1.13	72	1.16	99	1.16	316
3	1.30	83	1.35	115	1.35	368
4	1.51	97	1.58	134	1.58	430
5	1.75	112	1.85	157	1.85	504
6	2.05	131	2.18	185	2.18	594
7	2.40	154	2.57	218	2.57	700
8	—	—	3.10	264	3.10	844

Sources: For scale I, Israel Talavera and Juan Herrera, "La organización del trabajo y el salario en la agricultura," *Cuba Socialista*, 5 (May–June 1965), p. 70. For scales II and III, "Bases para la organización de los salarios y sueldos de los trabajadores," *Suplemento de la Revista Trabajo* (June 10, 1963), p. 10. For scale IV, estimates based on the methodology explained in Carmelo Mesa-Lago, *The Labor Sector and Socialist Distribution in Cuba* (New York, 1968), pp. 100–02, and explanations in the text.
Note: Rounded figures.

Within each scale there are seven or eight grades. These grades are determined by the degrees of complexity and precision of the job and, therefore, the skill required by the worker. The higher the grade, the more skill required by the job and the higher the wage to be paid. The relationship of each grade to the lowest in the scale is indicated by a coefficient.

By the end of 1963, the employed labor force was distributed among the various occupational sectors and wage scales as follows: (I) 41.9 percent were agricultural workers; (II) 42.6 percent were nonagricultural workers; (III) 10.7 percent were administrative employees; and (IV) 4.8 percent were technicians and executives. Information on the percentage distribution by wage *rate* within each scale is not available except for scale II. In this scale, 83 percent of the workers fell into the four lowest grades, that is, the worst paid, and the percentage of workers in the highest grades, or the best paid, was only 0.7 percent.[46] Commenting on this, Guevara stated in 1963: "The skills of our workers run so low, and, in general, such broad experience is necessary to reach the last levels or higher grades, that we can assume that it will take many years . . . before this situation is improved."[47]

There are four factors that introduce variations to the wages of workers falling under the same occupational sector and wage grade. These are labor conditions under which the work is performed, overfulfillment and nonfulfillment of work quotas, payments for overtime, and the survival of "historical" wages.

Wage rates for those performing their jobs under harmful conditions are increased by 20 percent, and for those laboring under extremely arduous or dangerous conditions, by 35 percent. According to the information available, these benefits apparently are not applicable to agricultural laborers.[48]

As explained before, there is a close relationship between wage scales and work quotas. A worker must fulfill his quota in order to be able to receive his full wages. The theory is that when a worker fails to fulfill the quota, his wage should be reduced in proportion to his nonfulfillment.[49] However, this criterion is not applied equally when the worker overfulfills the quota. At the time the system was established, a worker surpassing his work quota was to receive a wage bonus equivalent to only 50 percent of the overfulfillment. In addition, his basic wage combined with the bonus could not be higher than that of the wage rate for the next grade. The reason given by the Minister of Labor was that material incentives should neither undermine the workers' urge to increase his skills nor be more important than moral incentives in order to raise the consciousness of the working class.[50] As the official attitude toward material incentives became more and more negative, the approach toward bonuses for overfulfillment also changed. Between the end of 1967 and the end of 1969 it was publicly announced that overfulfillment bonuses as well as overtime payments were in the process of disappearing.[51] By 1970, bonuses had been completely eliminated.

Another factor that contributes to variations in wages is the so-called "historical" wage, that is, the difference resulting between the wage a worker received before wage scales were established and the new remuneration assigned to the same worker by the corresponding wage grade. As previously explained, in the early 1960s a campaign was initiated to encourage highly remunerated workers to give up part of their benefits in order to facilitate the establishment of the scales. However, the pressures exerted by the government were not entirely successful and Ernesto Guevara himself accepted the necessity of temporarily maintaining these higher wages:

> All those workers, whose actual wage is higher than the new average wages to be fixed, will receive their former remuneration in its entirety, but divided into two parts: that corresponding

to his true effort [as per wage scale], and as a gift the excess
wage maintained. This is done to show clearly that there is a
part of the wage given to him because of historical antecedents,
but . . . not because he is really entitled to it through his labor.[52]

This obstacle was possibly what made Guevara estimate that it would take
ten years for a full implementation of the wage scales, that is, to cut the
appendage of the historical wage. Originally, there was a plan to eliminate
such an appendage gradually by the normal process of retirement, promotion, and transfers. When a job was left vacant, the worker hired to the
post received just the wage established by the scale, without the additional
historical wage. However, the campaign of 1967–1969 against bonuses
and overtime pay has greatly accelerated the process of eliminating this
historical wage.

Let us now discuss wage and income differences. In 1963–1965, Cubans
closely followed the Soviet model in the matter of wage scales. This model
emphasized wage differences both in scales and grades, together with
bonuses for overfulfillment as economic incentives to increase national
production and workers' skills. Comparisons made by Carmelo Mesa-Lago
between Cuban and Soviet wage scales in the first half of the 1960s show
that, at that time, wage differences were larger in Cuba than in the USSR.[53]
According to table 2, for each peso earned by an agricultural worker of
the first grade of scale I, a nonagricultural worker of the eighth grade of
scale II earns four pesos. If the comparison is made between the two ex-
tremes of the table, that is, the minimum wage rate of agricultural workers
and the maximum wage rate of technical personnel, the ratio is 1:13.
This refers only to the basic wage without taking other additions into
account. Radoslav Selucky, a Czech economist who visited Cuba in 1964,
criticized the Cuban wage policy, saying that although he rejected egalitarianism, wage differences in Cuba were cruelly large, even in comparison
with the capitalist countries of Western Europe.[54] The reason for having
wider wage differences in Cuba than in the USSR, Czechoslovakia, or
East Germany, for example, could be that Cuba has a lower level of development and technology. It seems that the more industrialized a country
is (be it socialist or capitalist), the narrower its wage differences become.

However, Zeitlin has reported that in the summer of 1969, wage differences in two big Cuban plants—the textile factory Ariguanabo, and
the sugar mill Venezuela—were small: the lowest rate (for unskilled workers) was around $90 and the highest (for managers) was between $250
and $300. He also indicated that the typical wage of government officials
ranged from $200 to $250. (This could not be the result of the movement

begun in 1966 toward more egalitarianism because in 1969 the wage scale was still in force. Also, Zeitlin was referring to wage rates and not income in general.) Zeitlin apparently did not have an adequate background of the overall system of scales in view of his statement that the "newly established scales [in industry] will soon be extended throughout the occupational structure." Actually, the system of scales was established throughout all economic sectors in 1965, as we have seen. Based on his isolated observations and his inadequate knowledge of the overall system, Zeitlin then concluded: "The practice in Cuba, contrary to that in the Soviet Union, for example, is to keep the gap between the income of production workers, and clerical, administrative and technical personnel narrow. In fact, it may be more accurate to say that *there simply is not a gap along these lines at all, because there is as yet no systematic relationship between occupation and income*" [italics added].[55] In view of the previous discussion on the wage-scale system, the official data presented in table 2, and the comparisons made above, Zeitlin's conclusion seems to be incorrect.

In addition to monetary wages, top-ranking Cuban officials and highly specialized technicians enjoy benefits of various types that are not available to the rest of the population. Concerning these additional benefits, Adolfo Gilly, a South American journalist and sympathizer of the Revolution who was in Cuba in 1964, said, "The bureaucratic sectors exert [a permanent pressure] to increase their share by invisible means—these may be a series of privileges which go with the job or which are added arbitrarily: automobiles, apartments, trips, meals, etc."[56] Zeitlin has also acknowledged privileges such as cars and chauffeurs, as well as expense accounts, but has diminished the importance of housing, resorts, travel, and food.[57] René Dumont, however, after his visit to Cuba in 1969, reported a very large number of officials who owned Alfa Romeos, model 600. He also criticized other privileges of the leadership, as houses at Varadero Beach, luxury offices, and special food vis-à-vis the masses who are subjected to strict rationing.[58] Castro has referred to administrative officials that take advantage of their positions to get priorities in the allocation of extremely scarce housing.[59]

French Marxist Jacquers Valier maintains the thesis that the introduction of wage scales was a step forward in favor of egalitarianism because it reduced the differences in income that existed at the time in Cuba.[60] This thesis has also been supported by Cuban revolutionary officials who, nevertheless, stress that prior to the Revolution wage differences were not as large in Cuba as in most of Latin American due to the development, in Cuba, of organized labor and minimum wage legislation.[61] We generally agree with this thesis, but certain qualifications are necessary.

The only figures available prior to 1959 on Cuba's income distribution were of a very broad nature. One series published by the ILO referred to the percentage of national income paid out in wages, as opposed to the percentage represented by dividends, rent, interest, etc. This series indicated that the proportion of income accruing to the Cuban labor force rose steadily from 1948 to 1958, reaching a level by the latter year that was the fourth highest in the Western Hemisphere.[62] Other figures, released in 1958 by Cuba's National Economic Council, were based on a national sample systematically taken throughout the island between March 1956 and April 1957. Unfortunately, only two income categories were included: 62.2 percent of the labor force earned $75 or more monthly and 37.8 percent earned less than $75.[63] There were no overall statistics on average wages by occupational sectors. Therefore, it is not possible to establish exact comparisons on income distribution before and after 1959.

Yet, it is obvious that income differences existing in 1958 between, for example, a peasant and the best-paid public official, the president of the Republic (not to say the income of a sugar plantation owner, an industrialist, or a big businessman), were incomparably greater than current income differences between, for example, an agricultural peon and a minister of the government or a highly specialized technician. But it is one thing to acknowledge the evident process of income equalization and another to claim that today there is no significant gap between the income of production workers and technical or executive personnel. It is important to note also that in a situation of grave scarcity of essential consumer goods as that existing in Cuba, things such as cars, special food, travel, etc., acquire a very high value in relative terms.

If it is difficult to make comparisons on wage differentials before and after 1959, the situation is no better for the revolutionary period. Table 3 presents a wage index based on the only data on wages available. These are average wages resulting from dividing the wage fund (allocated to each state economic sector) by the number of employed workers in the same sector. It should be noted that because we are dealing here with averages, extreme differences (i.e., between the highest and the lowest wage rates) are not shown as in table 2. The first five columns of table 3 contrast the index of average wages in the various sectors with the national average, which is equal to 100 (or base). The final column of the table shows the percentage increase of the average wages (at current prices) of 1966 over that of 1962. Increases shown in this column may be partly the result of inflation, but the important thing is to establish the relationship of the increases among various sectors.

Since wage scales were introduced in 1963–1964, we should expect the table to show a noticeable change toward wage equalitarianism between 1962 and 1966. Indeed, there are changes, but no dramatic ones. The

TABLE 3
COMPARISON OF INDICES OF AVERAGE WAGES BY STATE ECONOMIC SECTORS IN CUBA: 1962–1966

Economic Sectors	1962	1963	1964	1965	1966	Percentage of Increase: 1966 Over 1962 (in Current Prices)
National Average, State Sector	100.0	100.0	100.0	100.0	100.0	3.5%
Productive Sectors	97.6	97.8	98.0	97.9	98.1	4.0
Agriculture	61.6	59.8	64.0	65.3	66.1	11.0
Sugar	61.4	54.7	63.3	64.4	63.7	7.4
Nonsugar crops	53.6	52.8	53.3	54.1	56.5	8.9
Cattle-raising	77.6	76.8	77.4	79.1	80.5	7.4
Forestry	71.3	73.9	81.4	85.4	70.7	2.6
Fishing	90.5	139.6	135.7	135.0	142.4	62.9
Services	96.9	113.2	119.4	117.3	116.9	24.8
Industry	125.5	127.8	128.3	130.8	128.9	6.3
Mining	129.8	129.3	127.2	126.7	131.4	4.8
Metallurgic & mechanic	123.3	124.6	122.7	122.2	124.9	4.8
Construction materials	103.5	100.3	105.8	113.1	121.5	21.5
Petroleum & derivatives	193.5	175.8	185.9	171.2	175.6	−6.1
Chemistry	125.5	134.8	129.0	127.7	126.7	4.5
Textile and leather	102.3	116.1	114.0	114.5	115.9	17.2
Sugar	148.9	146.4	143.9	150.2	141.8	−1.4
Food	115.8	125.9	125.4	128.1	123.0	9.9
Tobacco and beverages	116.7	126.8	126.6	127.7	127.7	13.2
Electric power	218.3	203.2	203.1	193.0	183.3	−13.1
Others	121.5	121.3	125.8	125.0	124.7	6.3
Construction	109.9	108.8	110.2	110.2	112.6	6.1
Transportation	144.0	142.4	181.5	141.4	145.9	4.9
Air	190.5	192.1	182.4	191.7	203.0	10.3
Maritime	176.1	175.3	172.8	171.7	188.9	11.0
Highway	138.0	136.7	136.0	134.3	136.9	2.7
Railroad	113.9	120.9	119.2	118.5	119.1	8.2
Communications	128.2	128.7	124.3	123.6	121.0	−2.3
Commerce	87.9	89.1	93.3	92.8	93.8	10.4
Domestic wholesale	114.3	113.1	120.5	125.5	106.9	−3.3
Domestic retail	71.9	75.4	79.0	79.1	88.3	27.0
Acopio and supplies	76.1	75.0	83.1	83.1	85.6	16.3
Foreign trade	129.7	129.3	145.7	144.3	138.7	10.7
Gastronomic services	93.3	98.2	102.5	102.3	101.2	12.3
Other Productive Activities	71.8	117.9	116.6	117.7	117.7	69.7
Nonproductive Sectors	110.0	108.6	108.3	108.3	107.5	1.0
Housing & communal services	91.3	89.8	71.9	68.9	58.7	−33.5
Education	108.1	106.1	103.4	103.6	106.9	2.3
Culture	119.2	117.4	119.7	119.5	118.6	3.0
Health & public assistance	105.7	105.0	104.3	105.8	109.3	4.9
Sports & recreation	108.3	106.7	110.3	110.5	106.7	2.0
Science and research	—	135.1	134.2	134.6	149.9	13.7
Administration & finance	118.0	117.7	132.1	131.6	120.4	5.6
Other nonproductive activities	—	—	—	112.9	118.1	—

Source: Based on raw data from JUCEPLAN, *Boletín Estadístico, 1966* (La Habana, n.d.), p. 26, table IV.3.

Note: Arithmetic averages were obtained by dividing the wage fund in each sector by the number of workers in the same sector.

average wage of the lowest paid occupation (nonsugar crops) shows very little improvement, and the same may be said of all agricultural activities. Fishing wages, however, show an astonishing improvement, 10 percent below the national average in 1962 and 42 percent above such average in 1966. Noticeable increases are also registered under "Other Productive Activities," *acopio* (under commerce), services (under agriculture), and construction materials (under industry). On the other hand, there has been a notable decline both in relative and absolute terms of average wages in housing, electric power, petroleum, retail trade, and communications. Extreme wage differences have continued throughout the period. In 1962 the average wages in air transportation, electric power, and petroleum almost quadrupled those in nonsugar crops. In 1966, the difference was somewhat reduced due to the wage decline in electric power and petroleum, but, on the other hand, the gap between average wages in nonsugar crops and air transportation expanded due to the increase in the latter.

A comparison of industrial average wages between Cuba and other Latin American countries prepared by JUCEPLAN in 1966 shows that Cuba had narrower wage differences than Venezuela and Colombia; wage differences similar to Mexico and Peru; and greater wage differences than in Chile and Brazil.[64] In all fairness, however, we should note that if the overall wage structure instead of the industrial average wages had been used in the comparison, Cuba would have been well ahead of all these countries in the matter of wage equalitarianism.

Since 1966, Cuba has accelerated the process of income equalization. This movement has been associated with Castro's decision, made public during the Twelfth National Congress of the CTC, to stress moral stimuli and deemphasize economic incentives. The climax of this movement took place with the Revolutionary Offensive launched by Castro in March 1968. Castro's strategy for the future was announced on July 26, 1968.[65] One characteristic of this strategy is the campaign already mentioned to waive bonuses for overfulfillment of work quotas, overtime pay, and the "historical" wage. Another feature is the gradual increase of social services conferred gratuitously by the state—the so-called social salary or collective consumption as opposed to monetary salary or individual consumption. All education, medical care, preventive vaccination, social security, public telephone calls, and burials, as well as some day-care centers, sports events and a large portion of housing are currently free and relatively equal to the population. Day-care centers are available only to certain persons and housing was available to one-fifth of the population in mid-1970. Castro has promised that in the near future, all housing, recreation, transportation, and public utilities will become free also. In a final step even food and clothing will be free, thus making money and wages unnecessary. In the meantime, Castro hopes to reduce wage differences in a gradual manner: lowest wages and pensions will be gradually increased in proportion to increases in production, while higher wages will be frozen. Ultimately, when the gap is closed, every worker would earn the same amount, whether he is a cane cutter or an engineer.[66]

Most of the steps summarized above have still to be taken. In the meantime, although wage scales continue in force, income differences among the masses are being lessened by the elimination of wage additions and the granting of free services, which operate as income equalizers. Income differences by 1970 are certainly narrower than in 1958. The leadership, however, maintains (at least as of 1970) important privileges in terms of consumer goods and services not available to the population. Unfortunately, no data is available to substantiate some of the previous hypotheses.

Socialist Emulation

The capitalist system is based on private property, individual interest, and competition. In theory, individual interest motivated by the desire for profits and wages promotes public welfare, even if not intentionally. Competition is the invisible hand that coordinates and converts private interest into public interest. Conversely, the socialist system is based on public property, collective interest, and emulation. Marxist-Leninist theory maintains that workers in a socialist state will maximize their efforts because they feel that they are the owners of all resources and the increase in production will be to their own benefit.[67]

Socialist emulation consists of the competition organized among individual workers and groups of workers to select and reward those who stand out according to a set of criteria previously established. The example of the winners (as well as that of workers who have negative attitudes) is presented to the masses, employing publicity as an important instrument to spread the vanguard experience. "Emulation," said Guevara, "is a weapon to increase production and an instrument to elevate the consciousness of the masses."[68]

Cuba began experimenting with emulation in early 1961, first among cane cutters, and, later, within some industries. Guevara, then minister of industries, sponsored the experiment and several sets of instructions were issued in order to regulate and expand it.[69] In 1961, the first national regulatory measures for socialist emulation were enacted, only to be superseded by new sets of regulations in 1963, 1964, and 1966.[70] During this period, two Festivals of Emulation (1962 and 1963) and two National Meetings of Emulation (1964 and 1965) were held. The overall impression received from official documents and self-criticism on the functioning of emulation

in Cuba is that it has been extremely rigid, complicated, formal, and bureaucratic and, hence, has not generated true mass support.[71] In 1967,
during the meetings of the CTC National Council, it was decided to divide
the year into four "emulation periods" and new changes were introduced
in relation to the "movement of vanguard workers." In 1969–1970, the
most important event was the establishment of merits and demerits, which
have to be included in the worker's personal file.

Workers emulate either on an individual or a collective basis. Individual
emulation involves the competition among workers performing a similar
chore in the same enterprise, farm, or field, either at a local, regional, or
national level. An example of the latter competition was the cane cutters
during the sugar crop. Collective emulation, favored by Cuban authorities,
particularly since 1966, takes place between teams of workers (e.g., sections of a factory or brigades in the fields) or among enterprises engaged
in similar productive tasks.

In order to determine the winner in emulation, a complex system of positive and negative indices and points (merits and demerits) has been established. Positive indices include: fulfillment of work quotas, reduction of
costs, improvement of quality, attendance and punctuality, professional
improvement, political education, voluntary work, reduction of occupational accidents, and participation in the militia or other defense activities.
Negative indices include absenteeism, nonfulfillment of work quotas, negligence, etc. Usually, negative indices are weighted more heavily (by sub-
tracting more points) than positive indices.

Control of emulation is exerted mainly by the management of the enterprise, with the help of the union section. Daily, monthly, quarterly, and annual checks are made depending upon the type of index. There was a period in which "contract forms" of emulation were handed to the workers
who made specific commitments in several aspects. These contracts, however, are no longer in effect. Revision meetings held at the enterprise publicly discuss emulation achievements and failures. The emulation plan, at
least until 1966, was prepared by JUCEPLAN, the Ministry of Labor, and
the central ministries under party guidance. A complex apparatus integrated by multiple commissions and councils (at the local, regional, provincial, and national level) composed of trade union, management, and
government representatives implemented and supervised the system.[72]

In the period 1963–1966, awards granted through emulation were primarily of a material nature, such as cash (a percentage of wages), consumer durable goods (e.g., refrigerators, motorcycles, houses, cars), and
vacation trips to Cuban resorts and socialist countries. The system faced
serious difficulties: the number of prizes was very small, hence generating
little incentive; problems with domestic output and delays in imports fre-

quently impeded the granting of durable consumer goods; and a number of workers that were granted trips rejected the award and requested consumer goods (that were not available) instead. Since mid-1966 (when the incentives controversy was apparently settled), practically all material awards were eliminated and emphasis placed on moral rewards. These rewards consist of diplomas, pennants, and flags. The most important awards are granted by the CTC, the Council of Ministers, or the prime minister himself in well-publicized meetings. Honorary titles are also granted, such as "Vanguard Worker," "National Work Hero," or "Heroes of the 1970 Sugar Crop." Diplomas and banners granted are given names of glorious revolutionary dates such as "Moncada Heroes," "May Day" or "July 26th." On the other hand, moral punishments constitute, for example, the selection of the laziest worker (or the least productive) in an enterprise and the exhibition of his name in a visible location.[73]

The movement of "vanguard workers" began in 1965, was regulated in 1967, and received a big push in mid-1969 with the campaign to waive bonuses, overtime pay, and historical wages. At this time, 113,043 workers participated in the movement, but the number rose to 285,000 by the end of 1969 and to 450,000 by mid-1970 or 17 percent of the labor force at that time. Vanguard workers are elected by their fellow workers in each enterprise in public meetings in which the merits of the candidates are discussed. Quarterly checks are made of the performance of selected vanguard workers to decide whether the title should be maintained or withdrawn. Although the award consists of a "moral" title, vanguard workers enjoy certain privileges, such as full payment of their wages when becoming sick, disabled, or retired, and priority in lists to buy scarce goods such as refrigerators, or to obtain transfers in housing.[74]

In mid-1969, Minister of Labor Risquet announced that the government had prepared a draft for the regulation of the "labor file" or identity card of each worker in the nation. Such a file would have a complete record of the worker's merits and demerits. "It will be like the workers' biography," said Risquet.[75] The draft was not discussed by the unions, and nothing else was published about it until it became law in September.[76] Nevertheless, in a meeting held ten months later (in which the CTC's executive bureau, members of the PCC Central Committee, and the minister of labor participated), it was announced that a chance would be given to the workers to discuss what kind of merits and demerits should be included in their own records.[77]

The previous announcement was immediately followed by an intense campaign in all the communications media. In July, it was disclosed that a project had been finally elaborated by the workers. Such a project, published in September, hardly changed the precedent practice of emulation.

Merits to be included in the workers' records are: election as vanguard worker or steward in the union section; participation in the sugar crop, overfulfillment of work quotas, overtime work without pay, or participation in labor mobilization programs; postponement of retirement to continue working; defense of socialist property; inventions, and other contributions to increase productivity; and a high level of political and labor consciousness. Demerits are defined as "activities that negatively affect production, disturb labor discipline, and show a low level of consciousness," and those to be included in the workers' records include absenteeism; negligence in handling equipment, raw materials, and fuel; nonfulfillment of work quotas; abandonment of the work in the enterprise without previous authorization; and desertion from labor camps (as during the sugar crop) before completing the term to which the worker has committed himself. The "labor file" will also register any sanction applied to the worker by Labor Councils, People's Courts, Revolutionary Tribunals, or Civil Courts.[78]

Workers' Participation in Decision-making and Regulating Labor Conditions

Theoretically, in a socialist country such as Cuba, the political power resides in the proletariat which is guided by the party. The proletariat, in turn, is composed of the vanguard or best representation of the working class. Data discussed in chapter 1 indicates that the participation of workers in the PCC is minimal. In this section, we will deal with the workers' participation in the decision-making process and in determining their own labor conditions, as well as with the workers' reaction to the government's direct fixing of wages and work quotas.

When central planning was about to be introduced in Cuba, Carlos Rafael Rodríguez assured that "each worker, each member of a farm will have an opportunity of expressing his opinion and directly intervening in national planning."[79] This opportunity arises when production plans prepared by central planners and the central ministries descend to the enterprise level in a process of disaggregation (see chapter 7). At that level, production meetings, organized by the union section and oriented by the party cell, should give to the workers a chance for "direct intervention" in planning.

However, according to Gilly's observations in 1964, the plan is viewed by the workers as a program that the leadership prepares "in discussion behind closed doors" and in which the masses participate only in "a formal and limited way." Because the plan appears to the workers as "a complete abstraction," they "show little interest in discussing it." Furthermore, workers "can discuss how much they will produce at such-and-such cost, but that kind of discussion certainly does not appeal to them. They feel they are learning absolutely nothing and have been asked to decide on nothing of any importance: they have been called to a purely schematic consultation paternalistically designed to arouse their interest." As a consequence, the masses "have no means of correcting the plan while it is being applied or for pointing out errors which have come to light."[80]

The former secretary general of the CTC, Miguel Martín, stated in 1966 in his official report to the Twelfth National Congress of that body: "Production meetings have been transformed into meetings where cold figures are released by officials without any participation or lively discussion among the workers. . . . The labor mass is becoming more and more separated from the solution of problems." Martín asserted that the workers' opinion was not heard and that bureaucrats and organizations assumed they had the right to think for the masses.[81] Four years later, the situation did not seem to have improved, according to the following statement signed by the CTC's executive bureau and the minister of labor, "[It is] frequent to hold production meetings at the enterprises in which arbitrary production targets are set without the real participation of the workers and in the absence of serious analysis of the requisites needed to fulfill such targets as manpower resources, raw material supply and the condition of the equipment and tools."[82]

It seems obvious that if the workers do not have a real chance to determine or modify production targets at the enterprise level, the less opportunity they will have to intervene directly in the actual formulation of the plan at the top level. After his visit to Cuba in 1969, Zeitlin commented on this topic:

> At present, despite the apparently ample participation of the workers in discussions and decisions concerning the *implementation* of the national economic plan set for their plant, the workers have no role whatsoever, to my knowledge, in determining the plan itself. They have nothing to say about investment priorities; the decision as to what and how much is to be produced is made by the central planning bodies of the Revolutionary Government responsible to the Council of Ministers.[83]

It could be argued that workers do not have the necessary knowledge to make decisions on technical matters such as the investment coefficient, selection of investment projects, or even aggregate targets of production. However, what about something more specific, such as the plan of manpower and wages? A government technician writing in the journal of the

Ministry of Industries, Fernando González, criticized in 1967 "the little or no participation that [managers and workers] at the enterprise level have in the preparation of the plan of labor and wages." González claimed that workers and local managers have concrete knowledge of the enterprise's real capabilities and needs, and because they were not consulted, such knowledge was wasted with a negative effect on the plan's accuracy and validity.[84]

As we have seen, work quotas and wage scales are centrally fixed by planners and central ministries. In view of the lack of precise data, it is impossible to determine in an accurate way the overall reaction of the working class to these measures. But scattered information suggests that resistance has been common, at least among a significant number of workers as to induce a public reaction from the government. The following statements cast doubt on the theory that Cuban workers feel that their interests are represented by the government. Furthermore, when confronted with a conflict between the claims of a sizable number of workers and a government decision, the local unions have occasionally sided with the workers, but the top hierarchy of the CTC has systematically backed the government.

Former Minister of Labor Martínez Sánchez said in 1963: "In the enterprise, there were workers who reacted in opposition to the work quotas. They said that the quota was high and that they were unable to fulfill it. This type of difficulty will always be present, because not everybody likes to be forcibly compelled."[85] An official publication of the Ministry of Labor acknowledged that in many enterprises work quotas had failed because they had been imposed without giving the workers an opportunity to express their point of view: "We asked the workers, and none of them knew what quotas were in force. Aren't we obliged to tell [the worker] in a meeting what is expected of him, and ask him for his views and approval?"[86] The late Che Guevara said in 1963 when he was the minister of industries: "At the beginning we encountered some difficulties. . . . The workers were not always in accord with the quotas set, and other times the local trade union gave in to the demands of the workers."[87] The minister of labor elaborated on the poor cooperation of the trade unions:

> The establishment of the system of work quotas has brought to light the deficient work of the local trade unions, which do not yet understand the importance of production, and balk when confronted with any organizational measure that may change the old working habits, remnants of capitalism. In many work centers, the local trade unions have not met the establishment of the quotas with the necessary revolutionary zeal.[88]

The secretary general of the CTC had previously acknowledged cases where certain workers believed work quotas to be high and that some local unions agreed with them. In view of this, he exhorted the workers to accept the system of quotas with "vivid interest and enthusiasm," and added, "In the name of the CTC, we recommend to all the workers, union leaders, to all levels, that they do not give in to the tendency to judge the work quotas as high."[89]

Three years later, in 1966, apparently there were workers that had not been convinced as yet. During a public speech, Premier Castro was interrupted by the audience requesting a reduction in the work quotas. Castro answered: "If we are going to win the economic battle, we cannot request the reduction of the quotas. . . . All, absolutely all must increase our physical effort so as to increase production and productivity."[90]

The same story repeated itself in the matter of wage scales. In late 1963, the minister of labor criticized local unions that had not given total cooperation to this plan, "Some have come to consider the plan not as a goal of the Revolution, but as a measure adopted by a Ministry."[91] The secretary general of the CTC answered this by explaining what the situation was among those whose wages were threatened by the new wage scales:

> Certain workers believe that their jobs have not been classified correctly or that they should be placed in a higher wage grade. We know that under capitalism there were individuals of very low skill working in profitable enterprises who received high wages. . . . This is an occurrence that has now been challenged and we must now go against the force of custom and habit.[92]

According to theory, socialist emulation should be a spontaneous movement developed from the rank and file. As was previously mentioned, the regulations of socialist emulation have been changed four times. On every occasion the official reason for the change given by the government has been the lack of enthusiasm from the workers who were compelled to accept a series of rules imposed from above. Criticizing the shortcomings of the first set of regulations, the minister of labor said: "It must be realized that in our country socialist emulation has not yet acquired its real meaning. The principal reason is that the working masses have not directly participated in emulation. This is why it has had a bureacratic character. We share in the blame for these errors."[93]

Similar criticisms were made in order to justify the abrogation of the second set of regulations. But after the third set was put into effect, the late César Escalante, a high member of the party, found out after conducting an investigation that workers still did not participate in the organization of emulation and, even worse, there were very few who actually emulated. He criticized such provisions saying, "The masses are not given a chance to express their opinions, to participate in discussions . . . workers have to remain silent and just say, 'All right, I agree,' and that's the end of that."[94]

After the fourth version of rules on emulation was published, problems seemed to persist. By mid-1966 the minister of labor admitted that they had not "yet been able to infuse into socialist emulation the movement of masses it requires . . . all formal or administrative concepts of same must be discarded."[95]

The best summary of the true role of the unions and workers in the process of decision-making in Cuba was given in 1969 by PCC Secretary of Organization Hart: "It is not a question of discussing all administrative decisions [with the workers]. The thing is that the enthusiasm of the workers must be obtained to support the principal measures of the administration."[96]

Conclusions

Let us now summarize our findings. Again, we must state that most of the following conclusions are tentative, but the evidence accumulated in this essay allows us to at least do this. According to socialist theory and practice, trade unions and collective bargaining in Cuba have changed their traditional role and objective of defense and regulation of the immediate interests of the workers (or better said, of groups of workers) to assume the role of defenders of collective national interests concretized around production and productivity. The benefits of national output are allocated and distributed by the leadership, following its criteria of what is better for the workers and the nation as a whole in the long run.

The channels for workers' and unions' regulation of labor conditions and conflicts have been gradually closed as the government has been increasingly reassuming its direct control over these matters. Work quotas and wage scales are part of the overall system of central palnning, of reward and punishment, of equilibrium between production and consumption. Indeed, they are tools for equalization, but also for control.

The potential disagreement and possibility of resistance of some groups of workers to these decisions and methods seems to be obstructed by the strict regimen of labor discipline, and if it becomes manifested, it is publicly criticized by the leadership. The worker's behavior is recorded in a labor file (which contains his merits and demerits), which is needed to obtain employment. Local unions that occasionally have sided with the workers have been admonished or disowned by the top union hierarchy, which, according to scattered evidence, seems to support the government in all its decisions. Socialist emulation reinforces the system by appraising and presenting as a model those workers who perform according to the established criteria, and by exerting pressure over those workers who do not comply with targets and expected attitudes, exposing them to public criticism.

Workers do not intervene effectively in planning or in the fixing of wage scales and work quotas. Emulation has been, at least up to 1966, formal and bureaucratic and does not stir up enough mass fervor and support. The whole system of targets-reward-stimuli is imposed from above with little or no chance for the workers to shape it or even voice their opinions about it.

And yet, the participation of workers in the decision-making process should be unavoidable for ideological, ethical, and pragmatic reasons:

1. Ideologically, the socialist state is the dictatorship of the proletariat and, therefore, workers should be in control of the decision-making process. Even if it is accepted that most workers do not have the necessary knowledge and expertise to intervene in technical decisions, some degree of proletariat participation should be allowed if the Marxist objective of withering away the state is ever to be accomplished. Yugoslavian Workers Councils, in spite of all difficulties, are a good trial in this direction. Cuban Labor Councils do not have voice in any significant matter of administration, planning, or distribution, and even their functions as judges of labor conflicts are limited by the powers entrusted to the Ministry of Labor.

2. Ethically, the workers are affected by the leaders' decisions due to the undesirable but allegedly short-run necessary sacrifices expected of them, such as the extraordinary labor effort and the deferment of present consumption (rationing) in view of the long-run expected achievements (economic growth, abundance). Therefore, it is only fair to give the workers a chance to participate somewhat in such decisions. This participation becomes even more justifiable when it is realized that planners, political leaders, and high-ranking technicians and executives—those making the crucial decisions—seem to be exempt from the short-run sacrifices imposed on the masses as a result of the chosen strategy. Furthermore, because government control is almost absolute, the decision makers are relatively well protected from the negative consequences of potential mistakes.

3. Pragmatically, the lack of workers' participation in planning results in the waste of the workers' knowledge of local conditions at the enterprise level, which is vital for the fixing of realistic output targets, estimates of manpower needs, etc. Finally, the isolation of the worker from the centers of decision-making may have induced a decay in his interest and enthusiasm for the centrally decided goals and a decline in his effort; this, in turn,

may have forced the administration to increase disciplinary and control measures.

In spite of the socialist theory, there are differences between the immediate interests of the working class and the leadership's long-run objectives. The fact that practically all means of production have become state or socialist property in Cuba does not necessarily result in a real collectivization of their use by the population. The administrators (or managers) of the means of production, appointed by the leadership, represent the interests and decisions of the latter, which are not necessarily equal to those of the masses. The workers have an abstract right over the collectivized means of production, whereas the leadership and managers have concrete power to manipulate such means. Hence, some mechanism has to be designed to give protection to the workers, be it traditional unions, workers' councils à la Yugoslavia, or new participatory bodies.

Epilogue

At the end of July 1970, when this essay was finished, important events took place that make the following epilogue necessary. In his speech of July 26, Premier Castro unveiled serious economic problems, saying that the leadership should be blamed for them and that the administration of the enterprises should not be the task of the manager alone. He suggested some changes to correct the situation, among them the establishment of a collective body that will direct the enterprise, presided over by a manager and comprising representatives of the vanguard workers, the party, and other mass organizations such as those made up of the youth and the women.[97]

A few days later, Minister of Labor Jorge Risquet referred to this proposition. Although he made it clear that the manager would continue to be the one controlling most directive functions, he admitted that the lack of workers' participation in management had produced negative consequences. Risquet's pronouncements reinforce the primary conclusions of this essay.

> Theoretically, the administrator represents the interest of the worker and peasant state, the interest of all the people. Theory is one thing and practice another. . . . The administrator may be making one mistake after the other, and this happens every day, everywhere. . . . The workers cannot do anything about it. . . . How can the worker be made to feel more involved with his workplace, with his production goal if he is only a pro-

ducer who never has any opinion, who cannot make any decision, who is never consulted about factory management? . . .
The worker may have a right established by the Revolution
[that is not respected or a complaint against the administration]
and there is no one to defend him. He does not know where to
turn. He turns to the party and it does not know [about the worker's right] or it is busy mobilizing people for production . . .
the party is so involved with the management that in many instances it has ceased to play its proper role, has become somewhat insensitive to the problems of the masses. . . . If the party
and the administration are one, then there is nowhere the worker
can take his problem. . . . The trade union either does not exist
or it has become the vanguard bureau [the organization that represents only the most conscientious workers]. . . . Local unions are weak, their importance has been downgraded.[98]

Risquet made several recommendations to solve some of the above-
described defects: (a) the unions should be given an opportunity to perform their role; their first duty should be to see that labor legislation is applied and workers' rights protected; (b) the elections to the directorate of
the union section should not be restricted; there should not be the slightest
fear that conditions would be placed on the election of the representatives;
there should be no doubt that the election will be free and open; and (c) an
investigation should be undertaken on the potential participation of the
workers in factory management so that output plans and long-term decisions could be discussed with the workers.[99]

It is premature to determine whether the above pronouncements are
mere rhetoric (a temporary tactic to compensate for the hardship of the
1969–1970 sugar crop mobilization) or would result in the factual implementation of workers' participation in management. As Risquet himself
pointed out, in 1962 technical advisory councils were set up, candidates
from the workers were selected, the council's functions were carefully regulated and, then, "the matter was shelved." Another attempt to establish
municipal participatory bodies in 1967, the well-publicized committees of
poder local ("local power"), was rapidly abandoned also.

Some events that took place in September 1970 could indicate what to
expect in the future. The announcements of trade union reform created
anticipations among the rank and file and confusion among labor leaders.
Risquet himself reported in September that strong criticism was being
voiced against trade union methods and that the leadership had been
caught by surprise and did not react. One labor leader said, "We turned the
rabbit loose before the hunter had his rifle ready." The minister of labor

explained that "counterrevolutionary elements" and "demagogues" had taken advantage of the situation, making attacks that were not opposed by the embarrassed labor leaders and party members: "This is a negative situation that has to be changed radically. . . . The fact that Fidel and I have suggested that the workers should be consulted does not mean that we are going to negate the vanguard role that the Party must play. . . . [There should not be] expectations or hope for magic solutions."[100]

NOTES

1. Cuban Economic Research Project, *Social Security in Cuba* (Coral Gables, 1964).

2. For documents, sources, and discussion see Cuban Economic Research Project, *Labor Conditions in Communist Cuba* (Coral Gables, 1963), pp. 112–18.

3. Blas Roca, "Planificación y los trabajadores," *Ocho conferencias revolucionarias* (La Habana, 1962), p. 17.

4. Law No. 962, August 1, 1961 in *Gaceta Oficial* (special edition), August 3, 1961.

5. "Declaración de principios y estatutos de la CTC," *El Mundo,* July 6, 1966, p. 6.

6. Blas Roca, *Hoy,* September 6, 1962.

7. Raúl Castro, *Revolución,* January 23, 1963.

8. Fidel Castro, *El Mundo,* July 18, 1962.

9. Miguel A. Martín, "Informe en el acto de apertura del XII Congreso de la CTC," *El Mundo,* August 26, 1966.

10. Maurice Zeitlin, "Inside Cuba: Workers and Revolution," *Ramparts,* 8 (March 1970), p. 20.

11. Joan Robinson, "Cuba-1965," *Monthly Review,* 17 (February 1966), p. 17.

12. Armando Hart, "Speech at the Graduation Ceremony for the 1963–1969 Course of the Department of Political Science," *Granma Weekly Review,* October 5, 1969, p. 6.

13. Quoted in Zeitlin, "Inside Cuba," p. 66.

14. UCLA, Latin American Center, *Statistical Abstract of Latin America: 1968* (Los Angeles, 1969), p. 94, table 22; and JUCEPLAN, *Boletín Estadístico, 1966* (La Habana, n.d.), p. 24, table IV.1.

15. Lázaro Peña, "Informe ante el XXVI Consejo Nacional de la CTC-R," *Revolución,* September 3, 1962.

16. Augusto Martínez Sánchez, "Información al pueblo sobre las normas de trabajo," *Hoy,* December 28, 1963, p. 5.

17. Law No. 678, December 23, 1959 in *Gaceta Oficial,* December 24, 1959.

18. For details concerning these laws, see Cuban Economic Research Project, *Labor Conditions,* pp. 145–52.

19. *Revolución,* September 2, 1962.

20. "Instrucciones sobre la concertación de los convenios colectivos de trabajo," *Revolución,* October 20, 1962.

21. Ibid.

22. Ernesto Guevara, *Revolución,* February 2, 1963.

23. For an explanation of the changes introduced by the first four laws, see Cuban Economic Research Project, *Labor Conditions,* pp. 129–43.

24. Law No. 1166, September 23, 1964 in *Gaceta Oficial,* October 3, 1964.

25. Ernesto Guevara, *Revolución,* June 27, 1961.

26. Roca, "Planificación y los trabajadores," pp. 18–19.

27. Guevara, *Revolución,* February 2, 1963.

28. Fidel Castro, *Revolución,* April 26, 1963. Minister of Domestic Trade Manuel Luzardo even criticized some commissions that have revoked administrators' decisions concerning the dismissal of a worker. Transcribed from "Radio Progreso," Santa Clara, August 26, 1963.

29. Augusto Martínez Sánchez, *El Mundo,* October 27, 1964, pp. 7–10.

30. Zeitlin, "Inside Cuba," pp. 1, 20.

31. Resolution of the Ministry of Labor, No. 76, August 1, 1966 in *El Mundo,* August 2, 1966, pp. 1, 6.

32. "En la clausura de la Plenaria Nacional de Justicia Laboral," *Granma Revista Semanal,* August 17, 1969, p. 2.

33. Ibid.

34. "Let's Fight Absenteeism, and Fight it Competently," *Granma Weekly Review,* November 9, 1969, p. 2.

35. For a detailed description of this process, see Cuban Economic Research Project, *Labor Conditions,* pp. 69–74.

36. A thorough study on wage scales and their theoretical antecedents, as well as their implementation in Cuba, is found in Carmelo Mesa-Lago, *The Labor Sector and Socialist Distribution in Cuba* (New York, 1968), pp. 74–115.

37. "Las normas de trabajo y la escala salarial," *Nuestra Industria,* 4 (October 1964), p. 42.

38. Augusto Martínez Sánchez, "A un mayor trabajo y una mayor calificación, un mayor salario," *Hoy,* May 16, 1964, p. 4.

39. *Ibid.* See also Mesa-Lago, *Labor Sector,* pp. 81–84.

40. Ernesto Guevara, *El Mundo,* May 5, 1962.

41. Partido Unido de la Revolución Socialista, "¿Qué son las normas de trabajo?" *Aclaraciones* (La Habana, 1962), pp. 31–34.

42. For a detailed study on work quotas, how they are computed and implemented in Cuba, see Mesa-Lago, *Labor Sector,* pp. 45–73.

43. "Establishment of Work Norms," *Granma Weekly Review,* October 19, 1969, p. 4.

44. "Bases para la organización de los salarios y sueldos de los trabajadores," *Suplemento de la Revista Trabajo* (June 19, 1963), p. 6.

45. Mesa-Lago, *Labor Sector,* pp. 100–02. The highest wage rate was obtained by Leo Huberman and Paul Sweezy in their latest visit to Cuba. See Huberman and Sweezy, *Socialism in Cuba* (New York, 1969), p. 118.

46. Ernesto Guevara in "Información al pueblo sobre las normas de trabajo," *Hoy,* December 28, 1963, p. 4.

47. Ibid.

48. Guevara in "Información al pueblo," p. 4; and Mesa-Lago, *Labor Sector,* p. 98.

49. Guevara in "Información al pueblo," p. 4.

50. Augusto Martínez Sánchez, "La implantación del nuevo sistema salarial en las industrias de Cuba," *Cuba Socialista,* 3 (October 1963), p. 16.

51. See as examples: *El Mundo,* November 28, 1967; and *Granma,* August 31, 1968, and September 2, 1969.

52. Ernesto Guevara, *El Mundo,* May 2, 1963.

53. See Mesa-Lago, *Labor Sector,* pp. 107–12. Peter J. Wiles and Stefan Markowski reach the same conclusions in an article (comparing income distribution in Cuba, Poland, United Kingdom, USA, and USSR) to be published in *Soviet Studies* (Glasgow) in 1971.

54. Radoslav Selucky, *Literarni Novini* (Prague), August 8, 1964.

55. Zeitlin, "Inside Cuba," pp. 11, 14.

56. Adolfo Gilly, "Inside the Cuban Revolution," *Monthly Review,* 16 (October 1964), p. 42.

57. Zeitlin, "Inside Cuba," p. 14.

58. René Dumont, *Cuba est-il socialiste?* (Paris, 1970), pp. 191–94, and "Il y a deux Castro," *L'Express* (July 20–26, 1970), p. 28. There are also reports that foreign technicians have special stores not open to the public. See John Clytus, *Black Man in Red Cuba* (Coral Gables, 1970), pp. 45–49.

59. Castro, "Discurso en la plenaria provincial de la CTC," *Granma,* September 10, 1970, p. 2.

60. Jacques Valier, "L'Économie Cubaine: Quelques problémes essentiels de son fonctionnement," *Les Temps Modernes,* 23 (March 1968), p. 1598.

61. "El desarrollo industrial de Cuba," *Cuba Socialista,* 6 (May 1966), p. 109.

62. ILO, *Yearbook of Labour Statistics, 1948–1958* (Geneva, 1948–1958).

63. Consejo Nacional de Economía, *El empleo, el sub-empleo y el desempleo en Cuba* (La Habana, 1958), table 3.

64. "El desarrollo industrial de Cuba," table 9.

65. On the Cuban controversy on incentives, see Carmelo Mesa-Lago, "Economic, Political and Ideological Factors in the Cuban Controversy on Material Versus Moral Incentives," (Paper presented at the Latin American Studies Association Second National Meeting, Washington, D.C., April 17–18, 1970).

66. Fidel Castro, "Discurso en conmemoración del 15° aniversario del ataque al Cuartel Moncada," *Granma Revista Semanal,* July 28, 1968, pp. 3–5.

67. See G. Glezerman, "Las relaciones económicas y los intereses personales en el socialismo," *Cuba Socialista,* 4 (November 1964), p. 93; and PURS, "Emulación socialista y competencia capitalista," *Aclaraciones* (La Habana, 1962), pp. 11–14.

68. Ernesto Guevara, "Plenaria obrera de Camagüey," *Obra Revolucionaria* (February 26, 1963), p. 13.

69. For a history of socialist emulation in Cuba, see "Un nuevo paso en el desarrollo de la emulación socialista," *Cuba Socialista,* 5 (August 1964), pp. 107 ff.

70. Official regulations of socialist emulation were published in *Gaceta Oficial,* February 7, 1963, and May 21, 1964, and Basilio Rodríguez, "Las nuevas normas de la emulación socialista," *Cuba Socialista,* 6 (April 1966), pp. 93–105.

71. A detailed discussion of these documents is made in Mesa-Lago, *Labor Sector,* pp. 131–33.

72. Ibid., pp. 136–45.

73. Ibid.

74. *Trabajo* (October 15, 1964), pp. 13–15; *Granma,* October 8, 1965 and September 2, 1969; and transcriptions from Radio Rebelde, August 30, 1969; and Radio Havana-Cuba, June 26, 1970.

75. Jorge Risquet, "En la clausura . . . ," *Granma Revista Semanal,* August 17, 1969, p. 2.

76. Law No. 1225, September 1, 1969. See Zeitlin, "Inside Cuba," p. 72.

77. "Decidida la clase obrera a convertir el revés en victoria," *Granma,* June 29, 1970, p. 1.

78. "Proyecto de evaluación laboral," *Granma,* July 8, 1970, p. 1; and "Proyecto de Resolución sobre méritos y deméritos laborales," *Granma,* September 12, 1970, p. 3.

79. Carlos Rafael Rodríguez, *Revolución,* August 15, 1961.

80. Gilly, "Inside the Revolution," pp. 34–35.

81. Miguel A. Martín, "Informe central al XII Congreso de la CTC," *El Mundo,* August 26, 1966, p. 6.

82. "Decidida la clase obrera a convertir el revés en victoria," p. 1.

83. Zeitlin, "Inside Cuba," p. 81. However, he suggests that workers' participation in planning at the enterprise level goes further than merely "implementing" the plan (pp. 66, 68).

84. González Quiñones, "Algunas experiencias acerca de la planificación de trabajo y salarios en nuestra industria," *Nuestra Industria Revista Económica,* 5 (August 1967), pp. 6–8, 15–16.

85. Martínez Sánchez in "Información al pueblo," p. 4.

86. "Salarios y normas en la construcción," *Trabajo,* 5 (March 1, 1964), pp. 29–30.

87. Guevara in "Información al pueblo," p. 4.

88. Martínez Sánchez, "La implantación del nuevo sistema salarial," pp. 9, 21.

89. Lázaro Peña in "Información al pueblo sobre las normas de trabajo," *Hoy,* December 28, 1963, p. 6.

90. Fidel Castro, "Discurso en la commemoración del VI aniversario de la fundación de los CDR," *El Mundo,* September 29, 1966, pp. 5–6.

91. Martínez Sánchez, "La implantación del nuevo sistema salarial," p. 19.

92. Lázaro Peña, "La clase obrera ha respaldado el plan," *Hoy,* December 28, 1963, p. 6.

93. Augusto Martínez Sánchez, *Revolución,* September 3, 1962, p. 4.

94. César Escalante, "Informe sobre la emulación," *Hoy,* October 18, 1964.

95. Basilio Rodríguez, *El Mundo,* June 23, 1966.

96. Hart, "Speech at the Graduation Ceremony," p. 6.

97. Fidel Castro, "Discurso en conmemoración del 17° aniversario del ataque al Cuartel Moncada," *Granma,* July 27, 1970.

98. Jorge Risquet, press conference transmitted by Havana television, July 31, 1970.

99. Ibid.

100. Jorge Risquet, "Palabras en la plenaria provincial de la CTC," *Granma,* September 9, 1970, pp. 4–5.

10 Eric N. Baklanoff

International Economic Relations

THIS chapter attempts to relate the significant changes that have taken place in Cuba's international economic relations during the first decade of the Revolution, that is, the direction, composition, and balance of trade; the sources and magnitude of foreign assistance and external debt; and the emigration of "human capital." This study is made in the light of the economic background of Cuba in the 1950s.

The writer has drawn on official statistics from JUCEPLAN and the Ministry of Foreign Trade (MINCEX), as well as on data compiled and analyzed by United Nations agencies, the World Bank, the International Monetary Fund, and the U.S. Commerce, Agriculture, and State departments. A number of publications and memoranda of the now dissolved Cuban Economic Research Project of the University of Miami have also been of valuable assistance in the discussion of the prerevolutionary period.

Cuba's foreign trade statistics are possibly the most comprehensive and accurate published by this nation. The need for precision in planning Cuban foreign trade with other socialist economies, together with a concentration of both foreign and domestic specialists in this sector, has resulted in the availability of high-quality data.[1] Furthermore, foreign trade data are generally recorded at a limited number of customhouses and can be cross-checked with information supplied by trading partners abroad. This happy conjunction permits the serious analysis of data, which is neither available nor accurate on other sectors of the Cuban economy.

The author acknowledges Carmelo Mesa-Lago's aid in providing statistical data, preparing and computing tables 3, 5, 6, and 7, and for numerous valuable recommendations that have been included in this essay. He is also grateful to the editors of the *Intercollegiate Review* and the *Annals of the South-Eastern Conference on Latin American Studies* for permission to include in this essay portions from his articles published by them.

251

The Prerevolutionary Situation

On the eve of the Cuban Revolution, the island essentially had an agricultural, semiindustrialized export economy with a strong orientation toward the United States—its principal trading partner and external source of development capital. In organization and structure, Cuba, until the early 1950s, typified what some economists have come to call an export economy.[2] Such an economy exhibits the following properties: a high ratio of export production to total output in the cash sector of the economy; a concentrated export structure; substantial inflow of long-term capital, including the presence of foreign-owned enterprises; and a high marginal propensity to import. Commonly, in such an economy government revenues are closely tied to the oscillations of export income. The export sector constitutes the dynamic, autonomous variable that powers the nation's development; it is also the short-run disturber. The sheer weight of exports in relation to total economic activity dictates that the external market, rather than private investment or government expenditures, exercises predominant influence on aggregate demand. Because of its specialized structure, the export economy is heavily dependent on foreign sources for many kinds of consumer and capital goods.

As Henry C. Wallich observed, the "main and very great advantage that underdeveloped export economies enjoy is precisely that they do not have to create a modern economy entirely out of their own resources—a process that took Europe centuries to accomplish."[3] His point applies with particular force to Cuba with its relatively small population and specialized tropical resources. On the negative side, because of the central position of sugar in Cuba's exports and GNP, the nation suffered from both economic instability resulting from sugar price variations and chronic seasonal unemployment.

Cuba's sugar sector, including cane-growing and the industrial and commercial income from milling and marketing of raw sugar, directly contributed between one-fourth and one-third of the national income in the post–World War II period. Sugar brought in between 75 percent and 85 percent of Cuba's external receipts from exports, and, thereby, constituted the "great independent variable," of the island's economy. Economic activity oscillated between the *zafra,* the four-month grinding period, and the dead season when unemployment normally reached a level of 20 percent and much capital equipment remained idle. On the other hand, by emphasizing specialization and extreme interdependence with the world economy (mainly the United States), Cuba was able to achieve what was probably the highest standard of living among tropical nations in the 1950s.

Foreign Trade

On the eve of the Cuban Revolution, in 1958, the United States was purchasing two-thirds of the island's exports and was supplying 70 percent of its imports. Next to Brazil, Cuba was the most important Latin American source of agricultural imports for the United States. During the five-year period 1954–1958, the United States purchased three-fourths of Cuba's tobacco and 60 percent of its sugar. Raw Cuban sugar was sold to the United States under a quota system at prices that in most years were substantially above the world price.[4] Both the quota and the more stable U.S. premium price helped to curb the annual fluctuations of Cuban sugar sales abroad.

Some 30 percent of Cuba's trade turnover in 1958 was carried on with nonsocialist nations other than the United States, while only 3 percent of the island's exports went to the Soviet bloc. The socialist nations in that year were an insignificant source of imports for Cuba. Next to the United States, Western Europe was Cuba's most important geographical trading area, purchasing 15 percent of its exports and supplying 14 percent of its purchases abroad.

The composition, by commodities, of Cuba's exports in 1958 revealed the following value shares: sugar and related products, 81 percent; tobacco, 7 percent; mineral products, 6 percent; and food and other products, 6 percent. In the same year, consumer goods comprised 39 percent, raw materials and fuels, 34 percent, and fixed capital goods, 27 percent of the value of Cuba's imports.[5]

Foreign Investment

Following World War II, Cuba's investment climate was one of the most favorable in Latin America. The constitution of 1940 guaranteed the protection of property and established the juridical procedure for special cases involving expropriation. Property could be expropriated only for just cause involving a public utility or social interest, and, then, only through prior indemnification of the owner in cash as determined by the courts.

In sharp contrast to the more general postwar experience in Latin America, Cuba enjoyed financial stability throughout the period analyzed. The cost of living remained stable, the peso continued at par with the U.S. dollar, and foreign exchange operations were free of control. The magnitude of the nation's external public debt and the debt-service ratio were of minor importance throughout the 1946–1958 period. Profits, interest, and other factor payments could be freely remitted abroad and the risk of currency devaluation was negligible.

Cuba was one of the most capitalized nations in Latin America. In the late 1940s, the World Bank report observed:

> In the 161 sugar centrales [mills], in the excellent central highway, in the extensive system of public and private railroads, in the harbor installations, in the cities and their utilities, Cuba has the basis of exceptionally fine equipment for modern economic activity and further development.[6]

From 1946 on, new U.S. investments in Cuba assumed a highly diversified pattern and flowed into a spectrum of Cuba's economic activities: infrastructure, manufacturing and commerce, petroleum refining, diversified agriculture, mining, and the tourist industry.[7] The augmented production capabilities represented by U.S. subsidiaries and branches in Cuba were primarily directed to meet the requirements of the local market. The $400 million increment of U.S. business investments between 1946 and 1959 both stimulated and responded to the postwar expansion of Cuba's economy. This was decisive in the growth of electric power and telephone service, in the rapid advance of petroleum refining, and the mining of nickel, and it helped pace the diversification and growth of manufacturing.

United States business investments in Cuba, which approached one billion dollars at the end of 1959, represented a significant participation in the nation's stock of productive capital. Cuba ranked second in Latin America (behind Venezuela) in the value of U.S. direct investments in 1959 and at the moment of expropriation, in 1960, they constituted one-eighth of total U.S. investments in the area.

A comprehensive survey of the impact of U.S. business investments on the Cuban economy was issued by the U.S. Department of Commerce late in 1960.[8] Among other things, the survey revealed the extent to which U.S. firms participated in the Cuban economy through production of their subsidiaries and branches for the island's market and exports. Total sales of Cuban subsidiaries and branches of U.S. companies were about $700 million in 1957. The value of their sales by major economic activity are given below, in descending order of magnitude: agriculture, $300 million; manufacturing, $150 million; public utilities, $130 million; and petroleum products, $120 million.

United States firms operating in Cuba also made critical contributions to the nation's balance of payments position in 1957 through export earnings ($273 million), net capital inflows ($88 million), and foreign exchange saved through import substitution ($130 million). Offsetting these contributions were income remittances plus fees and royalties (totalling $56 million) and imports (other than imports of trading companies or of petroleum to be processed in Cuba) amounting to roughly $100 million. By this calculation, U.S. companies accounted for a net foreign exchange gain or saving to Cuba on the order of $335 million.

The economic cost to Cuba of U.S. business holdings, measured by the rate of return (profit) on equity investment, appeared to be quite low when compared with U.S. direct investments in the rest of Latin America, in other parts of the world, and at home. Earnings for the 1950–1959 decade averaged $47 million, or 6.3 percent of book investment, 7 percent of exports, and 2 percent of the GNP, not a price too high to have paid for foreign capital.[9] Most profits did not leave the island but were reinvested.

Notwithstanding these large U.S. equity holdings in Cuba, it is important to observe that private Cuban groups succeeded in winning control over economic activities formerly dominated by the United States and other foreign investors. The outstanding cases of Cuban-controlled enterprises include sugar, banking, air transport, and insurance. From the 1930s on, Cubans purchased a large number of sugar mills from U.S., Canadian, Spanish, Dutch, and French interests.[10] In consequence, by 1958 Cuban capital controlled three-fourths of the sugar mills and these, in turn, accounted for 62 percent of the island's sugar production.[11] Transfer of these foreign assets into Cuban ownership proceeded through normal commercial channels and procedures—a manifestation of the progressive maturation of the island's business community and postwar prosperity.

Evaluation of Cuba's International Economic Relations in the 1950s

The diversification of Cuba's industrial park and a growing capacity to meet food requirements out of domestic production substantially lessened the island's dependence on world sugar markets in the postwar period. Not only did Cuban exports decline as a share of national income, but sugar played a diminishing role in commodity exports between the late 1940s and late 1950s. Sugar and its by-products constituted 89 percent of the value of Cuba's commodity exports during 1947–1949, compared to 80 percent during 1954–1958, and the ratio of total exports to national income declined from 41 percent to 33 percent for the same periods, respectively. Despite the stagnation in the value of sugar exports from the late 1940s to the late 1950s, the Cuban economy experienced a powerful upward trend in fixed capital formation, both private and public, signifying growing autonomy of this key variable from the exigencies of international trade.

Cuba's balance of payments position was materially strengthened in the 1950s by the development of the island's tourist industry and the growth of export earnings other than sugar. The expanded operations of the U.S.-government-constructed Nicaro Nickel Company and the Moa Bay Mining Company, a subsidiary of the Freeport Sulphur Company, assured Cuba a position as a major supplier of nickel in the world. Hotel construction from 1952 to 1958 almost doubled the existing hotel capacity and made available numerous large and modern hotels in Havana and other major cities. In addition, several hotels and motels were under construction in 1958, involving a total investment in excess of $90 million and a projected capacity of 6,066 rooms.[12] Foreign tourist expenditures in Cuba increased sharply from $19 million in 1952 to a yearly average of $60 million in 1957–1958. Local and foreign entrepreneurs were clearly mobilizing their resources in preparation for the anticipated Caribbean tourist boom of the 1960s. Two large hotels, the Havana Hilton and the Havana Riviera, figured importantly in the island's capacity to accommodate tourists seeking first-class service. Cuban agricultural diversification gained momentum after 1952 and was reflected in gains in exports of farm and livestock products other than sugar and its by-products and in a respectable increase in agricultural production for domestic consumption. Rice production, advancing from 118,000 tons in 1951 to 261,000 tons in 1957, was a notable case of foreign exchange savings.

Given the nature of the international sugar market and Cuba's substantial share as a world exporter, the nation's policy makers perceived that the sugar sector could no longer provide the stimulus for a further expansion of the economy.[13] As a consequence, the government organized a number of development banks and passed the Industrial Promotion Law of 1953, which granted, among other things, tax incentives to new industries. The implementation of these policy measures, together with a more aggressive use of the 1927 tariff, launched the Cuban economy on a new growth path via import substitution for the home market.

Industrial diversification gained momentum in the 1950s with particularly sharp increases registered between 1952 and 1957 in the output of cement (56 percent), rubber tires (66 percent), and chemical fertilizers (46 percent).[14] Production of electric energy grew at a cumulative annual rate of 10.6 percent from 1952 to 1957. Rapid advances were also made in the manufacture of paper from bagasse, in flour-milling and the dairy products industry, and in petroleum refining. Cuba achieved self-sufficiency in petroleum refining at the end of 1959 with a capacity of 83,000 barrels per day supplied exclusively by two U.S. subsidiaries, Texaco and Esso, and the Royal Dutch Shell group. In its review of Cuba's economy, the ECLA noted that a significant number of projects were underway in 1957:

> The purpose of these investment programs in the manufacturing sectors is to make Cuba completely self-sufficient at an early date in cement, tires and tubes, glass containers, aluminum sheet

and copper wire and cables, and relatively self-sufficient in light steel products.[15]

In addition to sugar mills and many traditional light industries, Cuba had in 1958 an impressive complex of intermediate capital goods industries producing sulphuric acid, fertilizer, cement, light steel products, paper, glass, nickel, and petroleum products. In many of the economic activities cited above, U.S. enterprises made valuable entrepreneurial and technical contributions. Cuba's steel mill (Antillana de Acero), for example, was mounted and operated with the technical assistance of the Republic Steel Corporation.

The accelerated capitalization of the Cuban economy in sectors other than sugar production is reflected in the changing composition of imports. The purchase abroad of fixed capital goods climbed steeply from less than $100 million (20 percent of total imports) in 1953 to $207 million annually (27 percent of imports) during the two years, 1957–1958.[16] These increases were achieved without creating an inflationary situation, as in most of South America, partly because Cuba was able to draw on its ample foreign exchange reserves. In mid-1957 Cuba's central bank possessed $535 million in gold and foreign exchange reserves. Among its sister republics, only Venezuela had larger accumulated reserves.

The picture presented above could seem excessively optimistic if the negative side of Cuba's international economic relations is not considered: (a) In spite of some diversification, Cuba was heavily dependent on sugar, tobacco, and minerals as the main sources for its exports and GNP. (b) More than two-thirds of Cuban trade was with the United States. In the period 1949–1958, the latter supplied Cuba with 75 percent of its imports, but only bought 69 percent of its exports. Hence, Cuba's cumulative trade balance with the United States showed a deficit of $350 million. (c) The above situation was partially the result of the diversification and industrialization drives of the 1950s, but also of the lack of a national merchant fleet and the fact that most U.S. plants operated with raw materials that were usually imported in a fabricated state. (d) A large percentage of imports went to luxuries (e.g., passenger cars represented some 4 percent of total imports in 1957) and still 20 percent to 25 percent of imports consisted of food that could be produced in Cuba.[17]

Some officials of the Cuban government and U.S. scholars have blamed "American imperialism" as the cause of the above national problems. They claim that the normal process of capitalist development in Cuba was interrupted by U.S. monopolies, which turned Cuba into a sugar plantation, prevented native industrialization, made Cuba a paradise for American tourists in search of pleasure, and transformed the island into a mere appendage of the U.S. economy. The only way out of this situation, these critics claim, was to achieve full independence from the United States through a socialist revolution.[18]

The data presented in the previous pages contradict some of the above charges. It could be argued also that (a) sugar development in Cuba preceded the U.S. inflow of investment and trade; (b) it was extremely difficult for a small island so close to the most powerful and efficient manufacturer-producer in the world to develop a large domestic industry; (c) development centered around sugar (which is not balanced development) was not the same as stagnation, and, according to the theory of the "big push," could have resulted in a more balanced development in the long run; (d) socialist countries, such as Yugoslavia, are resorting more and more to tourism as a relevant factor to improve their international economic position; and (e) it is doubtful that Cuba would have reached even the relative development that it did in fact achieve had it not been for the large U.S. capital investment.[19]

Still, some of the noted, most serious charges remain unchallenged. A socialist revolution, advocated by the above-mentioned critics, is now in progress. The question we must answer is whether the revolutionary government of Cuba has been able to change the prerevolutionary situation in the last twelve years by diversifying exports, solving the balance of trade problem, and achieving independence from a big economic power such as the United States.

Changes Under the Revolution

The appointment during November 1959 of Ernesto (Che) Guevara as president of the National Bank of Cuba portended a significant change in the island's international economic relations. Shortly after his appointment to this key post, payments to the American and British oil companies that supplied Cuba with petroleum were stopped. The Cuban government decided to import crude oil from the Soviet Union to take the place of that supplied to the companies by the United States. The companies, whose claim on the Cuban government for petroleum imports had risen to approximately $80 million, refused to refine petroleum supplied by the USSR. The Cuban government then proceeded to seize these refineries without offering indemnity.

The Eisenhower administration offered Cuba economic assistance during Premier Fidel Castro's visit to the United States in April 1959[20] and, nearly a year later, in January 1960, declared its willingness to negotiate all disputes, including those arising from Cuban seizure of American properties.[21] But the Cuban government never replied to these officially.

Cuba's signing of the trade and payments agreement with the USSR in February 1960 was followed shortly with similar bilateral agreements with other socialist nations. In July 1960, following the confiscation of most U.S. business holdings in Cuba, the U.S. Congress reduced the island's sugar quota and set it at zero for 1961 and following years. The USSR and most Eastern European nations rapidly offered to buy varying amounts of sugar from Cuba and a multilateral agreement was signed in 1960 regulating these purchases.

The revolutionary government declined to participate in the newly formed Inter-American Development Bank and, in late 1960, Cuba withdrew its representation from the World Bank. In 1960–1961, the USSR and Eastern Europe granted credits to Cuba totalling $357 million.

In January 1962, Cuba was excluded from the OAS, which also recommended the imposition of economic sanctions in retaliation for Cuba's alleged subversive activities in the Western Hemisphere. In accordance with the OAS decision, the United States imposed an embargo on U.S.–Cuban trade effective as of February 1962. During the following years, an intensification of the U.S.–OAS policy to isolate Cuba diplomatically and economically resulted in the breaking off of trade and diplomatic relations with Cuba by all Latin American nations except Mexico.

Cuba's trade with the United States was negligible in 1961–1962. There was a sudden but brief increase in U.S. exports to Cuba in 1963 as a result of the indemnization agreed upon between the Cuban and U.S. governments for the returning of Cuban exiles involved in the 1961 Bay of Pigs invasion. Thereafter, U.S.–Cuban trade ceased altogether. A boycott against merchant ships touching Cuban harbors, supported by the U.S. government, has resulted in a declining number of Western ships involved in trade with Cuba.

Direction of Trade

The realignment of Cuba's direction of trade since 1960 has been most striking, as may be seen in tables 1 and 2. In 1961–1968, the socialist countries as a group accounted for about three-fourths of Cuba's trade turnover, while nonsocialist nations supplied and purchased the remaining one-fourth of the island's trade. The USSR has replaced the United States as the island's major trading partner. In 1961–1968 Soviet purchases of Cuban exports averaged 44 percent, whereas imports from the USSR were 52 percent with a clear tendency to increase.

Next to the USSR, mainland China has been Cuba's most important

(*Text continued on page 262.*)

TABLE 1
CUBA'S EXPORTS BY AREA AND COUNTRY: 1960–1968
(Percentage of Value, FOB)

Countries	1960	1961	1962	1963	1964	1965	1966	1967	1968[a]
Socialist	24.2%	73.3%	82.0%	67.4%	59.2%	78.2%	81.4%	81.2%	74.7%
USSR	16.7	48.2	42.3	30.2	38.5	47.0	46.2	51.7	44.3
China	5.2	14.6	17.1	13.4	11.4	14.6	14.7	11.1	9.3
Czechoslovakia	0.2	2.7	7.1	7.0	2.1	6.6	7.8	5.8	6.3
E. Germany	0.1	1.2	4.7	7.4	2.2	4.1	5.2	5.1	5.5
Poland	1.6	4.6	3.6	3.3	1.1	0.6	2.1	0.9	1.1
Hungary	0.0	0.2	1.9	2.2	0.1	0.2	0.3	0.6	0.6
Bulgaria	0.0	1.0	2.6	1.7	2.1	3.0	3.2	3.4	3.8
Rumania	0.0	0.1	1.3	1.2	0.0	0.1	0.1	0.2	1.2
N. Korea	0.1	0.3	0.4	0.4	0.5	0.4	0.4	1.1	1.1
Others	0.3	0.4	1.0	0.6	1.2	1.6	0.4	1.3	1.5
Nonsocialist	75.8%	26.7%	18.0%	32.6%	40.8%	21.8%	18.6%	18.8%	25.3%
USA	52.8	4.8	0.8	0.0	0.0	0.0	0.0	0.0	0.0
Canada	1.3	0.7	0.5	2.5	0.4	0.7	0.8	0.7	0.6
U.K.	1.4	2.0	2.2	4.2	3.6	1.8	1.9	1.8	2.0
Spain	1.2	0.8	1.7	4.2	9.5	4.8	5.5	4.6	6.3
France	1.4	0.3	0.3	0.5	0.4	1.5	1.7	2.1	2.3
Japan	2.4	4.2	4.9	3.8	7.0	3.0	2.4	2.7	3.8
Others	15.3	13.9	7.6	17.4	19.9	10.0	6.3	6.9	10.3
Total	100.0%	100.0%	100.0%	100.0%	100.0%	100.0%	100.0%	100.0%	100.0%

Source: JUCEPLAN, Compendio Estadístico de Cuba, 1968 (La Habana, 1968), p. 26.
a. Preliminary.

TABLE 2
CUBA'S IMPORTS BY AREA AND COUNTRY: 1960–1968
(Percentage of Value, CIF)

Countries	1960[a]	1961[a]	1962	1963	1964	1965	1966	1967	1968[b]
Socialist	18.7%	70.2%	82.8%	81.8%	67.5%	76.0%	79.8%	79.1%	80.3%
USSR	13.8	41.1	54.2	53.1	40.2	49.5	56.3	58.3	60.9
China	1.7	13.9	11.8	10.5	10.7	14.2	9.3	7.3	7.0
Czechoslovakia	1.2	4.0	4.9	6.3	6.3	4.0	3.9	3.6	3.5
E. Germany	0.7	3.6	3.5	4.2	3.7	2.9	3.9	5.0	3.5
Poland	0.8	2.8	3.0	3.4	2.0	0.9	1.0	0.6	0.9
Hungary	0.2	1.3	1.7	1.4	1.5	1.0	0.8	0.4	0.3
Bulgaria	0.2	1.3	1.3	0.6	1.1	1.8	3.0	2.0	1.9
Rumania	0.0	1.1	1.8	0.8	0.8	0.4	0.3	0.1	0.8
N. Korea	0.0	0.1	0.3	0.3	0.5	0.3	0.2	1.0	0.9
Others	0.1	0.8	0.3	0.5	0.7	1.0	1.1	0.8	0.6
Nonsocialist	81.3%	30.0%	17.2%	18.9%	32.5%	24.0%	20.2%	20.9%	19.7%
USA	48.5	3.7	0.1	4.1	0.0	0.0	0.0	0.0	0.0
Canada	2.8	5.6	1.6	1.3	4.1	1.8	0.7	0.9	0.8
U.K.	3.6	2.4	1.5	1.2	3.7	5.8	2.7	2.9	2.7
Spain	2.1	0.8	0.2	1.6	3.8	5.4	8.1	2.9	1.8
France	2.0	1.1	0.2	0.7	1.8	2.2	1.4	4.1	6.2
Japan	1.6	1.6	1.4	0.6	4.0	0.5	0.5	0.9	0.3
Others	20.7	14.8	12.2	9.4	15.1	8.3	6.8	11.6	7.9
Total	100.0%	100.0%	100.0%	100.0%	100.0%	100.0%	100.0%	100.0%	100.0%

Source: JUCEPLAN, Compendio Estadístico de Cuba, 1968, p. 26.
a. Value FOB.
b. Preliminary.

trading country among centrally planned nations, followed by Czecho-slovakia and East Germany. Notwithstanding China's cancellation in 1964 of its five-year pact with Cuba and the quarrel between Cuba and China in 1966, trade between the two countries has continued on a reduced level.

The Communist bloc agreed in 1960–1961 to purchase 4.9 million tons of Cuban sugar annually, including three million tons by the Soviet Union, during the four-year period from 1961 to 1965.[22] Following, somewhat, the pattern set by the United States in earlier years, the Soviet Union entered in January 1964 into a new six-year agreement with Cuba to purchase a total of 24.1 million metric tons of sugar at a price of about six cents per pound. Shipments to the USSR failed to reach the agreed quantities in 1965–1969 (see chapter 11, table 8). It is interesting to point out that Soviet domestic sugar production has advanced rapidly, even as imports of raw sugar from Cuba have assumed growing importance. For example, Soviet sugar output, which averaged 6.2 million tons in 1959–1960, rose to a yearly average of 9.3 million tons in 1965–1967, a 50 percent gain.[23] Sugar output in the USSR has reached a level that will satisfy internal consumption and, since it can reexport only 1.25 million tons under the International Sugar Agreement, most of the Cuban sugar necessarily accumulates as stockpile—estimated at eleven million tons in 1968.[24]

In contrast to the U.S. quota system, however, only 20 percent of Cuba's sugar sales to the USSR were payable in dollars, with the balance in barter, including agricultural and industrial commodities. Since the main share of Cuba's trade with the Soviet Union and the other socialist countries is in terms of barter, there is considerable doubt with respect to actual price of imported items. The island's options as a trading nation have narrowed as the margin of convertible foreign exchange available to Cuba has greatly diminished.

The machinery and equipment available in the socialist nations was clearly incompatible with the prerevolutionary structure of Cuba's stock of physical capital. Most of Cuba's capital stock—equipment, machinery, and rolling stock—had originated in the United States. As these facilities began to wear out, Cuba after 1960 was unable to purchase in the United States spare parts for the maintenance of sugar mills, factories, refineries, railways, and automotive equipment. This serious problem resulted in stoppages and bottlenecks in the early 1960s. As a temporary device to solve these difficulties, Cuba had to resort to "cannibalization" or the dismantling of equipment (e.g., sugar mills) from one plant to use in the maintenance and operation of another. But the island was soon able to buy the necessary spare parts through triangular trade, particularly with Canada and some Western European nations. Indigenous inventiveness has been helpful in repairs and even duplication of nontechnologically complex spare parts. Soviet bloc and Western European vehicles have replaced in large degree U.S.-made vehicles (e.g., buses, trucks, trains), but replacement of machinery will take many years still.

Among nonsocialist nations, the European Economic Community, Canada, Spain, and the United Kingdom have been the most important sources of Cuban imports. Canada has been a major supplier of wheat and wheat flour, Spain and Japan of ships, and the United Kingdom of buses and a $50 million fertilizer plant. During 1967, Cuba purchased significant quantities of machinery from France and the United Kingdom, of chemicals from West Germany, Italy, and the Netherlands, and fertilizers from France and Italy.[25] Japan and Spain have been important buyers of Cuban exports. Cuba's trade with the Latin American area, which in 1958 had purchased 3 percent of the island's exports and supplied 11 percent of its imports, fell to insignificance after the economic boycott imposed in 1962. Venezuela, the principal source of crude petroleum for Cuba in the 1950s, was replaced in the 1960s by Soviet fuel shipments from distant Black Sea ports.

Previous data suggest that the U.S. embargo on Cuba, although successful in the early 1960s, has ceased to have true economic significance. Cuba has been able to obtain spare parts through triangular trade, Soviet oil has replaced U.S. and Venezuelan oil, transportation equipment has been imported from Western and Eastern Europe, and credit and machinery have been supplied also. Concerning the shipping boycott, the number of nonsocialist ships calling at Cuban ports has diminished steadily: from 394 in 1964 to 290 in 1965, 224 in 1966, 218 in 1967, and 152 in the first ten months of 1968.[26] But this gap has been filled with Soviet vessels and Cuba's own merchant marine. The Cuban merchant fleet reached 238,000 registered tons in 1968, a fivefold increase over the previous decade.[27]

Still, the boycott and the embargo may have had some effect, for example, increased transportation costs due to the distance of Cuban trade partners and slightly increased costs and more time to obtain spare parts. But these are minor economic problems. The embargo has served instead as a means to hide Cuba's internal difficulties by blaming the United States for them. In 1969, the Cuban delegate to the ECLA meeting held in Lima, Peru, Minister Carlos Rafael Rodríguez, stated: "The blockade that the U.S tried to impose upon us has totally failed. . . . It no longer has economic significance."[28]

Composition of Trade

The composition of Cuba's exports has changed little from the late 1950s to the late 1960s. As table 3 shows, sugar (both raw and refined) and related products have slightly increased to between 80 percent and 86 percent of the value of exports; the share of minerals, principally nickel,

TABLE 3
COMPOSITION OF CUBAN EXPORTS AND IMPORTS BY PRODUCT: 1959–1967
(Percentages of Value, FOB and CIF)

Products	1959	1960	1961	1962	1963	1964	1965	1966	1967[a]
Exports (FOB)									
Sugar and by-products	77%	80%	85%	83%	85%	86%	85%	84%	83%
Tobacco[b]	9	10	6	5	4	4	5	5	4
Minerals	2	1	6	7	7	6	7	8	8
Others[c]	12	9	3	5	4	4	3	3	5
Total	100%	100%	100%	100%	100%	100%	100%	100%	100%
Imports (CIF)									
Food[d]	27%	29%	22%	22%	24%	24%	23%	23%	24%
Raw materials[e]	4	3	4	3	3	4	3	4	4
Fuel and lubricants	9	—	—	—	9	8	10	10	9
Chemicals	9	—	—	—	6	6	5	7	10
Manufactured products	31	—	—	—	15	16	18	16	15
Machinery and transport	19	—	—	—	14	14	15	14	16
Others[f]	1	—	—	—	29	28	26	26	22
Total	100%	100%	100%	100%	100%	100%	100%	100%	100%

Sources: Export data are from Carmelo Mesa-Lago, "Availability and Reliability," p. 64, table 5, supplemented with JUCEPLAN, *Boletín Estadístico, 1966*, pp. 126–27, and JUCEPLAN, *Compendio Estadístico de Cuba, 1968*, p. 27. Import data are from Cuban Economic Research Project, *Cuba's Foreign Trade Before and After 1958*, p. 30; *Cuba Economic News*, 2 (April 1966), p. 9; JUCEPLAN, *Boletín Estadístico, 1966*, pp. 128–33; and JUCEPLAN, *Compendio Estadístico de Cuba, 1968*, p. 27.

a. Preliminary.

b. Includes beverages since 1963, which are included in "Others" in 1950–1961.

c. Fruits, vegetables, frozen fish, fibers, preserves, etc.

d. Includes edible oils and fats, and alcoholic beverages.

e. Crude, nonedible raw materials excluding fuel.

f. Due to different categorization criteria in 1959 and 1963–1967, this category becomes the most significant in the latter period, distorting the percent distribution.

has risen slowly, contributing 7 percent to 8 percent in the latter period; and tobacco's share has fluctuated between 4 percent and 5 percent of total export receipts. The ambiguous category "Others" has shown a tendency to decline. It is possible that increasing exports of fish have not been able to offset declining exports of fruits, vegetables, and preserves.

Any evaluation of the changes of Cuba's import composition should take into consideration the distortion in the table 3 percent distribution induced by the sharp increase in the ambiguous category of "Others." The possibility that this category includes the importation of weapons should be rejected in view of reiterated statements from Cuban leaders (Castro, Rodríguez) to the effect that military equipment has been supplied free of charge. With this caution in mind, it seems that the share of food imports has remained fairly stable in 1961–1967, although a decline is obvious relative to 1959 and 1960. This is reflected in the serious rationing of food in Cuba during the 1960s. Raw materials and fuel shares have remained stable even when compared with 1959. In chemicals, there was a decline with a clear trough in 1965 and a recuperation thereafter, which by 1967 had exceeded the 1959 level. The sharp decline in manufactured products is not a surprise, since consumer durables were being sacrificed in order to maintain or increase other more important lines of imports. On the other hand, the relative decline in machinery and transportation is surprising in view of the publicized socialist aid in terms of factories and equipment. The composition of transport-equipment imports has been notably altered. In 1952–1959, some 71 percent of these imports were passenger cars, 10 percent were trucks, and 19 percent, buses. These proportions have changed in 1960–1968 to 8 percent, 54 percent, and 38 percent, respectively.[29] These figures do not include shipyards of which there has also been a notable increase.

Balance of Trade

The decline in the output of the export sector of the Cuban economy (mainly sugar, tobacco, and minerals except nickel) has had a clear impact on foreign trade. As table 4 shows, exports began to decline in 1959 and reached a trough in 1962–1963, the worst agricultural years of the Revolution. In spite of some recuperation thereafter, the peak of 1967 was still below the 1957–1958 levels. On the other hand, imports, after a decline in 1959–1960, have increased steadily, reaching a record of more than one billion dollars in 1964. Cuba's year-end foreign reserves declined from $440 million in 1957 to $144 million in 1960, before the imbalance of trade became worse.[30]

The above-explained phenomenon has resulted in a growing trade deficit against Cuba. The cumulative trade deficit during the seven-year period

TABLE 4
CUBA'S FOREIGN TRADE: 1954–1967
(*In Millions of U.S. Dollars*)

Year	Volume	Exports (FOB)	Imports (CIF)	Trade Balance[a]
1954	1162	$563	$ 599	− $ 36
1955	1244	611	633	− 22
1956	1409	695	714	− 19
1957	1739	845	894	− 49
1958	1651	763	888	− 125
1959	1415	675	740	− 65
1960	1256	618	638	− 20
1961	1328	625	703	− 78
1962	1280	521	759	− 238
1963	1411	544	867	− 323
1964	1729	714	1,015	− 301
1965	1551	686	865	− 179
1966	1518	592	926	− 334
1967	1705	715	990	− 275

Source: International Monetary Fund, *International Financial Statistics: 1963, 1969*, January 1963 and July 1969.

a. The IMF series on trade balance for 1961–1967 does not coincide with the official Cuban series for the same period as shown in table 5.

from 1961 to 1967 is five times the largest foreign trade deficit accumulated in any similar period of Cuban prerevolutionary history.

As table 5 indicates, Cuba's cumulative trade deficit with the socialist countries reached $1,375.8 million in 1961–1967. The major creditor is the USSR (holding 83 percent of the trade deficit) followed by East Germany, China, and Czechoslovakia. Other important creditors are Hungary and Rumania, the latter becoming even more important in 1968–1969.

During the period 1961–1967, Cuba's cumulative trade deficit with nonsocialist countries reached $278.7 million. The major creditor nations were Canada, the European Economic Community (EEC), mainly France, and the United Kingdom. Cuba's trade with Japan and Morocco, on the other hand, has produced a remarkable export surplus. As for Spain, the trade has generally resulted in a surplus for Cuba with the notable exception of the year 1966 in which a large number of Spanish-made ships were bought by Cuba.

Foreign Aid

Table 6, although incomplete, provides a good picture of the extent of the socialist aid to Cuba. The USSR has provided $430 million in credit for development and possibly more than one billion dollars to finance

TABLE 5
CUBA'S BALANCE OF TRADE BY AREA AND COUNTRY: 1961–1967
(In Millions of U.S. Dollars)

Countries	1961	1962	1963	1964	1965	1966	1967	1961-1967
Socialist	+$11.4	-$211.9	-$330.0	-$264.7	-$122.3	-$256.7	-$201.6	-$1,375.8
USSR	+ 38.3	- 190.9	- 296.9	- 135.0	- 106.0	- 247.4	- 207.6	- 1,145.5
China	+ 3.0	- 0.8	- 18.1	- 28.3	- 22.9	+ 0.6	+ 7.1	- 59.4
Czechoslovakia	- 8.5	- 0.2	- 16.6	- 49.2	+ 10.1	+ 10.4	+ 5.9	- 48.1
E. Germany	- 14.8	- 2.4	+ 3.8	- 21.9	+ 3.3	+ 5.5	- 13.0	- 50.5
Poland	+ 10.7	- 4.1	- 10.8	- 12.3	- 4.2	+ 3.1	+ 0.5	- 17.1
Hungary	- 6.6	- 2.6	- 0.2	- 14.1	- 6.4	+ 5.8	+ 0.3	- 35.4
Bulgaria	- 2.4	+ 3.8	+ 4.0	+ 3.3	+ 4.8	+ 8.6	+ 4.5	+ 9.4
Rumania	- 6.5	- 7.1	- 0.4	- 7.8	+ 3.4	- 2.1	+ 0.4	- 26.9
Others	- 1.8	- 7.6	+ 5.2	- 0.6	+ 2.4	- 1.4	+ 0.3	- 3.5
Nonsocialist	- 60.9	+ 25.2	+ 62.2	- 43.5	- 57.3	- 99.0	- 105.4	- 278.7
USA	+ 20.0	- 8.0	- 40.1	- 0.1	—	- 0.1	—	- 28.2
Canada	- 30.0	- 8.9	- 4.8	- 59.3	- 48.8	- 57.7	- 37.5	- 247.0
EEC[a]	- 32.3	- 7.7	+ 30.9	- 44.0	- 9.3	- 23.2	- 86.7	- 172.3
U.K.	- 1.0	+ 10.0	+ 25.0	+ 6.9	- 33.1	- 13.2	+ 14.8	- 34.0
Spain	+ 3.6	+ 6.2	+ 9.5	+ 24.6	- 9.8	- 52.0	+ 3.8	- 14.1
Japan	+ 9.0	+ 20.7	+ 17.7	+ 10.4	+ 22.6	+ 13.2	+ 15.4	+ 109.0
Morocco	+ 3.1	+ 15.0	+ 14.0	+ 31.7	+ 24.3	+ 8.3	+ 7.1	+ 103.5
UAR[b]	- 1.6	+ 1.3	+ 1.5	+ 7.7	- 5.3	+ 8.7	+ 0.1	+ 8.6
Others	- 31.7	- 0.8	+ 11.4	+ 7.8	+ 2.1	+ 17.0	+ 7.2	+ 13.0

Sources: Data on socialist countries, 1961–1966, are from JUCEPLAN, *Boletín Estadístico, 1966,* pp. 124–25; and data on 1967 are from JUCE-PLAN, *Compendio Estadístico de Cuba, 1968,* p. 26. Data on nonsocialist countries are from International Monetary Fund, *Direction of Trade, Annual 1961–1965,* pp. 308–09, and *Annual 1963–1967,* pp. 377–78.

Note: Exports (FOB) minus imports (CIF).

  a. European Economic Community, mainly France.
  b. United Arab Republic.

TABLE 6
SOME CREDITS EXTENDED TO CUBA: 1960–1969

Country	Amount (in Millions of Dollars)	Amortization (Years)	Annual Interest Rate (Percentage)	Purpose
USSR				
1960	$100	12	2.5%	Development of metallurgy, electricity, petroleum
1961	100	10–12	2.5	Development of mining (nickel and cobalt)
1962	100	10–12	2–2.5	Chemical and fertilizer plants
1963	100–150	10–12	2–2.5	Finance trade deficit
1964	159	10–12	2–2.5	Finance trade deficit
1964	130	10–12	2–2.5	Development of sugar industry
1968	200	10–12	2–2.5	Finance trade deficit
China				
1960	60	10	0.0	Industrial plants and equipment
East Germany				
1960	10	10	2.5	Industrial plants and equipment
1963	10	10–12	2.5	Industrial plants and equipment
—[a]	40	10–12	2.5	Industrial plants, shipyard
Czechoslovakia				
1960	40	10	2.5	Electric plants, automotive industries
Rumania				
1961	15	10–12	2.5	Industrial plants, electricity
1968	30	10–12	2.5	Development of petroleum industry
1969	20	10–12	2.5	Development of mining (copper)
Hungary				
1961	15	10	2.5	Industrial plants and equipment
Poland				
1960	12	8	2.5	Industrial plants, shipyard
Bulgaria				
1961	5	10	2.5	Refrigerating and hydroelectric plants
France				
1968	36	—	—	Tractors
England				
1969	50	—	—	Fertilizer plant
Total	$1,232			

Sources: Robert S. Walters, unpub. app. to "Soviet Economic Aid to Cuba: 1959–1964," International Affairs, 42 (January 1966), p. 14, table 9; and Carlos Rafael Rodríguez, Cuba, ejemplo de América (Lima, 1969), pp. 99–102.
a. Date unavailable.

trade deficits. (The table does not provide information of trade-deficit credits for the period 1965–1967, but it is safe to estimate a $100 million to $200 million deficit for each year.) The total aid granted by the socialist bloc to Cuba in 1960–1969 may be close to $2 billion, about one-fifth of the sum made available by the U.S government to the Alliance for Progress for all of Latin America in this period. Typical credits extended by socialist nations to Cuba are for maturities of from ten to twelve years and carry an interest rate of from 2 percent to 2.5 percent. Assistance from nonsocialist countries takes the form of government-guaranteed medium-term supplier credits at the market interest rate. Table 6 gives information on the use of credit granted to Cuba. Not included are $1.5 billion in military aid granted by the Soviet Union alone.[31]

Aid granted to the development of heavy industry never materialized, and part of it was possibly wasted. However, there are visible positive results in other areas, such as electric power, dams, the new fishing fleet and fishing port near Havana, and the expansion of cement and fertilizer output capacity.

The Emigration of Human Capital

The socialization of the Cuban Revolution alienated the upper-income groups, the majority of the middle class, and significant segments of the workers (mainly urban, skilled organized labor). It is impossible to determine the size of the refugee outflow due to the lack of central filing and because the exiles have gone to many different countries. Yet, the overwhelming majority of emigrants are in the United States, with some 250,000 in the Miami area. There have been two waves of exiles. From 1959 to 1962, most came directly to the United States on commercial airlines. However, the missile crisis resulted in the closing of this channel of escape and, in 1962–1965, the exodus declined sharply, the only remaining exits being those of Spain and Mexico, which are quite expensive. The U.S.-government-sponsored airlift inaugurated in December 1965, with the approval of Cuba, is bringing to the United States some 1,000 exiles per week. Between 1959 and June 1965, an estimated 288,000 Cuban exiles came to the United States.[32] To this should be added 173,000 who came through the airlift from December 1965 to December 1969. In the period 1961–1968, about 10,600 exiles came to the United States through nonconventional means, that is, boats, rafts, etc.[33] Certainly, there are more than 30,000 exiles in Latin America and Europe. Therefore, giving proper allowance to double counting, a total estimate of more than half a million exiles at the end of 1969 seems accurate. This is equal to 6.5 percent of the Cuban population at the time and 8 percent of the population in 1958.

A large number of the exiles are well educated. According to a sample taken among exiles who arrived in Miami in 1959–1962, some 36 percent had either some years of college or had completed a professional degree.[34] An estimate made in 1965 based on data from the Refugee Center in Miami placed 28 percent of the exiles in this top educational category.[35] Table 7

TABLE 7

DISTRIBUTION OF CUBAN EXILES BY PREVIOUS OCCUPATION IN CUBA FOR SELECTED YEARS

(*In Percentages*)

	1959–1962	*1963*	*1965–1966*	*1961–1968*
Professionals, semiprofessionals, managers, and executives	37.2%	32.7%	22.2%	18.1%
Clerical and sales employees	30.9	35.5	30.6	11.7
Skilled and semiskilled workers	}31.9ᵃ	12.8	16.6	}70.2ᵃ
Unskilled workers		19.0	30.6	

Sources: 1959–1962: Richard R. Fagen and Richard A. Brody, "Cubans in Exile: A Demographic Analysis," *Social Problems*, 11 (Spring 1964), p. 391. *1963:* Florida Industrial Commission, "Characteristics of Cuban Refugees in Dade County, Florida," mimeographed (March 1963), table 7. *1965–1966:* Cuban Refugee Program, "Airlift Arrivals (December 1, 1965 to June 31, 1966)," mimeographed, July 1, 1966. *1961–1968:* Sample of Cuban exiles arriving in the United States by boats, rafts, etc., from John M. Clark, "Selected Types of Cuban Exiles Used as a Sample of the Cuban Population" (Paper presented at the meetings of the Rural Sociological Society, Washington, D.C., 1970).

Note: Limited to Dade County, Florida.

a. Clustering has been made to facilitate comparisons; the original categorization included: skilled, semiskilled, and unskilled workers; domestic service; and agriculture and fishing.

shows that in 1959–1963, about one-third of the exiles in the Miami–Dade County area were professionals or had managerial occupations in Cuba; another third were clerical or sales employees; and about one-seventh were skilled or semiskilled workers. However, it seems that Miami is not precisely a mecca for talented, challenging Cubans, and many preferred to go to other cities offering brighter opportunities. Therefore, the occupational composition of those exiles in Miami perhaps indicates a downward bias in favor of the less skilled groups.

Table 7 indicates that as time passes, the percentage of exiles in the professional-executive bracket diminishes, whereas that of those in the unskilled labor bracket increases. This phenomenon is a function of two factors: (a) the depletion of the former high- and middle-class groups within Cuba and (b) the restriction imposed by the Cuban government on technicians, professionals, and skilled workers who want to leave.

The seriousness of the brain drain induced the Cuban government in

May 1966 to stop the registration for the airlift. A total of 250,000 were registered by that date, and 80,000 are still waiting to leave. The last column of table 7 is derived from a sample of exiles arriving by boat and other similar means. The percentage of those in the top occupational categories is substantially below that of the previous columns. Out of the remaining 70 percent, 50 percent were *obreros* (nonagricultural workers), and 20 percent were fishermen, farmers, and domestic servants.

A crude estimate of Cuba's loss of "human capital" may be made by (a) using the estimated total exiled population of 500,000; (b) calculating one-third of it as the labor force (165,000) by using an average percentage derived from Cuban historical data; (c) using the percentage occupational distribution of 1963 (column 2 of table 7); and then (d) distributing the estimated labor force among this percentage distribution. The results, admittedly speculative, follow: 54,000 professionals, semiprofessionals, managers, and executives; 59,000 clerical and sales employees; 21,000 skilled and semiskilled workers; and 31,000 unskilled workers.

Whatever the exact figures are, there is no doubt that this exodus has created grave shortages in nearly all categories of trained personnel in Cuba: managers, engineers, physicians, agronomists, foremen, accountants, college teachers, mechanics, etc. The Cuban leaders have acknowledged on several occasions the impact of this outflow and even have accepted that in some cases it was unnecessarily aggravated by erroneous attitudes or decisions that alienated these groups. The government has tried to compensate the outflow of talent with a similar inflow from Latin America (mainly Chileans and Mexicans in the early period of the Revolution) and from Eastern Europe, but apparently this has not been sufficient to impede stoppages and management inefficiency. However, Cuban students have been sent to be trained abroad (mainly in the USSR and East Germany) and the recruitment of university students in technological careers and medicine has increased dramatically (see chapter 12).

The Cuban brain drain has been to the advantage of the United States (in the fields of medicine, college teaching, business, language skills) and of Latin America.[36] The Cubans' managerial skills have been in high demand, particularly in Puerto Rico, Venezuela, and Central America. International and inter-American specialized agencies have also benefited from the skills of Cuban exiles.

Conclusions

The profound recasting of Cuba's political economy after 1959 ruptured the web of economic ties with the United States that had endured for over half a century. As Cuba's market economy gave way to state ownership and central commands, its external economic posture shifted abruptly from the United States to the Soviet bloc.

The Revolution inherited an economy that was financially strong by Latin American standards and that depended heavily on the United States for capital and trade. The island reached a record sugar harvest in 1952 and in the 1950s was launched on a new growth path via import substitution for the home market. Industrial capacity advanced substantially in a number of branches, particularly electric power, glass containers, cement, oil-refining, chemicals, nickel-mining, paper, and light copper and steel products. Cuba's balance of payments position also drew support from the accelerated growth of the tourist industry in the 1950s and the replacement of food imports with domestic production. Inflation was not a problem and Cuba was able to keep a minimum of foreign reserve exchange. But, in spite of these advances, the Cuban economy was still depending mainly on the exportation of sugar and on other primary products such as tobacco and minerals, and two-thirds of its trade was with the United States, which usually ended in a trade deficit.

United States business investments in Cuba, through corporate subsidiaries and branches, reached a value of about one billion dollars at the end of 1959 and contributed markedly to Cuba's national income and net foreign exchange position. Apparently, U.S. profits in Cuba were below the average of U.S. profits in Latin America. New U.S. investments after World War II entered branches of activity that primarily served the national market and were often channels for the transmission of advanced technology. Many of the traditional U.S. holdings, that is, sugar mills and estates, insurance and banking, passed, from the 1930s on, into the hands of Cubans through negotiated purchases.

The structural changes that have taken place under the Revolution in Cuba's foreign trade sector involve primarily the direction of commodity flows rather than their composition. In the brief span of four years, from 1960 to 1964, Cuba's trade with the United States, its predominant trading partner, ceased altogether. The socialist countries have since 1961 accounted for about 75 percent of Cuba's trade turnover, of which about 50 percent is with the USSR. The rest of Cuba's trade is mainly with Canada, Western Europe, and Japan.

Cuba's external payments position since 1960 has been characterized by a widening trade gap, the consequence of stagnation, and even decline, in export values and a persistent rise in commodity imports. The associated explosive rise in external public debts during the 1960s has not been matched by growth in debt-service capacity, for exports have failed to expand. Of Cuba's cumulative trade deficit of nearly $1.7 billion for the period 1961–1967, more than four-fifths was held by the socialist countries, mainly the USSR.

Significant differences emerge when comparing Soviet economic involvement in Cuba vis-à-vis that of the United States. Prior to 1960, U.S. enterprises through direct investments, exercised managerial control over important segments of the Cuban economy, whereas U.S. official lending to Cuba played a relatively minor role. Since 1960, Cuba has become tied to the USSR and other centrally planned nations through barter arrangements, leaving Cuba a greatly reduced margin of convertible foreign exchange. Socialist economic aid to Cuba in 1960–1969 was possibly close to $2 billion. A large portion of this amount has been granted by the USSR to cover Cuba's trade deficit, the rest being developmental loans. The island has also received an estimated $1.5 billion worth of military equipment from the Soviet Union. Hence, although the USSR does not have direct economic control over Cuba, there is no doubt that its influence is enormous and that Cuba is heavily dependent on Soviet capital and trade.

Sugar and by-products made up between 80 percent to 86 percent of Cuba's exports in 1961–1967, showing a slight increase in this dependency. The share of minerals (mainly nickel) has risen slowly, that of tobacco is stagnant, and that of other exports (mainly agricultural products) has declined. The composition of Cuban imports is difficult to assess in view of available data, but it seems fair to say that food and manufactured products have been sacrificed in order to increase other import lines.

Cuba's economic reorientation since 1960 has induced serious adjustment problems. From a purely economic point of view, the trade relationship with the USSR, whose ports are 5,500 miles away, is an unnatural one and has resulted in an increase in freight cost. This problem does not have a clear solution at this time. The spare-parts crisis in those industries which utilize U.S.-made equipment and in transportation has been temporarily solved through triangular trade and the aid of transportation equipment from Western Europe and Czechoslovakia. In time, Cuba's capital stock could be reoriented to Eastern European and, to a lesser degree, Western European equipment specifications. The gap created by the ceased transfer of U.S. technology and the massive exodus of Cuban managers, professionals, and technicians has not been compensated for with technical assistance from the socialist bloc. Eventually, this gap may be filled because of the restrictions imposed upon technicians who want to leave the country, and because of the support of the current reorientation of Cuban education in favor of developmental-technological careers. Cuba has lost the opportunity to participate both in economic integration projects going forward in Central and South America and in the Caribbean tourist boom of the 1960s. Without doubt, Cuba would have captured the lion's share of this boom, which, instead, has benefited Puerto Rico, Jamaica, and the smaller Caribbean islands. Finally, the additional difficulties originally created by the U.S.-OAS economic embargo and shipping boycott seem to have lost much force by 1970.

On the other hand, important advances after 1960 have been made in the development of Cuba's merchant marine and fishing industry and the mining of nickel. Exports of nickel have continued the upward trend of the 1950s. All in all, Cuba's shift from the U.S. area to the Soviet area of economic influence has signified the exchange of one type of economic dependency for another, without essentially solving the malaise of Cuba's prerevolutionary export economy.

NOTES

1. Carmelo Mesa-Lago, "Availability and Reliability of Statistics in Socialist Cuba," *Latin American Research Review,* 4 (Spring 1969), pp. 61–62, and ibid. (Summer 1969), pp. 61–63, 76–77.

2. See, for example, Gerald M. Meier, *International Trade and Development* (New York, 1963), pp. 5–6.

3. Henry C. Wallich, *Monetary Problems of an Export Economy: The Cuban Experience, 1914–1947* (Cambridge, Mass., 1950), p. 26.

4. For example, in the five-year period from 1955 to 1959, the U.S. price averaged 5.2 cents per pound compared with the average world price of 3.7 cents. See International Monetary Fund, *International Financial Statistics, 1955–1959.*

5. Cuban Economic Research Project, *Study on Cuba* (Coral Gables, 1965), pp. 616–18, tables 462–64.

6. International Bank for Reconstruction and Development, Economic and Technical Mission to Cuba, *Report on Cuba* (Baltimore, Md., 1951), p. 72.

7. For a detailed discussion of U.S. investments in Cuba, see Eric Baklanoff's "Reflections on United States Investments in Cuba, 1929–1959," *Annals of the South-Eastern Conference on Latin American Studies* (March 1970), pp. 45–58.

8. U.S. Dept. of Commerce, *U.S. Business Investments in the Cuban Economy* (Washington, D.C., November 14, 1960).

9. Derived from *Survey of Current Business,* 1956–1961, August or September issues.

10. Between 1934 and 1951, Cubans purchased thirty-two mills from U.S. interests for about $35 million; nine from Canadians for $7.8 million and two each from Spanish, Netherlands, and French interests for a total of about $5 million. From 1952 to 1955, inclusive, five mills came under Cuban control. See U.S. Dept. of Commerce, *Investment in Cuba* (Washington, D.C., 1956), p. 37, n. 16.

11. *Anuario Azucarero de Cuba, 1959* cited in Cuban Economic Research Project, *Study on Cuba,* p. 523, table 360.

12. Cuban Economic Research Project, *Study on Cuba,* p. 569, table 428.

13. The Island produced approximately 15 percent of the global production and supplied one-third of the sugar sold in the international market. See, Cuban Economic Research Project, "Cuba's Foreign Trade Before and After 1958," mimeographed (Coral Gables, 1962).

14. ECLA, *Economic Survey of Latin America, 1957* (New York, 1959), pp. 190–93.

15. Ibid., pp. 190–91.

16. Cuban Economic Research Project, *Study on Cuba,* p. 618, table 464.

17. See Dudley Seers, ed., *Cuba: The Economic and Social Revolution* (Chapel Hill, 1964), pp. 7–20; and Edward Boorstein, *The Economic Transformation of Cuba* (New York, 1968), pp. 2–7.

18. For example, see Boorstein, *Economic Transformation,* p. 8.

19. See Boris Goldenberg, *The Cuban Revolution and Latin America* (New York, 1966), pp. 136–42.

20. Assistant secretary for Latin American Affairs, Roy Rubottom, invited Castro's aides to discuss Cuba's financial needs and offered help. See Robert F. Smith, *The United States and Cuba: Business and Diplomacy, 1917–1960* (New York, 1962), pp. 157–59.

21. Arthur P. Whitaker and David C. Jordan, *Nationalism in Contemporary Latin America* (New York, 1966), p. 156.

22. U.S. Dept. of Agriculture, *A Survey of Agriculture in Cuba* (Washington, D.C., June 1969), pp. 17–18.

23. UN, *Statistical Yearbook, 1968* (New York, 1969), p. 245, table 89.

24. Herbert G. Lawson, "Cuba's Economy," *Wall Street Journal,* 173, March 7, 1969, p. 20.

25. U.S. Dept. of State, Director of Intelligence and Research, Research Memorandum REU—71, December 26, 1968.

26. *The Morning Advocate* (Baton Rouge, La.), April 3, 1969, p. 12G.

27. UN, *Statistical Yearbook, 1968,* p. 418, table 156.

28. Carlos Rafael Rodríguez, *Cuba, ejemplo de América* (Lima, Peru, 1969), pp. 103–20.

29. Ibid., p. 40.

30. International Monetary Fund, *International Financial Statistics: 1957–1960.*

31. Fidel Castro, "Speech at the Ceremony to Commemorate the Centennial of the Birth of V. I. Lenin," *Granma Weekly Review,* May 3, 1970, p. 3.

32. Research Institute for Cuba and the Caribbean, *The Cuban Immigration 1959–1966 and Its Impact on Miami Dade County, Florida* (Coral Gables, 1967), app. B, table 1.

33. John M. Clark, "Selected Types of Cuban Exiles Used as a Sample of the Cuban Population" (Paper presented at the meeting of the Rural Sociological Society, Washington, D.C., 1970).

34. Richard R. Fagen et al., *Cubans in Exile* (Stanford, 1968), p. 28.

35. Research Institute for Cuba and the Caribbean, *Cuban Immigration,* p. 17.

36. See ibid., and John Thomas, "Cuban Refugees in the United States," *International Migration Review,* 1 (Spring 1967), pp. 47–57; "Cuban Success Story in the United States," *U.S. News and World Report* (March 20, 1967), pp. 104–06; "Cuban Shops an Asset to Miami," *New York Times,* August 26, 1969, pp. 53, 60; Raúl Moncarz, *A Study of the Effect of Environmental Change of Human Capital Among Selected Skilled Cubans,* published by the U.S. Department of Commerce,

Clearinghouse for Federal and Scientific and Technical Information, PB/186/396 (1969); Alejandro Portes, "Dilemmas of a Golden Exile: Integration of Cuban Refugee Families in Milwaukee," *American Sociological Review,* 34 (August 1969), pp. 505–18; and Harvey Rosenhouse, "El éxodo y el éxito de los cubanos," *Visión* (March 13, 1970), pp. 24–28, 33.

11 Carmelo Mesa-Lago

Economic Policies and Growth

THIS chapter describes the shifting economic policies applied by the Cuban government in successive stages during 1959–1970, and analyzes these policies in terms of their effectiveness in solving the structural problems of the prerevolutionary economy and their impact on production and economic growth.

The Structural Problems of the Prerevolutionary Economy

In the author's opinion the five crucial socioeconomic problems existing in Cuba in 1957–1958 were as follows: (a) the relatively small rate of economic growth, (b) the excessive significance of sugar in the generation of GNP and exports, (c) the overwhelming dependence on the United States in regard to capital and trade, (d) the high rates of unemployment and underemployment, and (e) the wide differences in standards of living between urban and rural areas. A brief discussion of these problems is necessary for a proper understanding of revolutionary economic policies.

Economic growth. Some economists, such as Dudley Seers and James O'Connor, have claimed that the Cuban economy was stagnant either since the 1920s or throughout the whole republican period beginning in 1902.[1] However, an analysis of the scarce available data does not seem to support the stagnation theory. National accounts began to be computed by the newly established National Bank of Cuba at the turn of the 1940s, and prior to this date there was a vacuum of reliable statistics in this field. Although a national income series was prepared for 1902–1948 by Julián

The author gratefully acknowledges several suggestions made by Professors William Dunn, University of Pittsburgh, and James O. Morris, Cornell University, who read and commented on an earlier version of this essay.

Alienes, he acknowledged its deficiencies and cautiously stated that his series was a "mere estimate" that had to be taken with "extreme reserve" and could not be used as "statistical proof."[2] In view of these problems, it is safer to concentrate our attention on the decade of the 1950s.

According to the National Bank, in 1950–1958 the Cuban GNP estimated at current prices grew at an average rate of 4.6 percent annually. The average population growth during this period was 2.5 percent annually, fixing the per capita growth of GNP at 2.1 percent.[3] The National Bank never published a deflated GNP series (at constant prices), perhaps because of the lack of an accurate wholesale price index. Nevertheless, various indices of consumer prices prepared during this period indicate that the cost of living in Havana (the most expensive city in the country) climbed by 1.1 percent annually, on the average. Therefore, it could be roughly said that the increase of GNP per capita in 1950–1958, at constant prices, was approximately 1 percent. The percentage of Cuba's GNP devoted to investment in 1950–1958 reached an average of 18 percent, and showed a steady tendency to climb, creating some hope that the rate of growth would rise in the 1960s. In summary, the Cuban economy was not stationary; indeed, it grew, but at a very slow rate, with some expectations for a higher rate in the future.

Importance of sugar. In the period 1949–1958, an average of from 28 percent to 29 percent of the GNP was generated by the sugar sector. However, a tendency toward the lessening of the importance of sugar was noticeable, not only during that period, but in comparison to the 1940s. Thus, in the years 1957–1958, sugar originated only 25 percent of the Cuban GNP. On the other hand, nonsugar industrial output grew 47 percent between 1947 and 1958. As a typical export economy, Cuba depended heavily on foreign trade; thus, in 1949–1958, some 36 percent of its GNP was generated by exports. Sugar and its by-products represented an average of 84 percent of the total exports, and the remaining exports were mainly tobacco and minerals. The price fluctuations of sugar on the international market, as well as the varying quota policies and prices of the United States, were exogenous factors that Cuba found impossible to control. As a result of the excessive importance of sugar, these fluctuations had a serious impact on the GNP, provoking a situation of instability and uncertainty.[4]

Dependence on the United States. United States investment in Cuba by 1958 was possibly the second largest in Latin America, and in the period 1949–1958, an average of 68.6 percent of Cuba's foreign trade was with the United States. This commercial dependence invariably resulted in a negative balance of trade for Cuba, building up an accumulative deficit of almost $350 million during that period.[5] Some scholars argue that the proximity of Cuba, an island, to the United States, the world's most powerful economy, resulted in a total integration of the Cuban economy into the American economy, and that because of this, the former could not achieve a satisfactory degree of independence or domestic integration.[6]

Unemployment and underemployment. The most serious socioeconomic problem of Cuba was unemployment. In the years 1956–1957, 39 percent of the labor force found employment in primary activities (agriculture, fishing, mining, cattle-ranching); 20 percent, in secondary activities (industry, construction, electricity); 36 percent, in tertiary activities (communications, commerce, services); and the rest had no specific occupation. Between 1919 and 1957, the percentage of the labor force employed in agriculture fell from 49 percent to 39 percent. The principal increases in employment were found in construction, commerce, and industry, in that order, but such increases were not high enough to absorb both the rapidly growing labor force and rural-to-urban migration. On the eve of the Revolution, 16.4 percent of the labor force was totally unemployed, and approximately 13.8 percent found itself in various forms of underemployment.

These figures represent annual averages, and they therefore do not reveal the fluctuations of unemployment during the year. From 20 percent to 25 percent of the labor force found work in the sugar sector, but due to the seasonal character of the sugar crop and its processing, this portion of the work force had stable work for only four months out of the year. During the "dead season" (May–December), the proportion of employment in the sugar sector fell to 4 percent or 5 percent. It is difficult to determine what percentage of the temporarily unemployed sugar workers worked on their own land or on other crop harvests during the dead season, although it is known that about one-third of the sugar workers found employment for another three months in the harvesting of the coffee crop. In any event, 1956–1957 statistics show that total unemployment increased from 200,-000 workers during the period of greatest activity in the sugar harvest (February–April) to 457,000 workers during the period of lowest activity (August–October). Although strict comparisons are not possible, statistics on unemployment calculated in 1943, 1953, and 1956–1957, suggest that this situation was becoming increasingly worse.[7]

Standards of living. An accurate study of differences in the standards of living among the Cuban population is impossible due to the absence of income distribution figures. Only a very general index exists, indicating how the national income was distributed within two large categories: remuneration for work (wages, fringe benefits, pensions), and remuneration for capital (rent, interest, dividends). Between 1949 and 1958, the average annual percentage of national income paid in workers' remuneration was 65 percent, and it showed a noticeable tendency to increase. Surprisingly, in 1958, Cuba's percentage was surpassed by only three developed Western countries: Great Britain, the United States, and Canada.[8] The *employed* labor force in Cuba had sufficient political and economic power to capture and increase its share of the national income, but it seems that this privileged status was obtained in large measure at the cost of the unemployed and the peasants.

In 1953, 43.7 percent of the Cuban population lived in rural areas, compared with 55.3 percent in 1919. During this lapse of time, legislation was enacted to better protect the peasants. (Good examples of these laws were the "right of permanency" introduced in 1937—squatters' rights—and the regulations of 1948 concerning sharecropping.) Nevertheless, growing urbanization was accompanied by preferential attention (in regard to state expenses) given to the urban areas and especially to the important cities such as Havana. In 1957–1958, national averages in the matter of education, public health, and social security placed Cuba among the top three Latin American countries: its literacy rate was the fourth highest, its percentage of the labor force covered by old-age, invalidity, and survivors social insurance was the second highest, its indices of number of inhabitants per doctor and hospital bed were the third lowest, its morbidity index was the second lowest, its death rate and infant mortality rate were the lowest, etc.[9] But social-service facilities were mainly concentrated in the capital city and urban areas, whereas their availability and quality declined sharply in the rural areas. A survey taken in 1956–1957 demonstrated that the position of the Cuban peasant in regard to caloric intake, diet, health, medical attention, housing, and income was very much below the national averages for 1953.[10]

The migratory movement from the countryside to the city was accentuated by the impoverished condition of the rural population, which soon made itself visible in Havana's shantytowns. However, the miserable condition of life in these quarters was still superior to the condition of many agricultural workers and peasants. A large number of these rural migrants found low paying work in the tertiary sector (e.g., domestic services, peddling) or they simply become beggars. The high and growing percentage of the work force engaged in tertiary activities in Cuba was a clear symptom of underemployment.

In summary, during the decade prior to the Revolution, the Cuban economy showed a small rate of growth and the government's policies did not manage to solve its structural problems. The employed labor force, organized into unions, absorbed a great part of the benefits of growth at the expense of the peasants and the unemployed groups devoid of union power. Even though a noteworthy advance in the development of the nonsugar sector was reported, the dependence on sugar was still enormous. Nor did the nation effect a substantial change in its dependency on and balance of trade with the United States.

The Shifting Revolutionary Economic Policy

The most important socioeconomic goals announced by the Revolution in its first year were related to the correction of the structural problems explained above: to reduce the dependence on sugar, diversify agricultural production, rapidly develop the industrial sector, and achieve a high rate of economic growth; to attain full employment, and improve the living conditions of the peasants and of the low-income workers in the cities; and to obtain more economic independence from the United States.

In the period 1959–1970, the Revolution frequently modified its economic policies in trying to implement the above-mentioned goals. Furthermore, some of the goals themselves were either changed or abandoned. Conflicts among alternative strategies and among organizational models were crucial in generating policy shifts: (a) the conflict between development based on industry and nonsugar agriculture (balanced-growth model), and development based on sugar and primary activities ("big-push" model); (b) the conflict between a "popular," short-term policy in favor of distribution and consumption, and a long-term policy in favor of capital accumulation necessary for development; and (c) the conflict between a model of economic organization characterized by decentralized planning, self-financed enterprise, and economic incentives, and another model typified by centralized planning, budgetary enterprise, and moral incentives. From 1959 to 1970 there was a shifting emphasis from the first toward the second alternative in each of the three conflicts presented.

Since other chapters of this book discuss in detail the shifts in the organization of the economy (chapters 7 and 8) and in distribution versus accumulation policies (chapter 2), this chapter will concentrate on the strategy for development, though not completely neglecting the other two areas. The period 1959–1963 was typified by an emphasis on industrialization and diversification of agricultural output with a strong bias against sugar. The 1964–1970 period was characterized by a return to sugar and the abandonment of the heavy industrialization plans. Both periods are discussed below, but the author has given more attention to the most recent and less-known period of 1964–1970. The policies of the Revolution directed to solve the structural problems of the country for each period are described and the results of such policies are evaluated.

The Industrialization Drive: 1959–1963

The revolutionary leaders were devoted to a philosophy of simplicity, and proposed the application of guerrilla techniques to Cuba's economy and administration. The logic of this attitude was that the guerrilla group had rapidly triumphed in the military camp using experimental, empirical methods against a supposedly "technical" army and the new leaders assumed, therefore, that similar methods should be used in other areas. The new leaders also had a special disdain for the bureaucrats whom they viewed with suspicion as opportunists who deliberately complicated administrative and economic matters in hopes of making themselves indispensable. It was thought that Cuba's economic and administrative problems would be rapidly resolved by the power of the Revolution, the zeal of the new leaders, the audacity of the improvisation, and the enthusiasm of the people.[11] In summary, "subjective" conditions (e.g., willingness, consciousness) were emphasized over "objective" conditions (e.g., expertise, knowledge, available resources).

The revolutionary theorem arrived at an erroneous conclusion based on two false premises. Castro's military victory was not so much the tactical defeat of a technical army, but, rather, the result of the demoralization of the corrupted armed forces, who did not decisively confront the guerrillas. The other false premise (which Lenin also mistakenly employed in his early days in the Soviet administration) was romantically to expect that a complex economy in a modern state could be managed with improvisation, audacity, and lack of knowledge.

Policies

The revolutionaries believed that a gradual collectivization of the means of production was a necessary first step if their goals were ever to be achieved. In the collectivization process, various means were used: confiscation of property and of goods obtained illegally by officials of the overthrown dictatorship, expropriation of the land for agrarian reform, expropriation of housing for urban reform, state intervention in enterprises alleging labor conflicts, confiscation of goods belonging to counterrevolutionaries or exiles, nationalization of all foreign properties and of medium- and large-sized domestic enterprises, nationalization of centers of private education, etc. In the majority of cases, the government confiscated goods without giving compensation.[12] The process of collectivization developed in Cuba with extraordinary velocity and scope (see table 1) without provoking violent reaction as had happened in other socialist countries.

The collectivization of agriculture in Cuba merits special attention. The First Agrarian Reform Law (1959) stipulated that a private farm could consist of no more than 400 hectares. Originally, it was announced that the large expropriated farms were to be divided and distributed, but later it was argued that land partitionment would result in a decline in productivity. By the end of 1961, many of the large farms were organized into cooperatives (600 units) or into state farms (500 units), the latter in a manner similar to that of the Soviet *sovkhozy*. In mid-1962, the cooperatives were

TABLE 1
PROGRESSIVE COLLECTIVIZATION OF THE MEANS OF
PRODUCTION IN CUBA: 1961, 1963, AND 1968
(*In Percentages*)

Sectors	1961	1963	1968
Agriculture	37%	70%	70%
Industry	85	95	100
Construction	80	98	100
Transportation	92	95	100
Retail trade	52	75	100
Wholesale and foreign trade	100	100	100
Banking	100	100	100
Education	100	100	100

Source: See Carmelo Mesa-Lago, "Ideological Radicalization and Economic Policy in Cuba," *Studies in Comparative International Development*, 5, no. 10 (1969–1970), p. 204, table 1.

transformed into state farms. The private sector was reduced to 30 percent in October 1963, when the Second Agrarian Reform Law expropriated all the farms having more than 67 hectares. (Private farms are mainly devoted to the cultivation of sugar, coffee, tobacco, fruits, vegetables, turbes, and beans.) The average size of the surviving private farms is 13.8 hectares and they are integrated into the ANAP. The ANAP is under the supervision of the INRA, which, in turn, controls the supplying of seeds, fertilizers, tools, and credit to the small farmers. Moreover, the INRA plans the type of crops that are to be planted, and controls the system of procurement quotas (*acopio*), that is, the compulsory sale of part of the crop to the state at prices set below the market prices. Thus, the private farm has been converted into a sort of Soviet *kolkhoz,* the only difference being that it is cultivated individually instead of collectively.[13]

In 1960, as part of the program of agrarian diversification to decrease dependence on sugar, large estates producing sugar cane were cleared off and replanted with rice, fruits, or vegetables. The total area planted in sugar cane was reduced from 1,414,000 hectares in 1958 to 1,064,037 hectares in 1963, a 25 percent decline.[14]

At the same time, a substantial part of the nation's investment was used for the purchase of manufacturing equipment from the USSR, Czechoslovakia, and East Germany. At the beginning of the 1960s, Minister of Industries Ernesto Guevara predicted that by 1965, Cuba's heavy industry would be very advanced, and Minister of Economy Regino Boti stated that on said date Cuba would lead Latin America in per capita output of electricity, steel, cement, tractors, and refined petroleum.[15]

In order to obtain economic independence from the United States, Cuba signed numerous commercial treaties and received credits from Eastern Europe and China. When, in July 1960, the United States suspended the Cuban sugar quota, the USSR and China committed themselves to buy one million and one-half million tons of sugar, respectively, between 1960 and 1965. Trade with the United States, which represented 66 percent of Cuba's trade in 1959, fell to 2 percent in 1962.[16]

Seasonal unemployment in agriculture was slowly reduced after 1960 due to various steps taken by the government: organization of the state farms that permanently absorbed manpower on a fixed-pay scale; rural-to-urban migration stimulated by popular mobilizations, the expansion of the army, and the attractiveness of city life; and an increase in the number of scholarships granted to rural youth. In 1962, overt unemployment had disappeared in the countryside. The tertiary sector had grown notably, as a new source of employment, due to the proliferation of organizations of the military (army, militia), of the masses (CTC, UJC, FMC, CDR), and the Communist party, as well as the expansion of social services controlled by the state and an increase of the bureaucracy of the planning apparatus. Potential unemployment in the secondary sector, resulting from the merging of enterprises into *consolidados* and the closing of some enterprises due to lack of spare parts created by the U.S. embargo, did not materialize because the surplus labor was not dismissed.[17]

In the first years of the Revolution (1959–1961), the government propitiated a definite policy for redistribution of the national income. The realization of full employment was a crucial step. Moreover, overall monetary wages were increased, and the minimum wage in agriculture and minimum pensions were also raised. Disposable income for the poorest sector was augmented as a result of the reduction of rent on dwellings and the cost of electricity, and the expansion of free public services such as medical care, education, recreation, and sports. A considerable amount of low-rent housing was constructed during the first two years of the Revolution. The government put special emphasis on extending essential services to the rural areas (see chapter 12). The economic policy in favor of consumption and distribution assured wide popular support for the Revolution during its first years in power (see chapter 2).

The almost total elimination of private ownership of the means of production and public services brought about the disappearance of the automatic mechanisms of a market economy. In other words, production and distribution of goods ceased being determined by the law of supply and demand. This situation became accentuated in 1961 because, by this time, the greater part of the nonagricultural sector already had been collectivized. The market system had been gradually replaced by administrative orders that set input and output quotas for state enterprises, fixed prices of primary, intermediate and final products, decided the number of workers in each unit of production, introduced labor norms and wage scales, and regulated foreign trade on the basis of quotas. All these measures were integrated by the annual plans of 1962 and 1963, and the long-run strategy for development was set by the four-year plan of 1962–1965. The system of production, distribution, and consumption was integrated under a hierarchical organization of pyramidal shape directed by JUCEPLAN (see chapter 7).

From what has been said, one could infer that, in 1961, the structural problems of the Cuban economy were either solved or on the way to being solved rapidly. However, in 1962–1963, alarming symptoms indicated that these solutions were more apparent than real and, in the meantime, new problems had come to the fore.

Results

The guerrilla mentality and the original animosity against technicians partly determined the alienation of this latter group, who were vital to the ambitious development plans and structural changes envisaged by the revolutionary leaders. The accelerated collectivization of the means of production antagonized the managerial class. Cuba did not follow the example of China, who, for more than a decade, flirted with management and technical personnel in order to make sure that a good number of these people stayed in business. China even offered compensation to the owners for their expropriated enterprises and a share of the profits. Cuba's technicians, managers, and administrators, the cadres that the Revolution was so soon and so desperately to need, fled the country (see chapter 10). The vacuum was filled with loyal revolutionaries, but incompetent administrators, who tried to improvise solutions under the prevailing guerrilla mentality.

State planners and managers without the pressure of market competition nor the fear of loss, and under the revolutionary enthusiasm, committed costly errors, brought about inefficiency and waste, and rapidly expanded the number of unproductive, bureaucratic jobs. The workers, especially on the state farms, with no fear of unemployment, with the stability of a job with a fixed income and the romantic idea that the means of production belonged to them, began to cut back their productive effort. The phenomenon of absenteeism appeared in 1962 and soon took on alarming dimensions.[18]

A large number of the jobs created by the Revolution were in the tertiary sector and of an unproductive nature. The interruption of trade with the United States and the embargo brought about initial difficulties in obtaining spare parts and raw materials, which resulted in the closing or diminishing of activities in various enterprises. As has been said, in the secondary sector the workers were not dismissed but were temporarily subsidized from a payroll (the labor reserve) supported by the affected enterprise. The leaders hoped to absorb part of the surplus labor through the process of industrialization. Seasonal, overt unemployment in agriculture was partly eliminated through subsidies for unnecessary workers in the secondary sector and disguised unemployment in the tertiary sector and in agriculture. For example, on the state farms, the workers received pay for eight hours of work, but only worked effectively for from four to five hours. The reduction of the work effort, combined with rural-to-urban migration and the absorption of the previously seasonal unemployed, induced a serious lack of manpower for the important crops, such as sugar cane and coffee.[19]

In order to resolve the above problem, Cuba resorted to a temporary transfer of manpower from the city to the country, referred to as voluntary (unpaid) labor, in some cases brought about under diverse forms of pressure. As many volunteers lacked experience and motivation, their work resulted in very low productivity. Crop damage and waste were negative side effects of the use of voluntary labor. Moreover, in certain cases, the cost of transferring the volunteers (work lost in the city, plus expenses of transportation and maintenance in the country) was greater than the product created by their work effort. The increase of employment, partially unproductive, the decrease of effort, and the inefficiency of the volunteers induced the decline of labor productivity.[20]

The reduction of sugar-cultivated area and the problems of labor and managerial organization occasioned a sharp decline in sugar output in the 1962–1963 harvests, as can be seen in table 2. The rapid increase of sugar output in 1959–1961 was possible because of the still large reserve of sugar cane planted and the underutilized equipment in the sugar mills. The harvest of 1961 was close to the record harvest of seven million tons in 1952. Sugar plantations and mills were nationalized in late 1960, but their organization was left almost unchanged for the 1961 harvest. Besides, the scarcity of manpower was not keenly felt until the harvest of 1962.

After attaining productive peaks between 1960 and 1961, agricultural production of a nonsugar nature (notably coffee, tobacco, rice, and beans) as well as dairy products (with the exception of eggs) became stagnant and then began to decline (see table 3). In 1961, the French agronomist and agricultural counselor to Cuba, René Dumont, reported that the productivity of the state farms was only 50 percent of that of the private farms.[21] Private incentive in agriculture was reduced even more substantially with the agrarian reform of 1963. According to figures of the UN Food and Agricultural Organization (FAO), total agricultural output in Cuba increased by 14 percent between 1958 and 1961 but declined by 27 percent between 1961 and 1963. Agricultural output in 1963 was 19 percent below the 1957 output (see table 11).

PHYSICAL OUTPUT OF SELECTED INDUSTRIAL PRODUCTS IN CUBA: 1957-1966

	1957	1958	1959	1960	1961	1962	1963	1964	1965	1966
Mining[a]										
Nickel ore	20.2	17.9	18.0	12.8	14.8	16.6	19.7	22.4	27.4	27.4
Copper ore	20.2	17.9	17.8	11.8	5.0	5.5	6.0	5.8	5.9	5.4
Manganese ore	59.9	28.9	25.0	8.2	10.0	33.0	33.3	33.3	33.0	33.0
Iron ore	8.0	6.0	5.0	5.0	5.0	5.0	5.0	5.0	5.0	5.0
Chrome ore	40.4	26.3	13.9	10.4	9.0	10.0	19.8	11.5	14.9	10.8
Salt	68.0	68.0	60.0	59.0	60.0	71.0	90.0	87.0	106.1	91.6
Sulphur	17.0	17.0	9.0	8.0	9.0	12.0	15.0	14.0	14.0	14.0
Crude petroleum	52.0	45.0	27.6	25.4	28.1	43.3	30.8	37.3	57.4	69.1
Energy										
Manufactured gas[b]	63.0	55.0	31.0	25.0	21.0	21.0	20.0	18.0	29.0	50.0
Electric power[c]	2,357.0	2,589.0	2,806.0	2,981.0	3,030.0	2,998.0	3,057.0	3,250.0	3,355.0	3,460.0
Manufacturing										
Cement[a]	672.6	735.6	672.7	813.3	870.9	778.9	811.6	805.3	801.1	750.4
Tires and tubes[d]	215.8	344.6	—	343.0	362.0	391.0	364.0	(451.0)	265.0	306.0
Paper and board[a]	—	(45.0)	65.0	64.0	87.1	90.7	95.9	94.5	100.0	105.0
Footwear[e]	—	20.0	16.7	14.1	7.1	11.9	18.7	18.8	16.2	17.0
Rayon & acetate filaments[a]	9.8	6.2	9.1	7.7	4.1	3.2	1.8	1.1	1.3	1.0
Food										
Sugar[a]	5,672.0	5,782.0	5,964.0	5,862.0	6,767.0	4,815.0	3,882.0	4,474.0	6,156.0	4,537.0
Fish[a]	22.0	21.9	28.2	31.2	30.4	35.5	35.5	36.4	40.2	43.2
Beer[f]	1,292.0	1,232.0	1,557.0	—	1,394.0	927.0	891.0	1,036.0	993.0	1,088.0
Evaporated milk[g]	319.0	336.0	129.0	214.0	314.0	360.0	267.0	223.0	(640.0)	—
Cigars[h]	—	628.0	591.0	—	—	—	369.0	616.0	655.0	622.0
Cigarettes[h]	9,803.0	10,197.0	11,434.0	—	13,611.3	14,400.2	15,346.8	16,015.3	16,462.3	18,455.0

Source: Based on official figures from Cuba (mainly JUCEPLAN, Boletín Estadístico, 1966 [La Habana, n.d.]) and from the United Nations FAO and ECLA. The original sources and discussion of reliability of the data can be found in Carmelo Mesa-Lago, "Availability and Reliability of Statistics in Socialist Cuba," Latin American Research Review, 4 (Spring and Summer 1969).

Note: Dashes indicate figures are not available. Figures in parentheses are doubtful.

a. Thousand metric tons.
b. Million cubic meters.
c. Million kwh.
d. Thousand units.
e. Million pairs (both rubber and leather).
f. Thousand hectolitres.
g. Thousand cases.
h. Millions.

TABLE 3
PHYSICAL OUTPUT OF SELECTED AGRICULTURAL-LIVESTOCK PRODUCTS IN CUBA: 1957–1966
(In Thousand Metric Tons)

	1957	1958	1959	1960	1961	1962	1963	1964	1965	1966
Industrial crops										
Sugar cane[a]	44.7	45.7	48.0	47.5	54.3	36.7	31.4	37.2	50.7	36.8
Tobacco	41.7	50.6	35.6	45.3	57.6	53.4	58.9	43.4	30.5	42.0
Coffee	43.7	29.5	48.0	42.0	48.0	39.0	28.5	36.0	27.6	32.0
Cotton (seed & lint)	—	0.2	4.3	21.7	14.1	10.8	12.0	12.0	12.0	12.0
Henequen	11.7	9.4	8.5	13.2	11.1	8.8	10.0	10.0	10.0	10.1
Cocoa beans	2.8	2.8	2.8	2.8	2.5	2.3	0.8	2.6	3.1	2.0
Peanuts	11.0	9.0	5.0	9.0	18.0	23.0	23.0	10.0	10.0	9.0
Cereals and pulse										
Rice	261.0	253.0	326.0	323.0	207.0	227.0	184.0	160.0	181.0	51.0
Maize	247.0	148.0	193.0	212.0	197.0	159.0	140.0	129.0	100.0	127.0
Dry beans	35.7	23.0	35.0	37.1	34.0	30.0	27.0	30.0	30.0	23.0
Yams and tubers										
Potatoes	94.3	70.6	63.5	97.4	88.4	92.4	86.0	75.0	83.0	104.0
Sweet potatoes and ñame	184.0	186.0	224.0	272.0	142.0	201.0	280.0	300.0	250.0	300.0
Cassava (yucca)	186.0	213.0	224.0	255.0	155.0	162.0	230.0	180.0	200.0	180.0
Malanga	91.0	226.0	240.0	257.0	77.0	61.0	—	—	—	—

Vegetables									
Tomatoes	43.9	55.2	65.0	116.3	109.2	140.4	103.0	103.0	118.0	119.0
Onions	1.3	7.8	11.1	18.0	6.0	16.1	12.0	8.0	10.0	11.0
Garlic	3.0	5.4	5.9	6.5	1.3	0.2	—	—	—	—
Fruits									
Citrus	111.3[b]	69.7	—	72.9	91.0	117.0	86.0	105.0	116.0	118.0
Bananas	42.0[b]	—	—	—	60.0	76.0	70.0	60.0	60.0	60.0
Pineapples	102.0[b]	—	—	—	87.0	100.0	100.0	100.0	100.0	100.0
Coconuts	10.0[b]	—	—	—	—	—	10.0	—	—	—
Meat and dairy products									
Beef	185.0	184.0	200.0	170.0	163.0	147.0	143.0	170.0	165.0	177.0
Pork	42.0	37.0	39.0	36.0	40.0	42.0	39.0	44.0	48.0	35.0
Poultry	47.0	—	—	—	45.0	47.0	48.0	48.0	48.0	—
Milk	806.0	765.0	770.0	767.0	706.0	690.0	695.0	715.0	—	575.0
Eggs[c]	275.0	315.0	341.2	429.0	580.0	660.0	750.0	830.0	920.3	1055.0

Sources: See table 2.

a. Unprocessed sugar cane; million metric tons.

b. 1957–1958 average.

c. Million units.

Mineral output was seriously affected by the nationalization of mines and refineries, that induced an exodus of technical personnel, and the U.S. embargo, which created a lack of spare parts. Consequently, there was a sharp decline in mineral output in 1959–1961 (see table 2). As soon as the Cubans managed to obtain the needed spare parts (through triangular trade with Canada and Western Europe) as well as technical aid from the socialist countries, some recuperation of mineral output took place. Nevertheless, with the exception of salt and nickel, the level of mineral output in 1963 was substantially below that of 1957–1958.

The decline in production had grave repercussions for domestic consumption. The increment in the population, employment, monetary income, and money in circulation brought about a considerable rise in demand, while the supply of consumer goods stagnated or declined. Thus, an imbalance quickly developed between the population's purchasing power and the consumer goods available for sale to the public.[22] In a market economy, such an imbalance would have corrected itself automatically through price increases. The Cuban planners only slightly increased the official price of consumer goods because they did not want to hurt the lower income groups of the population.[23] On the other hand, the prices of luxury goods and certain services, such as restaurant meals, were greatly increased (a good meal, for example, cost from $12 to $15). Nor was a sales tax (such as the Soviet "turnover tax") used, in lieu of price increases, to achieve equilibrium. Instead, there was an attempt to reduce the money in circulation through the change in currency effected in 1961, restrictions on bank withdrawals, and pressure on workers to save part of their wages with the object of reducing their purchasing power.

The above measures were not sufficient to achieve equilibrium; hence in March 1962, rationing was imposed and rapidly spread to practically all consumer goods (see table 4). Yearly quotas of some other manufactured goods not included in the table are two shirts (or blouses), two pairs of pants (or two skirts), one suit (or dress), and one pair of leather shoes.[24] These quotas are not always guaranteed to the population and depend on the availability of goods, which, in turn, is determined by domestic production, volume of imports, and commitment for exports. Hence, there are long queues in front of state stores, which supplement the allocation of consumer goods.

By resorting to the egalitarian rationing system, the revolutionaries tried to prevent the poorest sector of the population from becoming the most affected by the spiraling inflation.[25] However, this kind of discrimination was produced anyway since the government could not impede the establishment of the illegal black market. Here, rationed goods began to be sold at exhorbitant prices that only the upper- and middle-income groups of

TABLE 4
MONTHLY QUOTAS OF SELECTED RATIONED CONSUMER
GOODS IN CUBA: 1962–1969
(*In Pounds*)

	1962	1965–1967	1969
Per Capita			
Meat	3	3	3
Fish	1	1–8	2
Rice	6	3	4
Beans	1.5	3–9	1.5
Turbes	9	3–10	9
Fats	2	3	1
Milk (canned)[a]	free	2	2
Butter	0.125	0.125	0.125
Eggs (units)	4	12	15
Sugar	free	free	6
Coffee	free	0.375	0.375
Bread	free	free	15
Per Family			
Detergent (medium package)	1	1	1
Soap (cake)	2	2	2.5
Toilet paper (roll)	free	1	1
Toothpaste (small tube)	1	1	1
Cigars (units)	free	free	2
Malt (bottle)	free	free	2
Beer (bottle)	free	2	1

Sources: *1962:* Junta Nacional de Abastecimientos, as quoted in Cuban
Economic Research Project, *Cuba: Agriculture and Planning*, p. 37, table 11.
1965–1967: Rafael Rivas-Vázquez, "Consumer Goods in Cuba: Official
Quota and Official and Black-Market Prices," University of Miami Caribbean
Area Studies Seminar, mimeographed, Summer 1968. *1969:* René Dumont,
Cuba est-il socialiste? (Paris, 1970), p. 241, app. 1, and additional informa-
tion from recent visitors to Cuba.
    a. Children under eight have a daily ration of one quart of fresh milk.

the population could afford. Black-market prices of food exceeded official
prices from five to ten times. Secondhand manufactured products began
to be sold openly at incredible prices, for example, a Parker fountain pen
for $100, a man's suit for $200, a mixer for $300, an old refrigerator for
$2,000, and a 1960 car for $10,000.[26]
    The decline in production of the principal export articles (sugar, to-
bacco, minerals) also affected Cuba's balance of trade. With declining
exports and stagnant or increasing imports, the deficit in the balance of
trade was accentuated after 1961 and attained a record of $323 million
in 1963 (see chapter 10, table 4). The Soviet Union provided credit to
back up the deficits, but this has added the problem of repayment of loans

and the payment of interest to an increasingly worse financial situation. The public debt, therefore, has increased in a pattern parallel to the external deficit.

In 1962, 82 percent of Cuba's foreign trade was with the socialist bloc; 42 percent of its exports went to the USSR, and the latter provided 54 percent of Cuban imports (see chapter 10, tables 1 and 2). Furthermore, in that same year, 90 percent of the Cuban deficit of $211.9 million with the socialist bloc was held by the USSR (see chapter 10, table 5). The old dependence on the United States for capital and trade was substituted by a similar dependence on the Soviets. However, the new relationship has given Cuba relatively more independence because the USSR has no direct investment in the island as the United States had had. On the other hand, Cuba hardly could survive without Soviet credit and supplies, trade is more expensive with the Soviets due to higher transportation costs, and there are other inconveniences such as the greater length of time required for goods to reach Cuba, the inferior variety and quality of Soviet products as compared to American products, and the fact that terms of trade with the Soviets (in large manner, barter trade instead of cash trade) are more difficult to evaluate than those of the United States.

The deterioration of the economy and the shift to accumulative policies has affected the ambitious program of social services. Although it is certain that educational services, medical attention, and housing were increased remarkably between 1959 and 1961, there later occurred a decrease in the rate of their expansion. According to the ECLA, the percentage of investment that Cuba devoted to social services sharply declined from 48.5 percent in 1961 to 29.6 percent in 1963.[27] Cuban official data shown in table 5 does not include the year 1961, but the percentage of investment in social services (housing, education, health) for 1963 is set at 20.1 percent. In any event, the table shows the declining trend of investment in social services since 1962, which is also confirmed when comparing absolute figures.

The quality of educational and medical services suffered notably with the emigration of one-third of the doctors and of a great number of the university professors and teachers. In order to compensate this brain drain, the Ministry of Education and the universities considerably reduced the requirements for graduation of such professionals. This resulted in a far greater number of graduates accompanied by a sharp decline in the quality of their training. In the educational field, the advances in the number of teachers, registration of elementary and secondary school students, and the better distribution of facilities have partly offset the deterioration in quality, which is a difficult thing to measure in any case (see chapter 13). However, the situation in public health is not as good. Table 6 shows

TABLE 5

DISTRIBUTION OF STATE INVESTMENT BY SECTOR IN CUBA: 1962–1966
(Based on Current Prices)

Sectors	1962	1963	1964	1965	1966
Agriculture	29.4%	24.3%	30.5%	40.5%	40.4%
Industry	23.1	31.6	29.1	18.1	16.7
Construction	4.3	5.8	4.6	3.8	2.2
Transportation and communication	9.5	9.6	9.1	11.7	14.3
Commerce	4.4	3.3	3.5	4.6	3.2
Housing and community services	13.5	11.5	11.4	9.4	9.6
Education, culture, research	8.1	7.0	5.3	5.0	4.4
Health	2.0	1.6	1.9	1.6	1.2
Others[a]	5.7	5.3	4.6	5.3	8.0
Total	100.0%	100.0%	100.0%	100.0%	100.0%

Source: JUCEPLAN, *Boletín Estadístico, 1966* (La Habana, n.d.), p. 102, table VII.4.

a. Includes other activities in the productive sector, as well as sports and recreation, administration and finance, defense and internal security, and nonspecified activities.

how the number of people suffering from contagious diseases in relation to the number of inhabitants increased in 1959–1960 and reached a peak in 1963–1964. (In some cases, the rate continued growing, and in others it declined, but in general the rate of persons suffering from contagious diseases was much higher in 1966 than in 1957–1958.) Table 7 reflects an increase in the death rates; for example, the general death rate in 1957 was 6.3 deaths per 1,000 inhabitants, climbing to 7.3 in 1962, and in the same period, the infant death rate increased from 32.3 to 39.6 deaths per 1,000 babies born alive.

The introduction of a Soviet-style system of planning in Cuba met with serious obstacles, such as the lack of specialized personnel and the deficiency of the statistical system. The more complex and centralized the system of planning is, the greater is the necessity for accurate data and competent planners. In Cuba, the personnel was improvised and the figures were calculated in a haphazard manner, often in the heat and enthusiasm of production meetings. The optimism of the planners was reflected in unrealistically high production goals (see chapter 7). Thus, hopes were conceived that, in practice, never materialized and the production goals in 1962–1963 were left unfulfilled.

The mechanical application of the Soviet model of development based on accelerated industrialization did not produce the expected results in Cuba. In spite of the large investment in industry and the technical aid received from the socialist countries, the annual rate of industrial output in Cuba during 1960–1965 was the lowest within the socialist bloc.[28] An official Cuban report commented: "The success in the Soviet Union of the

TABLE 6
RATE OF CONTAGIOUS DISEASES IN CUBA: 1957–1966
(Per 100,000 Inhabitants)

Diseases	1957	1958	1959	1960	1961	1962	1963	1964	1965	1966
Brucellosis	. . .	. . .	0.1	. . .	0.2	0.5	0.5	0.7	—	—
Diptheria	3.5	2.4	4.7	8.1	19.2	19.4	12.8	8.6	8.2	4.6
Gastroenteritis	—	42.5	43.1	—	—	58.8	41.1	34.0	26.4	21.3
Hepatitis	—	—	—	—	5.0	51.1	64.4	70.6	115.8	115.1
Leprosy	0.5	0.4	2.9	2.0	1.8	4.1	2.2	2.1	—	—
Malaria	4.2	2.0	2.1	19.0	46.6	49.8	11.5	8.4	1.7	0.5
Measles	2.9	—	10.3	10.7	0.4	22.5	94.0	28.9	—	—
Polio	1.5	1.6	4.3	4.9	5.0	0.7	. . .	. . .	. . .	. . .
Syphilis	—	0.7	0.7	8.3	6.9	11.4	23.4	25.1	—	—
Tetanus	—	—	4.1	4.6	—	—	4.9	4.5	—	—
Tuberculosis	28.7	18.0	27.6	27.2	37.8	38.6	38.3	52.6	—	—
Typhoid	7.1	5.1	13.0	17.5	13.7	14.2	5.8	15.6	3.1	2.2

Source: See Mesa-Lago, "Availability and Reliability of Statistics in Socialist Cuba," table 7.
Note: Dashes indicate figures are not available. Ellipses indicate figures are minimal or null.

TABLE 7
VITAL STATISTICS OF CUBA: 1957–1968

Year	Population[a] (Thousands)	Live Births	Crude Live Birth Rates[b]	Infant Deaths[c]	Infant Mortality Rates[d]	Total Deaths	Death Rates[b]	Migration[e]	Rate of Population Growth[f]
1957	6,414.2	187,936	29.3	6,079	32.3	40,409	6.3	—	2.15%
1958	6,548.3	178,800	27.3	5,906	33.0	42,508	6.5	− 4,449	2.09
1959	6,692.7	192,400	28.7	6,646	34.5	44,043	6.6	−12,345	2.21
1960	6,825.8	214,900	31.5	7,604	35.4	43,164	6.3	−62,379	1.99
1961	6,938.7	234,600	33.8	8,717	37.2	45,945	6.6	−67,468	1.65
1962	7,068.4	260,900	36.9	10,350	39.6	51,579	7.3	−66,264	1.87
1963	7,235.8	256,900	35.5	9,666	37.6	49,624	6.8	−12,201	2.37
1964	7,434.2	264,300	35.6	9,994	37.8	47,922	6.4	−12,064	2.74
1965	7,630.7	263,975	34.6	9,965	37.7	49,279	6.5	−19,656	2.64
1966	7,799.6	255,413	32.7	9,597	37.6	50,472	6.5	−53,409	2.21
1967	7,937.2	232,027	29.2	9,221	39.7	50,442	6.4	−52,499	1.76
1968	8,074.1	233,418	28.9	9,489	40.7	53,569	6.6	−55,211	1.72

Sources: JUCEPLAN, *Boletín Estadístico, 1966* (La Habana, n.d.), pp. 9, 12, 13, tables 11.1, 11.7, and 11.7.1; and JUCEPLAN, *Compendio Estadístico de Cuba, 1968* (La Habana, 1968), pp. 3–6. The author has filled a few gaps in the table by deriving magnitudes from official percentages or vice versa.

a. Estimates at June 30.
b. Per 1,000 inhabitants.
c. Infants under one year of age.
d. Per 1,000 infants born alive.
e. Balance of migratory movement.
f. Percent.

model of economic development based on accelerated industrialization led us to identify economic development and industrialization. This conclusion did not take into consideration the especial characteristics of each country."[29]

The calamities of 1962–1963 made two points evident. First, the decline in the production of principal export goods made it impossible to sustain an ambitious effort for industrialization. Secondly, a policy of generous spending and emphasis on consumption was incompatible with the plan of development, which had to be based on the increase of savings and investment.

The economic deterioration was not the only cause for seriously reconsidering the program for industrialization. Various factors expounded by domestic economists and foreign advisors contributed to the decision: (a) Some of the manufacturing equipment for the new factories imported from the socialist bloc was obsolete, which made competition by Cuban manufactured products difficult on the international market. (b) The lack of technicians impeded the Cubans from installing the new equipment as quickly as it was received; hence, in some cases, machinery piled up on the docks and rusted while waiting to be put into use. (c) Some of the new factories (e.g., those that produced nails, screws, and tools) required raw materials that were not produced in Cuba and had to be imported from socialist countries, reinforcing Cuba's commercial dependence. (d) Petroleum explorations made by Soviet geologists did not give satisfactory results. The island lacks coal and the rivers do not have sufficient power to generate enough hydroelectric energy. The supply of oil from the USSR is very costly and requires the shipping of tankers every 2½ days, on the average. (Cuba relies on Eastern Europe for 98 percent of its oil supply.) (e) The island has a very small domestic market, and has almost no opportunity to export manufactured goods to the Western Hemisphere because of the economic sanctions imposed by the Organization of American States. Moreover, the nonindustrialized countries of the socialist bloc are very much involved in their own efforts to obtain balanced development and, therefore, are not logical buyers of Cuba's industrial surplus.[30]

The Revolution's initial strategy of following a policy with emphasis on distribution and consumption was gratified by the political support of the masses from the lower income levels and the formerly unemployed. The revolutionary leaders, however, did not seem to be aware that the large percentage of the GNP devoted to consumption made capital accumulation, investment, and development quite difficult. There is no doubt that the guerrilla mentality and the excessive confidence in the power of the Revolution were important factors in assuming that both the policy of consumption and that of development could be implemented simultaneously (see chapter 2).

The proportion of GNP devoted to investment, which had an annual average of 18 percent in 1950–1958, fell to 14 percent in 1959–1960. As a result of the control measures introduced by planning, the investment proportion increased somewhat, but in 1962 it only had reached 16.4 percent.[31] In the socialist countries, capital accumulation in the first years of planning had been very much higher than Cuba's, for example, 31 percent during the Soviet's first and second Five-Year Plan (1929–1937) and 25 percent during China's first Five-Year Plan (1953–1957).

However, policy oriented toward saving and investment at the cost of reducing consumption had been almost impossible in the first years of the Revolution. As has been discussed earlier in this chapter, the standard of living of the masses in Cuba was one of the highest in Latin America and, probably many times superior to that of the USSR in 1928 or to China in 1953. Also, the participation of the masses in the political process in Cuba was assured after the Revolution of 1933, whereas czarist Russia and imperialist China (including the period of the Kuo Ming Tang) were autocratic societies with little or no mass participation. The unions in Cuba were powerful and dominated by a materialist philosophy of economic class improvement. The revolutionary policy of 1959–1960, clearly oriented toward increasing the standard of living of the masses, could be partly explained by these facts. Before the possibility of reducing consumption was feasible, it had been necessary to control the unions, eliminate the remains of political parties, and liquidate all pressure groups.

The series of problems and difficulties faced in the implementation of the early revolutionary policy forced the Cuban leaders to a serious reconsideration in the second half of 1963. This eventually resulted in a new set of goals and policies.

The Return to Sugar: 1964–1970

Between 1960 an 1963, advisers and visitors to Cuba, such as the French Marxist agronomist René Dumont, the Czech economist Radoslav Selucky, and the American Marxist economist Edward Boorstein, recommended the postponement of the industrial program and advised a return to sugar. This recommendation was based on the well-known theory of Adam Smith and David Ricardo on comparative advantages and international division of labor. Due to the excellence of its soil and climate, it is much cheaper to produce sugar cane in Cuba than to cultivate sugar beet in the USSR, Czechoslovakia, or East Germany. In the latter three countries, technological advances, skilled personnel, and the existence of sources of energy make it more economical for them to produce machinery and equipment than the Cubans. Through specialization and trade, the socialist countries can mutually benefit from reduction of production costs without powerful nations taking advantage of poor ones.[32] As a Cuban report to the ECLA stated:

> The existence of an every-day increasing world socialist market permits economic cooperation and trade relations between developed and underdeveloped countries under conditions of independency. . . . [These relations] are very different than those existing between capitalist countries and their politico-economic colonies, as was the case of the United States and Cuba. In this case, economic relations only function in behalf of the interest of the powerful nation contributing to keep their partners in a situation of underdevelopment.[33]

Premier Castro traveled to Moscow in mid-1963 and early 1964 and the shift in policy was definitely an important item of discussion in his meetings with Khrushchev. The change in policy was publicly announced in Cuba after Castro's return from his first trip and was defined more concretely upon the return from his second trip.

Policies

The new program of development changed the order of importance of productive investment giving priority to sugar production. A second objective of the program was the development of agricultural premises: the expansion of land under cultivation and irrigation, mechanization, and fertilization in agriculture. A third concentration of the program was the development of cattle-raising through artificial insemination and of fishing through the expansion of the fishing fleet. (Grandiose targets set by the program for the end of the 1960s included the construction of small dams for the purpose of creating a total water reserve of one billion cubic meters; the cultivation of 90 percent of an estimated total of one million hectares of land that had been left idle by the mid-1960s; and an annual net increase of one million head of cattle, and a fourfold increase of milk production in a period of two years beginning in 1968.)[34] A fourth objective of the new program was to increase the production of electricity, nickel, and cement. Plans for developing heavy industry were postponed indefinitely.

The failure in implementing a highly centralized "macro" system of planning was one reason for developing a system of "miniplanning," that is, separate planning for the sectors of the economy that had received priority (see chapter 7). The most important of such sectorial plans was the Prospective Sugar Plan (1965–1970) developed for the sugar industry with a projected investment of more than one billion pesos. This plan included the substantial expansion of the area to be planted in sugar; the planting of improved sugar-cane varieties with higher productivity and different maturity; the almost total mechanization of the sugar harvest to solve the shortage of manpower; the irrigation and fertilization of sugar fields in order to increase their yield; and the expansion of the grinding capacity through the modernization of existing sugar mills and the construction of new sugar mills. The plan anticipated the gradual increase of sugar production from six million tons in 1965 to ten million tons in 1970 (see table 8). It was hoped that a 1971–1980 sugar plan would increase the sugar output to about eleven to twelve million tons. Production of molasses was expected to total from fourteen to fifteen million tons for use as cattle fodder and the development of sugar by-products.[35]

According to the new program, the increase in sugar output and of agricultural products in general would result in a sharp increase in exports with the consequent improvement of the balance of payments and the expansion of the country's capacity to import. This would make it possible to acquire fertilizer plants, irrigation equipment, and agricultural machinery (e.g., tractors, loaders); breeding bulls and artificial insemination equipment; fishing vessels; machinery for the extraction of minerals including petroleum; and electric-power and cement plants. In summary, Cuba was attempting to apply the "big push" or unbalanced economic development theory, centering all the nation's efforts around sugar production with the hope that the expansion of this sector would generate an overall development of agriculture and connected lines of industry.[36]

The USSR agreed to increase sugar purchases from Cuba from two million tons in 1965 to five million in the period 1968–1970, on the basis of a nominal price of 6.11 cents per pound (see table 8). In addition, the USSR, East Germany, Rumania and other countries of the socialist bloc committed themselves to supplying part of the imports necessary to implement the new Cuban economic policy. Also, it was hoped that with an improved situation of foreign exchange, Cuba would be able to buy from Western Europe (especially from Spain, Great Britain, and France), Japan, and Canada, other prerequisites for the success of the new program of development.[37]

One important aspect of the agreement, at least for the Cubans, was the assumption that the industrialized countries of the socialist bloc, and, in particular, the USSR, would not take advantage of their privileged position in order to benefit from their dealings with Cuba. If Cuba had accepted, with the consequent psychological and economic trauma, the new role of supplier of raw materials, it should, at least, be guaranteed fair prices and equipment of high quality.

The indefinite postponement of the plan for industrialization closed the doors on the hope that the excess of manpower in the cities might find productive employment in the new factories. On the other hand, the new emphasis on agriculture brought about an increase in the demand for manpower in the countryside. The government exerted pressure in order to rid itself of the surplus personnel, especially in the urban administrative and service sectors, and to transfer these workers to the countryside. A campaign against bureaucracy began at the end of 1964 with the establishment of the Commissions Against Bureaucracy. By 1967, more than 48,000 workers, some 2 percent of the labor force, had been "rationalized," that is, removed from their positions. In conjunction with this, a campaign for mobilization of excess workers and the youth, known as *De Cara al Campo* had been organized to direct labor toward agriculture. Nearly 40,000 youths were recruited and sent to the Isle of Pines and to the interior of Cuba in order to perform agricultural tasks for three years. Moreover, compulsory military service, introduced at the end of 1963, gradually absorbed, between 1964 and 1966, some 120,000 recruits from sixteen to twenty years of age, who otherwise would have entered and increased the labor force. These recruits perform agricultural labor for most of their terms in service. Finally, the mobilizations of voluntary workers were increased, especially during the sugar harvest.[38]

The new program of development envisaged a sharp increase in savings to be generated by reducing consumption through the expansion of rationing, the exporting of products previously set aside for internal consumption (e.g., meat, fruits, shoes, vegetables), and the considerable reduction of importation of products considered unnecessary (good examples are paper, cooking oils, and fats). In addition, the system of economic incentives (e.g., increases in salary, production bonuses) was practically replaced by the so-called system of moral incentives (flags, medals, honorable mentions, pennants, and other awards associated with socialist emulation). This last aspect requires special treatment.[39]

Between 1963 and 1965, two opposite lines of thought relative to the problem of incentives existed in Cuba. One, which defended the material incentives following the Soviet model, was represented by members of the PSP as well as by a few young revolutionaries. The other line of thought, which advocated moral incentives, was represented by a group of young Communists led by Guevara. Fidel Castro held an ambiguous position during this period, switching his support behind one line or the other. But, since August 1966, the system of moral incentives has been officially endorsed for Cuba, with the strong support of Castro. (There are increasing signs since mid-1970, and particularly in 1971, that suggest a return to economic incentives.)

In 1967, the peasants on the state farms were dispossessed of their tiny family plots where they could cultivate and do what they wished with their crops. Castro announced in late 1967 that "private land tenure would be honored only during the lifetime of the farmer," implying that this right could not be inherited. The premier also said that the state was to have priority to buy the land if the farmer wanted to sell it.[40] Material awards (trips, refrigerators, motorcycles) that had been offered to the sugar workers in 1965–1966 as incentives to increase production were eliminated in the harvest of 1967. Bonuses for overtime work and for overfulfillment of output goals were gradually abolished in the industrial sector. At the end of the year, the ANAP agreed not to sell agricultural surpluses from private farms on the free market, but to sell all that was produced to the INRA on the basis of the low official prices. The government began to pay salaries to the private farmers and to promote "collective work brigades" and "mutual aid groups," thereby putting manpower and equipment into common use.

The "Revolutionary Offensive," initiated in March of 1968, rapidly eliminated what remained of private property and economic incentives. Nearly 56,000 small businesses (e.g., retail food outlets, consumer services shops, restaurants and bars, small stores and handicraft shops) were confiscated by the government, completing the total collectivization of the nonagricultural sector (see table 1). The ANAP supported these confiscations, stating that these measures would eradicate the illicit purchases that the small merchants made from the farmers, purchases which had reduced the farmers' sales (*acopio*) to the INRA. The black market was substantially reduced by 1969, but barter transactions have become customary, especially in rural areas.[41] The Revolutionary Offensive also promoted gigantic labor mobilizations in order to increase agricultural production, and exhorted the masses to work harder and save more, and to accept the deprivations with revolutionary spirit without grumbling or weakness. As a result of these moves, it was hoped that the nation could substantially increase capital accumulation, even at the cost of further reducing consumption.[42]

Results: Sugar Sector

As table 8 shows, the Prospective Sugar Plan did not bring about the hoped-for results. Only in the first year, 1965, was the output target met, but sugar output in 1965 was 600,000 tons below the 1961 output. The percentage of the annual target left unfulfilled in 1966–1970 varied, reaching as high as one-half of the target in 1969. The actual accumulated out-

TABLE 8
THE PROSPECTIVE SUGAR PLAN: 1965-1970
(In Million Metric Tons)

Year	Plan Targets	Actual Output	Balance	Industrial Yields	Sugar Agreement with USSR			International Sugar Price Average (in Cents)
					Export Commitments	Actual Deliveries	Balance	
1965	6.0	6.2	+0.2	11.94	2.1	1.9	-0.2	2.12¢
1966	6.5	4.5	-2.0	12.09	3.0	2.2	-1.2	1.86
1967	7.5	6.2	-1.3	12.04	4.0	2.5	-1.5	1.99
1968	8.0	5.2	-2.8	11.97	5.0	1.7	-3.2	1.98
1969	9.0	4.5	-4.6	10.85	5.0	1.8[a]	-3.2	3.37
1970	10.0	8.5	-1.5	10.71	5.0	—	—	—
Total	47.0	35.1	-11.9	11.60	24.1	10.1[b]	-9.3[b]	2.26¢

Sources: Planned targets from Fidel Castro, Verde Olivo (June 20, 1965), p. 15; actual output from Fidel Castro, "Comparecencia sobre la zafra azucarera de 1970," Granma, May 21, 1970, p. 2, and Granma, July 27, 1970, p. 1; industrial yields from Castro, "Discurso con motivo de la fusión del Instituto de Recursos Hidráulicos y de Desarrollo Agropecuario," Granma Revista Semanal, June 1, 1969, p. 3; export commitments according to the January 20, 1964, Cuban-Soviet Agreement and actual deliveries are from Economic Research Bureau, Economic Intelligence Report: Cuba, II (April 30, 1969), p. 1. International sugar prices from the Journal of Commerce; Czarnikow-Rionda Co., Sugar Review; Merril Lynch, Sugar Weekly Letter; and Economic Intelligence Report.

a. Estimate.
b. 1965–1969.

put of 1965–1970 was 25 percent below the planned accumulated output. The well-publicized goal of ten million tons for 1970 was unfulfilled by 15 percent. Although Cuba broke the 1952 sugar output record in 1970 by more than one million tons, this was achieved by borrowing sugar cane scheduled for the 1969 crop (the annual average output of 1969–1970 was 6.5 million tons) and expanding the crop period to one full year. Furthermore, deployment of resources to achieve the 8.5 million tons induced a serious decline in practically all other productive sectors. Cuba's cumulative deficit in sugar exports to the USSR alone reached ten million tons by 1969. What were the causes of this failure?

Castro reasoned that the large trade deficit accumulated by Cuba with the USSR by the mid-1960s made the Prospective Sugar Plan and the 10-million-ton target necessary. Sugar was the only product for which output could be increased easily and rapidly. The initial plan called for a relatively small investment to support a gradual increase of sugar output up to 7 or 7.5 million tons, which would supply 3 million tons for exports to the USSR and generate a modest rate of economic growth. Castro has claimed that the decision to raise the output target to 10 million was not capricious, but was motivated by the desire to increase the rate of growth and by the fact that the Soviets were willing to buy as much as 5 million tons beginning in 1968.[43] Herbert Matthews, journalist and biographer of Castro, believes that the 10-million-ton goal was set by the premier without giving enough thought to the idea, and that the planning was hastily made later on by the Cuban technicians.[44] This hypothesis is confirmed by an early statement by Orlando Borrego, the first appointed minister of MINAZ, "We had no long-run plan in the sugar industry but as soon as the revolutionary government [led by the premier] disclosed the politico-economic directives to produce ten million tons of sugar in 1970, we set out to study a 1965–1970 Prospective Sugar Plan which would allow the industry to fulfill such directives."[45] The details of the plan did not become public until mid-1965 when Castro enthusiastically announced that the sugar target set by the plan had been fulfilled in its first year.[46]

The failure to fulfill the targets set by the plan for the following years (see table 8) was officially attributed to adverse weather conditions: excessive rainfall followed by drought in 1966; Hurricane Inez and drought in 1967; and the continuation of drought in 1968.[47] Castro announced that the 1952 sugar crop record would be surpassed in 1967, then in 1968, then in 1969.[48] These repeated disappointments were somewhat lessened by the solid promise that the ten-million-ton target would be fulfilled in 1970. Castro made it clear that this was a crucial test of the Revolution and that a crop of eight or nine million tons would be considered a "moral defeat."[49] As late as February 1970, the Cuban premier was still categorical in his statements: "We won't accept a pound less than ten million tons. . . . It would be incredibly humiliating if we were to produce anything less than ten million tons. We are defending the honor, the prestige, the safety and self-confidence of the country."[50] Thus, the year 1969 was named, "Year of the Decisive Effort," and 1970, "Year of the Ten Million Tons."

In the next paragraphs, a thorough analysis is made of several factors related to the 1970 sugar crop, and the role they played in its failure: weather; expansion of cultivated sugar land; use of improved sugar-cane varieties, irrigation, and fertilizers; manpower; mechanization of cane-cutting and loading; investment in expansion of existing grinding capacity and new sugar mills; transportation; and yields.[51]

The 1970 harvest began on July 17, 1969, and ended on July 26, 1970 (with a brief interruption in October). It lasted 334 days in contrast to an average crop period of 225 days in 1965–1969 and 100 days in the pre-revolutionary period (the 1952 crop lasted 132 days). There was a good rain pattern in 1969, some early rain in January 1970 (that had a very small adverse effect), and excellent weather (little rain) in January–July. Therefore, the weather was optimal.

Following the dictates of the plan, the area of cultivated land was increased from 1,038,552 hectares in late 1967 to some 1,500,000 hectares in mid-1969. It was estimated that this increase would yield enough cane to produce from 10.3 to 10.4 million tons of sugar. (The expansion of sugar-cultivated land was, in part, made at the cost of land devoted to other crops.) There are indications that the hastiness of planting some 500,000 hectares of cane in eighteen months resulted in some loss of the new seed (e.g., the seed was planted in the heat of the noonday sun or dried after days without water). Furthermore, the area of sugar-cultivated land in 1969 possibly did not exceed the existing area of 1952 (when the record crop of seven million tons was achieved), but the plan expected to reach the almost three-million-tons difference through increased yields resulting from intensive cultivation and new industrial equipment.

Most of the new cane planted was of improved varieties (e.g., Barbados, Cuba 8751) that reach higher yields than the traditional varieties previously used in Cuba. Prior to 1962, the cane was cut by an army of cane-cutters in January–April, the optimal time in terms of sugar content of the cane. Due to the manpower shortage since 1962, the crop period had to be expanded gradually; thus, the crop usually begins in November (when the cane is not yet ripe) and ends in July (rains starting in late April made cane-cutting a difficult task). The plan called for a time schedule to mature the new planted cane at different periods, not all at once. However, the new varieties needed a minimum period of eighteen months to mature; hence, most of the cane planted in 1969 could not reach an optimal yield until the second half of 1970 when the harvest was practically over. The plan also envisaged an area of irrigated sugar fields totalling 385,000 hectares, but in March 1969 there were no more than 140,000 hectares under irrigation. It is difficult to believe that the irrigated area was enlarged by 175 percent in the following four months. There were some problems also in fertilizing the cane fields, and the use of weed killers was very limited.

An estimated total labor force of 350,000 cane cutters participated in the sugar crop. The government suspended all traditional holiday festivities for one year beginning in July 1969 to assure maximum utilization of manpower. However, only 10 or 15 percent of the total labor force were professional cane cutters. The sharp decline in the number of these workers was the result of several factors: many of them retired, joined the rebel army or mass organizations, or moved to nonsugar jobs on state farms. The armed forces mobilized some 100,000 men for the sugar crop, 80 percent of whom worked in the field (with fair productivity) throughout the harvest and 20 percent of whom were held in reserve and worked in peak periods. Most of the men (from 55 percent to 67 percent of the total) were voluntary (unpaid) workers, mainly recruited in the cities. As previously mentioned, the productivity of these workers is very low. One problem was that the volunteers left a large amount of cane drying in the fields far too long before it was ground. If the cut cane is left in the field for ten days, for example, its sugar content diminishes 40 percent. In November 1969, Castro explained that an average delay of forty-eight hours in grinding all the cut cane would mean a loss of two million tons of sugar. Another problem was that most of the volunteers did not cut the stalk close enough to the ground, thus wasting the bottom segment of the cane, which contains the highest percentage of sugar. Also, a lack of organization resulted in waste of time and stoppages, creating disillusionment among mobilized workers. According to the plan, 200,000 cane cutters working eight hours a day could have easily cut all the cane needed to fulfill the target. Therefore, the crop failure may have been partially attributable to the low productivity of the volunteers.

The almost total mechanization of the harvest for 1970 was one of the conditions necessary to accomplish the ten-million-ton goal.[52] Plowing was relatively easy (2,000 Cuban-made sugar plowers—Herrera—were in operation in 1969), but mechanization of cutting and cleaning the cane became a difficult task. The terrain was irregular and required a previous leveling off with bulldozers. Cane-cutting combines began to be produced in the USSR and exported to Cuba in 1963. A total of 1,000 combines were imported, but in 1967 they had to be discarded because they were too heavy, complicated, and fragile. Cuban-made combines (Herderson, Libertadora) were developed and tested in 1967–1968, but the estimated number built in 1969 was only 150. The Cubans tried to repair old Soviet combines and to use them for the 1970 crop (with only some types of cane and in certain areas), but the worn-out equipment was not reliable, broke down frequently, and repairs had to wait for spare parts difficult to obtain.

Furthermore, the Cuban-made combines did not clean the cane of leaves and trash. Thus, "cane-conditioning centers" began to be tested in 1966 and, by 1970, some 300 of them were in operation. The cut cane is handled mainly in oxcarts in the field and sent to the centers where it is unloaded, cleaned of leaves and trash, recut into smaller pieces and then loaded onto trucks, trains, or oxcarts and delivered to the sugar mill. This process is an expensive one because it requires double hauling and transportation. It also requires a large number of lifters in the field. Soviet-made lifters began to be imported in the mid-1960s, but those ordered for the 1970 crop were just starting to arrive to Cuba in November 1969. Another problem faced was that the use of cane-lifting machines, cane-harvesting combines, tractors, bulldozers, and trucks requires skilled, disciplined workers who are in short supply in Cuba. Inexperienced personnel often harmed the delicate machinery and provoked stoppages. Also, inefficiency in cleaning of the cane later resulted in low industrial yields.

Preliminary estimates made by MINAZ in September 1965 called for a total investment of $1,020 million in order to reach the ten-million-ton sugar goal. An increase of sugar output from 7 to 8.5 million tons would have required an investment of only $300 million. Therefore, the additional increment of 1.5 million tons (from 8.5 to 10 million tons) would cost more than double the first 1.5-million-ton increment. The projected total investment of one billion pesos was higher than the total investment in the sugar industry (in both agricultural and industrial sectors) existing in 1965. The additional $720 million required to produce the last 1.5 million tons was larger than the total national investment in 1963 and close to that of 1964. The investment of one billion pesos was to be distributed as follows: $465 million for agriculture, $170 million for modernizing and expanding the existing sugar mills, $150 million for installing three modern, new sugar mills, $190 million for transportation, and $45 million for facilities in docks and ports.[53] The official report of the Cuban delegation to the ECLA meeting held in 1969 asserted that total investment in the sugar industry would reach a maximum of $400 million by the end of 1969, that is, only 40 percent of the initial estimate.[54]

The original plan to build three sugar mills was soon abandoned and, instead, the modest task of building one huge sugar mill, "Cauto Valley," was set. This, however, was also later discarded. It was said that this gap could be filled with a larger-than-planned increase in the milling capacity of the sugar mills already in existence.[55] However, according to official figures, total investment in modernizing and expanding the existing mills did not exceed the 1965 planned figure, that is, $170 million. Thus the actual installed capacity was about one-half of the planned capacity.

The above problem was compounded by the delays in receiving and installing the equipment for the modernization of the existing mills. Theoretically, the entire modernization process had to be completed by mid-1969. However, some of the installations had not been finished by December; in Camagüey some equipment was being installed in February 1970; and some of the equipment had not even arrived by late May. Even the already installed equipment required some time for adjustment, and its complexity made the training of personnel a slow process. Hence, practically all of the mills in the two eastern provinces of Cuba (Camagüey and Oriente), where three-fourths of the new equipment went, had serious operational problems, and the equipment, rather than helping, turned out to be a hindrance. Additional problems were that the repair and maintenance of the old equipment were seriously neglected (and when forced to do intensive and long work, it broke down), and many of the old experts and administrators in the mills had retired, leaving the new cadres who were not trained well enough to do the job. The seriousness of these problems forced Castro in February 1970 to stop all the operations in twenty mills of the two eastern provinces for several weeks. Teams of specialists from several government agencies (industry, universities, ministries) were urgently sent to help in the problematic mills. In view of the deterioration of the old equipment and the difficulties with the new installations, it is safe to conclude that the 1970 grinding capacity was possibly below that existing in 1952.

In March and May 1969, before the crop period began, Castro reported that the planned construction of new roads was encountering serious problems. There were 104 construction brigades involved in this work, but they were insufficient. For example, in the province of Camagüey, there were nineteen brigades where forty were needed.[56] Late in 1969, when the grinding operations in the mills with new equipment began to suffer serious delays, it became evident that the sugar cane in the fields surrounding these mills would be lost unless transferred to mills without such problems. (The troubled mills were precisely those on the largest sugar plantations.) The amount of cane to be transferred was 87.5 million cwt. Since the planned roads had initially encountered difficulties, the new transportation problem seemed insoluble at first. Enormous effort was exerted to solve this problem. From 4,000 to 5,000 kilometers of railways and highways began to be constructed; 800 trucks, other means of road transportation, and numerous passenger railways were mobilized; and hundreds of engineers, technicians, truck drivers, and students from technological schools, and thousands of construction and industrial workers were deployed from their jobs. (For example, the famous Construction Brigade of Cienfuegos, fourteen construction brigades from the western provinces, most workers building dams, and 18,000 workers from Havana industries were sent to the Camagüey and Oriente provinces.) Some 300 "links" had to be developed to transfer the cane; in some cases the complexity of the problem baffled accountants and, since they were not sure what was the optimal connection or the best possible route for trains, they resorted to computers. All of these problems must have created delays, which affected the sugar content of the cut cane. However, Castro asserted that transportation reserves were sufficient and the mobilization of vehicles and manpower would not affect other crops such as rice, citrus fruits, etc.

The percentage of sugar obtained in the mills in relation to the weight of the cut cane is called the industrial yield. Out of every 100 tons of sugar cane cut, from eight to fifteen tons of raw sugar are commonly squeezed in the industrial process.[57] The fluctuations in the yield are the result of various factors, such as the variety of sugar cane or seed, the period of the year in which the cane is cut in relation to cane maturity, the period of time it takes for the cut cane to be ground, the cleansing of the cane of leaves and trash, and the efficiency of the industrial equipment. The average prerevolutionary yield was systematically above 12.00; it was 12.46 in 1952 and 12.85 in 1957. Since 1962, with serious manpower and organizational problems, industrial yields began to decline. In spite of the fact that the average yield in 1965–1969 was 11.80 (see table 8), the plan originally set a yield of 12.36 for the 1970 harvest because of the expected increase in yields resulting from improved cane varieties, new equipment, and better organization. But none of these expectations materialized. By November 1969, Castro was hoping to have an average yield of 12.30 (at the time the yield was below 7.00) and, later, he said that the initially planned yield was overly ambitious. The average yield of the 1970 crop was 10.71, possibly the lowest in the last three decades. The actual cost of the pound of sugar produced at such low efficiency would have been higher than the international market price of 3.3 cents per pound of sugar paid in 1970. In 1966, the year of the highest industrial yield in the period 1965–1970, it was estimated that Cuba's production cost for sugar was $85 a ton. At 1966 international market prices (1.86 cents per pound), each ton of sugar could be sold at $41. The loss of $44 per ton could not be regained even by selling almost two million tons of sugar to the Soviet Union at the price of $137 per ton (6.11 cents per pound).[58]

Politically speaking, the 1970 sugar crop was but a forlorn hope because of the mistakes committed in overassuring the fulfillment of the target, considering a crop of eight or nine million tons a failure, and presenting the target as a test to the capability of the Revolution. Castro has also admitted that the failure to meet the ten-million-ton goal created irritation and discontent among the population (see below). Economically, it may be argued that the crop was a success because it broke the 1952 record production. And yet, there is enough evidence to prove that the crop was an economic failure because, by concentrating most scarce resources and energy on the 1970 sugar crop, Cuba seriously neglected the nonsugar sector.

The strategy of the Prospective Sugar Plan and the 1970 goal was to increase sugar output without affecting the nonsugar sector in which production should increase. In October 1969 Castro warned: "It is a matter not of winning this battle at any cost, but of doing so in an intelligent manner, nor of winning this battle while losing another, but of advancing on the sugar cane front and keeping up the effort on other fronts, which are also considered important."[59] At the beginning of 1970, Castro stated that production of nonsugar crops such as rice, turbes, vegetables, and citrus fruits was going along at an "excellent pace," but he warned that this effort had to continue and that cane-planting programs for the 1971 crop had to be implemented, "If we are not capable of simultaneously and efficiently tending to all agricultural fronts, the Battle of the Ten Million will be nothing but a Pyrrhic victory."[60]

In July 1970, however, Premier Castro reported that the extraordinary mobilization of the sugar harvest had required the deployment of manpower and transportation from all other sectors of the economy and this, in turn, had resulted in a substantial decline of production in most sectors.[61] The industrial output plan for the first half of 1970 was unfulfilled in the following proportions: steel ingots (38 percent), cement (23 percent), tires (50 percent), batteries (33 percent), fertilizers (32 percent), soap and detergents (32 percent), toothpaste (11 percent), bread and crackers (6 percent). The output of cement was 23 percent below that of 1968, and the output of steel, 38 percent less than in 1969. Production of paper and cardboard was 5,900 tons behind the plan, and the serious stoppages in the production of bottles cost Cuba $2 million worth of imports. The output plan of shoes had to be reduced from 15.6 million to 13.9 million pairs, and, in spite of this cut, production was one million pairs behind the target. There was also nonfulfillment in the output of fabrics equal to 16.3 million square meters. Other production declines of an undisclosed magnitude were reported in soft drinks, beer, alcoholic beverages, cigars, and cigarettes. The only sectors in which production was going according to schedule were nickel and electricity, but in the latter a serious deficit was reported due to an unexpected increase in demand.

The situation in agricultural output was equally serious. The *acopio* of milk declined by 25 percent in relation to 1969, and there also were declines in the *acopio* of poultry, turbes, vegetables, fruits, edible fats, and black beans. The *acopio* of beef was practically stagnant in relation to 1969 and was 5 percent below the 1968 level. The only products not affected were fish, eggs, and rice.

The mobilization of transportation equipment resulted in a 36 percent decline of railway transportation of passengers. Due to the lack of transportation, manufactured products badly needed by the population of the provinces piled up in MINCIN warehouses in Havana. The failure to transport necessary inputs (raw materials) to glass factories induced a decline of output of bottles and this, in turn, resulted in reduced beer and malt output. (The stoppage in the Santiago brewery caused a loss of seven million bottles of beer and malt.) Due to failures in the supply of sand, the largest Cuban cement factory, "Titán," suffered frequent stoppages and there was a loss of 50,000 metric tons of cement (from 5 percent to 6 percent of total Cuban output in 1968–1969). Deficiencies in the transportation of fodder impeded the proper feeding of cattle and poultry. Cattle to be slaughtered lost weight due to delays in transportation to slaughter houses. The deployment of manpower from industries not only resulted in output decline but also deterioration of quality (e.g., the production of shoes was defective, causing the soles to fall apart after ten days of wear).

After acknowledging these serious setbacks, Castro stated: "The enemy argued that the sugar crop of ten millions would cause these problems. We have not been able to avoid such difficulties. Our enemies say that we have problems, that there is irritation, that there is discontent. And in reality they are right." Then the premier blamed the leadership, including himself, for the failure: "We are paying the legacy of our own ignorance. We were not semi-literates, not illiterates, but ignorants. . . . In most cases we made the mistake of minimizing the difficulties or the complexity of the problems. . . . I am not an exception. . . . The leadership learning process has cost too much to the people." Finally, Castro said that the people could replace him whenever they wanted.[62] The only administrative official dismissed, however, was the minister of the sugar industry, engineer Francisco Padrón. Two months later, Castro held the planning apparatus and MINAZ responsible for the failure, forgetting his main responsibility in deciding on the ten-million-ton target (see above):

Those technocrats, geniuses, superscientists assured me that they knew what to do in order to produce the ten million tons. But it was proven, first that they did not know how to do it and, second, that they exploited the rest of the economy by receiving large amounts of resources. . . . With the excuse of the ten million tons, MINAZ, a single sector of the economy, served itself the largest allocations . . . while there are factories that could have improved with a better distribution of those resources that were allocated to the ten-million-ton plan.[63]

Results: Nonsugar Sector

Let us now examine in more detail the overall results of the new program of development in nonsugar agriculture, cattle, mining-manufacturing, and fishing. Irrigation, land under cultivation, mechanization, and use of fertilizers obviously had been accelerated in the second half of the 1960s. Some 360 dams (mainly small ones) had been built in the ten-year period 1959–1968, providing 862,000 cubic meters of water. This, although a remarkable achievement, was below the one-billion-cubic-meter target set for the five-year period 1965–1970 alone. The area of cultivated land in agriculture reportedly expanded by 369,000 hectares between 1965 and 1968. If these are accurate figures, they show another impressive accomplishment, but at that annual rate (123,000 hectares), only two-thirds of the target of 900,000 hectares would be fulfilled.[64]

According to Cuban figures, the number of tractors imported in 1950–1958 was 13,415, an annual average of 1,490 tractors. In 1959–1964, the total number of tractors imported was 19,051 (3,175 per year) and in 1965–1968, the number increased to 28,370 (7,092 per year).[65] Contradictions between official reports suggest that these figures should be taken with caution. For example, the number of tractors imported in 1965 was given as 4,282 by former President of INRA Carlos Rafael Rodríguez, whereas the Cuban delegation to the ECLA has reported a figure of 10,282 for the same year.[66] Rodríguez himself has given contradictory figures on the total number of tractors imported in 1960–1966. In his paper to the FAO in 1966, he reported 23,223 tractors, and in another publication he reported 29,478.[67] In spite of these problems of reliability, it is fair to say that the number of tractors imported increased substantially in 1959–1961, declined in 1962–1963, and then increased again since 1964, at higher levels than in the early years of the Revolution.

Consumption of fertilizers increased steadily in 1959–1962, but declined in the following two years. In 1965, however, fertilizer consumption was approximately of 581,000 metric tons, 75 percent more than in 1957–1958. Following the new program of development, internal production and imports of fertilizers have increased to 1,487,800 metric tons of consumption in 1968, a fourfold increase over the 1957–1958 figures.[68]

In spite of the advances in developing technological premises, output in the nonsugar agricultural sector does not seem to show a recuperation. Negative subjective factors that have offset the advances in the technological field are the excessive concentration in sugar, the frequent shifts in agricultural plans, and problems of labor and management organization, in part resulting from the reduction of economic incentives.

Although extensive sugar-plantings were replaced by other crops in 1959–1963 following the policy of agricultural diversification, the opposite occurred beginning in 1964–1965 in order to meet the goals of the Prospective Sugar Plan. Such a drastic change of policy occasioned a waste of manpower, capital, machinery, and seeds. The revolutionary logic to justify the new change was that it is cheaper to produce sugar than coffee or rice, and, thus, it is more economical to plant sugar and buy the other products on the international market. Unforeseen events, however, have frequently forced the leadership to alter this plan. Thus, in early 1966 when Cuba had a confrontation with China, the main supplier of rice (a crucial product in the Cuban diet), the Cubans were forced to prepare a rice plan to produce enough rice to meet consumption demands. Large, mechanized rice plantations were rapidly developed in 1966–1969.

The Second Agrarian Reform Law of late 1963 further reduced the private sector in agriculture. Traditionally, agriculture has been the Achilles' heel of the socialist countries and, only recently, when proper economic incentives have been provided (e.g., decollectivization of land in Poland and Yugoslavia, better prices to collective farmers in the USSR), has this situation changed somewhat. Cuba has been trying to develop its economy through the agricultural sector in which discipline and organization are difficult to impose. Furthermore, the leaders are doing this by neglecting economic stimuli. Table 3 shows that output of most agricultural products continued to decline or were stagnant in 1963–1966. Output in 1966 was below or stagnant in relation to the 1957–1958 output, with the exception of cotton, potatoes, sweet potatoes, tomatoes, citrus fruits, and eggs. Concerning the latter product, the Cubans have developed a very successful program.

The total elimination of economic incentives and the drought caused new decreases of agricultural production in 1967–1968. The state's supply of milk in January 1968 had fallen to 14 percent of the previous year's supply and declined even more at the beginning of the Revolutionary Offensive. This made it necessary to eliminate the quota of milk designated for the population above sixty-five years of age in Havana. In spite of the rice plan, the production of rice reached its lowest level in 1968, with only 50,000 tons, or 60 percent less than in 1966, and 85 percent less than in 1959. (However, according to official data, the output of rice increased in 1969.) Bread began to be rationed in 1968 and sugar in 1969. Other difficulties were reported in the supply of cooking oils, meat, and beans. Castro acknowledged publicly, in March 1968, that the problem of supplies was causing discontent, confusion, uneasiness, and protests. In September, the Cuban premier reported that counterrevolutionaries and *disgustados* ("the disillusioned") had committed eighty acts of sabotage against state property since April (that is, right after the inception of the Revolutionary Offensive), one-fourth of which were important and had caused millions of dollars in losses.[69] We have above referred to the negative impact that the deployment of resources for the 1970 sugar crop has had on the supply of turbes, vegetables, fruits, and black beans.

The results of the new plan of development in cattle-raising are not clear yet. According to the cattle census of 1952, there were 4,042,000 head of cattle.[70] This number increased to 5,700,000 in 1958.[71] The disorganization of the early years of the Revolution and the uncontrolled slaughtering of cattle kept the number of cattle stagnant in 1959–1961; in 1961, a new cattle census reported 5,776,000 head.[72] The introduction of rationing and the emphasis on artificial insemination apparently resulted in an increase of the number of cattle to 6,381,000 in 1963, 6,600,000 in 1964, and 6,700,-000 in 1965.[73] Nonofficial sources estimate that there were 6,750,000 head of cattle in 1966 and 6,800,000 in 1967.[74] Putting all these figures together, it is possible to estimate the following annual averages of increase in the number of cattle: 6.8 percent in 1952–1958; 0.3 percent in 1958–1961; and 4.0 percent in 1961–1965. (If the nonofficial figures of 1966–1967 are used, the increase in 1961–1967 was only 3.0 percent.) In summary, the annual rate of increase in 1952–1958 was at least 2.8 percent higher than the 1961–1965 rate (the 1961–1965 average rate excludes 1959–1961, because this was an abnormal period, and 1966–1967 because it is not based on official data). The originally planned goal of eight million head of cattle in 1970 seems to be unrealistic, as it is the goal to increase the herd by one million head of cattle annually. Even in the best years, the increase of cattle has not reached 250,000 head. As table 8 shows, the output of beef was practically stagnant in 1960–1966. It has already been said that the *acopio* of beef in 1970 was stagnant in relation to 1969 and 5 percent below the 1968 *acopio*. The ratio of cattle head per inhabitant in 1966–1967 was below the ratio of 1958. From 1962 to 1970, rationing of beef has been kept steady at a per capita rate of three-quarters of a pound per week (see table 4).

A second aspect of the cattle plan was to increase milk production by breeding Cuban native stock with imported bulls to develop a new breed —the F-1. Most Cuban cattle are Cebu or descendants of this breed, and they are poor milk producers. In order to develop the new breed, the Cubans mated the native stock with Holstein or Brown Swiss stock directly or by artificial insemination (two million cows had been inseminated by 1968). Official statistics claim that the F-1 gives a median of 2,723 kg. of milk per 300 days, with a maximum of 4,095 kg. This median is about four times the Cebu output median. A second generation of this hybrid (the so-called F-2) may show a twofold increase of F-1 milk output. However, at the First Congress of Animal Science held in Havana in 1969, a team of foreign advisors to the Cuban government, British geneticists J. Clark, M. B. Willis, and T. H. Preston, presented a report based on a scientific sample that showed that the milk output of the F-1 was only 16 percent of that of the Holstein and that the F-1 cows dried out after 100 days of nursing their calves.[75] Another report by Willis and Preston opposed the use of pastures and sugar molasses as cattle feed, insisting that corn was the best fodder for cattle. Preston also insinuated that political reasons had been an obstacle to choosing the proper fodder in Cuba. In his speech closing the Congress, Premier Castro strongly criticized the British scientists, and said that he was against corn as a fodder because it was very expensive to produce corn in Cuba, whereas it was very cheap to produce grass and sugar. Castro also attacked the report on the F-1, producing new data to show the inaccuracy of the report presented by the British team.[76]

As it has been said before, the ration of fresh milk to the elderly had to be cut in 1968, and the *acopio* of milk in the first half of 1970 was 25 percent below that of 1969. In September 1970, Castro acknowledged some of the flaws of the cattle plan but placed the blame on other factors:

> It will be difficult in the immediate future to increase the output of beef because . . . pasture lands have not received the necessary attention in the last few years, the birth rate [of cattle] has not been high enough, and due to the low weight of the cattle, the rate of slaughtering has increased. . . . There has been a genetic improvement of dairy cattle. We have the cows, and the equipment for mechanical milking is coming in. . . . The problem [now] lies in building the milking facilities and getting them in operation.[77]

The results of the new program of development in the mining-manufacturing sector are mixed, although, in general, are better than in agriculture. In most modern dynamic industries, which are highly concentrated and operate with a small number of skilled workers whose output can be carefully controlled, production has recuperated and, in some cases, increased over the 1957–1958 levels. On the other hand, traditional industries, which are dispersed and labor intensive, show a poor performance. According to table 2, the extraction of nickel, salt, and petroleum was higher in 1966 than in 1957–1958. But in the less technologically advanced mines, output in 1966 had not recuperated the 1957–1958 level. Production in the modern cigarette, electric, and paper-and-board industries has increased steadily, although at a slightly lower pace than in the 1950s. Production of cement, beer, and tires, which are also modern industries, declined after record achievements in the early 1960s. However, in the first two industries, the 1966 output was above the 1957–1958 output. Footwear and cigar output, mostly a handicraft type of operation and highly dispersed, has fluctuated, with 1966 production below the 1958 level. The three industries in which the Revolution has achieved its most notable success—nickel, electric, and fishing—merit more detailed consideration.

In 1958, the nickel industry had a relatively modern mine, the Nicaro Nickel Company, and a technologically advanced complex, the Moa Bay Mining Company, that was virtually ready to start production. When U.S. and Cuban technicians left, the Moa Bay mine could not be put into operation, and the Nicaro mine was temporarily closed in December 1960. With technical assistance from the socialist bloc, these two mines began operation and by 1963–1964 nickel output recuperated and surpassed the 1957 level of output. In 1967, output was 34,900 metric tons and in 1968 it rose to 37,000 tons, or some 10 percent of world output. Currently, Cuba has a total extractive capacity of some 40,000 metric tons of nickel and is the fourth largest nickel producer in the world. Due to the long strikes in Canadian nickel mines, the price of the metal increased sixfold in 1969 in relation to 1968. Cuba is mainly exporting raw nickel to the USSR, which refines the ore and reexports it to the socialist countries and the international market (the USSR is the primary nickel supplier in the international market).[78]

In 1958, the two largest thermoelectric plants were in Havana: Tallapiedra (450 million kwh) and Regla (150 million kwh); there was also a hydroelectric plant almost finished, the Hanabanilla (45 million kwh) in the Las Villas province. Under the Revolution, the latter plant was put into operation and two new thermoelectric plants were completed: Mariel (150 million kwh) in the Pinar del Rio province and Renté (100 million kwh) in Santiago, Oriente province. In 1968, construction of two new thermoelectric plants began: O'Bourke (210 million kwh) in Cienfuegos, Las Villas province, and Nuevitas (360 million kwh), Oriente province. The plan also called for an expansion of the capacity of the two plants in

Havana, to begin in 1971.[79] With the exception of the year 1962, electrical output increased steadily in 1959–1966 (see table 2) and, according to figures released by Castro, reached 3,733 million kwh in 1969, a 44 percent increase over 1958.[80] This is a significant achievement, but it should be said that in 1952–1958, the increase of electrical output was 77 percent.[81] The original plan envisaged a total electrical output of 10,870 million kwh by 1966, three times the actual output reached in that year.[82] Castro has referred to the neglect of maintenance of the old equipment as the cause of electrical shortages and frequent blackouts, which have created slowdowns and stoppages in factories, refrigeration plants, etc.[83]

Perhaps the most successful revolutionary program is that of fishing. Figures in table 2 show that the output of fish (including shellfish and other species of amphibians) doubled between 1957 and 1966. In 1968, fish output reached 62,800 metric tons, that is, three times the prerevolutionary output. This has been possible through an impressive expansion of the Cuban fishing fleet. The large vessels were bought from Spain, Japan, East Germany, and the USSR. Cuban shipyards produced 500 small wooden vessels in 1959–1968. (In 1968, the Cienfuegos shipyard launched its first all-metal fishing vessel.) Up to 1962, all fishing boats were rather small, mostly made of wood, and were organized into cooperatives; in 1962–1968, four state fishing fleets were put into operation. In 1968, cooperative vessels numbered 3,257 and they produced slightly above the 1961 output. State vessels numbered 249 in 1968, producing 42 percent of the total output.[84] Therefore, the expansion of fish output is the result of the tremendous growth of the state fleets, which are capital intensive, have a small number of units, and a relatively small number of well-disciplined and well-trained workers.

The state fleet—Flota Cubana—was established in 1962; it consists of long-range trawlers operating as far north as the Grand Banks and Greenland, as far east as West Africa, and south down to Patagonia. This fleet is mainly composed of twelve Soviet SRTMs and five East German vessels. The Flota del Golfo, officially started in 1963, actually grew out of the traditional Cuban fleet. It is equipped with some 100 wooden vessels that fish off Campeche and in the Yucatán Channel. The Flota Cayo Largo del Sur began operations in 1964; it is the smallest of the state fleets and is mainly devoted to fishing lobster, crab, etc., in nearby waters. The Flota Camaronera del Caribe began operations in 1968; it is composed of ninety Tasba-type vessels from Spain, and thirty French freezing vessels. This fleet fishes shrimp in the Caribbean Sea. Moreover, Cuban planners have ordered fifteen East German cutters for the manufacture of fish meal, which will be used as fertilizer.[85]

Results: Dependence on the Soviet Union

One of the targets of the new development program was to correct Cuba's imbalance of trade, but official data discussed in chapter 10 indicate that the situation has further deteriorated. Three factors have contributed to this impasse: the fall of sugar prices in the international market, the non-fulfillment of sugar output targets and trade commitments, and the continuing stagnation of the nonsugar agricultural export sector.

The sharp fall in sugar prices that took place in 1965 had not been anticipated by the Cuban planners. The fluctuations of sugar output in the island had repercussions on the supply and price of that product in the international market. The large harvests of 1957–1961 were followed by a gradual drop in the sugar price from 5.27 to 2.91 cents per pound. In turn, the drastic drop in the harvests of 1962–1963 resulted in an increase of the price to 8.48 cents in 1963, some months reaching almost 13 cents per pound, the highest price since the 1920 sugar boom. In the meantime, various Latin American countries had increased sugar production because of the newly enlarged American quota (the old quota for Cuba was divided among three or four countries) and the high prices on the international market. Moreover, Cuba gradually increased its production in the years 1964 and 1965, and the announcement of larger increases for the period 1966–1970 could have had a negative impact on prices. In January 1964, when Cuba began the return to sugar, the price of this product on the international market was 11.62 cents per pound, but the annual average for 1964 declined to 5.86 cents per pound. The price fell to 2.12 cents in 1965 and to 1.86 cents in 1966, the lowest since the Great Depression years of 1929–1940. Although there was a price recuperation to 1.99 cents per pound in 1967–1968, the price was much lower than the average price of 1958–1962. Cuba could not take full advantage of the excellent crops of 1965 and 1967 because of the deteriorated price of sugar. In 1969, the price rose to 3.37 cents per pound, but the 1969 Cuban crop was a poor one (see table 8 and its sources). In view of the decline of sugar prices in the international market, the Soviet Ministry of Foreign Trade suggested in 1969 that in future agreements with Cuba the Soviets could reduce the price assigned to Cuban sugar from six to four cents a pound.[86]

The inability to fulfill the Prospective Sugar Plan targets in 1966–1969 impeded Cuba in honoring its trade commitments, mainly with the USSR. The harvests of 1968 and 1969 were insufficient to cover the necessities of domestic consumption plus the export quota to the USSR, not counting Cuba's sugar obligations with other socialist and capitalist countries. In 1969, rationing of domestic sugar consumption was imposed in order to save 200,000 tons for exportation. The deficit in Cuban sugar deliveries to the USSR built up gradually, reaching ten million tons by 1969. The Soviet Union then deferred part of Cuba's sugar export obligations so that Cuba could fulfill some other commitments, but this deferment has resulted in an increase of Cuba's trade deficit and its debt with the USSR. It would be interesting to know why Cuba has preferred to increase its debt with the USSR in order to sell some sugar at two cents per pound in the international market, when the same sugar could have been sold at above six cents to the Soviets. One explanation could be that Cuba needed foreign exchange to buy products in Western markets that are not available in the socialist bloc. Another reason could be that, in the hope of increasing its sugar output in the 1970s, Cuba preferred to get Soviet credit (even at the cost of indebtedness) in order to fulfill its development program. Still a third cause could be that Cuba resented its barter agreement with the USSR in which the latter has had much to say regarding prices for capital goods. In mid-1968, Castro stated that numerous socialist countries maintain trade practices with the underdeveloped world similar to the practices used by the bourgeois, capitalist world.[87]

The increased Cuban exports of nickel, fish, and possibly citrus fruits in the second half of the 1960s could not compensate for the decline in exports of agricultural products and the fall in sugar prices. The value of Cuban exports in 1967 was 25 percent less than that of ten years before, although imports had increased 11 percent. In 1966, the deficit in the balance of trade reached the record sum of $334 million, and there is enough evidence to say that this record was broken again in 1968 and again in 1969. The cumulative 1959–1967 deficit in the balance of trade was close to $2 billion (see chapter 10, tables 4 and 5). Western estimates, adding the repayment of loans and the payment of interest, calculate Cuba's foreign debt in 1969 at $3 billion, most of which was owed to the USSR.[88]

The increase in the Cuban public debt in 1963–1965 is dramatically shown in table 9. In relative terms, all the categories of the state budget went down, while that earmarked for "payment of the public debt and reserve" gradually climbed. And this was before the record trade deficits of 1966 and 1968–1969. The situation is expected to become more acute by the mid-1970s, when most credits granted to Cuba will mature.

There has been some speculation on how much the record sugar harvest of 1970 could improve this gloomy situation. Our evaluation is pessimistic, not only because the export gains in sugar will be partially (or totally) offset by the losses in the nonsugar sector, but also because the failure to achieve the ten-million-ton target may have affected the long-term economic strategy of the Revolution. In 1970, Cuba had a commitment with the Soviet Union for the exportation of five million tons of sugar, plus one

TABLE 9
DISTRIBUTION OF EXPENDITURES IN THE STATE BUDGET OF CUBA:
1963–1966

Items in the Budget	1963	1964	1965	1966
Financing of the economy	41.6%	39.4%	35.0%	—
Social services	33.7	33.8	32.7	29.2%
Public administration	7.0	6.5	5.4	—
Defense and internal order	10.2	9.2	8.1	—
Payment of the public debt and reserve	8.5	11.1	18.8	—
Total	100.0%	100.0%	100.0%	100.0%

Sources: Law No. 1064, December 31, 1962, *La Tarde,* January 8, 1963; Law of December 27, 1963, *El Mundo,* January 10, 1964, p. 1; Law No. 1170, December 31, 1964, *Gaceta Oficial,* December 31, 1964, pp. 1–6; and JUCEPLAN, *Compendio Estadístico de Cuba, 1966* (Havana, n.d.), p. 13.

million tons committed to other socialist countries, and 1.9 million tons to the international market (a new international agreement signed in London in late 1968 assigned this quota to Cuba), and a domestic consumption of some 600,000 tons. These commitments totaled 8.5 million tons. The expectations were to have a sugar surplus of 1.5 million tons in 1970 (to reduce the sugar and trade deficit with the USSR) and to increase this sugar surplus in 1971–1980 to a maximum of twelve million tons of sugar and fifteen million tons of molasses. The fulfillment of these targets was important for the renegotiation of the sugar agreement with the USSR. The probability of achieving the ten-million-ton goal in the immediate future is doubtful, and the possibility of going beyond ten million tons is even more remote. (The target for the 1971 sugar crop was originally set at 7 million tons and later reduced to 6.5 million tons; actual production only reached 5.9 million.) Hence, Cuba's long-run strategy to solve its balance of payments problem with the USSR seems to be at stake, and Cuba's bargaining position for the negotiation of a 1971–1975 agreement appears to be weakened.

Cuba accepted a dependent status in its trade relations with the USSR with the hope of receiving fair treatment with respect to terms of trade with the Soviets. However, statistical investigation accumulated in the 1950s and the 1960s shows that the USSR has been giving preferential trade agreements to the countries of Western Europe as a result of benefits accrued from its trade with Eastern European countries.[89] Knowing this, Rumania resisted Soviet pressure to assign it the role of a producer of raw materials, which would obstruct its own industrialization plans. However, Rumania was able to do this by obtaining considerable aid from the United States and other Western countries. Cuba could not count on this. The only sign of Cuban independence in the matter of foreign trade relations is the expansion of the merchant marine. The number of Cuban ships increased from fourteen, with a deadweight of 56,740 tons in 1958, to thirty-five ships with 262,000 tons in 1968. This remarkable increase ranked Cuba's merchant fleet as the fifth largest in Latin America.[90]

Results: Employment

In 1964–1970, some correction was made in the inadequate distribution of the labor force (by transferring part of the urban labor surplus to the rural areas facing manpower shortages), but the disguised unemployment was still present, and the problems of waste of labor resources (including voluntary labor) due to organizational deficiencies and absenteeism became more acute. Measures announced by the leadership to solve these difficulties seem to be oriented toward tighter controls over the labor force.

The campaign to mobilize the surplus urban labor toward work in the countryside encountered certain difficulties at the beginning of 1967. The Commissions Against Bureaucracy, integrated by representatives of the trade unions, the administration of enterprises, and the government, were accused of having become guilty of the very vice that they tried to correct, that is, bureaucracy; this cost Basilio Rodríguez his post as minister of labor. The new minister, Captain Jorge Risquet, organized new commissions, this time integrated by young radicals coming from the Schools of Revolutionary Instruction (EIR). After these difficulties were overcome, the campaign proceeded without visible obstacles, and another 22,000 surplus workers were "rationalized." Most of these workers were transferred to agriculture, helping to correct the imbalance in the distribution of labor.[91]

On the other hand, studies conducted in 1968–1969 in more than 200 state enterprises showed that from one-fourth to one-half of the workday was still wasted in some places, for example, 27 percent lost in light industry, 40 percent in transportation, and 49 percent among cane-lifter operators. Causes of this phenomenon were stoppages provoked by lack of raw materials, tools, and electric power, and by broken equipment, but mainly by defects in labor organization and time lost in absenteeism, political activities, and malingering. As a result, more personnel and equipment were requested by managers than really was necessary. Among the losses reported due to waste in the workday were 779,752 pairs of shoes.[92] In a meeting of the CTC held in Havana in late 1970, there were reports of a large number of workers receiving wages without working, among them some 25,000 artists.[93] Referring to this problem, Castro admitted that Guevara's statement of the early 1960s was still valid in late 1970, "We have eradicated unemployment, but there are still many people without jobs that receive subsidies from the government."[94]

Mobilizations for voluntary labor reached a climax in 1968–1970, first as part of the Revolutionary Offensive, and then to face the enormous manpower needs to fulfill the 1970 sugar target. A few weeks after the announcement that the sugar target would not be reached, a CTC meeting released a document that (a) criticized the "generalized practice" among union leaders of pushing the workers for commitments to increase production based on prolonging working hours after the normal schedule of eight hours or on holidays; (b) stressed that after "eighteen long months of intensive work" in the sugar crop it was imperative to respect the workers' rest periods and vacations; and (c) exhorted managers, unions, and the government to obtain future increases in output by better organization of the work, full and rational utilization of the work schedule, and productivity increases, instead of waiving the necessary rest of the workers.[95] Three months later Castro acknowledged that poor organization of voluntary (unpaid) work had resulted in waste of time and effort with the consequent irritation of the volunteers. In some cases, many workers were mobilized without real need for it, whereas, in other situations, the volunteers spent hours waiting to be transported to the fields only to remain idle when arriving there because of a lack of tools necessary to do the job.[96] (We have commented above how the low productivity of the volunteers was a crucial factor in the failure of the 1970 sugar crop.)

It has been documented earlier (see chapter 9) that labor absenteeism has been increasing in Cuba, particularly since 1962. The most significant cause of this phenomenon, according to a report released in 1969 by the PCC Commission on Revolutionary Orientation, is that the socialist system in Cuba has not yet developed methods of its own to replace the market system of checks and incentives that was previously the motivating force behind production. Unemployment is no longer a fear and, due to the increasing scarcity of consumer goods, wages have ceased to be an incentive, "The workers' wage, as a result of present limitations in production, cannot be considered a real wage [in the sense that wages have purchasing power] since there is more money in circulation than things on which to spend it."[97] After the 1970 sugar crop was over, the government organized one week of festivities to provide some relaxation for the workers. In August, absenteeism increased enormously, perhaps reaching as much as 20 percent of the labor force, and the leadership realized that the task of reincorporating the workers to their jobs was a difficult one.[98]

In several meetings held by the CTC in September trying to cope with the problem of absenteeism, many harmful effects of absenteeism were pointed out: merchandise on the docks could not be loaded to the ships or trucks because of absenteeism among stowers (*estibadores*); the lack of transportation in the 1970 crop was in part induced by many drivers staying at home; some $70,000 in badly needed jute bags rotted in a warehouse due to absenteeism among employees in charge of distribution; cows were milked but the milk was not distributed to the consumers, also due to absenteeism. Union leaders at the meetings argued that, in many cases, the absentees were sick and, in other cases, they could not be blamed for their absenteeism—they didn't go to work because of the lack of facilities such as transportation and safety devices, and the bad physical conditions in the factories. A case was mentioned of a factory that had had large leaks in the roof for five years and when it rained 400 workers were soaked and raw materials and finished products were harmed and the machinery rusted.[99]

In one of the meetings, Castro posed the following question, "What should we promote first, the workers' spirit [to eliminate absenteeism] or the optimal conditions at the work place?" He answered that the former should be given priority because labor would eventually solve the lack of facilities. Minister of Labor Risquet added that it was not possible to improve facilities in most cases, and that, frequently, this was used as a mere excuse by the absentees. It was also said that many absentees simulated illnesses and that indolent physicians signed false certificates supporting those simulations.[100]

Minister Risquet stated that for several years the masses had exerted pressure upon the government to enact a severe law against absenteeism and vagrancy but that three steps had to be taken to have adequate control of the labor force and to avoid leaks: (a) the elimination of the nonagricultural private sector to avoid simulation of work (accomplished in mid-1968), (b) the implementation of the workers' labor file (in late 1969), and (c) the taking of a national population and housing census (effectuated in late 1970). Finally on March 16, 1971, the government enacted the law against loafing, which established the obligation of working upon all men from ages seventeen through sixty who are physically and mentally able. The law makes a distinction between the "precriminal stage of loafing" (applicable, for instance, to absentees of more than fifteen days) and the "crime of loafing" (incurred by recurrent incidents). Penalties fluctuate from house arrest to imprisonment in a rehabilitation center at forced labor for a period ranging from one to two years. As a result of the three-month campaign that preceded the enforcement of the law (in the midst of which mass organization such as CDR and ANAP detected and denounced men who were potential violators of the proposed law), more than 100,000 men were incorporated in the labor force, half of them in agriculture.[101]

Attempts have been made to solve problems of labor organization in the important agricultural sector by increasing militarization. After his 1969 visit to Cuba, Dumont reported that agriculture in Cuba is directed from a national command post, most state farms are headed by military men, military logistics and discipline are being used, and military labor brigades are being presented as models.[102]

Results: Capital Accumulation Versus Consumption

The restriction on consumption has allowed for a growing increment in capital accumulation in Cuba. However, table 10 figures showing produc-

TABLE 10

PRODUCTION, INVESTMENT, AND CONSUMPTION IN CUBA: 1962–1968

(1965 Pesos, Constant Prices)

Year	GMP[a] (in Millions)	Investment[b] (in Millions)	I/GMP[c]	Consumption per Capita[d]
1962	3,698.2	607.6	16.4%	352
1963	3,736.7	716.8	19.2	367
1964	4,074.6	794.9	19.5	374
1965	4,136.5	827.1	20.0	378
1966	3,985.5	909.8	22.8	355
1967	3,612.6[e]	979.0	27.1	338[e]
1968[f]	4,000.0[e]	1,240.0	31.0	329[e]

Sources: GMP, investment, and consumption per capita in 1962–1966 from JUCEPLAN, *Boletín Estadístico, 1966*, p. 20, table III.1. Investment data for 1967–1968 from Fidel Castro, "Speech on the Eleventh Anniversary of the Events of March 13, 1957," *Granma Weekly Review*, March 24, 1968, p. 5. GMP estimates in 1967–1968 have been derived by the author from data in ibid. Consumption per capita in 1967–1968 are conservative estimates made by the author by using investment and net-exports data for those years and extrapolations based on government-consumption and increase-in-stock data for 1962–1966.
    a. Gross Material Product, excluding nonmaterial services.
    b. Gross capital formation, including depreciation.
    c. Percentage of GMP devoted to gross capital formation.
    d. Per capita personal consumption.
    e. Estimates by the author.
    f. Official targets; should be taken as indicative only.

tion, investment, and consumption in 1962–1968 must be taken cautiously. Elsewhere, we have discussed the unreliability of Cuban national account figures, as well as the definitional problems of the socialist methodology in this matter.[103] It is sufficient to say here that GMP (close to the Western GNP concept) relates to "Gross Material Product," which in Marxist usage includes the value of material production plus services involved in such production, excluding the value or personal services and other services not linked with material production. "Personal consumption" (close to the Western concept of private consumption) excludes some social services granted to the public under the category of "collective consumption" (close to the Western concept of government consumption). Figures on gross domestic formation of capital do not present serious deviations from the Western use. If GMP and personal consumption figures in table 10 are accurate, they should be below actual GNP and private consumption figures, and the percentage of GNP devoted to gross capital formation should be smaller. Unfortunately, the lack of precise data precludes any computation directed at checking the reliability of the figures in table 10 or estimating Cuban GNP according to Western definitions in order to make a comparison with prerevolutionary figures. In spite of these problems, table 10 data can help indicate tendencies.

The percentage of GNP annually devoted to gross capital formation in 1952–1958 was about 18 percent.[104] The percentage of GMP going to gross capital formation rose steadily from 16 percent in 1962 to 27 percent in 1967. Goals for 1968 claimed another increase to 31 percent. In 1957–1958, private consumption was 75 percent of GNP, whereas in 1965–1966 personal consumption was 69 percent of GMP.[105] Personal consumption per capita reached a peak in 1964, became almost stagnant in 1965, and began to decline in 1966.

State investment devoted to social services (housing, education, health) that represented 23.6 percent of total state investment in 1962 declined to 15.2 percent in 1966 (see table 5). In 1958, some 65 percent of construction was in services and 35 percent was in the productive sector, but in 1968 the proportions had reversed themselves.[106] The percentage of state budget expenditures in social services declined from 34 percent in 1963 to 29 percent in 1966 (see table 9). Housing scarcity became crucial in 1969 with the practical paralyzation of housing construction, as acknowledged by the prime minister: "There are lists of houses to be delivered, but no houses. There are very few of them. . . . Thus, a worker who has headed the list for a year and a half and still has no house . . . loses all hopes of ever getting one."[107]

Restrictions on consumption have influenced the birth rate. In 1959–1962, there was a sharp increase in the birth rate, reaching a record of 36.9 per thousand in 1962 (see table 7). This was in large measure the result of rising standards of living among low-income groups and expectations about the future. (Other reasons were mobilizations, more sexual freedom among females, and a decline in the average age of those getting married.) After 1962, there was a gradual decline in the birth rate down to 28.9 percent in 1968, which was below the 1957 level. Reasons for the decline are rationing (which began in 1962), scarcity of housing, and a decline in consumption levels, as well as the increase of female participation in the labor force and improvement in education.[108]

The sacrifice in consumption has allowed the steady increase in investment, but, surprisingly, after reaching a peak in 1965, the GMP (see table 10) began to decline in 1966. (The 1968 goal for recuperating the GMP level of 1964 was probably not achieved because of the poor sugar crop.) Capital accumulation, which is usually assumed to be the main determinant of growth, does not guarantee economic growth by itself. Several reasons have contributed to a very low rate of investment productivity in Cuba, among them: poor management, lack of efficiency for investment allocation and use, frequent shifts in investment plans, and deficient training of the labor force.

The exodus of managerial personnel and technicians made it necessary to improvise with executive personnel lacking experience. Furthermore, loyalty has frequently received priority over expertise in the selection of managers of state enterprises and farms. Excessively large state farms (sometimes made up of hundreds of thousands of hectares) and overcentralization have required exceptional organizational skills, abilities Cuba lacks. Rapid and widespread collectivization of the means of production, before obtaining adequately trained personnel, has aggravated the managerial vacuum. For instance, most of the 56,000 small businesses nationalized in 1968 under the Revolutionary Offensive were turned over to inexperienced housewives who were members of the CDR. In 1970, Castro realized that under the market system 30,000 small groceries were operated with either primitive accounting methods or no accounting at all, but with high efficiency. This was because the owner knew all details on supply, demand, and distribution. When these small groceries were nationalized (most of them between 1961 and 1968), the state was unable to gather, aggregate, and use all the necessary information, new managers did not have adequate knowledge of local conditions, and, hence, inefficiencies rapidly appeared in the distribution system.[109]

The inefficiency of investment has been cited as one of the principal causes of the decrease in capital productivity in Cuba by the Cuban economist, Andrés Vilariño.[110] Capital should be allocated and used to increase productivity to the maximum degree. In Cuba, not only has the payment of interest been eliminated, but the Soviet "coefficient of relative effectiveness" has not been used as a substitute in order to assure at least a minimum of efficiency in the allocation of state investment. Cuban enterprises under the budgetary finance system have used capital gifts without taking into account the risk of losses and the possibility of increased profits, resulting in financial irresponsibility.

A former advisor to the Cuban government, Albán Lataste, has explained in detail some of the flaws of the investment plans in Cuba. Lataste states that allocation of resources according to political rather than economic criteria has resulted in serious failures or in nonprofitable ventures that later had to be abandoned or subsidized. Continuous use of special plans outside of the overall plan has created inconsistencies, bottlenecks, a shortage of funds, shutdowns, and the cutting off or abandonment of some projects. The provision of funds for initiating a project, without adequate allocation of funds for its completion, has proliferated uncompleted projects. Deficient construction plans have induced the piling up of costly imported equipment on the docks. And, finally, negligence in allocating funds for depreciation and repairs has caused factory stoppages.[111]

Occasional criticism from the Cubans themselves, but mainly from foreign advisors and sympathizers of the Revolution who have recently visited the island has provided dozens of examples of how capital has been wasted by mismanagement. In 1967, the newspaper *Juventud Rebelde,* for instance, referred to the goods piled up on the docks for a year, the undelivered cargoes of eighty-six ships, the 600 metric tons of butter that spoiled on the docks or in warehouses, and the half a million cans of ham that spoiled because of canning deficiencies.[112] In 1969, a visitor reported that several million dollars worth of pine seedlings were stored in a tobacco warehouse, forgotten, and then sprayed and killed. A UN expert worked for months on a new method to raise bananas, but a mayor in charge of the region decided to cut them down for consumption.[113] In his 1969 visit to Cuba, Dumont recorded numerous cases of mismanagement: hundreds of hectares of banana trees planted in Cauto Valley, Oriente province, and of pumpkins planted in Ciego de Avila, Camagüey province, were lost because the terrain was too wet and had very poor drainage. Millions of coffee bushes planted in the Havana Green Belt dried up because of poor soil and lack of water; many citrus trees have died also. Four tons of rice were lost in 1969 because of excessive water. Forty percent of the *malanga* (a turbe) crop in the same year could not be harvested due to lack of manpower. Vast stretches of land were cleared with bulldozers, leaving them unprotected against dangerous wind erosion and forcing the government to develop a costly curtain of wind-breaking trees.[114]

The emphasis on gross output has led the Cubans, as the Soviets before them, to fix output goals in physical quantities; this has induced a decline in the quality of goods and, in some cases, a total loss of goods due to serious deficiencies. These goods have been stockpiled, but nobody wants to buy them. Therefore, material inputs, labor, and warehouse space have been wasted. In other cases, the goods are sold, but their deficiencies have shortened their lifespan.[115]

Delicate and complex equipment has been frequently broken due to careless handling by operators or by lack of knowledge or expertise. The chief of a repair shop in Havana said at the end of 1969 that a lot of new equipment was sent to his shop practically wrecked. Batteries had been burned because of lack of proper maintenance, the devices to measure amperage had been taken out, and clutches had been burned due to excessive pressure: "We often found engines and batteries abandoned in the fields because the operator did not know how to fix them, became mad and threw them away. . . . We have repaired some equipment in the morning and that same night found it broken again."[116] Castro himself has commented on the losses caused by unskilled personnel, saying that in many cases costly imported equipment is placed in the hands of people who have no idea how to treat it, maintain it, and operate it; thus, a new machine that may have cost $25,000 soon becomes little more than scrap iron.[117] In late 1970, the Cuban premier sadly acknowledged the problem: "This country has means and resources, a good number of [them] have been obtained. But we must learn how to use these resources in the best, most effective manner possible."[118]

Evaluation of Policy Results and Their Impact on Growth

The preceding pages show that after twelve years of trials, experiments, and changes in policies and goals, the revolutionary government has not succeeded in solving most of the structural problems of the Cuban economy, perhaps, precisely because of the lack of a long-term consistent policy.

Plans for industrialization have been postponed and dependency on sugar has increased. Moreover, the failures of the 1965–1970 Prospective Sugar Plan have put the revolutionary strategy for development in jeopardy. In 1969, the accumulated deficit of sugar deliveries to the USSR had reached ten million tons, the equivalent of two good sugar crops.

United States capital investment in and trade with Cuba have been eradicated, only to be replaced by Cuban dependence on the USSR and the socialist bloc. By 1969, Cuba's accumulated deficit in the balance of trade was close to $2 billion, not counting the remittances for amortization of Soviet loans and payment of interest. Most of the Cuban deficit is held by the USSR, which also supplies Cuba with fuel, weapons, and most vital imports.

Seasonal unemployment in agriculture has disappeared, but problems of underemployment, deficient labor organization, and absenteeism have sprung up throughout the economy. The absorption of the former rural unemployed has created a scarcity of manpower during the important harvests, mainly sugar, which has brought about the campaigns to mobilize voluntary (unpaid) workers and to transfer the urban labor surplus to the countryside. The lack of expertise and low productivity of the volunteers, in turn, have had negative effects upon production.

The alienation of skilled personnel, the process of widespread and rapid collectivization, the lack of economic incentives, and the errors and frequent changes in planning and policy have induced a decline in output. On the other hand, the increase in employment, minimum wages, and free social services have generated an increase of monetary income. The imbalance between supply and demand forced the government to ration consumer goods in 1962 and gradually to expand rationing thereafter. The decline in exports affected negatively the balance of trade and expanded the public debt.

The policy in favor of capital accumulation that began in 1961–1962 and was accelerated in 1966 has been in large measure achieved at the cost of reducing consumption. This, together with the increasingly worse financial situation forced a cutback of the cherished program of social services, which includes housing, medical care, and public health, that had expanded rapidly during the early years of the Revolution. Increased capital accumulation has not succeeded in bringing about a substantial and sustained rate of economic growth due to the inexperience of managers and workers, the frequent shifts in investment plans, and the inefficiency in allocating and using capital.

Table 11 is an attempt to put together the scarce and difficult-to-check data on Cuban agricultural and industrial output. Space limitations impede a discussion here about the reliability of these data and the frequent contradictions among figures published by Cuban agencies and also between Cuban figures and those published by international agencies.[119] The FAO index of agricultural output, using Cuban data, is more favorable than the index computed by the U.S. Department of Agriculture. Both, however, show the general decline of agricultural output after 1961. According to the FAO index, output in 1969 was about 7 percent below the 1958 output and 21 percent below the 1961 level. If per capita figures are used, the decline is even more dramatic—29 percent and 33 percent, respectively.

The three indices of industrial output shown in table 11 are fairly similar, mainly because all of them are based on Cuban data.[120] The JUCEPLAN index embraces the state sector alone, but this sector was producing 95 percent of the total output by 1963. The index of industrial output shown in column 5 was prepared by the author by linking the annual percentage changes estimated by O'Connor for the periods 1958–1960 and 1962–1964.[121] The 1960 increase of 12.8 percent reported by the UN is substantially below the 29 percent rate given by O'Connor. He states that industrial output in 1961 possibly declined by a "fairly large magnitude," some 20 percent when proper links in his estimates are made. On the other hand, the UN originally reported an increase of 6.4 percent in 1961, although in the latest issue of the UN *Statistical Yearbook,* the in-

INDEX NUMBERS OF AGRICULTURAL AND INDUSTRIAL OUTPUT IN CUBA: 1957–1969

(1959 = 100)

Year	Agriculture — FAO Total	FAO Per Capita	U.S. Dept. Agric. Total	Per Capita	Industry Total, Excluding Sugar — O'Connor	UN	JUCE-PLAN (1963 = 100)	Agriculture and Industry — Total at Current Prices	Total at Constant (1957) Prices	Per Capita at Constant (1957) Prices
1957	96.4	100.0	—	—	—	—	—	114.9	94.6	98.7
1958	95.5	97.0	—	—	83	—	—	93.6	94.7	96.7
1959	100.0	100.0	100.0	100.0	100	100.0	—	100.0	100.0	100.0
1960	101.8	100.0	95.2	93.1	129	112.8	—	118.5	98.5	96.5
1961	109.0	105.0	97.1	93.1	109	(119.2)	—	126.9	105.5	101.8
1962	89.3	84.2	76.9	72.5	121	121.7	—	114.9	85.2	80.6
1963	76.8	71.3	67.3	61.8	129	128.2	100	107.7	75.9	70.2
1964	83.9	74.3	76.0	68.6	138[a]	137.2	109	118.5	85.7	77.1
1965	100.0	88.1	83.6	73.5	—	148.7	120	135.9	100.2	87.9
1966	83.9	71.3	72.1	61.8	—	—	116	129.4	93.6	80.3
1967	102.7	87.1	83.6	69.6	—	—	—	—	—	—
1968	94.6	78.2	76.9[a]	62.7[a]	—	—	—	—	—	—
1969	88.4	72.3	—	—	—	—	—	—	—	—

Sources: Agriculture, FAO: FAO, *Monthly Bulletin of Agricultural Economics and Statistics,* 19 (July–August 1970), pp. 14–17, tables 3A, 3B, 4A, 4B. The original base year, an average of 1952–1956, was changed to 1959 to allow comparisons. *Agriculture, U.S.:* U.S. Department of Agriculture, Economic Research Service, *Indices of Agricultural Production for the Western Hemisphere* (ERS Foreign 264, March 1969), p. 17, table 15. The original base year, an average of 1957–1959, was changed to 1959. *O'Connor:* Computed by the author based on scattered data supplied by James O'Connor, *The Origins of Socialism in Cuba* (Ithaca, N.Y., 1970), pp. 271–79, and table 6. *UN:* United Nations, *Statistical Yearbook, 1966* (New York, 1967), p. 155, table 50, and *1969* (New York, 1970), p. 142, table 49. The original base year, 1963, was changed to 1959. *JUCEPLAN:* JUCEPLAN, *Boletín Estadístico, 1966,* p. 78, table V.1. *Combined Totals:* Based on physical output as compiled in tables 2 and 3 of this chapter and shadow prices. Ernesto Quintanilla, "An Index of Economic Performance of Cuba: 1957–1966" (unpublished paper prepared under the supervision of the author, University of Pittsburgh, 1969).

a. Preliminary figure or estimate.

dex for this year was left blank. O'Connor reported a 12 percent increase for 1962, although the ECLA estimated it at 5 percent and the Chilean Max Nolff, at 7 percent.[122] Beginning in 1963, the three indices report similar increases. According to the UN index, industrial output increased in 1959–1965 at an annual average rate of 7.8 percent, whereas the index based on O'Connor's data shows a rate of 11 percent for 1958–1964. Compared with an average annual rate of 4.8 percent in 1952–1957, the revolutionary performance in the nonsugar industrial sector as judged by these data has been impressive.

The combined index of agricultural and industrial output shown in table 11 covers approximately one-half of the Cuban estimated GMP. One-fourth of the output in the combined index is generated by sugar. Correspondence of the combined index with the individual agricultural and industrial indices is fair, particularly with the FAO and UN indices. The only serious discrepancy appears in 1960, with either real industrial output overestimated by O'Connor and the UN or the figures of the combined index at constant prices underestimating real output. The table suggests that fluctuations shown in the combined index are mainly the result of variations in agricultural output (particularly sugar). According to the last column of the table, output per capita in constant prices declined by 21.5 percent between 1961 and 1966. The level of output per capita in the latter year was 16.4 percent below the 1958 level.

In spite of the reliability problems that Cuban national accounts present, it is fair to say that table 12 data show the magnitude of the economic deterioration of Cuba after 1961. First, it should be noted that the figures in the table begin in 1962, a year which, together with 1963, was the nadir of revolutionary economic performance. As previously mentioned, output declined sharply in 1962 and reached bottom in 1963. Therefore, growth shown in table 12 for 1964–1965 is relative to the recession year of 1962. The 1966–1967 decline of GMP and national income, both in total and per capita figures, is a dramatic one. GMP measured at constant prices was smaller in 1967 than in the recession year of 1962. Per capita GMP in 1967 was 13 percent below that of 1962 and 11.7 percent below that of 1963. In the period 1962–1966, per capita income declined at an average annual rate of minus one percent, whereas in 1962–1967 per capita GMP declined at an average annual rate of minus 2.6 percent.

Nevertheless, the above gloomy picture should be brightened somewhat by referring to the potentiality of the Cuban Revolution for economic growth in the future. Basically, the 1964 change in strategy was correct and, under the new program of development, important progress has been made in sugar, electricity, nickel, fishing, and perhaps in the artificial insemination of cattle. There is no doubt that the area of cultivated land has been

TABLE 12
NATIONAL INCOME AND GROSS MATERIAL PRODUCT IN CUBA: 1962–1967
(In Pesos and Index Numbers, 1962 = 100)

Year	National Income — Million Pesos Current Prices	National Income — Million Pesos 1965 Prices	National Income — Index Current Prices	National Income — Index 1965 Prices	Per Capita Income — Pesos Current Prices	Per Capita Income — Pesos 1965 Prices	Per Capita Income — Index Current Prices	Per Capita Income — Index 1965 Prices
1962	2,832.0	3,509.5	100.0	100.0	400.6	496.5	100.0	100.0
1963	3,256.0	3,544.2	114.9	101.1	450.0	489.8	112.3	98.6
1964	3,984.0	3,856.6	140.6	109.9	535.9	518.8	133.8	104.5
1965	3,886.0	3,888.2	137.2	110.8	509.2	509.5	127.1	102.6
1966	3,781.0	3,727.4	133.5	106.2	484.8	477.9	121.0	96.2
1967[a]	3,626.0	—	128.0	—	456.8	—	114.0	—

Year	Gross Material Product (GMP) — Million Pesos Current Prices	GMP — Million Pesos 1965 Prices	GMP — Index Current Prices	GMP — Index 1965 Prices	Per Capita GMP — Pesos Current Prices	Per Capita GMP — Pesos 1965 Prices	Per Capita GMP — Index Current Prices	Per Capita GMP — Index 1965 Prices
1962	3,079.0	3,698.2	100.0	100.0	435.6	523.2	100.0	100.0
1963	3,788.0	3,736.7	123.0	101.0	523.5	516.4	120.1	98.7
1964	4,202.0	4,074.6	136.5	110.2	565.2	548.1	129.7	104.8
1965	4,136.0	4,136.5	134.3	111.9	542.1	542.1	124.4	103.6
1966	4,039.0	3,985.5	131.2	107.8	517.8	510.9	118.8	97.6
1967[a]	—	3,612.6	—	97.7	—	455.2	—	87.0

Sources: Computations prepared by the author, based on Cuban official data: 1962–1966 at constant prices from JUCEPLAN, *Boletín Estadístico, 1966*, pp. 20–21, Tables III.1, III.2; 1962–1966 at current prices from *UN, Monthly Bulletin of Statistics*, 22 (June 1968), pp. 176, 182, 188, checked against JUCEPLAN, *Compendio Estadístico de Cuba, 1968*, p. 8.

a. Estimates.

substantially enlarged, and that the agricultural sector has made significant advances in the matter of mechanization, fertilization, and irrigation. The main problems in the current situation seem to be caused by the frequent shifts in policies, the grandiose targets that require enormous mobilization and strenuous effort (e.g., the ten-million-ton sugar goal), the excessive sacrifices imposed upon the population to increase capital accumulation, and the lack of efficiency and low productivity of capital and labor, partly due to the absence of proper incentives and market mechanisms. If the Revolution would become more institutionalized and would stabilize its economic policy; if the output targets were set by the planners at realistic levels; if the rate of capital accumulation were reduced to the more human level of some 25 percent; if proper incentives were given to managers, workers, and farmers, providing more consumer goods and allowing more initiative; and if market mechanisms were reintroduced, stressing efficiency, the economy would eventually recuperate and generate a modest rate of economic growth. By the end of 1970, however, two obstacles seem to obstruct the way for such necessary measures: the excessive concentration of power in the hands of the premier coupled with his constant intervention in economic affairs, and the old guerrilla mentality that still places more importance on consciousness and subjective conditions than on the real objective conditions of the Cuban economy.

NOTES

1. Dudley Seers, ed., *Cuba: The Economic and Social Revolution* (Chapel Hill, 1964), pp. 3–19; and James O'Connor, *The Origins of Socialism in Cuba* (Ithaca, N.Y., 1970), pp. 17–18.

2. Julián Alienes, *Características fundamentales de la economía cubana* (La Habana, 1950), pp. 51–53. For a detailed discussion of the reliability of Alienes's series and a refutation of the stagnation theory, see Carmelo Mesa-Lago's review of O'Connor's book in *Journal of Economic Literature,* 9 (June 1971), pp. 478–81.

3. Sources and a more detailed explanation of these and the following computations may be found in Carmelo Mesa-Lago, "Availability and Reliability of Statistics in Socialist Cuba," *Latin American Research Review,* 4, pt. 1 (Spring 1969), pp. 56–58, and pt. 2 (Summer 1969), pp. 48–49.

4. Cuban Economic Research Project, *Study on Cuba* (Coral Gables, 1965), pp. 477–574, 601–18; and "Informe de la Delegación de Cuba al XIII Período de Sesiones de CEPAL," Santiago de Chile, April 1969, pp. 3–8.

5. Cuban Economic Research Project, *Study on Cuba,* pp. 601–18. See also chapter 10, this volume.

6. For arguments in favor of and against this integration see Boris Goldenberg, *The Cuban Revolution and Latin America* (New York, 1966), pp. 136–42. For a Marxist viewpoint see Edward Boorstein, *The Economic Transformation of Cuba* (New York, 1968), pp. 1–16.

7. See Carmelo Mesa-Lago, "Unemployment in Socialist Countries: USSR, East

Europe, China and Cuba" (Ph.D. diss., Cornell University, 1968), pp. 346–98.

8. International Labour Office, *Yearbook of Labor Statistics*, issues from 1949 to 1959 (Geneva, 1949–1959).

9. Cuban Economic Research Project, *Social Security in Cuba* (Coral Gables, 1964), pp. 69–170.

10. Agrupación Católica Universitaria, Buró de Información y Propaganda, *¿Por qué reforma agraria?* (La Habana, 1958).

11. Charles Wright Mills summarized the early Cuban revolutionaries' philosophy in *Listen Yankee: The Revolution in Cuba* (New York, 1960), pp. 113–15. See also Herbert Matthews, *Fidel Castro* (New York, 1969), pp. 144, 356. In more recent times, the Cuban leaders acknowledged some of their previous misconceptions in this matter, e.g., Ernesto Guevara, "El cuadro, columna vertebral de la Revolución," *Cuba Socialista*, 2 (September 1962), pp. 17–22; and Fidel Castro, "El pueblo, la Revolución y el socialismo: los recursos superiores de nuestro país," *Cuba Socialista*, 10 (December 1964), p. 4, and "Combatamos el mal de burocratismo . . . ," *Revolución*, December 3, 1964, pp. 4–5.

12. For an enumeration of the various legal measures on collectivization, see Cuban Economic Research Project, *Labor Conditions in Communist Cuba* (Coral Gables, 1963), pp. 1–6.

13. Studies on Cuba's agrarian reform up to early 1964 include Jacques Chonchol, "Análisis crítico de la reforma agraria cubana," *El Trimestre Económico*, 30 (January–March 1963), pp. 69–143; Leon G. Mears, *Agriculture and Food Situation in Cuba* (Washington, D.C.: U.S. Department of Agriculture, 1962); Carlos Rafael Rodríguez, "Cuatro años de reforma agraria," *Cuba Socialista*, 3 (May 1963), pp. 1–30, and "El nuevo camino de la agricultura cubana," ibid., 3 (November 1963), pp. 71–98; Andrés Bianchi, "Agriculture," in *Cuba: The Economic and Social Revolution*, pp. 65–150; René Dumont, *Cuba, socialisme et développement* (Paris, 1964), pp. 35–93; Cuban Economic Research Project, *Cuba: Agriculture and Planning 1963–1964* (Miami, 1965); James O'Connor, "Agrarian Reform in Cuba, 1959–1963," *Science and Society*, 32 (Spring 1968), pp. 169–217; and Oscar A. Echevarría, "La reforma agraria en Cuba," *Problemas del Comunismo*, 24 (March–April 1967), pp. 85–92.

14. Ministerio de Comercio Exterior, *Anuario Azucarero de Cuba*, no. 26 (La Habana, 1962); and JUCEPLAN, *Compendio Estadístico de Cuba, 1967* (La Habana, 1967), p. 17.

15. Ernesto Guevara, *Revolución*, February 27, 1961; and Regino Boti, "El plan de desarrollo económico de 1962," *Cuba Socialista*, 1 (April 1961), p. 32.

16. Prensa Latina, *Panorama Económico Latinoamericano* (La Habana, 1967), p. 257.

17. Mesa-Lago, "Unemployment in Socialist Countries," pp. 400–22. See also Carlos Rafael Rodríguez's interview with Wassily Leontief in "Notes on a Visit to Cuba," *New York Review of Books*, 13 (August 21, 1969), p. 19.

18. See Carmelo Mesa-Lago, *The Labor Sector and Socialist Distribution in Cuba* (New York, 1968).

19. Mesa-Lago, "Unemployment in Socialist Countries," pp. 422–63.

20. Mesa-Lago, "Economic Significance of Unpaid Labor in Socialist Cuba," *Industrial and Labor Relations Review*, 22 (April, 1969), pp. 339–54.

21. Dumont, *Cuba, socialisme*, p. 71.

22. Andrés Vilariño, "Finanzas, dinero y circulación monetaria," *Teoría y Práctica*, 1 (February 1967), pp. 29–45.

23. For a comparison of official price increases between 1958 and 1963, see Cuban Economic Research Project, *Social Security in Cuba,* pp. 206–07.

24. René Dumont makes a pathetic description of the scarcity of consumer goods in 1969. See Dumont, *Cuba est-il socialiste?* (Paris, 1970), pp. 81–85.

25. In 1970, Castro announced a possible increase of the price of cigarettes and alcoholic beverages to discourage consumption, absorb part of the monetary surplus, and increase exports. He argued that this was not a discriminatory practice because these are not essential, but harmful, consumer goods. See Fidel Castro, "Discurso en la Plenaria Provincial de la CTC," *Granma,* September 10, 1970, p. 3.

26. The Cuban newspaper *El Mundo,* which rescinded publication in early 1969, used to publish a section of classified ads that provided information on prices of secondhand goods. See also Dumont, *Cuba est-il socialiste?,* p. 242, app. 2; and Paul Kidd, "The Price of Achievement Under Castro," *Saturday Review* (May 3, 1969), p. 25.

27. ECLA, *Economic Survey of Latin America, 1963* (New York, 1965), pp. 287–89.

28. Vassil Vassilev, *Policy in the Soviet Bloc on Aid to Developing Countries* (Paris, 1969), p. 21, table 1.

29. "Informe de la Delegación de Cuba," p. 45.

30. Irving Bellows, "Economic Aspects of the Cuban Revolution," *Political Affairs,* 43 (February 1964), pp. 49–51; Ernesto Guevara, "The Cuban Economy: Its Past and Its Present Importance," *International Affairs,* 40 (October 1964), pp. 589–99; and Carlos Romeo, "Acerca del desarrollo económico de Cuba," *Cuba Socialista,* 5 (December 1965), pp. 2–24. Little has been written on Cuba's industrialization: Max Nolff, "Industry," in *Cuba: The Economic and Social Revolution,* pp. 283–388; James O'Connor, "Industrial Organization in the Old and New Cubas," *Science and Society,* 30 (Spring 1966), pp. 149–90; Cuban Economic Research Project, *Stages and Problems of Industrial Development in Cuba* (Miami, 1965); and "El desarrollo industrial de Cuba," *Cuba Socialista,* 4 (April 1966), pp. 128–83, and ibid. (May 1966), pp. 94–127.

31. Mesa-Lago, "Availability and Reliability of Statistics in Socialist Cuba," pt. 2, pp. 48–51.

32. Dumont, *Cuba, socialisme,* pp. 126–27; Radoslav Selucky, "Spotlight on Cuba," *East Europe,* 13 (October 1964), pp. 20–21; Bellows, "Economic Aspects," pp. 49–51; and Boorstein, *Economic Transformation,* pp. 198–204. On comparative costs of sugar production within the socialist bloc, also see Leo Huberman and Paul Sweezy, *Socialism in Cuba* (New York, 1969), pp. 77–78.

33. "Informe de la Delegación de Cuba," pp. 49–50.

34. Ibid., pp. 18–27. See also Dumont, *Cuba est-il socialiste?,* pp. 86–87.

35. Fidel Castro, "Speech at the Graduation of Students of Agronomy . . . ," *Granma Weekly Review,* October 26, 1969, pp. 3–6.

36. A sympathetic discussion of the Cuban application of the unbalanced development theory has been made by David P. Barkin, "Agriculture: The Turnpike of Cuban Development" (unpublished paper, New York University, 1970).

37. Studies discussing the new agricultural plans are those by Michel Gutelman, *L'Agriculture socialisée a Cuba* (Paris, 1967); Isy Joshua, *Organization et rapports de production dans une economie de transition: Cuba* (Paris, 1968); and Sergio Aranda, *La revolución agraria en Cuba* (Mexico, 1969).

38. Mesa-Lago, "Unemployment in Socialist Countries," pp. 463–72.

39. For details and original sources in this matter, see Carmelo Mesa-Lago, "Cuba: teoría y práctica de los incentivos," *Aportes* (Paris), no. 20 (April 1971), pp. 70–112.

40. Fidel Castro, *Granma*, September 29, 1967.

41. There are contradicting versions from visitors to Cuba in 1969 on the complete disappearance of the black market: Gil Green, a member of the U.S. Communist Party, tried to discern signs of black-market activities without finding any evidence. See Gil Green, *Revolution Cuban Style* (New York, 1970), pp. 22. On the other hand, Dumont has published a list of price increases in the Havana black market during the first half of 1969. See Dumont, *Cuba est-il socialiste?*, p. 242, app. 2. As recently as 1971, Castro has accepted the fact that the black market continues to be a way out of rationing. See Castro, "Speech in the Rally to Celebrate May Day," *Granma Weekly Review*, May 16, 1971, p. 6.

42. On the Revolutionary Offensive see Carmelo Mesa-Lago, "The Revolutionary Offensive," *Trans-action*, 6 (April 1969), pp. 22–29, 62.

43. Fidel Castro, "Comparecencia sobre la zafra azucarera de 1970," *Granma*, May 21, 1970, p. 2.

44. Herbert Matthews, *Fidel Castro* (New York, 1969), pp. 237, 324.

45. "Informe del Ministro Orlando Borrego sobre el Plan Perspectivo Azucarero," *Hoy*, October 14, 1964, p. 1.

46. Castro announced the 1965–1970 targets in his speech of July 7, 1965, at the sugar mill "Antonio Guiteras." See *Verde Olivo*, June 20, 1965, p. 15.

47. For a detailed analysis of the 1966–1969 sugar crops, see Economic Research Bureau, *Economic Intelligence Report: Cuba*, 1966–1969 issues.

48. See Castro's speeches of June 7, 1965, January 2, and May 1, 1966, and January 30, 1967, all published in subsequent issues of *Granma*.

49. Castro, "Speech at the Graduation of Students of Agronomy," pp. 3–6.

50. Fidel Castro, "Report to the People on the Progress of the Sugar Harvest," *Granma Weekly Review*, February 9, 1970, pp. 3, 6.

51. Data come from the following Castro speeches: "Comparecencia sobre la zafra azucarera"; "Speech at the Graduation of Students of Agronomy"; "Report to the People"; and "Speech at the Meeting Marking the Beginning of the Mass-Scale Stage of the Sugar Harvest," *Granma Weekly Review*, November 2, 1969, pp. 2–5; "Speech to the Soldiers and Officers of the FAR Who Will Participate in the Ten-Million-Ton Harvest," ibid., November 16, 1969, pp. 2–4; and "The Progress of the Sugar Harvest," ibid., January 18, 1970, p. 3.

52. For additional information besides Castro's speeches, see "The Mechanization of the Sugar Crop," *Economic Intelligence Report: Cuba*, 1 (December 8, 1967), pp. 5–8; "Abreast of the Harvest," ibid. (January 26, 1968), p. 4; "Abreast of the Harvest," ibid. (April 19, 1968), p. 4; "Cubans to Mechanize Sugar Crop with Own Machine: La Libertadora," ibid. (May 31, 1968), pp. 1–3; "Total Sugar Mechanization Postponed Until 1975," ibid. (December 31, 1968), pp. 1–2; and "The 1970 Cuban Sugar Harvest," ibid. (July 18, 1969), p. 2.

53. Gutelman, *L'Agriculture*, pp. 204–06.

54. "Informe de la Delegación de Cuba," p. 28.

55. "What Happened to the Cauto Valley Sugar Mill?," *Economic Intelligence Report: Cuba* (September 30, 1968), pp. 3–4, and "The Gregorio A. Mañalich Sugar Mill," ibid. (January 31, 1969), pp. 1–2.

56. Transcription from Radio Havana broadcast of March 7, 1969; "Fidel Tours

Camagüey Province," *Granma Weekly Review,* March 30, 1969, pp. 1–3; and Fidel Castro, "Discurso con motivo de la fusión del Instituto de Recursos Hidráulicos y de Desarrollo Agropecuario," *Granma Revista Semanal,* June 1, 1969, p. 3.

57. If you have 100 tons of cane with a recovery of 12 tons of sugar at 96 degrees of polarization, the industrial yield is $(12 \times 100) \div 96 = 12.50$. See "¿Qué es el recobrado?" *Granma,* December 16, 1967, p. 4.

58. According to figures given by a former official of the Cuban government. See Economic Research Bureau, *Economic Intelligence Report: Cuba* (April 13, 1967). For 1970, see Juan de Onís, "Castro Seals Down his Fancy Blueprints," *New York Times,* August 2, 1970, p. 6E.

59. Castro, "Speech at the Meeting Marking the Beginning," pp. 3–4.

60. Castro, "The Progress of the Sugar Harvest," p. 3.

61. Castro, "Speech in Celebration of the 17th Anniversary of the Attack on the Moncada," *Granma Weekly Review,* August 2, 1970, pp. 2–6. The following statistics in the text are taken from this speech also.

62. Ibid.

63. Castro, "Discurso en la Plenaria Provincial de la CTC," p. 3.

64. JUCEPLAN, *Compendio Estadístico de Cuba, 1968* (La Habana, 1968), pp. 9–10, 20.

65. "Informe de la Delegación de Cuba," p. 19.

66. Ibid.; and Carlos Rafael Rodríguez, "Cuba en la Conferencia de la FAO," *Cuba Socialista,* 7 (February 1967), p. 29.

67. Rodríguez, "Cuba en la Conferencia de la FAO," p. 29, and "La situación económica en Cuba," *Panorama Económico Latinoamericano,* no. 242 (1967), p. 5, table 2.

68. Rodríguez, "Cuba en la Conferencia de la FAO," pp. 29–30; and "Informe de la Delegación de Cuba," p. 19.

69. For original sources and more details see Carmelo Mesa-Lago, "Ideological Radicalization and Economic Policy in Cuba," *Studies in Comparative International Development,* 5 (1969–1970), pp. 210–14.

70. Cuba, Ministerio de Agricultura, *Memoria del censo ganadero, 1952* (La Habana, 1953).

71. Raúl Cepero Bonilla, "Los problemas de la agricultura en América Latina y la reforma agraria cubana," *Cuba Socialista,* 3 (January 1963), p. 91.

72. Rodríguez, "Cuatro años de reforma agraria," p. 27.

73. Ibid.; and "Ganadería," *Panorama Económico Latinoamericano,* no. 233 (1967), pp. 6–7, tables 3–4.

74. Pan American Union, *América en cifras 1970,* 1 (Washington, D.C., 1970), p. 87, table 312–51. Rodríguez's figure for 1966 was 6,700,000; that is, 50,000 less than the PAU figure. See Rodríguez, "Cuba en la Conferencia de la FAO," p. 22.

75. "La ponencia de Clark, Willis y Preston sobre los F-1," *Granma Revista Semanal,* May 18, 1969, p. 6. See also Dumont, *Cuba est-il socialiste?,* pp. 87–88.

76. Fidel Castro, "Discurso en la clausura del Primer Congreso del Instituto de Ciencia Animal," *Granma Revista Semanal,* May 18, 1969, pp. 2–5.

77. Castro, "Discurso en la Plenaria Provincial de la CTC," pp. 2–3.

78. See "Cuba: ¿rey Midas del níquel?" *The Economist* (*para América Latina*), December 10, 1969, p. 26.

79. "Electricidad," *Bohemia,* 61 (January 17, 1969), pp. 18–19. These figures should be taken with caution because statistical contradictions are common. Thus

in mid-1971 Castro gave substantially less capacity for the following electric plants (in million kwh): Mariel, 150 (instead of 200); O'Burke, 60 (instead of 210); and Nuevitas, 120 (instead of 360). See Castro, "Speech at the Rally to Celebrate May Day," pp. 4–5.

80. Fidel Castro, "Discurso en el décimo aniversario de los CDR," *Granma,* September 29, 1970, p. 3. By comparing the output in the state sector in 1959 (about one-half of total output) with the output of the state sector in 1969 (which through nationalization has incorporated the former private sector), Castro came out with an increase of 150 percent, more than three times the actual percent increase in total electrical output. The United Nations has reported an electrical output of 4,250 million kwh in 1967, which is far above Castro's figure for 1969. See UN, *Statistical Yearbook, 1967* (New York, 1967), p. 357, table 144.

81. *Revista del Banco Nacional de Cuba,* 5 (May 1959).

82. "Electric Power," *Panorama Económico Latinoamericano: PEL 1964,* vol. 3 (La Habana, 1964), p. 153, table 5.

83. Castro, "Discurso en el Décimo Aniversario," p. 3.

84. JUCEPLAN, *Compendio estadístico de Cuba, 1968,* pp. 12–18.

85. Ibid.; and "Cuba: More Fish," *Latin America,* December 5, 1969, pp. 390–91.

86. I. Shwartsshtein ("The Sugar Market: The Problem is Overproduction") *Vneshnyaya Torgovlya* (Moscow), no. 2 (1969).

87. Fidel Castro, "Speech Analyzing Events in Czechoslovakia," *Granma Weekly Review,* August 25, 1968, p. 2.

88. "Cuba: The First Ten Years, Problems and Achievements," *Bank of London and South America Review,* 3 (June 1969), p. 363; and Herbert G. Lawson, "Cuba's Economy," *The Wall Street Journal,* March 7, 1969, pp. 1, 20.

89. See the pioneering work of Horst Mendershausen, "Terms of Trade Between USSR and Smaller Communist Countries, 1955–1957," *Review of Economics and Statistics,* 41 (May 1959), pp. 106–18.

90. "Development of Cuba's Merchant Marine," *Cuba Economic News,* 2 (July 1966), pp. 1–2; and "Informe de la Delegación de Cuba," p. 32.

91. Mesa-Lago, "Unemployment in Socialist Countries," pp. 472–78.

92. "Podemos aumentar la producción," *Bohemia,* 62 (May 1970), pp. 32–37.

93. "Franco debate obrero," *Granma,* September 8, 1970, p. 5.

94. Castro, "Discurso en la Plenaria Provincial de la CTC," p. 3.

95. "Decidida la clase obrera a convertir el revés en victoria," *Granma,* June 29, 1970, p. 2.

96. Castro, "Discurso en la Plenaria Provincial de la CTC," pp. 4–5.

97. "Let's Fight Absenteeism and Fight it Competently," *Granma Weekly Review,* November 9, 1969, p. 2. See also, "En la Clausura de la Plenaria Nacional de Justicia Laboral," ibid., August 17, 1969, p. 2.

98. Castro, "Discurso en la Plenaria Provincial de la CTC," pp. 2–4. This speech was given on September 2, but Castro said that he did not want it published. One week later, *Granma* obtained the premier's permission to print the speech.

99. "Franco debate obrero," pp. 4–5.

100. Ibid.; and Jorge Risquet, "Palabras en la Plenaria Provincial de la CTC," *Granma,* September 9, 1970, pp. 4–5.

101. Ibid. See also Law No. 1231, March 16, 1971, in "Text of the Law on Loafing," *Granma Weekly Review,* March 28, 1971, p. 2.

102. Dumont, *Cuba est-il socialiste?,* pp. 134–48.

103. Mesa-Lago, "Availability and Reliability," pt. 2, pp. 48–52.

104. Banco Nacional de Cuba, *Memoria del Banco Nacional de Cuba, 1958–1959* (La Habana, 1960).

105. Computations based on Cuban official figures. See Mesa-Lago, "Availability and Reliability," table 2.

106. "Informe de la Delegación de Cuba," p. 29.

107. Castro, "Speech in Celebration of the 17th Anniversary," p. 5.

108. Some of these causes are explained by Enrique González Manet, "Cuba y su población: perspectivas para 1980," *Granma*, February 5, 1970, p. 2.

109. Castro as quoted in "Franco debate obrero," p. 5.

110. Vilariño, "Finanzas."

111. Albán Lataste, *Cuba: ¿hacia una nueva economía política del socialismo?* (Santiago de Chile, 1968), p. 71.

112. As quoted by Elizabeth Sutherland, *The Youngest Revolution* (New York, 1969), p. 127.

113. John Corry, "Castro's Cuba: Drums, Guns and the New Man," *Harper's* (April 1969), p. 42.

114. Dumont, *Cuba est-il socialiste?*, pp. 87, 94–95, 112–13, 144, 152–61.

115. Juan M. Castiñeira, "La industria ligera en la etapa actual," *Cuba Socialista*, 4 (June 1964), pp. 4–5; Osvaldo Dorticós, "Tareas importantes de nuestros organismos económicos," ibid., 6 (March 1966), pp. 33–36; and "Notas Económicas," ibid., 6 (January 1966), pp. 127–28.

116. Transcription from Radio Habana-Cuba, December 11, 1969.

117. Fidel Castro, "Speech at the Graduation Ceremony at the University of Oriente," *Granma Weekly Review*, December 15, 1968, p. 3.

118. Castro, "Discurso en el Décimo Aniversario," p. 3.

119. Mesa-Lago, "Availability and Reliability," pt. 2, pp. 51–61.

120. JUCEPLAN has not published index numbers on aggregated industrial output for 1959–1962 and from 1967 on, but separate indices of output of most industrial products for 1963–1968 are available. See JUCEPLAN, *Compendio estadístico de Cuba, 1968*, pp. 18–19.

121. O'Connor, *The Origins of Socialism in Cuba*, p. 272. He asserts that the level of industrial output in 1960 did not recuperate until 1963 (p. 274). This information was the key to linking his two series of 1959–1960 and 1962–1964.

122. ECLA, *Economic Survey for Latin America, 1963*, p. 282; and Nolff "Industry," pp. 323–25.

III

Society

12 Nelson Amaro and Carmelo Mesa-Lago

Inequality and Classes

VERY little emphasis was put on the global study of classes in Cuba during the prerevolutionary period. Of the three works published about the middle class before the Revolution, two were of the historical type and highly speculative, and the third was an analysis based on figures of doubtful veracity and accuracy.[1] Another study carried out in the late 1940s by a North American academician, although excellent, dealt mainly with the rural sector.[2] After 1959, the Cubans have not made the necessary self-analysis of their class structure nor have they published figures on which a quantitative study could be based. Foreign academicians have devoted themselves fundamentally to discussing whether or not the middle class instigated the Revolution, in some cases producing interesting historical-sociological studies.[3] Only a few investigators have tried to discover what has happened to the social groups or classes after the Revolution: Zeitlin's 1962 study of the reaction of a sector of industrial workers in the light of the various aspects of the revolutionary process, and some theoretical works by Nelson Amaro.[4]

A conceptual problem must be added to the lack of a basis of reliable knowledge on this subject. It is generally conceded that no well-defined social classes existed in Cuba, but that they were amorphous, confused, fragmented, and heterogeneous, lacking consensus or class consciousness. In trying to overcome this problem, such terms as "quasi groups," "groups," "strata," "sectors," "segments," or "echelons" were employed. Some authors suggest that the Cuban "classes" were composed of groups without adequate integration or unity, and that they were not conscious of their position or role in society. Some ecological and ethnic variables (e.g., location, race), as well as employment, seem to be more significant in Cuba than class consciousness.

For these reasons, this paper has modest goals: (a) to study inequalities of location (urban or rural), race (whites, Negroes, or mulattoes), and occupation (employed, unemployed, underemployed) in prerevolutionary Cuba, and to discuss the Revolution's impact on these inequalities; and (b) to describe the characteristics of the interest groups or quasi groups in prerevolutionary Cuba, and to analyze how said groups have developed through the revolutionary process and how they have been affected with respect to these inequalities.

Inequalities

Urban-Rural Inequality

Just as in all Latin American countries, it was possible to note a great urban-rural difference in Cuba before 1959. This process was sustained by a constant and increasing migration toward Havana, the capital of the Republic. The population census of 1953 showed that 30 percent of the population coming from the provinces lived in Havana. In accordance with said census, 44 percent of the population was rural and 56 percent, urban.[5]

Resources were distributed unevenly between urban and rural areas. According to Harry T. Oshima's estimates, in 1953 the average national annual per capita income was not less than $430, but the per capita income of the nonagricultural labor force amounted to $1,600.[6] However, according to a private national survey undertaken in 1957, the average annual per capita income of agricultural workers was $92.[7] Although Oshima's estimates and the survey figures are not strictly comparable (the former made some allowances for nonwage income, while the latter did not make any allowance for nonwage income, e.g., the crops raised by the agricultural workers for their own consumption) the differences in income between rural and urban areas are obvious. The difference in the educational level was also noteworthy. For instance, in 1953, illiteracy reached 42 percent in the country, whereas it reached only 12 percent in the towns. School attendance of the population between five and twenty-four years of age was 45 percent in urban areas, but only 23 percent in rural areas. With regard to living conditions, 60 percent of the rural homes had wooden walls, straw roofs, and dirt floors, and only 9 percent had electric lights; whereas in the towns, only 14 percent of the homes were of wood and straw, and 87 percent had electric lights.[8]

The accelerated industrialization policy, recommended by the leaders of the Revolution from 1959 to 1963, was to bring about, as a corollary, the increase of urban societies. This idea was based on the socialist experience of other countries. Numerous unplanned social factors contributed to urban growth. The concentrations of large masses of peasants in the capital had a "demonstration effect" on them. The migration was also stimulated by the government, which created openings in the army, scholarships, and new clerical jobs.[9]

Table 1 shows the dramatic population increase of the city of Havana in 1959–1962, with a record of 67,600 people in 1960. After 1962, the growth rate began to decline rapidly. In 1965, the population increase was inferior to the annual average of the 1953–1958 period, and, in 1966, it was less than one-fourth of the growth of the year 1960. What were the causes of this change?

TABLE 1
EVOLUTION OF THE POPULATION IN GREATER HAVANA:
1953 AND 1958–1966

Year	Population (Thousands)	Yearly Growth (Thousands)	Percentage of Total (Cuban) Population
1953	1,224.2	—	21.0%
1958	1,361.6	27.5[a]	20.8
1959	1,392.5	30.9	20.8
1960	1,460.1	67.6	21.4
1961	1,520.4	60.3	21.9
1962	1,570.7	50.3	22.2
1963	1,606.7	36.0	22.2
1964	1,640.7	34.0	22.1
1965	1,665.7	25.0	21.8
1966	1,680.8	15.1	21.5

Source: JUCEPLAN, Boletín Estadístico, 1966 (La Habana, n.d.), p. 16, table 11.7.4.

Note: Greater Havana consists of the city of Havana and its outskirts: Marianao, Regla, Guanabacoa, Santiago de Las Vegas, and Santa María del Rosario.

a. Annual average of the 1953–1958 period.

When the industrialization plans were postponed after 1963–1964, and all efforts were again devoted to agriculture, the migration to the towns, especially to Havana, was discouraged. The monopoly of employment was one of the major means the government used to stop migration to the towns. Since 1962, the state has controlled almost all the means of production and employment. At the end of that year, the worker's identity card was introduced. This card, supplied by the Ministry of Labor, was an indispensable requisite for employment. Furthermore, the ministry was empowered to regulate employment transfers "on a national level as well as in regional sectors and among the different industries and different activities or specialties within a given activity."[10]

Another important means of migration control, started in 1962, was the establishment of the rationing system, which impeded freedom of movement. Some provisions aimed at assuring a supply of labor for the sugar harvest of 1962 made ration cards and residence permits valid only for one specific location.[11] Later, this system was generalized.

The policy of full employment, the granting of fixed and relatively high wages to agricultural workers, the stability of employment, and the expansion of rural services, also contributed to the slowdown of migration to the towns.

Beginning in 1964, the Compulsory Military Service Law (SMO) was enforced for persons between sixteen and twenty-two years of age. This resulted in another control to avoid rural-to-urban migration, since it is primarily among this age group that major migration takes place. It is estimated that between 84,000 and 120,000 persons are affected by the SMO.[12]

A factor that has contributed to the depopulation of the towns is the great number of emigrants or exiles coming principally from the urban zones most affected by the revolutionary process. According to official figures, the exterior migratory balance (emigration less immigration) in 1959–1968 amounted to 401,151 persons. The total migratory balance of 1966 amounted to 53,409, of which 32,574 were from Greater Havana.[13] Furthermore, those residents who apply for emigration increase the rural labor force, because, upon filing their applications to leave, except when they are necessary for production, they lose their jobs and have to perform agricultural tasks until emigration is granted. Thus, there is a forced inverse migration relative to that of 1959–1961. That is, a transfer of persons from urban areas to rural ones.

The mobilization campaigns to intensify voluntary labor, especially since 1964, by which the trade unions free service workers for agricultural assignments for several months, have had the same results. Since the middle of 1964, this system has become compulsory for students of elementary schools and high schools during vacation periods. Also, FMC frequently recruits numerous unemployed women, many from nearby villages, for the duration of the harvest.[14]

During the first years of the Revolution, social services in rural areas were extended significantly and the rationing system did not affect the country as much as the towns. In the country, some consumer goods can be produced and it is easier to evade governmental measures regarding rationing. Furthermore, there are people whose consumption of manufactured products (and of others, such as milk and meat) was lower before 1959—consequently, they have improved their level of consumption despite the rationing. State investment in agriculture increased from 29.4 percent of total investment in 1962 to 40.4 percent in 1966.[15] The temporary and permanent migrations also must have given a greater stimulus to the rural economy.

During the first years of the Revolution, great efforts were made to improve education, health, housing, and social services in general. Table 2 shows how health and education facilities increased in rural areas. Though this table has to be accepted with caution (for instance, the way "General Hospitals" in rural areas are defined seriously underestimates the number of these hospitals in 1958–1959), it is a fact that rural medical services were sharply increased. As regards elementary education, the results are even more obvious. Some 67 percent of those made literate during the

TABLE 2
THE GROWTH OF SOCIAL SERVICES IN RURAL AREAS IN
CUBA: 1958–1959 AND 1968–1969

	1958–1959	1968–1969
Elementary schools	4,889	12,353
Teaching personnel	5,336	18,637
Elementary school students	216,850	602,341
General hospitals	1	48
Beds in general hospitals	10	1,607

Source: JUCEPLAN, Compendio Estadístico de Cuba, 1968 (La Habana, 1968), pp. 29, 31, 43, 44.

1961 campaign were from rural areas. Nevertheless, the government has become continuously more aware of the need for more productive investment, and a reduction of investments with respect to social services can already be noted.[16]

Recent data show that as far as housing is concerned the desired goals have not been achieved. In the 1959–1963 period, 26,050 dwellings were built by the state in rural areas, a number similar to those erected in urban areas: 29,397. Since 1962 the construction of dwellings has decreased notably, especially in urban areas. At present, not as many dwellings are being built as in 1959–1961, but it seems that more are being erected in the rural areas than in the urban ones.[17] Practically all foreign visitors who have visited Havana during the last few years report unanimously on the physical deterioration of the city of Havana.

Some conclusions can be drawn from the above discussion. The migration toward the capital stopped and there is an inverse process in which persons from urban origin go to the country. This trend will be maintained for a long time. On the other hand, the city has been "ruralized" because of the tremendous importance of developmental goals assigned to the countryside. Numerous persons (e.g., voluntary workers) go to work in the country, but have permanent residences in town. Traditional rural-urban relations experienced a complete change fomented by the government according to the motto expressed by Fidel Castro in one of his speeches, "A minimum of urbanization and a maximum of ruralization."[18]

The distribution of the resources, which the urban areas benefited from under the former circumstances, has also changed, since the urban population has been most affected by the revolutionary process. Also, the rural population has been favored as regards employment and social services and has not suffered as much from the restrictions caused by economic deterioration, such as rationing.

Racial Inequality

Several factors in the history of racial relationships in Cuba make this country atypical, especially in comparison with the United States.[19] The Indians, whose initial number was small, disappeared rapidly, leaving almost no trace among the population. African slaves were introduced in the sixteenth century and slavery was not abolished until 1880. Contrary to the almost total power granted to the slaveholders in the United States, the Spanish legal system protected certain minor rights of the slave; for instance, the murder of a slave was a crime. Also, it was relatively easy for slaves to secure their liberty. Thus, in 1861, 43.2 percent of the population was Afro-Cuban (i.e., Negro or mulatto), 26.5 percent of whom held slave status and 16.7 percent, *liberto* status (former slaves who had bought their liberty or who had been emancipated by their owners).[20] The degree of ethnic mixture reached in colonial Cuba was noteworthy. The Spaniard was more inclined to a union with Negroes and mulattoes than the Anglo-Saxon, taking into account that the former did not usually bring his wife along with him to the New World, as the North American colonists did.

Among the first conspirators and martyrs in the fight for independence, the Afro-Cubans José Antonio Aponte and Gabriel de la Concepción Valdés held eminent positions. The Ten Years' War (1868–1878) was started by a white *hacendado* ("plantation owner"), Carlos Manuel de Céspedes, who freed all his slaves, exhorting them to fight with him for the independence of Cuba. The two main heroes of the War of Independence (1895–1898) were José Martí, a white poet, politician, and apostle of the struggle, and Antonio Maceo, a mulatto and legendary warrior who spread the war to the outskirts of the island. Other outstanding figures of the war were the Afro-Cubans Guillermo Moncada, Juan Gualberto Gómez, José Maceo, Flor Crombet, Quintín Banderas, Martín Morúa Delgado, and Quirino Zamora. Important Afro-Cuban figures in the fields of politics and arts had a remarkable impact in the first fifty years of the Republic. The

Afro-Cuban influence manifested itself mainly in music (e.g., Brindis de Salas, José White), dance, poetry, and the short story (e.g., Nicolás Guillén, Regino Pedroso, Rafaela Chacón, Renée Potts, Regino Boti), painting (e.g., Wilfredo Lam, Roberto Diago, Acosta León, Guido Llinás), religion, language, and cooking.

Whereas in 1899, 32.1 percent of the total population of Cuba was Negro or mulatto, in 1953 the Afro-Cuban group had decreased to 26.9 percent. The proportion of Negroes decreased from 14.9 percent in 1899 to 12.4 percent in 1953 whereas that of the mulattoes decreased from 17.2 percent to 14.5 percent.[21] This was the result of the white immigration in the beginning of the twentieth century and of steady interracial blending. This was also due to the fact that in Cuba light mulattoes have always been considered as whites and called themselves such in the census (or the persons filling out the census reported them as such), whereas light mulattoes are often considered as "Negroes," in the United States.

With regard to employment, the racial factor decreased in importance as soon as educational facilities were made available to Afro-Cubans. Whereas in 1907 only one percent of medical doctors was Afro-Cuban, in 1943 the proportion had increased to 20 percent.[22] The proportion of Afro-Cubans in the teaching profession and in the army exceeded the proportion of this ethnic group in the population. However, Afro-Cubans held, to a greater extent, menial jobs, for example, unqualified workers, domestic personnel, etc.[23] A law enacted in 1950 helped to secure equal employment for Afro-Cubans in certain jobs, as clerical employees in department stores and banks, which had been customarily closed to them.

The intensity of the racial discrimination varied according to geographical region and urban-rural location. The province of Oriente was characterized by a greater concentration of Afro-Cubans and interracial blending, followed by Havana, whereas the lowest concentration and blending was in Pinar del Río. Discrimination seemed lowest in Havana, and highest in the provinces of Las Villas and Camagüey where the Afro-Cubans used separate paths from those of the whites when strolling in public parks. In 1953, approximately two-thirds of the Afro-Cubans lived in urban zones and one-third in rural zones.[24]

Racial discrimination existed in a systematic form in exclusive social associations and in those places (e.g., fashionable hotels, restaurants, and nightclubs) frequented by persons belonging to the upper-class stratum. The successful Afro-Cubans established their own associations (the most remarkable of which was the sophisticated Club Atenas), avoiding an open conflict by trying to integrate the exclusive white associations. On the other hand, the majority of whites was also unable to get access to the exclusive white associations, either because income did not allow it, because they did not have the social status required, or because they lacked recommendations of members.

The majority of the private clubs that partitioned off the beaches in Havana did not admit Afro-Cubans. But there were some beaches, such as La Concha (adjacent to the most exclusive private club, the Yatch Club) to which whites and Negroes had access by paying a small admittance fee. The Club of the University of Havana and that of the professionals did not discriminate. During the 1950s with the expansion of better beaches to the east of the capital, various professional associations (e.g., physicians) set up clubs that admitted the Afro-Cuban members of said associations. The most beautiful beaches of Cuba, such as Varadero, Guanabo, and Santa María del Mar had public beaches that also did not discriminate.

In prerevolutionary Cuba, as one went down on the social scale, economic status became an important factor of discrimination difficult to separate from pure racial discrimination. For example, the Afro-Cuban was readily admitted to public free schools, elementary as well as secondary, and to public universities. However, in private schools, where the children of medium- and high-income groups were educated, there were few Afro-Cubans, since the enrollment fee was prohibitive. Some of these schools supported separate gratuitous schools where there was an adequate cross section of races.

A similar phenomenon could be noted in hospitals. Those of a public nature or of the free type were completely integrated, but the so-called *centros regionales* (cooperatives of medical services, founded by Spaniards and later opened to the middle strata) did not admit Afro-Cubans. Other medical cooperatives (which charged a small monthly contribution of three pesos) were open to the Afro-Cuban, but he remained practically excluded from private hospitals on account of their high prices.

No black neighborhoods as the typical ghettos of the United States existed in Cuba. In the urban areas of low income (e.g., Jesús María, Atarés, Luyanó, and El Cerro in Havana), whites and Negroes were neighbors, with a greater concentration of Afro-Cubans in low-income housing areas. However, the high-income residential areas (e.g., Miramar, Country Club, and Biltmore in Havana) were almost completely white.

The Afro-Cubans had the same right of access to cinemas, theaters, sport shows, buses, trains, and churches as the whites. It is important to point out that there were no black Christian churches, although those people practicing African rites were mainly Afro-Cubans. Numerous Afro-Cuban athletes were integrated into the national baseball teams and many represented Cuba abroad in such sports as baseball, track, and boxing.

Afro-Cuban participation in civil, military, and religious associations, trade unions, and political parties varied. For instance, participation was high in trade unions and in the army, and low in intellectual associations. From 1939 to 1947, the general secretary of the CTC, Lázaro Peña, was a Negro. In 1949, two Afro-Cubans, Generals Querejeta and Hernández Nardo were, respectively, head of the army and the police. During the dictatorial period prior to the Revolution, President Batista, as well as chief of the armed forces, General Francisco Tabernilla, were mulattoes and Minister of Justice Céspedes was a Negro. Also, a large number of congressmen (senators and representatives), as well as members of the judiciary, were Afro-Cubans.

The racial problem was never discussed in any revolutionary public document before the revolutionary take-over. In Castro's "History Will Absolve Me" speech, not a single paragraph was devoted to this subject. However, after the Revolution, the revolutionary government painted a picture of Negroes suffering more from discrimination than was actually the case. As Thomas stated, "Racial antagonism in Cuba in the past may have been overstated by the revolution."[25] But what was the revolutionary impact on racial relationships? The magazine *Cuba Socialista* is perhaps the only one that has published an extensive article on the subject. In this article it is stated that numerous revolutionary measures contributed to the elimination of cases of open discrimination that existed in Cuba—the nationalization of private schools and universities, the "intervention" of the *centros regionales* and private clinics, the suppression of the exclusive associations of the whites, and the opening to low-income people of the private beaches, luxury night clubs, and hotels.[26] At the same time, the standard of living of the Negro, as well as the low-income white, was improved through measures such as the urban reform (which reduced the rents and made it possible to acquire a dwelling); the agrarian reform (which supplied jobs to the seasonal rural unemployed); the increase of wages and of minimum pensions; and the reduction of the cost of certain public services (e.g., electricity, transportation) or the offering of services free of charge (e.g., medical services, education, public telephones, burials).

The campaign against illiteracy was particularly important for Afro-Cubans, because, previously, they were the largest group of illiterates. The establishment of compulsory elementary education, the expansion of elementary and secondary schools, boarding schools, and the large number of scholarships granted to Negro children, improved the education of this group notably. It is true that, prior to the Revolution, public education, including university education, was practically free and open to the blacks, but not too many Afro-Cuban families could afford to send their children to secondary school or college instead of working.

The urban reform did profit all low-income groups, but it has not substantially changed the racial distribution in housing. The majority of the urban population seems to live in the same type of residences as before. Nevertheless, the construction of dwellings by the state, the emigration of the majority of the high-income group and the subsequent nationalization of their houses, and the conversion of a large number of these houses into schools or residences for scholarship students allowed integration and eliminated, to a great extent, exclusive white neighborhoods.

The medical cooperatives continue to charge a modest monthly fee (which in inflationary times, is ridiculously low) to their members. But the rural medical services were greatly expanded and access of Afro-Cubans to private clinics has been assured.

Despite these remarkable improvements, four aspects of racial relationships in revolutionary Cuba do not seem to have improved conspicuously: job distribution, black-white aesthetic standards, the preservation of an Afro-Cuban culture, and sexual relationships. Some white North American academicians and activists, who paid a short visit to the island, were enthusiastic and did not seem to be aware of any serious racial problems. The following statement of the sociologist Joseph A. Kahl, who stayed for less than a month in Cuba at the beginning of 1969, is typical: *"For the first time* Cuba's Negroes share *equally* in the goods and services and the civic respect of their society. *They have been fully integrated* in the schools and on the job."* [italics added][27] Another sympathizer, Gil Green, a former member of the National Committee of the U.S. Communist Party, who stayed three weeks in Cuba also in 1969, pointed out that there are some racial problems, but did not explain their nature and underestimated their significance. Green quotes from an interview with a Negro who is presented as typical: "Sometimes we bump into individual cases of prejudice, but these are the exception. . . . When it comes to our rights and opportunities we now have them in *full*. . . . Also *we are now leaders in the party, militia and in industry."* [italics added][28]

In sharp contrast to these impressions are those of two U.S. black militants. Robert Williams and John Clytus spent several years in Cuba and then became disillusioned and bitterly critical of what they called the racial prejudices of the Revolution. Robert Williams, Negro leader and follower of the Maoist line, deserted the Revolution and went to China in 1966, although he has said little about the nature of the racial prejudice that caused his disillusionment. John Clytus has been more explicit. Clytus, a Communist sympathizer who went to Cuba in mid-1964 and worked there until 1967, was an English teacher at the University of Havana and the Ministry of Foreign Trade, and a translator for the newspaper *Granma.*[29] He noted racial discrimination in employment based on his own observation. Describing the racial composition of employment he said, "For every black face I saw there were at least fifty white faces." Then he added, "Of the seventeen or more Ministries in the country, the top two jobs in each were held by whites." He also stated that practically all supervisors in public offices were whites and that "none of the hotels or stores or restaurants had a black in a supervisory capacity. In fact, blacks were conspicuously absent from these places in any capacity."[30]

Commenting on "white supremacy in the Cuban power structure," Clytus referred to the almost unique case of Juan Almeida, a black who is one of the three vice ministers of the army: "He was a piece of window dressing so that the revolution could claim that his high position belied any accusation of racial prejudice."[31] Clytus also reported other discriminatory practices outside of jobs: "I looked at magazine covers and saw whites. I looked at newspapers and books and saw whites. . . . The 'queen' and her 'court' in the carnival were whites. . . . Ninety per cent of the students in my English class at the University of Havana were whites. . . . I constantly saw black women strolling with white men, but I saw no white women with black men."[32] He also reported the case of a black intellectual, writing on the role of the blacks in Cuban history who was told not to write about this theme by the government because his writing could cause division among the people, "There were no white Cubans or black Cubans, just Cubans, they told him."[33]

Apparently, Clytus's negative impressions on racial discrimination were shared by black students from Guinea, Sudan, Kenya, Rhodesia, South Africa, the Congo, and Angola who were in Cuba at the time. According to Clytus, in 1967, ninety Congolese students had demanded to be sent back to their country after some members of their group had fought with Cuban soldiers over some racist remarks that the latter had made to the African students.[34]

Clytus has been attacked by some as an unsophisticated black racist incapable of understanding some of the difficulties that impede a rapid and total abolition of racial discrimination, even within a revolutionary process. A more balanced, analytical view of the problem has been presented by Elizabeth Sutherland, an American mulatto writer and editor with the Black Liberation movement who spent the summer of 1967 in Cuba. After warning against outsiders and short-term visitors who easily make mistakes by generalizing from their partial experience and their own prejudices on this complex problem, she concludes that all traces of overt racism as they once existed in Cuba have been wiped out, but that certain forms of cultural racism still exist.[35]

Sutherland acknowledges that the top leadership of the government and the party is white, and that a disproportionately large number of blacks are still performing menial jobs as maids, street cleaners, and ditchdiggers.

She also says that in posters, magazines, television, movies, and theater, white faces are overwhelmingly predominant. (Sutherland tells the paradoxical story of a black actress, who was denied a role in a Spanish play because such a role was supposed to be performed by a white female, and of a play involving black characters that was performed by white actors in black painted faces, because of the alleged lack of black actors. This led a group of black actors to stage a play with a "black cast" and a "black plot.") Interracial marriage, particularly of a black man with a white woman is still rare, and often provokes a negative reaction.[36]

Sutherland agrees with Clytus on the revolutionary taboo on talking about racism, "Officially it doesn't exist any more." One of her interviewed blacks asserts that the Revolution has assumed a paternalistic attitude because it has given blacks "the right to enter the white society." Officials quoted by her forecast that the economic position of blacks, as well as their participation in leadership, will improve gradually, and that time will eliminate whatever vestiges of racism that remain. However, a group of Cuban black militants do not believe this can happen without a conscious effort, led by black intellectuals, to correct this problem.[37]

Carlos More, an Afro-Cuban militant who left the island because of his radical racial viewpoints, has referred to the problem of the systematic elimination of the Afro-Cuban culture through various methods: (a) the use in schools of history handbooks that underestimate the role of the Negro in the fight for Cuban independence; (b) the alteration of statistical figures regarding the ethnic composition of the population; (c) the systematic exclusion of Afro-Cubans from leading positions; and (d) the mocking of rites (songs, dances, ceremonies) of the African religion by transforming them into folklore. More explains that the Afro-Cubans are subjected to strong propaganda that shows them constantly the advantages they have received from the Revolution in contrast to the difficult situation of the Negroes in the United States and South Africa. Thus, it might seem that the Afro-Cubans will accept their situation and integrate themselves into the white value system.[38]

From what has been said, some tentative conclusions can be drawn. The vestiges of open racial discrimination that existed in Cuba in 1958 have disappeared together with the white high-income minority, which maintained exclusive associations. This was principally the indirect result of the structural changes undertaken by the government that forced these high-income groups to emigrate, destroying the discriminating institutions but it was not the result of direct measures that modified the prevailing ethnic relations substantially. The improvements experienced by Negroes under the Revolution (in education, medical services, full employment) are the result of social measures of an economic rather than ethnic nature, of which all low-income Cubans took advantage. Since the Negroes were predominately of this group, the revolutionary measures were of most profit to them. But less conspicuous vestiges of racial discrimination in the field of black-white aesthetic standards, employment, culture, and sexual relations still persist in Cuba.

Inequality in Access to Employment

The proportion of the labor force unemployed or underemployed in Cuba varied between approximately 20 percent and 30 percent, according to various censuses and samplings carried out between 1943 and 1957.[39] The structural causes of this unemployment included, (a) in the primary sector, the excessive dependence on sugar, which created a seasonal unemployment of eight months of "dead time"; (b) in the secondary sector, the relatively slow industrial growth, incapable of providing employment to the urban labor force, constantly increased by the migration from the country to the towns; and (c) in the tertiary sector, the "disguised" unemployment, formed by poorly paid and half-time working civil servants, hucksters, domestic personnel, bootblacks and others who performed tasks of this nature since they were unable to find adequate jobs (for more details on these aspects, see chapter 11). Those suffering most from the lack of jobs were the rural workers affected by seasonal unemployment and the urban, unskilled workers, usually underemployed, who came mainly from the country. The Negroes and mulattoes possibly constituted the majority of this latter group.

The leaders of the Revolution claim that they eliminated unemployment radically. Though this statement is correct, a thorough study of this field shows that overt seasonal unemployment has been eradicated partly by expanding "disguised" unemployment in the tertiary sector. This, in turn, has lowered labor productivity and created artificial manpower shortages.

In 1959–1960, overt unemployment reached a very high level, especially in the towns. This was due to the dismissal of civil servants for political reasons, the increase of urban labor on account of rural migration, the decrease of private investments due to the uncertainty of the revolutionary process, the closing of factories and businesses due to the scarcity of spare parts and raw materials, and the decline of U.S. imports.

In order to offset the old evil of unemployment, worsened by the structural transformation process, the revolutionary government prohibited all dismissals of workers for economic reasons, launched the agrarian reform, started an ambitious project of public works, opened the army to peasant groups, and set up an extensive program of scholarships for youths, especially those coming from rural zones.

Despite the fact that numerous industries and businesses remained paralyzed for the reasons explained, their employees were not dismissed. On the other hand, the integration of state enterprises into *consolidados* (see chapter 8) reduced labor requirements and the displaced workers started receiving state subsidies. The growth of new industry fell short of expectations and supplied few employment openings due to the relatively high degree of automatization of the new factories. In the meantime, the tertiary sector was expanding disproportionately as a result of the extension of social services and the official bureaucracy. On the other hand, the socialization of agriculture improved conditions and assured a stable employment for peasants. In fact, the agricultural sector began to lack manpower, especially during key harvests (e.g., sugar, coffee) because of the rural-urban migration and the absorption of former seasonal workers (e.g., cane cutters) by state farms.

In 1963–1964, when the projects of industrialization were postponed and emphasis was put on agriculture, it became obvious that there was a disproportionate distribution of labor, with a surplus in urban zones and a shortage in rural ones. A campaign against bureaucracy in civil service (1964–1967) was aimed at dismissal of surplus employees. These employees were transferred to a so-called "labor reserve," and were either used for agricultural work or were retrained. Another intensive campaign exerted pressure on nonproductive youths in urban areas (e.g., employees in services) to have them commit themselves to work for three years in agriculture. Finally, in 1964 the SMO started to recruit hundreds of youths of working age, blocking their access to urban labor markets in order to assure their availability for work in agriculture for three years.

The foregoing structural changes modified the former employment-unemployment relations profoundly and affected the various sectors that constitute the labor force in different ways, stirring up feelings of satisfaction and adhesion among some, and of dissatisfaction and estrangement among others. The majority of those who before the Revolution had stable, well-paid jobs with high status (e.g., in banks, insurance companies, legal professions, businesses, tourism), were affected negatively. Practically all jobholders of this type were urbanites and a great number of them chose exile. These people, having been removed from their former positions, would only have been satisfied if they had been given positions of equal status and remuneration. It is obvious, however, that this desire could not be satisfied, because the only real employment market in Cuba was in agriculture. On the other hand, a great many of the people who found temporary employment in 1959–1964 in the tertiary sector, also urban, and who had improved their living standard and status considerably, were transferred back to the country. Finally, there is a sector of highly educated youths recruited by the army, whose future is essentially in rural areas. This group is facing an employment structure characterized by the relatively low age of bureaucrats in key positions, whose essential merits are not of a technical nature but of a political one (loyalty, party spirit, membership in the Sierra group).

Another different group consists of the former unemployed and underemployed who secured steady, relatively well-paid jobs with higher status, such as the former seasonal agricultural workers, many of whom are now employed in state farms and some of whom had been underemployed in the tertiary sector before the Revolution and now hold urban jobs. Zeitlin's 1962 survey shows the importance of employment as an alienating or supporting factor to the revolutionary process. In general, the unemployed and underemployed who had more stable employment after 1959, were in favor of the Revolution; those who had had stable jobs before 1959 showed less enthusiasm for and even opposition to the Revolution.[40] If this was true in 1962 on the eve of the radical change in the employment structure, these attitudes, other factors being equal, may be even more evident now. Unfortunately, there is no later survey that could help document these speculations.

Interest Groups and Quasi Groups

In every society there are relations between pople based on the role that they play or the position that they hold. A landowner exerts authority (or domination in Weber's terms) over the peasant, the manager of a factory over his employees. When there is an awareness of being the dominator or the dominated, often group peers seek mutual solidarity in order to increase their bargaining position against the opposite group. Thus, interest groups such as trade unions, peasant leagues, associations of landowners, and chambers of commerce and industry emerge. On the other hand, when an awareness of these relationships is lacking, members of the peer group are not organized in a structural manner and remain as quasi groups. Members of these quasi groups could eventually take common action (a riot of blacks, a student demonstration, a general strike), but often it is of a temporary nature. Finally, there is an intermediate sector in a situation difficult to define, being sometimes dominant, dominated, or independent. This model has been applied by Dahrendorf to industrial societies with some success.[41] However, this model is not as easily applicable to agricultural, semiindustrialized societies such as Cuba, where intermediate, not clearly defined situations are common.

First we will describe interest groups and quasi groups in the rural sector, explaining the changes they underwent during the first decade of the Revolution (especially in fields of employment, income, the living standard, organization, and conscience or awareness) and, thereafter, we shall make the same analysis of these groups and quasi groups in the urban sector.

Rural Sector

This sector comprised the dominant prerevolutionary groups of *hacendados* (sugar plantation owners), *colonos* (sugar growers), and cattlemen (herders); and the dominated quasi groups of small landowners, peasants, and agricultural wage-earning workers.

The *hacendados* were a mixture of landowners and capitalists. They were the owners of the sugar mills and of the nearby land in which sugar cane was cultivated. This was possibly the group that earned the highest income in Cuba. The plantation owners were usually absentees, that is, they lived in the capital or in big towns, and kept administrators at the mills and plantations. In 1946, 25.6 percent of the cultivated land was entrusted to administrative nonowners and, in general, two-thirds of the total land was cultivated by nonowners.[42] The majority of the sugar mills was not owned by individuals, but by enterprises or corporations. In 1959, nine of these enterprises controlled about 40 percent of the sugar-sown land, and about 10 percent of the surface of all cultivable lands in the country.[43]

The *colonos* were linked to the sugar mills. Their job consisted of cultivating sugar cane on their own or on rented lands, and then selling the cut cane to the plantation owner or to a sugar mill. The riches of the planter depended on the extension of his plot of land and on the size of the production quota of cane allotted to him. In 1951, 14 percent of the cane growers controlled 35 percent of the ground cane, whereas 80 percent of the growers controlled only 16 percent of the cane.[44] Although the big sugar growers were also absentees, the greater part of this group lived on their farms or *colonias*.

The cattlemen appeared as a consequence of the decline of the sugar industry in 1920–1930, which coincided with a government policy that stressed domestic production. As was the case with sugar, the cattlemen controlled vast rural properties, but there were differences among them. The small rancher had the cattle up to the first year; the "improver" up to three years; and the *cebador* ("feeder"), with much more land and better pastures, cared for the animals up to their slaughter age, between thirty-six and forty months. The latter was the big owner. According to the 1952 cattle census, 3 percent of the ranches owned 43 percent of the cattle.[45]

Hacendados, colonos, and cattlemen were organized into interest groups called "associations." In the associations of sugar growers and cattlemen there were medium-sized and small-sized landowners. Control was in the hands of those who had the largest extensions of land. But, generally, the dominant rural groups had little or no class consciousness. They were organized with regard to the type of crops they cultivated and no common bond existed between them. In fact, there were often conflicts among these groups, for example, between *hacendados* and *colonos*. Sugar production did not constitute an agglutinating factor as it might have, because of its seasonal and unstable nature, because it has as many characteristics of an industrial process as an agricultural one, and because the Cuban appropriation of the sugar sector was relatively recent (1930–1940). This impeded the crystallization in Cuba of rural classes so common in Latin America, where there is a long family tradition pertaining to the land, and more structured interest groups allowing varying degrees of political control.[46] In Cuba, the dominant rural groups despised politics as an activity of "gangsters and thieves." Therefore, they exerted pressure only when their interests required it, without participating directly in the governing process.

The small landowners and the tenants or peasants (e.g., lessees, sublessees, sharecroppers, squatters, and tobacco sharecroppers) devoted themselves principally to cultivating cane (usually in association with a *colono*), tobacco, coffee, vegetables, and cattle-breeding. The reduced size of their farms, the general lack of property, the predominance of extensive cultivation and inefficiency in production, and the presence of intermediaries between producer and consumer were the principal differentiating characteristics of these quasi groups. The instability of the tenants and the threat of eviction were notably reduced by the so-called right of permanency granted by a 1937 law protecting even squatters in sugar fields, and by the regulation of share cropping and lease contracts introduced by a law enacted in 1948. Before 1959, there were about 150,000 estates operated by small farmers and peasants.[47] Approximately 100,000 were tenants or peasants who worked the land of others.[48] Their standard of living depended on the product they cultivated, declining gradually from dependence on a crop for export to one intended for domestic consumption. It is quite possible that a good number of small landowners and tenants suffered from underemployment. Some of them were members of associations (e.g., rice growers, tobacco growers), but, in general, they were not as organized as the previously mentioned groups.

The agricultural workers, a kind of rural proletariat, were connected either with the large plantations (sugar, tobacco, coffee) or with vast rural ranches on a daily-wage basis. The majority were itinerant workers who moved from one place to another following the harvest, though some also had a small plot that they owned or occupied. This was the quasi group that was most affected by seasonal unemployment and underemployment, and, probably, that which fed the streams of migrants from the country to the towns. Before 1959, there were from 500,000 to 600,000 agricultural workers, either permanent or itinerant.[49] Trade union organization among workers in export cultivations (sugar, tobacco) was strong but unstable due to the seasonal character of these crops. This instability and the mixture of proletarian and peasant features among this group impeded the development of a true class consciousness. The remaining workers were poorly organized or unorganized and had little class consciousness, constituting quasi groups. They probably had the lowest income. The sugar worker was the best paid and protected, followed by the tobacco worker and the coffee worker.

Negroes and mulattoes were evenly represented among agricultural workers, but they were less well represented among the small landowners, and grossly underrepresented among the *hacendados, colonos,* and cattlemen. In 1931 only 11.2 percent of the total number of estates and 7.8 percent of the value of these estates belonged to Negroes. In 1943, only 8.7 percent of the administrators of estates were black, but 26.8 percent of the agricultural workers were black.[50]

The Revolution confiscated at once most property acquired unlawfully by persons connected with the former regime. Thus, some cattle ranches, sugar plantations, and agricultural endeavors were taken over by the government. This action did not provoke a visible reaction among the dominant rural groups, since the majority considered it a legitimate, individualistic type of action that did not hurt their interests.

In general, the dominant rural groups supported the beginning phase of the Revolution. Various factors explain this position: the collective atmosphere of enthusiasm, hope, and popular support; the repeated promises of the revolutionaries to eradicate the vices of the past (e.g., corruption, bribery) and to enforce law and order under honest public administration; and the objective of economic development and the declaration in favor of national enterprise. These factors were fully compatible with the capitalistic values of the dominant rural groups. Those groups supported the government and even contributed generously of lands, cattle, and equipment, as long as their interests were not affected.

The first Agrarian Reform Law was the first alienating factor involving the leading rural groups. The associations of *Hacendados* and Cattlemen protested immediately. Some leaders of said associations, united with adherents of Batista and Trujillo, participated in a frustrated plot to overthrow Castro. As a result, the majority of the Cuban population rejected these groups even more. On the other hand, in 1959 the Association of *Colonos* requested the government to "intervene" in forty-three sugar mills on the grounds that they were delaying payments from that year's crop. The agrarian collectivization was carried out rapidly and peacefully, despite many arbitrary cases of intervention (nonformal confiscation or expropriation) by the INRA.[51] These characteristics of the process can be explained by the limited class consciousness and power of the dominant groups, and by the fact that many members left their property to go abroad with the illusion that the revolutionary process would be aborted by the United States. The Association of *Hacendados* was dissolved in October 1960, and the Association of *Colonos,* in January of 1961 after various confrontations with the government.[52]

The small farmers and peasants have experienced many ups and downs. The first Agrarian Reform Law brought about the parceling out of the land and the transformation of the tenant (who cultivated the land without ownership deed) into landowner. Though the INRA granted only about 31,500 ownership deeds up to 1961, the number of *de facto* owners (that is, those tenants who received the land they were cultivating without a formal ownership deed) was from 100,000 to 150,000 early in 1962 and rose to 200,-000 in 1964.[53] These owners devoted themselves principally to growing tobacco, sugar, turbes, coffee, and raising cattle. In 1961, the small farmers were integrated into the ANAP, which replaced the Association of *Colonos.* In theory, ANAP is an interest group, but it is obvious from its bylaws that it is integrated into the INRA and serves, rather, as an agency of state control. The small farmer has to obtain credit, seeds, machinery, and technical assistance through the ANAP. On the other hand, the majority (or the totality) of the crops of these small farmers have to be sold to the *acopio* (INRA's procurement agency) at official prices.

In 1961–1962, some dissatisfied farmers, located in Matanzas and the hilly region of Las Villas, rebelled against the government. The outburst was controlled rapidly and the estates of all those involved were confiscated. According to spokesmen of the government, many injustices were committed during this process. In March 1962, when faced with serious supply problems and declining sugar production, the government assured the small farmers that it would respect their property and enacted measures to repair the injustices committed. At the same time, intermediaries were eliminated and a policy of official prices for state purchases was established.

The second Agrarian Reform Law, passed in October 1963, reduced the maximum size of private lands, expropriating (promising indemnization payment) some 2.1 million hectares from 11,215 landowners. After this, the state controlled 70 percent of the cultivable land. Another movement to integrate the private sector was started in 1967 and reached its climax in mid-1968 with the Revolutionary Offensive. This movement has had several consequences: some 12,000 farms were sold to the state;[54] the system of *acopio* was extended in some areas to embrace an entire crop; the government began to pay wages and build houses for former landowners (who continued to operate their holdings as administrators); the black market that encouraged the private sale of agricultural products at high prices to private buyers was substantially reduced; brigades of mutual assistance among the small landowners were organized; and there was a campaign to eliminate wage-earning workers on private farms.

The income of the small farmers still varies according to the specific crop to which they devote themselves. Huberman and Sweezy have stated that, in the second half of the 1960s, there were private farmers earning $10,000 and even $20,000 a year, much more than the annual income of a minister of the government ($8,400).[55] However, in the mid-1960s, Rodríguez reported that the average payment for INRA purchases from small farms was $1,500 annually. To this had to be added an average amount of $500 for direct sales to consumers, trade among farmers, and direct consumption of the producer. A survey taken at the time among 92,000 private farmers showed that tobacco growers had the highest state payment: $350 per hectare (with a maximum of seven hectares) for an annual payment of $2,450. Even when an allowance of $800 is added for other trade operations and the producer's own consumption, it is clear that the average income among the best-paid private farmers in the mid-1960s was less than one-half a minister's salary. The poorest among the small farmers, some 40,000 of them, have very small plots and do not produce a surplus; hence, they are engaged in subsistence agriculture.[56]

There are three other types of associations of small farmers besides the ANAP. The peasant associations were composed of 121,833 farmers by the mid-1960s (that is 60 percent of the total number of small farmers). Members keep cultivating their farms and selling their output individually, but participate, theoretically at least, in the administration of annual output plans, *acopio,* etc. The credit-and-service cooperatives embrace small farmers who mainly grow tobacco and sugar cane. Among them, individual cultivation of land is also the rule, but the cooperative facilitates credit and sells their products in a collective way, although the distribution of profit is made on an individual basis. In 1963, there were 527 of these cooperatives with a membership of 46,133 farmers; in the mid-1960s, the number had risen to 884 and 55,069 respectively, or 28 percent of the total.

In the agricultural-livestock societies, land is worked collectively and distribution is made in a communal manner according to the amount of work each member contributes. The number of these societies, in contrast to the other two types of associations, has been declining, from 328 with 3,884 members in 1963 to 270 with 3,200 members by the mid-1960s, or only 3 percent of the total.[57] This has happened in spite of government exhortations addressed to the farmers to enter these societies, which are considered better in terms of the socialist organization of property. The farmers' opposition to follow this exhortation could be interpreted as a rejection of these quasi groups to a form of integration contrary to their interests. Nine percent of the small farmers do not belong to a production association.

It is difficult to weigh the changes experienced by these quasi groups. The former landowners and tenants who had medium-sized farms, especially those who devoted themselves to export crops, have probably suffered a decline in their incomes and consumption levels. On the other hand, the majority of land tenants (especially the squatters and sublessees) have probably improved their stability, income, consumption, and standard of living. Tobacco growers seem to have the highest income.

As regards the agricultural wage workers, almost all are hired by state farms. In 1961 a large number of these workers belonged to sugar-cane cooperatives or worked for medium- and small-sized landowners. The transformation of the cooperatives into state farms (1962), the elimination of the medium-sized landowner (1963), and the campaign to reduce the number of wage-earning laborers in the small private farm (1967–1968) gradually transferred this segment to the state sector. Whereas in 1962 there were only 297,000 agricultural workers in the state sector, the number had increased to 447,400 in 1966, of which one-half belonged to the sugar sector.[58] There still remains, according to nonofficial estimates, from 36,000 to 60,000 wage-earning workers in the private sector.[59]

Trade unionization among these workers is almost total. Most of them are affiliated to the National Trade Union of Agricultural Workers. These workers do not suffer any longer from seasonal unemployment, and the majority have stable employment on the same farm during the whole year. (A segment that was still moving from one harvest to another, mainly cane cutters, has become permanently settled since the sugar crop of 1969.) It can be asserted that the worker's income has been considerably improved through full employment, enforcement of minimum wages, and the expansion of free medical services and education. In 1957, the monthly income of an average family of six members, of which all those of working age had an agricultural job for twenty-three hours a week, was $46, including the food produced by themselves in their plot or vegetable garden.[60] The average monthly wage of the agricultural worker (not of his family) was $80 in 1962 and increased to $88 in 1966. These figures show the remarkable improvement in income achieved by this group, but suggest that the majority is still concentrated in the lower income bracket of the wage scale. Cattle workers have the highest wage average followed by that of sugar workers.[61] Therefore, though these quasi groups probably gained the greatest benefits from the Revolution, they are still at the bottom of the social and economic scale.

Any judgment as to whether the quasi groups of small farmers and wage-earning workers have an improved class consciousness is somewhat speculative. The literacy campaign, the expansion of education for children as well as adults, the organization of militias, the peasant meetings in cities, the improvement of rural communications, the contact of leaders with rural areas, the sharply increased contacts between peasants and urban workers, and the activities of political and economic organizations have probably broken the previous isolation of the peasant. It is also possible that such changes have made the peasant more aware of the national goals and the previous situation of domination under which he lived in the past. It seems that there has been a movement of former quasi groups, which constituted a large proportion of the population, into interest groups organized into associations and trade unions. In spite of government exhortation (and economic incentives such as lower interest rates charged to loans), some of these groups have rejected associational forms highly praised by the state. On the other hand, it is quite difficult to think that these groups can develop a class consciousness because of the tremendous state pressures in favor of goals that go beyond class boundaries, such as the defense of the fatherland against foreign enemies or the fulfillment of national output targets under the unifying charismatic leadership of Fidel Castro. Nevertheless, the low increase, stagnation, or decline of production in most of the agricultural sector might be an indication that, in spite of all pressure and indoctrination, little has been achieved in developing social consciousness and solidarity over individual and group interest among small farmers and agricultural workers.

Urban Sector

This sector includes the dominant groups of industrialists, financiers, and big merchants; the intermediate groups of professionals, the self-employed, and clerical employees; the dominated groups of skilled and semiskilled workers; and those dominated quasi groups made up of unskilled, nonorganized workers, the underemployed, and the unemployed.

The industrialists, except for those of the sugar industry, which have already been studied, were involved in the production and refining of metals (e.g., nickel, copper, manganese); metallurgy; oil extraction and refining; electricity and telephones; cigars, cigarettes, and matches; textiles; synthetic fibers; leather and garments; cosmetics (soap, detergent, toothpaste, perfumes); paint; tires; glass and ceramics; construction materials; plastics and chemicals; paper, cardboard and newsprint; dairy products, soda pop, and beer; and canning of food. In 1957 there was a total of 38,384 industrial enterprises employing 960,770 workers.[62] An important industrial sector was in the hands of, or controlled by, subsidiaries of North American corporations (e.g., Esso Standard Oil, International Telephone and Telegraph, Goodrich, Firestone, Goodyear, Colgate Palmolive, United Fruit,

Freeport Sulphur, Owen Illinois), or was in partnership with domestic capital.

A large number of banking institutions were controlled by branches of U.S., British, and Canadian banks, although national banks developed rapidly from 1940 to 1950. State banks and financial institutions that emerged in the decade prior to the Revolution included the National Bank, the Agricultural and Industrial Development Bank, the Economic and Social Development Bank, the Cuban Bank for Foreign Trade, the Cuban Finance Company, and the Insured Mortgage Fund. Most of the insurance companies were American or British, but the national social-security funds were quite extensive and their enormous capital was partially utilized for financing.

Big merchants were mainly involved in the import-export field. Manufactured goods such as automobiles and consumer durables were generally imported from the United States and distributed through concessions. Another trade sector of importance was that of the large department stores built with national capital (with the exception of Sears and Roebuck, and Woolworth's), but which were largely dependent on imported products. Warehouses and wholesale enterprises dealt, for the most part, in foodstuffs (some of them imported), liquor, hardware, and textiles. We may also include those businesses connected with tourism (mostly emanating from the United States), such as hotels, casinos, nightclubs, and restaurants.

Dominant urban groups began to form in the second half of the 1920s when the Machado regime stimulated domestic industry and signed a tariff agreement with the United States. Nevertheless, the crash of 1929, the Great Depression, the reciprocity treaty (which gave preferential treatment to some 400 articles, principally of U.S. manufacture), and the institutional instability of the 1930s delayed this evolution. In the 1940s, however, with greater political stability, the scarcity of manufactured products due to the war, high sugar prices, and the general expansion of markets, forward movement resumed. This continued in the 1950s, aided by the creation of state banks and finance institutions aimed at development, by American investment, and a new tariff agreement with the United States, which was more beneficial to domestic industry. The dominant urban groups organized themselves into associations, one of the oldest being the Chamber of Commerce. Later, there appeared the Association of Cuban Banks, the Association of Cuban Industrialists and the newer Cuban Management Confederation. In 1943, only 15 percent of the owners and major executives were Negro or mulatto, which indicates an underrepresentation of this ethnic group in the dominant urban groups.

The studies done by Boorstein, Wood, and Ruiz suggest that Cuban dependence on U.S. capital and commerce, as well as the physical nearness of the great American consumer market, impeded the formation of class consciousness and of a cohesive set of values within the dominant groups. These authors also maintain that these groups had no unity and no real independent power.[63] However, these evaluations cannot be accepted completely because a segment of the industrialist group was domestically oriented. Another characteristic of those groups (mainly of the domestically oriented industrialist) was their dependence on the state: financing through state banks or parastate banks, tax exemptions and import tariffs for protection of new industries, auditing through the Central Bank and the General Comptroller's Office, etc. Bribery was frequently used in obtaining government licenses for operation and importation, for tax evasion, to bring in contraband, and to obtain privileges. A large number of native capitalists made their fortunes through fraudulent manipulation of public funds, but the political instability in Cuba (in contrast to Mexico) did not favor the total reinvestment of these funds in the country. A significant part of these funds were deposited or invested in foreign countries.

Intermediate groups were composed of professionals, small businessmen and merchants, real estate owners, some clerical, sales, and banking employees who could not enter trade unions because of the nature of their work, and civil servants. Negroes and mulattos were underrepresented among professionals, semiprofessionals, and clerical and banking employees. According to the 1943 census, they comprised only 15 to 16 percent of those working in these occupations. (They were, however, overrepresented in skilled and semiskilled occupations.) Association among these groups was strong but segmented. Almost every profession was organized into its own association (*colegio*) with obligatory membership.

Before the Revolution, there had been a strong desire for national change and a high potential for radicalism among some professionals and members of the intermediate groups. Politics was generally considered something dirty and dishonest, but from time to time this segment enthusiastically supported movements or political parties that proposed structural changes, such as the *ABC* party in the 1930s, the *Auténticos* in the 1940s, and the *Ortodoxos* at the end of the 1940s and beginning of the 1950s. The main leaders of the Revolution emerged from this segment, which was also responsible for organizing the urban underground that gave such vital support to the revolutionary triumph. A large number of these professionals (doctors and lawyers) were underemployed due to oversaturation within their field and the lack of adequate employment opportunities. An extraordinary number of lawyers were involved in politics, government, and the official bureaucracy. Lawyers predominated in the first revolutionary cabinet of 1959. We may speculate on the conflict faced by lawyers in the decade of the 1950s, a conflict involving theoretical training that emphasized the optimum regulation of society through legislation, and the reality of an imperfect society needing reforms that were not effected by what they thought of as an illegitimate and corrupt government. Avenues of access and possibilities to effect change were closed because of the saturation of the market, the elimination of the free play of politics, and the control of the best positions by a small group of law firms. The lawyer's frustration was either channeled into acceptance of a badly paid bureaucratic post or into rebellion.

The skilled and semiskilled workers and trade unionized clerical and banking employees had quite a superior position with respect to income and status when compared with agricultural workers. This was a result of the labor unions' conquests, which began with the revolution of 1933, and which were consolidated in the 1940 constitution and expanded in legislation passed in the 1940s and 1950s. The degree of unionization in Cuba may have been the highest in Latin America. The Confederation of Cuban Workers (CTC), founded in 1939 with Communist initiative, was the only union confederation in the country. Due to legislative and union protection, the worker was given stability of employment, a minimum wage, and social security. Up to 1960, 47 percent of the workers in the manufacturing and service sectors earned between $81 and $500 per month.[64] Wages depended on type of occupation, degree of unionization, and the concentration of capital in the enterprise. Power and telephone workers' unions, bank employees' unions, and gastronomic workers' (tourism, hotels, nightclubs, restaurants) unions were related to firms with significant U.S. investment and were probably the best organized and the richest. The workers had little or no active role in the insurrectional stage of the Revolution. The CTC and most of the unions were on good terms with the Batista government, which was careful not to interfere with the unionized workers' interests. A proposed law authorizing dismissal with indemnization was quickly withdrawn under pressure from the CTC. A 1958 law authorized a generous increase in minimum wages. Social-security funds grew in the 1950s. The only attempt by organized workers to oppose the dictatorship was a general strike in April 1958, which was a total disaster.

The urban quasi groups of lowest income and poorest living conditions were unskilled workers (generally not organized into unions), domestics, the underemployed, and the unemployed. Passage from one of these positions to another was common (e.g., public servant to unemployed), and rural-urban migration constantly increased the numbers of these groups. According to the 1943 census, the proportion of Negroes and mulattoes in the unskilled labor market (e.g., street cleaners, garbagemen, ditchdiggers) and in the domestic servant category was from 8 percent to 10 percent greater than their proportional representation in the total population. Lack of class consciousness and organization was characteristic of these quasi groups.

The dominant urban groups did not initially oppose the revolutionary process. The segment directly connected with U.S. investment was the first to be affected by nationalization (such as the telephone enterprise and oil refineries) and by the cessation of importation. The segment involved in domestic industry (highly dependent on state protection) welcomed the Revolution, with its plans for diversification, industrialization, nationalism, fiscal reform, administrative honesty, and expansion of the internal market. Government measures such as the campaigns to reduce importation of foreign products and to increase consumption of domestic products also raised hopes among native industrialists. These hopes that this segment had, along with fears of sanctions, explain the massive payments of back taxes or taxes previously evaded that took place in the first months of 1959. These record tax collections were of great help in the financing of government plans for public works and agrarian reform. Some well-known Cuban bankers who had financially aided the guerrillas in the Sierra were given government jobs. For example, the president of the Continental Bank became president of the Cuban Social Security Bank. The owner of an important beer factory publicly supported the Revolution by joining the militia. At the beginning of 1960, Ernesto Guevara acknowledged the support given to the Revolution by numerous native industrialists.[65]

The first friction between government and the industrialists arose when the Ministry of Labor took control of enterprises facing labor conflicts in 1960 (see chapter 9). The first nationalization of U.S. companies took place in July and August of that year, and the banks were nationalized in September. In October, not only were the remaining American companies nationalized, but also most domestic industries, businesses, and banks. The directional change taken by the Revolution excluded the possibility of co-operation with domestic businessmen and entrepreneurs. Surprisingly, the dominant groups did not raise much opposition, but chose exile, thinking that the Revolution would soon be destroyed by the United States. An analysis of exiles made in Miami in 1962 based on the figures provided by the Refugee Center shows that, in the third quarter of 1960, the number of exiles suddenly increased by more than 200 percent (in relation to the second quarter) and in the final quarter there was a similar increase. The most notable increase was in exiles with managerial occupations, followed by professionals, and clerical employees.[66] The dominant urban groups' associations were abolished without relevant opposition in 1960–1961.

The intermediate sector found itself divided with respect to the radicalization of the Revolution. Most chose exile (see chapter 10, table 7), especially after the massive confiscation of property in the second half of

1960. The rest either became part of the governing elite (occupying positions that were vacated by the exodus of technicians, managers, bureaucrats, and university professors) or they retired. In the second half of 1960 and the first half of 1961, obligatory professional associations were taken over by the government. Later, their research functions were integrated into the National Cuban Academy of Sciences (e.g., research in medicine) and their membership was integrated into various unions.[67] Obviously, some professionals left Cuba because the 1960 confiscations affected their source of employment, but it is probable that the majority went into exile because of the attack on their set of values (private property, liberal democracy, religion), the hostile governmental attitude, and their belief that the Revolution would fail. It is interesting to speculate as to how many professionals would have stayed in Cuba had they known that the Revolution would consolidate itself or if the government had tried to entice them to remain.

The Revolution has had diverse effects on the skilled workers, but generally this group must have been harmed. Those in occupations connected with American investment or with the market system must have suffered a decline in their standard of living. In the oil, electricity, telephone and wholesale-trade fields, the average salary in 1962 was greater than that of 1966.[68] The rest possibly have continued to earn the same amount or have received a slight salarial increment, but there is not much on which to spend it. Most of these workers in the prerevolutionary period could afford to live modestly, paying for adequate medical and educational services. They were also protected by social security and were not noticeably affected by unemployment. Others in this segment, especially those in administrative positions, must have suffered from the consolidation of industry in 1961 and the antibureaucracy campaign of 1964–1967. It is possible that many of them were transferred to other positions or to agriculture. They must also have felt more strongly the pressures of the campaign against individualism, the restrictions of consumption, and the social pressure to do voluntary labor. This explains the growth in the number of exiles in this category as seen in chapter 10, table 7. On the other hand, it is possible that some of these workers achieved higher status within their enterprises. The small number of air and maritime transport workers not only had their wages significantly increased between 1962 and 1966 (perhaps because of the importance of and demand for their services on the part of the government), but also were not greatly affected by rationing and internal pressures because they spent most of their time abroad.

Undoubtedly, those quasi groups of urban unskilled workers, unemployed, and underemployed have reaped the greatest benefits from the Revolution because of the guarantee of stable employment and the increases in income, and the provision of free medical and educational services, including scholarships for their children and the establishment of day-care centers. They also benefited from the lowering or elimination of rent, social security protection, reduced costs for electricity and for transportation, and free burials. This segment probably predominates in mass organizations such as the CDR. Unionization must also have increased significantly among them. On the other hand, restrictions on consumption probably have not had much effect on this segment, considering the low nutritional indices they must have had before 1959. In some cases, their level of consumption may have risen in spite of rationing.

It is difficult to make an accurate judgment about the present state of class consciousness and the degree of association among the urban groups and quasi groups remaining in Cuba. Industrial, commercial, financial, and professional associations have been abolished and their members integrated into unions. The function of the union has changed from that of defending the interest of the group to that of a transmission belt for increased national production and productivity. Zeitlin notes that the specific social function of the union as an organization of workers devoted to protecting and advancing their immediate interests has disappeared; and suggests that this is a consequence of the identity of interests that the workers have established among themselves, the administration of the enterprise, and the state.[69] As in the case of the agricultural workers, if it is true that there is no conflict between the workers and the state enterprises because the workers feel that they are the owners of those enterprises, how does one explain the increased absenteeism, worker negligence, and the decline in productivity? Are these defects the result of the weakening of authority and the fact that there is no longer a fear of unemployment, or are they due to the fact that the worker still maintains some individuality and does not accept in practice the theoretical argument that working to his utmost capacity for the enterprise (and the state) is really to his own benefit?

Conclusions

Much of the material analyzed above lacks sufficient precision to reach concrete conclusions, not to mention quantitative ones. It does, however, permit us to make educated guesses and to indicate tendencies. There is no doubt that the Revolution has greatly reduced the inequalities that existed in prerevolutionary Cuba in terms of urban-rural location, race, and access to employment. In chapter 9, we saw that the inequalities of income have also been noticeably reduced.

Rural migration to the city has reversed itself. The countryside has accrued the benefits of larger state investment, full employment, and the expansion of social services. The rural areas have been less affected by rationing than the cities. On the other hand, the cities, especially Havana, seem to have fallen into decay because of emigration, decline in construction, rationing, mobilizations of the citizenry to the countryside, and the deemphasis on industrial investment. It would seem that the rural areas have forged ahead at the expense of the cities.

Although cases of racial discrimination existed in prerevolutionary Cuba, their number was very small when compared with the discrimination existing in the United States, even in the most integrated regions. The Revolution has eliminated the sources of discrimination remaining in Cuba by opening beaches, clubs, schools, and private hospitals to the public and by alienating the dominant groups who had lived in exclusive neighborhoods and then confiscating their homes. The expansion of income, education, medical services and the lowering of rents and utilities has favored the lowest income groups in which Afro-Cubans predominated. Nevertheless, there are still reports of discrimination in the distribution of employment, participation in political decision-making, and interracial sexual relations. The Revolution claims that racial problems no longer exist, but militant Negroes insist that the government is trying to integrate the Afro-Cubans into the white value system, thus eliminating black culture.

Seasonal unemployment in agriculture has been eliminated; in fact, there is a manpower shortage during the important harvests (e.g., sugar) as a result of the creation of jobs on state farms, the rural-urban migration, and the granting of fellowships to rural youth of working age, all of which took place during the first years of the Revolution. At the same time, underemployment and, possibly, unemployment increased in the cities. The government hoped to absorb the urban jobless through expansion of employment resulting from plans for industrialization. When this plan was abandoned in 1963–1964, the return to agriculture made it evident that there was an urban labor surplus and a rural labor shortage. The antibureaucracy campaign, the Compulsory Military Service Law, the mobilizations for voluntary labor, and the transfers have been aimed at bettering the distribution of manpower. These changes favor the seasonally unemployed agricultural workers and the underemployed urban workers who have accepted jobs in agriculture or in the tertiary sector. On the other hand, most of those who had stable employment of high status (as in American companies) have left the country. Probably, the skilled workers have experienced no change in this sense.

The dominant rural groups have lost their power and property, their associations have been dissolved, and almost all their members have left the country. Those who owned medium-sized farms before the Revolution have been affected by total or partial confiscation of land (for example, the agrarian reform of 1963 affected some 10 percent of the total number of farmers), by the obligation to sell all or part of their crop to the INRA, and by the restrictions on credit, machinery, and salaried labor. The former peasants have now become small farmers, and their condition has been improved by the granting of land (whether *de facto* or *de jure*) and by the provision of social services. Some, such as tobacco farmers, are probably enjoying greater incomes. But the sector is being submitted to restrictions and to increasing state control. Their sales on the open market have been drastically reduced, and they must sell almost all their crops to the INRA at official prices. As a result of this, some 5 percent of these farmers have sold their farms to the state. On the other hand, about 20 percent of the small landowners do not generate any surplus and only produce for their own subsistence. Apart from the ANAP, farmers are part of various productive associations, in decreasing proportion according to their degree of socialization: 60 percent in individual planting, sales, and distribution; 28 percent in individual planting, collective sales, and distribution; and 3 percent in communal planting, sales, and distribution. (Proportions are based on earlier discussion in the text—see also note 57.) Ninety-two percent of salaried agricultural workers are employed on state farms. They have benefited from full employment, increased income, and social services. But in spite of these improvements, they are still at the bottom of the wage ladder. Those receiving higher salaries are the cattle and sugar workers. Unionization, apart from the sugar and tobacco sectors, must have increased greatly among this group.

The dominant urban groups have undergone the same fate as their rural counterparts. Most professionals and members of intermediate groups have also taken the road of exile, their associations have been dissolved, and their members integrated into unions. Some who have stayed in Cuba (apart from those who are retired) have possibly filled some vacant positions and have higher status and income than before. Most skilled workers have probably been affected because revolutionary social measures have not improved their previous living standard, and they may suffer from restriction of consumption, from transfers, and from sociopolitical pressures to which they were not previously subjected. Their unions, although they have not been abolished, no longer function in the defense of the workers' interests. Unskilled urban workers and previously unemployed and underemployed workers have reaped the greatest benefits through full employment, increased wages, and free social services. Their degree of unionization must have increased notably and most of them are possibly members of mass associations like the CDR.

One can only make conjectures as to the Revolution's effect on the class consciousness of these groups. Mobilizations, political education, propaganda and the work of mass organizations have probably made the former peasant, the former unemployed worker, and the former unskilled worker aware of the privations, injustices, and abandonment that existed for them in the past. It is also clear that existing organizations such as the unions do not have their former function of acting in solidarity against the dominant groups for the defense of the dominated. These organizations now seem to be parastate agencies responsible for mass mobilization, control of production, and productivity.

Decisions made in the past by the dominant groups are now the responsibility of the government. If most of the groups and quasi groups of the past lacked class consciousness and a definite ideology, the present leadership certainly lacks neither ideology nor concrete objectives. In chapters 1, 7, and 9, it was proved that power is concentrated in a small coterie, which allows little or no mass participation in decision-making. Existing associations of farmers and workers have little or no participation in the development of plans and goals on the national level. Rather, they function as agencies that mobilize their membership in the direction of facilitating the acceptance of already-made decisions and the execution of already-made plans. The sacrifices imposed on the people are compensated for by those benefits mentioned: more equality, free social services, and employment security. There also exists the promise of the Communist millennium in which a society of abundance will make current deprivations unnecessary.

The hardest question to answer is whether the farmers and workers have accepted the national goals as their own by identifying their individual interests with those of the state. Because they do not really participate in decisions about national production plans (or in setting their own work quotas or *acopio* prices), it is entirely possible that they do not actually see the connection between their own labor effort and national production. Another important problem is that those receiving benefits through the egalitarian process apparently have not substituted a higher grade of consciousness and social responsibility for the system of economic incentives and checks typical of the disappeared market economy. Money is not an incentive if there are no consumer goods to buy, and unemployment is no longer a threat. This might explain poor productivity on state farms, the absenteeism among urban workers, and the decline of output in important production sectors. The small farmers' resistance to integration into state-supported associations (which are considered the most advanced in the socialist system) is another indication that individual self-interest continues to play a relevant role.

NOTES

1. Juan F. Carvajal, "Observaciones sobre la clase media en Cuba"; Carlos M. Raggi Ageo, "Contribución al estudio de las clases medias en Cuba," in *Materiales para el estudio de la clase media en la América Latina,* ed. Theodore R. Cravenna (Washington, D.C., 1950); and Publicidad Fergo Arregui, S.A., *La clase media en Cuba: factor de progreso económico* (La Habana, 1958).

2. Lowry Nelson, *Rural Cuba* (Minneapolis, Minn., 1950).

3. Theodore Draper started the polemic with *Castro's Revolution: Myths and Realities* (New York, 1962), expanded in his *Castroism: Theory and Practice* (New York, 1965), pp. 57–134. For divergent viewpoints see Hugh Thomas, "Middle Class Politics and the Cuban Revolution," in *The Politics of Conformity in Latin America,* ed. Claudio Véliz (New York, 1967), pp. 249–77; G. C. Alroy, "The Peasantry in the Cuban Revolution," *Review of Politics* (January 1967), pp. 87–99; Ramón E. Ruiz, *Cuba: The Making of a Revolution* (Amherst, Mass., 1968), pp. 13, 15, 142–66; and Dennis B. Wood, "Las relaciones revolucionarias de clase y los conflictos políticos en Cuba: 1868–1968," *Revista Latinoamericana de Sociología,* 5 (March 1969), pp. 40–79.

4. Maurice Zeitlin, *Revolutionary Politics and the Cuban Working Class* (Princeton, N.J., 1967); and Nelson Amaro, "Mass and Class in the Origins of the Cuban Revolution," *Studies in Comparative International Development,* 4 (1968–1969).

5. Oficina Nacional de los Censos Demográfico y Electoral, *Censo de población, viviendas y electoral, 1953* (La Habana, 1955).

6. Harry T. Oshima, "A New Estimate of the National Income and Product of Cuba in 1953," *Food Research Institute Series,* 2 (November 1961), p. 214.

7. Buró de Información y Propaganda de la Agrupación Católica Universitaria, *Por qué reforma agraria* (La Habana, 1958), pp. 1–3.

8. *Censo de población, 1953.*

9. René Dumont, *Cuba, intento de crítica constructiva* (Barcelona, 1964), pp. 85–86.

10. Cuban Economic Research Project, *Labor Conditions in Communist Cuba* (Coral Gables, 1963), p. 15.

11. Ibid.

12. Carmelo Mesa-Lago, "Economic Significance of Unpaid Labor in Socialist Cuba," *Industrial and Labor Relations Review,* 22 (April 1969), p. 345.

13. JUCEPLAN, *Boletín Estadístico, 1966* (La Habana, n.d.), pp. 12, 16, tables 11.7 and 11.7.4.

14. Mesa-Lago, "Economic Significance," pp. 342–43.

15. JUCEPLAN, *Boletín Estadístico, 1966,* p. 102, table VII.4. For 1961–1963 figures see ECLA, *Economic Survey for Latin America, 1963* (New York, 1965), pp. 287–89; and Michel Gutelman, *La Agriculture socialisée à Cuba* (Paris, 1967), p. 187.

16. See chapter 11, this volume.

17. Alberto Arrinda, "El problema de la vivienda en Cuba," *Cuba Socialista,* 4 (December 1964), p. 16, table 4.

18. Quoted in Carlos Rafael Rodríguez, *Cuba, ejemplo de América* (Lima, Perú, 1969), p. 125.

19. For statistics and different viewpoints see Alberto Arredondo, *El negro en Cuba* (La Habana, 1939), and *El negro cubano socio-económicamente considerado* (La Habana, 1958); Blas Roca, *Los fundamentos del socialismo en Cuba* (La Ha-

bana, 1961), pp. 91–105; Carlos More, "Le Peuple noir a-t-il sa place dans la revolution cubaine?" *Présence Africaine*, no. 4 (1964), pp. 177–230; Cuban Economic Research Project, *Study on Cuba* (Coral Gables, 1965), pp. 6–13, 203–05, 303–05, 425–26; and Claude Lightfoot, *Ghetto Rebellion to Black Liberation* (New York, 1968), pp. 152–82.

20. Cuban Economic Research Project, *Study on Cuba*, p. 11.
21. Ibid., pp. 11 and 426.
22. Thomas, "Middle Class Politics," p. 263.
23. Ibid., and Lowry Nelson, "The Social Class Structure in Cuba," in *Materiales para el estudio de la clase media en la América Latina*, ed. Theodore R. Cravenna (Washington, D.C., 1950).
24. *Censo de población, 1953.*
25. Thomas, "Middle Class Politics," p. 263.
26. J. F. Carneado, "La discriminación racial en Cuba no volverá jamás," *Cuba Socialista*, 2 (January 1962), pp. 54–67.
27. Joseph A. Kahl, "The Moral Economy of a Revolutionary Society," *Transaction*, 6 (April 1969), p. 33.
28. Gil Green, *Revolution Cuban Style* (New York, 1970), p. 93.
29. John Clytus, *Black Man in Red Cuba* (Coral Gables, 1970).
30. Ibid., pp. 23–24.
31. Ibid., pp. 41–42. See also More, "Le Peuple noir," pp. 211–12.
32. Clytus, *Black Man*, pp. 24, 49, 132.
33. Ibid., p. 76. More also reports the case of another Afro-Cuban writer who was accused of being counterrevolutionary and an "agent of imperialism" because he wrote on racial themes. See More, "Le Peuple noir," pp. 182, 185, 208.
34. Clytus, *Black Man*, pp. 42, 152. A similar confrontation that occurred in 1963 between Guevara and a group of Afro-Americans is reported by More, "Le Peuple noir," pp. 216–17.
35. Elizabeth Sutherland, *The Youngest Revolution* (New York, 1969), pp. 138–39.
36. Ibid., pp. 141–42, 148–49, 153.
37. Ibid., pp. 146–49, 159.
38. More, "Le Peuple noir," pp. 212–20.
39. Material in this section mainly comes from Carmelo Mesa-Lago, "Unemployment in Socialist Countries: USSR, East Europe, China and Cuba," mimeographed (Ph.D. diss., Cornell University, Ithaca, N.Y., 1968).
40. Maurice Zeitlin, "Political Generations in the Cuban Working Class," *American Journal of Sociology*, 81 (March 1966), p. 506.
41. Ralph Dahrendorf, *Las clases sociales y su conflicto en la sociedad industrial* (Madrid, 1962), p. 260.
42. Ministerio de Agricultura, *Memoria del censo agrícola nacional, 1946* (La Habana, 1951).
43. Jacques Chonchol, "Análisis crítico de la reforma agraria cubana," *El Trimestre Económico*, 30 (January–March 1963), p. 76.
44. Aureliano Sánchez Arango, *Reforma Agraria* (La Habana, 1959), p. 39.
45. Chonchol, "Análisis crítico," p. 77; Ministerio de Agricultura, *Memoria del censo ganadero, 1952* (La Habana, 1953).
46. Wood, "La relaciones revolucionarias," p. 58.
47. Carlos Rafael Rodríguez, "Cuatro años de reforma agraria," *Cuba Socialista*, 3 (May 1963), p. 10.

48. Carlos Rafael Rodríguez, "El nuevo camino de la agricultura cubana," *Cuba Socialista,* 3 (November 1963), p. 95.

49. These estimates are based on figures from *Censo de población, 1953* and *Memoria del censo agrícola nacional, 1946.*

50. Roca, *Los fundamentos del socialismo,* pp. 92–93; and Cuba, Dirección General del Censo, *Informe general del censo de 1943* (La Habana, 1945).

51. Juan Martínez-Alier, *The Peasantry and the Cuban Revolution from the Spring of 1959 to the End of 1960,* St. Anthony Papers: Latin American Affairs, no. 22, (Oxford, 1970), pp. 137, 157. This author makes a deep study of conflicts among landowners, tenants, and workers in this period.

52. Cuban Economic Research Project, *Labor Conditions,* pp. 124–25.

53. For different estimates see Chonchol, "Análisis crítico," p. 116; Antonio Núñez Jiménez, "Dos años de reforma agraria," *Bohemia* (Havana), May 28, 1961; *Hoy,* May 20, 1962; Cuban Economic Research Project, *Cuba: Agriculture and Planning* (Miami, 1965), p. 225; and Antero Regalado, "El camino de la cooperación agraria en Cuba," *Cuba Socialista,* 3 (June 1963), p. 47.

54. Farmers selling their land to INRA could get total payment in cash or on an installment basis or they can join a pension plan that provides from $40 to $120 monthly. Most farmers prefer the latter arrangement. See Green, *Revolution Cuban Style,* pp. 107–08.

55. Leo Huberman and Paul Sweezy, *Socialism in Cuba* (New York, 1969), p. 118.

56. Carlos Rafael Rodríguez, "The Cuban Revolution and the Peasantry," *World Marxist Review,* 8 (October 1965), p. 14.

57. Data from 1963 comes from Regalado, "El camino de la cooperación," pp. 48–54; data for late 1960s from Sergio Aranda, *La revolución agraria en Cuba* (Mexico, 1968), pp. 157–60.

58. JUCEPLAN, *Boletín Estadístico, 1966,* p. 24, table IV.1.

59. Aranda, *La revolución agraria,* p. 148; Huberman and Sweezy, *Socialism in Cuba,* p. 118.

60. Buró de Información y Propaganda de la Agrupación Católica Universitaria, *Por qué reforma agraria.*

61. JUCEPLAN, *Boletín Estadístico, 1966,* p. 26, table IV.3.

62. For a full list of these enterprises, their value and employment in 1957 see Cuban Economic Research Project, *Stages and Problems of Industrial Development in Cuba* (Coral Gables, 1965), pp. 67–83.

63. Edward Boorstein, *The Economic Transformation of Cuba* (New York, 1968), ch. 1; Ruiz, *Cuba,* pp. 142–43; and Wood, "Las relaciones revolucionarias," p. 49.

64. Labor census of 1960, quoted in Seers, ed., *Cuba,* p. 23.

65. Ernesto Guevara as quoted in C. Wright Mills, *Los Marxistas* (México, 1966), p. 416.

66. Richard Fagen and Richard Brody, "Cubans in Exile: A Demographic Analysis," *Social Problems,* 11 (Spring 1964), p. 395, table 5.

67. Cuban Economic Research Project, *Labor Conditions,* pp. 126–27.

68. JUCEPLAN, *Boletín Estadístico, 1966,* p. 26, table IV.3.

69. Maurice Zeitlin, "Inside Cuba: Workers and Revolution," *Ramparts,* 8 (March 1970), p. 20.

13 Rolland G. Paulston

Education

THE purpose of this chapter is to examine the background, aims, and process of educational change in Cuba during the past decade. In order to put such an analysis in perspective, it will also be necessary to adumbrate something of the development of educational structures and services during the prerevolutionary republican era as well. A diachronic approach is useful in that it facilitates comparison of the formal educational systems before and after the Revolution and, by way of contrast, indicates the truly revolutionary nature of educational change since 1959.

The study is organized into three broad sections: The first covers the change in social organization and in educational functions during the periods of Spanish and North American influence. The second describes revolutionary educational innovation and change after 1959. The third examines some of the characteristics, problems, and trends of the current educational system. We have used a wide variety of primary source material from Cuba in the preparation of this study, especially reports of the Cuban UNESCO delegation.[1] We have also drawn heavily on the work of U.S. and European social scientists, such as Richard Jolly, Richard Fagen, Carmelo Mesa-Lago, and other notable scholars on revolutionary change in Cuba.

We are primarily concerned here with the role of education in social development. The new field of development education is diagnostic in that it seeks to understand educational problems in their larger social context. It is also professional and applied in that its practitioners, if requested, undertake directed-change activities. At best, these interventions are guided by relevant knowledge from the social sciences concerning cause-and-effect relationships, as well as more normative considerations of ends and means.

Obstacles to Educational Change

The author's experiences as a technical consultant to Latin American ministries of education, most recently to Venezuela and Peru, have provided vivid lessons of the staggering obstacles to qualitative educational change, or reform, if you will, in traditional Latin American societies. These essentially sociocultural obstacles have been well documented by Seymour Lipset and Aldo Solari, Ivan Illich, John Gillin, Richard Adams, and others.[2] These authors all stress that prominent social values in terms of a power function continue to be those of the upper class, and large segments of the middle sectors tend to identify (if only in terms of social aspiration) with the upper class and, therefore, to accept and defend upper-class values. According to the Brazilian sociologist Floristán Fernández, because of the differentiation of social and educational structures over time, the democratization of schooling (i.e., the creation of a mass educational system) has resulted in the spreading of the aristocratic school of the past throughout much of Latin American society.[3]

Throughout Latin America, this process has in varying degrees created public-school systems inculcating traditional, neocolonial, aristocratic, upper-class values that are for the greatest part highly dysfunctional for the individual's economic and social development. Theoretical, humanistic, and gentlemanly studies are seen as rewarding and desirable, whereas practical, technical, and work-related activities are largely rejected. Thus, Latin America, as Burns has observed, faces a paradox: to improve education, it must first change its social order; to change its social order, it must develop and distribute its economic resources. But the educational systems capable of providing sufficient technically qualified personnel to do the job are not forthcoming because of existing aristocratic value constructs that teach children to reject physical work and social responsibility.[4] Moreover, as the Alliance for Progress has discovered, Latin American elites have shown no more than a superficial interest in reforming their educational, economic, or social institutions, which are highly functional for the maintenance of privileged elites, if not for national development.

The United States, nevertheless, remains committed to the *Alianza* (Alliance for Progress) model that seeks evolutionary change, or gradual reform. But because existing elites are unwilling or unable to relinquish their monopoly on power and privilege, little basic change in social and economic structures has resulted. As Ortega y Gasset observed, "The tiger does not detigerize itself." In marked contrast, Cuba has had undeniable success in "detigerizing the tiger" by creating new social institutions and a basic social and cultural realignment that totally rejects the egocentric "gentlemanly" model for a more "societalcentric" exemplar that morally rewards the doer—the cane cutter, the rural teacher, or the technician. In the following section, more will be said on the extent to which prerevolutionary Cuban upper- and middle-sector values coincided with the Hispanic-American value construct, still dominant today throughout most of Latin America.

The Prerevolutionary Educational Situation

As Spain's last colony in the Americas, along with Puerto Rico, Cuba shared little in the widespread creation of public-schooling that took place in many Latin American republics during the last half of the nineteenth century. Instead, Cuban education continued to follow the colonial pattern in which a relatively small elite of plantation owners, bureaucrats, and professionals educated their children in private schools or abroad. A few public, religious, and charity schools existed for the urban, middle strata, leaving children of the large rural lower class unschooled, as had always been the case. Public primary education in colonial Cuba began in 1857 with the *Ley Española de Instrucción Pública*. Public secondary education came into being in 1880 with the *Plan de Instrucción Pública de la Colonia*, which founded eighty urban secondary schools (*bachillerato*) exclusively dedicated to preuniversity studies. In 1898, the total enrollment of all these schools did not exceed 30,000 students. Less than one-third of the total population could be classified as literate.[5]

Following independence in 1898 and two periods of U.S. intervention, from 1898 to 1902 and from 1906 to 1909, Cuba entered an era of forced modernization and Americanization. It may be recalled that in 1898 the United States became, almost overnight, a leading colonial power. In that momentous year, Americans annexed Hawaii and, following a short and successful war with Spain, found Puerto Rico, the Philippine Islands, and Cuba on their hands as well. In a rather vague manner, President William McKinley instructed the commander of the U.S. military forces occupying Cuba to prepare the people for independence and, more specifically, to conduct the occupation "in the interest and for the benefit of the people of Cuba and those possessed of rights and property in the Island."[6] General Leonard Wood, who directed the first occupation, remarked that he viewed his task as one of the building up of a republic "modeled closely upon the lines of our great Republic . . . by Anglo-Saxons in a Latin country where over 70 percent of the population is illiterate."[7]

In applying the U.S. development model to Cuba, public-schooling, along with the construction of sewers and roads, public health, and commercial development, became an area of intense activity. Because American policy makers viewed literacy as the prime requisite for any sort of a stable government, public primary-schooling became the chief educational aim of the occupation.

A new school law based on that of the state of Ohio created local boards of education, called for compulsory school attendance, teacher-training institutions, textbooks, and curricula. Cuba, however, is not Ohio and the law lasted only as long as American troops occupied the island.

During this period, nevertheless, Cubans were exposed to a number of new educational ideas—manual training, kindergartens, modern school construction, citizenship education, and numerous other practices reflecting the middle-class values imbedded in the American public-school model.[8]

In quantitative terms, the U.S. contribution was impressive. Thousands of public schools were built, and school enrollment, mostly urban, increased by three times the preindependence peak. Still, less than one-half of all school-age children attended classes and most left before attaining literacy. In the United States, the American policy of seeking a democratic government through literacy was criticized as being both naïve and unrealistic. It was suggested, instead, that Cubans really needed practical education designed to help them adapt to their rural agricultural environment.[9]

With the termination of U.S. military control, Cuban educators adapted a number of American practices and sought to extend the fledgling public-school system. Enrique José Varona, minister of education and proponent of neopositivism, struggled, largely in vain, to reorient the secondary-school curriculum from a classical humanistic cast to one with more scientific emphasis. The teacher certification law of 1909 sought to put the training, placement, and supervision of teachers on a more professional basis. Schools for training teachers were created in 1915 and schools for training accountants and clerical employees were founded in 1927.[10]

Following the World War I sugar boom, public-schooling reached a qualitative and quantitative highpoint. As table 1 shows, the number of teachers and students in primary education increased twofold between 1902 and 1925. Furthermore, between 1902 and 1927, the state expenditures in education increased fourfold and per capita expenditures rose from $2.01 to $4.19 (table 2). Enrollment of school-age children (five to fourteen years) increased from 46 percent in 1901–1902 to 63 percent in 1925–1926, a larger percentage than in any other Spanish-speaking republic at that time. This meant that in 1926 Cuba led all other Latin American countries in the percentage of children in school. During the late 1920s, Cuban educators with U.S. support offered technical assistance on teacher-training to a number of South American countries, most notably to Venezuela. Also during the 1920s, Cuban public education retained a good deal of U.S. influence in organization and content and until the 1930s conformed more closely to the U.S. educational system than did that of any other Latin American country.[11]

Nevertheless, serious shortcomings affected the system. Nelson has noted that graft and corruption plagued school administration, that the compulsory education requirement soon became a dead issue, that originally locally elected communal school boards came to be appointed from Havana, and that because the public-school system never was able to afford its own buildings, most classes took place in substandard rented or loaned structures.[12] Perhaps the most serious defect, however, was that the Cuban school system had totally failed to meet the educational needs of the rural population.[13] The vast majority of Cubans lived in what can best be described as a backward, impoverished world centuries apart from modern, urban Cuba.

With the world depression and the political and social turmoil of the 1930s and after, the percentage of school-age children enrolled in public schools dropped from 63 percent in 1925–1926 to 35 percent in 1942–1943. With war and postwar recuperation, between 1939 and 1955, the number of public primary schools and their enrollment grew by 80 percent and 70 percent respectively. Some emphasis was given also to rural schools under a sort of military organization. But the growing population and the general rural neglect during the 1930s were counteracting factors. Thus, although the illiteracy rate dropped to 23 percent in 1953 (a remarkable achievement), primary school enrollment of school-age children was only 36 percent, or some 10 percent below the enrollment figure at the beginning of the Republic. Moreover, enrollment ratios in secondary schools in 1953 were only 12 percent of the number of adolescents from fifteen to nineteen years of age. In marked contrast to Cuba's leading position in the 1920s, all but three Latin American countries claimed higher primary-school enrollment ratios than those of Cuba in the early 1950s.

The authoritative *Report on Cuba* sponsored by the World Bank describes public schooling at the beginning of the 1950s as being in a state of disquieting deterioration. The report notes that, although some progress toward developing a public secondary-school system and specialized types of schools was made during the 1940s, the general trend since the late 1920s had been one of retrogression. Fewer school-age children attended school and the number of hours of instruction a day had dropped to four hours—in many districts it dropped to only two hours a day. Only about one-half or less of the school-age children attended school, and of some 180,000 children entering the first grade, less than 5,000 reached the eighth grade. Apathy and absenteeism prevailed among teachers. Public-school administration was described as being afflicted by overcentralization

TABLE 1
NUMBER OF SCHOOLS, TEACHERS, AND STUDENTS IN PRIVATE AND PUBLIC EDUCATION IN CUBA: SELECTED YEARS, 1902 to 1968

Primary Schools

Year[a]	Public			Private		
	Schools	Teachers	Students	Schools	Teachers	Students
1902	3,474	3,583	163,348	—	—	—
1912	3,916	4,055	234,625	—	—	—
1925	3,627	6,898	388,349	575	1,956	38,064
1931	3,816	7,567	452,016	568	1,668	32,450
1939	4,386	9,386	424,094	360	1,906	31,023
1950	7,614	21,148	593,361	—	—	79,645
1955	7,905	20,119	728,087	—	6,619	107,000
1958	7,567	17,355	717,417	665	7,000	120,000
1962	13,780	36,613	1,207,286	0	0	0
1968	14,807	48,994	1,460,754	0	0	0

| | Secondary Schools | | | | | | Universities | | |
| | Public | | | Private[d] | | | Public and Private[e] | | |
Year[a]	Schools	Teachers	Students	Schools	Teachers	Students	Schools	Teachers	Students
1902	—	—	—	—	—	—	1	—	—
1912	—	—	—	—	—	—	1	—	—
1925	—	—	—	—	—	—	1	—	—
1931	—	—	—	—	—	—	1	—	—
1939	—	—	—	—	—	—	1	—	—
1950	119[b]	1,952[b]	26,413[b]	—	—	—	4[b]	711[b]	20,971[b]
1955	116	1,963	46,914	165[c]	850	13,459[c]	7	975	24,273
1958	184	2,580	63,526	168	—	14,850	6	1,053	25,514
1962	335	7,380	123,118	0	0	0	3	1,987	20,537
1968	434	10,703	186,358	0	0	0	3	4,151	27,523

Sources: Cuban Economic Research Project, Study on Cuba (Coral Gables, 1965); UNESCO, Statistical Yearbook, 1963–1968 (Louvain, Belgium, 1963–1968); and Carmelo Mesa-Lago, "Availability and Reliability of Statistics in Socialist Cuba," Latin American Research Review, 4 (Summer 1969), pp. 72–74.

a. School year begins in September and ends in June.
b. 1952.
c. 1956.
d. High schools only.
e. Until 1962 when all were public.

TABLE 2
STATE EXPENDITURE IN PUBLIC EDUCATION IN CUBA: SELECTED
YEARS, 1902 TO 1966
(*In Millions of Pesos at Current Prices*)

Year[a]	State Budget	Educational Expenditures	Percentage of State Budget in Education	Expenditures Per Capita (in Pesos)
1902	17.5	3.7	21.2%	2.01
1906	24.2	4.2	17.4	2.09
1921	62.7	10.4	16.6	3.37
1927	81.0	15.1	18.6	4.19
1940	79.0	11.4	14.4	2.66
1952	299.8	58.2	19.4	10.07
1958	382.0	75.5	19.8	11.53
1962	1,853.9	221.2	11.9	31.30
1966	2,717.9	272.3	10.0	34.91

Sources: Mercedes García Tudurí, "La enseñanza en Cuba en los primeros cincuenta años de independencia," *Historia de la nación cubana*, 10 (La Habana,
1952); Cuban Economic Research Project, *Study on Cuba* (Coral Gables, 1965);
and JUCEPLAN, *Boletín Estadístico, 1966* (La Habana, n.d.), p. 20.

Note: Comparisons between prerevolutionary and revolutionary figures are
misleading. For 1902–1958, data refer to the expenditures of the Ministry of Education, excluding those of the provinces, municipalities, and special funds, as well
as those of universities and private schools. Data for 1962–1966 embrace all educational expenses.

a. Refers to the financial year: July 1 to June 30.

in the Ministry of Education in Havana, discontinuity due to rapid political
shifts, lack of professionalism and any sort of civil-service system, and a
demoralizing heritage of patronage and graft.[14]

The problem of graft in school administration reached something of an
all-time high under the administration of President Grau San Martín
(1944–1948), when Minister of Education Alemán during his term of office literally stole millions of dollars from educational budget allocations
and rapidly became one of Cuba's richest men.[15] His brazen theft of public
funds allocated to education deprived public schools of badly needed resources. In 1952 and 1958 nearly one-fifth of the total state expenditure
went to public education and, theoretically, expenditures per capita were
above ten dollars, more than twice the figure of the golden 1920s. Thus, at
the same time that Cuba ranked nearly last in Latin America in terms of
the percentage of school-age children enrolled, only two or three Latin
American countries "spent" more public funds on education than Cuba.

Because Cuban teachers held life tenure as government officials and received full salary whether they taught or not, teacher appointments became
a major focus of patronage. Not infrequently, appointments were purchased

outright at prices ranging from $500 to $2,000. The higher fees usually secured appointments as "specialists" who received the same salaries as full-time teachers, but who taught subjects as music, art, or English—often without proper knowledge of their specialties—for only two or three hours a week. As the World Bank report caustically observed, "Some specialists were too incompetent even for such efforts and were made inspectors, usually in Havana, where most job holders preferred to live."[16]

It would be difficult to overstate the adverse effects of patronage practices and outright theft on educational standards and the morale of many dedicated teachers. Absenteeism, apathy, and social antagonisms especially among teachers assigned to rural primary schools (secondary schools in rural areas were practically nonexistent) further intensified the marked differences between urban and rural education. Several Cuban educators have candidly commented on this problem:

> Most teachers and inspectors live in the capital city or an important provincial city. They commute each day and from the moment they arrive at their respective schools, they have only one thought in mind—to leave in time for the last vehicle that will take them back home. The work performed by these teachers is worthless and their school is of absolutely no use!

Another Cuban writer has stated:

> If you take the early morning train from Havana to Matanzas, some 60 miles distant, you will notice how well-dressed people get off a few at a time at each stop along the line. These are teachers living in Havana and going out by train to their teaching posts. They hate their jobs, hate the towns where they teach, hate the pupils and the parents. Whenever they can, they say they are ill, they do not go. They do everything they can to get transferred to Havana.

A distinguished Cuban with intimate knowledge of Cuban schools since the early days of the Republic has also commented on the perceived qualitative decline of public schools vis-à-vis private schools:

> All of my children went to public schools. I knew the teachers and the schools and knew that the public schools were better than the private ones. But not one of my grandchildren is in a public school, though some of their mothers are themselves pub-

lic school teachers. The reason is that they know and I know that the public schools today are not good.[17]

The quantitative and qualitative decline of Cuban schooling during the prerevolutionary decades might be due not only to gross fluctuations of income from sugar, the influence of dictatorships, graft, patronage, and political turmoil, but it might also be the result of social differentiation following independence. With increased urbanization and commercial activity, Cuban society by the 1950s had gradually changed from the essentially dual colonial social organization into something of a three-tier hierarchy: an upper elite composed of plantation owners, businessmen, some successful professionals, politicians, and merchants; a middle stratum composed of most professional men, skilled workers, clerical employees, medium-sized farmers, and military men; and a lower stratum of unskilled urban workers, the rural proletariat, peasants, and the unemployed.

As new social groups emerged, the educational system also differentiated and provided something of a parallel educational hierarchy of social-class-linked schools. The upper group, for example, continued to educate their children in elite private schools or abroad—usually in the United States. The expanding middle sectors, from which came most of the teachers and administrators for the urban and rural public schools, for the most part moved their children into private schools after the 1930s as increasing numbers of working-class children entered the public-school system. In 1939, private secondary schools were "incorporated" into the public system, and in 1950 the establishment of private universities was approved.

As table 1 shows, the number of private primary schools increased almost twofold between 1939 and 1958 and enrollment increased almost threefold in the same period. Prior to the 1950s, there was only one university and it was public, but in 1955 there were seven, four of which were private. Politics and violence in public and secondary schools and in the university were also significant causes for the expansion of private schools. On the eve of the Cuban Revolution, some 15 percent of total enrollment in primary education, about 25 percent of that in secondary education, and 20 percent in college education were in private schools. The rapid growth of private schools, many of which were unauthorized and unregistered with the Ministry of Education, reflected a greatly increased middle-sector demand for this type of more prestigious, elite-oriented schooling. Throughout the island, families of even quite modest means who could little afford it would scrimp to put their children in private schools.[18] In the lowest stratum, the majority of the urban proletariat sent their children to the urban public schools, whereas children of the rural proletariat and related groups attended the grossly inferior rural public schools, or went un-schooled.

In sum, at the time of the Revolution, the Cuban school system provided strikingly unequal educational opportunities to students according to their socioeconomic status and place of residence. The system intensified rural-urban divisions and inculcated upper-class values and fostered aspirations that were simply unrealistic for the vast majority of Cuban children and largely dysfunctional for national development. In commenting on this problem, the World Bank report stressed that "unless Cuba greatly im-proves her public educational system within a short time, it is impossible to be optimistic about her chances of successful economic development."[19] It might also be added that given the upper-class value orientation of Cu-ban public schools in 1958, the chances for social and political develop-ment appeared to be equally discouraging. Rather, schooling functioned principally to dispense *cultura,* or status. It was divorced from life and rooted in transcendental values stressing the *pensador* ("man of letters") tradition. It reinforced belief in *personalismo* ("personalism"), in the strength of family ties, and in the importance of hierarchy. The Cuban edu-cational system during the late 1950s, to paraphrase Rudolph Atcon, had become a fragmented microcosm faithfully reflecting the fragmented mac-rocosm of society at large.

Innovations in Cuban Education Under the Revolution

Even before the guerrillas took power, the central role that formal schooling would play in creating a new, more equitable society had been clearly spelled out by Castro and several of his supporters. They strongly criticized the existence of private schools, which they claimed discriminated with a social-class bias and were commercially exploitive. They character-ized education, and rightly so, as verbalistic, falsely intellectual, unscien-tific, disassociated from life, and suffering from open divorce between theory and practice. They also took note of education's lack of relevance to manpower needs for economic development and, especially, to its con-tinuing U.S. influences and linkages, which gave the system a neocolonial cast.[20] In his famous *La historia me absolverá* speech fully six years before the revolutionary take-over, Castro flatly stated that a revolutionary gov-ernment would undertake the integral reform of the Cuban educational sys-tem so as to remove the deficiencies noted and to hasten the creation of the new society.[21]

Accordingly, with the victory of the revolutionary forces in January 1959, educational crash programs received high priority to carry the educational and sociopolitical revolution to the traditionally neglected rural areas and to the urban slums and shantytowns. In the first year, the government built more than 3,000 new public schools, and 7,000 additional teachers entered classrooms to teach more than 300,000 children attending school for the first time. Educational expansion on this scale was only made possible by creating greater efficiency in the existing school system and by enlisting young volunteer teachers, such as the "Frank Pais" Brigade, which taught in the most remote areas of the mountains, areas that in 1957–1958 had sustained the guerrilla forces.

The quantitative gains claimed for Cuban education during the past decade are truly impressive regardless of how one views Castro and his revolution. In 1958–1968, the number of primary and secondary public schools nearly doubled and accessibility to schooling in rural areas was much improved. The number of teachers tripled and working hours nearly doubled. Matriculation of students showed a twofold increase in primary school and a threefold increase in secondary school. In 1958–1966, state expenditures in education increased almost fourfold, and per capita expenditures, more than threefold. Even if proper allowance is given to such factors as the incorporation of private schools into the state system (which resulted in an impressive statistical increase in 1962 without an actual expansion of services) and increasing inflation, there is no doubt that the improvement has been considerable. The Ministry of Education proudly claims that "no Cuban child or young person lacks schools today" and that "attendance is reflected in the following figures: 93 percent [of school-age children] are attending primary schools and 95 percent, secondary schools."[22] Greatly facilitating expansion of this magnitude, some 240,000 full scholarships were awarded in 1968. Preschool education, special education for handicapped children, and school health services have, in like manner, also made impressive gains.

Differences in educational services according to income have been eliminated. Some military buildings and many houses of upper- and middle-strata families fleeing the Revolution have been converted for educational purposes. All private schools were nationalized on July 6, 1961, shortly after the unsuccessful invasion at Playa Girón (Bay of Pigs).

In summarizing the educational changes occurring during the first revolutionary years, Jolly has observed that (a) a high value has been placed on a variety of formal and nonformal educational programs both as an item of basic consumption and as a good investment for economic development; (b) the large exodus of technically qualified refugees, as well as the rush to industrialize before 1964, placed a high priority on technical education programs; (c) the inequalities, privileges, and distinctions fostered by the prerevolutionary society were attacked and, if possible, eliminated by the new educational system, especially with the nationalization of private schools; and (d) the introduction of a new political culture placed a heavy ideological burden on education to teach the Cuban variant of Marxist-Leninism.[23]

During the first revolutionary decade—and especially after 1964—the government's educational goals gradually took a more distinct form and specific programs were created in schools to operationalize objectives. The dual objectives of adult literacy and involvement of youth in volunteer rural development work had previously been well served by the 1961 National Literacy Campaign. Over 100,000 volunteer students and workers lived with rural families for six months, taught the value of literacy and revolution, and apparently reduced illiteracy from 23.6 percent (of the population ten years of age and over) in 1953 to 3.9 percent in 1961.[24]

Following this vast undertaking, the government launched the "Battle of the Sixth Grade" to improve the educational level of the more than 700,000 adults claimed to have been made literate during the "Year of Education" in 1961. The worker-farmer education program since then has annually enrolled more than a half-million adults. More than one-third of a million have already received their sixth-grade certificates.[25]

The need to involve students continually in productive work while continuing formal studies has been met by the establishment of a variety of programs. Most important of these is the Schools to the Countryside program, which seeks to involve youth in a revolutionary experience aimed at rural development. Begun in the 1965–1966 school year, 20,000 secondary school students donated free labor in productive agricultural activities—picking coffee, planting fruit trees, and other socially and economically useful tasks. In 1966–1967, 140,000 students participated; in 1967–1968, 160,000; and in 1970, nearly all secondary school students from all provinces were involved in some part-time agricultural activity.[26]

The need to provide increased numbers of technically qualified students to support agricultural and industrial development has led to vastly expanded technical and professional education programs. For example, during the past decade, the Cuban government founded thirteen industrial-technological institutes to train scarce medium-level specialists in thirty-three fields related to engineering. Forty-five technical institutes to prepare skilled workers and agricultural technicians were established, along with a number of fishing schools to prepare skilled workers for the new and rapidly growing fishing fleet.

In an attempt to integrate the school and work experience, the so-called Six by Six program seeks to increase output of medium-level technicians and skilled workers in production centers and service industries through the application of polytechnical educational concepts. After a short period of theoretical training, students alternately spend six months working in industry and six months studying in school. The program began with over 8,000 students in 1966–1967, but without explanation, the number of participants fell to only 300 or so the following year.[27]

The *Mínimo Técnico* program, begun in 1962, seeks to give workers in industry, agriculture, and business a minimum technical understanding of their work and machines. Classes take place on the job and seek to increase productivity and responsibility by explaining to workers how their contribution relates to the total production process.

During the first years of the Revolution, special training programs were developed to give large numbers of prostitutes and domestic workers (many of their employers had fled the country) new skills that would enable them to engage in new, more ideologically acceptable occupations.[28] In the Ministry of Armed Forces, a technological education section was established in late 1963. The enrollment increased from 4,115 in 1964 to 32,966 in 1968.[29]

A new campaign to upgrade in-service schoolteachers as one means of increasing effectiveness or expertise in system cadre has received highest priority. On February 16, 1970, a long, prominent official announcement of the *Plan de titulación de maestros* appeared in *Granma*. The plan presents the rationale and tactics for certification of some 26,031 primary and secondary schoolteachers, or some 40 percent of the existing teaching corps. Objectives of the plan, in what seems in part to be something of a harking back to John Dewey, are to prepare "teachers who understand the essence of the educational process and who are able to dominate this process; teachers with a mastery of the subjects they teach; and teachers capable of teaching children not encyclopedic facts, but how to learn."[30]

Cuba's universities, it might be noted, have also been profoundly altered by sweeping university reforms. With the nationalization of private schools, the previous seven universities were concentrated into three: one for the western part of the island (University of Havana), another for the central part (University of Las Villas), and the third for the eastern part (University of Oriente). New departments, schools, and chairs have been created and others have been eliminated or reorganized. Faculty tenure has ended. The university has been made more open than before through a remarkable expansion of the fellowship program. Student enrollment declined in the early years of the Revolution, but in 1968 had surpassed the 1958 level by 2,000 students. The number of professors, in contrast, has increased fourfold (see table 1).

Moreover, the basic orientation of higher education has been truly revolutionized. Where the traditional prerevolutionary university was essentially divorced from national development needs and emphasized humanistic, legal, and social-science careers, the university today has been harnessed to national manpower requirements. (According to the 1953 census, the number of lawyers was higher than the combined number of engineers, agronomists, veterinarians, and teachers with a university degree.) A comparison of enrollment shifts in key curriculum areas of study between 1959 and 1967, as shown in table 3, gives telling evidence of this reorientation. The proportion of enrollment in humanities and law, for example, has declined from 15.5 percent to 2.9 percent, whereas that in engineering and the natural and agricultural sciences has increased from 24 percent to 43.2 percent. Notable enrollment increases have also been achieved in the medical sciences and in education. Table 3 also reflects Cuba's changing strategy for development. When the emphasis was on rapid industrialization (1959–1963), the most remarkable enrollment increase was registered in engineering, whereas in the agricultural sciences, there was a relative decline. As emphasis shifted to agriculture, a decline in engineering enrollment was more than offset by an increase in agricultural sciences enrollment. In the social sciences, the decline is explained by the fact that, in 1959, the school of commerce (later to become economics) enrolled quite a large number of students, actually 95 percent of the total, whereas in 1967 the figure had declined to 70 percent (with only one-fifth of the 1959 enrollment). Cuba's deemphasis of the self-finance system of management has resulted in a strong pressure to suppress the professional careers of public accounting and commerce, which explains the decline in enrollment in economics.[31] At the same time, some modest increases have been registered in history, sociology, and political science enrollment.

A significant innovation at the university level is the *Facultad Preparatoria Obrero-Campesina* ("Preparatory School for Peasants and Workers"), which attempts to link farming, industry, and higher education more closely. The program seeks to prepare industrial workers and peasants aged eighteen through forty for university study. After several years of preparatory courses held at the universities, the candidates begin a regular program of studies. Enrollment in this strikingly innovative program increased from eighty-five students in 1959–1960 to 8,156 in 1967–1968.[32] (These data have been excluded from table 1 as well as table 3 since this is a special program.)

Current Characteristics, Problems, and Trends

During the past decade, attempts to implement and consolidate the Revolution in and through educational activities have created what Cuban leaders like to call a genuine teaching state. Educational authorities point out that the Revolution has been both the prime motivating source for edu-

TABLE 3
DISTRIBUTION OF UNIVERSITY ENROLLMENT BY DISCIPLINE IN CUBA: 1959–1967

Year[a]	Humanities[b]	Law	Education	Social Sciences[c]	Natural Sciences[d]	Engineering, Architecture	Medical Sciences	Agricultural Sciences[e]
1959	4.3%	11.2%	19.7%	25.3%	6.3%	13.0%	15.5%	4.7%
1961	3.1	3.9	18.5	21.8	3.7	25.4	19.2	4.3
1963	3.0	1.7	15.4	25.3	6.2	21.0	23.1	4.3
1965	2.5	1.4	24.4	13.1	6.6	24.0	22.8	5.2
1967	2.1	0.8	26.0	7.1	9.5	23.7	20.8	10.0

Source: Computations based on rough data from JUCEPLAN, *Compendio Estadístico de Cuba, 1968* (La Habana, 1968), pp. 34–35.

Note: Enrollment in the Preparatory School for Peasants and Workers has been excluded.

a. School year begins in September and ends in July of the next year.
b. Philosophy and literature.
c. Mainly economics (commerce in 1959), and political science, history, and sociology.
d. Mathematics, physics, chemistry, biology, geology, pharmacy, psychology, and geography.
e. Agronomy, veterinary medicine, and animal husbandry.

cational innovation and change and also has constituted the educational or ideological message par excellence. The constant stress placed on educational-ideological activities, be they in the schools, in the factories, or in the field, as the central means of creating both the material abundance and social consciousness required by the sought-after ideal Communist society is, perhaps, the most salient feature of the Cuban educational revolution.

The counterpoint of the ideological emphasis in education is the constant stress on technology and modern science as key elements in improving agricultural and industrial production. This emphasis permeates not only the teaching of skills in vocational training but also formal education courses in which students are taught better to appreciate the role of science and technology in the entire development process. The educational system is guided by an overriding concern to produce students who know how to learn, and who understand the scientific approach to problem-solving and how things work. Castro has stated the issue on a number of occasions when he has asked, "What place can the scientifically illiterate man, the technologically illiterate man, possibly have in the community of the future?"[33] For anyone familiar with the general partiality of Latin Americans to more traditional, even mystical ways of knowing, this stress on science and empiricism as a way of knowing is truly, epistemologically revolutionary.

The strong emphasis placed by Cuban revolutionary leaders on the work ethic is another constantly recurring theme. Work, according to Ernesto (Che) Guevara, brings out the best in man. Castro says that work is the great teacher of youth. Cuban education reflects the belief that youth's moral and ideological formation flows out of their participation in socially valuable work. It is claimed that contributing through work activities, especially in manual tasks, to national development transformation, the youth are also developed and transformed. Here again, the educational system's attempts to alter traditional Latin American values concerning the dignity of physical work and the individual's responsibility to others is revolutionary in the extreme.

Egalitarian emphasis in the educational system has become increasingly apparent. Every year, the government gives more students full support for their studies. Opportunities for advanced studies are now almost entirely based on ideological commitment and achievement, whereas before, socioeconomic criteria were paramount in educational selection processes. The pronounced symbology of antispecial privileges in schools and in society at large underscores the pervasive emphasis on the social equality of the common man. The socialization of the means of production and property, and the elimination of glaring disparities of wealth as well, offers concrete evidence of the government's commitment to change relations radically between people and between people and property. Unfortunately, we have no data on to what extent social solidarity has replaced individual and family egoism nor on the effectiveness of educational activities in achieving this basic reorientation.

Another recurring aspect of Cuban revolutionary education is its mobilizational character. The literacy campaign, especially with its brigades, literacy army, battles, marches, and the like, resembled a classical military offensive. Other mass mobilization efforts, as the Schools to the Countryside program, exhibit similar military aspects. Campaigns are viewed as powerful socializing and motivating experiences that are seen as a means of strengthening personal identification and understanding of the larger revolutionary effort.

The considerable progress achieved by the Revolution in Cuba's educational system is beyond doubt. This is not to ignore, however, the existence of a number of serious problems, which continue to limit the achievement of educational objectives and to circumscribe to varying degrees the impact of education on the overall transformation process. Quite clearly, the system does have a number of inherent contradictions that may breed antagonism and induce difficulties.

Perhaps the most serious continuing problem in education is that of quality. Emphasis on the right of all children to schooling and all adults to literacy and a sixth-grade level of education took place in the Revolution's first years. Programs expanded far faster than the supply of teachers and facilities. The exodus abroad of thousands of teachers aggravated this shortage. Nationalization of the private educational sector, the confiscation of refugee housing, and, above all, the crash program to graduate teachers and the use of volunteer teachers all helped to bridge the gap. However, standards fell in many instances, most notably with regard to the skill levels and economic potential of school graduates. Quality in the formal school system has also quite likely suffered as a result of excessive student participation in mobilizational activities that take them into agricultural work for extended periods.

The extent to which higher education can adjust to the ideologically inspired *Facultad Preparatoria Obrero-Campesina* programs, bringing industrial workers and peasants into universities, is not kown. Nor do Cuban educational planners seem able to resolve the more general conflict involved in attempts to develop a high level of scientific and technological competence without creating a new privileged technical and scientific elite, as in the USSR and Eastern Europe. In this regard, the Communist Chinese state the need for education to be both "red" and "expert," that is, education must teach both ideological correctness and technical expertise.

But, as the Chinese and Cubans are learning, it is extremely difficult to seek these objectives simultaneously and rationally.

The heavy emphasis on ideology may have induced negative effects in matters of scientific inquiry, pluralism of ideas, and freedom of entry to higher education. As Elizabeth Sutherland indicates, "The Revolution seemed to expect new men with a creative, nonconformist mentality to emerge from an educational experience that was not nonconformist."[34] The mobilization-militarization model held up to Cuban youth seems to give excellent results in discipline, solidarity, and commitment to national tasks, but may well hamper development of initiative and originality in the search for alternative solutions to complex problems.

Ideology has also been a deterrent to nonpolitically committed students who want to pursue advanced studies. As Sutherland points out, experts are needed in production, "yet promising students are not considered sufficiently pro-Revolutionary to be trained. Students have been refused entrance to the university for that reason. Doesn't Cuba's development require their skills more than their political loyalty?"[35]

All fellowships granted by the Ministry of Education to study abroad (with the exception of two for Mexico up to 1965) are for study in socialist countries, mainly the USSR and East Germany. Fellowships for Yugoslavia were cut altogether in 1967, and those for Czechoslovakia declined from 296 in 1963–1964 to 72 in 1968–1969.[36] Therefore, the Cuban student trained abroad has practically no possibility of being exposed to divergent points of view, even within the socialist camp.

Another continuing obstacle to revolutionary educational programs is found in widespread resistance to cultural change. Despite the slogans, the activities, and many revolutionary changes, Cubans have not within a decade been able to overcome entirely either individually or collectively the burden of their past. As Fagen notes, one of the developmental lessons the Cubans have been longest in learning is that cultural systems have very great inertia and tenaciously resist change.[37] And, when the attempted changes are in nearly complete discontinuity with the traditional, established ways of knowing, with the world view, cultural organization, and traditional value systems, as has been the case in Cuba, the persistence of old values and patterns of behavior, even among the most revolutionary Cubans, is a serious and not altogether understood problem. To wit, over one-half of a million mostly upper- and middle-class Cubans have left their homeland rather than embrace the new value system. Although many Cubans who grew up in the prerevolutionary society have become loyal citizens of the new state, the children growing up in the emerging revolutionary environment only now taking form are the only ones seen as being sufficiently pure and uncorrupted by egoism, capitalism, and elitism to be formed into the "integral man" or true Communist.

Cuba's educational strategy for the 1970s, as described in the 1968 national educational report to UNESCO, calls for a continued dual emphasis on ideology and technology, on being both red and expert. Castro explains the rationale for this strategy as follows:

> No social revolution can lead to socialism without a technical revolution . . . nor can communism be achieved only through abundance. It can be reached only through education and abundance. Abundance cannot be achieved without technology, and technology cannot be achieved without massive education of the people.[38]

Another constantly recurring theme is the need for greater unity between schools and society and between theory and practice. As noted by Castro, Cuba today is "one large school." According to the Cuban UNESCO report, Castro says that in the future, the schools' sphere of action will expand and be more closely related to life so that the entire national atmosphere will be one of education and learning. The Cuban report to UNESCO also predicts that the time will soon come when today's extracurricular activities will become a part of scholastic activities and that the boundaries between the two will fade away. Moreover, by combining physical and intellectual labor, it is claimed, every citizen will be able, with the assistance of technology, to carry out both intellectual and manual activities.

The government also claims that by 1975 all children and youth will receive not just free education and books, but free food and clothing as well. Compulsory education of a general and polytechnical nature will be extended up to and including basic secondary school. Higher-education enrollments will grow rapidly and universities will be decentralized with branches in the rural, industrial, and research and production centers of the country. Adult education will continue to stress the "Battle of the Sixth Grade" until all educational deficits from the previous regime are eradicated and all citizens are given the minimum level of knowledge necessary to participate successfully in the technical advancements of industry and agriculture.

It is extremely difficult to determine the degree to which the Cuban educational revolution has succeeded in accomplishing its at times utopian objectives. It is clear that education has played a central role in replacing the old elitist, hierarchical society with a new social order dedicated to egalitarianism and development. However, how effectively the schools have been in changing attitudes, let alone deep-seated values, and in securing desired behavioral capabilities we simply will not know until extensive research on these problems is carried out and published.

We do know, nevertheless, that as Cuba seeks to prepare the groundwork for the Communist millenium through mass mobilization, mass education, and other activities based on the revolutionary model, Cuba's educational system has become increasingly functional with regard to national development. If we compare it to the aims of the Alliance for Progress program of educational reform needed in Latin America, that is, eradication of illiteracy, reduced dropouts, expanded technical education, efficient administration, improved science and rural education, it is evident that Cuba is among the leaders in Latin America in successfully implementing these called-for reforms. Cuba is, moreover, the only Latin American country in which the privileged elites and the value system supporting them have been eradicated as an essential prerequisite for economic development, sociocultural integration, and educational reform.

In conclusion, we might note Comitas's observation that in any social system, educational institutions have two major functions: to maintain and facilitate the existing social order and, more rarely, to promote and secure the restructuring of a given society through the deliberate introduction of a type of education significantly different from that offered to the older generation.[39] Cuban education before 1959 was clearly preoccupied with the first function, that is, maintaining the *status quo*. Since 1959, the educational system, in its efforts to reformulate the structure and to change the values of society, has presented an example of the second, or revolutionary function. Quite clearly, a true social revolution requires the development of a new educational system to help build the new society as well as to safeguard against the possible collapse of the new system and the rejection of the revolutionary value construct.

As Cuba ends a decade of revolutionary change and as Cuban education begins to shift from its revolutionary function back to one of maintaining the new social order, other third-world countries, and especially those in Latin America, continue to watch Cuba with its promise of rapid and thoroughgoing sociocultural and economic reformation. Although *Fidelismo* and the Cuban model may well be unique—as claimed by Fagen and others—there can be little doubt that Cuba has undergone a profound transformation in which both formal and nonformal educational activities have played an increasingly crucial role in securing a radically new *status quo*.[40]

NOTES

1. Misión Nacional de la UNESCO, *Cuba: educación y cultura* (La Habana, 1963); Ministerio de Educación, *Informe a la XXIX Conferencia Internacional de Instrucción Pública convocada por el OIE y la UNESCO, Ginebra, 1966* (La Habana, 1966); and Ministry of Education, *Report to the Thirty-First International Conference on Public Instruction Convened by the OIE and UNESCO* (Havana, 1968).

2. This work is reviewed in Rolland G. Paulston, "Estratificación social, poder y organización educacional," *Aportes,* 16 (April 1970), pp. 91–111.

3. Cited in Seymour Lipset and Aldo Solari, eds., *Elites in Latin America* (New York, 1967), p. 19.

4. Hobert W. Burns, "Social Values and Education in Latin America," *Phi Delta Kappan,* 45 (January 1964), p. 200.

5. For an account of educational development during the prerevolutionary period, see Mercedes García Tudurí, "La enseñanza en Cuba en los primeros cincuenta años de independencia," in *Historia de la Nación Cubana,* eds. Pérez Cabrera, Remos and Santovenia, vol. 10 (La Habana, 1952).

6. Quoted in Charles S. Olcott, *Life of William McKinley* (New York, 1916), p. 196.

7. Quoted in Merle Curti and Kendall Birr, *Prelude to Point Four: American Technical Missions Overseas, 1838–1938* (Madison, Wis., 1954), p. 83.

8. Ibid., pp. 90–92.

9. Foreign Policy Association, Commission on Cuban Affairs, *Problems of the New Cuba* (New York, 1935), p. 138.

10. Mercedes García Tudurí, "Resumen de la historia de la educación en Cuba: su evaluación, problemas y soluciones del futuro," *Temática cubana: primera reunion de estudios cubanos* (New York, 1970), pp. 108–42.

11. See Leland H. Jenks, *Our Cuban Colony: A Study in Sugar* (New York, 1928); Lowry Nelson, *Rural Cuba* (Minneapolis, Minn., 1950), pp. 61, 186, 235, 239–44; and Carleton Beals, *The Crime of Cuba* (New York, 1933), pp. 281–94, 297. See also Richard Jolly's chapter on "Education: Pre-Revolutionary Background," in *Cuba: The Economic and Social Revolution,* ed. Dudley Seers (Chapel Hill, N.C., 1964).

12. Nelson, *Rural Cuba,* pp. 61, 186.

13. Foreign Policy Association, *Problems of Cuba,* pp. 130–31, 134.

14. International Bank for Reconstruction and Development, Economic and Technical Mission to Cuba, *Report on Cuba* (Baltimore, Md., 1952), p. 404.

15. Private information from Carmelo Mesa-Lago, May 1970.

16. *Report on Cuba,* p. 426.

17. As quoted in ibid., pp. 414–29.

18. Ibid., p. 414.

19. Ibid., pp. 434–35.

20. *Revolución,* September 7, 1961, p. 6.

21. Fidel Castro, *La historia me absolverá* (La Habana, 1961), pp. 60–71.

22. Ministry of Education, *Report to the Thirty-First Conference,* p. 157.

23. Jolly, "Education."

24. For what appear to be objective evaluations of the campaign's impact, see the reports of UNESCO experts Anna Lorenzetto and Karl Neys in Ministry of Education, *Report on the Method and Means Utilized in Cuba to Eliminate Illiteracy*

(Havana, 1965), pp. 17–18, and in the UNESCO Spanish version, pp. 53–128. The multifaceted role of the literacy campaign in teaching, mass mobilization, internalizing new values, and as a leadership learning experience is treated at length by Richard R. Fagen in *The Transformation of Political Culture in Cuba* (Stanford, Calif., 1969), ch. 3.

25. Ministry of Education, *Report to the Thirty-First Conference*, p. 165.

26. See Ministry of Education, *Report on the Method and Means;* Elizabeth Sutherland, *The Youngest Revolution* (New York, 1969); Arlie Hochschild, "Student Power in Action," *Trans-action*, 6 (April 1969), pp. 16–21; José Yglesias, "Cuba Report," *New York Times Magazine*, January 12, 1968; and " 'Column' of 40,000 Aids Cuban Farms: An Army of Young People Is Deployed in Camagüey," *New York Times*, April 26, 1970.

27. Ministry of Education, *Report to the Thirty-First Conference*, p. 167.

28. Jolly, "Education," pp. 209–19.

29. JUCEPLAN, *Compendio Estadístico de Cuba, 1968* (La Habana, 1968), p. 40.

30. "Directivas del MINDED sobre el plan de titulación de maestros," *Granma*, February 16, 1970.

31. Albán Lataste, *Cuba: ¿hacia una nueva economía política del socialismo?* (Santiago de Chile, 1968), p. 20.

32. JUCEPLAN, *Compendio Estadístico*, pp. 34–35.

33. Fidel Castro, *Speech to the Closing Session of Trade Unions of Cuban Workers, August 30, 1966* (Havana, 1966).

34. Sutherland, *Youngest Revolution*, p. 129.

35. Ibid., p. 136. See also Jaime Suchlicki, *University Students and Revolution in Cuba* (Coral Gables, 1969), pp. 100 ff.

36. JUCEPLAN, *Compendio Estadístico*, p. 39.

37. Fagen, *Transformation of Culture*, pp. 147–52.

38. Ministry of Education, *Report to the Thirty-First Conference*, p. 165.

39. Lambros Comitas, "Education and Social Stratification in Contemporary Bolivia," *Transactions of the New York Academy of Sciences*, 2d ser. 29, no. 7 (May 1967), pp. 935–48.

40. See Richard R. Fagen, "Revolution: For Internal Consumption Only," *Trans-action*, 6 (April 1969), pp. 10–15.

14 Mateo Jover Marimón

The Church

THE subject of religion has aroused little interest among the social scientists who have studied the Cuban Revolution. Worse still, the majority of those few published works that deal with this theme are obscured by sectarian passion. Other works, such as journalistic reports, deal merely with anecdotal matter or with purely "folkloric" aspects and still expect to draw general conclusions on the basis of weak data. The present chapter aspires to more modest and more concrete goals, that is, to provide a description, a causal analysis, and a prediction of future relations and conflict between the revolutionary government and the Catholic church.

There are two reasons for our concentration on the Catholic church. First, Catholicism has been the principal religion among the Cubans, the result being that the church has possessed the most extensive and best-organized prerevolutionary institutional apparatus in the country. Second, available bibliographic sources refer almost exclusively to the Catholic church. In spite of these factors, this chapter will make a brief reference to the reactions of various Protestant sects to the Cuban Revolution. Actually, most of the conclusions to be drawn herein with regard to the Catholic church may also be applied to the Protestant sects. Almost nothing has been published on this topic with regard to Judaism.[1]

Due to limitations of space, two aspects relative to the origin of the conflict have been excluded from this study: the analysis of the forces in conflict and the various strategies these forces employed.[2] Therefore, in the analytic section of this study, attention shall be focused on the origins of

The author wishes to thank Manuel Fernández, Carlos Germán Renes, Carmelo Mesa-Lago, and James Monell, as well as a team of students from the University of Puerto Rico, Colegio Regional Humacao, for their assistance in obtaining bibliographic material.

the conflict and on the many hypotheses formulated about its remote or immediate causes. In the section dealing with the future, three aspects of the problem shall be discussed: future relations between church and state, the renovative role that the Catholic church may perform in various areas, and the characterization of the church's new image. Although this author has been personally involved in the events (1959–1966) described and analyzed herein, it is hoped that through a conscious effort to maintain minimal objectivity, an impartial treatment of the subject has been achieved.

Relations Between the Catholic Church and the Revolutionary Government

Historical Antecedents

A dearth of knowledge exists with respect to the church in prerevolutionary Cuba. What is lacking is a historical-sociological study of such important topics as (a) the type of institutionalization of the religious educational system in Cuba and its effects as a force for socialization; (b) the institutional apparatus of the church in the colonial and republican periods; (c) the role of the clergy with respect to such variables as the world image of the church in the process of Cuban history, vocations, and rational utilization of human and economic resources; and (d) the role of intellectual elites and organized minorities such as Catholic Action with respect to the church and its evolution. Further knowledge of these matters must be provided in order to investigate zealously their influence in the historical development of the conflict between the church and the revolutionary government. In a study of such limited proportions as this one, it is impossible to rectify completely this deficiency, so that we must be satisfied with some summary observations and some limited statistical data.

Table 1 data, taken from a 1954 survey by the Association of Catholic University Students (ACU—*Agrupación Católica Universitaria*), show the predominance of Catholicism in prerevolutionary Cuba, but suggest that the Cuban people, although claiming to be faithful, did not actively practice their professed religion. According to the survey, only 16 percent of all marriages were formalized in the church. Although 91 percent of all Cuban children were baptized, merely 50 percent of those baptized received first communion. In rural areas, only 52 percent of those interviewed declared themselves to be Catholics, whereas fully 41 percent declared themselves "indifferent" as to religious affiliation. Even among those calling themselves Catholics, 27 percent admitted that they had never seen a priest.[3]

We may conclude, then, with Ramón E. Ruiz, that with the exception of a small group of regular participants, "most Cubans paid no more than lipservice to the Church."[4] In view of other data available, Ruiz seems to be

TABLE 1
RELIGIOUS ATTITUDES OF CUBANS: 1954

Query	Percentage
Existence of God	
Exists	96.5%
Does not exist	1.5
Does not know	2.0
Religion	
Claims no religion	19.0
Catholics	72.5
Protestants	6.0
Jews	0.5
Spiritists	1.0
Afro-Cuban faith	0.5
Freemasons	0.5
Church attendance (Catholic)	
Regularly attend Sunday mass	24.0
Irregularly attend	42.0
May go every few years	31.0
Has never attended mass	3.0
Church attendance (all religions)	
Regularly attends services	17.0
Irregularly attends	30.0
Almost never attends	53.0
Church's attitude	
Toward the workers	
Good	57.0
Bad	3.5
Indifferent	11.5
No opinion	28.0
Toward rich and poor	
Not concerned with the poor	2.0
More interested in the rich	
than in the poor	14.0
Same for both	42.0
More concerned with the poor	26.0
Question was not asked	16.0

Source: Agrupación Católica Universitaria, "Encuesta nacional sobre el sentimiento religioso en el pueblo de Cuba" (La Habana, 1954), table quoted in Manuel Fernández, "Esbozos para la pastoral en un medio revolucionario," *Mensaje Iberoamericano,* no. 32–33 (June–July 1968), pp. 6–7.

correct also in his statements that the Catholic church was largely dependent on the Spanish clergy and that its influence in rural areas and among black Cubans was especially weak.

The data in table 2 demonstrate the startling changes in the ecclesiastical

TABLE 2
THE CATHOLIC CHURCH IN CUBA: 1945–1966

	1945	1950	1955	1960	1965	1966
Ecclesiastic districts	6	6	6	6	6	6
Inhabitants per district	822	918	1,021	1,132	1,253	1,279
Parishes	191	199	206	210	226	227
Inhabitants per parish	25,800	27,600	29,700	32,300	33,200	33,800
Secular priests[a]	182	186	229	240	100	99
Inhabitants per secular priest	27,100	29,600	26,700	28,300	75,200	77,500
Regular priests[b]	336	353	464	483	120	129
Inhabitants per regular priest	14,600	15,600	13,200	14,100	62,700	59,500
Total of priests	518	539	693	723	220	228
Inhabitants per priest (total)	9,500	10,200	8,800	9,400	34,200	33,700
Nuns	1,772	2,004	2,484	2,225	191	198
Inhabitants per nun	2,800	2,700	2,500	3,000	39,400	38,300

Source: Isidoro Alonso, "Estadísticas religiosas de América Latina," *Social Compas*, 14 (1967), pp. 5–6, table quoted in Manuel Fernández, "Cuba: exigencias pastorales en una sociedad revolucionaria," *Mensaje Iberoamericano*, no. 30 (April 1968), p. 5.
  a. Those under the bishop or diocese hierarchy.
  b. Those belonging to religious orders, e.g., Jesuits.

structure brought about by only six years of ongoing revolution. Between 1955 and 1966, the total number of priests decreased by about 70 percent, and, of greater significance, the priest-inhabitant ratio shrank from 1:9,000 to 1:34,000. Another outstanding indicator of the changes taking place is shown by the decrease of more than 90 percent of the number of nuns for the period indicated above.

The Church and Batista's Dictatorship

After the fall of his regime, Batista's name was linked with those of former Cardinal Manuel Arteaga, archbishop of Havana, and with the former bishop of Cienfuegos, implying hierarchical support of the dictatorial regime. However, objective study of the situation makes clear that the general attitude of organized Catholicism was first opposed to the usurpation of power by force, and later opposed to the exercise of that power by illegal means and by increasing violence.[5]

In support of this statement, we cite the following: the frequent public denunciations of the Batista regime by Catholic Youth; the similar but private attitude of nearly all the secular clergy and of many groups of regular clergy (i.e., the Franciscans); the active militancy of Catholic students, leaders in the Federation of University Students (FEU) and later in the National Student Front (FEN), as well as the militancy of Catholic workers, leaders in the National Workers' Front (FON); the participation of

Catholic professionals in the Civic Resistance movement; and, finally, the participation of Catholic Youth in the Alliance of Civic Institutions. The opposition in question took all possible forms, including financial cooperation with the forces of the Revolution, aid to fugitives, the obtainment and transmission of arms and medicines, and public moral condemnation of the dictatorial regime. Such active participation was officially recognized by Prime Minister Fidel Castro soon after the triumph of the Revolution when he said in reply to a question on this subject: "The Catholics of Cuba have lent their most dedicated co-operation to the cause of liberty."[6]

The Conflict Between the Church and the Revolutionary Government

We may distinguish five distinct stages in the relations between church and state in the first eleven years of the Revolution: (a) reciprocal acceptance and cordiality (1959), (b) confrontation (1960–1961), (c) decreasing tension (1962–1964), (d) coexistence (1965–1968), and (e) opening of the church to dialogue (1969–). We shall briefly discuss the first three stages in this section, and later give special attention to the latter two stages.

During the so-called "honeymoon" of the Revolution, cordial relations existed between church and state. Various Catholic leaders were named to key government posts, while the Vatican promoted various members of the clergy sympathetic to the Revolution. Public support for certain revolutionary programs, such as the agrarian reform, was given by prelates, by secular associations, and by national and international Catholic personalities. The government was receptive to this support and public functionaries of highest rank, as the president and the prime minister, openly participated in religious ceremonies. The culmination of this first stage occurred on the anniversary of the birth of the Cuban patriot José Martí on January 28, 1960. The archbishop of Havana, Evelio Díaz, invited to participate in the act of homage, was photographed shaking hands with Premier Castro. The photograph was widely disseminated by the press.

The first friction between the church and the government was created by isolated cases of intervention by prelates in controversial national issues. Outstanding among these prelates was the archbishop of Santiago de Cuba, Monsignor Pérez Serantes. Forms of intervention included requests for mercy in behalf of those condemned to the firing squad; defense of the Catholic University in the face of attacks through certain legislative measures; and the proclamation of the necessity for freedom of education and freedom of expression vis-à-vis state control.

The National Catholic Congress, which met at the end of 1959, lent full support to those principles. In 1960, Catholic personalities and some publications began a campaign against the rise of communism in Cuba, which evoked replies from governmental ranks. For example, one such publication, giving the campaign momentum, was the "Pastoral Letter from the Cuban Episcopate" of August 7, 1960, which criticized the rise of communism in Cuba. This was followed by many disorders, by verbal attacks in the churches, and even by some arrests. On August 10, Premier Castro made a direct attack upon the hierarchy, followed by an intensive backup campaign in the government press. Various Catholic radio and television programs were forced to close. There was a government-supported attempt to create an organization parallel but opposed to the church line, which was called "With Cross and with Country." A priest presided over this organization. On October 30, national Catholic organizations took a position by supporting the church in this conflict. On November 20, the premier again criticized the church. The bishops, on December 4, answered with an "Open Letter to the Prime Minister" in which they denounced the governmental attacks on the church and defended their own position. On December 31, Premier Castro announced that an invasion of Cuba was imminent. A general mobilization followed immediately, and included the temporary military occupation of some churches and Catholic schools. The minister of the armed forces and the minister of education accused the church of sponsoring acts of terrorism.

In the Bay of Pigs invasion of April 17, 1961, two Catholic priests accompanied the invaders as chaplains. During the following few days, two prelates and dozens of priests were arrested or taken into custody by the revolutionary government, many churches were temporarily closed, and offices of Catholic organizations were occupied. Cardinal Arteaga took asylum in the Argentinian embassy. Among those shot at the beginning of the invasion were some members of Catholic organizations. On June 6, the government nationalized private education, attaching the property of the two Catholic universities and all of the 324 primary and secondary church schools. Following months saw the exodus of hundreds of priests and nuns. In September, serious disturbances took place and a layman was killed while participating in a religious procession. The government placed the responsibility for these acts on the church, expelling Monsignor Eduardo Boza, a bishop, along with 120 priests, both Cuban and foreign. Dozens of Catholic leaders were imprisoned. Castro forbade religious processions and announced that any priest involved in politics would be deported. On September 20, Pope John XXIII made reference to these events, deploring their occurrence and hoping for improvement in the future.

By the end of the confrontation stage, the church had lost all attributes of power and all chance to mobilize public opinion. Previously available Catholic education no longer existed; the number of priests had been reduced to a third of its former size, the number of nuns to a tenth; teaching orders of nuns had left the country; Catholic organizations had been dissolved; and there was a dearth of means of both written and oral expression. Soon it became clear that the church no longer constituted a threat to the revolutionary government and pressure began to diminish noticeably. The transition was facilitated by the substitution of Chargé D'Affaires Monsignor Cesare Zacchi for Papal Nuncio Monsignor Luigi Centoz in 1962. "Here, my principle task is to reduce the distrust between the Cuban clergy and the government."[7] This statement by Monsignor Zacchi seems to signify the development of a program by the Chargé D'Affaires of the Holy See. A few Vatican officials even attended the reception of the Cuban embassy at the Holy See in commemoration of the anniversary of Cuban independence from Spain.

Some minor signs of tolerance on the part of the government toward the church began to be evident. Premier Castro made two visits to the Nunciate in Havana, one in 1963 on the occasion of the Pope's Day, and another in December 1967, when Monsignor Zacchi was elevated to the rank of bishop. Also, the government granted authorization to Cuban prelates to attend the second Vatican Council, although the government continued to maintain an attitude of suspicion and distrust with respect to future behavior of the hierarchy. The church accepted this *modus vivendi* and attempted to adapt to the new situation. There were no uniform norms handed down by the hierarchy to the dioceses and parishes, and there were contradictory norms in the various dioceses. On the local church level, two trends became obvious: (a) quietism and wait-and-see attitudes mixed with private verbal aggressiveness; and (b) the beginning of an acceptance by a small minority of the values put forth by the second Vatican Council, including liturgical and catechismic renovation, and receptivity and a spirit of dialogue with the world.[8]

Period of Coexistence and the Church Alternatives

The lessening of tension became quite noticeable during the coexistence stage (1965–1968). The depreciatory or condemnatory allusions to the church and to the bishops, previously a mandatory part of any revolutionary speech, completely disappeared. Four priests imprisoned for alleged counterrevolutionary activities were freed under the condition of leaving the country. The Catholic Action, its membership depleted, weak in organizational structure, and under continuous surveillance as a suspect group, nevertheless was able to function in four dioceses. In two other dioceses, Catholic Action was replaced by other secular bodies by a decision of the bishops.[9] The hierarchy, most of the local leadership, and a small part of the lay base had begun to realize that the new situation was irreversible.

However, the revolutionary government continued to follow a policy of brusque change and showed unexpected twists of intention in its relations with the Catholic church. The government concession permitting national and foreign priests, both secular and regular, to enter the country, has been rescinded many times. The same can be said of the drafting of seminary students into the Compulsory Military Service (SMO). There have been sporadic interruptions of religious classes and of Sunday mass by the so-called Street Plan under the direction of the National Institute of Sports, Physical Education, and Recreation (INDER). There also has been use of "filtering and selection processes" connected with university admissions procedures of Catholic students. At the end of 1965, there were mass arrests and priest consignments carried out by the Military Production Aid Teams (UMAP).[10] In 1966, the El Buen Pastor Seminary in Havana was confiscated by the government. Two Franciscan priests were accused of giving asylum to two counterrevolutionary fugitives; this resulted in the occupation of the church and convent and the condemnation of one of the priests to thirty years in prison.

Although not attempting to explain these policies, we can point out four general tendencies that emphasize and exemplify them.[11] The tendencies in question can best be characterized through the enumeration of the following variables:

1. *Rural-urban differences.* Generally speaking, the absence of limitations on the church is much more evident in the cities than in the rural areas, and becomes still more palpable in direct proportion to the size of the city.

2. *Priestly behavior.* The priest who shuts himself in his church, refusing all contact with the local authorities, is immediately classified as "suspect." On the other hand, the priest who is open stands to gain from maintaining good relations with the local authorities, and stands to avoid many difficulties and misunderstandings.

3. *Location and visibility of religious rites.* All activities taking place inside the church building (e.g., masses, liturgical acts, catechizing of children or of adults, retreats) while the doors are open meet with no difficulty. This holds true only as long as such activities stay within the limits of what may be designated as "religious," and do not venture into those areas that the government has labeled "political."

4. *Fulfillment of labor duties.* In certain cases, the believer will be tolerated and possibly even respected for his belief provided that he maintains an intellectual level in his faith along with the fulfillment and overfulfillment of his duties as a worker.

For the duration of the stage of peaceful coexistence, the Cuban church was faced with three alternatives: defiance—that is, to begin the polemic once again, to mount a frontal attack on the government; abstention—to shut itself off completely from all things originating with the regime; or collaboration—either pragmatic (i.e., suiting behavior to the situation, putting principles aside) or based on grounds of moral or ideological reasoning.

Denied access to the first alternative because of its impractical nature, and to the collaborationist-pragmatic alternative due to its unacceptability on ideological grounds, Cuban theologists (both within the country and outside of its borders) focused their attention on the possible adoption of the only remaining choices—abstention or collaboration with ideological limitations. They concentrated most heavily on the latter, in the light of the orientations emerging from the second Vatican Council.[12]

Perhaps these alternatives merge in one respect: faith may still provide answers in a revolutionary society. What are these answers?[13] For some people, especially for the youth, a fundamental similarity exists between the ideal that the revolutionary Cuban society proposes to create for and with its members and the ideal that the church has today reclaimed for Christians. This fundamental similarity may be found on two levels: final goals and concrete moral options.

The group who finds similarities based on final goals asks, "Is not present-day Cuba a prophetic, utopian charismatic society, seeking to build a better future? Is this not also the message of the documents which emerged from the second Vatican Council? Where, then, lies the discrepancy?" Although they may not say it precisely this way, this group of young Christians feels that human hope lies in the same direction as Christian hope. The latter in no way contradicts the former, rather it "carries it farther along the same road."[14]

The similarities between evangelical values and socialistic concrete moral options may be seen more clearly. These similarities, in spite of the self-proclaimed materialistic and atheistic nature of socialism, are more pronounced than those that exist between evangelical values and the pragmatic materialism of capitalism. The similarities are found at four points: (a) in the rejection of material incentives and the promotion of moral incentives to motivate men to produce goods and services, together with the will and desire to avoid becoming a consumption-oriented socialist society, which would be the equivalent of the capitalist consumption-oriented society; (b) in the dignification of work as an instrument of human development, and not merely as a means of earning a living; (c) in the formulation of an egalitarian policy, firmly based on the use of ration books (guaranteeing that all are fed equally), in the redistribution of educational and health facilities throughout the entire island, in the desire to create an equality between urban and rural workers' consumption levels, etc.; and (d) in the emphasis upon cooperation rather than competition (e.g., in the meaning of the word *campañero,* and in mutual aid) and in the practical promotion of an elevation of the masses ("cheap books and expensive beer" and closing of nightclubs and casinos).

On the other hand, there are basic discrepancies between the revolutionary ideal and the Christian ideal in the minds of most adults involved. As regards final goals, the ideal of present-day Cuba is, after all, to build a Communist society, which will be both materialistic and atheistic. Although this ideal may be more in evidence at some times than at others, the reality of its existence cannot be denied. Many adults also argue that the Leninist distinction between religious neutrality on the part of the state and the more or less militant doctrinaire materialism of the party is nothing more than a smoke screen designed to deceive "useful fools."

Discrepancies are also basic in regard to concrete moral options. Some feel that a Catholic could never collaborate with a regime that "converts hatred into a fighting force" and violates the most elemental individual freedoms (freedoms of the press, of assembly, of speech, to petition, judicial guarantees against arbitrary arrest, etc.). Those who take this attitude point to the continuing discrimination in education—now such discrimination is based upon ideology rather than upon social class or wealth. They indicate the huge gap that stretches between the beautiful promises and the sad realities. In summary, even if an agreement might be possible on the final ends involved, an agreement could never be reached as to the means used to attain those ends.[15]

The Cuban bishops found themselves caught between the alternatives of a pastoral of preservation and a pastoral of participation. They chose the second after deep meditation, repeated conferences, and many preliminary projects. They took this action, convinced of the need for the church to present a testimony of faith when Cuban history is in the making.[16]

In making that choice, the bishops have decided that the church shall be a vital presence in the new society, even at the risk of scandalizing thousands of the faithful in an ideologically divided environment, and at the risk of ceasing to be for many—at least for a while—a "symbol of unity."[17] Furthermore, the church has been running the risk of completely alienating the vast majority of Cubans living in exile, who may well see in the church attitude an unconditional surrender, a submission. However, by acting as they have, the Cuban bishops have demonstrated their recognition of the irreversible nature of the revolutionary process under which their homeland exists. They have cast their lot with the future.

The Church Takes a Step Toward Dialogue

On April 20, 1969, the Cuban bishops asked all the priests to read the "Communiqué from the Cuban Episcopal Conference to Our Priests and

Laity" at that day's Sunday mass.[18] That document followed the line adopted by the Meeting of the Episcopal Conference for Latin America (CELAM), which had taken place a few months earlier in Medellín, Colombia. It was the first of a series of reflections on themes discussed at the Colombian meeting. The communiqué called for conversion of the Christian community, on both a social and an individual basis, to a position of being able to account for the revealed truth (ethics) on the one hand, and, on the other, the adaptation of those ethics to the signs of the times.

> Those ethics today places the responsibility upon each man to fulfill his vocation for development. . . . The attitude of the Christian implies a renovation of his social ethics, especially when he exists in a reality such as ours, wherein he himself is a fundamental part of the problem of development. . . . The importance of work in the perspective of a renovated ethics of development must force us to renew our spirituality as well.

The communiqué then quoted Pope Paul VI in the encyclical *Populorum Progressio,* adding, "Work has been beloved and blessed by God [because] every worker is a creator." Later, the faithful are advised, "We are not unaware of the implications and sacrifices this Christian attitude calls for," but they are exhorted to be a "light for the world."[19]

In the most significant part, the communiqué discussed the U.S. embargo, saying, "Are not many of our ills due to the situation of concrete isolation in which we have been living for the past several years?" After explaining how the embargo affects workers, housewives, children, the sick, and families separated from their loved ones, it concludes,

> Looking out for the welfare of our people, and remaining faithful to the service of the poorest as Jesus Christ has ordered us, and in line with the newly proclaimed compromise of Medellín, *we denounce this injust act of embargo* which contributes to unnecessary suffering and to making the search for development more difficult than it already is. *Therefore, we appeal to those in a position to assuage these conditions, asking that they undertake decided and effective actions to put an end to this measure.* [italics added][20]

The reactions of Cuban Catholics toward the communiqué were divergent, as the two following private letters show:

> There has been an uproar from the priests on down . . . actually, *only a minority have understood and approved.* I under-

stand that the diocese most receptive to the message is Matanzas because they have a majority of young clergy. . . . Here there are priests who simply did not read the Communiqué, as in my parish, or who skipped that part about the blockade, which has evoked the strongest reaction. [italics added][21]

I, personally, enjoyed the document very much, for it serves as a jumping-off point for another stage in this already long history. However, it effectively kills the few remaining hopes harbored by the more conservative elements for something that would seem like a return to the past. Many of them in their inability to comprehend the new wave still see the Church as their final psychic refuge, and this act of opening of itself, and of an invitation to the construction of a new era on the part of the Church . . . must have been terribly shocking to them.[22]

No exiles' collective document condemning the communiqué has been brought to our attention. However, individual reaction made known to us either through publications, direct knowledge, or acceptable testimony reflects, with some few exceptions, a generally negative attitude, stretching from mere surprise to incredulity to bitterness and frustration.[23] This being the case, it is incumbent upon us to ask the following questions: Was the communiqué opportune? Did it reflect the attitudes of the Cuban Christian community? Should the priests and the laity have been gradually prepared so that they might understand such a document? Whatever the answers, the one thing that is certain is that the communiqué lies at the center of the controversy that has aroused and divided Cuban Catholicism since the beginning of 1962, when the stage of decreasing tensions began.

It is significant to note that the average age of Cuban Catholic bishops in 1961 was sixty-one but had dropped to fifty-five in 1969, and continues to decline with every new appointment.[24] This progressively rejuvenated Episcopal Conference has captured the essence of the new breed of Christian in Cuba. We are speaking here of young people, from eighteen to twenty-two years of age, who are not marked by the battle that, in 1960 and 1961, pitted the Catholic church against the revolutionary government. They have survived a series of educational and labor experiences, together with their peer-group comrades, which has involved them totally (in the sense of the French engagé) in the Revolution, a revolution that they feel is their own. They would be disposed to fight for it, if need be, and yet they are extremely critical of it. As a function of their system of Christian legitimation, and of their involvement with the Revolution, they are quick to censure all that might be termed unauthentic, corrupt, false, and inefficient in their school, their work, their scholarship students' dormitories, and even in their families. This spirit occasionally leads them into confrontations with official directives (such as those that reach them through the channels of the UJC) or with their Christian comrades who cling to a counterrevolutionary attitude.

On the other hand, the Cuban bishops have not failed to perceive the significant decline in the number of "participants," basically due to the exodus, which has been inexorably shrinking, bit by bit, the ranks of the faithful, and death, whose effects are strongly felt in a community whose age structure is dominated by the elderly. Is this loss compensated for by an influx of young people? Early in 1970, a young priest answered this question for us, saying, "In my parish, one new member is taken in for each ten who leave." He added, however, "That doesn't matter to me, as long as the one person is a guiding light."[25] This seems to be one of the assumptions implied in the choice made by the bishops to participate, that is, in the face of the decrease in present membership, it is necessary that they direct themselves toward potential membership.

The manifest function of the authors of the communiqué was pastoral, but the latent function certainly comprised obvious political implications. The sad thing for the Cuban church is that only the latter function seems to have been perceived by much of the clergy and lay membership, both inside and outside of the country. It should be noted that a later communiqué dealing with the "problematic nature of faith" and its repercussions in the liturgy, the Bible, the catechism, and with practical choices in the daily life of the Christian, seems to have gone by completely unnoticed by exiled Cubans as well as by the membership actually living in Cuba.[26]

Not one major official of the revolutionary government has made a statement with respect to the controversial communiqué. It is, however, significant—mainly because of the infrequency with which such things occur—that shortly after its circulation, Radio Havana granted an interview to Monsignor Francisco Oves on the eve of his consecration as auxiliary bishop of Cienfuegos. This interview revolved, almost in its entirety, about the main theme of the communiqué—development. Monsignor Oves had been deported in 1961 and returned to Cuba in 1964 after a period of study in Rome. In 1970, the archbishop of Havana resigned and Monsignor Oves was appointed as his successor.[27]

The Church in Cuba in 1970

The following is a brief overview, with bibliographic data and other material from sources reliable through mid-1970, of the present status of the

Cuban church (see note 12). We refer the reader seeking more recent information, along with various, often contradictory, points of view, to the bibliographic notes at the end of this chapter.[28]

1. *The hierarchy.* At present there are nine bishops in Cuba, one at the head of each of the six dioceses, and three auxiliary bishops. During the revolutionary decade, the cardinal and two bishops died, one bishop was expelled and two resigned. Eight were consecrated. All of the present bishops are Cubans.

2. *Priests.* There are currently 228 priests in Cuba, 99 of whom are secular priests and 129 of whom are regular priests. This yields an average of 35,400 inhabitants per priest in 1968, the highest ratio in Latin America; the next highest is 11,700 to one in Honduras. There are, in addition, 198 nuns.[29]

3. *Seminarists.* There are more than seventy-five seminarists in the San Carlos and San Ambrosio Seminary in Havana, and about twenty-five more in the San Basilio Magno Seminary in Santiago de Cuba. Sixteen Cubans were ordained in 1971. That figure is unprecedented, even in the best days of the prerevolutionary period.[30] Among those sixteen there are seminarists who are more revolutionary than others, but not one is a counterrevolutionary. From time to time, all of them have done unpaid labor in agriculture voluntarily, without being forced to do so by either the government or by the rector of the seminary. They insist that their actions have no political implications. They feel that their work in the fields has two pastoral functions. First, it bears witness to a love of work and to a desire to aid in national development. Secondly, it provides them with an opportunity to become acquainted with the life-style and thought patterns of the people they will eventually be serving as priests. The seminarists all apparently agree on the necessity of the predominance of the task of "evangelization" over the task of "sacramentalization."

4. *Laity.* Although constantly decreasing in number, the intensity of their participation increases apace.[31] There is an increasing number of converted Christians who have made a self-discovery of faith and who adhere to it without reservation in all aspects of life. If this can be called "purification," then we may say that the Cuban church has purified itself in the last ten years.

5. *Ecumenism.* The Center for Ecumenic Studies has been adjoined to the San Carlos and San Ambrosio Seminary. Catholic laymen, as well as clergymen of different Protestant denominations are active in the center. An introductory course was held from October 1969 to January 1970, attended by fifty seminarists and forty laymen of diverse religious alliances.

At present, an analagous center has been projected for establishment in the province of Camagüey.

6. *Protestant attitudes.* While confronted with the same division of criteria that affects the Catholic church, the Protestant denominations seem to be more receptive to change. The leaders of this movement are the theologians Cepeda and Arce.[32] Cepeda is the executive secretary of the Council of Cuban Evangelical Churches, and Arce is rector of the United Evangelical Seminary. The Protestant-affiliated Christian Student Movement (MEC) declared its unreserved support of the revolutionary process following a meeting which dealt with the creation of the "New Man" in Cuba.[33]

On the other hand, the Jehovah's Witnesses, the Seventh-Day Adventists, and the Evangelical Gideon's Society all show great reticence with respect to dialogue and collaboration. They have had serious difficulties with government authorities due to their refusal, on the grounds of religious prohibition, to work on Saturday or to wear prison garb or to give military salutes to the custodians of the rehabilitation farms.[34]

7. *Relations with the revolutionary government.* The most vital relations are maintained through the Office of Ecclesiastic Affairs under the auspices of the Chargé D'Affaires of the Holy See. In routine matters, priests consult directly with official agencies (as the Ministry of Domestic Trade) or with mass organizations such as the CDR.

In an article written in 1969, Anne Power accurately states, "There is no propaganda against the Church or against religion, either in the press or on radio or television. There is rather a general neglect."[35] In effect, the current official line with respect to the internal affairs of the Cuban church is one of utter silence. However, the mass media provide frequent information and commentary on internal dissent among the various lines of thought within the church in Latin America,[36] and also on the positions taken by rebellious priests.[37] Finally, whatever propaganda that does exist tends to show that the faithful in socialist countries are guaranteed free exercise of their religion.[38]

Anne Power in the above-mentioned article also discusses a slightly caricatured portrait of what she calls "the three Churches in Cuba."[39] This portrait, although accurate in its general outlines, includes what is described as "the structured Church, the Church that survives the Revolution without changing its beliefs or its practices." However, in reality, the church is much more open to change, as we have already seen. After the publication of that article, French theologian-sociologist Fernand Boulard and sociologist Aldo Buntig visited Cuba. Visits to Cuba of leaders of religious orders and infrequent travel of some Cuban prelates abroad have contributed to a general acceptance of change also by exposing the Cubans to new ideas. The panorama that Anne Power presents as a rigid entity is actually evolving into a spirit of tolerance on the part of the church.

Hypotheses Explaining the Initial Conflict

In this section we will present hypotheses that will attempt to explain the initial conflict between church and state.[40] It will be useful to summarize the attitudes of both church and state prior to the conflict in order to try to locate the point at which this conflict began.

The most common attitude, both public and private, of government leaders was antagonistic toward the church. This was due to two preconceptions: the church is responsible for the evils of the past because of its alliance (real or symbolic) with the moral corruption of Cuban politics, and the church has always been a traditional ally of the bourgeoisie and big capitalists and the enemy of socialism.

In their own sphere, the members of the church also shared some preconceptions: the unconditional condemnation of Marxism and socialism by the encyclicals *Rerum Novarum* (1891), *Quadragesimo Anno* (1931), and *Divini Redemptoris* (1937); and the persecutions, both open and clandestine, bloody and bloodless, that the church has suffered in China and in parts of Eastern Europe under this form of government.

If we ask who started it, we will immediately be given two contradictory answers. The revolutionary government would say that measures were taken against the church because it planned and carried out counterrevolutionary activity. The church would say that the position it has taken has been purely ideological, that it has never attacked the Revolution, but rather the Communist influence within the Revolution, and, as for the rest, each Christian is free to take whatever position his conscience may dictate in temporal matters.

It is almost impossible to determine who cast the first stone.[41] In the light of the prejudices on both sides, and within the context of deteriorating relations and growing reciprocal mistrust, the most minor incident could have set off the chain reaction that set into motion a circular causality, feeding, in its turn, on the conflict.

Four causative hypotheses of the conflict will be discussed: (a) the one commonly presented by the church or its supporters, attributing the cause of the conflict to the Marxist-Leninist character of the Revolution; (b) the one held by some officials of the government, accusing the church of being a counterrevolutionary group of conspirators, in alliance with external forces that tried to overthrow the regime; (c) the one that charges the origin of the conflict to a reviving anticlerical movement; and (d) the one that considers the church as a pressure group that, presenting a threat to a totalitarian regime, was deemed to be disposed of all its power.

The Marxist-Leninist Character of the Government

This hypothesis requires us to differentiate between the theory and the practice of Marxism-Leninism. In theory, the forces of production (that is, the economic variable) constitute the structure that, in its turn, determines the nature of the entire superstructure (law, politics, morality, art, religion, etc.). Therefore, it should be necessary only to modify the structure, and, in virtue of this act, to have the consequent changes in the superstructure take place automatically. In other words, within the format of orthodox Marxism, it should never be necessary to attack religion as such, it will disappear naturally.[42] Also, in theory, the Leninist principle of separation between party and state is very clear with respect to religion. The state shall respect the law of religious neutrality because it officially recognizes the freedom of the individual conscience of each citizen; the party, on the other hand, as an instrument of mass education, must preach militant atheism.[43]

In a socialist country, however, it is difficult to make a practical distinction between state and party when a specific policy has been prepared for implementation. On the other hand, some socialist experts on atheism and religion hold that church and religion act as a counterforce to the acquisition of the new type of consciousness based on the changes produced in the economic structure. Even in the socialist stage, religion continues to function as "an instrument of alienation" of the laboring masses in whose name it is necessary to mount a frontal attack on the institution.[44]

Those who are of this persuasion feel that it was the revolutionary government that first attacked the church, that the same thing would have happened even if the church had not issued formal condemnations of communism, and that such action is a result of the Marxist-Leninist character of the regime.

Others, without entering into theoretical discussions, take it for granted that the "persecution" was initiated by the revolutionary government, which was either following the Chinese Communist model found in the pamphlet, "Cuba and the Catholic Church: Program of Action" by Li Wei Han, published in Peking in 1959, or was under the direction of the Czechoslovakian Wladimir Paulicek, an expert in the fight against religion.[45] We lack sufficient information to enable us to confirm or deny these hypotheses.

Counterbalancing these criteria is the fact that the Cuban Revolution spans a first stage in which its character was basically that of a popular democratic nationalist revolution, a second stage as a social, antiimperialist revolution, and finally, a third stage in which it took on its Marxist-Leninist character.[46] The state's conflict with the church must be chronologically located between the first and second stages, when the Marxist-Leninist character of the regime was far from definite. This, then, would appear as a justification ex post facto.

The International Capitalist Conspiracy

This hypothesis is rooted in the existence of Criminal Case No. 428 of 1961, adjudicated as a crime of conspiracy against the national sovereignty by the revolutionary tribunal of Havana. An archbishop, a bishop, and various leaders of Catholic organizations were incriminated in this case. In the trial, there were several references to the existence of a supposed plot conjured up by the government of the United States, the OAS, and the Cuban Catholic church. The goal of this plot was to spread international propaganda about the alleged religious persecution in Cuba. This would provide a valid moral argument to those who were hoping to see the successful acceptance of the doctrine of "multilateral intervention" with respect to the problem of Cuba by the General Council of the OAS.[47]

Without debating the margin of credibility that such statements may have had in government spheres at any given moment, we may note that there is a series of circumstances that would tend to deprive this explanation of credence. Since the middle of 1961, the government has been completely aware of the church's nearly total inability to influence public opinion (Catholic educational institutions had been nationalized, Catholic organizations had fallen apart, etc.). Since the beginning of 1961, the church itself had proclaimed that so-called street activities (e.g., processions), which the government might classify as "provocations," were to be avoided. Therefore, such incidents were limited in number and in their propagandistic consequences. Even before April 1961, the government had officially received Monsignor Oddi, special envoy from the Holy See, on several occasions, trying to establish a basis for compromise in the face of the existing conflict. Finally, the attacks on the church had started long before the government began to mention any international conspiracy. Therefore, this hypothesis also turns out to be an a posteriori justification rather than a causal explanation of the conflict.

The Rebirth of Anticlericism

In order to understand this hypothesis, it must be recalled that during the entire colonial period, the church and the state were united and Catholicism was the official religion, taught in the public schools. Almost all priests were Spaniards, and with very few exceptions, they aligned themselves with Spain in the War of Independence.

When independence was proclaimed in 1902, it was decreed that church and state would henceforth be separate, and Catholic religious education was taken out of the public schools. Some Spanish priests, especially noted for their antiindependence sentiments, left Cuba. All of this contributed to the formation of a strong anticlerical movement, centered in the Masonic lodges.[48] This feeling lasted, with varying degrees of intensity, for decades. By 1940, however, it had largely disappeared except for sporadic occurrences.

Those who support this hypothesis feel that when the revolutionary government came to power and first began its clash with the church, anticlerical elements, which had been pushed aside for want of an appropriate emotional climate, felt that the moment had arrived for them to get back into action.

This hypothesis seems completely unfounded for several reasons. The old anticlerical tradition had its point of origin in the Masonic lodges, and these were attacked by the government along with the church. Some lodges were closed down and many Freemasons were arrested. The young Masons of the new order not only participated in dialogue, but also grew closer to the church and to Catholic organizations both before and after the Revolution. The two collaborated, for example, in the National Federation of Cuban Youth organizations. Long before 1959, the old quarrel about clergy that had divided the country at one time had lost much of its importance, both as a concrete conflict and as a philosophical point of dispute. Along with all other quarrels, this one gave way to the real cleavage in Cuban society: that between revolutionaries and counterrevolutionaries.

The Church Is Attacked as a Pressure Group

The best of the available hypotheses is based on the theoretical reflections of more than a century ago of Alexis de Tocqueville[49] on the importance of "intermediate bodies or groups" in a democracy, and, more recently on the work of two theoreticians of mass society, Philip Selznick and William Kornhauser.[50] These writers delineate a double movement: one that may lead a mass society to a totalitarian state and one that leads a totalitarian society to direct and maintain its citizens in a state of massification.

By a totalitarian state, we mean one in which the mechanism of executive, judicial, and legislative power are concentrated in the hands of a relatively small number of leaders, and in which the instrument of social control expands to encompass the personal life of the citizen.

The project of establishing a totalitarian state forces those in power to take two simultaneous actions: to destroy the so-called intermediate groups, such as organizations, social movements, and pressure groups that may serve to protect the citizen from the will of the state; and to create (as a substitute) state-dependent organizations and movements capable of supervising those persons not wholly in agreement with the government, and to mobilize the faithful.

It is our opinion that this is just what has happened in Cuba. Without becoming enmeshed in the question of whether or not the revolutionary government was Marxist-Leninist from the beginning, it was soon clear that the government's intention was to establish a political regime quite different from a representative democracy. In other words, a regime which would not permit the formation of legal opposition in the form of political parties, of more or less articulate social movements, or of pressure groups. The supportive reasoning was simple: the revolutionary power embodied the popular will in bringing about the legitimate transformations to which the people were entitled and to which they aspired. Therefore, if one tried to slow the process down, or sidetrack it, or oppose it, one would be threatening the common good and would have to be stopped.

According to the hypothesis being examined, the church was not so much attacked as a transmitter of cultural values or of ideologies distinct from those of the dominating group, but rather as a pressure group. The attack was part of a general endeavor geared to remove all existing or potential organized opposition to the regime.[51]

We may cite various arguments in support of this hypothesis. The church was not the only social institution to be attacked. The church suffered along with labor and management organizations, radio and television broadcasting groups, the written press, and the Masonic lodges. In the first years of the Revolution all were subjected to a consecutive process: systematic penetration of the highest ranks by revolutionary elements; dissolution by virtue of law, decree, or ministerial resolution; creation of parallel organizations with similar goals to replace them; and absorption of those members who were prepared to "integrate themselves into the revolutionary process." Together with the disappearance or "reconversion" of those organizations mentioned, therefore, there appeared the so-called mass organizations. Thus, the National Pioneer Union replaced the Boy Scouts, the militia partially replaced the army, the ANAP replaced the associations of *Hacendados, Colonos,* and Cattlemen; the Association of Young Rebels (which later became the UJC) replaced various student, religious, and youth organizations, the FMC replaced numerous women's social groups, and so forth. Other *ad hoc* organizations such as the CDR assumed a number of disperse functions—social functions of the former neighborhood clubs, political functions of the now defunct municipal committees of the political parties, and the function of police informers.

The pressure-group hypothesis also explains the longevity of the conflict with the church. Open conflict began a few weeks after the last mass concentration the church was able to organize in Cuba—the National Catholic Congress, held in November 1959. The more acute aspects of the conflict ended in September 1961, when the church no longer represented a powerful or organized pressure group, as explained above. The pressure on the church was reduced only when this institution became unable to exercise any real sway over public opinion.

An Attempt at Prospective Analysis

The final section of the present study will attempt to answer three questions: What can we look for in future church-state relations? What renovating roles could the church play in the future? What will be the new image of the Cuban Church? (See note 12.)

Future Church-State Relations

Three basic variables can influence church-state relations: the pastoral attitude projected by the church, the government's attitude toward the church, and the international political situation.

The church's attitude. We have seen that the church hierarchy has taken the first step toward dialogue with the government. The government's acceptance of this opening to dialogue will depend upon the overall image that the church may project in the future, not merely the hierarchy, but also the community of Christians.

Regardless of anything the bishops have said or may say, as long as the majority of the Christian community in Cuba remains at the level of political confrontation with the regime (i.e., denying its legitimacy, challenging its authority, and refusing all collaboration), an atmosphere conducive to meaningful dialogue will not be feasible. On the other hand, as the target for confrontation moves from the political to the ideological, that is, to that which both separates and unites Christian and Marxist in their concept of God, of man, of nature, of history, and of science, chances for creating a meaningful dialogue will improve.[52] It must be remembered that all dialogue rests on a common set of value referents, and that a valid speaker is one who argues with but respects his adversary within his area of competence.[53]

Assuming that the Christian community decides to follow the path marked by the bishops, moving within the dictates of the imperative of existing in and for the present, then it will eventually find itself competing with the government for the loyalty of the young people of Cuba. A brief glance at the situation would tend to convince us that the government must win this battle of ideologies. It is no secret that the government controls the instruments of socialization, that it has repeatedly brought pressure on the young to separate them effectively from the church, or that it has tried to undermine their religious faith.[54] The "politics of silence" also works in the government's favor.[55]

But we must not become overly simplistic in our analysis. For one thing, schooling in dialectic materialism helps to cause religious inquietude among the young, paradoxical though this may seem. Furthermore, the government lacks qualified teachers for these courses, which may continue in the future. In fact, the government removed these courses from basic high school and preuniversity institute curricula in the 1968–1969 school year. The courses had begun to amount to nothing more than a poorly recited and poorly learned "catechism" due to the lack of qualified teachers. At present, those few capable teachers are concentrated in the preuniversity scholarship boarding schools, where most of the promising students are trained.

It would seem, then, that the ideological battle between atheism and religious belief is far from over. The question remains, will the young Cubans evolve in the direction of ideological-religious indifference so typical today in the socialist nations of Eastern Europe?[56] Only the passage of time will reveal the answer.

The government's attitude.   In studying the Cuban church, we must deal with its two facets—that of an ideological force, and that of a pressure group. We have already seen that the church has lost its efficacy as a pressure group. On the other hand, as an ideological force, it continues to transmit cultural values accepted by a fairly large part of the population. As a consequence, as the government increasingly relies on the church's ideological support, and at the same time has less and less to fear from the church as a powerful pressure group, it will be more likely to liberalize its relations with the church.

This was expressed by one of the notables of the regime: "We have no problems with the current Church. What we don't want is a flourishing Church. We are convinced that the exodus is slowly killing it. Why create a bad image in the press by attacking the Church unnecessarily, when the more flights there are [from Cuba to the outside world], the less Catholics the Church will have?" (See note 12.)

At this point, we must consider whether or not the government would allow the Christian community to integrate itself with the rest of the society. Kenneth Howard relates the following illustrative anecdote: "There is a story about a young [Christian] doctor who wanted to specialize, and was given the following answer: 'You Christians are all potential counterrevolutionaries. Money is scarce and we don't want to waste it training a specialist who might leave at any time. . . . It's a luxury we can't afford right now'." Howard then puts his finger on the problem: "It is all very well that the bishops or Christians of other countries talk about the participation of Cuban Christians in the ongoing society, but this is not a matter of one-sided good will. *The road is blocked from the other side as well"* [italics added].[57] There is no doubt about this. Important positions (some high-level professional posts, certain positions of political responsibility, educational posts) are closed to Christians in Cuba.

As long as the government persists in allowing its developmental role (e.g., that of a technician essentially oriented toward the production of goods and services) to coincide with its political role (e.g., that of a party member whose goal is the ideological orientation of the masses), the Christian will find it difficult to become integrated into the revolutionary ranks on any significant level.[58] As long as the regime insists that only Marxists can be part of the revolutionary process (in terms of the system of values and legitimatization), integration will be forbidden to the Christian, as this would entail a renunciation of his own value system. However, we should point out that this is really a problem of the future. Today, the revolutionary quality of a Cuban is measured by "the amount of cane he cuts and of fruit he picks."[59] In other words, the practical has absolute dominance over the ideological.

The international political situation. Without enmeshing ourselves in international politics, we can point out two alternatives open to Cuba in its orientation to the rest of the hemisphere: (a) reestablishment of diplomatic —or at least commercial—relations with the rest of Latin America without necessarily rejoining the OAS. In this case, the revolutionary government would need the help of the Christian Democrats on the continent, especially those in Venezuela and Chile, as they could help in the eventual initiation of unilateral relations; or (b) reestablishment of support of guerrilla movements in Latin America. In this instance as well, Cuba would need the support of the non-Communist socialist forces and of the so-called leftist Christians.[60]

If the above alternatives are to be considered seriously, then Cuba needs Christian support for whatever foreign policy it chooses to follow. To gain this support, it would be opportune for the government to reinforce its policy of liberalization as regards the Cuban church.

Renovative Functions Available to the Church

The sociocultural changes following the triumph of the Cuban Revolution, along with the results of the second Vatican Council, have forced the Cuban church to redefine itself. This slow and painful process is far from complete. Below we discuss five areas in which the Church could assume renovative attitudes.

1. In a country in which the central fact of life is work, and in which the government is striving to consolidate production, consumption, and education around the work centers (e.g., state enterprises, state farms, government agencies), it may be feasible to consider the possibility of creating worker priests, while still maintaining some priests who devote full time to the pastoral function.

2. In the face of the increasing scarcity of priests (who will be scarcer by the nature of the age pyramid and in spite of the projected ordinations for 1971), this may be an opportune time to consider the possibility of ordaining carefully selected and trained married men. It may also be opportune to give the deaconate a role of its own, with specific duties, within the redistribution of clergy and also to give greater responsibility to the layman.

3. Considering the continuing exhaustion, both physical and emotional, of priests involved in such demanding work, it may be wise to lend great importance to communal life and discussion. It may be possible to provide one day a week for this obligatory measure, even at the risk of neglecting certain pastoral functions. Considering the isolation in which many priests exist, it may be wise to pay more attention, in the future, to the team aspects of priestly life.

4. Cuban socialism aspires to the creation of a "New Man": unselfish, involved, faithful to the cause, competent, responsible, humble, loving to give and to sacrifice. Without discussing the failure of initial efforts (e.g., the Isle of Pines pilot project), does this not offer to the Christian as a human being, and to the church as an institution, a challenge to be a guiding light for these men who seek—in their own often fumbling way—to create a new man in a new society? Perhaps this would force the Cuban church to insist with increasing frequency on a return to Christianity as practiced by the primitive Christian communities. That would seem to be one way to squelch the criticism from both government authorities and from the conservative faction within the Christian community that the renovation of the church is an example of opportunism or a purely tactical manuever.

5. Finally, taking into account the political and generational division of the two groups comprising the Christian communities in Cuba, it would be convenient to find the means whereby young people who feel disillusioned and misunderstood in their own parishes may establish contact with other young people facing similar problems to share their inquietudes and their wish to carry on a style of life quite different from that of the adult Christian community.

The New Image of the Church

The new image of the church is characterized by its leaders through two movements—one involves selection and purification and the other, an expansion of purpose or intention. There is a slow but inexorable movement toward the creation of a church with fewer members, but with those who do remain becoming increasingly purer in their faith. On the other hand, the "ghetto" feeling has begun to disappear. There is a receptivity to the nation's problems (development, the embargo, work) and to the problems of the world (wars in Vietnam and in the Middle East, the Dutch Synod, social change in Latin America, the racial problem in the United States, etc.). There is, in all, a deeper sense of belonging to the universal church.

Does this image correspond to reality? For the moment, the Cuban ecclesiastic hierarchy seems to have decided not to go backward. Aware of both their enormous limitations and of their future possibilities, they want to plan ahead to make optimum use of available resources, maintaining a constant attitude of self-criticism and renovation. To what extent the Christian community will go along with this endeavor and to what extent they will be hindered by external limitations resulting from the political environment are the two questions which remain to be answered in the early years of this decade.

NOTES

1. One exception is "Holy Days in Havana," CIDOC, Doc 69/133, reprint from *Conservative Judaism*, 23 (Winter 1969), pp. 15–24. The number of Jews declined from 8,000 in 1961 to 2,400 in 1966. See UCLA, Latin American Center, *Statistical Abstract of Latin America, 1968* (Los Angeles, 1969), p. 186.

2. The author has dealt with this material in another work. See Mateo Jover Marimón, "Presencia de la Iglesia en una sociedad en transformación revolucionaria: la experiencia cubana," in *Temática cubana: primera reunión de estudios cubanos* (New York, 1970), pp. 218–53.

3. Oscar Tiseyra, *Cuba Marxista vista por un Católico* (Buenos Aires, 1964), pp. 69–70.

4. Ramón Eduardo Ruiz, *Cuba: The Making of a Revolution* (Amherst, Mass., 1968), pp. 160–63, 167.

5. Against this opinion, see Ruiz, *Cuba*, p. 162.

6. Leslie Dewart, *Christianity and Revolution: The Lesson of Cuba* (New York, 1963), p. 115, quoting Fidel Castro, *Bohemia* (Havana), January 18, 1959. Dewart makes a detailed relation of these events in pp. 103–15.

7. Quoted in Carlos María Gutiérrez, "La Iglesia Católica y Fidel: entrevista exclusiva al Nuncio Apostólico," *Presencia Latinoamericana* (March 1968), p. 4.

8. For more information and for data sources summarized in this section, see *Pasión de Cristo en Cuba* (Santiago de Chile, 1962), pp. 7–70; Manuel Fernández, "La Iglesia en Cuba a los diez años de la Revolución," *Mensaje Iberoamericano* (April 1969), pp. 10–13, and "Cuba: ¿una nueva frontera para la Iglesia?" ibid. (April 1970), pp. 12–13.

9. Acción Católica Cubana, "Informe a la Comisión Episcopal de Apostolado

Seglar sobre la Organización del Apostolado Seglar y Renovación de la Acción Católica," mimeographed (La Habana, February 2, 1967).

10. Jover, "Presencia de la Iglesia," pp. 16–19.

11. The author is aware that certain statements found in this section are highly controversial. Written evidence on which these statements are based is available to all responsible researchers interested in the scientific study of this subject by contacting this author.

12. For a theological reflection on these and other questions affecting the pastoral function in a revolutionary environment, see Carlos Germán Renes, "Sugerencias para un diálogo, la Iglesia cubana: ¿Tragedia o esperanza?" *Mensaje Iberoamericano* (June 1969), pp. 4–7, and "Respuesta de la Teología," ibid. (July–August 1969), pp. 16–19.

13. For a deeper discussion of this problem, see Manuel Fernández, "Esbozos para la pastoral en un medio revolucionario," *Mensaje Iberoamericano* (June–July 1968), pp. 6–7; and Jover, "Presencia de la Iglesia," pp. 21–38.

14. "Le réveil du prophétisme," *Informations Catholiques Internationales* (January 1, 1968), pp. 8, 12.

15. It should be understood that the two positions we have described here do not necessarily refer to any individual Christian, even the educated one, on a conscious and explicit level. Nevertheless, both divergent and convergent opinions do exist, and it is from the fact of this existence that all would-be analysts of the phenomenon in question, as well as those charged with pastoral responsibility, must begin their work.

16. Fernández, "Esbozos," pp. 6–8; Jover, "Presencia de la Iglesia," p. 29.

17. Constitución Dogmática sobre la Iglesia, *Concilio Vaticano II: Constituciones, Decretos, Declaraciones* (Madrid, 1965), p. 9.

18. *Vida Cristiana* (La Habana, April 27, 1969).

19. Ibid., pp. 2–3.

20. Ibid., p. 3.

21. Private correspondence, Havana, April 28, 1969.

22. Private correspondence, Havana, April 23, 1969.

23. See, for example, some writings published in the *Diario Las Américas,* April–May 1969.

24. Author's own figures; and Fernández, "La Iglesia en Cuba," p. 10.

25. Private correspondence, Havana, February 14, 1970.

26. "Comunicado de la Conferencia Episcopal de Cuba a nuestros sacerdotes y fieles," mimeographed (La Habana, September 1969).

27. Orlando Contreras, "La Iglesia en Cuba, reportaje a un nuevo obispo: Monseñor Oves," CIDOC Doc 69/153, from *Cristianismo y Revolución* (Buenos Aires, 1969), pp. 36–38; and Fernández, "Cuba: ¿una nueva frontera?" p. 12.

28. See especially Everett E. Gendler, "Cuba and Religion: Challenge and Response," *The Christian Century,* 86 (July 30, 1969), pp. 1013–16; Braulio Morán and Leslie Dewart, "An Exchange of Views: Cuba and the Church," *Commonweal,* 79 (March 13, 1969), pp. 717–19; James Harvey, "The View from Cuba," *Commonweal,* 91 (December 12, 1969), pp. 360–61; Kenneth Howard, "En Cuba: ¿entrarán los cristianos en la revolución?" *Informaciones Católicas Internacionales* (August 1969), pp. 16–19; Eduardo Novoa, "La situación religiosa en Cuba," *Mensaje,* 17 (March–April 1968), pp. 104–07.

29. Most of the figures in this section are taken from Fernández, "La Iglesia en Cuba," pp. 10–13.

30. Harvey, "View from Cuba," p. 360.

31. Howard, "En Cuba," p. 19.

32. Rafael Cepeda, "La conducta cristiana en una sociedad revolucionaria," CIDOC, III (March 16, 1966), pp. 101–05.

33. Movimiento Estudiantil de Cuba, "Declaración general sobre la reunión del hombre nuevo," mimeographed (La Habana, September 5, 1968).

34. Fernández, "La Iglesia en Cuba," p. 13. See also Rev. Domingo Fernández (Baptist minister), "Informe . . . sobre la situación de los protestantes en Cuba," mimeographed (Miami, 1966).

35. Anne Power, "The Church in Cuba," *Commonweal*, 89 (March 7, 1969), p. 704.

36. "Hemisferio 69: brusco viraje de la Iglesia argentina," *Bohemia* (Havana), May 23, 1969, p. 87. See also Miles Wolpin, "Izquierda chilena: factores estructurales que impiden su victoria en 1970," *Pensamiento Crítico* (May 1969), pp. 27–57, for a detailed analysis of the role played by the Chilean Catholic church and its support of the Christian Democrats.

37. Abel Sardiña, "Camilo Torres y la Iglesia," *Bohemia* (Havana), February 13, 1970, pp. 60–61; "América Latina: la rebelión de las sotanas," CIDOC, Doc 69/187, taken from *Tricontinental*, 6 (1969), pp. 19–30.

38. Jesús Martí, "Vietnam: vivo en una sociedad humana," *Bohemia* (Havana), February 13, 1970, pp. 90–92.

39. Power, "Church in Cuba," pp. 704–05. As an example of the many comments provoked by this article, see Rafael Durbán, "Las tres iglesias de Cuba," *Indice* (August 1, 1969), pp. 30–32; and W. del Prado, Jr., "Respuesta a Rafael Durbán: sobre las tres iglesias de Cuba," *Indice* (September 25, 1969), p. 19.

40. Throughout this section, especially where there is no annotation, the author has used his personal notes from First Cuban Studies Meeting, Washington, D.C., April 1969; seminar on "Problèmes Politiques de l'Amérique Latine," held in 1968–1969 at the Institut des Sciences Politiques et Sociales, Université Catholique de Louvain, Belgium; and symposium on "Eglise et Révolution en Amérique Latine," held in January–February 1969 at the Centre International des Etudiants Etrangers, Université Catholique de Louvain, Belgium.

41. Some authors hold the government responsible for this. See *Pasión de Cristo*, p. 6; and Angel Aparicio Laurencio, *Donde está el cadáver . . . se reúnen los buitres* (Santiago de Chile, 1963).

42. Karl Marx and Frederick Engles, *Sobre la religión* (La Habana, 1963), pp. 70, 82, 117–19, 129, 161.

43. V. I. Lenin, *Oeuvres completes*, vol. 15 (Moscow, 1956), pp. 382–93.

44. "Informe sobre los errores en la conducción de la propaganda ateísta científica entre la población, de 10 de noviembre de 1954," quoted in V. Kelle and M. Kovalzon, *Formas de la conciencia social* (Buenos Aires, 1967), p. 136.

45. Aparicio, *Donde está el cadáver*, pp. 57–65, 101–02, and biblio. n. 200; *Pasión de Cristo*, p. 55.

46. See Luis Aguilar León, "La proyección internacional de la Revolución Cubana," in *Temática Cubana*, pp. 90–92. For a different chronological classification that also supports this hypothesis, see Nelson Amaro, "Mass and Class in the Origins of the Cuban Revolution," *Studies in Comparative International Development*, 4 (1968–1969), pp. 229–34.

47. Ramiro Valdés, Minister of the Interior, Havana television, September 12, 1961.

48. Ruiz takes these antecedents back to Martí and his controversial "Hombre del

Campo" and feels that the "anticlericalism and the weakness of the Church . . .
played their respective parts in the rise of Marxism and the Communist party." See
Ruiz, *Cuba,* pp. 67–68, 117.

49. Alexis de Tocqueville, *De la démocratie en Amérique,* vol. 2 (Paris, 1961),
pp. 295–428.

50. Philip Selznick, *Institutional Vulnerability in Mass Society,* Bobbs-Merrill Reprint Series in the Social Sciences (London, 1967–1968); and William Kornhauser,
The Politics of Mass Society, 3d ed. (London, 1968), pp. 74–75, 83–84, 179–82.

51. In support of this hypothesis, see Edward B. Click, "End of a Hope: Castro
and the Church," *Commonweal,* 75 (October 13, 1961), pp. 67–69.

52. Jover, "Presencia de la Iglesia," pp. 29–30.

53. Jean Lacroix, "Las condiciones del diálogo," CIDOC, IV (April 15, 1967),
taken from *Criterio,* no. 1463 [no other data given] (Buenos Aires); and Jover,
"Presencia de la Iglesia," p. 30.

54. Private correspondence, Santiago de Cuba, March 12, 1970.

55. Power, "Church in Cuba," p. 95.

56. Laslo Nagy, *Démocraties Populaires* (Paris, 1968), pp. 326–27.

57. Howard, "En Cuba," pp. 17–18.

58. Jacques Valier, "L'Économie Cubaine: Quelques problèmes essentiels de son
fonctionnement," *Les Temps Modernes,* 23 (March 1968), pp. 1624–25.

59. Jover, "Presencia de la Iglesia," p. 42.

60. Fidel Castro, "Discurso pronunciado el 5 de enero de 1969, en la inauguración
de un semi-internado de primaria y un policlínico en el Cangre," *Granma Revista
Semanal,* January 12, 1969, p. 5.

15 Julio Matas

Theater and Cinematography

IN this chapter, the evolution of theater and cinematography in Cuba before and after 1959 is described. This division is used in view of the thematic emphasis of this book on revolutionary change. Nevertheless, the author wants to warn the reader against the common tendency of some scholars to divide Cuban cultural history in a Manichean way, that is, into two sharply distinct periods—prerevolutionary and revolutionary. This approach has led such scholars (aligned to the Right or the Left in a rather narrow way) to offer a very simplistic account of facts and history. The confusion is increased by often reducing prerevolutionary Cuba, with exceedingly somber tones, to the period of the dictatorial regime that ended with the year 1958.

Typical assertions often made by the Left are that no books were published in Cuba prior to 1959,[1] that artists were not motivated to work, and that "inculture was the most noticeable of Cuban endowments."[2] By the same token, to deny—as some people on the Right do—that artists and intellectuals had to overcome many difficulties during the fifty-seven years of republican, prerevolutionary Cuba and that there was a general indifference to serious work in art and literature would be equally misleading and dishonest. Certainly, many good job prospects in the artistic and intellectual fields were turned down in exchange for more secure and profitable ways of earning a living—as bureaucrats, journalists, professionals, politicians, advertising executives, consultants, decorators, or designers. Nevertheless, dedication and endurance surmounted the obstacles in numerous instances as the long list of writers and artists who had attained, prior to the Revolution, domestic reputation and international recognition testifies.[3]

It is true that during the twenties, thirties, and forties, Cuban artistic and intellectual groups appeared as small armies of quixotic knights-errant, but

427

the scene presented a noticeable change at the turn of the 1940s. Politically, the country was under the government of the *Auténtico* party. No matter how disappointing the experience with this party had been—public administration had not ceased to be a means to build personal fortunes for the politicians in power—a more or less democratic structure had been established. Furthermore, the labor laws passed in the thirties and forties, the stabilization and development of the economy during and immediately after World War II, and the fast growth of Cuban-owned business enterprises had originated a wave of optimism and, consequently, had generated a desire for new activities that were at the base of the new cultural expansion. From this effervescence, which continued with relative vigor in spite of Batista's *coup d'état* in 1952, sprung the theater movement and, in due time, the film industry as they exist now in Cuba.

Theater

The Prerevolutionary Period

The theater was, as it may be supposed, one of the main sources of entertainment for all social classes in the cities during the colonial period, although it was not until the end of the eighteenth century that the first fine coliseum appeared in Havana. In the early years of the nineteenth century, other theaters were established in Santiago de Cuba and Puerto Príncipe (today Camagüey). The players—actors or opera singers—were then primarily peninsular, and the theater proper had a repertory similar to that of the contemporary Spanish stage: adaptations of Golden Age plays or works by Spanish or foreign playwrights of the period. Occasionally Cuban plays were also staged.[4]

Parallel to this type of theatrical entertainment, a "vernacular" theater—wider in its range of popularity—was born in the first half of the nineteenth century. This type of theater was, essentially, part of the nationalistic affirmation that eventually led to independence in 1898. Comic sketches with Cuban popular characters, which dealt with national subjects, contained native songs and dances, and sometimes took the line of humorous political comment, were the substance of this long-lived genre. Cuban players were its natural or born interpreters, establishing an acting tradition in the national stage that has counted scores of idolized performers.[5] This movement was significant in that it attracted generations of Cuban theatergoers, making possible through this continuous mobilization a more or less sustained popular interest in similar artistic expressions, such as opera, musical plays of the genre called "lyrical" (in the line of the Spanish operetta or *zar-*

zuela), and, finally, the wave of national theater productions of first-rate plays in the universal repertoire which has developed in the last thirty years. The vernacular genre attained its climax in the 1920s with the establishment of the Alhambra Theater Repertory Company.

During the first quarter of this century, the most important theatrical activities, besides the vernacular just described, consisted of foreign opera, light opera, and dramatic touring companies, predominantly those from Spain.[6] Around 1925, a native musical theater came to life. This should be considered as a sort of forerunner of later good dramatic works dealing with national themes. Some of these musical plays became very popular and have been revived several times in recent years.[7]

The first attempts to establish a type of theater in pace with the trends of modern European drama go as far back as the year 1910, with the founding of the Association for the Fomentation of the Theater under the direction of the Dominican scholar Max Henríquez Ureña and the Cuban playwright José Antonio Ramos, among others. In 1915, the Pro-Cuban Theater Organization started a campaign in favor of the inclusion of Cuban playwrights in the repertory of foreign visiting companies. At the University of Havana, professor of Spanish literature, Salvador Salazar, inspired a university theater group in 1920: *Institución Cubana Pro-Arte Dramático*. In the late twenties, a real breakthrough from a rather provincial (and at times chauvinistic) attitude took place, with the performance of plays by world-renowned authors, such as Synge, Evreinoff, Sacha Guitry, and Valle-Inclán. The musical society *Pro-Arte Musical* gave support to the theatrical movement. These activities and experiments (briefly interrupted by the turmoil during Machado's dictatorship) led to the founding in 1936 of the first Cuban repertory company to perform both domestic and foreign plays with rigorous artistic criteria. This company, called "The Cave" (*La Cueva*), was headed by the then young playwright Luis A. Baralt, who, years later, become the director of the University of Havana Theater (*Teatro Universitario*).

After 1936, external circumstances helped to strengthen these efforts. The Spanish Civil War and the outbreak of World War II provoked the emigration of reputed European intellectuals and artists, among whom were several well-known Spanish figures who settled for some time in Cuba. The director and writer Cipriano Rivas Cheriff, and the eminent Spanish actress Margarita Xirgu staged plays by Shaw, Lorca, Hoffmansthatl, and Lenormand. In 1941, Spaniards Rubia Barcia and Martínez Allende and the Austrian Ludwig Shajowicz (a member of the Vienese Reinhardt Seminar) founded the first school of drama, the Academy of Dramatic Art (ADA—*Academia de Artes Dramáticas*). The famous troupe of Louis

Jouvet, on tour around the New World, also visited Havana at this time. The 1940s witnessed the multiplication of theatrical activities inspired by the above-mentioned events.

In 1940, the People's Theater Library (*Teatro-Biblioteca del Pueblo*) was organized by the Spanish exile Rafael Marquina under the government's auspices, following the model of the Student Cultural Missions of the Spanish Republic led by Federico García Lorca. (This experiment was repeated in Cuba some years later by the Ministry of Education through the permanent Cultural Brigades, created around 1950, which exposed countryside communities to theater, music, and dance.) In 1941, the University of Havana Theater and its adjoining school of drama, the University Seminar of Dramatic Arts, were also established, under the direction of Shajowicz. The theater began staging three major productions a year, primarily Greek tragedies or Spanish classical plays, but later adding an experimental theater, which produced a large annual number of short plays directed and acted by the students of the school of drama. In 1942, the *Patronato del Teatro,* a private association sponsored by patrons of the theater, was founded and began to offer, together with the school of drama, monthly performances.

Soon, various high schools and vocational schools created their own dramatic clubs, while several other semiamateur, semicommercial theater groups started to work (e.g., *Prometeo, Teatro Popular, Teatralia,* and *Farseros*). These offered performances in Havana and in other important cities of the island. Finally, in 1947, the first official (government accredited) drama school, the Municipal Academy of Dramatic Art, was founded in the capital city, directed and staffed by former members of its predecessor, the unofficial ADA.[8]

Between 1951 and 1954 a new theatrical wave was ready to take over the scene. A recently created group was transformed into a repertory company called *Las Máscaras,* which was led by Andrés Castro. This company started offering "seasons" in the small auditorium of the Mason Workers Union building. This attempt superseded similar experiments done in the past, and its success was as impressive as it was, perhaps, unforeseen. García Lorca's *Yerma,* directed by Castro and interpreted by the Spanish actress Adela Escartín (trained in New York in the Piscator Workshop and in Stella Adler's Studio), established the reputation of this troupe. *Arena,* a repertory company founded by this author, gave performances of Euripides's *Medea,* which met with good response in the theater of the Cigar Workers Union building. The *Teatro Experimental de Arte* (TEDA), directed by Erik Santamaría, presented Jean Paul Sartre's *Respectful Prostitute* in the building of the Odonthologist's Social Security Fund, attracting audiences for a long period of time. Francisco Morín produced and directed Jean Genet's *The Maids* in the theater of the Reporters Association building, also with a warm response. Giving depth to these new achievements, the theater section of the cultural society *Nuestro Tiempo,* under the guidance of actor and director Vicente Revuelta, was engaged in a serious program of research.

The time was then ripe for something more ambitious and durable, and a number of permanent little theaters, comparable in size and organization to the North American off-Broadway playhouses or community dramatic centers, came successively to life between 1954 and 1958. Some of the existing theater groups followed this trend, and new playhouses were established: *Talía, Hubert de Blanck, Atelier, El Sótano, Arlequín, Idal,* and *Arcoiris.* Although the repertory or the performances were not always similar in quality, and at times rather commercial plays were shown, the best of contemporary European or North American dramatic literature was staged.[9] The audiences largely consisted of elements of the middle class: businessmen, professionals, students, clerical employees, and technical workers. The visits in the early 1950s of the Spanish company *Lope de Vega* and the one led by the reputed Argentine movie and theater actor Francisco Petrone were also landmarks in the formation of a new "taste" among Cuban audiences.

The Cuban artists who undertook the task of developing this movement were either the old members of the first serious dramatic schools already mentioned or the disciples of those who had learned their techniques abroad. Dramatic workshops were opened and their influence was soon felt by the two existing dramatic schools, which improved their curricula.[10] In the provinces, particularly those of Camagüey and Oriente, the ferment was also apparent at this time. The University of Oriente, for example, organized a university theater from which several talented actors emerged.

It should also be mentioned that the Department of Culture of the Ministry of Education presented, since around 1954, performances of plays at popular prices—either originally produced for this department or selected among those staged by the playhouses—in the auditorium of the Museum of Fine Arts. The auditorium held 500 seats, and low-income groups acquired the habit of attending these shows.

Some obstacles, mainly of an economic nature (but also as a result of increasing terrorism and the boycott of public spectacles near the end of Batista's dictatorship), hindered the growth of the independent theaters beyond certain limits. The playhouses were generally small (the largest would hold around 400 seats) and the price of admission, considering the Cuban consuming capabilities, could not exceed much more than a dollar per seat. The playhouses were, thus, unable to pay adequate salaries to their actors and technicians, a circumstance that forced these people to devote most of their time to well-remunerated jobs in radio or television. Participating in the production of plays was spiritually rewarding but usually represented hard physical work.

By contrast, the movie houses, as well as the vernacular or musical shows (national or foreign) that were presented in the few big theaters still in operation (e.g., *Martí, Nacional, Payret*), charged about the same price or even less. The capacity of the theaters allowed, naturally, a good profit for the impresario and a decent income for the performers, musicians, technicians, and stagehands, since they were all syndicated professionals and, consequently, had the customary advantages provided by the labor unions—minimum wages to start with. Large audiences (attracted by the popular and easy to understand themes) attended this type of theater entertainment regularly.

For some time before the advent of the revolutionary regime in January 1959, the most alert people in the playhouse theater movement thought that generous state support would be the only helpful solution to their economic problems. However, given the heightening political crisis, this was nothing more than an impossible dream. The government did almost finish the building of what was to be the National Theater of Cuba in the Plaza Cívica (today, Plaza de la Revolución). But it was felt by those concerned with the arts that the theater was going to be exploited politically and placed, most probably, in inept hands.

The Revolutionary Period

The opening of the National Theater of Cuba at the end of 1959 and the support received from the government by existing or newly created groups brought high hopes for most theater people. The frantic enthusiasm that shook the majority of Cubans from their routine during the early years of the revolutionary era was strongly felt by those active in the arts. There was a sense that things never done before could and should be done now. A theater boom never equalled before was the natural consequence of this. But the feverish theatrical activity engendered by that civic ardor cooled down in 1961. With the structural changes taking place, the arts, as several activities in the nation, were to be pervaded by the bureaucratic apparatus stemming from the new political structure.

Cultural activities were assigned to an autonomous organism many times the size of the former Department of Culture in the Ministry of Education called the National Council of Culture (*Consejo Nacional de Cultura*). By mid-1961, the politico-ideological objectives of the council were revealed by its support of the ban on the film *P.M.,* of which more will be said later.

The policy of the government concerning creative art was precisely established at this time by Fidel Castro at a meeting held with the artists and intellectuals in the National Library in June 1961 (see chapter 16). This policy has been often summarized with a quote from Castro's closing speech to this meeting, "Inside the Revolution, everything; against it, nothing." Because of its vagueness, this statement has been interpreted in various ways, going from flexible to hard lines vis-à-vis the intellectuals, according to the changing political trends set throughout the Revolution.

One of the missions of the council at the moment of its creation was to reorganize the exuberant (since 1959) theatrical activities. Disregarding the political side, the measures taken were needed and altogether beneficial because the prevailing disorder was causing a regrettable waste of talent and money. A large number of the state-supported theatrical groups were preserved so as to provide a variety of entertainment and artistic competition, which ultimately resulted in better quality. The National Theater, originally selected by the theatrical groups for their headquarters, soon had to be abandoned because of technical inconveniences. (The original project could never be completed for lack of equipment.)

To provide the groups with a large-capacity house as well as a proper stage for certain major productions, a big movie house was converted into a theater auditorium. To give a popular foundation to the professional theater by means of conditioning (which also meant ensuring) new and larger audiences, groups of amateurs (*aficionados*) were organized in labor centers or schools all over the island.

Another aspect of the cultural reorganization was the creation of the School of Art Instructors, which has a theater section. The missions of the art instructor were (a) to help develop an interest in the different art forms among not formally educated people, (b) to stimulate individuals with creative talent, and (c) to assist in the organization and activities of the performing groups of *aficionados*.

Concerning the several private playhouses still in operation, the official policy at the time was one of wait and see—an intervention or confiscation was to be decreed only if its owners or directors had left the country. Two playhouses were appropriated by the government in 1961 and a third one was donated by its owner, playwright, actor, and director Paco Alfonso, an old member of the Communist party.

By 1962, the new cultural machinery was working very well in the theater. There was considerable freedom in the selection of the repertory to be performed by the official groups, and a central warehouse and workshop served them with professional efficiency. The only handicap of the theater system was, perhaps, the total centralization of budgeting and technical services and supplies, but this was later corrected by giving greater financial independence to the groups. Two new groups were founded in 1962, the

Lyrical Theater (devoted to *zarzuelas,* operas, and operettas) and the Musical Theater (devoted to foreign or national contemporary musical plays). Both had a high budget because of the special requirements of those genres; each group had, to start with, its own orchestra. Two old theater houses were adapted to the needs of these two ensembles. The Lyrical Theater has been particularly successful since its founding, for it provided the light and colorful entertainment so much favored by Cuban audiences. The government has also revived, with enthusiastic response, the old vernacular genre in one of its popular theaters of yesterday, the *Martí.*

And yet, theater activities began to decrease substantially in 1962. Understandably, theatrical reorganization had to lead to a reduction in the number of works performed, especially in contrast with the outburst of the first two years of the Revolution. However, instead of keeping the pace set in 1961 or, as was to be expected, increasing the activities step by step as part of the much publicized cultural growth in Cuba, theater activities apparently collapsed by the late 1960s. Two important testimonies from sympathizers of the Revolution support the previous assertion. Rine Leal, a Cuban theater critic, in a collection of his reviews published in Havana in 1967, states:

> From that point on [1963], the theater movement starts to slow down (let us be more sincere, to be slowed down), slides along a dangerous slope which soon becomes a ditch and in the end is threatened with annihilation. There is a moment in which all theaters are paralyzed, the new actors do not find jobs and new playwrights seem reluctant to reveal their talent. This last aspect is the most painful and deplorable. Between 1959 and 1963 appear Triana, Arrufat, Reguera Saumell, Brene, Estorino and Nicolás Dorr. Between 1963 and 1966 only one name deserves attention, Héctor Quintero. Between 1959 and 1963 the groups are formed and organized, ambitious projects are devised, new playhouses are adapted, the state budgets are generous, there is confidence in the cultural work. From 1963 to this date these words can be substituted by their opposites and the resulting image will be close to reality. . . .
>
> There is much to say about the moralistic persecution of the artists, which reminds one so much of the stream of puritanism that brought the closing of the theaters in London in 1642. The wave of the so-called sexual morality, the tendency of certain bureaucrats to see in the artists the worst kind of social illnesses, the idea that the theater is a place for sin, improvisation or easy

living, have hit with such a strength, that a long time will elapse before the theater recovers from so big an infamy. To this let us add a malignant discrimination on the part of some cultural sectors against the artist in general, who is seen as an evil to be tolerated while necessary, instead of an active member of the society of men. And, finally, let us refer to the abuse of power, the bureaucratic impositions, the poor taste and the theatrical demagogy.[11]

Mario Benedetti, an Uruguayan leftist intellectual writing in 1968, presents a briefer but similarly gloomy picture, "Of all cultural sectors in Cuba, it is perhaps the theater which undergoes a serious crisis at present . . . the theatrical activity in Havana is almost nonexistent today."[12]

Besides the explanations for the decline of the theater advanced by Leal, other circumstances should be taken into consideration. First, around 1963, a great part of the middle class that provided a permanent audience for the playhouse since its establishment had left or was in the process of leaving the country. Secondly, the present theater audiences are more inclined to attend simple, light, relaxing types of amusement (musical comedy or vernacular variety shows). And thirdly, it is quite difficult to educate a mass of people in a single decade for the absorption of sophisticated cultural activities.

In spite of the above facts, it is only fair to say that positive and very important accomplishments have taken place in the theater during the early sixties. First, the revolutionary government gave the necessary support for a good professional theater, providing salaries for all people involved in this activity—artists, technicians, stagehands, laborers—and the funds to obtain the required equipment or materials. This allowed the staging of some productions which were highly impressive, the more so when the shortcomings of the Cuban economy of these years is considered.[13]

The second and most important achievement of this period has been the opportunity and stimulus it has offered to the Cuban playwrights. Before the Revolution, many people wrote for the theater, but very few actually would consider this their profession, mainly because it was absolutely unprofitable. Only four names from the prerevolutionary period deserve full critical consideration: José Antonio Ramos, Virgilio Piñera, Carlos Felipe, and Rolando Ferrer (in order of age). During the early years of the Revolution, new names have been added and some with important contributions to Cuban dramatic literature: Matías Montes Huidobro, José Triana, Manuel Reguera Saumell, José Brene, Antón Arrufat, Abelardo Estorino, José Ignacio Gutiérrez, Nicolás Dorr, and Héctor Quintero (Felipe, Piñera, and Ferrer have been active during this period also).

In contrast, the present ideological pressures, reflected in the official condemnation of several literary works (among them the plays *Cain's Mangoes* by Abelardo Estorino and *The Seven Against Thebes* by Antón Arrufat), apparently have led to a decline of good dramatic literature. If this is true, it is not adventurous to predict that in the immediate future only politically palatable plays will be accepted by the Cuban authorities and staged.

One theater experiment, which may prove successful under present conditions, was on its way in 1970 under the direction of the most talented Vicente Revuelta. The experiment consists of the adaptation of the interesting ideas on the theater expounded by the Polish *metteur en scène* Jerzy Grotowski, which is addressed to small audiences for a deep emotional involvement.[14]

Cinema

The Prerevolutionary Period

It is somehow surprising to find out how much of a creative spirit was generated by movie shows in Cuba from 1897 (when a Frenchman named Gabriel Veyre projected in Havana the first films by the Lumière brothers) to the 1930s.[15] This fact certainly increases the sadness derived from the realization of the very poor accomplishments, not to say the void, of the Cuban cinema during the thirty years preceding the revolutionary decade. One would expect a progressive evolution, as that of the theater, from the melodramas filmed by Enrique Díaz Quesada between 1906 and 1919 to some of the finest productions of today. From 1920 to 1930 an imaginative director, Ramón Peón, produced some interesting films influenced by the then popular Hollywood passionate love stories—among them the celebrated *Our Lady of Charity*—which were the last promising pictures to be made in Cuba for a long time. After 1930 there was a remarkable decrease in the quantity and quality of films due to several causes, which are explained below.

A few poor musical films starring popular theater and radio singing artists were the only films to appear in the 1930s. By the end of that decade and during the following one, the invasion of the Cuban market by Argentine and Mexican pictures, the products of a prosperous movie industry in both of these countries, was a terrible blow to the development of a solid national film enterprise. Of course, Mexico and Argentina, countries with large populations, had the basic numerical power to develop their cinema as a profitable business. Cuba, with a population of only around four million at the time, was, by contrast, in a very unfavorable position. Large audiences, made up mostly of poorly educated people, loved these foreign films in Spanish, Mexican films in particular, and the competing Cuban films of the period were box-office failures. Other circumstances that worked against the Cuban movie industry were the graveness of the economic depression combined with the revolutionary turmoil of the 1930s, as well as the competition of Hollywood-made films.

From 1950 to 1959 the only major production of certain value was *Seven Deaths in the Installment Plan* (*Siete muertes a plazo fijo*) directed by Manuel Alonso, the producer of a weekly newsreel shown regularly in Cuban movie houses during those years. The film, a police thriller that followed the formula of similar North American pictures, was a success in terms of moviemaking technique (rather naïve up to that point), much of it due to the assistance of foreign technicians hired for the occasion. Paradoxically, a film bank for the financing of national motion pictures was established by the government during this decade. And it was through the aid provided by this bank that the first properly equipped studios were built. But the studios soon fell into the hands of persons linked with the distribution of foreign films and who, therefore, were not interested in the consolidation of the Cuban film industry. Several deplorable movies, some of them Cuban-Mexican coproductions put on the Latin American market by Cub-Mex Films—a company led by the Cuban radio and television writer of soap operas, Felix B. Caignet—were the monstrous offspring of this era. The irony of it all was that, contrary to the case of the theater at that time, a real financial aid from the state finally had been granted, just to be wasted by inefficiency and greed.

Nevertheless, during the culturally alive period of the early fifties, several unofficial activities somewhat compensated for official dilapidation and infertility. Art-film clubs obtained the favor of progressively growing audiences, especially in the capital. The University of Havana Cinema Club and the Film Library of Cuba were directed by the film critic José Manuel Valdés Rodríguez, who also taught a regular cinema course at the university. The Film Library of Cuba, founded originally as the Cine-Club of Havana at the end of the 1940s by Germán Puig and the late Ricardo Vigín and reorganized in 1951, offered successive cycles of art films borrowed from the Cinematheque Française and the New York Museum of Modern Art Film Library. The Catholic Center of Film Orientation established two cinema clubs in Havana and promoted others in the provinces. Finally, there were the movie-debate sessions sponsored by the film section of the cultural society *Nuestro Tiempo*.

Another important activity in the field during the fifties was that of the amateur film makers, which could be traced back to 1943 when the first national contest of amateur films was sponsored by the Photography Club of Cuba. Many interesting short films, either documentary or purely artistic were made by these amateur cinematographers, some of whom later became the most outstanding professionals of the revolutionary era. Plácido González and Walfrido Piñera should be given special attention as being among the pioneers in the making of short art films shown in the mid-1940s. And after them, without going in strict chronological order, were film makers Néstor Almendros and Ramón F. Suárez, both successful cameramen in Europe today who individually or jointly made several remarkable experiments, such as a Hamlet monologue in big closeup. Also to be included in this list are Paúl Villanueva, organizer of a group called "Tecnifilm," Germán Puig, Julio García Espinosa, and Tomás Gutiérrez Alea. The last two studied for two years at the famous Experimental Center of Cinematography founded in Rome by De Sicca and Zavattini. On their return to Cuba, they made a film entitled *El Mégano* in the mid-fifties which denounced the poor living conditions endured by the vegetable-coal workers in the swampy land of Batabanó, located at the south of Havana. In view of the political nature of the film and the existing censorship practices of the government, the film was confiscated by Batista's secret police and only recovered in 1959. Although its artistic value is of a very relative nature, it stands as the first wave of social documentary films that emerged after the revolutionary victory. The last of the short films of certain importance to be made in Cuba before the Revolution was José Massip's *The Life of Young Martí,* started in 1958 and finished after the revolutionary take-over.

The Revolutionary Period

The Cuban Institute of Cinema Arts (ICAIC—*Instituto Cubano del Arte e Industria Cinematográficas*), created in March of 1959, has been the official organization in charge of the film industry. This organization soon absorbed all Cuban film activities, providing proper equipment and training for those interested in the cinema. It expropriated the existing studios and the movie houses, employed almost all the potential young talents mentioned above, many of whom were being wasted in making commercial advertising films, and began publishing a serious film magazine, *Cine Cubano,* which has appeared to this date.

Among the newcomers that joined the staff of ICAIC were the cinema critic and writer Guillermo Cabrera Infante, and Santiago Alvarez, much praised during the past ten years for his dynamic weekly newsreel. Alfredo Guevara, former student leader and amateur of the arts, was appointed director of the institution and still holds the post.

In the beginning, the creative enthusiasm referred to above materialized in several interesting documentary films and continues to the present time, always showing great propriety and sometimes attaining a mark of excellence. There was no hard political line to follow at first, and the revolutionary themes that appeared in these first documentaries really manifested the sincere beliefs of the film makers, who saw in the new aggressive appeal for political independence the way toward a genuine national expression.

The year 1961, the starting point of stricter control of all national activities (we have seen the results of it in the theater), also marked the outbreak of carefully conducted film censorship. The realization that things had begun to change had a rather dramatic effect, since it came on the eve of the first conference of writers and artists through the above-mentioned banning of the film *P.M.* (Post Meridian). This short film was made by the painter Sabá Cabrera Infante and by Orlando Jiménez in the free-cinema style. It presents groups of people in search of amusement on a particular Saturday evening in the waterfront area of the capital. Images of people cheerfully drinking, dancing, and joking against the background of Afro-Cuban music offers a fresh, unprejudiced view of town dwellers of the working class during their leisure time. The film was shown during a television program sponsored by the literary magazine *Lunes de Revolución,* winning the applause of many artists, intellectuals, and cinema fans. The makers of the film asked the ICAIC to schedule its projection in a Havana movie house. To their surprise ICAIC not only rejected the request, but confiscated the film on the grounds that it had features that were demeaning to the Revolution, its deeds and ideals. ICAIC officials claimed that no image of a militiaman or of the new political face of the island appeared in the film. They also asserted that *P.M.* created the impression of a people that had not acquired any consciousness of the national problems and preferred to dance, get drunk, and forget. A long and violent debate on this action took place in the *Casa de las Américas,* an inter-American cultural agency that publishes a magazine under the same name, with the participation of a large number of artists and intellectuals. However, ICAIC officials, supported by the upper hierarchy of the National Council of Culture and against the feeling of the majority of those present, reinforced their early decision to ban the film.

Since then, it was clear that the cinema would have to follow certain lines or, at least, to adapt to patterns determined by the policies of the revolutionary government. Since the cinema is an important means of communication, it is easy to understand that it (together with television) has been the form of art most subject to direct, precise control. The pressures have hardened or softened according to the development of political events in the national or international scene. In latest years, the trend, as it has been explained in connection with the theater, has been one of extreme caution and, naturally, has been a hindrance to the creators (something that can also be observed in the general field of literature—see chapter

16). A new tolerance is not to be discarded as a possibility for the future. Nevertheless, the continuous tension deriving from the struggle of the artist for his freedom against the pressures of a highly politicized organization such as the ICAIC became intolerable for some of the talents formed or developed under the tutelage of the revolutionary government, and many have chosen to live in exile. Such is the case of Almendros, Suárez, Canel, Jiménez, Sabá Cabrera Infante, Fernando Villaverde, and Roberto Fandiño. The latter, now in Spain, is the director of an excellent short film entitled *People of Moscow*—a sort of Russian *P.M.*, made on location in the Soviet capital.

According to Fandiño, since 1968 movie production has decreased considerably because of the shortage of raw film.[16] This material handicap may have contributed to the strengthening of dogmatism, for the government has felt that film should be saved for the primary need of political propaganda. Therefore, documentary films have had primacy since 1968.

Nevertheless, some of the most important film makers of this era have chosen to remain in Cuba, and have been producing regularly in the latest years: Gutiérrez Alea, García Espinosa, Alvarez, Massip, Enrique Pineda Barnet, Jorge Fraga, Manuel Octavio Gómez, Octavio Cortázar, and Humberto Solás. The latter reflects very well an attitude that is, perhaps, typical among all of them. Solás firmly supports the Revolution but has not given up his belief that true artistic revolutionary values are to be found in dialogue and not in dogmatic conception. He hopes that his view will finally win over the dogmatist position or hard line, but if this does not happen, he will not leave Cuba but will wait until things improve.[17]

The achievements of the Cuban film industry in the last ten years are certainly outstanding. According to Fandiño, up to March 1969, the ICAIC has produced 45 full- or medium-length films, 210 documentaries, 85 educational short films, 49 animated cartoons, 94 film sketches for a popular scientific movie encyclopedia, and 446 editions of the Latin American Newsreel. The number of awards received by the ICAIC has reached a respectable cipher: 22 as of March 1969.[18]

Documentaries could be classified into three broad categories: internal politics and mobilization, international relations, and customs and folklore. The first two types are highly politicized and often of poor cinematographic quality. Those of the third type (which includes some color films) usually have little political content and, conversely, show high artistic quality and sophistication in some cases. The following is a very incomplete sample, based essentially on the availability of these documentaries abroad. Many of these films are available with English subtitles.

1. *Internal politics and mobilization.* These may describe socioeconomic achievements of the Revolution, for example, *The Isle of Youth* (Isle of

Pines development), *Los niños* (day-care centers), and *Nuestra olimpiada en la Habana* (sports); or national mobilization in case of emergencies or for developmental purposes, for example, *Ciclón* (Hurricane Flora in 1963), *Historia de una batalla* (illiteracy campaign in 1961), *Men of Canefields* (student team working in the sugar harvest), and *Cuban Teachers* (young volunteers teaching in rural communities).

2. *International relations.* These may be related to guerrilla warfare in Latin America, for instance, *Golpeando en la selva* (Colombia) and *Hasta la victoria siempre* (Bolivia); may be a denunciation of U.S. military intervention, such as *Muerte al invasor* (Bay of Pigs invasion in 1961), *L.B.J., Hanoi 13,* and *La muerte de Joe E. Jones* (Vietnam war); or may attack social conditions in the United States, for example, *Now* and *La hora de los hornos* (mainly on racial discrimination).

3. *Customs and folklore.* These include such films as *Historia de un ballet* (national ballet, based on Afro-Cuban dances), *Y tenemos sabor* (music), *Color de Cuba* (paintings), *O ciel de Toa* (Afro-Cuban folklore), *San Lázaro y Babalú* (religion and superstition), and *Por primera vez* (reaction of a formerly isolated village to the first film they see—an old Charlie Chaplin movie).

Several full-length movies have shown remarkable artistic quality, as *La muerte de un burócrata* (1966) and *Memorias del subdesarrollo* (1968) by Tomás Gutiérrez Alea, and *Lucía* (1968) by Humberto Solás. The last two are considered by one foreign film critic as representative of the coming maturity of the Cuban cinema, now able to compete on equal terms with any other country.[19]

The three films mentioned above offer a sincere, critical view of problematic aspects of the Revolution. *La muerte de un burócrata* is a denunciation of the evils of bureaucratism resulting from the socialist administrative apparatus. It tells the story of a young man who tries to recover his dead uncle's identification card (buried with the corpse) so that the widow can claim her pension. After much arguing with obstinate officials, the nephew, driven to despair, ends by killing a bureaucrat. The nephew is taken away in a strait jacket and the final scenes on the film show the "bureaucratic" ceremony accompanying the burial of the assassinated bureaucrat.

Memorias del subdesarrollo, based on the novel of the same title by Edmundo Desnoes (published in English in the United States as *Inconsolable Memories*), tells the story of a counterrevolutionary who has chosen to remain in Cuba and analyzes the present situation and his own with the prejudice of a high-middle-class background.

Lucía (the most awarded Cuban film in history) is composed of three stories of women who bear that name during three crucial periods of Cuban history: the 1895 War of Independence, the tyranny of Machado, and the present day. The three women have to make important social decisions, which conflict with their affections or the prejudices of their milieu. The present-day Lucía abandons her husband, who is still haunted by the traditional Spanish *machismo* and, through her emancipation, is able to devote herself properly to her revolutionary tasks.

Other full-length films recently produced in Cuba are *Manuela, La primera carga al machete,* and *La odisea del General José.* The last two are historical movies set at the time of the War of Independence.

Conclusions

Cuba's national art theater had attained a considerable degree of professional efficiency as well as certain stability before Castro's take-over. A large number of playhouses patronized by large segments of the middle class operated in the capital city, where the Municipal Academy of Dramatic Arts, the University Seminar of Dramatic Art, and other independent groups or individual artists trained the future theater professionals. Although some theatrical activity existed in the provinces, it could never match that of the capital, due to a great extent to the dominant role of Havana—the only really cosmopolitan city of the island—in every aspect of the national life, but especially in the cultural and educational fields. The playhouses operating in Havana faced, nevertheless, a serious economic problem, which limited their possibilities in every sense and was the main obstacle to their growth and, in some cases, to their survival.

The Revolution absorbed step by step all forms of theatrical entertainment. The art theater became part of the official cultural structure built up around the National Council of Culture. Theater artists and technicians have been granted a stable occupation and native playwrights have been properly stimulated. A program to develop independent groups in the provinces has met with certain success, but Havana remains, for the still valid reasons stated above, the vital center for the theater. The experiment of the groups of *aficionados* has been a promising project of the revolutionary government, but the results are not clear yet. Moral and political restraint in the last few years has contributed greatly to a noticeable slack of activities. But the massive exodus of middle-class people, who provided most of the theater audiences in the past, is also to be taken into consideration in the present crisis. The process of shaping new audiences for a theater that goes beyond mere entertainment cannot be sped up and this might be another important cause of this recession. New experiments are now under way, some remarkable talents are still working in the Cuban theater, and the present outlook could change for the better in the near future.

After a rather strong impulse given to movie production by some film makers during the 1910s and 1920s, there was a recession, which lasted until the official organization of the industry in 1959. The competition of Hollywood, Argentine, and Mexican films was the most apparent cause of the poor accomplishments of the Cuban film enterprises for about thirty years. When a government film bank was established in the fifties to stimulate the production of pictures, inefficiency and administrative corruption, plus the interference of foreign film-distributing organizations, soon frustrated all hopes for a brighter outlook. However, as part of the prevalent cultural ebullience of those years, several amateur film makers produced interesting experiments that served as their first training experience in the field, for many of them became the first professionals of the revolutionary period.

In 1959, the ICAIC—the state agency in charge of film production and cinema art in general—was founded. In recent years, the ICAIC has turned out several first-rate full-length movies, as well as a large number of documentaries, some of undisputed artistic value. The lack of raw materials and the need for ideological propaganda have caused the ICAIC to favor documentary against full-length film production at present, but this situation might be improved if the prevailing circumstances (economic or ideological) change.

NOTES

1. Take, for example, this statement by the Spanish writer Jesús López Pacheco, "Before the Revolution, there was not a single publishing house in the island." See "Cuba entrevista," in *Cuba: una revolución en marcha* (Paris, 1967), p. 503.

2. Natividad González Freire, *Teatro cubano, 1927–1961* (Havana, 1961), Introduction. Despite its bias, this is the only scholarly work done on this period of the Cuban theater and has been a source of primary importance in the preparation of this paper.

3. A few names will suffice to give an idea: poets Nicolás Guillén, Mariano Brull, Eugenio Florit, Emilio Ballagas, José Lezama Lima, Cintio Vitier; novelist Alejo Carpentier; storytellers Carlos Montenegro, Lino Novás Calvo, Lydia Cabrera, and Virgilio Piñera (the latter an outstanding playwright as well); painters Fidelio Ponce, Wilfredo Lam, Amelia Peláez, Cundo Bermúdez, Mario Carreño, René Portocarrero; symphonic music composers Alejandro García Caturla and Amadeo Roldán; and composers of stylized folkloric music Eduardo Sánchez de Fuentes, Moisés Simmons, Ernesto Lecuona, Gonzalo Roig, and Eliseo Grenet.

4. For a complete, well-documented account of theater events and dramatic literature in colonial Cuba, see Juan José Arrom, *Historia de la literatura cubana* (New Haven, Conn., 1944).

5. One of its first interpreters and playwrights, Francisco Covarrubias (1775–1850), has become a sort of legendary hero for Cuban theater people. His plays have unfortunately disappeared.

6. During the first quarter of this century, Enrico Caruso, Sarah Bernhardt, and Eleonora Duse visited Cuba, which was considered an important center for their American *tournées.*

7. Two of them, at least, are now part of the Cuban tradition: *Cecilia Valdés,* based on a Cuban historical nineteenth-century novel with music by Gonzalo Roig, and *María la O,* with music by Ernesto Lecuona.

8. Leading commercial theatrical enterprises of those years included the company led by the Cuban actor Otto Sirgo and the Mexican actress Magda Haller, which performed mainly Spanish dramas; the French vaudeville company of Mario Martínez Casado; and the seasons of *zarzuelas* and operettas, especially those sponsored by Maestro Lecuona. The customary Spanish repertory companies also paid their visits, as well as those of the Mexican actress María Teresa Montoya and the Argentine comedienne Paulina Singerman.

Other activities should also be mentioned here, for they contributed to the favor received by the public of a cultural nature. One was the stability attained by the Havana Symphony Orchestra, which had been reorganized in the early 1940s by the famous conductor Erich Kleiber. The orchestra played every summer in the late 1940s and early 1950s—through the sponsorship of the Ministry of Education—in the Plaza of the Cathedral at the low price of twenty cents, and had massive attendance. Another was that of the Ballet of Cuba, led by prima ballerina Alicia Alonso, which performed with the help of a permanent grant of the government (maintained through 1958) in theaters and parks across the island.

9. Remarkable were the productions of *The Crucible,* directed by Andrés Castro; *South* and *Electra Garrigó,* staged by Francisco Morín; *Gigi,* directed by Reynaldo de Zúñiga; *An October Day,* by Adolfo De Luis; *A Long Day's Journey Into Night,* by Vicente Revuelta; and *The Bald Soprano,* directed by this author.

10. By Adela Escartín, Andrés Castro, Adolfo De Luis, and Vicente Revuelta (the first three studied with several teachers in New York, among them Erwin Piscator, and Revuelta attended a small theater laboratory in Paris).

11. Rine Leal, *En primera persona: 1954–1966* (Havana, 1967), pp. 334–35, trans. by this author.

12. Mario Benedetti, "Situación actual de la cultura cubana," *Marcha* (Montevideo), December 27, 1968, p. 18, trans. by this author.

13. Memorable for their spectacular qualities, in some cases accompanied by fine interpretations, were the following productions: Brecht's *Mother Courage, The Caucasian Chalk Circle,* and *The Mother;* Lope de Vega's *Fuenteovejuna* and *The Dog in the Manger;* Lorca's *Doña Rosita, the Spinster;* and Shakespeare's *Romeo and Juliet,* staged by the Czech director Otomar Krejcha. Other plays successful from every point of view have been Virgilio Piñera's *Cold Air* and *Electra Garrigó;* José Brene's *St. Camille of Old Havana;* Abelardo Estorino's *Stolen Hog;* Jose Triana's *Night of the Assassins;* Albee's *Zoo Story;* and Ruiz de Alarcón's *Suspected Truth.* Well-staged and well-accepted plays presented by private playhouses during this period were Tennessee Williams's *Sweet Bird of Youth;* Reguera Saumell's *Tulipa's Memories;* Ionesco's *Lesson;* and Aristophanes's *Lysistrata.*

14. About this experiment and the work of some of the groups operating today, see Karl A. Tunberg, "The New Cuban Theatre: A Report," *The Drama Review,* 14 (Winter 1970), pp. 43–53. In spite of the somewhat excessive optimism of his view, the author of this article provides valuable information on the plans and performances of these groups, as well as on the reactions of the audiences. Tunberg refers several times to negative audience reactions, as the one he witnessed toward LeRoi Jones's

Dutchman: "Approximately one-half of this audience walked out, which indicated to me that they were offended by the language or the mediocre acting or did not appreciate either the subject matter or Jones's style" (p. 46).

15. For a detailed history of prerevolutionary cinema in Cuba, see Faustino Canel, "Breve historia de un cine," *Lunes de Revolución* (Havana), February 6, 1961, pp. 54–57. A good survey for the revolutionary period can be found in Mario Rodríguez Alemán, "Cine cubano retrospectiva," *Vida Universitaria* (Havana), August 1967, pp. 12–15.

16. Personal letter from Fandiño dated October 22, 1969. Data on this section have been supplied by Fandiño.

17. See Solás as quoted in Renata Adler, "Cultural Life in Cuba Thriving Despite Rein," *New York Times,* February 10, 1969, p. 42.

18. Personal letter from Fandiño dated October 22, 1969.

19. See Andi Engel, "Solidarity and Violence," *Sight and Sound,* 38 (Autumn 1969), pp. 196–200.

16 Lourdes Casal

Literature and Society

TWO major questions are to be considered in this chapter. One is to what extent and in what way "revolutionary" literature differs from "prerevolutionary" literature. In comparing the two, three literary areas (poetry, the short story and the novel) will be analyzed according to several criteria—volume of output, quality, content, and characteristics of the authors.

The second question pertains to the major changes that have taken place under the Revolution in the sociopolitical context of literature. In other words, what have been the changes, not in the society at large, which are impossible to document in an essay of this nature, but in the areas immediately affecting the literary community, that is, in publishing facilities, in the relationships between the revolutionary government and the writers (with special discussion of control mechanisms), and in the government's definition of the writer's role and the function of literature in society.

A Comparison of Literature Before and After 1959

Poetry

The predominant literary genre in prerevolutionary Cuba (in terms of volume of output, amount of critical attention, number of anthologies, and international interest and impact) was poetry. Already at the close of the nineteenth century, Cuban poets (José Martí, Julián del Casal) were among the originators and most influential figures of the Modernist movement in Spanish America.[1] The evolution of poetry during the republican period could be traced through a number of significant anthologies.[2] However, such an analysis is clearly beyond the scope of this study.[3] It is necessary, however, to survey the situation of Cuban poetry on the threshold of the Revolution.

Most poetry was generated, or at least published, in Havana. During the fifties, the most persistent and influential group of poets was associated with the magazine *Orígenes* (1944–1957) and one of its founders, José Lezama Lima.[4] Its volume and quality of production made it the most important group in the Cuban literary scene of the forties and fifties. The ten main *Orígenes* poets published over thirty books of poetry between 1937 and 1958, plus thirteen years of uninterrupted publication of their literary magazine—a Cuban record—and many books of essays and criticism. This group has been characterized as "transcendentalist," hermetic, and evasive.[5] Fernández Retamar characterized these poets as "transcendentalist" in 1954, because of their conception of poetry as an instrument for the apprehension and naming of the essential, hidden reality beneath the superficial texture of things and historical accident.[6] The poets of *Orígenes* never became popular;[7] their baroque style, the accumulations of metaphors, the unexpected associations, the convoluted allusions, the richness of their language and imagery made them very difficult reading. However, the quality and persistence of their poetic work left a strong imprint upon the younger generations of Cuban poets. Their body of work and its formal sophistication constituted the standards against which the younger generations pitted themselves. The so-called "first generation of the Revolution" will later reject the *Orígenes* group's hermetism and elitism, and its lack of involvement with social and political realities.[8] However, the influence of the *Orígenes* group is recognizable in the work of many of its representative authors, especially Fayad Jamís, R. Fernández Retamar, and Pablo A. Fernández.

José Rodríguez Feo, co-founder of *Orígenes,* broke off from the group in 1955 and started a new magazine, *Ciclón* (1955–1959), in an attempt to create a more socially involved publication. Most of Cuba's intellectual Left was associated with a cultural society called *Nuestro Tiempo,* which published a magazine of the same name (1951–1959), but poetry was not among its predominant interests. "Social" poetry was written mainly by José Z. Tallet (b. 1893), Nicolás Guillén (b. 1902), and others.[9]

There were also a number of poets who could be classified as "independents."[10] This group was not associated with the *Orígenes* poets nor with the "social" poets and, thus, remained marginal to the major established tendencies.

Outside of Havana, there was a group of poets in the province of Las Villas composed of Samuel Feijóo (b. 1914), Alcides Iznaga (b. 1914) and Aldo Menéndez (b. 1918). At first, the work of this fairly cohesive group was similar to that of the *Orígenes* poets in terms of thematic and stylistic concerns, but soon their work manifested a conscious and careful incorporation of folkloric elements into their themes, and a greater simplicity of language and obvious preoccupation with the immediate socio-political milieu. The Las Villas poets in general and Samuel Feijóo in particular were very productive during the forties and fifties, publishing over fifteen books of poetry between 1944 and 1958, plus several books of criticism and folkloric research and one novel. Feijóo's influential work as director of the publishing program of Las Villas University must also be mentioned.

After the triumph of the Revolution, most of the above-mentioned groups continued to be active.[11] The "social" poets, faced with the revolutionary experience, have shown a strong tendency to become unabashed propagandists, in most cases to the detriment of quality.[12] The *Orígenes* group, as indicated above, continues to be very influential and its representatives are extremely productive.[13] However, the Revolution has not affected their themes or concerns, although a certain distillation and simplification of their poetic language is observable. Some of the original ten members of the group have become exiles, continuing their poetic activity abroad.[14] The group of independent poets has split apart, most remaining in Cuba but, with the exception of Hurtado, they have not been very productive.[15] Although the poets of Las Villas remain prolific, they moved away from poetry and into other literary genres after 1959.[16]

The dominant literary group within the Cuban literary scene today is the so-called first generation of the Revolution. This group of writers were approximately thirty years of age as of 1959, and, although they had started to publish during the fifties, they came to maturity, so to speak, with the advent of the Revolution. In poetry, members of this generation are represented by Roberto Fernández Retamar (b. 1930),[17] Fayad Jamis (b. 1930), Heberto Padilla (b. 1932),[18] Pablo Armando Fernández (b. 1930), and the now deceased Rolando T. Escardó (1925–1960) and José Alvarez Baragaño (1932–1962). The list is, of course, not meant to be comprehensive; however, the authors listed are considered to be the most representative poets within this age group.[19]

Most of the poets of this generation lived abroad for some time during the fifties and thus were acquainted firsthand with other literatures and were affected by the many sociopolitical and cultural transformations of the decade. After 1959, many of them returned to Cuba and became involved with the Revolution. "Involved" is perhaps not an adequate word. They became part of the Revolution and the Revolution part of them, and their poetry was transfigured by the sudden invasion of history. However, because they had not been directly engaged in the anti-Batista struggle, the process of learning how to relate to the political vanguard of their generation was rather tumultuous. Having been widely scattered geographically in their formative years, this generation also lacked cohesiveness.

Nevertheless, these poets constitute the major force within the literary establishment in post-1959 Cuba. In terms of their control of major magazines, cultural institutions, and literary prizes, they were undoubtedly the most dominant, at least until 1968. But their claim to dominance can best be substantiated by reference to their productiveness. The fourteen poets referred to as most representative of this generation by López (see n. 19) have published an average of three books of poetry per capita in the decade between 1959 and 1969, not counting anthologies, poems in magazines, and books better classified in literary genres other than poetry. Quality is more difficult to discuss because of temporal proximity, relative unavailability of their books abroad, scarcity of critical accounts, and politically originated distortions present in available critical account. However, R. Fernández Retamar, H. Padilla, J. A. Baragaño, P. A. Fernández and C. López are unquestionably poets of lasting significance. Of six poets selected to represent Cuba in an ambitious anthology of contemporary Spanish-American literature published in Italy, four belong to the first generation of the Revolution.[20]

A new generation of poets, which could be called the second generation of the Revolution (composed of writers born between 1940 and 1946) has already come of age.[21] It first became known with the establishment of the publishing house El Puente (1960–1965). El Puente published poetry primarily although its list of works also included short stories and plays. It was privately financed and, thus, represented the major literary outlet not controlled by a governmental agency or writer's union. The El Puente writers constituted a heterogeneous group; the major unifying characteristics were perhaps a rejection, open or implicit, of engaged literature and an obvious debt to the *Orígenes* group.

Members of this group have been accused of a number of aesthetic (transcendentalism), moral (homosexualism), and, primarily, political (being unreliable as revolutionaries) sins.[22] The group as such, disappeared in 1965 when José Mario (b. 1940), founder of the publishing house, was sent to a labor camp. Several of these writers (including Mario himself, Mercedes Cortázar, and Isel Rivero) have become exiles.[23] Other authors originally associated with El Puente (e.g., Belkis Cuza Malé, Nancy Morejón, Miguel Barnet) remain in Cuba and are still active in the literary scene.[24]

These poets really represented (whether openly committed to the Revolution, lukewarm, ambivalent, or opposed) a new wave in Cuban literature and were characterized by their openness to all kinds of experimentation: formal, thematic, and personal (i.e., in terms of their own life-styles). Inevitably, many of them collided with the formulations being elaborated and redefined regarding the role of the writer in the revolutionary process as well as with the perceived survival needs of the Revolution. They did not feel compelled to make the Revolution central to their poetic concerns as did their elders of the first generation of the Revolution; in a very radical sense, many of them took the Revolution for granted—perhaps prematurely—and launched a search for their own origins and identity (hence, a new look at the past) and their liberation, not only from family, bourgeois morality and mentality, but also from the literary and political tutelage of their immediate elders.

This is obvious even in the politically committed sector within this second generation, that is, the group of writers associated with the literary magazine *El Caimán Barbudo*. Representative names are Víctor Casaús, Luis Rogelio Nogueras, and Jesús Díaz Rodríguez, among others.

This group atttempted to identify themselves with a critical tendency within the Cuban cultural scene, pitting themselves against what Díaz labeled the "hysterical-liberal" and the "terrorist-dogmatic" tendencies within contemporary Cuban literature. The *El Caimán Barbudo* writers rejected the "terrorist-dogmatic" tendency representing those who demanded pledges of allegiance to the Revolution in every work, and who insisted on the didactic, popular character of revolutionary works of art. (Hence the label "populist" also applied to these poets and critics). Thus, the writer was required to become a publicist for the Revolution and to use a simplified language to reach the "level of the masses." On the other hand, the *El Caimán Barbudo* writers also rejected the "hysterical-liberal" tendency which they identified as being represented openly by the El Puente group and covertly by some poets of the preceding generation. The El Puente group is rejected ostensibly because of the "metaphysical" and "escapist" nature of their poetry. But the "hysterical-liberal" label clearly implies the true origins of the rejection: they are seen as being afflicted by individualism and liberalism, two unforgivable sins for a true revolutionary writer.

As a result, members of the *El Caimán Barbudo* group have been involved in a number of intense controversies, for example, Díaz against Jesús Orta and the "populist" poets; Díaz against El Puente; César López against the whole *El Caimán Barbudo* group and their overall stance; and the whole editorial board of *El Caimán Barbudo* in the Padilla-Otero controversy of 1967–1968.[25] They claimed for themselves the right to write not *against* or *for* but *from within* the Revolution. Thus, they could present a critical view of the Revolution and of the problems of constructing socialism, taking for granted their involvement with and loyalty to revolutionary principles.

In the aftermath of the Padilla-Otero controversy (see the section on "The Role of the Writer"), the *El Caimán Barbudo* editorial board had to resign, and the magazine stopped publication for several months (1968) until a new editorial board was appointed. In spite of this, all of the original members of the group are still active in the Cuban literary scene.

Recently, a group of even younger poets, associated neither with El Puente nor with *El Caimán Barbudo,* has started to publish. Among these independents, Lina de Feria (b. 1945), who became editor of *El Caimán Barbudo* in its second period, and Excilia Saldaña (b. 1946) must be mentioned.

Cuban poetry after the Revolution has maintained and perhaps even surpassed its traditional levels of productivity and quality. Members of the prerevolutionary generations in their various groupings continue to produce. The dominant first generation of the Revolution has been challenged by newer groups of poets, who, in turn, have been split and shaken by the revolutionary experience. Poetry, more than the short story or the novel, has been able to reflect accurately the tensions and conflicts generated by the Revolution. This is not only true of the work of such poets as Padilla and Pablo A. Fernández (who have been criticized by the government), or of the younger generation; but also of the work of poets well entrenched in the cultural establishment, such as Fernández Retamar and Jamis. Thematically, poetry has evolved from the transcendentalist concerns of the *Orígenes* group and members of their generation to the very immediate worries of the revolutionary society (the insurrection, the poet in the "New Society," the pressures for conformity, international conflict, voluntary work, sectarism, the exiles, military duty, the rebellion against the bourgeois family, etc.), very much intermingled with the traditional themes of lyrical poetry. Formally, there has been a strong trend toward a new poetic language, much more colloquial and almost conversational, and which, at its worst, has frequently fallen into vulgarity and prosaism.

The Short Story

On the eve of the Revolution, the short story was the predominant narrative genre, surpassing the novel, which had been decaying since the powerful work of the first generation of republican writers.[26] One factor encouraging this favored status of the short story was the establishment of the Hernández Catá awards in 1942.[27] The awards were a significant stimulus which fostered the development of a young and heterogeneous group of writers. Influential authors from previous generations were Lino Novás Calvo (b. 1905), Carlos Montenegro (b. 1900), Enrique Labrador Ruiz (b. 1902) and Lydia Cabrera (b. 1900). The short stories of the *Orígenes* group (V. Piñera, E. Diego, J. Lezama Lima) reflected a reaction against the naturalism, realism, and folklorism that had prevailed up to this time in Cuban narrative literature. However, members of the *Orígenes* group, with the exception of V. Piñera, did not cultivate the genre assiduously.

The new short-story writers who appeared during the fifties were a very mixed group, difficult to classify in terms of schools or tendencies, although the tradition of the "rural" short story remained strong (O. J. Cardoso, D. Alonso, R. González de Cascorro). However, it is possible to identify a group of young writers, the most notable of whom was Guillermo Cabrera Infante (b. 1929) whose work represented a new mode in Cuban storytelling, strongly influenced by contemporary British and North American models. These young writers did not represent an absolute break with tradition, but were different enough to be recognizable as a new wave: a definite trend toward stories with urban settings, away from the patterns of the traditional rural short story; thematically, a trend toward the exploration of the worlds of the bourgeoisie and petite bourgeoisie; and an obvious concern with stylistic questions and formal experimentation, as opposed to the formal carelessness so frequently encountered among writers of previous generations. These new writers would later constitute the first generation of the Revolution. During the fifties they published relatively few books—even G. Cabrera Infante did not publish his stories in book form until after the Revolution.

After 1959, the short story form was cultivated assiduously and no less than ten anthologies[28] and approximately seventy books by individual authors have been published from 1959 to 1969.[29] Furthermore, popular and literary magazines (e.g., *Bohemia* and *Cuba,* and *Casa de las Américas, Unión* and *El Caimán Barbudo*) have frequently published short stories by Cuban writers.

Thematically, there has been a strong tendency to exorcise prerevolutionary society and middle-class values, which were typical of most, if not all, of these writers.[30] Some of the most remarkable books of postrevolutionary short stories fall into this category, for example, those of Cabrera Infante, Calvert Casey (1923–1969), Onelio Jorge Cardoso (b. 1914), and Humberto Arenal (b. 1927), among others.[31] A sizable group of authors (e.g., Piñera, Ezequiel Vieta, Ana María Simo) has cultivated the fantastic short story in its different forms, including the black-humor short story, producing a minor boom in the field.[32] Science fiction has also received attention.

Guerrilla, terrorist, and counterguerrilla (i.e., the fight against anti-Castroists in the Escambray Mountains) activities have provided major themes for some significant new writers, in particular, Jesús Diaz and Norberto Fuentes.[33] These new writers, together with others of the previous generation (e.g., David Buzzi and Edmundo Desnoes) have started to face some of the thorny issues of the revolutionary period.[34] For example, topics for stories include the alienation of some people by the Revolution, revolutionary solidarity, voluntary work, etc. However, the fact remains that most revolutionary narrative fiction does not contend with contemporary Cuban society and its transformations and problems. Furthermore, it is possible that the trend toward fantastic, science-fiction, and black-humor stories (a new development in Cuban literary history) represents an evasion from contemporary themes and their attendant dangers.

Generationally, most of the above-mentioned short-story writers belong to the first generation of the Revolution. However, the second generation in its three groups, the El Puente, the *Caimán Barbudo,* and the independents, is as well represented in this genre as it is in poetry. A large number of short-story writers have chosen exile, some of them of the early prerevolutionary period (Novás Calvo, Montenegro, L. Cabrera), but also some of the members of the first generation of the Revolution (Cabrera Infante, Masó, and the now deceased Casey). Most of them have continued to write and publish outside of Cuba.

The Novel

During the fifties, the number and quality of Cuban novels written probably reached the lowest point in republican history. Established authors, for example, Alejo Carpentier, Labrador Ruiz, Novás Calvo, and Enrique Serpa, wrote important works, but practically all of them were published outside of Cuba, and few new novelists emerged during the decade.[35] The Cuban Revolution of 1933 provided the theme for the most representative novels of the period.

After 1959, the novel in Cuba underwent a true revival. Over sixty novels (excluding posthumous editions and émigré novels) have been published during the sixties.[36] Most of these novels have been written by members of the first generation of the Revolution, for example, Cabrera Infante, Arenal, Desnoes, and Otero.[37] Members of previous generations (Carpentier, Piñera, López-Nussa), however, are still active.[38] Other established writers who had not been known as novelists before the Revolution (e.g., Lezama Lima and Feijóo) have since moved into this genre.[39] The second generation of the Revolution has also started to publish novels, most of them of an astonishingly high quality.[40]

Thematically, most post-1959 novels have been concerned with prerevolutionary society and/or the insurrectional struggle. Only a few works, and not precisely the best, have dealt directly with the changes occurring after the triumph of the Revolution.[41] The image of prerevolutionary society reflected in these novels has been officially criticized because of its lack of depth and simplistic characterization of the bourgeoisie.[42] (On the other hand, many significant writers, e.g., Lezama Lima, P. A. Fernández, Sarduy, and Arenas, have rejected the pedestrian realism that characterized so much of prerevolutionary fiction.)[43] José A. Portuondo, one of these critics, has also accused Cuban novelists of being more attentive to the most irrelevant statements of well-known literary figures abroad, than to the "hard and constant battles in the cities and in the countryside to establish socialism."[44]

A similar criticism has been made by the government's official critic who writes under the pseudonym of Leopoldo Avila for the magazine of the armed forces, *Verde Olivo:*

> One of the most interesting and surprising characteristics of Cuban literary criticism, and Cuban literature in general, is its apparent depoliticization. Except for producing an occasional essay —very often dealing with the past—those who most consistently contribute to our cultural publications very seldom make their evaluations or write their works with a revolutionary approach uppermost in their mind. . . . The dumping of the so-called pamphlet [political propaganda] has not been accompanied by the study of the themes and possibilities of revolutionary literature.[45]

The most recent novels published in Cuba by the second generation represent a significant growth in the thematic repertoire of the post-1959 novel (e.g., parent-child relationships, a Cuban version of the Odyssey, love) and a definite improvement in the average level of quality, but no move has been made toward the politicization of literature or a greater willingness to handle the conflicts and problems of the revolutionary society.

Changes in the Sociopolitical Context of Literary Life

Publishing Facilities and Incentives

Before the Revolution, there was a dearth of publishers and those which existed (Cultural, Lex, Montero, Martí) were primarily concerned with school texts and technical and professional books. Most authors took their books directly to the printer, paid for their editions, and distributed them as best they could. An exiled Cuban writer, José A. Arcocha, has described the situation with great clarity:

> extremely limited editions, paid for by the author, national distribution limited to a few bookstores in the old quarter of Havana, inter-American and Spanish distribution nil; that is to say, the book which was the product of long months of writing, revising and distributing, was finally read by the friends of the author

or, if he was lucky, by an occasional reader attracted by a more
or less original title or by a more or less attractive cover.[46]

Incentives to writers were almost nonexistent. Only the Hernández Catá
short-story contest was consistently and fairly run and writers awarded.
Literature found no support among the masses and the middle and upper
sectors of society who could have fostered it, with some notable exceptions
(e.g., the Lyceum Society and some private *mecenas* ["patrons"] such as
José Rodríguez Feo and Víctor Batista). Most of these people looked at
literature with disdain, as a pastime for good-for-nothings and homosexuals. A few groups, as the one clustered around the magazine *Orígenes,*
took literature as a serious pursuit and survived, with the spirit of an underground organization, in the midst of this hostile environment.

The Revolution brought immediate material changes to the literary
scene. The Imprenta Nacional (government press) was organized in 1959
and an ambitious publications program was started. A number of publishing houses, some private (e.g., La Tertulia and El Puente, which survived
until 1965) and others with official sponsorship (e.g., Ediciones Revolución, Granma, Unión) coexisted during the first few years of the Revolution. In 1967, the overall publishing system was restructured and integrated under the state agency Instituto del Libro. Official figures from this
agency report eight million books produced in 1967 and over thirteen million in 1968, representing roughly from 600 to 700 different titles.[47] This
new central publishing agency also became the international distributor of
Cuban books and now has agents in all socialist countries, as well as in a
number of nonsocialist countries that do not participate in the U.S. embargo, such as Mexico, France, Spain, and England.

Periodicals for literary works were also created. *Lunes de Revolución*
(1959–1961) was the first cultural magazine established in the history of
Cuba to be distributed in runs at the hundreds-of-thousands level. Its influence is still felt today, nine years after it disappeared in the aftermath of the
first major confrontation between the revolutionary government and the literary community (for details, see the section, "The Role of the Writer").
Other significant literary outlets have been the magazines *Casa de las
Américas* (published by the inter-American cultural agency of the same
title), the *Unión* and *La Gaceta de Cuba* (both published by UNEAC—
the National Union of Writers and Artists of Cuba), and *El Caimán Barbudo* (literary supplement of *Juventud Rebelde,* the newspaper of the
UJC). Furthermore, such mass magazines as *Bohemia* and *Cuba* regularly
publish articles, poems, and short stories by contemporary Cuban authors.
Other journals, such as *Pensamiento Crítico* and *Universidad de La Ha-*

bana, although not primarily concerned with current literature, do publish translations of theoretical articles, criticism, etc.

A most important factor in stimulating literary production has been a great number of literary contests, among the most prestigious, the *Casa de las Américas* yearly awards, open to international competition and judged by international juries. UNEAC sponsors two yearly contests, one of them for unpublished writers. Other publishing houses (e.g., Ediciones Revolución and Granma) and official organizations (e.g., the armed forces) have also sponsored literary contests.

International attention, manifested by special issues devoted to Cuban literature by prestigious foreign magazines (e.g., *Insula, Les Lettres Nouvelles, El Corno Emplumado, Imagen* and *Cuadernos Hispanoamericanos*)[48] and the reprinting of Cuban works by foreign publishing houses (e.g., Ediciones Alfa of Montevideo; Era of Mexico City; and De la Flor, Jorge Alvarez, and Centro Editor de América Latina of Buenos Aires), has probably been an additional stimulating factor.

Another change in publishing conditions has been the rejection of the copyright since April 1967. Authors receive no royalties for their works, thus eliminating the possibility of an author's earning an independent income. However, the importance of such a change can be easily overestimated abroad, where royalties are an essential part of the writer's incentive system. In Cuba, even after the new publishing structures eliminated the need (and later even the opportunity) for self-financed editions, royalties did not represent a significant income for most authors.

Government and the Writers: Control Mechanisms

Before 1959, there was little attempt by the state to control literary production, but, rather than a virtue, this was the result of government indifference to this type of activity. Some indirect influences were exerted, however, through the granting of government sinecures to a very limited number of writers who often were characterized by their mediocrity.

After 1959, with the dramatic increase of state sponsorship of literary activities and the Revolution's concern for politics, several techniques of control had been developed by the government. The elimination of royalties mentioned above has been a key element in the government strategy since all authors had to be employed by or be dependent on the state in order to survive.

Withholding of publication and the thematic restriction of literary contests (see the next section) have been other methods used in an attempt to manipulate intellectual life.[49] At another level, the curtailment of trips abroad and the quality and influence of the jobs awarded to a writer (or lack of jobs) have been important elements of the carrot-and-stick system.[50]

Writers accused of serious "deviations" (e.g., homosexuality in 1966) or those who have attempted to leave the country (e.g., Luis Agüero) were sent to labor camps to be reeducated.[51] More serious political sins (as suspected association with counterrevolutionaries or foreign agents) have led to imprisonment (see the next section). However, these methods have not been constantly or consistently used. As will be mentioned later, there have been different stages in the evolution of the relationship between the writers and the government, and it is only since 1968 that more stringent controls have been applied.

The Role of the Writer and the Function of Literature in Society

Any presentation of the panorama of the first ten years of the Revolution as a paradise of freedom for writers and artists is false.[52] However, it is also false to maintain a negative view of the impact of the Revolution on literature and culture in general.[53]

It is obvious that "freedom of expression" does not exist in Cuba. In the words of a Puerto Rican social scientist sympathetic to the Revolution: "If we apply to Cuba the criteria about freedom of expression which prevail in capitalist countries, there is no doubt that, in that sense, freedom of expression does not exist there. But then, the Revolutionary Government has never claimed for itself the title of representative democracy."[54] However, it is also obvious that, given the scope and variety of the works that have been produced, there has been considerable leeway given to literary expression during the first ten years of the Revolution.[55]

Initially there was a "honeymoon" period in which many writers who had been living abroad during the fifties returned to Cuba. There were many signs of effervescence and vitality during this period: *Casa de las Américas* was organized, *Lunes de Revolución* started publication, the Cuban Institute of Cinema Arts (see chapter 15) was founded, and the Imprenta Nacional initiated its activities. This early period came to a close during the second half of 1961 with the *P.M.* affair and the demise of *Lunes de Revolución.*

The banning of *P.M.,* a film on Havana's night life, triggered a crisis that had been brewing since 1960. This crisis was induced by the intolerance of dogmatic elements (militants of the PSP, which was rapidly rising in influence due to Cuba's closer ties to the USSR) and their mistrust of *Lunes de Revolución,* which sponsored the television program on which the film was seen, and its director, Guillermo Cabrera Infante. The crisis was also fueled by existing rivalries between the leadership of the Cuban Institute of Cinema Arts, in particular, its director Alfredo Guevara, and the leadership of *Lunes de Revolución,* particularly Cabrera Infante. (A more detailed discussion of the *P.M.* affair can be found in chapter 15.)

In June 1961, the *Lunes de Revolución* group, plus most Cuban writers and intellectuals, were invited to a series of meetings at the National Library. At these meetings, the leaders of the PSP, particularly Edith García Buchaca, accused the *Lunes de Revolución* group of fostering division within the revolutionary camp and not being truly socialist.[56] The confrontation was long and heated and Fidel Castro himself had to appear on June 30, 1961, to end the debate. Castro's speech established the outlines of the government's cultural policy for the following years.[57] Until 1968, at least, this policy was characterized by tolerance toward all forms of artistic expression as long as there was a basic acceptance and support of the Revolution.

However, this confrontation provoked a restructuring of the literary establishment: *Lunes de Revolución* was closed, the showing of the film *P.M.* was forbidden, Antón Arrufat, director of the magazine *Casa de las Américas,* was dismissed, a convention of writers was called, and the UNEAC was established.

In the following years, the underlying tension between cultural bureaucrats and most of the Cuban writers and artists was manifested in different ways, as in the controversy between socialist realism (or at least a strong populist line) and didacticism (which most of the writers violently opposed).[58] Ernesto (Che) Guevara, writing in 1965, accused most writers and artists of not being authentic revolutionaries because of their bourgeois and petit bourgeois origins. But he also rejected simple-minded attempts at dirigibility and expressed his belief that a new type of writer would eventually appear, "The revolutionaries which will intone the songs of the New Man with the legitimate voice of the people shall come."[59]

During the second half of 1965, a new crisis developed. Superficially an attempt to rehabilitate antisocial elements (e.g., people who did not work, homosexuals), militarily organized labor camps were created (UMAP— *Unidades Militares de Ayuda a la Producción*). Large numbers of Cuban writers and artists were sent to those camps, and some institutions (e.g., Havana University) were purged. *Paradiso,* José Lezama Lima's novel with its obvious homosexual references, almost did not get published. The resultant international uproar, the counterproductive effects of the camps, and the intervention of the UNEAC led to the eventual elimination of the labor camps, although the political-cultural scene remained very tense.

Toward the end of 1967, a debate over *Pasión de Urbino,* a novel by Lisandro Otero (a high-ranking cultural official) began in *El Caimán Barbudo.* Heberto Padilla sent a letter that debunked Otero's novel and praised Guillermo Cabrera Infante's *Tres tristes tigres.* This controversy ended with the resignation of the editorial board of *El Caimán Barbudo,*

Padilla's loss of his job and the withdrawal of his permission to travel to Italy.[60] In August 1968, an interview with Cabrera Infante was printed in the Argentinian magazine *Primera Plana*.[61] Although Cabrera Infante had been living abroad with no ties to the Cuban government since 1965, it was in this 1968 interview that he, for the first time, publicly attacked the Revolution and denounced the condition of the writers within Cuba. This left Padilla in the dangerous position of having been on the side of a now public "traitor to the Revolution."[62]

When Padilla was awarded the 1968 UNEAC prize for his book of critical poems, *Fuera del juego,* and Antón Arrufat was awarded the theater prize for his play, *Los siete contra Tebas,* by an international jury, UNEAC officials strongly criticized the decision. Although the decision of the jury was respected and the books published, the editions were printed with the political disclaimer of UNEAC. A series of articles published in the magazine of the armed forces, *Verde Olivo,* under the pseudonym of Leopoldo Avila strongly criticized Padilla and Arrufat.[63] But more than a criticism of the two individual writers, the articles were an indication of a new offensive on the cultural front.[64]

UNEAC's stance and government criticism manifested by Avila's articles reflected a cultural policy established by a declaration of principles approved at the October 1968 Congress of Writers and Artists held in Cienfuegos. The declaration stated that "the writer must contribute to the Revolution through his work and this involves conceiving of literature as a means of struggle, a weapon against weaknesses and problems which, directly or indirectly, could hinder this advance."[65]

In order to prevent writers who did not fulfill their obligations to the Revolution from receiving contest prizes in the future, Haydeé Santamaría, director of the inter-American cultural agency *Casa de las Américas,* suggested that the juries for future UNEAC contests should consist only of Cuban authors. The advice was heeded during the 1969 contest, and the awards were predictably safe.[66] Nicolás Guillén, president of UNEAC, in his speech during the award ceremony reminded all that "these contests have taken place during an era of acute political crisis, one from which creative intelligence cannot—or rather, should not—consider to keep itself divorced. . . . Cuban writers and artists have the same responsibilities as our soldiers, with respect to the defense of the nation. . . . He who does not [fulfill his duty] regardless of his position, will receive the most severe revolutionary punishment for his fault."[67]

Guillén's speech came in the aftermath of the expulsion from UNEAC of José Lorenzo Fuentes, a winner of the 1967 annual literature contest with his novel *Viento de enero*. Fuentes was expelled from the UNEAC on September 22, 1969, because of his alleged involvement with H. Carrillo

Colón, accused by the Cubans of being a CIA agent employed by the Mexican embassy in Havana. Carrillo Colón was supposedly in charge of penetrating intellectual circles and fostering defections. The expulsion decision was accompanied by an appeal by UNEAC's executive board, which addressed itself "to all Cuban writers and artists exhorting them to increase revolutionary vigilance, to avoid all forms of weakness and liberalism, and to denounce all attempts at ideological penetration and counterrevolutionary activity, faithful to the principle which gave birth to the Writers' Union: to defend the Revolution is to defend Culture."[68]

In general, then, there has been a new emphasis on an attempt to stimulate authors to produce works that are revolutionary in content: one aspect of this effort has been the nomination of more militant juries for the various literary contests; another aspect has been the thematic manipulation of the contests. For example, Haydeé Santamaría announced during the ceremonies in which the 1969 juries were installed that future juries would favor Latin Americans residing in their own countries instead of Latin Americans residing in Europe.[69] The 1969 David Award, established by UNEAC for unpublished writers, had markedly militant juries, mostly composed of party members: Portuondo, Guillén, Félix Pita Rodríguez, César Leante, Luis Marré and Raúl Luis. The short-story prize was awarded in 1969 to Hugo Chinea, also a member of the party.[70]

Perhaps it is not accidental that in the 1969 *Casa de las Américas* contest, none of the awards went to Cubans. Two of the chosen works dealt specifically with the guerrilla experience: *Los fundadores del alba,* a novel by Bolivian writer Renato Prada Oropeza, and *Perú 1965: una experiencia guerrillera,* an essay by the then jailed Peruvian guerrilla leader Héctor Béjar Rivera. Furthermore, the 1970 *Casa de las Américas* contests added a new category, "Testimony," restricted to books offering firsthand documentation of the present Latin American reality.[71] One of the objectives of the revolutionary armed forces contests is to stimulate the production of "works useful to the effort of constructing socialism in our country."[72] As another example of this trend, Nicolás Guillén, in a speech given during the 1969 David Award ceremonies, announced that the 1970 award "will be limited to works on a single theme . . . all the works must deal with the decisive effort of our country, of all of us, in the agricultural tasks."[73]

This new policy of revolutionary vigilance became even more evident when the director of *Casa de las Américas* withdrew an invitation to Nicanor Parra, a Chilean socialist poet, to be a juror of the 1970 *Casa de las Américas* contest because he had attended a reception at the White House.[74] Haydeé Santamaría, during the ceremonies in which the literary contest juries were installed, said: "This year we will be able to say that the awards have grown much greater and much more revolutionary, because there are only two roads open to us: the revolutionary and the non-revolutionary one. . . . *Casa de las Américas* has the right and the duty to make the awards more revolutionary."[75] Practically all 1970 awards were granted to authors of "revolutionary" works, for example, the Uruguayans María Ester Gilio, for *La guerrilla tupamara,* and Carlos María Gutiérrez, for *Diario del cuartel* (both writing on the guerrilla in their country); and the Cubans Miguel Cossío, for *Sacchario* (a novel on the Revolution and the sugar crop) and Víctor Casaús, for *Girón en la memoria* (on the Bay of Pigs invasion).[76]

During 1971, the above-mentioned trends seem to have become stronger, and the overall cultural policy of the Revolution has hardened even further. On March 20, 1971, Heberto Padilla, whose various difficulties since 1967 have been discussed above, was jailed, to be released thirty-seven days later. Before his release, Padilla signed a long statement of self-criticism which he personally delivered at a meeting of the UNEAC, where he exhorted other writers present (among them Pablo A. Fernández, César López, Manuel Díaz Martínez, and Padilla's wife, Belkis Cuza) to follow his example. This new "Padilla affair" provoked a strong international reaction. A large group of European and Latin American intellectuals (among them, Jean-Paul Sartre, Hans-Magnus Enzensberger, Gabriel García Márquez, Octavio Paz, Carlos Fuentes, and Mario Vargas Llosa) addressed a letter to Fidel Castro on April 9, 1971, expressing concern about Padilla's imprisonment. A second letter, dated May 20, protested Padilla's confession, pointing out the similarity of these proceedings with the worst moments of the Stalinist era.[77]

The Declaration of the First National Congress on Education and Culture and Castro's speech during the closing session of the Congress on April 30, 1971, further emphasized the new hard line on cultural affairs: (a) the primacy of political and ideological factors in staffing universities, mass media, and artistic institutions, (b) the barring of homosexuals from these institutions, (c) tighter controls on literary contests to assure that judges, authors, and topics are truly revolutionary, (d) more control on subjects of publication, giving higher priority to textbooks than to literary works, (e) the elimination of foreign tendencies in cultural affairs in order to wipe out "cultural imperialism," and (f) a violent attack against the "pseudoleftist bourgeois intellectuals" from abroad who had dared to criticize the Revolution on the Padilla issue.[78]

Conclusions

Three generations of Cuban writers are active in literature with varying degrees of output and influence. The prerevolutionary generation, which became well known in the 1940s, is represented mainly by the *Orígenes* and *Nuestro Tiempo* groups, plus a number of less influential groups and independent writers. This generation has possibly produced the finest literary work, but seems to be declining in terms of output and influence. The first generation of the Revolution constitutes a generational transition; its members began to work (and a few of them to publish) in the 1950s, but came to maturity and became known after the revolutionary take-over. This is the most influential group (at least in 1959–1970), although the group has split apart, with some of its members choosing exile. The second generation of the Revolution is composed of young writers born in the 1940s who began to publish mainly in the second half of the 1960s, challenging the dominant first generation. They have been involved in several literary-political controversies and the volume and quality of their literary work is rapidly increasing.

The predominant literary genre in prerevolutionary Cuba was poetry, followed by the short story and the novel. Under the Revolution, an opposite trend can be observed: the largest increase of literary output has taken the form of the novel, followed by the short story, whereas poetry is just maintaining (or perhaps slightly increasing) the prerevolutionary volume. Thematically, literature has not reflected much of an interest in the revolutionary process itself, but rather in criticizing the prerevolutionary society (with some simplistic views), in glorifying the insurrectional struggle, or in using escapist fictional themes. A few short stories and novels, but mainly poems, have reflected a concern for current problems and conflicts or have appraised revolutionary changes. Many of these works tend to be propagandistic in nature and of poor literary quality.

The Revolution has substantially increased publishing facilities, both for books and magazines, has established well-funded and prestigious contests, and has subsidized most writers. On the other hand, the abolition of royalties, the nationalization of publishing houses and newspapers, the abolition of some journals, the organization of UNEAC under government auspices, and the integration of all publishing activities into the state agency Instituto del Libro have made the writer totally dependent on the state. The state has used this power to manipulate the writers by granting or withholding publication, using (temporarily) labor camps against some of them, hiring and dismissing them from state jobs, and pressuring them by criticism and appraisal through communications media. This process has not been exempt from tension and conflict, as the several controversies and polemics among the writers testify. In 1961, the official policy of the government vis-à-vis the writers was defined by Castro, and until 1968 there was relative tolerance toward those who accepted the Revolution.

To stimulate the creation of literature concerned with the problems of a revolutionary society, the state has exerted pressure through various channels (e.g., granting of awards, exhortations). In spite of these efforts, until the turn of the 1960s the content of literary work had failed to become markedly militant.

As the first decade of the Revolution came to an end, there was evidence of a strict tightening of controls, an emphasis not only on revolutionary loyalty, but also on revolutionary themes and concerns, and a concerted attempt to direct intellectual life toward a greater militancy.

NOTES

1. Ivan A. Schulman and Manuel Pedro González, *Martí: Darío y el modernismo* (Madrid, 1969).
2. Anthologies of prerevolutionary poetry include *Arpas cubanas* (La Habana, 1904); José María Chacón y Calvo, *Las cien mejores poesías cubanas* (Madrid, 1922); José A. Fernández de Castro and Félix Lizaso, *La poesía moderna en Cuba (1882–1925)* (Madrid, 1926); Juan Ramón Jiménez, José M. Chacón y Calvo, and Camila Henríquez Ureña, *La poesía cubana en 1936* (La Habana, 1937); Rafael Esténger, *Cien de las mejores poesías cubanas* (La Habana, 1948); Cintio Vitier, *Cincuenta años de poesía cubana: 1902–1952* (La Habana, 1952); and José Lezama Lima, *Antología de la poesía cubana,* 3 vols. (La Habana, 1965). Critical works include Cintio Vitier, *Lo cubano en la poesía* (La Habana, 1958); and Otto Olivera, *Cuba en su poesía* (Mexico, 1965).
3. The interested reader should consult Max Henríquez Ureña, *Panorama histórico de la literatura cubana: 1492–1952,* 2 vols. (Puerto Rico, 1963).
4. The *Orígenes* group includes José Lezama Lima (b. 1910), Angel Gaztelu (b. 1914), Justo Rodríguez Santos (b. 1915), Virgilio Piñera (b. 1912), Gastón Baquero (b. 1916), Cintio Vitier (b. 1921), Eliseo Diego (b. 1920), Octavio Smith (b. 1921), Lorenzo García Vega (b. 1926), and Fina García Marruz (b. 1923). See Cintio Vitier, *Diez poetas cubanos, 1938–1947* (La Habana, 1948).
5. Roberto Fernández Retamar, *La poesía contemporánea en Cuba: 1927–1953* (La Habana, 1954); and Raimundo Lazo *Historia de la literatura cubana* (La Habana, 1967), pp. 220–21.
6. Roberto Fernández Retamar, *La poesía contemporánea,* quoted by Max Henríquez Ureña, *Panorama histórico,* vol. 2, pp. 431–32.
7. Truly "popular" poetry in Cuba before 1959 was a world apart from the work of "serious" poets, whether by the *Orígenes* group or others. Its main representatives include José Angel Buesa (b. 1910) with his unabashed sentimentalism; Jesús Orta, known as Indio Naborí (b. 1923), who followed the traditional forms of Cuban *guajiro* ("peasant") poetry; and a number of popular interpreters, adaptors, and imitators of Cuban negroid poets, as Luis Carbonell.
8. Ambrosio Fornet, *Antología del cuento cubano contemporáneo* (Mexico, 1967), p. 40.
9. For example, Manuel Navarro Luna (1894–1966), Regino Pedroso (b. 1897), and Félix Pita Rodríguez (b. 1909).
10. Such as Eugenio Florit (b. 1903), Oscar Hurtado (b. 1919), and Rafaela Chacón Nardi (b. 1926).
11. Anthologies and samples of postrevolutionary poetry besides Lezama Lima's

(see n. 2) include Fajad Jamis and Fernández Retamar, *Poesía joven de Cuba* (Lima–La Habana, 1959); Heberto Padilla and Luis Suardíaz, *Cuban Poetry: 1959–1966* (La Habana, 1967); *El Corno Emplumado* (July 1967); Nathaniel Tarn, *Con Cuba* (New York, 1969); *Tri-Quarterly*, (Fall/Winter, 1968–1969); José Agustín Goytisolo, *Nueva poesía cubana* (Barcelona, 1970); Félix Grande, "Selección de poesía cubana," *Cuadernos Hispanoamericanos,* (August–September 1968), pp. 375–410; *El Corno Emplumado,* (October 1968), pp. 8–32; and Francisco Fernández Santos and José Martínez, eds., *Cuba: una revolución en marcha* (Paris, 1967), pp. 368–400.

12. Nicolás Guillén has published *Tengo* (La Habana, 1964) and *El gran zoo* (La Habana, 1967). The first is of very poor quality and very politicized, but in the second his poetry returns to its highest levels. See also Manuel Navarro Luna, *Obra poética* (La Habana, 1963), and Félix Pita Rodríguez, *Las crónicas: poesía bajo consigna* (La Habana, 1960).

13. See José Lezama Lima, *Dador* (La Habana, 1960); Armando Alvarez Bravo, *Orbita de Lezama Lima* (La Habana, 1966); Eliseo Diego, *El oscuro esplendor* (La Habana, 1966) and *Muestrario del mundo o Libro de las maravillas de Bolona* (La Habana, 1968); and Cintio Vitier, *Testimonios* (La Habana, 1968).

14. Lorenzo García Vega, "Tres poemas," *Exilio,* 3 (Summer 1969), pp. 14–16; and Gastón Baquero, *Poemas escritos en España* (Madrid, 1960) and *Memorial de un testigo* (Madrid, 1966).

15. Florit has continued to publish in exile, but the most prolific of this group is Oscar Hurtado who remains in Cuba. He is the author of one original and surprising good work: *La ciudad muerta de Korad* (La Habana, 1964).

16. Feijóo has published over a dozen books since 1959, mostly on folklore and literary criticism, and also a novel (see n. 39). Alcides Iznaga has published two volumes of poetry: *Patria imperecedera* (La Habana, 1959) and *La roca y la espuma* (La Habana, 1965), and in 1969 won UNEAC's novel prize for *Las cercas caminaban.*

17. Already a respected poet during the fifties (*Elegía como un himno* [La Habana, 1950]; *Patrias* [La Habana, 1952]; *Alabanzas, conversaciones* [Mexico, 1955]), Fernández Retamar has published several books of poems since 1959: *Vuelta de la antigua esperanza* (La Habana, 1959); *Con las mismas manos* (La Habana, 1962); *Historia antigua* (La Habana, 1965); *Poesía reunida* (La Habana, 1966); *Buena suerte viviendo* (Mexico, 1967); and *Algo semejante a los monstruos antediluvianos* (Barcelona, 1970), besides several books of essays and literary criticism. Since 1961, he has been director of the influential *Casa de las Américas* magazine, and has written a serious essay analyzing the evolution of literature under the Revolution: "Hacia una intelectualidad revolucionaria en Cuba," in *Ensayo de otro mundo* (La Habana, 1967), pp. 159–88.

18. Padilla's early book, *El justo tiempo humano* (La Habana, 1962), is remarkable because of its polished quality and the economy of its poetic language. His recent book, *Fuera del juego* (La Habana, 1969), received UNEAC's poetry prize in 1968 and was the center of a heated controversy (for details, see the section, "The Role of the Writer").

19. Other important poets include Rafael Alcides, Armando Alvarez Bravo, Antón Arrufat, Roberto Branly, Manuel Díaz Martínez, Luis Marré, and Luis Suardíaz. See César López, "En torno a la poesía cubana actual," *Unión,* 6 (December 1967), p. 191.

20. Marcelo Ravoni and Antonio Porta, *Poeti ispanoamericani contemporanei* (Milano, 1970).

21. See José Mario, "Novísima poesía cubana," *Mundo Nuevo* (August 1969), pp. 63–69; and Víctor Casaús, "La más joven poesía: seis comentarios y un prólogo," *Unión*, 6 (July–September 1967), pp. 5–15.

22. See Casaús, "La más joven poesía," p. 10; and José Mario, "Allen Ginsberg en La Habana," *Mundo Nuevo* (April 1969), pp. 48–54.

23. See Mercedes Cortázar and Isaac Goldenberg, "La joven poesía latinoamericana en Nueva York," *Mundo Nuevo* (April 1969), pp. 55–58.

24. Miguel Barnet, author of two books of poetry—*La piedrafina y el pavorreal* (La Habana, 1963) and *La sagrada familia* (La Habana, 1967)—has become known abroad with his *Biografía de un cimarrón* (La Habana, 1966), an ethnographic story, published in the United States as *The Autobiography of a Runaway Slave* (New York, 1968).

25. Casaús, "La más joven poesía," p. 11; Mario, "Novísima poesía cubana," p. 69; and López, "En torno a la poesía," pp. 195–98.

26. Anthologies of short stories covering the prerevolutionary period include Federico de Ibarzábal, *Cuentos contemporáneos* (La Habana, 1937); Manuel Pedro González and Margaret S. Husson, *Cuban Short Stories* (New York, 1942); Emma Pérez Telles, *Cuentos cubanos: antología* (La Habana, 1945); José A. Portuondo, *Cuentos cubanos contemporáneos* (Mexico, 1946); and Salvador Bueno, *Antología del cuento en Cuba: 1902–1952* (La Habana, 1953).

27. See Max Henríquez Ureña, *Panorama histórico*, vol. 2, pp. 405, 413–14; and Bueno, *Antología del cuento*, p. 13.

28. Antón Arrufat and Fausto Masó, *Nuevos cuentistas cubanos* (La Habana, 1961); UNEAC, *Nuevos cuentos cubanos* (La Habana, 1964); Oscar Hurtado, *Cuentos de ciencia-ficción: Cabada, Herrero, Martí* (La Habana, 1964); José Rodríguez Feo, *Cuentos: antología* (La Habana, 1967); *Aquí, once cubanos cuentan* (Montevideo, 1967); J. M. Cohen, *Writers in the New Cuba* (Baltimore, 1967); Ambrosio Fornet, *Antología del cuento cubano contemporáneo* (Mexico, 1967); José M. Caballero Bonald, *Narrativa cubana de la revolución* (Madrid, 1968); Rogelio Llópis, *Cuentos cubanos de lo fantástico y lo extraordinario* (La Habana, 1968); José Miguel Oviedo, *Antología del cuento cubano* (Lima, 1968); and Rodolfo Walsh, *Crónicas de Cuba* (Buenos Aires, 1969).

29. Federico Alvarez, "Literatura y Revolución," *Casa de las Américas* (November 1968–January 1969), p. 187. For a bibliography of short stories in 1959–1969, see Seymour Menton, *La novela y el cuento de la revolución cubana, 1959–1969: bibliografía* (Cuernavaca, Mexico, 1969).

30. See José Rodríguez Feo, "Breve recuento de la narrativa cubana," *Unión*, 6 (December 1967), p. 131.

31. Cabrera Infante, *Así en la paz como en la guerra* (La Habana, 1960); Calvert Casey, *El regreso* (La Habana, 1963); Onelio Jorge Cardoso, *Cuentos completos* (La Habana, 1964); Humberto Arenal, *El tiempo ha descendido* (La Habana, 1964), and *La vuelta en redondo* (La Habana, 1962).

32. Rogelio Llopis, *El fabulista* (La Habana, 1963); Antonio Benítez, *Tute de Reyes* (La Habana, 1967); José Lorenzo Fuentes, *Después de la gaviota* (La Habana, 1968); Ana María Simo, *Las fábulas* (La Habana, 1962). On black humor, see Evora Tamayo, *Cuentos para abuelas enfermas* (La Habana, 1964); and Angela Martínez, *Memorias de un decapitado* (La Habana, 1965).

33. Jesús Díaz, *Los años duros* (La Habana, 1966); and Norberto Fuentes, *Condenados de Condado* (La Habana, 1968).

34. See "Aquí me pongo" in Edmundo Desnoes, *Punto de vista* (La Habana, 1967), pp. 109–25.

35. Labrador Ruiz, *La sangre hambrienta* (La Habana, 1950); Lorenzo García Vega, *Espirales del Cuje* (La Habana, 1951); Piñera, *La carne de René* (La Habana, 1952); Surama Ferrer, *Romelia Vargas* (La Habana, 1952); Alejo Carpentier, *Los pasos perdidos* (Mexico, 1953) and *El acoso* (Buenos Aires, 1956); Alcides Iznaga, *Los valedontes* (La Habana, 1953); Rafael Esténger, *El pulpo de oro* (Mexico, 1954); Novás Calvo, *Pedro Blanco: el negrero* (Buenos Aires, 1955); Enrique Serpa, *La trampa* (Buenos Aires, 1956); and Gregorio Ortega, *Una de cal y otra de arena* (La Habana, 1957).

36. Bibliographies of the Cuban novel in 1959–1969, besides that of Menton, include Rosa M. Abella, "Bibliografía de la novela publicada en Cuba y en el extranjero por cubanos, desde 1959 hasta 1965," *Revista Iberoamericana,* 30 (July–December 1966), pp. 307–11; and Lourdes Casal, "The Cuban Novel, 1959–1969: An Annotated Bibliography," *Abraxas,* 1 (Fall 1970), pp. 77–92. Critical reviews include Seymour Menton, "La novela de la revolución en Cuba," *Cuadernos Americanos,* 23 (January–February 1964), pp. 231–41; Rosa M. Abella, "Five Years of the Cuban Novel," *The Carrell,* 7 (June 1966), pp. 17–21; Salvador Bueno, "La nueva (y actual) novela cubana," in *Cuba una revolución en marcha,* pp. 401–07, and "Cuba hoy: novela," *Insula,* 23 (July–August 1968), p. 1; and José Rodríguez Feo, "Breve recuento de la narrativa cubana," *Unión,* 11 (December 1967), pp. 131–36.

37. Edmundo Desnoes, *No hay problema* (La Habana, 1961), *El cataclismo* (La Habana, 1965), and *Memorias del subdesarrollo* (La Habana, 1965); Lisandro Otero, *La situación* (La Habana, 1963), and *Pasión de Urbino* (La Habana, 1967); Severo Sarduy, *Gestos* (Barcelona, 1963); Arenal, *Los animales sagrados* (La Habana, 1967); Cabrera Infante, *Tres tristes tigres* (Barcelona, 1967); and Pablo A. Fernández, *Los niños se despiden* (La Habana, 1968).

38. The best novel of all produced by this group is Alejo Carpentier's *El siglo de las luces* (Mexico, 1962).

39. José Lezama Lima, *Paradiso* (La Habana, 1966); and Samuel Feijóo, *Juan Quinquín en Pueblo Mocho* (Santa Clara, 1964).

40. Luis Agüero, *La vida en dos* (La Habana, 1967); Reynaldo Arenas, *Celestino antes del alba* (La Habana, 1967), and *El mundo alucinante: una novela de aventuras* (Mexico, 1969); Jaime Sarusky, *Rebelión en la octava casa* (La Habana, 1967); Reynaldo González, *Siempre la muerte, su paso breve* (La Habana, 1968); Noel Navarro, *El plano inclinado* (La Habana, 1968); Francisco Chofre, *La Odilea* (La Habana, 1969); and Miguel Barnet, *Canción de Rachel* (La Habana, 1969).

41. Examples of this kind of literature are José Soler Puig, *En el año de enero* (La Habana, 1963), and *El derrumbe* (La Habana, 1964); Daura Olema García, *Maestra voluntaria* (La Habana, 1962); and David Buzzi, *Los desnudos* (La Habana, 1967). Although Edmundo Desnoes's *El cataclismo* must be included in this group, his *Memorias del subdesarrollo* is possibly the only exception of a "revolutionary" novel of high quality. The latter has been published in the United States as *Inconsolable Memories* (New York, 1967).

42. An example of these defects is Juan Arcocha's early work, *Los muertos andan solos* (La Habana, 1962). The only attempt at a proletarian novel, Abelardo Piñeiro's *El descanso* (La Habana, 1962), also fails because of the unidimensionality of its characters and its naïve Manicheism.

43. See Reynaldo Arenas, "Celestino y yo," *Unión,* 6 (July–September 1967), pp. 117–22.

44. José A. Portuondo, "José Soler Puig y la novela de la revolución cubana," *Crítica de la época y otros ensayos* (Las Villas, 1965), p. 201.

45. Leopoldo Avila, "Sobre algunas corrientes de la crítica y la literatura en Cuba,"

Verde Olivo (November 24, 1968), pp. 14–18. Translated as "Concerning Some Currents in Cuban Criticism and Literature," in *Granma Weekly Review,* November 24, 1968, p. 11.

46. José A. Arcocha, "Dicotomías: Lezama Lima y Cabrera Infante," *Aportes* (January 1969), pp. 59–65, trans. by this author. Other testimonies concerning the publishing situation in prerevolutionary Cuba can be found in Manuel Maldonado-Denis, "Documentos de un viaje a Cuba en 1967," *Caribbean Studies,* 7 (January 1968), p. 20; and Piñera, *Cuentos* (La Habana, 1964), p. 7.

47. *Cuba* (July 1969), p. 9. For American views of the Cuban publishing scene see Andre Schiffrin, "Publishing in Cuba," *New York Times Book Review,* March 17, 1968, pp. 40–42, 44–45; and "Report from Cuba," *Library Journal,* 93 (May 1, 1968), pp. 1865–67.

48. See *Insula,* 23 (July–August 1968); *Les Lettres Nouvelles* (December 1967–January 1968); *Imagen,* no. 4 (July 1967), no. 20 (March 1968), no. 32 (September 1968); *El Corno Emplumado,* no. 23 (July 1967); *Tri-Quarterly,* no. 28 (October 1968).

49. Fausto Masó's novel *La sangre de los buenos* received a mention in the *Casa de las Américas* contest. It was never published because he left the country. Other examples of withholding of publication among authors still in Cuba include the delayed publication of Rafael Alcides, *Contracastro;* and Reynaldo Arenas, *El mundo alucinante.* See Claude Couffon, "Reinaldo Arenas," *Le Monde* (supplement), March 22, 1969.

50. For example, Heberto Padilla lost his job with *Granma* after his involvement in the 1968 controversy with Lisandro Otero in *El Caimán Barbudo.* His planned trip to Italy was also cancelled.

51. See Mario, "Allen Ginsberg."

52. See as examples of this attitude Bueno's articles (see n. 36) which mention only the positive achievements with no reference to the controversies or conflicts; Margaret Randall, "A Poet Looks at Cuba Eight Years After the Triumph of the Revolution," *Ikon,* 1 (July 1968), pp. 5–10; and Filiberto Díaz, "Cuba y su literatura," *Mundo Nuevo* (September–October 1969), pp. 83–86.

53. Examples are Carlos Ripoll, "Coacción y creación en la literatura cubana actual," *Zona Franca,* 5 (October 1968), pp. 38–41; Masó, "Literatura y revolución en Cuba," *Mundo Nuevo* (February 1969), pp. 50–54; and Federico Hasse (pseudonym), "Filiberto o el último compilador," *Mundo Nuevo* (April 1970), pp. 63–74.

54. Maldonado-Denis, "Documentos de un viaje," p. 17, trans. by this author.

55. For more realistic, although still strongly partisan, appraisals of revolutionary Cuban literature and the situation of the writer, see Mario Benedetti, "Situación actual de la cultura cubana," in *Cuaderno cubano* (Montevideo, 1969), pp. 80–112; and José Mario, "La narrativa cubana de la Revolución," *Mundo Nuevo* (November 1969), pp. 75–79.

56. A lucid account of this crisis is given by K. S. Karol, *Les Guerrilleros au pouvoir* (Paris, 1970), pp. 237–44.

57. Fidel Castro, *Palabras a los intelectuales* (La Habana, 1961).

58. See Lisandro Otero, "El escritor en la Revolución cubana," *Casa de las Américas,* 6 (May–August 1966), reproduced in Francisco Fernández Santos and José Martínez, eds., *Cuba: una revolución,* pp. 299–308; also see Ambrosio Fornet, "La crítica literaria, aquí y ahora," in *En tres y dos* (La Habana, 1964), pp. 13–34.

59. Ernesto Guevara, "El socialismo y el hombre en Cuba," in *Obra Revolucionaria* (Mexico, 1967), p. 636.

60. For a view from abroad, see *Times Literary Supplement,* July 11, 1968, p. 735, and August 22, 1968, p. 903.

61. Tomás Martínez, "América: los novelistas exiliados," *Primera Plana* (July 30–August 5, 1968), pp. 40–50.

62. See Heberto Padilla, "Respuesta a Cabrera Infante," *Primera Plana* (December 24–30, 1968), pp. 88–89; Cabrera Infante, "La confundida lengua del poeta," ibid. (January 14–20, 1969), pp. 64–65.

63. Leopoldo Avila, "Las respuestas de Caín," *Verde Olivo* (November 3, 1968), pp. 17–18; "Las provocaciones de Padilla," ibid. (November 10, 1968), pp. 17–18; "Antón se va a la guerra," ibid. (November 17, 1968), pp. 16–18; "Sobre algunas corrientes de la crítica y la literatura en Cuba," ibid. (November 24, 1968), pp. 14–18; and "El pueblo es el forjador, defensor y sostén de la cultura," ibid. (December 3, 1968), pp. 16–17.

64. See I. S., "Cuba: ¿Fin de una tregua?," *Mundo Nuevo* (February 1969), pp. 80–84; *Times Literary Supplement* (January 5, 1969), p. 464. For comprehensive summaries of the controversy, see *Carte Segrete* (April–June 1969), pp. 230–39; and Gabriel Coulthard, "Cuban Literature and Politics," *Caribbean Monthly Bulletin,* 6 (March 1969), pp. 5–8.

65. *Granma Weekly Review,* October 27, 1968, p. 8.

66. For the composition of the juries, comments on the prizes, etc., see *Cuba International,* 2 (February 1970), pp. 36–39.

67. Nicolás Guillén, "Speech delivered at the awarding of prizes to winners of the Annual Literature Contest," *Granma Weekly Review,* December 7, 1969, p. 9.

68. *Bohemia,* supplement, October 3, 1969, p. 9, trans. by this author.

69. Ibid., January 24, 1969, pp. 44–49.

70. Ibid., August 1, 1969, p. 54.

71. *Granma Weekly Review,* March 8, 1970, p. 11.

72. *Bohemia,* August 8, 1969, p. 62.

73. Ibid., August 1, 1969, p. 54.

74. Radio Habana-Cuba broadcast, May 13 and 28, 1970, and *Granma,* June 13, 1970.

75. *Granma Weekly Review,* July 5, 1970, p. 4.

76. *Granma Weekly Review,* July 26, 1970, p. 1.

77. Padilla's statement of self-criticism was released by the Cuban press agency, *Prensa Latina,* in Paris. Excerpts were published in *Le Monde,* April 29, 1971. The texts of the intellectuals' letters were published in *Le Monde,* April 9 and May 20, 1971. For more details see Marcel Niedergang, "Le poète Heberto Padilla à été libéré a La Havane," and Juan Arcocha, "Le poète et le commissaire," *Le Monde,* April 29, 1971, p. 2; and José Yglesias, "A Cuban Poet in Trouble," *New York Review of Books,* June 3, 1971, pp. 3–8.

78. See *Granma Weekly Review,* May 9, 1971. Practically the whole issue is devoted to the Congress.

17 José A. Moreno

From Traditional to Modern Values

IT is quite apparent that prerevolutionary Cuba was highly misdeveloped or unevenly developed, although the country in some ways had attained a certain degree of relative development.[1] Some geographical areas, some business and industrial sectors, and some population groups were highly developed and could easily compete in modernity with their counterparts in other parts of the world. The country as a whole, however, with its economy dependent on one agricultural product, subject to the fluctuations of the world market, and furnishing a large sector of the labor force with only seasonal employment, resembled in its social structure and political governance social conditions found only in underdeveloped countries. As in other countries of the third world, so-called pockets of modernity could be found in Cuba within the overall framework of a traditional society. Such pockets of modernity were not, however, acting as catalysts of modernization upon the whole society with the speed and thoroughness that was desired. On the contrary, the ever-widening gap between the modern and the traditional sectors could lead one to believe that the goals and progress of the former were alien, if not in conflict with those of the latter.

The level of development of the economic and social structure was supported by and, in turn, helped to produce a set of social values, the goal of which was to maintain the coexistence of the traditional and modern structures. Central to such a matrix of values was a hierarchical conception of society and a deep feeling of individualism. A firm belief that each man occupied a position in society according to a set of characteristics that were often beyond his control seemed to justify the lack of mobility in a system in which opportunities were unevenly distributed. On the other hand, emphasis on the worth and rights of the individual above and beyond those of

471

the collectivity helped set the stage for those in privileged positions to take the leading roles for themselves to the exclusion of others. In such circumstances, individuals, groups, or classes, not the whole of society, became the recipients of whatever benefits were brought about by the process of development. The value system of the society sought to justify and perpetuate this state of affairs.

With the advent of the Revolution in 1959, the whole Cuban society was suddenly faced with a fundamental overhaul not only of its economic and political structure, but also of its social organization and cultural values. For many people who fought against Batista, particularly the middle class, the Revolution was over as soon as the dictator was overthrown, and some changes in the political structure were introduced. These were the people who cried that their revolution had been betrayed when Fidel Castro began to implement changes, such as the agrarian reform or the laws reducing rents and telephone rates by 50 percent.[2] The first reforms, revolutionary as they seemed, were not as radical as sometimes depicted.[3] Castro, however, made it clear from the beginning that for a revolutionary process as deep as the one Cuba had started, it was not possible to stop halfway, and that a compromise between the past and the present was not possible.[4]

The past, with which the Revolution could not compromise, was characterized by a traditional society with from 16 percent to 27 percent of the total labor force either unemployed or underemployed, dependence on foreign capital and markets, landless peasants, institutionalized political corruption and patronage, *latifundia* and foreign monopolies, and an institutionalized system of alternative democracy and dictatorship that was functional to the interest of particular groups of the population, often at the expense of the majority.[5] The present (or, to be exact, the future) envisaged by Castro was a society in which the injustices, prejudices and selfishness of the past would be substituted by equality and unselfish dedication to the community. These goals would be achieved only after the Revolution could secure work, bread, health, and education for every citizen.[6] To reach this stage, however, the Revolution had to overcome many obstacles, undergo the opposition of many, impose painful sacrifices on its own followers, and be ready to pay the high costs of development and modernization.

The goals of modernity and an egalitarian society were present in Castro's mind since 1953 when he attacked the Moncada barracks (this was the action that started the July 26 movement), although more as a utopia than as a concrete reality. The means to attain such goals or the path the Revolution should follow to achieve them were not clear at the start. Through a painful process of trial and error, the means were found and the route to modernity was delineated.[7] That route was socialism. However, it was only in his May Day speech of 1961, after the victory of Playa Girón, that Castro proclaimed that the Revolution had chosen the socialist path. In that speech he made it clear that the petit bourgeois constitution of 1940 was no longer appropriate to the needs of Cuban society and that a new socialist constitution would be promulgated that would not sanction the domination of man by man or the exploitation of one class by another.[8]

The new constitution is still to be drafted.[9] That the revolutionary government has not enacted a socialist constitution in over ten years is somewhat unique in the socialist world. The reason may be that the Cuban leaders have been engaged all this time (particularly since 1965) in the creation of a "New Man" and a "New Society." Ernesto (Che) Guevara has said that the New Man is to be brought about not purely by producing changes in his patterns of behavior or by the passive acceptance and compliance with laws and regulations alien to himself, but by the creation in man of a new set of values and attitudes that will dictate norms to regulate his actions in society. Unless such values and attitudes are created in a sizeable majority of the population, the New Society could not come into being. Until then, he said that it will be the task of the leaders to function as catalysts in the midst of the masses who still operate under the influence of the old value system.[10]

Of the matrix of values that will have to exist in a full socialist society, the Cuban leaders chose equalitarianism (in opposition to elitism and hierarchical stratification) and unselfish dedication to the community (a collectivistic orientation versus individualism) as the cornerstones to be used in building the New Man.[11] In a speech made early in 1959, Castro pointed out that the first rights of man were the right to live by his own labors, the right to have bread for his children, and the right to have his own culture. In the same speech, he also said, "We have dreamed, and continue to dream, of a Revolution where a majority of the people overrule a minority of egotists, status seekers and all those unadaptable to the revolutionary reality of the country."[12] Nine years later, after launching the Revolution in the path of socialism, when Cubans were fully engaged in the difficult task of exercising their right to create their own culture, after pointing out that illiteracy had been eliminated, that every young person had the opportunity to study, that everybody had the opportunity to work, and to have decent housing and good health, Fidel Castro was able to say:

> We cannot encourage or even permit selfish attitudes among men if we don't want man to be guided by the instinct of selfishness, of individuality. . . . The concept of socialism and communism, the concept of a higher society, implies a man devoid of those feelings; a man who has overcome such instincts at any cost;

placing, above everything, his sense of solidarity and brother-
hood among men.[13]

Whereas in 1959, the values of equalitarianism and unselfishness were
as a dream (even in the minds of the top leaders), in 1968, such values
were concrete guidelines that clearly indicated to the leaders and the masses
at large the path they had to follow in building the New Society. It is impossible at this point to attempt to measure the degree to which various
sectors of the population have internalized such values. Apart from the
fact that no such sociological study has been conducted, it is clear that any
findings at such an early stage could only be tentative, since ten years is indeed a short period of time for such a complex process as value changes in
an overall society to take place.[14]

Therefore, the purpose of this chapter is only to explore various areas
of social interaction that will help us to detect whether or not these value
changes have been introduced. This may allow us to suggest that greater
equalitarianism and a collectivistic orientation are more likely to exist now
than before the Revolution. Even though the depth and breadth of such
changes cannot be indicated, the mere presence of such qualitative changes
would be an indication that a breakthrough has taken place and that the
value system under construction is more conducive to modernization than
the former system.[15]

Equalitarianism Versus Hierarchical Elitism

Although, in principle, prerevolutionary Cuban society was open and all
citizens were equal before the law, in practice, many inequalities existed
that were prejudicial to some groups of the population. Such an institutionalized system of inequalities was not sanctioned by the constitution. The
social system, however, by emphasizing certain things, by granting certain
privileges, by advocating certain principles, and imposing certain restrictions, clearly favored some groups and handicapped others. Such discriminatory practices, institutionalized as they were in the system, had been
reinforced by a set of elitist values advocated by the upper groups as the
values of the society. At the root of the elitist orientation is the belief that
men have different abilities and, consequently, that society will have to be
stratified either through a caste system or through a system of initiative
and competition.[16] Elitism in Cuba had produced a semicompetitive, stratified society in which certain individuals or groups of individuals entered
the so-called arena of competition with all the characteristics of those who
are predetermined to be the winners.

In the next paragraphs, an attempt will be made to show how, with the advent of the Revolution, hierarchical elitism has been superseded as a social value by equalitarianism. As values are not tangible, concrete realities, but are inferred from actions, choices, and behavioral patterns, the most we can do at this point is to compare actions, choices, and behavioral patterns of prerevolutionary Cuba with those introduced during the Revolution. Certain areas of study have been selected here in which the contrast between the past and the present seems to be greatest. The past represented a traditional, capitalist society based on hierarchical elitism, which was functional to those at the top or to the so-called modernizing entrepreneurial elite, but dysfunctional to the total society. The present represents a socialist society founded on equalitarianism, which purports to serve the interest of all people in an equal way, although it might turn out to be dysfunctional to some groups or individuals of that society.

Poor Versus Rich

It would be platitudinous to say that the rich enjoyed all kinds of privileges in prerevolutionary Cuba or that they lost them with the Revolution. However, it is fair to say that, as in most underdeveloped countries, elitism in Cuba gave the rich all the advantages of participation in the competitive arena of capitalism, that it modified and adjusted the system to serve the purposes of the rich, and that the system was quite conducive to allowing their mistakes in economic, political, and moral matters to be forgotten and even condoned. The rich were at the top of the social pyramid and they ran the government or had it run for them. They initiated economic and political actions and were the main beneficiaries of such actions.

On the other hand it, perhaps, is not platitudinous to say that the poor in Cuba were truly dispossessed. By poor is meant that large percentage of the total population made up of peasants, the underemployed, and the unemployed city and slum dwellers. It is not the purpose of this paper to furnish statistical data. Thus, it is sufficient to mention that this group included the permanent unemployed and underemployed and the illiterate, and those with no social security or health compensation. Also, those who were not culturally and politically integrated into, but who were economically alienated from, the rest of society could be included in this group. The most salient characteristics of the poor were their powerlessness and their lack of participation in economic, political, and cultural matters. The only relationship that existed between the poor and the rich were those of a hierarchical subordination of the former to the latter.

With the advent of the Revolution, a clear policy of equalization was established. From the signing of the first Agrarian Reform Law on May 17, 1959, to the launching of the Revolutionary Offensive on March 13, 1968, a series of laws and policies were formulated and implemented to curb the privileges of the rich and to allow the poor to enjoy a larger share of social and economic rewards. Other chapters in this book describe in detail some of the equalizing effects of the revolutionary measures. By 1962 Castro claimed that rural unemployment had been eliminated, that illiteracy had been eradicated, and that all Cubans had been freed from exploitation and from social inequality.[17]

There is little doubt that full employment in Cuba brought some kind of income security that not all Cubans enjoyed before the Revolution. Wage scales were devised to close the gap of income differentials between various kinds of occupations.[18] However, in a speech made in 1968 Castro conceded that in Cuba there were still many inequalities of income, some of them quite considerable, but that the Revolution could not equalize incomes overnight. He pointed out that the aspiration of the Revolution was to arrive eventually at equal incomes, starting from the bottom up, not from the top down.[19]

Although income differences still exist, other inequalities have been completely wiped out. Education is the same for all, universal, free, and compulsory for all children under the age of fourteen. Day-care centers are available for children of working mothers. Health services, public telephones, burials, and sports are available free of charge to all citizens. Rationing of food is also used as an equalizing mechanism.[20]

According to Castro, the goals of equalization will only be achieved when the use of money is entirely dispensed with; when all workers—the canecutter and the engineer—receive the same pay for the same amount of work; and finally, when wealth created through everyone's efforts is equally shared by all.[21] Such are the long-range goals of the Communist society for which Cubans are encouraged to prepare themselves. These goals can be achieved by creating a social structure and a set of cultural values that resemble, as closely as possible, the structure and values of the New Society.

Rural Versus Urban

The traditional society in Cuba had institutionalized relations based on the subordination of the countryside to the urban centers. The economy depended basically on three agrarian products: sugar, tobacco, and cattle. Over 40 percent of the total population lived in rural areas, and 39 percent of the labor force was engaged in agricultural production. And yet, conditions of underdevelopment, traditionalism, and inequality were highest in the countryside. With few exceptions, sugar plantations still used labor intensive forms of production with outmoded technology, and a low ratio of yield per acre and per man-hour was used in agriculture.[22]

The single most impressive document about social conditions in the Cuban countryside was one put out by the Association of Catholic University

Students (ACU), a conservative organization, prepared from a fairly re-liable survey conducted in 1957. To quote one of the opening remarks: "The city of Havana is going through a period of extraordinary prosperity, while the countryside, especially its working people, is living in unbelievable conditions of stagnation, misery and despair."[23] The survey estimates that the families of agricultural workers enjoyed a per capita income of $91.56 a year, and, despite the fact that they made up about one-third of the popu-lation (an estimated 2.1 million persons), they received only 10 percent of the national income. The survey also showed that the diet of the agricul-tural workers was deficient in calories (about 1,000 calories short of the estimated minimum requirements) and in proteins (only 4 percent ate meat, 2 percent ate eggs, and 11 percent drank milk as part of their regular diet). Some 36 percent of the agricultural workers had worms, 13 percent had had typhoid fever, 14 percent had had tuberculosis, and 31 percent had had malaria. Only 8 percent reported receiving free medical aid from the state, and another 8 percent from charitable or trade union medical centers. About 43 percent of the agricultural workers were illiterate. Sixty-four per-cent of their houses did not have toilet facilities, 60 percent had dirt floors, 83 percent lacked shower or bath facilities, and 42 percent had only one bedroom for the whole family, which averaged approximately six persons. Interesting information is furnished by the survey's questions tapping atti-tudes of the agricultural workers with regard to possible ways of solving their problems. An overwhelming majority of the agricultural workers (73 percent) thought that the solution was to open new sources of work. Again, an overwhelming majority (69 percent) placed the responsibility of provid-ing new work opportunities on the government.[24]

This situation contrasts sharply with the conditions created by the Rev-olution from the start. If the agrarian reform had an equalizing effect on the rich and the poor, it was also meant to level off differences particularly be-tween the *latifundista* (rich landowner living in the city) and the impov-erished landless peasant. The goal of the first Agrarian Reform Law was to eliminate the *latifundia* and to distribute land to tenant farmers or landless peasants. Consequently, land-holdings of more than 1,000 acres were expropriated and plots of land were distributed to the landless. In 1963, the second Agrarian Reform Law was implemented to further reduce the size of estates, owned by medium-sized farmers to a maximum of 160 acres. By the mid-1960s, the average size of the private farm was 33 acres.[25]

The second big step toward eliminating inequalities between the urban and rural areas was the literacy campaign. Whereas the overall illiteracy rate for the whole population was estimated at 23 percent, for the rural areas, it was as high as 42 percent. The literacy campaign was an organized attempt to bring urban people into the countryside. Out of a total of 707,-

212 people who were made literate during the campaign, 67 percent were from rural areas. At the end of 1961, it was estimated that only 3.6 percent of the total population was illiterate.[26]

It is clear that the purpose of the literacy campaign was not only to bring the countryside closer to the city by educating the peasants, but also to bring the city closer to the countryside by exposing the boys and girls of the city to the life, misery, deprivations, and sacrifices of the peasants. In his speech to the brigades of makeshift teachers departing for the countryside, Fidel Castro emphasized that by living with the peasants they would achieve a better understanding of the relationship between the country and the city and would realize how it was impossible for the city to progress any further unless the countryside was developed. In the same speech, he said:

> You are going to teach, but as you teach, you will also learn. You are going to learn much more that you can possibly teach, and in the end you will feel as grateful to the *campensinos* as the *campesinos* will feel to you for teaching them to read and write. They will teach you the "why" of the Revolution better than any speech. They will show you what life has been like in the country-side and how our *campesinos* have lived deprived of everything.[27]

The process of equalization between rural and urban areas has been remarkable in expansion of social services and social security benefits. With the emphasis on modernizing agriculture, roads, dams, and bridges have been built and electric power has been significantly expanded in the countryside. Hospitals and schools have been built to dispense free medical assistance and to continue the education of the peasants. All graduating physicians must spend the first two years of practice in the countryside.[28] State stores were set up from the start to make consumer goods available to the peasants at the same rates they are sold in the cities. In fact, some observers have pointed out that scarcity is less dire in the countryside than in the cities.[29] Finally, it should be emphasized that the choice of the agricultural sector as the economic sector that the revolutionary government sought to develop more than any other was not made purely for economic reasons. Actually, as Jacques Valier has suggested, the Cuban revolutionary leaders have always manifested a desire to eliminate the imbalance between the rich modern city and the impoverished underdeveloped countryside.[30]

Female Versus Male

Perhaps in no other Latin American country, with the exception of Argentina and Uruguay, had women achieved such a high level of equality as they had in Cuba. Women had obtained the right to vote in Cuba in 1934, before the women of most countries of the hemisphere. According to the 1953 census, the percentage of illiterates among females (21 percent) was smaller than among men (26 percent) and the percentage of females attending school, from five to twenty-four years of age, was almost equal to that of men. Percentages of women in the labor force and of those attending school were probably higher in Cuba than in most Latin American countries, as were the number of women possibly practicing birth control and the rates of abortions and divorces. Cuba's fertility rate was the third lowest in Latin America. However, these data should not give the impression that inequalities between the sexes did not exist. Indeed, the traditional Cuban society was far from bestowing the same rights and privileges upon woman as it granted its men. On the contrary, in the traditional Catholic mainstream of Spanish culture, norms and values had been elaborated to a point at which a double standard was definitely present.

Lack of egalitarianism was manifested by the small percentage of women in the labor force. Although, in 1943, the percentage of women in the total population was 48 percent, only 10 percent of the labor force was composed of females. The percentage increased to 13 percent in 1953 and to 14 percent in 1956–1957. Females were well represented (46 percent) in the professions and semiprofessions (overrepresented in teaching, philosophy, and nursing), underrepresented (from 15 percent to 20 percent) among white-collar workers, and grossly underrepresented (from 2 percent to 10 percent) among blue-collar workers. The largest concentration of women was in the service occupations (from 41 percent to 48 percent in 1943–1957). Far below followed industry (from 15 percent to 19 percent) and commerce (from 6 percent to 9 percent). Female participation in agriculture, fishing, mining, construction, and transport was below 3 percent. However, in 1956–1957, women enjoyed more stability in employment than men and were less affected by unemployment than men.[31]

Female participation in cultural activities was relatively high, particularly in poetry and the novel, ballet and modern dance, sculpture and painting, theater, radio, and television. But their lack of participation in the political life of the nation was obvious. In traditional Cuban society, the place for the women was at home. The roles of mother, wife, and housekeeper were particularly emphasized, with the functions of child-bearing and child-rearing receiving the usual prominence within the Spanish Catholic tradition. Religious, social, cultural, and philanthropic values and participation were encouraged. Whereas boys were encouraged from early childhood to behave with *machismo* (male chauvinism), girls were instilled from an early age with the joys of femininity, to make them gracious and particularly attractive to men.

A natural by-product of a double standard system in sexual norms is prostitution. Some estimates gave as many as 270 whorehouses in Havana alone, not counting the number of prostitutes working in bars and *posadas* (a hotel that rents rooms for a few hours to couples).[32] As soon as the Revolution took over in 1959, an attack was launched against prostitution. Soon the streets in Havana were cleared of pimps and many brothels began to close. In 1960–1961 hundreds of prostitutes were sent to training schools (driving, sewing) or to work in the countryside.

In 1961, during the literacy campaign, about 90,000 women participated in the movement. The role of women was particularly important in convincing recalcitrant, illiterate women to receive instruction. Out of those made "literate" by the campaign, 67 percent were women. The fact that many city girls went unchaperoned to the countryside to teach peasants was an experience never heard of in Cuba and was to contribute to the emancipation of the new generation of women.[33]

To defend the Revolution against the old order, the Committees for the Defense of the Revolution (CDR) were created in 1960. By the end of 1963, the CDR was a mass organization in which all sectors of society were represented. Women were highly represented in all sectors. Moreover, a special category for "housewives" made up 26 percent of the total organization.[34] Women also participated actively in the militias in which they received military training and participated in drills and sentry duties. Although the Compulsory Military Service Law of 1963 opened the door to the recruitment of women, practically none were called into service by 1968. At that time, the vice minister of the armed forces announced that measures were under study to organize a course for female command cadres, and that women would progressively form part of the armed forces.[35] However, no further data has been published on this matter.

Another way of mobilizing women to partake in revolutionary action was the creation in 1960 of the FMC. Women of all ages, occupations, and strata were recruited into the organization. Membership in the FMC has grown quite rapidly during the last ten years, from 376,571 in 1961 (11 percent of the total female population) to 750,000 in 1967 (19 percent) and to 1,132,000 in 1969 (28 percent). The FMC membership participates in emulation, school and special courses, Red Cross brigades, mutual-aid agricultural teams, vaccination, and voluntary work programs.[36]

Participation of women in the labor force has continued to grow as it did between 1943 and 1957. Thus, it increased from 14.2 percent on the eve of the Revolution to 15.6 percent in 1968 and 17.7 percent in 1969. The government expects, however, to increase female participation in the labor force sharply during the 1970s and hopes to reach one-third or about 33 percent of the labor force by 1980. As part of this plan, the FMC recruited about 94,000 women into the labor force between November 1968 and August 1969. When comparing the distribution of these new female workers by occupation in 1969 with that of the 1943–1957 period, significant differences appear: participation in agriculture increased sharply to almost 16 percent; there was a continued increase in service occupations, to 52 percent, but a decline in commerce, and, in the other occupations, the percentages remained fairly stable.[37] New opportunities have been opened up for women in the poultry combine, coffee crop, planting of seedlings, health centers, day-care nurseries, etc. At the same time, the closing of department stores and the decline in commerce has reduced a traditional source of female employment. Castro has reported that women are turning out to be workers of high efficiency and that they are highly conscious of their responsibilities.[38]

It seems, however, that traditional attitudes among both men and women prevent the latter from fully participating in productive tasks. Thus, in the 1968–1969 drive, only one woman out of four responded to the FMC's exhortation to join the labor ranks. Out of the 300,000 women who were unresponsive, 59 percent alleged family obligations or lack of facilities (e.g., day-care centers that are mostly free of charge but not available in certain areas), but the remaining 41 percent were idle women who had no family responsibilities. In explaining the reasons for this attitude, an official report mentioned "obstacles of an ideological nature" and "the weight of tradition." Some of the excuses were: "The place of women is at home" or "A woman's career is marriage." The report also referred to several cases of discriminatory practices in state agriculture, industry and services.[39]

Women also contribute to the various campaigns of voluntary labor, particularly in agriculture. They are recruited and organized into work groups by either the CDR or the FMC to work in the Green Belt around Havana or in various other projects, particularly in the coffee fields. It was estimated that in 1967 they contributed from about 5,000 to 10,000 man-years of work.[40]

Although data are not available, the number of girls enrolled in elementary schools has probably sharply increased, especially in rural areas. But available official figures on female enrollment in secondary and vocational schools are contradictory: enrollment in basic-secondary, teaching, and technological schools declined between 1958–1959 and 1966–1967, whereas that in preuniversity and administration schools increased. In 1966–1967, women were not enrolled in the agricultural schools, and their proportion in art and language schools (traditional fields of women) was below the proportion of women in the population.[41] Unfortunately, there are no statistics available on the enrollment of women in higher education.

Participation of women in politics and government positions is not as impressive as in other activities. Besides Celia Sánchez (Secretary to the

Presidency), Vilma Espín (president of the FMC), Haydée Santamaría (director of the literary institution *Casa de las Américas*), and Clementina Serra (director of Day-Care Centers), it is difficult to find women in top government positions. It should be noted that the first three women mentioned were in the Sierra close to Castro, and that two of them are the wives of leading government figures (i.e., Armando Hart and Raúl Castro), whereas the fourth is an old member of the party. All of them are over forty years of age and their positions are in typically feminine fields. With the exception of Celia Sánchez's job, women are conspicuously absent in the cabinet, the leadership of the trade unions, and the Politburo, the Secretariat, the auxiliary commissions and the provincial branches of the PCC. Out of 100 members of the Central Committee, only five are women, four of whom include those mentioned above. In spite of the overwhelmingly majority of women in the CDR, its head has always been a man. In the 1967 election of delegates for the local government, out of 21,838 delegates only 2,380 (or 10.9 percent) were women.[42] Vilma Espín has conceded that it would be unrealistic to expect women to have been totally emancipated.[43]

Concerning sexual mores, in spite of relevant changes, some traditional customs still persist. The number of annual marriages legally registered has increased almost threefold, from 30,658 in 1958 to 84,620 in 1968. This is mainly the result of several revolutionary laws that have simplified the requirements for and ceremony of weddings, which are now administered free of charge. The government has also opened several *Palacios de Matrimonios* throughout the island where wedding ceremonies can take place. Exhortations to legalize common-law marriages resulted in more than 100,-000 marriages in 1959–1963. The annual number of divorces has shown a sixfold increase, from 2,251 in 1958 to 15,357 in 1968. Causes for this increase include the greater freedom enjoyed by women and political disagreements among middle-age couples.[44]

Some foreign observers report that a high value is still placed by males on the virginity of their wives-to-be and that, on the other hand, *machismo* still has a firm grip. But the situation seems to be slowly changing, particularly in big cities. Thus, a survey conducted in 1967 in Havana by *Juventud Rebelde* showed that half of those interviewed (both male and female) agreed that virginity did not have to be a prerequisite for marriage.[45]

Castro has expressed his opposition to Malthusianism. The revolutionary government does not support birth control for mere economic reasons, rejecting the capitalist theory that the population explosion is the main cause of people's misery. In fact, Cuban infant-maternity centers encourage married couples to have several children. However, contraceptives are available (e.g., diaphragm, intrauterine loop) for those women who want them. Although there is no sex education program, occasionally the newspapers publish information on birth control, mobile units go to rural districts to explain how to use contraceptives, and the FMC supports these activities. Induced abortion is legal and free if there is sufficient reason for asking for it. There are, however, numerous cases of abortions operated illegally and, reportedly, the death rate from such operations is very high.[46]

Blacks Versus Whites

Another area of social interaction in which the old order maintained traditional elitist relations of subordination of one group to another was that of relations between whites and blacks. It has been said that racial discrimination did not exist in Cuba as it exists in the United States. Indeed, institutionalized racism (United States style) did not exist in Cuba, but racial prejudice did exist, and manifested itself in various ways. The best clubs, clinics, schools, beaches, and parks were reserved exclusively for the whites. Blacks were heavily underrepresented in the professions and better paid occupations.[47] Despite the fact that blacks made up nearly one-third of the total population and had participated fully in the war of liberation against Spain, they were not represented among the bankers, sugar-mill owners, cattle-ranch owners or the *latifundista* class. Although they were well represented among some of the skilled blue-collar jobs and in the army, they were underrepresented in the professions and in the police force (see chapter 12). It is interesting to note that the same problems of representation in such groups is found in the United States. Perhaps the strongest prejudice was that against interracial marriage, particularly among the middle class.

By the end of 1959, beaches, nightclubs, and public parks were desegregated, and work opportunities were open to all, regardless of color.[48] It would be unrealistic, however, to think that all inequalities and manifestations of prejudice have been eliminated. In fact, the imbalance that existed in 1959, because the traditional system did not give the blacks equal opportunities for education and for developing and acquiring abilities, is still bound to manifest itself among those that are in their thirties and older. It is probably that the old ingrained prejudice against interracial marriage still exists, since a set of values operating for so many years cannot be supplanted by contradictory ones in less than a generation. However, it is quite possible that by institutionalizing equality, not only in the law, but in actual practice, Cuban society may rapidly erode the foundations of the old system and create, at the same time, a social structure and a value system founded upon racial equality.

Manual Versus Mental Work

The way most Cubans, particularly those of the middle class, looked down on manual labor, was no different from that of other Latin American countries.[49] To prove this point, let me draw upon the general orientation of the emerging middle class and of the educational system in particular. The middle class, including the large petite bourgeoisie, was oriented toward the professions, the bureaucracy, and business occupations. The white-collar mentality was a product of the old, traditional value: "Don't work with your hands if you can work with your mind." Many petite bourgeoisie who could not enter the bureaucracy or get a white-collar job, would rather set up a stand to sell candy, coffee, refreshments, cigarettes, or toothbrushes than take a menial job as a dishwasher or as a janitor.[50]

The orientation of the whole educational system was toward careers in the liberal arts. This was so not only at the university, but at the secondary and primary levels, not only in the better private schools frequented by the rich and the middle class, but also in the public schools run by the government.[51] The high school was oriented to produce "bachelors in letters or in science," that is, the foundations for a liberal arts career at the university. No orientation was given at this stage to stimulate students to become technicians for industry or agriculture. Seventy-three percent of the total student body at the University of Havana in 1959 was enrolled in medicine, education, law, and commerce. Also in 1959, there were as many students studying the humanities, that is, law and literature, as there were engineers, architects, veterinarians, and agronomists put together.[52] This, of course, was not because there were more work opportunities for lawyers than for members of other professions, but because, in the traditional Spanish value system, such a profession is considered manipulative and craftlike.

The egalitarian ethos of the Revolution addressed itself to eliminate such manifestations of the elitist traditional system. The Revolution made it clear that there is no reason to favor mental labor over manual labor. The goal is that, in the future, a cane cutter and an engineer will receive the same wages for his work.[53] The Revolution has made a special effort to create an ideology of work by showing its worth, its rewards, its role in the realization of man and in the construction of the New Society. According to Guevara, "man needs to undergo a complete spiritual rebirth in his attitude towards his work."[54] Probably the only word that is repeated more often than *work* in the rhetoric of the Revolution is the word *conciencia* (in broad terms, "consciousness"—this term is defined in detail later). The only way to overcome underdevelopment and to build the socialist society is with *work* and *conciencia*. It seems that the puritanic ideology of the Protestant ethnic has finally arrived in Latin America. In this case, however, the fruits of labor are not a symbol of individualistic achievement and justification but of self-realization in the collectivity. In his May Day parade speech of 1966, Fidel Castro addressed himself to the cane cutters of the Millionaire Brigades—the workers who had cut over one million *arrobas* of sugar cane that year:

> For the masses of our country the concept of work and of the worker has changed profoundly. To the same extent that the revolutionary consciousness of our people has grown, the idea of work and the honor of being a worker are felt and understood by ever-growing sectors of our population.[55]

In 1963–1967, a vigorous campaign was launched to free the Revolution of bureaucratism in the administrative machinery and the service sector. As a consequence of this campaign, many bureaucrats and white-collar workers changed their occupations to productive (nonservice) jobs.[56] Since 1962, many bureaucrats and intellectual workers have spent several days or weeks of each year helping with the harvesting of various crops (particularly sugar cane) or doing menial jobs. Prime Minister Castro and other cabinet members are no exception to this rule. The function of such symbolic actions is not only to show the workers that their leaders do not think it unworthy of their positions to engage in manual labor, but also to make the leaders aware of the hardships of productive work.

The ultimate goal of complete equality in all occupations (in terms of status, remuneration, etc.) should not be confused with Marx's idea that the same person could perform several occupations in his lifetime. In today's world of complex technology, this appears as a utopian idea, and Cuban leaders have not referred to it. Yet, they do believe that total occupational equality could be achieved in the future through education, mechanization of agriculture and other manual jobs, and automation. The emphasis on technological careers and vocational training is a sign of this preoccupation. At the same time, prerevolutionary primary occupations, such as law, literature, philosophy, and commerce, have declined both in university enrollment and in social status. By stressing craftlike occupations (e.g., agronomy, engineering, architecture, veterinary), deemphasizing humanistic, liberal occupations, and by upgrading manual tasks (e.g., cut sugar cane is now loaded by machines, sugar bags are being gradually eliminated by sugar tanks), the Cuban leadership is reducing the equality gap between manual and mental work.

Collectivistic Orientation Versus Individualism

The other major value orientation chosen by the Revolution to implement a matrix of values conducive to and supportive of a socialist structure is one that emphasizes the worth, rights, and functions of the collectivity above (not in opposition to) those of the individual. This orientation does not attempt to deprive the individual of his rights, but operates on the assumption that individual rights are best pursued and can only be fulfilled in the context of, and in agreement with, the rights of the collectivity.

This conception of society was clearly in opposition to the values of liberal capitalism that Cuban society subscribed to before the Revolution. Such a value system emphasized primarily the rights of the individual, particularly his political freedom, his right to private property, and his right to compete with others in a situation of relative deprivation. The rights of the collectivity were recognized inasmuch as they helped to preserve and further the rights of the individual. Laws, constitutions, and policies were established to protect the rights of the individual within the competitive framework of a market situation. One needs only to observe various by-products of the capitalist system of free enterprise to understand how deeply ingrained individualism was in Cuba's social structure. Let me mention only a few:

1. the high concentration of wealth, particularly of land, in the hands of a few,

2. the concentration of production in one seasonal product and the lack of diversification,

3. the high rates of unemployment and underemployment,

4. the dependence on foreign markets for exporting its main products and for importing commodities that could be produced within the country (including vegetables!),

5. the unequal distribution of economic production in the various geographic areas of the country,

6. the inequalities in the distribution of income, and

7. the inequalities in the distribution of services and utilities.

These are some manifestations in the social structure of a value orientation that emphasizes individualism. One could also mention the inadequacy of the tax system, the social security system, or the health and educational system.

Individualism also manifested itself in Cuban politics. The alienation from and disgust of most Cubans with politics was partly due to a long tradition of self-seeking politicians who sought power only for the purpose of enriching themselves. Such dissatisfaction with self-seeking politicians grew still greater with the failure of the so-called "middle-class revolution" of the 1930s, which was characterized by wholesale graft and corruption during the *Auténtico* governments of Grau San Martín and Prío Socarrás.[57]

Finally, it may have been the staunch individualism of the value system that curbed the growth of solidarity among the Cuban middle class, both before and after the Revolution. For seven years, the middle class was fragmented in its fight against Batista, whom it only managed to overthrow by accepting the directives of Fidel Castro.[58] The same lack of solidarity among the middle class has been apparent in the lack of agreement of the various exiled groups fighting Castro for the last ten years or so.

In the remaining pages of this essay an attempt will be made to show how individualism is being substituted by a collectivistic orientation. Again, data about attitudes or value change in Cuba are not available. However, I will again attempt to show how the Revolution has undertaken the double task of changing the social organization and the value system of the society.

Collectivization Versus Private Ownership

The first Agrarian Reform Law was the first serious step taken by the Revolution in 1959 to protect the rights of the collectivity vis-à-vis the rights of the individual. As it has been said, restrictions were placed on the amount of land each individual could have, since many others were land-less. Some of the leftover land was given to those who had none, some was turned into cooperatives, and some was kept for state farms. The latter grew in scope and significance in the following years. Economic and ideo-logical reasons were adduced by the Cuban leaders for keeping the large sugar plantations and cattle ranches as state farms rather than distributing them to the peasants. Eventually, most cooperatives were to become state farms. "The day will come [Castro said] when no one will want to work for a boss, when all farmers will move toward the state farms, to remunera-tive work and to all the benefits of the state farm. The life in these com-munities will, in every way, be comparable to life in the cities."[59]

With the second Agrarian Reform Law in 1963, the proportion of land in state hands rose to around 70 percent. By this time, most other produc-tive sectors were also collectivized: industry, trade, banking, education, etc. The collectivization process was completed in 1968 with the Revolutionary Offensive when all retail stores and small businesses were nationalized.[60] By doing so, the Cuban leaders were trying to extirpate all remnants of the old system of private property and profit-making. Today, Cuba is the so-cialist country with the highest degree of collectivization of the means of production. The process took place at the highest speed and without pro-ducing as violent a reaction as in other socialist nations. From a purely economic point of view, perhaps, it would have been better if Cuba had maintained the level of agricultural collectivization attained in mid-1963, and, perhaps, still better with the level of 1961. Why did the government expropriate farms with over 160 acres? Why did it collectivize small shops, fruit stands, and barbershops in 1968? Castro responded bluntly:

We did not make a Revolution here to establish the right to trade. Such a revolution took place in 1789; it was the revolution of the merchants, of the bourgeois. This is a Socialist Revolution! . . . The communist man cannot be developed by encouraging man's ambition, man's individualism, man's individual desires. If we are going to fail because we believe in man's ability to improve, then we will fail, but we will never renounce our faith in mankind![61]

In the opinion of the Cuban leaders, all forms of self-employment, competitive trade, business, and private industry direct man's motivation toward individualistic and selfish goals. Those who engage in such actions practice various forms of exploitation and become parasites of society. They are an obstacle in the construction of socialism and they should be given a chance either to incorporate themselves into productive tasks oriented toward the collectivity or should be separated from the society. Indeed, many middle-class and petit bourgeois Cubans have incorporated themselves into the Revolution. Others have migrated to Miami or are waiting to depart. However, those who stayed may have found that collectivization of production helps to create a commonality of interests rather than competitiveness, solidarity rather than alienation, and *conciencia* rather than selfishness.

Unselfishness Versus Selfishness

Probably the most frequently used term in the rhetoric of the Revolution and the most efficient method used in Cuba to build socialism is *conciencia*. Joseph Kahl describes *conciencia* as an amalgam of consciousness, conscience, conscientiousness, and commitment.[62] One has *conciencia* if one is aware (at least vaguely) of what the Revolution is all about, what the Revolution has done for him and for society, what he or others should do for the Revolution, and what are the goals of the Revolution. Such awareness is more than pure intellectual perception. It also conveys the idea of commitment to action in the pursuance of certain goals.

Evidently, not all people in Cuba today act with *conciencia*.[63] Only those who are actively committed to implementing the Revolution have *conciencia*. And even among these, *conciencia* exists in various degrees. No survey has been conducted to measure various degrees of *conciencia* in various sectors of the population. We would hypothesize that it is highest among the following groups or categories of people: the top leaders, the cadres, members of the PCC, the armed forces, the youth, active members of mass organizations (e.g., CDR, CTC, FMC, UJC), members of voluntary labor brigades, and members of groups that participated in the literacy campaign, the militias, or in the Schools for Revolutionary Instruction (EIR). Again, I would hypothesize that *conciencia* is lowest among those who do not belong in any of the above-mentioned categories and are over forty-five years of age, or are among those who engage in heavy manual labor (e.g., agricultural laborers), or among those whose economic status has deteriorated with the advent of the Revolution.

Perhaps, one of the characteristics of those who act with *conciencia* is the eradication of selfish attitudes that were fostered under capitalism. Society now provides them with work and a decent salary, with free schools, health services, and with housing and utilities at a fraction of their cost. They, in turn, are expected to work not for the selfish motivation of profit-making in a spirit of competition, but with the fullest dedication and maximum effort to produce the material goods that are needed to create a society of abundance and solidarity.[64]

Revolutionary rhetoric about unselfish motivation has opened up an ideological controversy within the ranks of the rebel leadership. There is no room in this chapter to deal extensively with the controversy over what types of incentives should be used to accelerate development.[65] However, let me point out briefly that the Cuban leaders' choice of a policy of moral over material incentives used by other socialist countries cannot be evaluated, judged, and its results predicted in purely economic terms. It is true that the use of incentives bears directly on production. However, the Revolution is not primarily interested in production, but in the creation of a New Man and a New Society. Consequently, to evaluate whether or not the use of moral incentives is succeeding in producing the expected results, one would have to determine to what degree this New Man has been developed, not how much this or that economic measurement has increased or decreased over the last five years. Fidel Castro was quite aware of this when he said: "Communism cannot be established if we do not create abundant wealth. But the way to do this, in our opinion, is not by creating wealth with political awareness, but more and more collective wealth, with more and more collective political awareness."[66] To quote Zeitlin's impression after his last visit to Cuba in 1969:

> This conception of socialist morality is at the heart of the Cuban revolution's uniqueness among Communist states, because it is combined with an egalitarian practice and a rejection of individual and material incentives in favor of collective and moral ones. Talking to Cuban workers throughout the country, it is quickly apparent that these are not mere slogans, but commitments deeply felt by many.[67]

The use of voluntary unpaid labor has probably been one of the most efficient methods used by the Revolution to stimulate the growth of *conciencia* and to demonstrate, in practice, that people indeed are guided by moral incentives. According to Guevara, voluntary unpaid labor is based on the appreciation of the fact that man reaches a full human condition when he produces without being driven by the physical need to sell his labor as a commodity.[68]

Voluntary unpaid labor began in 1962 under the auspices of the UJC, when students began to help with agricultural work during the summer months. By 1967, voluntary labor had been institutionalized and most sectors of the population were contributing their time and effort to the common task of production. It is estimated that in 1967 unpaid labor comprised from 8 percent to 12 percent of the total labor force.[69] Voluntary workers are recruited from all walks of life, the young and the old, male and female, students and working people, government officials and bureaucrats. The goal is not only to have people working without pay, but also to bring the city to the countryside, and to bring blacks and whites, intellectuals and manual workers, and men and women together in a united effort to create wealth with *conciencia.*

There is little doubt that all who contribute their unpaid labor do not do so of their own free will or because they have a high degree of *conciencia.* Indeed, many of these people act under coercion and moral pressures of the society. A person who refuses to participate in some kind of voluntary task will encounter the criticism of his peers, of the members of his work group, of his neighbors, and even of his own relatives. In some circumstances, this person might find it harder than others to get access to some limited facilities or to get hold of some scarce commodities. All of these pressures, however, are mechanisms of the social structure that in various ways induce, coerce, and help produce a kind of behavior to which neither the social organization nor the value system are as yet conducive. As Guevara has said, this change in consciousness cannot take place automatically in the economy.[70]

Mass Mobilization Versus Indifference

Another method used by the revolutionary government to eradicate individualistic values of the traditional system is to promote participation in mass movements, rallies, campaigns, parades, organizations, and various other forms of mobilization. Since Castro arrived in Havana on January 8, 1959, various kinds of collective behavior such as rallies, parades, public trials, and television appearances began to take place, some of which were spontaneous, but others, no doubt, were organized by the leaders in order to establish closer contact between themselves and the masses.

It is not my intention to discuss how much participation the Cuban masses have in the decision-making process. However, I will try to show how participation of the people in various kinds of mass movements and government programs can contribute to the creation of a new value orientation centered around the collectivity. Again, participation in such programs was and is, in many cases, the product of *conciencia.* In other cases, however, it is the result of moral pressures of the social structure that help design the course of action for the individual. To what extent individualistic values have been replaced by those of the New Man no one can tell at this point. It is the assumption of the Cuban leaders, however, that participation in such mass movements is conducive to creating the values of the New Man within each member of the population. As in the theory of guerrilla warfare in which Guevara maintains that the *foco* is the school of true revolutionaries, in the same manner, it is only through mobilization into collectively oriented movements that the masses at large will internalize the values of the New Man.[71]

No sociological study has been undertaken to evaluate the roles, functions, and significance of mass organizations and state programs of such variety as the CDR, PCC, UJC, FMC, CTC, ANAP, the militia, and the disappeared EIR, ORI, and PURS. Two of these organizations, the CDR and EIR, together with the literacy campaign, were studied recently by Professor Richard Fagen in an attempt to show the role played by such movements in the transformation of political culture. After studying each of these movements in considerable detail, he concludes that, although there is a great deal of revolutionary behavior that does not stem from the internalization of new values, the modification of some aspects of the traditional value system is the most important long-term consequence of attempts to transform the political culture.[72]

Cubans were highly amused during World War II when stories were told about the German colony in Cuba collecting empty toothpaste containers to help Germany with the war effort, or when war propaganda showed the British or the Americans tilling vegetables in their "victory gardens" to help ease the war economy. Perhaps, the reason for this amusement was that Cubans did not understand the meaning of solidarity or of participating in a cause common to all. Today, the Germans and Americans may be amused when they hear that housewives and bureaucrats from Havana go to work in the Green Belt around Havana to contribute unpaid voluntary labor. Cubans have contributed to the Revolution by donating their jewels, their private collections, and their properties. Today, they contribute with their time and their effort, participating in the common tasks to free the country from underdevelopment and to build the New Society of the twenty-first century. In order to achieve this goal, society as a whole has been turned into a gigantic school. People in Cuba today can learn the values of the New Man not only in the schools, but also by participating in various common tasks and by getting involved in different mass programs that pursue the common good. "Education [according to Guevara] takes hold of the masses and the new attitude tends to become a habit; the masses continue to absorb it and to influence those who have not yet educated themselves. This is the indirect form of educating the masses."[73]

Of the many projects into which people are mobilized to work for the collectivity, I will mention only three, perhaps because they seem to be the most important in terms of the involvement of sectors of the population that are central to the national life. The first is the Green Belt project around Havana where fruit trees, coffee, and vegetables are cultivated to make the capital city self-sufficient in such products. Before the Revolution, oranges, lettuce, and tomatoes, if not imported from the United States, came to Havana from places as far as 600 miles away. After 1959, when many peasants began to consume some of these products, the city began to suffer the pinch of scarcity. The Green Belt project is an attempt to solve that need. However, what is more important is that Havana's future supply of fruits and vegetables will depend on the *habaneros* and not on the peasants of the interior. Office workers, government officials, and housewives spend their weekends irrigating beds of lettuce or picking coffee beans while their children play around them in the fields.[74]

The second project of particular relevance is that of the Isle of Youth project (formerly, Isle of Pines), in which several thousand young people work in an almost communistic way. These young people, under the direction of the party, are implementing a serious experiment in an attempt to create the New Man within themselves. Each young person, on a voluntary basis, agrees to work on the island for two years. Wages are paid not according to ability, but according to the needs of the workers. The life is generally communal and everybody participates in the same tasks.[75]

The third and, perhaps, most important project, because of the commitment of the whole nation, was the sugar harvest of 1970 with its ten-million-ton goal. This is the most important experiment of mass mobilization undertaken by the Revolution because it touches, in a decisive manner, all aspects of Cuban society. In my opinion, it is entirely unrealistic to evaluate the experiment in purely economic terms. The ten-million-ton figure was a quantitative goal that all could understand and work for. However, can one set such goals for awareness, unselfishness, or commitment? Yet, when the sociologist looks at the experiment as a whole, he cannot fail to understand that although quantitative targets cannot be set for such values, still their achievement is as important and genuine to the goals of the

Revolution as the economic targets. Regardless of the relative failure to achieve the economic goal, achievements in terms of mobilization and solidarity must have been remarkable. Day by day for almost ten months the drive was publicized in the press, radio, and television. It became a preoccupation not only in Cuba but abroad, as U.S., Korean, and Japanese brigades demonstrated. Almost everyone in Cuba, in one way or another, was involved in the mobilization.

Conclusions

An attempt is made in this chapter to show that the main task the Revolution faced in 1959 was to bring Cuba from underdevelopment and traditionalism to development and modernity. Underlying the traditional structure of underdevelopment in a capitalist system was a set of value orientations that stressed hierarchical elitism and individualism. With the advent of the Revolution, an attempt was made to change these values for others more conducive to modernity, such as equalitarianism and orientation to the collectivity. The rebel leaders decided to seek such values in the path of socialism.

This chapter has tried to show what methods the Revolution has used to eliminate hierarchical elitism and individualism and to implement equalitarianism and a collectivistic orientation. Since no survey data are available to show to what extent the traditional values have been superseded by the new, I have made use of the speeches and writings of the leaders and have observed the changes that actually have been implemented in the social structure. I hope that by observing closely the scope and depth of the changes in this structure, the direction toward which cultural values are changing has been indicated.

No single piece of evidence presented in this chapter demonstrates that Cubans today are less selfish, less prejudiced, or more equalitarian than those who lived in the traditional system. Indeed, what this chapter has presented is that the changes introduced in the social structure and the motivations emphasized by the current leaders make it more conducive for Cubans today to act unselfishly, without prejudice, and in an equalitarian manner. What this chapter also suggests is that some, perhaps many, Cubans today may have internalized the values of equalitarianism and the collectivistic orientation. However, it is not known how widespread or how deep this internalization has gone. This chapter also shows that, over the last ten years or so, the Revolution has eliminated internal structural obstacles that hindered the development of socialism. With the emergence of the new social structure, the leaders want to build a cultural system that would be conducive to and supportive of the new structure. Such a cultural system is what the theory of the New Man is all about. The Cuban people are moving fast in that direction, in a program more radical than that of any other socialist nation.

NOTES

1. Defending the thesis of relative development are Boris Goldenberg, *The Cuban Revolution and Latin America* (New York, 1965); Theodore Draper, *Castro's Revolution: Myths and Realities* (New York, 1962); and Cuban Economic Research Project, *Study on Cuba* (Coral Gables, 1965). For data on underdevelopment, see Herbert L. Matthews, "Fidel Castro Revisited," *War and Peace* (December 1967), p. 5; and Dudley Seers, ed., *Cuba: The Economic and Social Revolution* (Chapel Hill, 1964). On uneven development, see Richard Fagen, *The Transformation of Political Culture in Cuba* (Stanford, Calif., 1969), p. 23.

2. Herbert L. Matthews, *Fidel Castro* (New York, 1969), p. 134.

3. Fidel Castro, speech delivered at the General Assembly of the United Nations, September 26, 1960, in Martin Kenner and James Petras, eds., *Fidel Castro Speaks* (New York, 1970), p. 11.

4. Castro, speech delivered on February 6, 1959, in *Fidel Castro: pensamiento político* (La Habana, 1959), p. 109.

5. For an assessment of democracy in Cuba prior to the Revolution, see Hugh Thomas, "Middle Class Politics and the Cuban Revolution," in *The Politics of Conformity in Latin America,* ed. Claudio Véliz (New York, 1967), pp. 257–58.

6. Fidel Castro, *La historia me absolverá* (La Habana, 1961) and his speech on the first anniversary of the CDR delivered on September 28, 1961, in *Revolución,* September 30, 1961, pp. 12–14.

7. There is little doubt that all during 1959 the Revolution was merely a nationalist, petit bourgeois revolution. Castro himself defined it as "neither capitalist nor communist" since "our Revolution is not red but olive green, the color of the rebel army that emerged from the heart of the Sierra Maestra." Kenner and Petras, *Fidel Castro Speaks,* p. 67.

8. Ibid., pp. 79–81.

9. This is against the common Latin American practice of promulgating a new constitution after every *coup d'etat* or "revolution." Such constitutions usually pay lip service to democratic principles and ideals, which, in fact, are never implemented.

10. Ernesto (Che) Guevara, "El cuadro, columna vertebral de la revolución," *Cuba Socialista,* 2 (September 1962), pp. 17–22.

11. See S. M. Lipset, *"Values, Education and Entrepreneurialship,"* in *Elites in Latin America,* eds. S. M. Lipset and A. Solari (New York, 1967), p. 6. On the decision of the Cuban leaders, see Castro, speech delivered on July 26, 1968, in *Granma Revista Semanal,* July 28, 1968, pp. 3–5.

12. Castro, speech delivered on October 26, 1959, in Kenner and Petras, *Fidel Castro Speaks,* p. 64. It is interesting to note that the two basic values of equalitarianism and collectivistic orientation are also advocated here, although within a general capitalist framework.

13. Kenner and Petras, *Fidel Castro Speaks,* pp. 270–78.

14. For an excellent discussion of this problem see Fagen, *Transformation of Culture,* pp. 157–58.

15. See Lipset, "Values, Education and Entrepreneurialship," p. 49.

16. See Ernesto Guevara, "Notes on Man and Socialism in Cuba," in *Che Guevara Speaks,* ed. George Lavan (New York, 1968), p. 127.

17. "The Second Declaration of Havana," in Kenner and Petras, *Fidel Castro Speaks,* pp. 96–97.

18. See Carmelo Mesa-Lago, *The Labor Sector and Socialist Distribution in Cuba* (New York, 1968), pp. 94–101, and his more recent "Economic, Political and Ideological Factors in the Cuban Controversy on Material Versus Moral Incentives" (Paper delivered to the Latin American Studies Association Second National Meeting, Washington, D.C., April 17–18, 1970), which stress the relevance of wage differentials in Cuba. For an account of a recent observer who emphasizes wage equalization, see Maurice Zeitlin, "Inside Cuba: Workers and Revolution," *Ramparts,* 8 (March 1970), pp. 11–14.

19. Castro, speech delivered on July 26, 1968, in Kenner and Petras, *Fidel Castro Speaks,* p. 288.

20. Jacques Valier, "L'Économie Cubaine: Quelques problémes essentiels de son functionnement," *Les Temps Modernes,* 23 (March 1968), p. 1613.

21. Castro, speech delivered on July 26, 1969, in Kenner and Petras, *Fidel Castro Speaks,* pp. 293–95.

22. Carlos Rafael Rodríguez, *Cuba, ejemplo de América* (Lima, 1969), p. 12.

23. Buró de Información y Propaganda de la Agrupación Católica Universitaria, *Por qué reforma agraria* (La Habana, 1958). Excerpts of the survey are reproduced in *Cuba Socialista,* 1 (December 1961), pp. 71–72.

24. Ibid.

25. For a discussion of this matter, see chapter 11, this volume. The economic and social functions of private farmers in a socialist state are discussed by Leo Huberman and Paul Sweezy in *Socialism in Cuba* (New York, 1969), pp. 113–30.

26. Ibid., pp. 26–27.

27. Castro, speech to departing brigadistas on May 14, 1961, reproduced in Fagen, *Transformation of Culture,* p. 183.

28. Jacques Valier reports that free medical attention is given to everyone in Cuba, but drugs are given free only in the rural areas. See Valier, "L'Économie Cubaine," pp. 1604–05.

29. Adam Hochschild, "Cuba: Notes on a Revolution," *The Progressive* (May 1970), pp. 29–32.

30. Valier, "L'Économie Cubaine," p. 1629.

31. Oficina Nacional de los Censos Demográfico y Electoral, *Censo de población, viviendas y electoral, 1953* (La Habana, 1955); Cuba, Dirección General del Censo, *Informe general del censo de 1943* (La Habana, 1945); and Consejo Nacional de Economía, *El empleo, el subempleo y el desempleo en Cuba* (La Habana, 1958).

32. Anne Loesch, *Jeune Afrique* (February 19–25, 1968), pp. 46, 47. See also C. W. R. Mills, *Listen Yankee* (New York, 1960), p. 15.

33. Elizabeth Sutherland, *The Youngest Revolution* (New York, 1969), p. 173; and Loesch, *Jeune Afrique,* pp. 46–47.

34. Fagen, *Transformation of Culture,* pp. 48, 60, 83.

35. Major Belarmino Castilla Mas, "Discurso clausurando la Asamblea del Partido en el Ejército del Centro," *Verde Olivo* (March 3, 1968), pp. 8–14.

36. Vilma Espín, "Speech in the Celebration of the 9th Anniversary of the FMC," *Granma Weekly Review,* August 31, 1969, p. 5; Sutherland, *Youngest Revolution,* p. 173; and Loesch, *Jeune Afrique,* pp. 46–47.

37. Rodríguez, *Cuba,* p. 61; and *Granma Weekly Review,* August 31, 1969, p. 4.

38. Castro, speech delivered on May 1, 1966, in Kenner and Petras, *Fidel Castro Speaks,* p. 187.

39. "Without the Women of Our Country . . . ," *Granma Weekly Review,* August 31, 1969, p. 4. See also Gil Green, *Revolution Cuban Style* (New York, 1970), pp. 102–03; and Sutherland, *Youngest Revolution,* pp. 175–76.

40. Carmelo Mesa-Lago, "Economic Significance of Unpaid Labor in Socialist Cuba," *Industrial and Labor Relations Review,* 22 (April 1969), p. 340.

41. JUCEPLAN, *Boletín Estadístico, 1966* (La Habana, n.d.), pp. 138–47.

42. "Results of Election of Delegates to Local Government," *Granma Weekly Review,* October 8, 1967, p. 3.

43. Vilma Espín, "La mujer en la revolución cubana," *Cuba Socialista,* 1 (December 1961), pp. 59–61.

44. JUCEPLAN, *Compendio Estadístico de Cuba, 1968* (La Habana, 1968), pp. 5–6; and "Weddings and the Revolution," *Granma Weekly Review,* May 26, 1968, p. 7.

45. Sutherland, *Youngest Revolution,* pp. 176–83; Joan Robinson, "Cuba—1965," *Monthly Review,* 17 (February 1966), p. 17.

46. Ibid.; Loesch, *Jeune Afrique,* pp. 46–47; and "On the Use of Contraceptives," *Granma Weekly Review,* July 9, 1967, p. 11.

47. Here I draw upon my own experience of twenty-one years lived in Cuba. I was educated in the Jesuit-run *Colegio de Belén* at the same time that Fidel Castro attended that school. Out of a total of approximately 1,200 students and about 100 teachers of middle- and upper-class extraction, I only recall one or two mulattoes, but not a single black. Next to the college, the Jesuits ran a small preelementary school for the poor—entirely segregated from the luxurious buildings of the college—in which the majority of the children were black.

48. Castro, speech delivered on October 26, 1959, in Kenner and Petras, *Fidel Castro Speaks,* p. 54.

49. See John P. Gillin, "Some Signposts for Policy," in *Social Change in Latin America Today,* eds. R. Adams et al. (New York, 1960).

50. It is hard to evaluate how much of this was due to lack of opportunity, insecurity, and the poor pay of such jobs and how much was due to the reluctance of the middle class to take menial jobs.

51. Here, again, I draw from my own experience as a Cuban student both in public and private schools. I do not recall a single teacher mentioning to me or to other students that it would be worthwhile for one of us to think of becoming a carpenter or a mechanic, but *all of us* were encouraged to dream of becoming doctors, lawyers, or architects.

52. See JUCEPLAN, *Compendio Estadístico de Cuba, 1968,* pp. 34–35.

53. Castro, speech delivered on July 26, 1968, in Kenner and Petras, *Fidel Castro Speaks,* p. 294. See also Guevara's "On Creating a New Attitude," in *Venceremos,* ed. John Gerassi (New York, 1968), p. 338.

54. Guevara, "Notes on Man and Socialism in Cuba," p. 130.

55. Castro, speech on socialist consciousness, in Kenner and Petras, *Fidel Castro Speaks,* p. 183.

56. Guevara, "Against Bureaucratism," in *Venceremos,* pp. 220–26. For a full

treatment of the topic see Carmelo Mesa-Lago, "Unemployment in Socialist Countries: Soviet Union, East Europe, China and Cuba" (Ph.D. diss., Cornell University, 1968), pp. 463–78.

57. Thomas, "Middle Class Politics," p. 257.

58. José Moreno, "Che Guevara on Guerrilla Warfare: Doctrine, Practice and Evaluation," *Comparative Studies in Society and History,* 12 (April 1970), p. 128.

59. Castro, speech to the National Congress of Cane Cooperatives, August 18, 1962, in Kenner and Petras, *Fidel Castro Speaks,* pp. 45–47.

60. Carmelo Mesa-Lago, "Ideological Radicalization and Economic Policy in Cuba," *Studies in Comparative International Development,* 5, no. 10 (1970), p. 204, table 1.

61. Castro, speech on the Revolutionary Offensive, in Kenner and Petras, *Fidel Castro Speaks,* pp. 276–78.

62. Joseph Kahl, "The Moral Economy of a Revolutionary Society," *Trans-action,* 6 (April 1969), p. 30.

63. Mesa-Lago has studied manifestations of lack of consciousness among three groups—the youth, the intellectuals, and the workers. This study, illuminating as it is, only shows that some individuals, not the whole group, lack consciousness. See Mesa-Lago, "Economic, Political and Ideological Factors," pp. 37–44.

64. Castro, speech on intellectual property, in Kenner and Petras, *Fidel Castro Speaks,* p. 220.

65. For an extensive treatment of the subject, see Valier, "L'Économie Cubaine," pp. 1590–1649; and Mesa-Lago, "Economic, Political and Ideological Factors."

66. Castro, speech on political awareness, July 26, 1965, in Kenner and Petras, *Fidel Castro Speaks,* p. 294.

67. Zeitlin, "Inside Cuba," p. 68.

68. Guevara, "Notes on Man and Socialism in Cuba," p. 130. See also Guevara, "On Creating a New Attitude," p. 337.

69. Mesa-Lago, "Economic Significance of Unpaid Labor," pp. 339–57.

70. Guevara, "Notes on Man and Socialism in Cuba," p. 131.

71. Moreno, "Che Guevara on Guerrilla Warfare," p. 119.

72. Fagen, *Transformation of Culture,* pp. 151–53.

73. Guevara, "Notes on Man and Socialism in Cuba," p. 127.

74. Kahl, "Moral Economy," pp. 34–36.

75. Fagen, *Transformation of Culture,* pp. 175–79.

IV
Conclusions

18 Carmelo Mesa-Lago

Present and Future
of the Revolution

THIS chapter consists of two sections: the first attempts to balance the revolutionary performance as of 1970; the second explores the future path of the Revolution. Although these two sections are mainly based on the material presented in the preceding seventeen chapters, the author uses his own scheme, selects the variables that he considers most relevant to the revolutionary process, and provides his own judgment in the evaluation.

The first section attempts to summarize, in a coordinated manner, the results of the structural transformation that has taken place in Cuba in the last twelve years. It analyzes revolutionary achievements and failures (or the positive and negative effects of the process) in the fields of polity, economy, and society, trying to show their interrelationship.

The second section begins by presenting a model that compares the principal features of Cuban socialism at the end of the 1960s with those of the Soviet, Chinese, and Yugoslav systems. Then, the author tries to predict what might occur in Cuba in the 1970s if the Revolution continues on its current path or moves in a different direction, be it toward moderation following the Soviet type, toward increasing radicalization à la China, or toward a dramatic change in strategy by using features of the Yugoslav system.

An Attempt to Balance the Present

Polity

Perhaps the most significant achievement of the Revolution is the fact that it is still in power. In view of the proximity and power of the United

501

States and the pressures exerted by it, and the relative isolation of Cuba from the Western Hemisphere and the innumerable conflicts that Cuba has had with other socialist countries (such as the USSR, China, Yugoslavia, and Czechoslovakia), it is truly remarkable that the revolutionary leaders have been able to remain in power. In large measure, this has been possible because of Castro's charisma, audacity, unpredictability, and pragmatism. Castro has frequently shifted ideology, policy, and strategy to develop his bargaining power to the utmost. He has been able to do this by centralizing power and controlling key executive, army, party, and economic posts. The substantial support received from the socialist bloc, and essentially from the USSR, has been another factor in keeping the Revolution in power.

The radical transformation of the prerevolutionary to the revolutionary structure was accomplished in a rather short period, with relatively little bloodshed, and without destroying the main resources of the country. Reasons for this could be the relative development of Cuba in 1959 (particularly that of its infrastructure and communications system), the vacuum of power at the onset of the revolutionary take-over, filled by Castro and his inner circle, the lack of solid institutions that could have opposed the Revolution, and the relative ease with which opponents were able to leave the country.

The revolutionary leaders have used their unrestricted power over national resources to pursue national independency, egalitarianism, and economic development. Centralization and control have been instrumental in mobilizing the population to defend the Revolution in the military field and to help the government in its developmental plans. Corruption and bribery, typical of previous administrations, have been conspicuously absent from the revolutionary administration.

Cuba is less politically dependent on the Soviet Union than it was on the United States. United States political influence and involvement in Cuba was a natural outgrowth of the former's investment and economic interests in the latter. Conversely, USSR involvement in Cuba is a result of international politics, and Soviet economic aid is granted to keep Cuba a socialist country in the Western Hemisphere. Because of the physical distance between Cuba and the USSR, the absence of direct Soviet investment in the island, and the Soviet political concern to save socialism in Cuba (and avoid a direct confrontation with Castro), there has been a high degree of independence in Cuba, at least compared with that allowed by the USSR to other socialist allies. In this process, Cuba has become one of the best known, best watched and most ideologically influential countries in the world. It has had and still has a significant role to play in the U.S.–

USSR confrontation, the socialist-camp controversy, and the third-world search for a new path.

However, some of the variables discussed above also have a negative side. Let us refer first to the concentration of power. The political structure of Cuba is characterized by personalism, autocracy, and paternalism. Castro and his small clique of loyal supporters control the political functions of rule-making, adjudication, and application. Despite several promises, a political constitution that could have defined and restricted the powers of this group has not been enacted. Political rights considered essential in the West, such as freedom of expression, publication or dissent, or even public constructive criticism from within the Revolution, are nonexistent or at least greatly reduced, particularly in the last few years. There is no real protection given to the politically dissenting citizen by the judiciary process (controlled by revolutionary courts) and the number of political prisoners is high. The only political party allowed, the PCC, does not have real power, has a small membership, does not have regulations or bylaws, and has held no congresses. There are no truly associational interest groups. Organizations such as the CTC, ANAP, FMC, UJC, and CDR do not participate in decision-making (e.g., political decisions, planning, fixing production targets), but mobilize their memberships to support decisions made by the leaders. The absence of a system of evaluation and checks from below have led to unrealistic targets, excessive optimism, and serious mistakes among the top hierarchy, and perhaps indifference among the masses.

As the Cuban Revolution has evolved throughout the years, means of generating popular support have gradually changed from demand satisfaction and affectivity to coercion. Social costs of the revolutionary process initially borne by foreign interests, and next by domestic upper- and middle-income groups, are now borne by the lower strata of the population. (This tendency may be related to the shifting composition of the exile population, now reaching 7 percent of the total population. Although there was initially a very small percentage of unskilled workers, fishermen, and agricultural workers among the exiles, this percentage has been gradually increasing and is now even larger among those who leave the island by illegal means.) The leaders have resorted to moral stimulation as a new way to generate popular support, but there is no evidence as yet that this method is producing results. This could explain the increasing trend toward the militarization of the economy and the regimentation of society in general. In this process, the power of the armed forces has been considerably augmented, with members holding control of most crucial posts in the cabinet, important state enterprises and farms, and even in the party.

Serious flaws of the Revolution include the lack of institutionalization and the problems of continuity and succession. On several occasions, steps taken by the revolutionary leaders have created hope of institutionalization —for example, the establishment of the PCC and the announcement of a political constitution in 1965, and the election of the commissions of local power in 1966–1967. (New promises to democratize the unions, allow mass organizations to check the party, and generate collective management in state enterprises were made in late 1970.) However, these hopes have not materialized, and the Revolution's constant changes in structure, ideology, and policy have impeded consolidation, maturation, and the possibility of each new round of changes bearing fruit. During the twelve years of Revolution, practically nothing has been done to decentralize and delegate the power concentrated at the top. The enormous role played by Castro and the lack of institutions (besides the armed forces) create concern about the future. One question often raised is what would happen to the Revolution if Castro would suddenly disappear. Although Raúl Castro has been appointed official successor in the hierarchical line, he does not have the charismatic appeal of his brother. Charisma has been a crucial element in keeping the Revolution in power and in avoiding bloody factional struggles. The question is whether the increasingly powerful armed forces could be strong enough in such a case to save the Revolution.

Cuba's efforts to export the Revolution's model to Latin America through subversion and guerrilla warfare have failed up to now. This fact together with Guevara's death in 1967, the need to concentrate on domestic economic problems, and Soviet pressures have induced Cuba to slow down such efforts. In the meantime, Cuba has accepted other alternatives (such as peaceful democratic elections and *coups d'état* by progressive military men) to Latin American problems. The election of a socialist president in Chile has resulted in the reestablishment of diplomatic relations between the two countries. On the other hand, in spite of informal cordial relations with Peru and to lesser extent with Bolivia, these two countries had not followed the Chilean example by mid-1971. Also, trade between Cuba and Mexico, Jamaica, and Trinidad-Tobago has been almost nonexistent and has been relatively small even with Chile. Hence, Cuba continues to be isolated within Latin America.

Economy

Through collectivization of the means of production, the Cuban state achieved almost total control of all the nation's resources. This permitted the early consumptionist policy of the Revolution that was essential in the consolidation of popular support. Later on, control of national resources and unions allowed the steady increase in capital accumulation (from some 14 percent of GNP in 1959 to some 31 percent of GMP in 1968) and the redirection of investment toward the "productive" sector of the economy. Control over resources and the educational system has permitted the reorientation of the latter away from nonfunctional humanistic careers and toward technological and vocational training that has helped the development effort.

After applying the initial erroneous strategy of "balanced development," which emphasized heavy industrialization and neglected primary activities (1959–1963), a dramatic shift was made in favor of the "big push" development strategy based on primary activities, particularly those of sugar, and cattle, mining, and fishing. Besides the expansion of cultivated land, the premises for intensive agricultural development (i.e., fertilization, irrigation, improved seed, mechanization) have been substantially enlarged. The new program of development has had remarkable success in the capital intensive, highly technological and concentrated industries that use a small number of skilled workers whose output and productivity is easy to control. Thus, nickel output has increased twofold in 1957–1969, and fish output has increased threefold in the same period. Output of electricity, cigarettes, and eggs also shows substantial increases.

The combination of rural-to-urban migration, expansion of employment in the state bureaucracy, farms, and social services, army recruitment, and the program of fellowships for rural youngsters of working age has eliminated seasonal, overt unemployment in agriculture. The urban labor surplus is being transferred to the countryside through the campaign against bureaucracy, compulsory military service (in which recruits perform agricultural tasks), and the mobilization of youngsters.

The nation has become economically independent of the United States. Cuba's percentage of trade with the USSR is smaller than it had been formerly with the United States, and there is no direct Soviet investment in the island. United States economic actions (e.g., the cut of the sugar quota) and the embargo against Cuba have failed because the latter has been able to obtain needed spare parts from triangular trade, transportation equipment from Western Europe, and fuel, military equipment, machinery, and credit from the USSR and the socialist countries. The latter, in turn, have made agreements to buy Cuban products, mainly sugar. Also, Cuba's merchant marine rapidly expanded in the second half of the 1960s and today is one of the largest in Latin America.

In spite of the achievements mentioned above, the negative effects of the revolutionary economic process far outweigh the positive. The initial guerrilla mentality and excessive and rapid collectivization alienated technicians and managers who left the country before the Revolution could have had a chance to train its own cadres. Possibly, the centralization of political power has been a determinant of the type of economic organization chosen—the possibility of market socialism received very little consideration, and soon the leadership decided to eliminate totally or partially self-financed enterprises, economic incentives, and monetary and mercantile relations. There seems to be some relationship between political centralization, militarization, and the Guevarist dream of a cybernetic, computerized economy for Cuba.

Despite the high rate of capital accumulation, the scarcity of skilled personnel, the constant changes in investment plans, costly economic experiments, and the lack of market mechanisms (e.g., interest rate) and their substitutes in an efficiently handled command economy (e.g., the coefficient of relative effectiveness) have induced waste of investment resources and low capital productivity.

Manpower shortages at the peak of the harvest season (resulting mainly from the transformation of seasonal unemployment into various forms of underemployment) have been alleviated by the use of unpaid labor recruited in the cities, but at the cost of very low productivity. This fact together with the lack of economic incentives, poor utilization of the work schedule, bad organization, rising absenteeism, and frequent shifts in economic policy have induced either stagnation or decline of output both in agriculture and in the traditional (labor-intensive) industrial sector. Combined agricultural and industrial output per capita in 1966 was substantially below that of 1958.

Domestically, the decline in output accentuated by an increase of disposable income made the introduction and rapid expansion of rationing necessary. Scarcity of resources and the emphasis on capital accumulation since 1962 were determinants in the gradual cut of investment in social services and housing. These restrictions have possibly operated as disincentives for the labor force, which has reduced its productive effort even more.

Externally, the reduction in exports at the same time that imports have increased resulted in a growing deficit in the trade balance. The USSR has provided credit to temporarily cover this deficit, but this has put Cuba in debt. In 1969, the deficit in Cuba's balance of payments was possibly above $3 billion, most of it held by the USSR. Cuba's trade with the Soviets is mainly barter trade and is thus difficult to evaluate, resulting in small convertible foreign exchange for Cuba. The enormous distance between the two countries has induced higher freight costs. Although Soviet political influence in Cuba is much smaller than that previously exerted by the United States, Cuba is heavily dependent on the USSR for capital, trade, fuel, machinery, and military equipment. There has been very little change in the composition of Cuban exports; sugar and minerals increasing slightly at the cost of tobacco and miscellaneous exports.

The Prospective Sugar Plan (1965–1970) was unfulfilled by 25 percent, and there were years in which nonfulfillment reached as high as 50 percent. Cuba's failure to honor its sugar commitments with the USSR has led to an accumulated deficit of ten million tons of sugar. Although the 1970 sugar harvest set a new output record (1.3 million tons above the 1952 record, but 1.5 millions below the 1970 target), this was partly achieved by neglecting the 1969 harvest and by deploying resources from the nonsugar sector, which resulted in a general decline of output in the first half of 1970. After satisfying previous export commitments and domestic needs, no surplus was left over from Cuba's 1970 sugar harvest to reduce its accumulated deficit in both sugar deliveries and balance of payments. Furthermore, the new breeding program for cattle expansion apparently has not yielded the expected results neither in birth rate nor in milk output.

Cuban national income probably increased in 1959–1961, declined in 1962–1963, a period of serious recession, and then recuperated in 1964–1965, only to decline again in 1966–1969 to lower levels than those of 1962–1963. Per capita income in 1962–1967 declined at an average annual rate of minus 2.6 percent.

As far as labor is concerned, Cuban trade unions are no longer defenders of the individual worker's interests, but of the interests of the collectivity centered around production and productivity. The government has direct control over the regulation of labor conditions, but the unions have no real participation in the administration of socialist property, planning, and managerial decision-making, all of which seem to be under the exclusive control of the political leadership. There are differences between the immediate interests of the proletariat and the leadership's long-run national objectives. The managers of the means of production appointed by the leadership represent the interests and decision-making policies of the latter, which are not necessarily the same as those of the masses. The freedom to express potential disagreement by workers and unions seems to be obstructed by CTC hierarchical control over local unions, by the strict regime of labor discipline in the enterprises, the system of state control over employment, the labor record of the worker, etc. This overall situation has been an important cause of the planning of unrealistic output targets and probably of the declining labor effort.

Society

The emphasis on egalitarianism is one of the most significant accomplishments of the Revolution. Class distinctions, institutionalized racial discrimination, income differentials, the gulf between urban and rural living standards, and some of the barriers that impeded the integration of women into the labor force have been totally or partially eliminated. Principally, this has been a result of the revolutionary policies in favor of full employment, enforcement of minimum wages for the occupations at the bottom of the social ladder, reduction of the cost of housing, utilities and transportation, expansion of free social services (e.g., education, public health, burials) particularly in rural areas, increased investment in agriculture, and expansion of the social security system and of day-care centers. A factor that has helped in the egalitarian trend has been the exodus of the former upper- and middle-income groups of society.

The government has given special attention to education and culture by using its centralized control over national resources. Achievements in this field include the campaign against illiteracy, the enormous increase of schools, personnel, and enrollment in elementary, secondary, and vocational schools, the ambitious program of fellowships, and the redirection of higher education in favor of new careers committed to development. The publication of books and specialized journals has increased tremendously, and government agencies encourage literary and artistic production by facilitating publication, the staging of plays and exhibits, giving stable occupation and paying salaries to artists, and by stimulating these artists through international contests. The development of the cinema has followed a similar path and, for the first time, Cuban films are competing in the international arena for cinematographic quality and plots. Theatrical activities also had increased notably in the early years of the Revolution.

Changes introduced in the social structure have played down the pre-revolutionary values that stressed hierarchical elitism and individualism, and both the revolutionary leaders and the communications media now encourage a new set of motivations, stressing equalitarianism and collectivity orientation.

The almost absolute state control of resources and employment, however, has resulted in the reinforcing of a unique line of thought, gradually eliminating pluralism and initiative in society. Thus, the abolition of royalties, nationalization of the publishing houses and news media, the organization of the writers union under government auspices, and the integration of all publishing activities into a single state agency (Instituto del Libro) have made the writer totally dependent on the state. Theater has become part of the official cultural structure controlled by the National Council of Culture, whereas the cinema has been brought under the control of the Cuban Institute of Cinema Arts. Thematically, literature (as well as the arts) has not shown too much interest in the revolutionary process itself.

But the state is increasingly tightening its control, emphasizing not only revolutionary loyalty but also thematic concern in an attempt to direct intellectual life toward greater militancy.

Pluralism in education came to an end with the nationalization of private schools in 1961. Politicization of education, the granting of fellowships to study abroad only in orthodox socialist countries, control over the use of textbooks and other educational materials and the suspension of several important journals in 1965–1967, in which several controversies were publicized, have reinforced the official viewpoint.

Religious freedom has been affected also, although there has been a noticeable decline in tension between church and state since the mid-1960s. Through both compulsory and voluntary exile, the number of priests has declined to one-third of its former size and that of nuns to one-tenth. Also, government concessions permitting entry and exit of priests have been rescinded many times; religious associations have been dissolved; religious schools (and even seminaries) have been confiscated; religious communications media have been suspended; there have been sporadic interruptions of religious services; priests have been occasionally imprisoned or sent to labor camps; and there is discrimination against students with strong religious beliefs in university admission policies.

In spite of the remarkable advances in equalitarianism, racial and sexual discrimination are still strong in the distribution of employment, participation in political decision-making and in sexual mores. Rural areas have apparently forged ahead at the expense of the cities (especially Havana), which have fallen into decay due to emigration, decline in construction, rationing, mobilization of the citizenry to the countryside, and deemphasis on industrial investment. Finally, the leadership seems to enjoy a privileged position because it is not affected by rationing, housing scarcity, and other restrictions imposed on the general population.

The Revolution has affected various social groups in different ways. The large masses of former peasants (most of whom are now small private farmers) have benefited from land grants and the provision of free social services. Possibly, the living conditions of salaried agricultural workers and unskilled urban workers have improved most, with full employment, increased income, and free social services. Also, these two groups (peasants and workers) probably have not been seriously affected by rationing because their previous level of consumption was very low. Conversely, most members of the former dominant urban and rural groups (and of intermediate groups such as professionals) have left the country and lost all their possessions. Owners of medium-sized farms have been affected by land confiscation, compulsory *acopio,* and state control. (The last two measures have also affected small farmers.) Possibly, most skilled workers have not improved their previous status and have been affected by restrictions on consumption, transfers, and pressures to do unpaid labor.

At the risk of oversimplification, the above discussion of revolutionary performance to date allows us to make a general statement regarding the revolutionary changes that have taken place in the fields of polity, economy, and society. In politics, the revolutionary performance has been more positive in external matters than in domestic ones. Overall performance in economics seems to be on the negative side, whereas most revolutionary achievements can be recorded in social matters. In order to keep and improve its accomplishments in the social sphere, the Revolution must generate a minimum of political support and consensus, and this in turn will depend in large measure on its future economic performance. The two crucial problems that are challenging the Revolution and may have to be solved in the 1970s are (a) excessive centralization of power, lack of participation of the masses in the decision-making process, and the need for institutionalization and (b) stagnation or decline of output, very low capital and labor productivity, and lack of continuity in economic policy. In the following pages, some alternative solutions to these problems are discussed.

An Attempt to Explore the Future

Based on the material presented on Cuba in this book as well as on our knowledge of the experience of other socialist countries and resorting somewhat to speculation, an exploration of the possible alternatives open to the Cuban Revolution will be made. For simplicity, such alternatives or variables have been integrated into types, which are summarized in table 1.[1] However, this does not preclude a different combination of the variables of each type into an infinite number of types.

First of all, the author wants to warn the reader that the table requires further refinement and, hence, should be taken with caution. In many cases, the evaluation of the variables has been made by rule of thumb rather than by the use of supporting quantitative data, which are often simply nonexistent. Ranking of variables could be modified as a result of better measurement. The purpose of using the table is to show the differences between the Cuban type and those of other socialist countries. This will help us to explore the future path of the Cuban Revolution.

In the table, Cuba's fifteen variables are compared with those of China, the USSR, and Yugoslavia as of 1968. These three latter countries have been selected because their types are probably the most influential within the socialist world. The need to specify the year is important because these countries have frequently changed important variables over time. The So-

TABLE 1
FOUR TYPES IN THE SOCIALIST WORLD, CIRCA 1968

Predominance of	China	Cuba	USSR	Yugoslavia
Subjective over objective conditions	Very strong	Very strong	Weak	Very weak
Equality over stratification	Very strong	Strong	Weak	Very weak
Moral over material incentives	Strong	Very strong	Weak	Very weak
Mobilization over institutionalization	Very strong	Strong	Very weak	Weak
Mass participation in economic decision-making over power clique	Strong	Very weak	Weak	Very strong
Political indoctrination over non-politicized education	Very strong	Strong	Medium	Weak
Tight control over flexibility in artistic expression	Very strong	Medium	Strong	Weak
Decentralized over centralized planning	Strong	Weak	Medium	Very strong
Communes and state farms over collective and private farms	Very strong	Strong	Medium	Very weak
Budgetary finance over self-finance	Very strong	Very strong	Weak	Very weak
Loyalty over expertise in manager selection	Very strong	Strong	Medium	Weak
Production of capital goods over consumer goods	Very strong	Very strong	Strong	Weak
Investment in agriculture over heavy industry	Strong	Very strong	Very weak	Weak
Full employment over high labor productivity	Strong	Very strong	Strong	Weak
Commitment to world revolution over coexistence	Very strong	Strong	Medium	Very weak

viet type or War Communism (1918–1920), for instance, is dramatically different from that of the New Economic Policy (1921–1928), the Stalinist (1929–1953), and from the economic reform type of the 1960s. On the other hand, the Chinese, Yugoslavian, and Cuban types applied under the first long-range plans in all of these countries were similar to the Stalinist type. The Chinese types of the Great Leap Forward (1958–1960) and the Great Proletarian Cultural Revolution (1966–1968) show strong similarities with the Cuban type of the Revolutionary Offensive of 1968.

In the table, China represents the extreme-left stand, an attempt to skip the socialist transitional stage (or at least go rapidly through it) and go directly to communism. This type (followed closely by Cuba) is an amalgam of ideas from Marx in his younger years, Trotsky, Mao, Guevara, and Castro. Conversely, Yugoslavia is the best representative of the so-called revisionist or liberal stand. This is a pragmatic realization of the need of the transitional stage. The type, commonly called market socialism, results from the ideas of Marx, Lange, Taylor, and Lerner, as well as from Yugoslav experimentation. In the table, the USSR is much closer to Yugoslavia than to China, although the mild reforms introduced in the Soviet Union after Stalin's death hardly integrate a market-socialism type. The Cuban brief testing of some market-socialism features (e.g., self-financed enterprise) in 1964–1965 was even milder than current Soviet reforms. With increasing emphasis on moral incentives after 1966 and the climactic Revolutionary Offensive of 1968, Cuba moved closer and closer to the Chinese type although with some significant differences.

The fifteen variables in the table measure the degree of radicalization of each type. A ranking of fifteen "very strong's" would mean a pure extreme-left type. In practice, this does not exist, but China and Cuba are very close to such an ideal type. Conversely, a ranking of fifteen "very weak's" would mean a pure type of market socialism, approximated by Yugoslavia. (In this case the opposite variable, e.g., institutionalization over permanent revolution, actually receives a grading of "very strong.") By "medium," a situation is indicated in which none of the two opposite variables is strong enough to constitute a predominant feature of the type.

Some of the variables in the table may appear too vague and require clarification. The first one refers to the Sino-Cuban belief that subjective conditions (willingness) are more important than objective conditions. The guerrilla spirit of Yenan and the Sierra Maestra has been an important determinant in this attitude. Both Mao and Guevara have claimed that it is possible to change the superstructure first (e.g., ideology) in order to facilitate the transformation of the structure or mode of production (i.e., economy).

The third variable—moral over material incentives—refers to the ambitious attempt of China and Cuba to develop rapidly a new man, characterized by asceticism, collective, spirit, self-discipline, and selflessness. The fourth variable presents the opposition between "permanent revolution" on the one hand (characterized by constant changes, experimentation, and mobilization to avoid the cooling off of revolutionary fervor), and institutionalization, bureaucratization, or routinization on the other. The sixth variable could also present the dilemma of isolation over the exposure of a socialist country to foreign ideas, measured by the exchange of publications, students and technicians, the facilities for travel, the screening of foreign scholars, etc.

Since there are only small differences in the degree of collectivization of the nonagricultural sector within the socialist world, the ninth variable concentrates on the degree of collectivization of agriculture. China has a very strong ranking in this variable with its communal system, whereas Yugoslavia's percentage of collectivized agriculture is very small. In the

USSR, the proportion of land organized into state farms and collective farms is about equal and there is no private agriculture, whereas in Cuba, 70 percent of agriculture is organized into state farms and, although the rest is cultivated by private farmers, they are as controlled as the Soviet collective farms. In the tenth variable, the budgetary finance system is not only characterized by capital allocation through the central budget but also by the use of nonrepayable capital gifts that are exempted from interest charges. The self-financed enterprise, on the other hand, is based on repayable loans and interest charges.

The eleventh variable presents the traditional controversy of "red versus expert," accentuated in the Sino-Cuban model by the guerrilla leaders' distrust of and distaste for bureaucrats, technicians, and academicians. This frequently has resulted in placing inexperienced laymen, but loyal revolutionaries, in charge of important specialized jobs. The twelfth variable could similarly measure capital accumulation versus consumption or percentage of state investment in the productive sector vis-à-vis the social services.

Concerning the thirteenth variable, it could be argued that the direction of state investment toward industry or agriculture is determined in most cases by national conditions and needs. Some sociologists, however, claim that the rural base of Chinese and Cuban guerrillas has been the main reason for the priority granted to agriculture. Finally, the fifteenth variable also refers to the controversy of whether universal socialism is a prerequisite for full development of socialism in one single country. Presented in another way, it could also measure the degree of commitment in the exportation of the socialist revolution versus nonalignment in blocs. The Soviet ranking as medium in this variable is explained by a contradictory attitude; for instance, the Soviet invasion of Czechoslovakia but support of Latin American orthodox Communist parties that have rejected Cuban-based guerrillas.

China and Cuba are both ranked "very strong" in three variables, whereas in another nine variables one of the countries is ranked "very strong" and the other as "strong." But there are a few significant differences between the two types. In China, mass participation in economic decision-making (fifth variable) has been typical of both the Great Leap Forward and the Great Proletarian Cultural Revolution periods, but the high centralization of decision-making power has been a constant in Castro's Cuba. Another discrepancy is clear in the eighth variable in which China seems to be closer to Yugoslavia (although following a different decentralizing scheme) than to Cuba.

The effects of the Great Proletarian Cultural Revolution in China and of the Revolutionary Offensive in Cuba have been fairly similar. This is consistent with the similarity of their types. For instance, excessive emphasis on "willingness" and moral incentives on the one hand, and serious negligence of real conditions and economic incentives, on the other, have induced in both countries a slowdown of labor effort, absenteeism, and declines in output and productivity. Interestingly enough, the two variables in which China and Cuba show a noticeably divergent performance could have induced different results. Thus, economic chaos, labor indiscipline, and factional struggle have been considerably higher in China than in Cuba. This could be partially explained by the prevalence of a strong and united power elite (controlled by Castro) and centralization in Cuba as opposed to mass participation in decision-making and decentralization in China.

Let us now analyze the action that Cuba might take if it continues to follow its current path or moves toward any of the three alternative types presented in the table.

Continuation of the Cuban Type

It is very unlikely that Cuba will continue on its present path. The nonfulfillment of the 1970 sugar-crop target could be a turning point for a reconsideration of policy. The population was enduring sacrifices in the second half of the 1960s with the promise of a better decade in the 1970s. The long-range economic strategy of the country, the expectations to reduce the foreign debt, and the hopes to alleviate rationing all were based on the epic achievement of the ten-million-ton sugar goal. The year 1970 is also crucial because it marks the end of the Soviet-Cuban sugar agreement that began in 1965.

The official target for the 1971 sugar harvest was originally set at 7 million tons and later reduced to 6.5 million tons; the actual output was only 5.9 million. The time period for the 1971 harvest was half of the 1970 time period and labor mobilization was considerably smaller. There have been official reports that the replanting and fertilization of the cane was considerably delayed. The strenuous effort to which the old equipment was submitted in 1970 may have resulted in the breakdown of machinery difficult to replace. A new method of burning the sugar fields to ease the cutting process was tested in 1971 with apparently poor results. In addition, Castro claimed that there was a severe drought.[2]

Cuba could try to produce ten million tons in the 1970s. If this target is achieved, it could help solve Cuba's foreign debt and provide more resources for developing the nonsugar sector, particularly cattle-raising, mining, and fishing. But the possibility that this ambitious target will even be tried seems to be very small. First, the country lacks the material and human resources to pursue this grandiose sugar policy and to keep up output in the nonsugar sector. Second, it is unlikely that the Cuban government can continue to mobilize the population in the 1970s as it did in the 1960s. The costs of economic and political deterioration might be too high. This mobilization problem, however, could be overcome by increasing the current process of militarization and the role of the armed forces. By the end of 1970, twelve out of twenty-three ministerial posts in the cabinet (including the most strategic ones dealing with defense, interior, communications, agriculture, labor, education, internal distribution, etc.) were occupied by military officers. Six out of eight members of the PCC politbureau were army majors. In the July–August 1970 changes in the cabinet, two new ministries went to the military. In chapters 9 and 11, it has been indicated that control measures over the labor force and against absenteeism have been increasing recently. The question is how long the Cuban leaders may go on requesting sacrifices from the population and tightening control.

In any event, what would Cuba's long-range strategy be if it is able to produce steadily ten million tons of sugar (or more) per year? The USSR is self-sufficient with its domestic production of ten million tons, and U.S. specialists affirm that the Soviets have been storing part of the Cuban sugar bought in the past to avoid a major decline in prices.[3] On the other hand, in 1966 the USSR exported almost as much sugar as it imported from Cuba, whereas in 1967, Soviet sugar exports totalled about half the amount imported from Cuba.[4] The probability that Cuba can substantially expand the sale of sugar in other countries, socialist and nonsocialist, is small due to the current system of bilateral and international quotas. Another possibility, although with poor chance of implementation is that Cuba—with or without Soviet aid—will attempt a "dumping" of sugar to bring about a serious drop in prices. This, in turn, would eliminate various sugar producers, leaving Cuba in control of the international market.[5]

Change Toward the Soviet Type

Guevara's death and reversals in guerrilla warfare in Latin America, as well as events in Peru and Bolivia and the democratic election of socialist Salvador Allende as president of Chile, have weakened Cuba's hard line in Latin America (i.e., armed struggle as the only solution) and bolstered the milder Soviet line that propounds a variety of solutions, including peaceful ones. As has been explained in chapters 4 and 5, Castro has given priority to domestic problems, diminishing considerably his effort to export his type of Revolution, while accepting the Peruvian model as a suitable alternative. He has done this even at the cost of being criticized by the Venezuelan guerrilla leader Douglas Bravo and abandoning to their fate various guerrilla fighters in Peru and Bolivia.

Since Castro's support of the Soviet invasion of Czechoslovakia in August 1968, Cuban relations with the Soviet Union have improved considerably after mutual concessions and signs of friendship. In October, Ramiro Valdés was removed from his post as minister of the interior, a post that he held since 1959. He was the leading accuser of the pro-Soviet "microfaction" purged in February of 1968. Soviet Vice President Vladimir Novikov visited Cuba in January 1969. The 1969 trade protocol between the two countries was signed without any difficulties in February. The Association of Cuban-Soviet Friendship was established in April. Cuba sent two observers (one of them was Carlos Rafael Rodríguez, a member of the old Communist guard) to the World Communist Conference held in Moscow in June, a Soviet attempt to isolate China. (The latter, together with Albania, North Korea, and North Vietnam did not attend the conference. Cuba had refused to send a delegate to the preparatory conference held in Budapest in February 1968.) Soviet warships paid a visit to the Havana harbor in July 1969, and Russian sailors went to the countryside to cut sugar cane in a friendship gesture. Soviet Defense Minister Marshall Andrei Grechko visited Cuba in November.

In his speech during the centennial commemoration of Lenin's birth in April 1970, Castro accused "pseudo-leftists" and "superrevolutionaries" that had criticized the Soviet invasion of Czechoslovakia of being either idiots or CIA agents. He also showed eagerness to increase Cuba's military links with the USSR. This was also the occasion chosen by Castro to answer Douglas Bravo's criticism of Cuba's abandonment of guerrilla warfare, and to proclaim the acceptance of the Peruvian model.[6] *Fidelista* periodicals in Latin America published the previously cited speech with annotations criticizing Trotsky, Mao, Sartre, and Marcuse, and their followers, as divisionist agents who actually serve U.S. imperialism by taking an extremist position.[7]

President Dorticós, Minister of Armed Forces Raúl Castro, and Minister of the Interior Major Sergio del Valle went to Moscow in April–May 1970 to attend the festivities in commemoration of Lenin's birth. Dorticós had a well-publicized interview with Brezhnev. Raúl Castro discussed Soviet arms supplies for the Cuban armed forces and was honored by being chosen as one of the dignataries to preside over the May-Day parade in Moscow. Also, in October, Castro's brother went back to Moscow, held an interview with Brezhnev, and attended military exercises of the Warsaw-Pact forces in East Germany.[8]

Two Cuban intelligence agents and two military men that defected from Cuba in the second half of 1969 have stated that Soviet influence over Cuba has increased substantially. One of the intelligence agents, Orlando Castro, asserted that in early 1969 Cuba had signed an agreement with the USSR by which the former would cease its criticism against Moscow and the Latin

American Communist parties that follow the Soviet line. In reciprocity, the Soviets would continue their economic aid to Cuba, send 5,000 technicians to Cuba (in agriculture, mining, fishing, atomic energy, military-training, and internal security), increase oil supplies, and buy higher quantities of Cuban nickel.[9] Whether this agreement is real or not, it is evident that Soviet pressures and Cuba's domestic problems have made the Cubans move closer to the Soviet line, at least in foreign policy. The point is whether the Russians will take advantage of the impending negotiation of the sugar agreement and the weakened bargaining position of Castro to pull the Cubans into line economically and politically.

If Cuba yields to Soviet pressures, significant changes might result (as in the direction indicated in table 1 when moving from the Cuban to the Soviet types). Politically, there would be an attempt to institutionalize the Revolution, possibly enacting a socialist constitution (which would define the political structure and its functions and put limits to Castro's power) and making the PCC stronger. Economically, the experiment of moral incentives would be suspended and economic incentives gradually reintroduced (there have been signs in 1970–1971 that Cuba is moving in this direction), the economic organization and decision-making apparatus would be decentralized somewhat, the system of self-finance would be partly reestablished, the *acopio* requested from private farmers would be reduced and prices of farm products increased, there would be a trend toward professionalization in management, and both the percentage of GMP devoted to consumption and that of investment directed toward consumer-goods production and social services would increase somewhat. Possibly, the strategy of development based on primary activities would continue, but the goals for sugar output would be less spectacular (e.g., from six to seven million tons) with increased emphasis placed on cattle-raising, fishing, and mining, as well as on the fertilization, irrigation, and mechanization of agriculture.

This change would increase Cuba's economic dependence on the Soviet Union. (For the possibility of Cuba following the Soviet type but reaching an agreement with the United States, see the next section.) If everything were to function adequately, however, the change would result in some improvements in domestic production and the balance of payments. Cuba would put aside its policy of external subversion in Latin America. Castro would relinquish part of his power to the party, the army, and the managerial bureaucracy and, hence, erode his charismatic appeal. (Another alternative would be for Castro to follow the Stalinist type of tight control in ideology and internal politics, together with pragmatism in economics and international relations. This path, however, would be blocked by Soviet pressure for institutionalization.) The Castroite model would lose its originality and relative independence and thus would lose its attractiveness to other countries of the third world.

Change Toward the Yugoslav Type

This alternative depends on the intensity of Cuba's desire for independence from the USSR and the changing role that both the latter and the United States could play in their future relations with Cuba. The application of the Yugoslav type would be a drastic retreat in the ideological stand that Cuba maintained in 1966–1970, in favor of a position that it has criticized vehemently. And yet, Castro has gone through so many ideological shifts that a new one would not be surprising.

The acceptance of the Yugoslav type (see table 1) would imply a step forward in the application of the measures already discussed in the previous section. Pragmatism being accentuated, professionalization in management and education would follow. Possibly, part of the land would be decollectivized, that is, a large number of state farms would be transformed into cooperatives or divided into private-holdings, as occurred in Poland and Yugoslavia in the mid-1950s. One would also have to expect greater private initiative in other sectors, such as trade, handicrafts, and services. Emphasis on productivity and economic incentives might result in some unemployment and a reverse in the tendencies toward equalitarianism. Decentralization in planning and economic decision-making would be accelerated, perhaps, with the introduction of a system of workers' participation in management. Political decentralization would result in the delegation of responsibilities to local authorities, perhaps by reviving the commissions of local power. Cuba would attempt to increase its independence of the USSR and attach itself to the peaceful coexistence line in the hemisphere.

An important factor that would help to bring about this change would be the willingness of the United States to lift the embargo and resume trade relations with Cuba. By doing this, the United States would accept socialism in the island in order to make the Cuban regime more liberal domestically and independent externally. United States involvement in this way could be caused by either a confrontation between Cuba and the Soviets or, more possibly, by mutual agreement among the three countries.

The latent Cuban-Soviet frictions might be exacerbated by discrepancies induced by the negotiation of the new sugar agreement, Castro's reluctance to yield to Soviet pressures to institutionalize his regime, Soviet withdrawal of the allegedly installed submarine base in Cienfuegos without consulting Cuba, or by other similar causes. More realistic is the possibility that the USSR, facing a deteriorating economic situation in Cuba, would negotiate with the United States a greater politico-economic independence for Cuba in order to consolidate socialism in the island and save itself from the financial burden that Cuba represents. In this kind of situation, American and Soviet interests would coincide in the matter of Cuba suspending armed subversion in the hemisphere. (The possibility of a Cuban-American *rapprochement,* at least in trade matters, is a variable that could also fit in the case that Cuba would move toward the Soviet type.)

Currently, neither the United States, most Latin American countries, nor Cuba seem to favor the reestablishment of diplomatic and trade relations among themselves. In spite of recent moves among U.S. intellectual circles in favor of a *rapprochement* with Cuba,[10] the Nixon administration has not changed its stand. Declarations made in 1969–1970 (some of them at the OAS) by Chile, Venezuela, and Peru supporting the reintegration of Cuba to the inter-American system did not produce results. On two occasions in 1970, Assistant Secretary of State for Inter-American Affairs Robert A. Hurtwitch defended the maintenance of the U.S. embargo and OAS sanctions upon Cuba and reiterated the previous policy that the renewal of diplomatic and trade relations with Cuba was not possible unless the latter would cut its ties with the USSR and cease its subversive activities in the hemisphere.[11] In June, the Chilean Christian-Democrat government announced that a two-year trade agreement had been signed with Cuba to sell it $11 million in Chilean foodstuffs. A few weeks later, spokesmen of the Nixon administration revealed that in March the U.S. government had sent a report to the OAS and all Latin American foreign ministers attempting to prove that Cuba's subversion was still a threat to the hemisphere and urging them not to relax the diplomatic and economic boycott against Cuba. According to the U.S. spokesmen, Peru and Bolivia had agreed with this report and were discouraged from renewing relations with Cuba.[12] In November, however, Cuba and the newly elected socialist government of Chile reestablished diplomatic relations. It is too soon to judge whether the movement will encourage other Latin American countries to follow the Chilean example in spite of U.S. opposition.

The Cuban position is not encouraging either, although recently there has been some softening. In July 1969, Castro said that in order to reestablish diplomatic relations with Cuba any country in Latin America must begin by rejecting the OAS measures taken against it and condemning the "crime" committed by "Yankee imperialism." The prime minister also declared that his country would wait as long as necessary (ten, twenty, thirty years) until all of Latin America revolts: "Our country will never set foot in that putrid, revolting den of corruption called the OAS. Some day we will belong to the Organization of Revolutionary States of Latin America."[13] But in April 1970 Castro changed his stand somewhat by saying that Cuba would not reenter the OAS (unless the United States is expelled), but that it would be willing to reestablish relations on an individual basis with countries that would behave independently of the United States.[14] Just a few weeks before, Carlos Rafael Rodríguez had declared in a press conference at the United Nations that Cuba would accept relations with Latin American countries if no preconditions were set, but that Cuba could neither consider nor was interested in reestablishing diplomatic relations with the United States.[15]

At the beginning of the 1950s, the United States was willing to help Yugoslavia economically and to respect its commitment to the socialist system in order to gain at least the relative independence of a former Soviet satellite. The American-Yugoslav relationship was beneficial for both countries. Yugoslavia was able to survive the embargo imposed by the Soviet Union and the socialist bloc and consolidate its independence. The United States saw with satisfaction how the Yugoslav system was liberalized, expanding its communications with the Western world and influencing the Eastern European reforms. Conversely, Cuba had been under the U.S. sphere of influence until the early 1960s, and broke the inter-American embargo and gained independence from the United States with aid from the Soviet Union and the socialist bloc. A *rapprochement* between Cuba and the United States might pose threats for both countries. Cuba would be apprehensive of returning to its former status of dependency, and would not be likely to enter into negotiations with the United States at the price of cutting its protective ties with the Soviet Union. (This could change if there is an internal revolt in Cuba or a grave confrontation between Castro and the Soviets.) Cuban revolutionaries also would be fearful that reopening communications with the great consumer society of the United States would stimulate the appetite of the Cuban citizens, cool off revolutionary fervor, and either soften the Revolution (as happened in Mexico) or kill it (as in Bolivia). On the other hand, the United States would be concerned that acceptance of socialism in Cuba, could set an example for other Latin American countries, especially taking into account the fact that Cuba confiscated one billion dollars worth of U.S. investments. The vested interests of various Latin American countries (including Mexico) that received a portion of the former U.S. sugar quota to Cuba would be jeopardized. Finally, there would be strong opposition of anti-Castro, conservative regimes in Latin America.

Change Toward the Chinese Type

The possibility of Cuba moving even further toward the Chinese type was strong in 1966–1968 but, thereafter, seems to have weakened considerably. Nevertheless, in May 1970 there was a spurt of radicalization when eleven Cuban fishermen were captured by exile forces apparently operating from the United States and the Bahamas. Castro mobilized a huge crowd in front of the former building of the U.S. embassy in Havana, now occupied by the Swiss embassy. There, he accused "British imperialism" of cooperating with the exiles, the Swiss minister of foreign relations of being a "CIA spokesman," and French journalists of being spies. The Cuban premier threatened to cut the "thin protection of diplomatic immunity" in Cuba and to get the means (a vague reference to missiles) to pass from a defensive to an offensive position.[16] But this action has been regarded by "Cubanologists" as a diversionary tactic of Castro's to arouse Cuban nationalistic feelings behind him at a time when he had the embarrassing task of explaining the failure of the 1970 sugar harvest to the population.

In the unlikely case that Castro would decide to move closer to the Chinese type (see table 1), the event would probably be preceded by the launching of a Cuban "cultural revolution" similar to the Revolutionary Offensive of early 1968. Several steps could follow: collectivization of the remaining private farms; expansion of the system of communes now being experimented with in San Andrés and the Isle of Youth; an increase in the mobilization of unpaid workers to be used in labor-intensive projects that require little capital, such as road construction, and clearing, planting, and irrigation of fields, as well as handicrafts projects; setting of grandiose output targets of from ten to twelve million tons of sugar; and acceleration of the use of moral incentives by encouraging wage equalitarianism, gradually eliminating money and mercantile relations, and intensifying ideological indoctrination. Some scheme for economic decentralization and mass participation in decision-making would be attempted and the armed forces would become more powerful and the only arbiter in case of factional struggle. Diplomatic relations with both Soviet-bloc countries and some nonsocialist countries could either be cut or become cold. Being more isolated, Cuba would be forced to reactivate its support of guerrilla warfare in Latin America.

In anticipation of Soviet retaliatory measures, Cuba would have to be assured beforehand a lifeline of oil, credit, technical aid, machinery, and military equipment. This would come from China, North Korea, the Arab world, Rumania, and, perhaps, also from Japan, Canada, and some Western European countries. However, this is not an easy arrangement to make; otherwise, Cuba might have tried it in 1966–1968. The alternative of getting U.S. support (as in the case of Chinese-sympathizer but Soviet-dissident Rumania) would be even less likely than in the case of a Cuba following the Soviet or Yugoslav types. Radical internal policies and external subversion would make a *rapprochement* with the main enemy impossible. In a situation such as this, the United States would possibly have the tacit approval of the USSR to crush a revolting Cuba.

In his October 1970 speech celebrating the tenth anniversary of the establishment of the CDR, Castro said that a "tremendous battle to overcome the vices that still exist" was being fought. Among those vices, he included "bureaucratic and administrative methods" and the backwardness and weakness of the unions. He then announced that Cuba was entering a "most important decisive phase of the democratization of the revolutionary process." Through organizations such as the CTC, CDR, FMC, ANAP, and UJC, Castro said it will be possible to bring about

> a more direct participation by the masses in decision making and in the solution of problems [so that] nothing will escape supervision and control by the masses. . . . And our Party's role—let this be perfectly understood—cannot be, nor can it be, that of replacing the administration or the mass organizations. . . . It is impossible to control the Party's work through inspectors. . . . Who could better supervise our Party than the masses?[17]

Features of the previous statement, such as the attack against bureaucratic methods, and the use of the masses to control the party are indeed against Soviet practice and could suggest that the Cuban leaders are perhaps considering some variables of the Chinese type. And yet, in other statements made by Castro and Minister of Labor Risquet (discussed in chapter 9) pointing to the democratization and strengthening of the unions and the need to have collective rather than exclusive managerial decisions in the enterprises, traces of a Yugoslav influence could be found. The chances are, however, that this is another of Castro's stratagems to gain time, rebuild his charismatic appeal (somewhat eroded after the 1970 sugar harvest failure), provide some hope to the masses, and improve his bargaining power with the USSR.

In summary, the most probable alternative open to Cuba under the current situation seems to be to yield to Soviet pressure. However, Castro is still capable of reaching a compromise with the Soviets which would allow him to keep his tight control over internal politics, at the expense of increasing pragmatism in economics and acceptance of Soviet requests on international relations. The application of the Yugoslav type would not be possible unless an unforeseen change in U.S. and Soviet attitudes occurs.

Could Socialism Be Eliminated in Cuba?

The structural changes (political, economical, social) introduced by socialist revolutions are transformed into institutions difficult to eliminate, although susceptible to evolution as the Yugoslav experience proves. There are no historical examples of a consolidated socialist revolution that has been completely eradicated. In the case of Bela Kun in Hungary, Arbenz in Guatemala, Nkrumah in Ghana, and Sukarno in Indonesia, either their revolutions were not defined as socialist or they had not had time to place themselves securely in power. The Cuban Revolution has now been in power for more than one decade and has proclaimed itself socialist since 1961. But domestic factors (the lack of institutionalization and poor economic performance) and geopolitical factors (the proximity to the United States and the distance from the USSR) seems to be unique in the Cuban case. Are there prospects for the elimination of socialism in Cuba?

A change of this kind could be generated by external or internal forces, or by a combination of the two. The present conditions appear to dismiss the possibility of an American invasion as well as a seizure of power by Cuban exiles. The clandestine antisocialist movement was practically destroyed after the invasion of Playa Girón, and several guerrilla *focos* with the same ideology (e.g., in Escambray) were later eradicated. It is difficult to imagine that Castro would forsake the socialist ideology and transform his Revolution into a nationalist-democratic movement.[18] The possibilities of an internal anti-Castro and antisocialist movement are very slim since the political and military figures who espoused a democratic way of thinking at the beginning of the Revolution have either been physically eliminated or are in prison or in exile.

An anti-Castro movement originating within the socialist ranks would have greater probabilities for success. It is difficult to believe that the ideology of such a movement could be to the left of Castro, at least at the present time. It would, most likely, follow the Soviet or Yugoslavian types. In reference to the previous discussion of these types, if triumphant, a move in this direction would probably emphasize peaceful coexistence, especially in this hemisphere (a Yugoslav movement would also stress independence of both the USSR and the United States) and might change the current attitude of the American government.

On the other hand, changes in the present conditions could engender new alternatives. A new attempt by the USSR to place long-range missiles in Cuba or an invasion by the Cubans of a Latin American country could open the doors to American intervention. But these contingencies are highly improbable. An aggravation of the current economic and political conditions in Cuba, together with Castro's resistance to any strategic change, could provoke the type of reaction that occurred in Hungary in 1956. In this case, Cuba's proximity to the United States could impede Soviet intervention. A world war, an armed conflict between the USSR and China (which might facilitate an understanding between the Soviets and the Americans), or the conversion of other important Latin American countries (e.g., Argentina, Brazil, Venezuela) to socialism, would be factors capable of promoting change under the present conditions.

After twelve years of revolution, a radical transformation of the nation's structure, and after innumerable changes in ideology and policy, the unpredictable and powerful Cuban premier continues to be the key factor in shaping the future of his country.

NOTES

1. Based on Carmelo Mesa-Lago, "A Model to Measure Ideological Radicalization Over Economic Pragmatism in Socialist Countries," Commentary presented at the Fourteenth Conference of the Southern Economic Association, Atlanta, Georgia, November 13, 1970.

2. Most information comes from reports and statistics published in *Granma* or broadcast on Radio Habana-Cuba in the period January–July 1971.

3. Herbert G. Lawson, "Cuba's Economy," *Wall Street Journal,* March 7, 1969, p. 20.

4. Kathryn H. Wylie, *A Survey of Agriculture in Cuba* (Washington, D.C., U.S. Department of Agriculture, June 1969), p. 18.

5. Fidel Castro referred to this strategy as a possibility in his televised speech after his 1964 visit to the USSR. See *Bohemia,* January 24, 1964, pp. 44–45.

6. Fidel Castro, "Discurso en conmemoración del Centenario del Natalicio de Lenín," *Granma,* April 23, 1970, pp. 2–4.

7. See Malcolm W. Browne, "To Some Latin American Revolutionaries It Is Marxism Si! Castro No!" *New York Times,* July 26, 1970, section 1, p. 1.

8. *Granma,* April 30, May 2, and October 28, 1970, p. 1.

9. "Defectors Charge Sovietization of Cuba" and "Soviet-Cuban Relations Show Warning Trend," *Christian Science Monitor,* November 13, 1969, pp. 1, 6.

10. For example, the 1968 conversations between Antonio Núñez Jiménez, president of the Academy of Sciences of Cuba, and American intellectuals who are trying to facilitate the interchange of scholars and publications; the 1968–1969 agreements of the Hispanic Foundation, Library of Congress in Washington, and of the Latin American Studies Association in order to promote intellectual interchange between the two countries; the seminars held from November 1968 to February 1969 by the Center for Inter-American Relations of New York with the purpose of recommending to the U.S. government a new policy with respect to Cuba; the 1969 Ford Foundation grants made available for field research in Cuba; and the article by John Plank of the Brookings Institution proposing a *rapprochement* between the United States and Cuba.

11. In February 1970, in the television program "The Advocates" that discussed the lifting of the U.S. embargo, and also in July before the House Foreign Affairs Committee.

12. Henry Raymont, "U.S. Urges Latin Countries Not to Relax Boycott of Cuban Regime," *New York Times,* July 13, 1970, section 1, p. 1.

13. Castro, "Speech at the Close of the Main Rally Marking the Beginning of the Ten-million-ton Sugar Harvest," *Granma Weekly Review,* July 20, 1969, p. 5.

14. Castro, "Discurso en conmemoración del Centenario," pp. 2–4. In April 1971, President Nixon's China policy showed the first sign of success with the visit of the U.S. table tennis team to the mainland. At that time, the American president stated that if Cuban policy toward the United States would change, then the U.S. government would consider changing its policy toward Castro. The Cuban premier reacted violently to Nixon's gesture, saying that the OAS should be dissolved and a *Union* of American States should follow a successful revolution in every Latin American country. See Fidel Castro, "Speech at the Main Event in Commemoration of the Victory of Playa Giron," *Granma Weekly Review,* May 2, 1971, pp. 5–6.

15. Carlos Rafael Rodríguez, transcription from Radio Habana-Cuba, March 25, 1970.

16. Fidel Castro, "Discurso pronunciado en el recibimiento a los once pescadores secuestrados," *Granma,* May 20, 1970, pp. 2–4. See also the diplomatic note of Chancellor Raúl Roa in ibid., May 22, 1970, p. 7.

17. Fidel Castro, "Speech on the Tenth Anniversary of the Committees for the Defense of the Revolution," *Granma Weekly Review,* October 4, 1970, pp. 2–3.

18. Herbert Matthews, however, believes that Castro's pragmatism may lead to surprising changes: "The man who took the Cuban Revolution into Communism could conceivably take it out one of these days. He has the power to do it, should the practical possibility arise" (Matthews, *Fidel Castro* [New York, 1969], pp. 318–19).

Biographical Notes
Bibliographical Notes
Index

Biographical Notes

Nelson Amaro is Chief of Social Research of the Central-American Institute of Population and Family which is part of the Institute for the Economic and Social Development of Central America (DESAC), and a Professor of Sociology at the University Rafael Landivar, Guatemala City. He received his Licenciatura in sociology from the Catholic University of Chile and has also studied at the University of Havana, the Institute of Social Studies at the Hague, MIT, and the University of Wisconsin. He has conducted or worked in various surveys dealing with marginal groups in Guatemala. Mr. Amaro is the author of "Mass and Class in the Origins of the Cuban Revolution," *Studies in Comparative International Development* (1969), "Fases de la Revolución Cubana," *Aportes* (1968), and *La Revolución Cubana ¿por qué?* (1967), and the editor and a contributor of *Panorama del desarrollo social de Guatemala* (1970).

Eric N. Baklanoff is Dean for International Programs and Professor of Economics at the University of Alabama. He received his Ph.D. from Ohio State University and has taught at OSU, Vanderbilt University, and Louisiana State University, and also directed Vanderbilt's Graduate Center for Latin American Studies and LSU's Latin American Studies Institute. He has worked on research or in a technical capacity in Chile, Puerto Rico, and Spain. Dr. Baklanoff edited and contributed to *New Perspectives of Brazil* (1966) and *The Shaping of Modern Brazil* (1969); he has also contributed chapters to six volumes, including *Money and Banking Casebook*, ed. Lewis E. Davids. His articles have appeared in *Economic Development and Cultural Change, National Tax Journal, Journal of Inter-American Studies, Mining Engineering*, and *Revista Brasileira de Economia.*

Roberto M. Bernardo is Associate Professor of Economics at the University of Guelph, Canada. He received his M.A. from Stanford and his Ph.D. from Berkeley, and has also studied at the University of Salamanca, Spain. He has taught at San Francisco State College and the University of Philippines. Professor Bernardo is the author of *The Theory of Moral Incentives in Cuba* (1971) and "Moral Stimulation as a Nonmarket Mode of Labor Allocation in Cuba," *Studies in Comparative International Development* (1971), and has contributions in *Journal of Political Economy, International Social Science Journal*, and *Problems of Communism.*

Ernesto F. Betancourt has been a high official of the Pan American Union since 1960. He participated in the activities leading to the start of the Alliance for Progress in Punta del Este and its implementation thereafter. Currently he is Development Administrator in Residence at the Graduate School of Public and International Affairs, University of Pittsburgh. He was an activist of the 26th of July movement and in 1959 became associated with Cuba's National Bank and the Bank of Foreign Trade. He has written articles on Cuban affairs for the *New Republic* and the *Washington Post,* and has lectured at several universities on guerrilla warfare, the Cuban Revolution, and the Alliance for Progress.

Cole Blasier is Professor of Political Science and Director of the Center for Latin American Studies, University of Pittsburgh. He received his M.A. and Ph.D from Columbia University. Dr. Blasier has taught at Universidad del Valle, Cali, and Colgate University, and served as foreign service officer in Belgrade, Bonn, Moscow and the U.S. Department of State. Professor Blasier is the author of "The United States and the Revolution, 1952–1964," in *Beyond the Revolution: Bolivia Since 1952,* eds. James Malloy and Richard Thorn (1971), "Studies of Social Revolution: Origins in Mexico, Bolivia and Cuba," *Latin American Research Review* (1967), and *Chile in Transition* (1966); the editor of *Constructive Change in Latin America* (1969); and has other contributions in *Journal of Inter-American Studies, Political Science Quarterly,* and *Estudios de Comunismo.*

Lourdes Casal is Lecturer in Psychology at Brooklyn College of the City University of New York and has been a lecturer at Hofstra University and Chairman of Social Sciences, Dominican College at Blauvelt, New York. She received her M.A. and is completing her Ph.D. from the New School for Social Research. Miss Casal has done research work at the Bureau of Applied Social Research, Columbia University, and at the New York Medical College. Her publications include: "The Cuban Novel, 1959–1969: An Annotated Bibliography," *Abraxas* (1970), "La novela en Cuba, 1959–1967: una introducción," *Temática Cubana* (1970), and contributions to *Child Welfare, Developmental Psychology,* and *Cuba Nueva.*

Edward Gonzalez is Assistant Professor of Political Science at the University of California, Los Angeles. He received his M.A. and Ph.D. from UCLA. Dr. Gonzalez has been a Research Fellow at the Brookings Institution and a Consultant of the Hispanic Foundation and Library of Congress. He was in Cuba doing research in 1967 and 1968, and is the author of "Castro: The Limits of Charisma," *Problems of Communism* (1970), and "Castro's Revolution, Cuban Communist Appeals, and the Soviet Response," *World Politics* (1968). He is the author of *Cuba Under Castro: The Troubled Revolution,* to be published by Houghton Mifflin in 1972.

Roberto E. Hernández is Research Associate, Institute for Cuba and the Caribbean, Center for Advanced International Studies, University of Miami, and

Assistant Professor, Dade County College. A graduate from the School of Law and the School of Social Sciences at the University of Havana, he received his M.A. and is completing his Ph.D. at the University of Miami. He was a professor at La Salle University in Havana and a top official at the Cuban Bank of Social Insurances under the revolutionary government. He is the author of "La atención médica en Cuba hasta 1958," *Journal of Inter-American Studies* (1969), and a co-author with the Cuban Economic Research Project of *A Study on Cuba* (1965), *Social Security in Cuba* (1964), and *Labor Conditions in Communist Cuba* (1963).

Irving Louis Horowitz is Professor and Chairman of the Sociology Department at Rutgers University, editor-in-chief of *Trans-action,* and director of *Studies in Comparative International Development.* He has worked extensively in Latin American affairs. Among his recent works in this field are: *Masses in Latin America* (1969), *Latin American Radicalism,* co-edited with John Gerassi and Josue de Castro (1969), *The Rise and Fall of Project Camelot* (1967), *Three Worlds of Development* (1966), and *Revolution in Brazil: Politics and Society in a Developing Nation* (1964). Professor Horowitz has published various articles on Cuba in *Trans-action* and is editor of and contributor to *Cuban Communism* (1970) and *Cuba: diez años después* (1970).

Mateo Jover Marimón is Lecturer in Sociology, University of Puerto Rico at Humacao. A graduate of the School of Law at the University of Havana he was a national leader of the Catholic Action in Cuba and a state lawyer under the revolutionary government. He received his Master in Religious Sociology from the Catholic University of Louvain, Belgium. Mr. Jover is the author of "Présence de l'Eglise dans une societé en transformation révolutionaire: L'Experience Cubaine" (Switzerland, 1970) and "Presencia de la Iglesia en una sociedad en transformación revolucionaria: la experiencia cubana," *Temática Cubana* (1970), and a contributor to the Bulletin of the International Federation of Institutes for Social and Socio-Religious Research (FERES).

James M. Malloy is Associate Professor of Political Science, University of Pittsburgh. He received his M.A. and Ph.D. from Pitt and has done extensive research in Bolivia and other Andean countries. Professor Malloy is author of *Bolivia: The Uncompleted Revolution* (1970), co-editor of and contributor to *Beyond the Revolution: Bolivia Since 1952* (1971), author of "El MNR Boliviano: estudio de un movimiento popular nacionalista en América Latina," *Estudios Andinos* (1970), "Revolution and Development in Bolivia," in *Constructive Change in Latin America,* ed. Cole Blasier (1968), and co-author of *Political Elites: A Mode of Analysis* (1964).

Julio Matas is Associate Professor of Hispanic Languages and Literatures at the University of Pittsburgh. A graduate of the School of Law and the School of Dramatic Arts in Havana he received his M.A. and Ph.D. degrees from Harvard University. Dr. Matas has been active in the Cuban theater and cinema for more than fifteen years. He was one of the founders of the *Cinemateca de Cuba* and was its secretary from 1955 to 1957. Under the Revolution he became one of the Directors of the National Theater of Cuba. He is the author of a book of poetry *Retrato de tiempo* (1959), a volume of short stories *Catálogo de imprevistos* (1963), a play *La crónica y el suceso* (1964) and articles in several literary and scholarly journals in Cuba and abroad.

Carmelo Mesa-Lago is Associate Professor of Economics and Associate Director of the Center for Latin American Studies, University of Pittsburgh. He has law degrees from the Universities of Havana and Madrid, an M.A. from the University of Miami and Ph.D. from Cornell. A former professor at the Universities of Madrid and Villanueva (Havana) and a former research associate at the University of Miami, he has made field research in Argentina, Chile, Cuba, Dominican Republic, Mexico, Peru, Spain, Uruguay and Venezuela. He is the author of seven books and two dozen articles, among them: *The Labor Sector and Socialist Distribution in Cuba* (1968), *Planificación de la seguridad social: análisis especial de la problemática cubana* (1960), "Economic Policy and Ideological Radicalization in Cuba," *Studies in Comparative International Development* (1970), "Availability and Reliability of Statistics in Socialist Cuba," *Latin American Research Review* (1969), "Economic Significance of Unpaid Labor in Socialist Cuba," *Industrial and Labor Relations Review* (1969), "The Revolutionary Offensive," *Trans-action* (1969), and other contributions in such journals as *Problems of Communism, Economic Development and Cultural Change, Industrial Relations, Aportes, Annales, Seguridad Social, Revista Cubana de Derecho,* and *Revista de Política Social.* Dr. Mesa-hago is also the editor of *Cuban Studies Newsletter.*

José A. Moreno is Associate Professor of Sociology, University of Pittsburgh. He received his M.A. from St. Mary's University, Halifax, his Ph.D. from Cornell, and also has studied at Comillas University, Spain; Heythrop College, Oxford; and Regis College, Canada. Professor Moreno has taught in Guatemala and Puerto Rico, worked as a counselor in Cuba, New York, Rochester, and Detroit, and done extensive research in the Dominican Republic, Guatemala, Colombia and Cuba. His publications include "Che Guevara on Guerrilla Warfare: Doctrine, Practice and Evaluation," *Comparative Studies in Society and History* (1970), "What Made the Rebels Different," in *Political Power in Latin America,* eds. Richard Fagen & Wayne Cornelius (1970), *Barrios in Arms* (1970), *Sociological Aspects of the Dominican Revolution* (1967), and contributions in *Economic Development and Cultural Change* and other journals.

Rolland G. Paulston is Associate Professor in the International and Development Education Program, School of Education, University of Pittsburgh. He received his M.S.Sc. degree from the University of Stockholm and a doctorate from Columbia University. He visited Cuba in late 1970 and has been Advisor in Educational Planning and Research with the Columbia University Advisory Team in Peru, and consultant to UNESCO and USAID on various educational change projects in Latin America. Publications resulting from this and related work include *Society, Schools, and Progress in Peru* (1971), *Educación en el cambio dirigido de la comunidad* (1969), *Educational Change in Sweden* (1968), *Desarrollo somático y rendimiento físico del escolar peruano* (1968). His articles have been published in *Aportes, Comparative Education Review, International Review of Education, School and Society,* and *Mundo Nuevo,* among other journals.

Andrés Suárez is Professor of Latin American Studies at the University of Florida, and has been Associate Researcher at the Center for International Studies at MIT. A graduate of the School of Law at the University of Havana, Professor Suárez was a participant in student movements and revolutionary politics in Cuba. He held several positions in the revolutionary government (1959–1960), including Undersecretary of the Ministry of Treasury. He is the author of *Cuba: Castroism and Communism, 1959–1966* (1967) and articles in *Problems of Communism* and other professional journals.

Luc Zephirin is a Ph.D. candidate at the School of Public and International Affairs, University of Pittsburgh. He visited Cuba in 1959, was a student in Paris of René Dumont and Charles Bettelheim (former advisors of the Cuban government), and assisted Dr. Mesa-Lago in the Pitt seminar "Cuba: A Decade of Revolution, 1959–1968." Mr. Zephirin has studied at Fundação Getúlio Vargas, Rio de Janeiro, National University of Mexico, Institute Lebret, Paris, and Northeastern University.

Bibliographical Notes

BECAUSE of space limitations it is not possible to list here the numerous books, articles, reports, and statistical works consulted in the preparation of this study, much less to include a general bibliography of the Cuban Revolution. This note is a guide to the most valuable and recently published bibliographies on the subject.

The best general bibliography available, containing almost four thousand entries meticulously classified (some briefly annotated), is Nelson P. Valdés and Edwin Lieuwen's *The Cuban Revolution: A Research-Study Guide (1959–1969)* (Albuquerque: University of New Mexico Press, 1971), 230 pp. A previous and more modest effort, although richer in annotations, is that edited by Gilberto V. Fort, *The Cuban Revolution of Fidel Castro: An Annotated Bibliography* (Lawrence: University of Kansas Libraries, 1969), 140 pp. Pioneering work in this area was done by the late Fermín Peraza Sarausa, who published an annual bibliography for many years; his last work was *Revolutionary Cuba: A Bibliographical Guide* (Coral Gables: University of Miami Press, 1970), 262 pp. The most comprehensive bibliography of books and pamphlets put together in Cuba is the one edited by Marta Dulzaides Serrate and Marta Bidot Pérez, *Bibliografía cubana, 1959–,* Biblioteca Nacional José Martí (La Habana: Consejo Nacional de Cultura, 1967, 1968–), six vols. A brief work, but useful because of its annotations, is Joseph A. Kahl, *Annotated Bibliography on Cuba* (Cornell University, December 1969), mimeo., 6 pp.

An outstanding listing of documents has been prepared by Jaime Suchlicki, *The Cuban Revolution: A Documentary Bibliography, 1952–1968* (Coral Gables: Center for Advanced International Studies, University of Miami, 1968), 83 pp. The two most comprehensive collections of statistics available are Junta Central de Planificación, Dirección Central de Estadística, *BE Boletín estadístico 1968* (La Habana: JUCEPLAN, 1970), 225 pp., and C. Paul Roberts and Mukhtar Hamour, *Cuba 1968: Supplement to the Statistical Abstract of Latin America* (Los Angeles: UCLA Latin American Center, 1970), 213 pp. For additional sources and an evaluation of accuracy the reader may check Carmelo Mesa-Lago, "Availability and Reliability of Statistics in Socialist Cuba," *Latin American Research Review,* 4 (Spring and Summer 1969), pp. 53–91 and 47–81. An index of more than one hundred Cuban

535

journals, magazines, and newspapers with information on the publication agency, period, content, regularity, price, and availability in U.S. libraries is "Cuban Periodicals, 1959–1970," *Cuban Studies Newsletter,* 1 (May 1971), pp. 1–10.

The two most important and productive leaders of the Revolution, Castro and Guevara, have been the object of numerous studies. The best bibliographical compilations are Rolando E. Bonachea and Nelson P. Valdés, "The Making of a Revolutionary: A Fidel Castro Bibliography (1947–1958)," *Latin American Research Review,* 5 (Summer 1970), pp. 83–88, and "Documento: una bibliografía de Fidel Castro," *Aportes,* no. 18 (October 1970), 120–30, and Robert J. Scauzillo, "Ernesto Guevara: A Research Bibliography," *Latin American Research Review,* 5 (Summer 1970), pp. 53–82. Compilations of writings and speeches are Bonachea and Valdés, eds., *The Selected Works of Fidel Castro,* 3 vols. (Cambridge: MIT Press, 1971–); James Petras and Martin Kenner, eds., *Fidel Castro Speaks* (New York: Grove Press, 1969), 332 pp.; John Gerassi, ed., *Venceremos! The Speeches and Writings of Che Guevara* (New York: The Macmillan Co., 1968), 442 pp.; and Bonachea and Valdés, eds., *Che: Selected Works of Ernesto Guevara* (Cambridge: MIT Press, 1969), 456 pp.

Specialized, topical bibliographies are scarce; some of them may be found in footnotes and bibliographical notes in books on Cuba. In addition to the bibliographical information in the footnotes of this book, a selection of "hidden bibliographies" follows. Hugh Thomas's monumental work, *Cuba: The Pursuit of Freedom* (New York: Harper & Row, 1971), footnotes and pp. 1573–99, includes an outstanding listing of historical sources. On the origins of the revolution see Cole Blasier's "Studies of Social Revolution: Origins in Mexico, Bolivia and Cuba," *Latin American Research Review,* 2 (Summer 1967), pp. 28–64. On politics the reader should check the footnotes of Andrés Suárez's *Cuba, Castroism and Communism, 1959–1966* (Cambridge, Mass.: MIT Press, 1967), 266 pp., and Richard R. Fagen, *The Transformation of Political Culture in Cuba* (Stanford, Calif.: Stanford University Press, 1969), 271 pp. Good sources for economic materials are Cuban Economic Research Project, *Study on Cuba* (Coral Gables: University of Miami Press, 1965), 774 pp.; Dudley Seers et al., *Cuba: The Economic and Social Revolution* (Chapel Hill, N.C.: University of North Carolina Press, 1964), 432 pp.; and Roberto M. Bernardo, *The Theory of Moral Incentives in Cuba* (University, Ala.: University of Alabama Press, 1971), 159 pp. On labor see Cuban Economic Research Project, *Labor Conditions in Communist Cuba* (Coral Gables: University of Miami Press, 1963), 158 pp., and Carmelo Mesa-Lago, *The Labor Sector and Socialist Distribution in Cuba* (New York: Praeger, 1968), pp. 187–250. Bibliographies of Cuban creative literature are Rosa M. Abella, "Bibliografía de la novela publicada en Cuba y en el extranjero por cubanos, desde 1959 hasta 1965," *Revista Iberoamericana,* 30 (July–December 1966), pp. 307–11; Seymour Menton, *La novela y el cuento de la revolución cubana: 1959–1969. Bibliografía* (Cuernavaca: Centro Intercultural de Documentación, July 1969), DOC 69/151, 10 pp.; and Lourdes Casal, "The

Cuban Novel, 1959–1969: An Annotated Bibliography," *Abraxas,* 1 (Fall 1970), pp. 77–92.

The increasing number of listings of Cuban collections in U.S. and foreign libraries are useful as bibliographies. Earl J. Pariseau has edited several essays evaluating the Library of Congress's collection as well as other Cuban sources in England, Germany, Spain, and the United States: *Cuban Acquisitions and Bibliography* (Washington, D.C.: Library of Congress, 1970), 164 pp. See also Rosa Quintero Mesa, *Latin American Serial Documents* (Ann Arbor, Mich.: University Microfilms, 1969), vol. 3, *Cuba;* University of Texas Library, *Catalogue of the Latin American Collection* (Boston: G. K. Hall, 1969), 31 vols., section on Cuba; University of Pittsburgh Libraries, *Recent Acquisitions in Latin American Studies, 1967–1970* (University of Pittsburgh, 1968–1971), mimeo., 5 vols., section on Cuba; Ana Guerra Duarte, *The Cuban Collection at UCLA* (Los Angeles, n.d.), mimeo.; and Yale University Library, *Cuban Imprints Acquired by Yale University Library 1969–1970* (New Haven, n.d.), mimeo.

Cataloguing and annotation of current publications on Cuba are done systematically by three periodicals: *Cuban Studies Newsletter,* published biannually by the Center for Latin American Studies, University of Pittsburgh; *Caribbean Studies,* published quarterly by the Institute of Caribbean Studies, University of Puerto Rico; and *Handbook of Latin American Studies,* published annually by the Hispanic Foundation, Library of Congress.

Index

NOTE: This index includes the names of some of the authors whose works are cited in the notes.